T0388134

Protestant Resistance in Counterreformation Austria

Protestant Resistance in Counterreformation Austria examines Austrian Protestants who actively resisted the Habsburg Counterreformation in the early seventeenth century. While a determined few decided early on that only military means could combat the growing pressure to conform, many more did not reach that conclusion until they had been forced into exile. Since the climax of their activism coincided with the Swedish intervention in the Thirty Years' War, the study also analyzes contemporary Swedish policy and the resulting Austro-Swedish interrelationship. Thus, a history of state and religion in the early modern Habsburg Monarchy evolves into a prime example of *histoire croisée*, of historical experiences and traditions that transcend political borders.

The book does not only explore the historical conflict itself, however, but also uses it as a case study on societal recollection. Austrian nation-building, which tenuously commenced in the interwar era but was fully implemented after the restoration of Austrian statehood in 1945, was anchored in a conservative ideological tradition with strong sympathies for the Habsburg legacy. This ideological perspective also influenced the assessment of the confessional period. The modern representation of early modern conflicts reveals the selectivity of historical memory.

Peter Thaler is Associate Professor of History at the University of Southern Denmark. He holds a Ph.D. in history and a Ph.D. in Scandinavian Studies from the University of Minnesota as well as a doctorate of law from the University of Vienna.

Routledge Research in Early Modern History

Maurits of Nassau and the Survival of the Dutch Revolt
Comparative Insurgences
Nick Ridley

The Economic Causes of the English Civil War
Freedom of Trade and the English Revolution
George Yerby

Edwin Sandys and the Reform of English Religion
Sarah L. Bastow

Murder, Justice, and Harmony in an Eighteenth-Century French Village
Nancy Locklin

The Dirty Secret of Early Modern Capitalism
The Global Reach of the Dutch Arms Trade, Warfare and Mercenaries
in the Seventeenth Century
Kees Boterbloem

Languages of Reform in the Eighteenth Century
When Europe Lost Its Fear of Change
Edited by Susan Richter, Thomas Maissen, and Manuela Albertone

Religious Tolerance from Renaissance to Enlightenment
Atheist's Progress
Eric MacPhail

Protestant Resistance in Counterreformation Austria
Peter Thaler

For more information about this series, please visit: www.routledge.com/
Routledge-Research-in-Early-Modern-History/book-series/RREMH

Protestant Resistance in Counterreformation Austria

Peter Thaler

NEW YORK AND LONDON

First published 2020
by Routledge
52 Vanderbilt Avenue, New York, NY 10017

and by Routledge
2 Park Square, Milton Park, Abingdon, Oxon, OX14 4RN

Routledge is an imprint of the Taylor & Francis Group, an informa business

© 2020 Taylor & Francis

The right of Peter Thaler to be identified as author of this work
has been asserted in accordance with sections 77 and 78 of the
Copyright, Designs and Patents Act 1988.

All rights reserved. No part of this book may be reprinted
or reproduced or utilised in any form or by any electronic,
mechanical, or other means, now known or hereafter invented,
including photocopying and recording, or in any information
storage or retrieval system, without permission in writing from
the publishers.

Trademark notice: Product or corporate names may be
trademarks or registered trademarks, and are used only for
identification and explanation without intent to infringe.

Library of Congress Cataloging-in-Publication Data
Names: Thaler, Peter, author.
Title: Protestant resistance in Counterreformation Austria / Peter
  Thaler.
Description: New York, NY : Routledge, 2020. | Series: Routledge
  research in early modern history | Includes bibliographical
  references and index.
Identifiers: LCCN 2019055328 (print) | LCCN 2019055329 (ebook) |
  ISBN 9780367429348 (hardback) | ISBN 9781003000235 (ebook) |
  ISBN 9781000766844 (adobe pdf) | ISBN 9781000767131 (mobi) |
  ISBN 9781000767421 (epub)
Subjects: LCSH: Counter-Reformation—Austria—History—17th
  century. | Protestants—Austria—History—17th century. | Thirty
  Years' War, 1618–1648. | Habsburg, House of. | Austria—
  History—17th century. | Church and state—Austria—History—
  17th century.
Classification: LCC BX1516 .T55 2020 (print) | LCC BX1516
  (ebook) | DDC 274.36/06—dc23
LC record available at https://lccn.loc.gov/2019055328
LC ebook record available at https://lccn.loc.gov/2019055329

ISBN: 978-0-367-42934-8 (hbk)
ISBN: 978-1-003-00023-5 (ebk)

Typeset in Sabon
by Apex CoVantage, LLC

Contents

	List of Illustrations	vi
	Preface and Acknowledgments	vii
1	Old Conflicts and Modern Interpretations: An Introduction	1
2	A House Dividing: The Rise of Confessions in Early Modern Austria	27
3	Last Estate Standing: Representative Government and Catholic Restoration	70
4	The Thinker: Georg Erasmus von Tschernembl and the Ideology of Resistance	111
5	The Noble Warriors: Austrian Protestants in Swedish Services	150
6	The Peasants: When Humble Subjects Mar the Mighty's Sleep	192
7	Beyond Habsburg: A Conclusion	230
8	Historiographical Essay: An Introduction to Historical Writing on Austria's Confessional Age	269
	Bibliography	282
	Index	326

Illustrations

Figure

0.1 Habsburg Empire 1648–1795 (exclusive of Italian
possessions and the Austrian Netherlands)   ix

Tables

1.1 Structure of the Austrianist Conception of Identity
according to Reiterer   17
6.1 Subject Hearths according to Category of Landlord in
Upper Austria 1620–1625 (Property Registry)   195
6.2 Subject Hearths according to Category of Landlord in
Upper Austria 1750 (Tax Rolls)   196

Preface and Acknowledgments

Protestant Resistance in Counterreformation Austria examines the minority of Austrian Protestants who actively resisted the Habsburg Counterreformation in the early seventeenth century. Since the climax of their activism coincided with the Swedish intervention in the Thirty Years' War, the study also analyzes contemporary Swedish policy and the resulting Austro-Swedish interrelationship. Thus, a history of state and religion in the early modern Habsburg Monarchy evolves into a prime example of *histoire croisée*, of historical experiences and traditions that transcend political borders.

I hope that the book will be able to satisfy its diverse audiences. It is directed at readers with an interest in Central and Northern European history, but it also examines the role of religion in early modern society. By applying a transnational approach and anchoring the analysis in a framework of historical recollection, the study also tries to illuminate the role of history in the creation of collective identities.

During my work on this study, I have profited from the help of many. Generous editors permitted me to incorporate individual components of the research, which I continually published during the long writing process, into the overall study. This allowed me to develop and challenge my argument along the way and thus contributed to a more refined final product. The libraries at the University of Southern Denmark fulfilled my never-ending requests for additional materials. The Austrian National Archives, the provincial archives of Carinthia, Upper Austria, and Saxony, the Vienna Museum of Applied Arts, the Swedish National Archives and Military Archives, the archives at Julita Castle, and the private Pauli family archives supplied most of the primary sources. Joakim Pauli of the Pauli family association and my colleagues Werner Wilhelm Schnabel at the University of Erlangen, Arno Strohmeyer at the University of

viii   *Preface and Acknowledgments*

Salzburg, the late Jan Glete at the University of Stockholm, and Wilhelm Wadl at the Provincial Archives of Carinthia generously shared their extensive knowledge about important aspects of the subject. The insightful comments by R. J. W. Evans, James D. Tracy, Thomas Winkelbauer, and Tina Thaler improved the study in content and style. I am glad to be able to acknowledge these contributions.

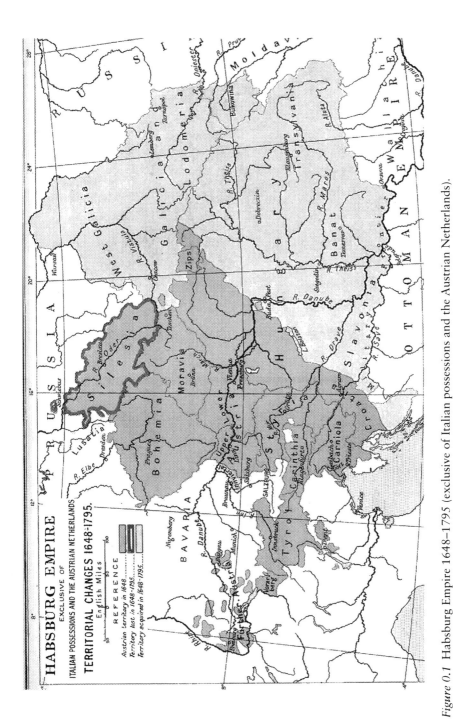

Figure 0.1 Habsburg Empire 1648–1795 (exclusive of Italian possessions and the Austrian Netherlands).
Source: Adapted from Adolphus William Ward and others, eds., *The Cambridge Modern History Atlas* (London, 1912).

1 Old Conflicts and Modern Interpretations

An Introduction

In spite of the territorial, cultural, and constitutional chasm that separated the Habsburg Monarchy from all its successor states, the Austrian republic largely assumed its legacy. Dominant opinion saw the Alpine populace as the rightful successor to the deposed dynasty and its multicultural empire.[1] Diverse historic expressions of Austrianness merged into the genealogy of a new state.[2]

This retroactive identification also surfaced in portrayals of the confessional era. In popular historical imagery, the Habsburg perspective represented the country's natural point of reference. From this angle, resistance to the dynasty appeared suspect and latently anti-Austrian.[3] The political confrontations of the early modern period cannot be described with a terminology developed for democratic nation-states, however. Religion and social standing competed with political affiliation. In dynastic conglomerates such as the Habsburg Monarchy, this conflict of loyalties was exacerbated by the clash between the estatist tradition of individual territories and the nascent absolutism of Habsburg rulers. Whereas the dynasty tried to impose a more homogenous and centralized form of government, the estates strove for regional autonomy and aristocratic co-dominion. When the preexisting rivalry between monarchy and territorial aristocracy was reinforced by denominational differences, open conflict seemed unavoidable.

This study examines Austrian Protestants who actively resisted the Habsburg Counterreformation in the early seventeenth century, focusing particularly on those who ventured or at least contemplated the use of arms. While a determined few decided early on that only military means could combat the growing pressure to conform, many more did not reach that conclusion until they had been forced into exile. Since the climax of their activism coincided with the Swedish intervention in the Thirty Years' War, the study also analyzes contemporary Swedish policy and the resulting Austro-Swedish interrelationship. Thus, a history of state and

2 Old Conflicts and Modern Interpretations

religion in the early modern Habsburg Monarchy evolves into a prime example of *histoire croisée*, of historical experiences and traditions that transcend political borders.

Protestant Resistance in Counterreformation Austria not only explores the historical conflict itself, however, but also uses it as a case study on societal recollection. Austrian nation-building, which tenuously commenced in the interwar era but was fully implemented after the restoration of Austrian statehood in 1945, was anchored in a conservative ideological tradition with strong sympathies for the Habsburg legacy. This ideological perspective also influenced the assessment of the confessional period. The modern representation of early modern conflicts reveals the selectivity of historical memory.

The Rise of the Habsburg Dynasty and the Challenge of the Protestant Reformation

After Martin Luther's "Ninety-five Theses on the Power of Indulgences" had triggered a religious upheaval in 1517, most Western European monarchs experienced its impact. No major dynasty, however, was touched more immediately and comprehensively than the House of Habsburg. The Habsburgs had established themselves as the leading princely family of the Holy Roman Empire, whose crown they had worn without interruption since the election of Albrecht II in 1438.[4] It was right at the heart of this empire that the reformist ideas came to fruition. At the same time, the Habsburgs had consistently expanded their dynastic patrimony throughout Europe, which subjected their religious decision-making to considerations of foreign policy.

When the imperial electors had chosen the Swabian count Rudolf of Habsburg as King of the Romans and thus ruler of Germany in 1273, they had hardly foreseen this development.[5] The Habsburgs had built up a solid power base in the southwest of the empire, where they had also profited from the demise of the formerly domineering Hohenstaufen family. Nonetheless, they did not measure up to such powerful houses as the Guelphs, long-time rivals of the Hohenstaufens with extensive landholdings in the German north and a previous spell as Roman-German emperors. In fact, they were hardly considered equals by the influential king of Bohemia Přemysl Otakar II, who openly questioned Rudolf's qualifications and repudiated his election.

Yet Otakar's defiance turned into a political windfall for the Habsburgs. Soon after the battlefield death of the last Babenberg duke of Austria in 1246, the Bohemian king had stepped into the resulting power vacuum.

Since the empire experienced an interregnum of its own, Otakar relied more on his regional dominance and on domestic Austrian collaborators than on legally secured mandates. When Rudolf challenged territorial transactions that had taken place during the interregnum, Otakar initially refused to comply and was placed under the ban of the empire in 1276. Although the two rivals reached a temporary compromise, the conflict was eventually settled by military means. Otakar's defeat and death in the Battle on the Marchfeld in 1278 proved decisive for the future of Austria and the Habsburg dynasty.

Rudolf I did not hesitate to exploit the renewed uncertainty in the Austrian lands for the benefit of his own family. In 1282 he enfeoffed his sons Albrecht and Rudolf with Austria, Styria, and Carniola, thereby fundamentally transforming the stature of the dynasty. Henceforth, the Habsburgs controlled territories straddling the southwestern as well as the southeastern rim of the empire. Regardless of their still fluctuating success in imperial elections, they had become a force to be reckoned with in German politics. During subsequent centuries, they strove to consolidate their geographically disjunct possessions. This policy integrated much of Carinthia and Tyrol into their patrimony and created a territorial configuration that began to display early similarities with the twentieth-century Republic of Austria.

The regency of Rudolf I did not yet establish the Habsburgs as the undisputed imperial dynasty. For more than a century they had to share this distinction with several competitors, among whom the houses of Wittelsbach and especially Luxemburg seemed to have superior prospects. When John the Blind was elected to the Bohemian throne in 1310, the Luxemburgs even eclipsed their Austrian rivals in their own backyard. For more than a century they controlled Bohemia, which, under the able rule of Charles IV, developed into an imperial center of power. But when Charles' second surviving son Sigismund, Holy Roman Emperor as well as king of Bohemia, Hungary, and Croatia, passed away in 1437 without leaving a legitimate heir, the way was finally clear for Habsburg supremacy. The Holy Roman Empire transformed into a quasi-hereditary monarchy under Habsburg leadership. Although the emperor was elected and not determined by hereditary succession, the dynasty ruled the polity all but continuously between 1438 and 1806.[6] Austria changed from periphery to core; Vienna turned into imperial residence and important center of German cultural and political life.

At the same time, the Habsburgs determinedly expanded their dynastic patrimony. In the late 1400s Frederick III secured the rich Burgundian inheritance for his son Maximilian. As emperor, the latter devised a web of

4 Old Conflicts and Modern Interpretations

additional marital unions that soon came to benefit the dynasty. The marriage of Maximilian's son Philip the Fair with Joanna of Castile allowed their son Charles to succeed not only in the empire, where he ruled from 1519 to 1556 as Charles V, but also in the far-flung Spanish possessions, where he had already acceded to the throne as Charles I three years earlier. Although the family split into a Spanish and a German or Austrian branch in the subsequent generation, the dynastic bonds remained important and exerted considerable influence on imperial politics.

Their location at the southeastern frontier of the empire also involved the Habsburgs in the political affairs of East Central Europe. Encouraged by the successful Burgundian experience of his son, Maximilian I arranged the double wedding of his grandchildren, Ferdinand and Maria, with the children of the Hungarian and Bohemian king Vladislav II Jagiello, Louis and Anna. The Jagiellonians desired the support of influential Christian neighbors against the Ottoman Empire, which was persistently expanding its hold over the Balkans. To Vladislav, the Habsburgs could seem an obvious choice. Through his father Casimir IV Jagiello, the grandson of Emperor Albrecht II, he was already related to the dynasty; in addition, members of the family had held the Bohemian throne in the past. When King Louis II subsequently perished in August 1526 while attempting to escape the triumphant Turkish army after the Battle of Mohács, Archduke Ferdinand claimed his succession in the lands of the Bohemian and Hungarian crowns.

If Ferdinand had hoped that his marital compact would give him an indisputable right to the throne, he stood to be disappointed. The Bohemian estates adamantly rejected any claim to hereditary succession and insisted on their prerogative of electing a king. This posed a serious challenge to Ferdinand. As a native Spaniard who could not speak Czech, he was considered alien to the country's cultural and religious environment. As a Habsburg, he might also entangle Bohemia in foreign wars. In consequence, there were other contenders to the throne, not least of all the Bavarian Wittelsbachs. To secure his accession, Ferdinand had to strike a compromise. He was forced to concede the elective nature of Bohemian kingship, uphold the Compacts of Basel that assured religious equilibrium, and guarantee the established prerogatives of the native nobility in the governing of the country. In return, the estates reluctantly granted Ferdinand the right to have his son designated king and successor during his own lifetime. Under those terms, the Bohemian diet unanimously elected Ferdinand king of Bohemia, and he was crowned in Prague in February 1527. Stung by their exclusion from the negotiations, the representatives of Moravia and Silesia directly accepted Ferdinand as their ruler.[7]

Old Conflicts and Modern Interpretations 5

In Hungary, Ferdinand encountered even more resistance. His claim to the throne, based on his marriage to the previous king's daughter and the Habsburg-Jagiello marital treaty, was countered by the Transylvanian voivode János Szapolyai, who invoked a 1505 resolution by the Hungarian diet calling for the succession of a native king. Szapolyai initially enjoyed broad support and was elected as King John I in Székesfehérvár, the country's historical place of coronation, in November 1526. Ferdinand had to content himself with being chosen by a rump diet assembled in the western city of Pressburg (Pozsony; now Bratislava in Slovakia) the following month. Aided by his brother Charles, Ferdinand eventually defeated his rival on the battlefield, but the intervention of the de facto masters of central Hungary, the Ottomans, restored John's control over much of the country. In time, this established a triple partition of the old Hungarian kingdom, which left the heart of the country in Ottoman hands, established a semi-independent Transylvanian principality, and restricted Habsburg rule to the western and northern borderlands. The conquest of the remainder of Hungary from the Turks represented a dominant aspect of Austrian foreign and military policy during the subsequent centuries and eventually turned the Habsburg Monarchy into the prevalent force of the European southeast. This victorious conclusion only took shape at the end of the seventeenth century, however. During the main years of Reformation and Counterreformation, the Habsburgs had to tread more lightly in Hungary than in other possessions if they wanted to retain any hope of eventually reunifying the kingdom under their scepter. They had to respect the constitutional privileges of the estates and the political and economic power of the great magnate families.[8]

This was the framework in which the Habsburg response to Luther's theses was placed. When the nineteen-year-old Charles followed his grandfather Maximilian to the imperial throne in 1519, he had much more than German politics with which to contend.[9] Charles was born and raised in the Low Countries, the Burgundian dominion of his father, whom he also succeeded there in 1506. Upon the death of his maternal grandfather Ferdinand II in 1516, he also assumed the throne of Aragon and, for all practical reasons, power over the Spanish empire.[10] Since the Iberian Peninsula remained almost untouched by the religious reform movement, Charles could but fear any ecclesial schism that would alienate his imperial from his Spanish possessions. At the same time, he rejected any denominational diversification within individual territories, in full agreement with contemporary political philosophy, which considered religious homogeneity a prerequisite of social stability.

In consequence, Charles initially tried to reconcile the divergent tendencies under the roof of Reform Catholicism and tolerated negotiations

6 *Old Conflicts and Modern Interpretations*

between Luther and the imperial estates.[11] When he recognized the futility of these efforts, he resolved to enforce religious conformity. Yet the monarch was soon confronted with the realities of imperial politics. Raised with notions of royal supremacy and universal monarchy, Charles hoped to establish himself as undisputed ruler of matters political as well as religious in Germany. Yet the Holy Roman Emperor did not enjoy the constitutional stature of French or Spanish kings. Most importantly, he needed to secure his own accession to the throne. Succession in the empire was not determined by birth and inheritance but by the vote of seven imperial princes. The Golden Bull of 1356 had granted the king of Bohemia, the count palatine of the Rhine, the duke of Saxony, the margrave of Brandenburg, and the archbishops of Mainz, Trier, and Cologne the privilege to elect the imperial ruler. This statute formalized a development in which the suffrage had gradually been restricted from extending originally, at least in name, to the tribal assemblies of free men to subsequently a shrinking number of prominent nobles and ultimately a predetermined circle of electors, even if none of these shifting bodies disregarded lineage and other established principles of royal succession.[12]

In a political system of that nature, the emperor had to share his power with the leading princes of the realm. The electors, especially, enjoyed a high degree of autonomy, which they determinedly protected with the help of charters termed election capitulations. In these preelection accords, the electors made full use of their temporarily enhanced position to limit the prerogatives of the future monarch. The Golden Bull had already noted the monarch's obligation to immediately confirm the electoral privileges. Yet it was the contentious election of Charles V that formalized the practice of sworn concessions. Monarchs regularly succeeded at preempting the electoral vote by having their preferred successor confirmed as Roman kings during their own reign, when they were able to apply their full authority to influence the outcome. Emperor Maximilian I died before he could arrange for the succession of his grandson, however, and outside contenders eyed a realistic chance at breaking the Habsburgs' hold over the imperial throne. Since the choice stood between the reigning kings of Spain and France, many German princes harbored concerns about the implications of these international entanglements for the politics and administration of the empire. Charles successfully invoked his credentials as the scion of the foremost imperial dynasty, but he also had to subscribe to a detailed list of constitutional safeguards.

Many of these concessions concerned the rights of the electors and other princes.[13] The monarch pledged to uphold the electoral process designed in the Golden Bull and refrain from trying to make succession inheritable. He was to respect the rights of the electors and enforce them against third parties. And he was to consult these electors on questions of fundamental importance, not least of all in regard to foreign policy. Yet there were also stipulations that expressed national concerns. Charles promised to install a regency council of suitable Germans only. Other imperial offices, too, would be filled with German-born nobles. German and Latin were the only languages permissible in official government business; exceptions could only be made for regions of the empire where other languages had traditionally been in use. Finally, the monarch had to assure the electors that he would personally accept the crown at his earliest convenience and also subsequently spend as much time as possible within the borders of the empire.

Charles V took an oath on the charter on the day of his coronation in Aachen.[14] Two years later, during the diet of Worms in 1521, he personally experienced the substantive limitations of his authority. Not only did he have to relinquish ambitious designs for imperial reform, which would have facilitated the closer amalgamation of his diverse realms. Even on the matter of religious compliance, where the electoral capitulation had granted him substantial prerogatives as protector of church and pope, he met aristocratic resistance. His Edict of Worms, in which he labeled Luther a heretic and outlawed him as well as his teachings, was not enforced by high-ranking princes such as the Elector of Saxony. Within the constitutional framework of the empire, the widespread support for Luther among German princes became decisive for the outcome of the religious conflict. To be sure, the Reformation in Germany was a mass phenomenon and spread rapidly throughout the country. Yet the abject failure of more revolutionary-minded reformers such as Thomas Müntzer, as well as the subsequent advances of the Counterreformation in the Alpine hereditary lands, make it doubtful that this popular movement could have survived a coordinated assault by the authorities.[15] In so politically multicephalic a structure as the Holy Roman Empire, the conversion of territorial princes, by contrast, undermined any attempts by the emperor to suppress the reform movement.

Having failed at Worms, Charles V was soon distracted by more pressing matters of state. The need to consolidate his rule in Spain, where he was, if anything, considered more foreign than in the German lands, and the protracted conflict with France demanded his full attention. Charles found himself at war during more than half of his long reign, with Francis I and his successor Henry II of France alone accounting for 16 years of military confrontation. He was also forever traveling between his domains; between 1517 and 1555 he spent a quarter of his time on the

8 *Old Conflicts and Modern Interpretations*

move.[16] To redress the ensuing problems, he entrusted his brother Ferdinand, married to the daughter of Vladislas II of Hungary and Bohemia, with the adjacent Austrian segment of the vast Habsburg inheritance.[17] He also appointed Ferdinand to head a regency council for the time of his absence from the empire. In 1531 he even had him confirmed as Roman king and thus successor designate.

When a temporary cessation of hostilities with Francis I allowed for it, Charles—urged by his brother to combat the dual menace of Turks and Protestants—returned to Germany and called a meeting of the imperial diet at Augsburg in 1530. If the emperor had hoped that his personal presence could settle the religious disagreements, he soon learned otherwise. Instead, the Protestant princes in the assembly submitted the Augsburg Confession, which formalized their creed and subsequently became the theological foundation of a separate Lutheran church. The imperial diet, historically divided into electoral, princely, and urban curiae, fractured along religious lines. The division into Catholic and Protestant corporations evolved into a central fault line in the assembly, which subsequently also obtained constitutional status.[18]

When reconciliation proved elusive at Augsburg, the emperor reaffirmed his edicts against heresy. In response, major Protestant princes and towns founded the League of Schmalkalden, with the express purpose of providing military support against imperial encroachments in matters of faith.[19] Far from being resolved, the theological conflict had taken on political and military overtones. Confronted with such vigorous opposition, Charles reverted to a more conciliatory stance. Without formally recognizing their status or withdrawing his proclamations against them, Charles invited Protestants to join in a national peace and held out the prospect of a general church council. While this left the future resolution of the empire's denominational disagreements purposely undecided, it ended any illusions the emperor may have had about a speedy return of the dissenters to the Catholic fold. When Charles was called back to Spain in 1533, Protestantism stood more securely in the empire than it had three years prior.

For the next decade and a half, the religious conflict in Germany simmered without erupting into full-blown war. Protestantism further consolidated its position, helped by the conversion of such significant territories as Württemberg, Mecklenburg, Pomerania, and Brandenburg. In the German north and east, Catholic holdouts became increasingly rare. Monarchy and church did not consent and never withdrew the decrees and resolutions against religious heterodoxy. The papal curia

Old Conflicts and Modern Interpretations 9

adamantly called for decisive action, but not until 1546 did Charles, who had recently made peace with France and returned to the empire, regard it as opportune to resort to arms. Rather than challenging German Protestantism in its entirety, Charles decided to frame his intervention as an imperial measure to discipline rebellious princes. By subduing two central pillars of the League of Schmalkalden, Elector John Frederick of Saxony and Landgrave Philip of Hesse, the emperor hoped to domesticate the remaining Protestant estates without having to confront them in battle. Charles even succeeded at drawing Duke Moritz of Saxony over to his side by opening up the possibility of transferring electoral status from the older, Ernestine branch of the House of Wettin to Moritz's Albertine cadet branch.

Charles prevailed in the first Schmalkaldic War, which permitted him to influence Lutheran ecclesial life through the Augsburg Interim of 1548 and sealed the transfer of the Saxon electorate to his ally Moritz.[20] The Interim delineated the extent of deviation from Catholic orthodoxy permissible for the time being, that is, until a general council of the church would permanently resolve the matter.[21] It proved difficult to enforce and galvanized renewed Protestant opposition. North German princes allied themselves with Henry II of France, and even Moritz of Saxony saw it in his own best interest to rejoin the Protestant bloc to secure his recent gains. Pressured from all sides, Charles reluctantly acceded to the Treaty of Passau, in which King Ferdinand and the Protestant princes had agreed on another temporary compromise that largely vacated the Interim in August 1552.

The outcome of the Second Schmalkaldic War had shown that Protestantism could no longer be eradicated in the Holy Roman Empire by military means. This opened the door for a genuine resolution of the denominational impasse. Under the chairmanship of Ferdinand, whom Charles instructed to act in his role as king of the Romans and not as personal representative of the emperor, the imperial diet assembled at Augsburg in February 1555. Although its fundamental principles had already been established at Passau, disagreements on the exact provisions of a lasting compromise remained. The negotiations were primarily in the hands of lawyers and diplomats rather than princes and clerics, and their objectives were modeled on the Perpetual Public Peace of 1495 and similar general pacifications that had outlawed feuds and established the rule of law.

In the end, a resolution could only be reached with the help of procedural subtleties. On 25 September 1555 Ferdinand signed the imperial

10   *Old Conflicts and Modern Interpretations*

recess, which, next to a number of constitutional reforms, also included the religious accord.[22] Its pivotal clause stipulated the principle subsequently summarized as *cuius regio, eius religio*, in other words, that the individual estates of the empire held the right to determine the religion of their territory and its inhabitants. This prerogative only extended to Catholic and Lutheran estates, however; other confessions, including Calvinism, were expressly excluded. Imperial estates adhering to the two recognized confessions should not intervene in each other's internal religious affairs, which entailed that the historic ecclesiastical rights of Catholic clerics as well as previous statutes and edicts against heresy no longer applied in reformed territories.

Although it instituted denominational dualism within the Holy Roman Empire, the concord did not introduce popular freedom of religion for the adherents of the two privileged faiths. The right to choose largely remained the privilege of territorial princes. There were only glimpses of individual religious liberty. In free imperial cities that contained supporters of both churches, biconfessional tolerance was to be upheld. And in a provision that appeared more benevolent in the eyes of contemporaries than it does in retrospect, the subjects of imperial estates who adhered to the locally proscribed denominational alternative were granted the privilege to sell their property and emigrate, provided the financial interests of seigniorial lords were respected.

Two stipulations proved so controversial that they remained outside the consensual text. The most intractable problem concerned the status of ecclesiastical estates whose ruler converted to Lutheranism. Ferdinand could not but concede the factual secularization of such territories in the past, but he adamantly opposed any continuation of this practice. The Lutheran estates refused to consent officially but indicated their willingness to accept an imperial directive. As a consequence, Ferdinand inserted the so-called ecclesiastical reservation into the diet's final document, the recess, which clarified that clerical rulers were not entitled to reform their territories and would forfeit their offices if they left the Catholic Church.[23] In return, the king conceded in a secret declaration that knights and towns in ecclesiastical principalities could maintain their Lutheran faith if they had been practicing it for an extended period.[24]

The Peace of Augsburg remained contingent on a future resolution of the confessional discord, but it marked a decisive change in the empire's ecclesial law. By leaving the negotiations to his brother, the emperor had already foreshadowed his further course of action. Charles was not ready to condone the official legalization of Lutheranism in his empire, even if he recognized its inevitability.[25] His stubborn effort to preserve a unified

Old Conflicts and Modern Interpretations   11

dynastic realm was failing as well, as he could not secure the imperial succession after Ferdinand for his own son Philip. Increasingly disillusioned, Charles began his withdrawal from office. He would have preferred to resign the imperial crown prior to the confessional compromise, but Ferdinand convinced him to wait. In September 1556, Charles—who had already been succeeded by Philip in his Spanish, Burgundian, and Italian possessions—transferred the administration of the Holy Roman Empire to his brother, whom the electors formally confirmed as emperor two years later.

Thus, Ferdinand, who had been raised on the Iberian Peninsula and arrived in Vienna with a Spanish entourage that was no less disparaged than were Charles' Flemings in Madrid, had secured the imperial crown for himself and his progeny. Even though he had initially tried to uproot heresy as determinedly as his older brother, his long and continuous presence in the empire had given him a finer ear for the realities of German politics. He retained a belief in the eventual reconciliation of the religious differences through a general council of the church and was willing to compromise on form and ritual. By the time of Charles' resignation, it was Philip who was seen as the Spaniard unfamiliar with conditions in Germany, whereas Ferdinand and his oldest son Maximilian had established themselves as the dynasty's native contenders.

With the Peace of Augsburg, the initial phase of the Reformation in the Holy Roman Empire had come to an end. The medieval unity of the church had splintered and proven impossible to restore. The foundations for a coexistence of Catholicism and Protestantism had been laid. Significant disagreements remained, to be true, and it took a devastating war during the subsequent century to resolve them. Yet on the imperial level, at least, the principle of religious toleration had been introduced. Within individual territories, in contrast, homogeneity remained the norm. To which extent this could also be enforced in the Habsburgs' patrimonial lands was to become a pivotal question of Austrian and Central European history.

Historical Memory in Theory and Practice

This book examines a crucial turning point in Austrian history, but it also traces its afterlife in societal recollection. The public imagery of contemporary Austria remains tied to a dynastic legacy even at historical junctures in which that dynasty stood in opposition to large sectors of the populace. At first sight, it may seem difficult to explain the divergence between historical experience and historical representation. Theorists

12 Old Conflicts and Modern Interpretations

have long pointed to the disparity between event and remembrance, however, and the relationship between history, memory, and myth has become an important topic of theoretical debate.

A central model of collective memory owes its foundations to the French sociologist Maurice Halbwachs. As early as the 1920s, Halbwachs—a follower of Émile Durkheim—began to develop his concept of *mémoire collective*, in which he underscored the social nature of memory.[26] It is individuals who remember, but they call recollections to mind by relying on the framework of social memory. Social entities can always reconstruct their past, but in the act of reconstructing they also distort it.[27] As a consequence, collective memory is tied to the groups that share in it and determine what they regard as memorable. There are as many social memories as there are groups, and the memories they share are essential for their coherence and identity.

This view of collective memory has tangible significance for the relationship between history and memory. Halbwachs conceived of history as the opposite of memory.[28] History not only takes its starting point where living memory ends but also removes memory from the past. Whereas history is a portrayal of changes, collective memory is a portrayal of similarities.[29] Memory connects past and present; history sets them apart.

Half a century later, French historian Pierre Nora expanded on Halbwachs to emphasize the intrinsic chasm between memory and history. In Nora's view, real memory is the hallmark of archaic societies, where it expresses a commanding, unwitting, spontaneous recollection that is part of a collective experience. Its counterpart is the discipline of history, which characterizes changeable modern societies in search of a means to record and structure a rapidly disappearing past. The two are not identical but rather are in outright opposition to each other. Whereas memory is unconsciously alive, history is a reconstruction of the dead. Memory binds groups together, as it is directed at one alone. History, in contrast, endeavors to be rational and analytical. Therefore, it distrusts memory and tries to supplant it.[30] In fact, even what we call memory today, such as the places, monuments, and artifacts of the past, is merely the result of a conscious process of collection and preservation and thus yet another form of history.[31]

The impulses that emanated from those works produced a wealth of new scholarship. Patrick Hutton defined its essence as a reckoning with the present as a privileged moment of time.[32] To Hutton himself, history forms an art of memory because it connects the latter's central facets: repetition and recollection.[33] Repetitions are living traditions, whereas recollections are conscious reconstructions. Their intersection allows for historical thinking.

Old Conflicts and Modern Interpretations   13

French historian Jacques Le Goff divided the development of collective, or historical, memory into consecutive stages. The ethnic memory of preliterate societies was transformed by the arrival and constant expansion of written memories, culminating in the overflow of memory characteristic of contemporary societies.[34] To Le Goff, memory seeks to save the past for the sake of its current and future benefits; in this process, it both informs and is informed by history.[35] American sociologist Barry Schwartz, in turn, based collective memory on both history and commemoration and defined it as a representation of the past embodied in both historical evidence and commemorative symbolism.[36] Whereas commemoration mobilizes symbols to evoke sentiments about the past, history is objectively conceived and sustained by evidence.[37] Yet at the same time, both phenomena are highly interdependent, with commemoration relying on historical evidence and history reflecting the sentiments expressed by commemoration.[38]

The sociologist Paul Connerton complemented the study of social memory with a physical dimension.[39] Connerton affirms that the human experience of the present is informed by knowledge of the past and that images of the past legitimate the existing social order. Yet he is most concerned with the mechanisms through which communities convey and sustain memory, and assigns them to the realm of collective performances. In Connerton's eyes, societies remember through commemorative ceremonies and interrelated bodily practices and are therefore more inert than commonly understood.

Together with his wife Aleida, the German Egyptologist and cultural theorist Jan Assmann developed the concept of cultural memory.[40] Assmann concedes that his term also covers elements commonly referred to as tradition, but he argues that the latter leaves out the essential twin phenomena of reception and amnesia. As a conscious process to invoke the past, it is commemoration that sets cultural memory apart from tradition. In a critical differentiation, Assmann distinguishes communicative from cultural memory. The former relies on recollections that are shared by contemporaries; they are orally transmitted and fade out after three to four generations. Cultural memory, by contrast, is willfully created by specialized carriers of tradition. It expresses itself in ritual and performance, not least of all in the shape of celebration, and integrates a community through references to an absolute past. The past only comes into being by being referred to, and cultural memory only recognizes commemorated history. Through commemoration, in turn, history becomes myth.[41]

In a somewhat different manner, Eric Hobsbawm and Terrence Ranger examined the relationship between the past and its recollection, for which

14 *Old Conflicts and Modern Interpretations*

they popularized the concept of invented traditions. They highlighted the novel and constructed nature of purportedly ancient practices and emphasized the ideological interests that guided their conception.[42] Hobsbawm, in particular, deconstructs such tradition-carrying symbols by pointing to their conscious creation or transformation and applies the implicit lesson to the concept of the nation.[43] Much of the subjective content of national identity is the outcome of careful social engineering. The underlying motivation of this invention of tradition lies in the political and economic interests of ruling elites. In this approach, Hobsbawm and his associates replaced a Durkheimian interest in collective recollection with a functionalist focus on political actors and their conscious control and instrumentalization of memory.

The new interpretation of history and memory presented by Halbwachs and Nora has been enormously influential, but it has not gone unchallenged. Historian and geographer David Lowenthal accepted the paradigmatic dichotomy of these phenomena but took a more negative view of collective memory, for which he preferred the term heritage.[44] To Lowenthal, it is heritage that forms the conceptual counterpart to history, as a subjective representation of the past that is not beholden to accepted tenets of evidence. Even if history cannot fully escape bias, it at least attempts to, whereas heritage has no such aspirations. In fact, in order to be exclusive to its own community, heritage requires a shared misreading of the past. Whereas history is universal, heritage is group-specific.

Historian Amos Funkenstein anchored his objections in a different aspect of the paradigm. While acknowledging the significance of Halbwachs, he expressed reservations about his rigid juxtaposing of professional history and collective memory.[45] Although it was nineteenth-century scholarship that canonized historicism, earlier writers were no strangers to the concept. Modern historians, in turn, are not intrinsically detached from collective memory and the societal norms and perceptions that surround them. Even atomized memory employs the milestones of national history to reconstruct the past, argued Hue-Tam Ho Tai.[46] Peter Novick, in turn, doubted if the organic metaphor of collective memory is still suitable for the fragmented and rapidly changing societies of the late twentieth century.[47] And Stefan Berger rejected a generalized premise that memory is group-specific and history universal.[48]

Berger's critique of Halbwachs and Nora simultaneously broadened the challenge to history as a scientifically superior reflection of the past.[49] Like Funkenstein before him, Berger questioned the intrinsic opposition of history and collective memory, as he found their respective assignment to individual and collective experiences unsubstantiated. Instead,

Old Conflicts and Modern Interpretations 15

the German historian placed them in a triangular relationship that also includes myth.[50] By admitting the latter among legitimate representations of the past, however, he undermined another pillar in the established self-understanding of scientific history. Berger used national pedigrees and myths of origins as examples of the overlap between history and myth. As the foremost writers of grand national narratives desired to extend the lineage of the nation as far back in time as possible, they found themselves dependent on established myths of origin. Rather than rejecting them, they attempted to reformulate their core findings in the language of modern scientificity.

To establish the nation's credentials, historians drew on a wide imagery. Berger described the Whig interpretation of England as the vanguard of liberty.[51] The emulation of heroic figures such as Arminius in Germany or Vercingétorix in France.[52] The invocation of past suffering in the historiographies of Poland and Hungary.[53] The glorification of peasant life as the retainer of indigenous culture in the history of stateless nations.[54] The aggrandizing of borderlands and cultural missions.[55] The amalgamation of national and Christian images in the histories of communities in which political and denominational demarcations coincided.[56] The latter experience was especially pronounced in European territories at the intersection with Islam, giving rise to a variety of historiographies that depicted their nation as Europe's bulwark against the infidels.[57]

Not least of all, Berger pointed to national historiographies that tried to establish their perennial attachment to the territory that the national populace currently inhabited or coveted.[58] This construction of continuities extends over centuries and connects the poleis of ancient Greece with the modern Greek nation-state, undiminished by intermediate periods of foreign settlement and rule. In its most far-reaching form, it preserves this continuity through extended periods of exile, as exemplified by Zionist historiography. As a consequence, Berger encouraged historians to surrender unrealistic expectations about the superiority of historical writings and open themselves to a broad variety of textual representations of the past.[59]

This criticism of national historiographies supports divergent conclusions. It can reaffirm and even expand Hayden White's postmodern critique, which highlighted the role of literary techniques in historiography.[60] The American literary scholar observed a continuum ranging from historical evidence via the narrative interpretation of such evidence to imaginative literature inspired by such evidence. Whereas this continuum demystified the distinctions between different styles of history-based discourse, however, it did not automatically validate White's equation of

16 Old Conflicts and Modern Interpretations

historical writing and fictional literature. Most historians who challenged the purely rational nature of historical writing did not subscribe to all of White's conclusions. Even if Stefan Berger aligned the grand narratives of national history with mythology, he defined his personal objective as demythologization and thus reintroduced the conceptual distinction between myth and history.[61]

By the end of the 1900s, the definition of myth itself was undergoing a transformation. Whereas the pioneers of modern historiography, informed by the ancient Greek dichotomy of *mythos* and *logos*, had characterized myth as erroneous representation of the past and thus yet another opposite of history, their late twentieth-century successors were redefining the term to convey the notion of meaningful history, in other words, of representations of the past that create meaning and identity for a community. Based on his study of ancient cultures, Jan Assmann described myths as foundational narratives that strive to illuminate the present through an account of the past.[62] In this constellation, history and myth are no longer antonyms but functional complements.

Austria

In Austria, the collapse of the Third Reich offered a Catholic conservatism with strong roots in Habsburg dynasticism a unique chance at reestablishing itself in public discourse. This intellectual tradition was not new; it originated in the erstwhile monarchy and segments of the Christian Social Party, the pre- and interwar representative of one of Austria's central ideological tendencies.[63] Following the disintegration of its imperial frame of reference, it had faced stiff challenges from National Liberal and Social Democratic alternatives. After Austria's incorporation into the Third Reich, it seemed destined for oblivion. In the early postwar era, however, it promised to distance reemerged Austria from the misery and isolation of its northern neighbor.

Political scientist Albert Reiterer developed a systematic overview of the national ideology that gained currency in postwar Austria. This ideology perpetuated older self-representations of Habsburg rulers as integrative figures in a world of national strife, deeply intertwined with the Catholic Church and its universalist legacy. Not until the late 1920s did small circles of Habsburg legitimists adapt this historical imagery to the altered political environment of the Alpine republic.[64] In the course of the postwar decades, however, its major conceptions spread to initially resistant sectors of society and established themselves as the preeminent expression of Austrian historical identity.

Old Conflicts and Modern Interpretations   17

Table 1.1 Structure of the Austrianist Conception of Identity according to Reiterer[70]

Issue/statement	Conservatives	Communists
	Leopold Figl, Felix Hurdes, Alfred Missong, Wilhelm Böhm, Ernst Joseph Görlich	Ernst Fischer
Descent		
Austrians are an ethnic mixture	+	+
Core sequence: Illyrians—Celts— Romans—Slavs—Teutons	+	+
Side sequence: Latins—Jews	+	+
Culture		
Baroque	+	+
Phaeacian-Epicurean stereotype versus Prussian militarism	+	+
History		
Germany was part of Austria, not vice versa	+	+
Habsburgs	+	(+)
Maria Theresa versus Frederick II	+	+
Resistance to the Turks (and by extrapolation Nazis)	+	+
Positive evaluation of the consequences of 1866	+	+
Austria has European/global role, is anational	+	(–)
Political attitudes		
Conciliation	+	(–)
Tolerance	+	+
Conservative	+	–
Progressive	–	+
Synthesizing-musical	+	+
Catholic	+	(–)
Personification	mainly Alpine Austrian	Viennese

Source: Albert Reiterer, "Die konservative Chance: Österreichbewußtsein im bürgerlichen Lager nach 1945," *Zeitgeschichte* 14 (1986/87): 380f.

This emergent national conception emphasized the country's long historical roots.[65] Many authors traced Austrian separateness back to the *privilegium minus* in 1156; others chose the early modern consolidation of the Alpine hereditary lands or dissolution of the Holy Roman Empire in

18 Old Conflicts and Modern Interpretations

1806.[66] Austrian identity was formed by the Counterreformation and the Baroque and represented a Catholic antipode to Protestant Germany.[67] History had given rise to a distinct human type, *homo austriacus*, which was described as a supranational mediator between nationalities, as well as polylingual, adaptable, art-loving, and deeply immersed in the traditions of the Habsburg empire.[68] And perhaps most importantly, at the historic juncture when this imagery established itself in public discourse, the Austrians had been incorporated into Germany against their will in 1938. They had resisted to their best ability but had been abandoned by the international community.[69]

Core aspects of this historical interpretation have come under scrutiny in recent decades. The millennial underpinnings of postwar Austrian nationalism formed one centerpiece of investigation.[71] The Austrian recollection of World War II constituted another.[72] Tied to the debate about the wartime past of Kurt Waldheim, who had risen to both secretary general of the United Nations and president of Austria, the international critique of this state historiography reflected a rare cooperation among scholars, journalists, and politicians that altered entrenched historical interpretations.[73] Starting in the 1980s, the focus on Austrian victimization was gradually replaced with an acceptance of co-responsibility for National Socialist crimes.[74] This politically induced revisionism was in itself an intriguing demonstration of the interplay of politics, memory, and history.

In regard to more distant historical periods, the conservative paradigm largely held sway. An important element of this paradigm, with deep roots in Habsburg tradition, anchored Austria's very essence in its Catholic legacy and saw the Counterreformation as essential for the country's survival. The interwar president Wilhelm Miklas explained that "Catholic faith in the hearts and souls of the Viennese is inseparably intertwined with true Austrianness, with a love for the fatherland that cannot be separated from Catholic belief and truly Catholic convictions."[75] The Christian Social politician and historian Ernst Karl Winter wrote of an *Austria Sancta*, which, as the representation of Austria's Catholic saints, should guide the country and its people.[76] Oscar Schmitz argued that in "almost every Austrian, something of the binding powers of the Catholic Church, of the baroque urge to sensualize the sublime and to sublime the sensual, of the harmony of Haydn, Mozart, and Schubert, became flesh and blood, whereas in almost every German there is something of Luther's negation of form."[77] And in his *Österreichische Staats- und Kulturgeschichte*, Ludwig Reiter concluded simply that "the Austrians formed their national culture in resistance to Luther's reformation."[78]

If Catholicism forms an intrinsic attribute of Austria's historical identity, its one-time opponents are placed firmly outside the country's collective legacy. In an increasingly secular and diverse society, it proved impossible to maintain such an explicit equation of national and confessional identity, and political declarations of this nature have become the exception. Nonetheless, the residual identification with Habsburg confessional policy owes some of its endurance to postwar nation-building. National ideology informs the public assessment of historical conflict. The present provides the measure of the past.

Sources and Structure

This book is based on archival and printed sources primarily from what is today Austria, Sweden, Germany, and the Czech Republic. Among published sources, contemporary or near-contemporary chronicles and source collections such as Franz Christoph Khevenhüller's *Annales Ferdinandei* and Bernhard Raupach's *Evangelisches Oesterreich* play an important part, as do original prints of speeches, treaties, and collections of papers such as Georg Erasmus von Tschernembl's *Consultationes*.[79] Select theological and philosophical works were also available in modern editions. Among the archives consulted, the Carinthian Provincial Archives with their recently acquired Khevenhüller collection proved especially rewarding, providing deep insights into the fortunes of an Austrian noble family in both its Carinthian homeland and its Franconian and Swedish exile. Yet also the Swedish National and Military Archives, the archives at Julita castle, the Saxon State Archives, the Austrian National Archives, the Vienna Museum of Applied Arts, and the Upper Austrian Provincial Archives supplied valuable source material on the nature and motives of Austrian resistance to dynastic policy. Finally, a number of documents were only available in private collections, such as the archives of the Swedish Pauli family, whose ancestors had to leave Austria in the 1600s. Together these collections provided a broad and multifaceted picture of both the history and the worldview of Protestant activism in counterreformation Austria.

The study itself is divided into seven chapters. Following the delineation of the historical, historiographical, and theoretical context in the introduction, Chapter 2 describes the reception of Luther's reform in the Austrian lands. It traces the initial spread of the new impulses in different parts of society and the increasing interconnection of religious and political conflict. The firm support of the dynasty allowed the established church to rejuvenate and initiate a determined effort at Catholic restoration.

20   *Old Conflicts and Modern Interpretations*

Chapter 3 focuses on the position of the nobility in Austrian society. It examines the nature of the estate system in an international context and evaluates the implications of the religious schism for the relationship between monarchs and nobles. Thwarted in their efforts to enforce confessional orthodoxy in the Holy Roman Empire, the Habsburgs were determined to retain control of their patrimonial lands. The Protestant nobility found itself increasingly isolated politically and confessionally.

The subsequent three chapters zoom in on different aspects of Protestant resistance to the dynasty. Chapter 4 traces the philosophy of state developed by Austria's estatist opposition during the early decades of the seventeenth century. Inspired by international currents, but relying primarily on indigenous legal and societal traditions, aristocratic activists confronted the renewed emphasis on monarchic sovereignty. In the writings of Georg Erasmus von Tschernembl, especially, an alternative vision of state and governance took shape, whose implementation would have transformed the history of Central Europe.

Chapter 5 shows the increasing confluence of national and international politics. Both the Habsburgs and their domestic opponents relied on cross-border alliances. Aided primarily by Spanish and Bavarian support, Ferdinand II established full control over the Austro-Bohemian lands. Exiled nobles were drawn to the army of Sweden's King Gustavus Adolphus, who promised to restore their constitutional and religious prerogatives. National histories intertwined, and concepts of allegiance began to blur.

In Chapter 6, the analysis moves from the political elites to the rural core of the populace. The early Reformation in the Holy Roman Empire was a popular movement that contained both spiritual and social components. This duality already surfaced in the peasants' wars of the 1520s but also characterized later periods of confessional strife. Even after the fading of reformist mass activism in the Habsburg lands, popular resistance to the state church remained significant. At the apex of Catholic restoration in the dynasty's patrimony, the peasantry evolved into the most enduring obstacle to confessional homogenization.

In its conclusion, the study merges the individual findings and puts them into their comparative and theoretical context. It examines the reasons for the decline of Austrian Protestantism and traces its submerged continuities in Alpine society. It highlights the repercussions of Habsburg confessional policies for the dynasty's international standing. Most comprehensively, however, the chapter examines the societal recollection of dynastic policy in both Austria and other Habsburg successor states. As

Old Conflicts and Modern Interpretations 21

much as they share a historical legacy, these countries remain divided in its interpretation.

Notes

1. This tendency intensified over time, with Social Democrats and some National-Liberals still distinguishing more clearly between the Habsburg polity and its inhabitants in the interwar era, whereas most Catholic-Conservatives always emphasized the continuities.
2. This conflation of different notions of Austrianness also surfaces in such popular expressions as "when Bohemia still was a part of Austria," which are widely (but of course anachronistically) understood as expressing a historical subjugation of Bohemia to the territory of the modern Republic of Austria.
3. See Karl Eichmeyer, Helmuth Feigel, and Rudolf Walter Litschel, *Weilß gilt die Seel und auch das Guet: Oberösterreichische Bauernaufstände und Bauernkriege im 16. und 17. Jahrhundert* (Linz, 1976), 167.
4. In a number of English-language works, the Albrechts of the Habsburg family are translated as Alberts.
5. For English-language overviews of the history of the dynasty, see Paula Sutter Fichtner, *The Habsburgs: Dynasty, Culture and Politics* (London, 2014); Benjamin Curtis, *The Habsburgs: The History of a Dynasty* (London, 2013); Andrew Wheatcroft, *The Habsburgs: Embodying Empire* (London, 1995); Dorothy Gies McGuigan, *The Habsburgs* (Garden City, NJ, 1966); and Adam Wandruszka, *The House of Habsburg: Six Hundred Years of a European Dynasty* (New York, 1964).
6. After the Habsburg Charles VI had died without leaving a male heir in 1740, a Bavarian Wittelsbach was elected emperor in 1742. Yet the untimely death of Charles VII in 1745 allowed Maria Theresa's husband Francis Stephen of Lorraine to rise to the throne and restore Habsburg imperial leadership.
7. For a closer investigation of the establishment of Habsburg rule in Bohemia, see Kenneth J. Dillon, *King and Estates in the Bohemian Lands, 1526–1564* (Brussels, 1976), and Joachim Bahlcke, *Regionalismus und Staatsintegration im Widerstreit: Die Länder der Böhmischen Krone im ersten Jahrhundert der Habsburgerherrschaft (1526–1619)* (Munich, 1994).
8. For a closer look at Hungary during the period of Ottoman and Habsburg intervention, see Géza Pálffy, *The Kingdom of Hungary and the Habsburg Monarchy in the Sixteenth Century* (New York, 2009); Géza Perjés, *The Fall of the Medieval Kingdom of Hungary: Mohacs 1526-Buda 1541* (Boulder, CO, 1989); and Géza Dávid and Pál Fodor, eds., *Ottomans, Hungarians, and Habsburgs in Central Europe: The Military Confines in the Era of Ottoman Conquest* (Leiden, 2000).
9. For a more contemporary Central European biography of Charles V than Karl Brandi's classic *Karl V.: Werden und Schicksal einer Persönlichkeit und eines Weltreichs*, 2 vols. (Munich, 1937–1941), see Alfred Kohler, *Karl V. 1500–1558: Eine Biographie* (Munich, 2001). For an up-to-date contribution by a leading Spanish expert, see Manuel Fernández Álvarez, *Carlos V: El*

22   Old Conflicts and Modern Interpretations

césar y el hombre (Madrid, 1999). For recent introductions in English, see William Maltby, *The Reign of Charles V* (Houndmills, England, 2002), and Wim Blockmans, *Emperor Charles V: 1500–1558* (London, 2002), the latter a translation from the original Dutch.

10. For a recent biography of Ferdinand II of Aragon, also called the Catholic, see Luis Suárez Fernández, *Fernando el Católico* (Barcelona, 2004).

11. Heinrich Lutz, *Reformation und Gegenreformation*, 5th ed. (Munich, 2002), 26.

12. For the early history of royal election in Germany, see Heinrich Mitteis, *Die deutsche Königswahl und ihre Rechtsgrundlagen bis zur goldenen Bulle*, 2nd ed. (Brünn, 1944). See also Franz-Reiner Emkens, "*Multi* oder *pauci?* Überlegungen zur fürstlichen Wahlbeteiligung an den Königswahlen der staufischen Epoche," in *Von Sacerdotium und Regnum: Geistliche und weltliche Gewalt im frühen und hohen Mittelalter*, ed. Franz-Reiner Emkens and Hartmut Wolff (Cologne, 2002), 136–152.

13. See Alfred Kohler, ed., *Quellen zur Geschichte Karls V.* (Darmstadt, 1990), 53–58.

14. Gerd Kleinheyer, *Die kaiserlichen Wahlkapitulationen* (Karlsruhe, 1968), 11.

15. For more recent studies of Müntzer available in English, see Hans-Jürgen Goertz, *Thomas Müntzer: Apocalyptic, Mystic, and Revolutionary* (Edinburgh, 1993); Tom Scott, *Thomas Müntzer: Theology and Revolution in the German Reformation* (New York, 1989); Eric W. Gritsch, *Thomas Müntzer: A Tragedy of Errors* (Minneapolis, MN, 1989); and Abraham Friesen, *Thomas Müntzer, a Destroyer of the Godless: The Making of a Sixteenth-Century Revolutionary* (Berkeley, CA, 1990).

  In accordance with Anglophone practice and in the interest of simplicity, this study also addresses the Habsburgs' traditional Austrian patrimony collectively as the Alpine hereditary lands rather than as the Alpine and Danubian hereditary lands.

16. Wim Blockmans, *Emperor Charles V: 1500–1558* (London, 2002), 34.

17. This step was also intended to enhance Ferdinand's stature as a potential spouse.

18. See Fritz Wolff, *Corpus Evangelicorum und Corpus Catholicorum auf dem westfälischen Friedenskongreß: Die Einfügung der konfessionellen Ständeverbindungen in die Reichsverfassung* (Münster, 1966).

19. For the League of Schmalkalden, see Gabriele Haug-Moritz, *Der Schmalkaldische Bund 1530–1541/42: Eine Studie zu den genossenschaftlichen Strukturelementen der politischen Ordnung des Heiligen Römischen Reiches Deutscher Nation* (Leinfelden-Echterdingen, Germany, 2002).

20. For a summarization of the Schmalkaldic Wars, consult James Tracy, *Emperor Charles V, Impresario of War: Campaign Strategy, International Finance, and Domestic Politics* (Cambridge, England, 2002), 204–248.

21. For the text of the Interim, see Joachim Mehlhausen, ed., *Das Augsburger Interim von 1548*, 2nd ed. (Neukirchen-Vluyn, Germany, 1996). For the ensuing controversy, see also the contemporary texts printed in Irene Dingel, ed., *Reaktionen auf das Augsburger Interim: Der Interimistische Streit (1548–1549)* (Göttingen, 2010).

Old Conflicts and Modern Interpretations 23

22. For the text of the Peace of Augsburg, see Karl Brandi, ed., *Der Augsburger Religionsfriede vom 25. September 1555: Kritische Ausgabe mit den Entwürfen und der königlichen Deklaration*, 2nd ed. (Leipzig, 1927), and Ernst Walder, ed., *Religionsvergleiche des 16. Jahrhunderts*, vol. 1, 2nd ed. (Bern, 1960), 41–68. For a recent examination of the accord, see Axel Gotthard, *Der Augsburger Religionsfrieden* (Münster, 2004).

23. Ernst Walder, ed., *Religionsvergleiche des 16. Jahrhunderts*, vol. 1, 2nd ed. (Bern, 1960), 49. The so-called *Reichsabschied*, or imperial recess, summed up the decisions taken by the imperial diet.

24. Ibid., 68f.

25. As Charles wrote to Ferdinand in June 1554: "You should act as Roman king in my absence and in the same way as you would act if I were in Spain. To give you my honest reasons for this, as is appropriate among brothers (and you should suspect no other motives): only religious considerations give me scruples." See Alfred Kohler, ed., *Quellen zur Geschichte Karls V.* (Darmstadt, 1990), 455.

26. His central works on the topic were *Les cadres sociaux de la mémoire* (Paris, 1925), *La Topographie légendaire des Évangiles den Terre Sainte: Étude de mémoire collective* (Paris, 1941), and the posthumously published *La mémoire collective* (Paris, 1950). In English, see Maurice Halbwachs, *On Collective Memory*, ed. and translated by Lewis A. Coser (Chicago, 1992). For a recent assessment of Durkheim's influence, see Barbara A. Misztal, "Durkheim on Collective Memory," *Journal of Classical Sociology* 3:2 (2003): 123–143.

27. Maurice Halbwachs, *On Collective Memory*, ed. and translated by Lewis A. Coser (Chicago, 1992), 182.

28. See ibid., 68–74.

29. See ibid., 77f.

30. For the content of this paragraph, see Pierre Nora, "Between Memory and History: *Les Lieux de Mémoire*," *Representations* 26 (1989): 8f. For Nora's comprehensive description of places of memory, see idem, *Les lieux de mémoire*, 3 vols. (Paris, 1984–1992).

31. Pierre Nora, "Between Memory and History: *Les Lieux de Mémoire*," *Representations* 26 (1989): 13.

32. Patrick Hutton, "Recent Scholarship on Memory and History," *The History Teacher* 33 (2000): 533–548.

33. Patrick Hutton, *History as an Art of Memory* (Hanover, NH, 1993), xx–xxi.

34. Jacques Le Goff, *History and Memory* (New York, 1992), 54.

35. Ibid., 99.

36. Barry Schwartz, *Abraham Lincoln and the Forge of National Memory* (Chicago, 2000), 9.

37. Ibid., 10.

38. Ibid., 12.

39. For the following, see Paul Connerton, *How Societies Remember* (Cambridge, England, 1989).

40. See especially Jan Assmann, *Das kulturelle Gedächtnis: Schrift, Erinnerung und politische Identität in frühen Hochkulturen* (Munich, 1992), and Aleida

24 Old Conflicts and Modern Interpretations

Assmann, *Erinnerungsräume: Formen und Wandlungen des kulturellen Gedächtnisses* (Munich, 1999).

41. For a schematic juxtapostion of communicative and cultural memory, see especially Jan Assmann, *Das kulturelle Gedächtnis: Schrift, Erinnerung und politische Identität in frühen Hochkulturen* (Munich, 1992), 56.

42. Eric Hobsbawm and Terence Ranger, eds., *The Invention of Tradition* (Cambridge, England, 1983).

43. Eric Hobsbawm, *Nations and Nationalism since 1780* (Cambridge, England, 1990).

44. See David Lowenthal, "Fabricating Heritage," *History and Memory* 10:1 (1998): 5–24, as well as idem, *The Past is a Foreign Country* (Cambridge, England, 1985), and idem, *The Heritage Crusade and the Spoils of History* (Cambridge, England, 1997).

45. Amos Funkenstein, "Collective Memory and Historical Consciousness," *History and Memory* 1 (1989): 5–26.

46. Hue-Tam Ho Tai, "Remembered Realms: Pierre Nora and French National Memory," *American Historical Review* 106 (2001): 920.

47. Peter Novick, *The Holocaust in American Life* (Boston, 1999), 267f.

48. Stefan Berger, "On the Role of Myths and History in the Construction of National Identity in Modern Europe," *European History Quarterly* 39 (2009): 492.

49. For the following, see Stefan Berger, "On the Role of Myths and History in the Construction of National Identity in Modern Europe," *European History Quarterly* 39 (2009): 409–502.

50. Berger spent much of his scholarly career in Britain.

51. Stefan Berger, "On the Role of Myths and History in the Construction of National Identity in Modern Europe," *European History Quarterly* 39 (2009): 497.

52. Ibid., 495.

53. Ibid., 494.

54. Ibid., 495.

55. Ibid., 497.

56. Ibid., 496.

57. Ibid., 497.

58. Ibid., 494.

59. Numerous additional examples of mythical representations of the national past can be found in Monika Flacke, ed., *Mythen der Nationen: 1945—Arena der Erinnerungen* (Mainz, 2004). See also Stefan Berger, Mark Donovan, and Kevin Passmore, eds., *Writing National Histories: Western Europe since 1800* (London, 1999).

60. Some of White's foremost contributions to this topic are collected in Hayden White, *Tropics of Discourse: Essays in Cultural Criticism* (Baltimore, 1978). See also Hayden White, *Metahistory: The Historical Imagination in Nineteenth-Century Europe* (Baltimore, 1973).

61. Stefan Berger, "On the Role of Myths and History in the Construction of National Identity in Modern Europe," *European History Quarterly* 39 (2009): 497.

62. Jan Assmann, *Das kulturelle Gedächtnis: Schrift, Erinnerung und politische Identität in frühen Hochkulturen* (Munich, 1992), 52.

Old Conflicts and Modern Interpretations 25

63. Still paradigmatic for the origins of the Austrian party system is Adam Wandruszka, "Österreichs politische Struktur," in *Geschichte der Republik Österreich*, ed. Heinrich Benedikt (Munich, 1954), 289–485.

64. For an early expression of this ideological innovation, see August Maria Knoll et al., *Die Österreichische Aktion: Programmatische Studien* (Vienna, 1927).

65. See, *inter alia*, Wilhelm Böhm in Bundesministerium für Unterricht, ed., *Österreichische Zeitgeschichte im Geschichtsunterricht* (Vienna, 1961), 151; Ernst Fischer, *Der österreichische Volks-Charakter* (London, 1944).

66. See, *inter alia*, Ernst Görlich, *Handbuch des Österreichers* (Vienna, 1949), advancing the *privilegium minus*; Felix Kreissler, *Der Österreicher und seine Nation* (Vienna, 1984), stressing 1806.

67. Almost all conservative Austrianists supported this proposition, among them Ludwig Reiter in his *Österreichische Staats- und Kulturgeschichte* (Klagenfurt, 1947).

68. Descriptions of this Austrian Man can be found in Oscar Schmitz, *Der österreichische Mensch* (Vienna, 1924), and, retrospectively, in Alphons Lhotsky, "Das Problem des österreichischen Menschen," in *Aufsätze und Vorträge*, vol. 4 (Munich, 1976), 308–331.

69. This view was official public policy from the very beginning of the Second Republic; it had a prominent place in the country's Declaration of Independence. [*Proklamation über die Selbständigkeit Österreichs, Staatsgesetzblatt für die Republik Österreich 1945*, Stück 1, Nr. 1.] It was presented in detailed scholarly form in Karl Stadler, *Österreich 1938–1945* (Vienna, 1966), and in Felix Kreissler, *Der Österreicher und seine Nation* (Vienna, 1984).

70. Leopold Figl, Felix Hurdes, and Ernst Missong were Conservative political figures; Wilhelm Böhm and Ernst Joseph Görlich were Conservative historians and publicists; Ernst Fischer was a leading Communist politician. A plus sign indicates the clear presence of those arguments; a minus its clear absence. Signs in parenthesis indicate a weaker expression of the respective attitude.

71. See Peter Thaler, *The Ambivalence of Identity: The Austrian Experience of Nation-Building in a Modern Society* (West Lafayette, IN, 2001); Ernst Bruckmüller, *Nation Österreich: Sozialhistorische Aspekte ihrer Entwicklung*, 2nd enlarged ed. (Vienna, 1996).

72. For discussions of the victim theory, see Heidemarie Uhl, *Zwischen Versöhnung und Verstörung: Eine Kontroverse um Österreichs historische Identität fünfzig Jahre nach dem "Anschluß"* (Vienna, 1992); Peter Utgaard, *Remembering and Forgetting Nazism: Education, National Identity, and the Victim Myth in Postwar Austria* (New York, 2003).

73. For an introduction to the Waldheim debate in an Austrian context, see Richard Mitten, *The Politics of Antisemitic Prejudice: The Waldheim-Phenomenon in Austria* (Boulder, CO, 1992).

74. See Heidemarie Uhl, "From Victim Myth to Co-Responsibility Thesis: Nazi Rule, World War II, and the Holocaust in Austrian Memory," in *The Politics of Memory in Postwar Europe*, ed. Richard Ned Lebow, Wulf Kansteiner, and Claudio Fogu (Durham, NC, 2006), 40–72.

75. "Würdevolle Feier in Mariazell," *Wiener Zeitung*, 8 July 1935, 2.

26 Old Conflicts and Modern Interpretations

76. Ernst Karl Winter, "Austria Sancta," in *Ernst Karl Winter—Bahnbrecher des Dialogs*, ed. Ernst Florian Winter (Vienna, 1969), 95.
77. Oscar Schmitz, *Der österreichische Mensch* (Vienna, 1924), 8.
78. Ludwig Reiter, *Österreichische Staats- und Kulturgeschichte* (Klagenfurt, 1947), 122. For a similar interpretation, see also Wilhelm Böhm, "Oesterreich," *Wiener Zeitung*, Beilage der Wiener Zeitung, 30 October 1946, 3.
79. For an evaluation of these works, see Kurt Peball, "Zur Quellenlage der 'Annales Ferdinandei' des Grafen Franz Christoph Khevenhüller-Frankenburg," *Mitteilungen des Österreichischen Staatsarchivs* 9 (1956): 1–22; and Karl Eder, "Bernhard Raupach (1682–1745): Ein Beitrag zur Historiographie der österreichischen Reformationsgeschichte," in *Festschrift zur Feier des zweihundertjährigen Bestandes des Haus-, Hof- und Staatsarchivs*, ed. Leo Santifaller, vol. 1 (Vienna, 1949), 714–725. The *Consultationes* are discussed in greater detail in Chapter 4.

2 A House Dividing
The Rise of Confessions in Early Modern Austria

History progresses continually but not evenly. Periods of relative stability alternate with periods of profound change. In Western Europe, medieval societies rested on several core foundations. Politically, the epoch witnessed the universal (re-)establishment of territorial polities. The associations of people that dominated the period of migration were increasingly superseded by spatially defined entities. This was also reflected in the legal systems, ever the bellwether of societal power structures. The tribal laws of the sixth to eighth century, such as the *lex salica* or the *lex baiuvariorum*, were first supplemented and subsequently replaced with statutes and codes that covered more clearly circumscribed areas, such as the royal statutes of the Roman-German kings or the territorial laws of individual political entities. At the same time, the era experienced further social diversification and the replacement of popular assemblies with diets and estates. A landowning nobility, at times in conjunction with the leadership of the local Catholic hierarchy and the urban patriciate, evolved into the last remaining political counterweight to the monarch.

On the religious level, which played a key role in society's moral and ideological sense of self, the period witnessed the institution of Roman Catholicism as the sole legitimate expression of metaphysical thought. The remaining pagan holdouts in northern and eastern Europe were converted by force unless their political elites had sensed sufficiently early that religious adaptation formed the only alternative to political subjugation. Polities that were dominated by non-Christians, such as the Islamic entities of the Iberian peninsula, were by definition not a part of the Western community, whose preferred self-designation was Christendom; they could, however, be seen as *terrae irredentae* to be liberated. Yet also Christian heterodoxy was successfully suppressed or marginalized, and non-Christian minorities such as Jews could be tolerated as guests, but

28 A House Dividing

not as integral parts of society. Notwithstanding social and regional idiosyncrasies, Western Europe has never been more cohesive in public religious expression.[1]

These fundamental parameters of medieval society were neither immutable nor immune from challenge. Nonetheless, they held sway over most of Western Europe until the 1400s. At the end of that century, however, the continent entered a period of accelerated change. New geographic and scientific discoveries, together with a stagnation of established institutions of power, questioned the status quo. Intellectually, this development had been foreshadowed by the rediscovery of classical art and philosophy in the Italian renaissance. Its secular approach and humanist focus on the individual defied the medieval unity of church and state, and its interest in the pre-Christian writings of ancient Rome and Greece undermined the monopoly of Catholic dogma and scholarship.

Humanist thought also played a role in the spread of religious dissent.[2] Even if the leading reformers tended to be rooted more deeply in the theological tradition of the Christian church, many of their intellectual supporters held humanist views. In more respects than one, the Protestant Reformation cannot be explained solely on religious terms. Widespread dissatisfaction in the rural underclass erupted in repeated peasant uprisings, which also invoked reformist theology. At the opposite end of the social spectrum, many princes and nobles judged the new ideas from a utilitarian standpoint, seeing them either as a welcome instrument for expanding their own influence at the expense of a once omnipotent church or as a dangerous challenge to an established symbiosis of worldly and spiritual power.

Religion and politics remained deeply intertwined, as monarchs became of paramount significance for the ultimate success or failure of Protestant movements in much of Western Europe.[3] In the southern outskirts of the continent, neither the monarchy nor the broader populace were appreciably touched by the new religious currents.[4] As the heartland of Catholicism and seat of its spiritual leader, who at the same time ruled his own not insignificant political entity, Italy did not offer fertile ground for religious upheaval. Spain and Portugal were far removed, both geographically and culturally, from the Central European cradles of the Reformation. Moreover, their political history had been shaped by a protracted struggle with Islam, in which they relied on support from the papacy and Catholic allies. As among the Croatians along another frontier of western Christianity, Catholicism had entrenched itself in public imagery and identity.[5] The few dissenting voices were easily silenced through traditional means.

In the very north of Europe, by contrast, rulers and subjects converged on the inverse resolution. The monarchs proved decisive for the conversion of Sweden, Denmark, and England to Protestant polities, but they did not act in isolation. Reformist ideas had already penetrated those countries prior to royal intervention. Not even in England, whose religious reorientation under Henry VIII in the 1530s most openly bore the mark of monarchic self-interest, did the king impose the new creed on a reluctant population. In fact, the monarch's theological standpoint remained ambiguous, and it was parliament that implemented and expanded the shift to Protestantism, which it also defended against subsequent attempts at Catholic restoration.[6] In Sweden, and even more so in Denmark, Luther's ideas had arrived via German pastors and merchants, as well as Scandinavian students returning from Central European universities, long before the local kings saw it in their own best interest to back this development. There was resistance, to be sure, not only in segments of the church hierarchy but also in more remote pockets of rural Sweden and especially in Danish-ruled Norway and Iceland. But this resistance did not articulate a popular mass rejection of the religious transformation. In northern Europe, the monarchs tended to attach themselves to a movement that was spreading rapidly in the general public, and even though official support was instrumental in crushing Catholic holdouts, it was not the government that implanted the Reformation in the bulk of the populace.[7]

Whereas religious homogeneity and denominational congruence between ruler and ruled was largely retained on the northern and southern edges of Western Christianity, albeit in diametrically opposed forms, the confessional differentiation proceeded more contentiously in the core of the continent. Although similar developments occurred in other countries, notably in France, where a sizable Calvinist minority long resisted the Catholic monarchy, the archetypical expression of denominational division was found in the Holy Roman Empire and especially its Habsburg patrimony. It is there one repeatedly encounters a divergence of popular and dynastic interests and an interweaving of religious and political disagreement. The nature of this conflictual confluence of matters worldly and spiritual will be examined in this chapter.

The Advent of the Reformation in the Alpine Hereditary Lands

When the new religious currents stirred up the Holy Roman Empire in the early sixteenth century, they easily transgressed territorial borders.

30 *A House Dividing*

More so than in subsequently thoroughly Protestantized countries such as Sweden, the Reformation in Germany started as a genuine popular movement. After all, Luther taught, preached, and published in Germany and—just as importantly—the German language. The fresh emphasis on the vernacular, which amplified the calls for religious change, gave the Reformation a more immediate impact in its cultural sphere of origin. Aided by the recently established art of printing, the arguments of Luther and his followers were distributed rapidly throughout Central Europe. With their higher rates of literacy, urban areas proved especially susceptible, and none more so than the free imperial cities, which had no territorial prince with which to contend.

Within few years, the impact of the reform movement had reached the Habsburg domains, much to the dismay of the dynasty. The Catholic affiliation of the House of Habsburg was beyond doubt, even if individual members may have held more complex views.[8] This affiliation was reinforced by the historical ties between pope and emperor and the encompassing cooperation with the Spanish branch of the family, in whose core domains Catholicism not only reigned supreme but had during the *reconquista* developed into a virtual ideology of state. But the social and cultural conditions that advanced the spread of Luther's teachings throughout the empire were no different in the emperor's patrimonial lands. In the German-speaking provinces, the linguistic commonalities provided immediate access to the ubiquitous printed sermons and pamphlets that promoted the reformist message. By 1519, approximately 250,000 copies of Luther's writings had been distributed throughout Europe; by 1525, this number had exploded to 1.7 million.[9] Even though the Habsburg authorities soon outlawed the printing and distributing of reformist publications, it proved impossible to prevent their continued import. Before long, the struggle between different scriptural interpretations had triggered a propagandistic effort in which the printing industry demonstrated its full potential. Reformation and Counterreformation witnessed early expressions of a comprehensive struggle for control of the societal debate, of a contest for public opinion based on both the printed and spoken word.

Yet the Habsburg Monarchy also contained the one region within Western Christendom in which religious heterodoxy had already established a foothold. Even after the religious reformer Jan Hus had been burned at the stake during the Council of Constance in 1415, support for his ideas continued to grow. In 1419 incensed followers stormed the city hall of Prague's New Town and introduced the defenestration of unpopular councilors into the region's symbolic repertoire. For almost two decades, Bohemia's religious dissenters waged war against the Catholic world that surrounded them. Repeated crusades by Emperor Sigismund and his allies could not subjugate the Hussites, who enjoyed broad support in the Czech population and were led by able military commanders such as Jan Žižka of Trocnov and Prokop the Great.

The apparent futility of coercive measures finally resulted in the Compacts of Basel in 1436, which provided for the toleration of select Hussite practices. This compromise with moderate Hussitism established the Utraquist confession, named for its insistence on dispensing the Eucharist to the congregation under both kinds.[10] After renewed tensions, the peace of Kutná Hora (Kuttenberg) confirmed the status quo in 1485. Thus, Bohemia held a unique position within Western Europe by containing an autonomous ecclesial body with its own liturgy and teachings, even if formally still under the roof of the one and catholic church.[11]

Although the Habsburgs strongly backed Catholicism following their assumption of the Crown of St. Wenceslas in 1526, their initial successes were limited. Many of the remaining Catholic populations, especially in German-speaking districts, embraced Lutheranism, and the Utraquists began to define themselves more openly as a distinct religious body. In 1575 they joined Lutherans and the Unity of Brethren, historically connected to the more radical strain of the Hussite movement, in support of the Bohemian Confession, which formed a compromise between the individual theological traditions on distinctly Protestant ground.[12]

Due to these cultural and historical preconditions, the Habsburg lands proved highly susceptible to the new religious currents. Their reception was furthered by longstanding grievances against the Catholic hierarchy and its perceived wealth and corruption. Renegade members of mendicant orders surfaced repeatedly among the most passionate advocates of reform. Their sermons popularized the religious message and were frequently accompanied by public agitation. Especially receptive to the new ideas were the mining communities. Their members were not only educated and well-organized but also geographically mobile and integrated into a cross-border flow of information. Personal and professional ties connected them to Saxony and other centers of the industry. Alpine communities such as Hall und Schwaz in Tyrol, Schladming in Styria, and Gastein in neighboring Salzburg witnessed early expressions of a Protestant public sphere, in which miners represented a close-knit, activist core. At the same time, the economic importance of the industry triggered harsh governmental countermeasures, particularly in Tyrol, where both

32   A House Dividing

Lutherans and Anabaptists were suppressed effectively. The latter paid the heaviest price—by 1539, approximately 600 had been executed in the western provinces alone.[13]

In general, however, the towns provided fertile ground for continued religious reform. Even the capital of Vienna was touched early on. Its first reformatory sermon is documented for January 1522, when the married preacher and theologian Paul Speratus challenged the local church establishment from the pulpit of St. Stephen's Cathedral with a fervent attack on prevailing teachings and practices.[14] Speratus was quickly excommunicated and continued onward to Hungary and Moravia, only to conclude his life as a Lutheran bishop in Prussia. In spite of repeated edicts by Archduke Ferdinand, the implantation of reformist thought could not be prevented. By 1524 Protestant activism had become so commonplace that the authorities decided to employ harsher methods. To set an example, they arrested known dissenters and had the prominent Viennese cloth merchant Kaspar Tauber beheaded and burned for violating the Edict of Worms. Tauber was a devout Christian who had even joined the guild of Corpus Christi, one of the foremost institutions of lay Catholicism in the archduchy's capital. The numerous Lutheran tracts that circulated in the city and his personal reading of the Bible impacted him deeply, and by 1522 he had become estranged enough from the church to cease paying his membership dues to the guild. He invoked the general priesthood of believers and openly displayed his reformist beliefs as a lay preacher. Even though the city council intervened on his behalf, a theological commission initially pressured him to recant and—following Tauber's public refusal—submitted him to the secular authorities for execution.[15]

An edict of 20 August 1527 summarized the transgressions that were to be punished as heresy. Next to practical offenses, such as the distribution of heretical writings and the non-observance of fasting regulations, it also listed such doctrinal deviations as an erroneous conception of the nature of Christ, the denial of Mary's perpetual virginity and assumption, the denial of the merits and intercession of the saints, the rejection of purgatory, the rejection of such sacraments as Holy Orders and the anointment of the sick, and the taking of communion under both kinds.[16] The local citizenry was not deterred for long, however, and recurring edicts against the preaching of heresy and the distribution of Lutheran books proved futile. While common citizens were prohibited from forming heterodox congregations, aristocrats claimed the right to hold Lutheran services in their city manors. To put an end to this custom, Emperor Maximilian II orally conceded the estates the exercise of their faith in the Estates Building, temporarily instituting one semiauthorized place of

Protestant worship in the city.[17] When Rudolf II had this Protestant center closed in 1578, however, time was running out for the public practice of Lutheranism in Vienna. Since they were unable to maintain houses of worship within city walls, the Protestant inhabitants frequented churches on protected estates in the countryside. Every Sunday throngs of Viennese pilgrimaged to surrounding communities such as Hernals or Vösendorf.

In many other urban centers, the gradually Protestantizing citizenry did not have to escape to the country but acquired its own places of worship. With the reformation of its parish church in 1526, the Carinthian city of Villach stood in the vanguard of this development.[18] As a regional trading center, the town was intimately tied in with the larger stream of information in German Central Europe. Through its feudal overlord, the prince-bishop of Bamberg, it was connected to this important Franconian territory close to the heartland of the early Reformation. Local merchants and artisans regularly attended to business in the free imperial cities of southern Germany. Their sons attended universities throughout the empire. Among those students one finds the subsequent pastor of nearby Maria Gail, Georg Krainer, who personally experienced the early Reformation in Wittenberg in 1517.[19]

In September 1526 Baron Sigmund von Dietrichstein transferred his right of presentation and guardianship over the parish church of St. James to the city and its representatives. What made this act so noteworthy were the motives and conditions listed in the deed of gift.[20] Dietrichstein clarified that mayor, council, and congregation were transmitting the gospel in true Christian interpretation and insisting on hearing the word of God clearly, purely, and without human additions.[21] The wording typified contemporary Protestant diction, and Dietrichstein included a provision that obliged the council to ensure continued adherence to these principles. The deed confirms that the local inhabitants had already embraced Luther's teachings, so that the Protestant church patron could safely forego his own right of presentation and entrust it to the city.

In the subsequent period, religious conditions in Villach displayed the ambiguity that characterized the Habsburg domains. For several decades, Lutheran and Catholic rituals coexisted. By the middle of the century, however, St. James had turned into a purely Lutheran congregation, and the later cardinal Giovanni Francesco Commendone reported in 1563 that there were few Catholics left in the city.[22] St. James remained Lutheran until 1594, when Bamberg's local vice-dominus Johann Georg von Stadion, acting on behalf of Patriarch Francesco Barbaro, had the building forced open and surrendered to Catholic clergy. Even then, the citizens continued to resist, with factual control of the church repeatedly

34 A House Dividing

changing hands until the general advance of Catholicism resolved the dispute in 1600.

The Upper Austrian city of Steyr offers another informative case study. Located at the confluence of the rivers Enns and Steyr, the settlement developed into a major trading and refining center for iron. The metal passed through the city on its journey from the mines of Upper Styria to the Danube, the principal waterway for further domestic and international distribution. Skillful artisans and ironworkers turned Steyr into the nucleus of an early protoindustrial region and contributed to its rapid growth in wealth and population; in 1576, town and suburbs contained 702 inhabited houses and thus far surpassed the rivaling centers of Wels and Linz, which were limited to 453 and 252 houses, respectively.[23]

Its stature and connections exposed Steyr to international currents, and anticlerical sermons were heard as early as 1520.[24] In 1525 the council employed a reformist Viennese monk and fought to retain him against the wishes of the bishop in Passau—albeit unsuccessfully. Yet also his properly appointed successor Michael Forster, a member of the nearby monastery in Garsten, subscribed to Lutheran tenets, as did many of his fellow brethren.[25] His forced removal antagonized the congregation and continued a pattern in which the church hierarchy defended orthodoxy, whereas a growing segment of citizenry and lower clergy demanded reform. The subsequent decades mirrored the resulting stalemate: Catholic form was offset by Lutheran content. By 1545 the Protestantization of religious life in Steyr had become unmistakable, and even the dismissal of openly Lutheran pastors only resulted in their succession by coreligionists. During the second half of the sixteenth century, Steyr was for all major purposes a Protestant community, although its status remained vulnerable to challenges by political and ecclesial authorities.

Established interactions with the early centers of the Reformation spread Lutheran ideas as well. Austrian students at reforming universities in the empire were touched by the new religious spirit and transmitted it to friends and families. We can follow this development in the chronicle of Hans Herzheimer, who administered the salt works of Bad Aussee.[26] Two of his sons were enrolled at the University of Wittenberg in 1512.[27] They were not alone. From the same modest town in the Salzkammergut, the regalian salt domains in modern-day Upper Austria and Styria, the matriculation register includes Thomas Aman in 1514 as well as Leonhard Trauner, Christoph Isenbunt, and Wolfgang Dimpel the year thereafter.[28]

Following his retirement from the salt works in 1518, Herzheimer decided to visit his sons, whom he had not seen for more than a decade.

A House Dividing 35

During his journey, he crossed paths with the papal nuncio Karl von Miltitz, who had been entrusted with letters from Pope Leo X, in which the head of the Catholic Church warned Elector Frederick III of Saxony against the harmful teachings of Luther. In Saxony, Herzheimer became acquainted with Martin Luther, Philipp Melanchton, and especially Georg Spalatin, who supported the Reformation as court chaplain and personal confidante of the elector. These encounters left a deep impression on Herzheimer, who—much against his original intention—returned a champion of Lutheranism, which his son Hans Jordan also attempted to introduce on the family's Bavarian estates.[29]

As a consequence of the religious transformation, Protestant German universities attracted ever more students from Habsburg territories. Of the 131 natives of Villach documented at German-speaking institutions of higher learning prior to 1518, 90 percent attended the University of Vienna. In the subsequent decades, Vienna's share fell to approximately one-third of the total, with the remainder drawn primarily to Protestant universities such as Tübingen, Wittenberg, and Leipzig.[30] A similar picture emerges among the nobility. In the second half of the sixteenth century, one even encounters Austrian rectors in Wittenberg, Jena, and Rostock.[31] It was only consistent that monarch and Catholic Church viewed the attendance of Protestant universities with particular displeasure and did whatever possible to restrict and eventually prohibit it.[32]

The great landowners held special significance for the implantation of the new creed because they enjoyed the right of presentation over the parishes in their domains, as well as judicial and administrative control over ecclesiastical property. In wealth and influence, few Austrian nobles could measure themselves with the Jörgers of Tollet in Upper Austria. Even though they belonged to the old aristocracy and traced their presence in the territory to the 1200s, their status reached its high point in the sixteenth and seventeenth century, until the victory of the Catholic armies during the initial phase of the Thirty Years' War sent many of them into exile.[33] During this period of ascent, the Jörgers not only expanded their landholdings but also rose to important office. They were appointed to the local governorship and treasury as well as entrusted with the hereditary post of territorial court chamberlain.[34]

This elevated position brought extensive contacts throughout the Holy Roman Empire. In the fall of 1522, Wolfgang Jörger, recently retired as governor of Upper Austria, dispatched his twenty-year-old son Christoph to the court of Elector Frederick III of Saxony. In the stylized retrospect contained in the family chronicle, Christoph II Jörger reports to have affirmed his Catholic conviction upon arrival at the Saxon border.[35] At

36   A House Dividing

his destination, however, he was soon engulfed in the theological and intellectual debates and deeply impressed by Luther. Jörger visited the reformer in Wittenberg and established a close relationship that continued long past his return to Upper Austria in 1524.[36] Also Christoph's mother Dorothea stood in regular contact with the reformer, whose 13 surviving letters to her form one of the largest bodies of Luther's correspondence with women.

As soon as Christoph Jörger had taken possession of his estates, he invited his spiritual mentor to recommend a suitable pastor. Upon Luther's advice, he called the Swabian-born theologian Michael Stiefel to his castle Tollet near the town of Grieskirchen. For two years Stiefel served as minister and tutor and attracted communicants from throughout the region, until the increasing pressure from the bishop of Passau—who had Stiefel's colleague and friend Leonhard Kaiser executed for heresy in nearby Bavaria—drove him out of the country again in 1527.[37] This setback did not discourage Christoph Jörger and his mother, however, who clung tenaciously to their convictions and implanted them in both their family and their subjects. To secure their Protestant orientation, Christoph sent his son Helmhard to the court of Elector John Frederick of Saxony and his son Abraham to the University of Wittenberg.[38] To embed the new creed in the local population, the Jörgers consistently invested Lutheran pastors with the parishes over which the family held the right of presentation.

The right of presentation proved a particularly effective as well as controversial instrument. It derived from the institution of patronage, which could be exercised by ecclesiastical bodies such as monasteries, but also by laymen. In the case of the latter, the right of patronage tended to stem from the historic foundation or endowment of a place of worship. Feudal lords and urban municipalities regularly erected proprietary churches on private lands. The donors retained proprietary interests but also obligations; they were responsible for the maintenance of buildings and occasionally also of clerics. At the same time, they were entrusted with upholding law and order. Similar responsibilities derived from the instrument of ecclesial guardianship, which had originally designated secular protectors for parishes or monasteries but subsequently provided the guardian ample opportunity to intervene in the administration of these institutions. As a consequence, many ecclesial bodies strove to shake off these unwanted intrusions, and some of the more powerful ones also succeeded.[39]

Patronage offered a variety of privileges. Some were primarily symbolic, such as seats of honor in the proprietary church. Others provided genuine influence, and none more so than the right of presentation. The precise content of this privilege varied, but it always included the authority to nominate a candidate for ecclesiastical office. More so than in territories in which the religion of rulers and subjects coincided, this prerogative influenced confessional developments in the Habsburg domains. After all, the right of patronage was typically exercised by towns and noblemen, the two sectors of Austrian society in which Lutheranism had taken hold most firmly. Its impact, in turn, was greatest among the very populations that had initially remained beyond the reach of reformist thought. Burghers, miners, and nobles were integrated in a larger circle of information, which had rapidly transmitted the Protestant message. They were also more likely to be literate and thus receptive to the burgeoning pamphlet literature. The common populace of outlying rural areas was largely bypassed. Following the conversion of their manorial seigneurs, however, this isolation was broken decisively.

Proprietorial nobles could utilize their position in different manners. Sometimes, they succeeded at directly investing reformist theologians with the ecclesial offices under their jurisdiction. At other times, they sheltered sitting clerics who had embraced the new creed from retaliatory measures by their superiors. Where it proved impossible to confirm pastors in public congregations, nobles employed them in their manorial chapels. In time, they also sponsored new places of worship on patrimonial lands, thus in essence creating additional Lutheran proprietary churches.

The well-organized miners of Schladming and Schwaz, the internationally connected merchants of Villach and Steyr, the Viennese burghers who read reformatorial pamphlets and listened to the sermons of itinerant preachers, the noble students at Protestant universities, and the agricultural subjects of Protestant feudal lords exemplified the diverse patterns of religious reorientation in the Alpine hereditary lands. By the middle of the sixteenth century, the new ideas had taken hold in a large segment of the Austrian populace. This remarkable advance occurred under constant threat of governmental interference, however. As long as the monarch possessed the unabridged authority to regulate religious practice, the fate of heterodoxy remained imperiled. Therefore, politically connected Protestants persistently strove to secure a legal foundation for the exercise of their faith. The most natural arena for these attempts were the territorial estates.

The Austrian Reformation Between Monarchy and Estates

At a General Diet in 1526, the Austrian estates moved for the toleration of Lutheran principles.[40] Although this demand remained unheeded,

38   A House Dividing

Lutheranism continued to proliferate in the region. It would be deceptive, therefore, to project the modern-day distribution of Catholicism and Protestantism in Central Europe back into the sixteenth century. What did begin to take root, however, was a division between territories with Catholic and territories with Protestant rulers. Considering that the compromise reached in Augsburg in 1555 invested the territorial rulers with the authority to determine the religious practice of their subjects, the stalwart Catholicism of the Habsburgs was ominous for the future of Protestantism in Austria.

Several factors help explain why it nonetheless took over a century for the Habsburgs to reestablish Catholic supremacy in their hereditary lands. The Reformation had taken deeper roots in the Habsburg Monarchy than in neighboring Bavaria. Within the narrower confines of their patrimony, the Wittelsbach dukes in Munich proved more successful at implementing imperial and territorial prohibitions against the new creed.[41] Only during the middle of the century, encouraged by the legalization of Lutheranism in both the empire and adjacent Austria, segments of the nobility made a serious bid for confessional tolerance. The uncompromising stance of the dukes won out, however, and Bavaria cemented its role as the vanguard of Catholic restoration in Germany. The Society of Jesus established important bridgeheads and gained pivotal influence on the territorial university at Ingolstadt, whereas Lutheranism was increasingly restricted to political enclaves such as the free imperial city of Regensburg and the sovereign domains of the counts of Ortenburg. In time, Bavaria even managed to export its policies and exert great influence on the confessional structure of neighboring territories, not least of all the emperor's hereditary lands.

Many authors ascribe the initial moderation of the Habsburgs to their financial dependency on the estates in an era of international tensions. "The Turk is the Lutherans' blessing," quipped their detractors, and later observers saw some truth in this statement.[42] Yet foreign policy considerations also induced the estates to seek compromise and conciliation, as can be seen in a letter by the Styrian deputies to their Carinthian and Carniolian counterparts during the early phase of the Ferdinandean counterreformation in 1599. In spite of their profound disagreement with his religious policies, the Styrians advised against withholding military assistance from the archduke. Not only would this expose their own territories and the rest of the empire to devastating attacks by "the highly superior archenemy."[43] Local recalcitrance would also allow the monarch to post foreign mercenaries along the border, which could hardly be in the estates' interest.

The constitutional complexity of the Habsburg empire, by contrast, has not always received sufficient attention. The Peace of Augsburg only covered territories within the Holy Roman Empire. In addition, the Habsburgs' position was as yet more fragile in the lands of the Hungarian and Bohemian crowns than in their more established domains. Especially in Hungary, the Habsburgs, who initially only controlled a minor part of the kingdom, faced an in part religiously motivated resistance that could instrumentalize the conflict between sultan and emperor for its own objectives. The Austrian estates, in turn, paid close attention to the concessions granted to their Hungarian and Bohemian peers, with whom the geographically adjacent Danubian territories repeatedly cooperated as well.[44]

Confessional conditions in other Habsburg domains provided concrete arguments for debates with the monarch. When the archduke and subsequent emperor Matthias contended in 1609 that his religious conscience would not allow him to accommodate the estates' confessional demands, the Upper Austrian nobleman Erasmus von Tschernembl replied tersely that the much farther-reaching concessions recently granted to the Hungarians apparently had been reconcilable with the princely conscience.[45] Thus, the position of the Habsburgs differed from those of minor imperial princes who tried to impress their religious orientation onto a relatively small and homogenous populace. Not until the peak of their power in the 1620s did the Habsburgs feel strong enough to remove the last relevant religious liberties in the Austrian and Bohemian lands. In Silesia, this proved impossible even then.

A coordinated suppression of religious dissent was further impeded by the administrative division of the hereditary lands. During the late 1500s and early 1600s, in part even beyond, the Habsburgs' Alpine and Danubian provinces were divided among different branches of the family. The archduchy of Austria (below and above the Enns) comprised modernday Lower and Upper Austria, while Styria, Carinthia, and Carniola—together with Gorizia and parts of the Adriatic littoral—formed an entity called Inner Austria, or Austria Interior, with Graz as its capital. Finally, the later provinces of Tyrol and Vorarlberg were ruled from Innsbruck together with the old Habsburg domains in southwestern Germany; they were known as Tyrol and the *Vorlande*, or Austria Anterior.

These subdivisions also surfaced in the region's religious history. After its predominantly urban Lutheranism and comparatively strong Anabaptist movement had been suppressed, Tyrol and much of the remainder of Austria Anterior developed into a Catholic confessional territory reminiscent of Bavaria.[46] In noticeable contrast to their Austrian peers, the nobles

40 *A House Dividing*

of Tyrol never turned into a vanguard of Protestantism. Among possible explanations for this divergence, one may cite the area's geographical, political, and cultural closeness to both Bavaria and the Italian-speaking south, where reformist ideas failed to establish a lasting foothold. In general, the nobility in the Tyrolean territories was politically weak and overshadowed by the monarch; in the area that developed into modern-day Vorarlberg, it did not even form an estate of its own.[47] The violence associated with the peasant uprising of 1525, combined with the prevalence of Anabaptism and its more radical challenge to the existing social order, further reinforced the identification of Tyrolean elites with the dynasty's uncompromising denominational policy.[48] The confessional offensive that also reached Austria Anterior in the second half of the sixteenth century could therefore focus most of its attention on the reinvigoration of popular piety and its adaptation to Tridentine doctrine rather than on the subjugation and conversion of Protestant recalcitrants.

In the remaining subdivisions of the Habsburgs' Alpine patrimony, Protestantism became the majority religion, even if exact numbers are difficult to ascertain and the initial lack of a Protestant church structure delayed a clear-cut denominational break. A sizeable segment of the population held intermediary or ambivalent religious views, which bridged the theological divide. With the gradual formation of parallel ecclesiastical spheres, however, this group was shrinking.

The archduchy of Austria formed the cradle and core of the hereditary lands, which gave it special significance and visibility to the dynasty. All the more notable was the breakthrough of Protestantism in large parts of the territory.[49] Due to the harsh edicts and prohibitions against heterodoxy, religious dissenters proceeded cautiously, which made the passage from reformist Catholicism to explicit Protestantism almost imperceptible. Since it occurred under the roof of the established church, doctrinal differentiation proved difficult to control, unlike the clear break with ecclesial institutions undertaken by the Anabaptists. Even if pastors openly or implicitly preached Lutheran doctrine, they formally remained within the existing church structure and subordinate to the sitting Catholic bishop. Most of them continued to define themselves as proponents of the one and catholic church, albeit in its true and unadulterated form; at the same time, many pre-Tridentine Catholics adopted individual symbols of reform as well. The absence of separate ecclesial structures with firm hierarchies and ordinances allowed broad doctrinal diversity among self-declared followers of the new creed. The resulting openness constituted both a strength and a weakness. On the one hand, it provided ample room for individual identification with the reform movement. On the other, it presaged the internal conflicts and fissures that weakened Austrian Protestantism in later decades, not least of all between doctrinal moderates and the more fundamentalist followers of Matthias Flacius and other so-called Gnesio-Lutherans.[50]

By the middle of the century, however, a dissimilation into separate confessional communities was well on its way. At territorial diets, demands to hear the pure gospel gave way to demands to legalize the Augsburg Confession.[51] In this process, most nobles and municipalities of the archduchy chose Lutheranism, and at least half of the local parishes can be identified with the new creed.[52] This Protestant culture also expressed itself in well-reputed educational institutions, such as the grammar schools in Lower Austrian Horn and Loosdorf and the estates school in Linz.[53] Conditions in Upper Austria proved especially conducive to religious reform since the region strove to secure its independent territorial status. Geographically removed from the court in Vienna and administered by an autonomous governor and diet, the territory could chart its political and religious course more independently from the dynasty than the Lower Austrian heartland. The territorial estates also exploited the latent rivalry between the bishop of Passau, frequently beholden to the Wittelsbach dukes in Munich, and the Habsburg court. By the middle of the sixteenth century, Upper Austria had become so predominantly Lutheran that the local prelates appealed to Ferdinand to permit the utraquist communion and lift the provision of celibacy so as not to lose the remaining Catholics in clergy and populace.[54]

In the German-speaking regions of Inner Austria, religious conditions resembled those in the archduchy. Whereas the Latin and Slavic districts in the south largely remained Catholic, much of Styria and Carinthia turned Lutheran. This was especially pronounced among nobles and burghers but also among the German-speaking peasants of Carinthia and Upper Styria, even if the Reformation made some inroads among Slavophones as well.[55] Foreign Catholics repeatedly expressed their dismay at local religious conditions. At his arrival in Graz in 1580, the papal nuncio Germanico Malaspina found but five Catholic aristocrats in the duchies of Inner Austria.[56] As late as 1604, Bishop Martin Brenner of Seckau reported that only three of Klagenfurt's established citizens adhered to Catholicism.[57] Even though the specifics of these alarmist assessments are open to question, the basic outlines are confirmed by other indicators, not least of all by the subsequent course of recatholization. One has to remember, however, that denominational boundaries formed in a gradual manner. The duality of Catholic ruler and predominantly Protestant estates delayed the institutionalization of religious heterodoxy.

42 A House Dividing

One cannot talk of a distinct Lutheran church in Carinthia until 1566; in Styria, its establishment did not antedate the religious concessions of 1572 and 1578.

Even then, this institutionalization commenced on a minimalist level. In order to refute incriminations of sectarianism, the Carinthian estates commissioned a statement of belief, which 26 Lutheran pastors formulated in 1566. Since the Peace of Augsburg had restricted toleration to adherents of the Augustana, the *Confessio Carinthica* emphasized the Lutheran orthodoxy of Protestant ecclesial life in Carinthia.[58] It countered accusations of sewing discord among the faithful by defining Lutheranism as an expression of the ancient apostolic and truly catholic creed. Far from being apostates, Protestants were espousing the gospel in its original form.[59] Lutheran assemblies also began to develop a provincial superstructure, which was cemented further through the Inner Austrian church and school ordinance of 1578. This ecclesial constitution homogenized doctrine as well as ritual and devised institutional structures and procedures, including regulations for the selection and appointment of clergy. To supervise ecclesiastic life, the ordinance instituted provincial church ministries, but the diets also retained considerable influence.

Ecclesial consolidation was only possible because Austrian Protestants had secured a judicial basis for exercising their faith. At no other time during the century did conditions seem so conducive. Ferdinand I was to be succeeded by his son Maximilian in the Holy Roman Empire and the archduchy, albeit not in Inner Austria and Tyrol, which were to go to his brothers Charles and Ferdinand, respectively.[60] As a rare exception among leading Habsburgs, Maximilian II was rumored to harbor Lutheran sympathies.[61] He engaged in reformist conduct, such as taking the Eucharist under both kinds. He also cultivated good relations with Protestant princes in the empire, especially the new elector Moritz of Saxony. His court chaplain Johann Pfauser regularly criticized the church and moved from Catholic irenicism to a more openly Lutheran position after Ferdinand had forced his resignation in 1560.[62]

The entire dynasty was worried. The Spanish relatives kept a close eye on the heir apparent and repeatedly intervened in Vienna. Ferdinand himself may have become less uncompromising than his Iberian cousins, but he, too, was convinced that the established faith had served the Habsburgs well. Faced with intense pressure to conform to Catholic orthodoxy, Maximilian at some point contemplated taking refuge with Protestant princes, but the latter proved so unreceptive to a step of this magnitude that the seriousness of the plan was not put to the test.[63] In the end, Maximilian became more mindful of the political realities and

A House Dividing   43

disillusioned with the internal disunity of German Protestantism. To assuage his father, he took an oath to remain within the Catholic Church in 1562.[64] By the time he acceded to the imperial throne two years later, any inclination toward outright conversion had passed, even if he continued to question Catholic dogma and criticize the curia's reluctance to reform.

During the first diet of Maximilian's regency in 1564, the Protestant estates of Lower Austria invoked his father's intention to resolve the religious conflict and requested toleration of the pure and true religion of the Augsburg Confession.[65] Maximilian responded in the evasive manner of his predecessor, triggering an increasingly irritated exchange that continued for several years. By 1568, however, the emperor had begun to reconsider his stance. The war against the Turks proceeded costly and ineffectually, and the imperial court had amassed substantial debts. In the Netherlands, the coercive confessional policies of his cousin Philip had provoked open rebellion, whereas France and Poland-Lithuania were experimenting with limited tolerance for religious dissenters. Maximilian's relationship with Spain and the curia was strained, as these two most rigid proponents of Catholic orthodoxy proved more generous with uninvited advice and admonitions than with financial and military assistance.

The Protestant estates grasped the opportunity. They declared their willingness to assume Maximilian's debts in the amount of 2.5 million florins but indicated that they expected palpable religious concessions in return. In view of his financial calamities and the elusiveness of religious rapprochement, Maximilian granted the Lower Austrian aristocracy the freedom to practice Lutheranism on their estates and in the towns and villages subject to them. In the wording of the assurance of 1571, which confirmed and specified the concessions, members of the noble estates were entitled to use the Augsburg Confession "for themselves and their households on their estates and in their palaces and houses (but not inside our own towns and market towns); in the countryside and in their patrimonial churches, for their subjects as well."[66] The Upper Austrian nobles received corresponding rights in exchange for a separate contribution of 1.2 million florins.[67]

These concessions marked a breakthrough in the legal status of Austrian Lutherans, but they did not establish unrestricted freedom of worship. Not only were there enough qualifications and imprecisions to leave ample room for conflicting interpretation. In a step that proved ominous for the long-time preservation of religious privileges, Maximilian had already separated the urban curia from the other estates in 1566.[68] Thus,

44 A House Dividing

the territorial municipalities of Lower Austria were not covered by the privileges granted to the nobles and subsequently served as convenient launching grounds of recatholization.

In Inner Austria, legalization encountered even more resistance. Archduke Charles II was a committed Catholic who personally opposed concessions to religious heterodoxy; his marriage to a Wittelsbach princess linked him to the Bavarian heartland of Catholic restoration. Yet Charles, too, suffered from a chronic shortness of funds, which only the estates could remedy. The latter had closely followed the historic developments in the archduchy; it was no coincidence that matters came to a head in Graz shortly after Maximilian's assurance of 1571. When the archduke invoked his prerogatives as delineated in the Peace of Augsburg, the Inner Austrian estates pointedly cited the concessions in the archduchy. If the emperor had granted the nobles of Upper and Lower Austria the right to practice Lutheranism, they could see no reason why they themselves needed to be treated differently.[69] Faced with massive opposition, Charles had to relent and make comparable concessions in what came to be known as the Pacification of Graz.

Based on their improved legal status, the estates established a separate Lutheran church structure. Since the archduke's financial liabilities quickly increased again, he had to confirm and slightly expand his concessions at the diet of 1578.[70] During this territorial assembly in the Styrian city of Bruck, the archduke assured the estates not only that they and their subjects would not be prevented from exercising their Lutheran faith on their patrimonial lands but also that he had no intention of expelling Lutheran preachers and educators from the provincial capitals of Graz, Klagenfurt, and Ljubljana or the regional center of Judenburg.[71] Charles refused to confirm his declaration in writing, however, and before long conflicting versions of its content were in circulation. As in Lower Austria, the disagreements primarily concerned the status of territorial towns and market towns. Many had a Protestant majority, whose legal position remained vulnerable. In the end, the interpretation of the pacification came to depend on the respective distribution of power rather than its wording.

Catholic Reform and Counterreformation in Austria

The Lutheran ecclesiastical structure in the Alpine hereditary lands was formalized at a time when the official church had recovered and laid the foundations for a counteroffensive. In the Protestant Reformation, the Catholic Church faced a profound challenge, which it met in different ways. In the beginning, the curia tried to squelch dissent with the instruments historically applied against heretics. Lacking the power to directly enforce its prescriptions, it depended on secular rulers. In this respect, however, the religious reform movement of the 1500s differed from its predecessors, as important princes refused to execute papal bulls against the new teachings and their protagonists. A troubled church hierarchy watched with dismay as a growing number of monarchs came out in support of the religious rebellion.

Yet outright rejection of the reformers was not the only course available. Within the clergy, too, there was an awareness of spiritual and structural deficits. The need for ecclesial reform was not only raised from the outside but also had many champions within the church. In fact, the founding fathers of Protestantism originated within the Catholic Church and initially saw it as their mission to reform their established spiritual home. Long after the chasm between Protestant reformers and Rome had become unmistakable, there were still those who hoped that moderate concessions, such as the dispensing of communion in both kinds, could facilitate the eventual reintegration of break-away forces into the Catholic Church. Emperor Charles V, who had a compelling personal interest in pacifying the emergent conflict within his realm, promoted these efforts, which were also supported by such influential clerics as the Venetian-born cardinal Gasparo Contarini.[72]

In the end, the Catholic leadership chose a different path. At the Council of Trent, it promoted doctrinal purity and refused to compromise with the reform movements.[73] When it was first conceived, the great council of the church reflected a different ambition. It was Charles V who hoped that this assembly could assuage the calls for a national council that were sounding throughout Germany and resolve the religious schism that had torn western Christianity apart. Therefore, the council was to be held on imperial soil and strive for reconciliation within a reformed Catholic Church. By the time it finally opened in 1545, however, much of the impetus for rapprochement had faded. Protestants were no longer interested in negotiating under the leadership of the pope, and the curia had given up any hope for an amicable return of the heretics to the fold. Even though the council convened within the borders of the Holy Roman Empire, it was dominated by clerics from Italy and southern Europe. Its agenda was set by the curia, which called for a reaffirmation of Catholic doctrine and its demarcation from heresy. Protestantism was to be confronted head-on by a reinvigorated Catholicism rather than appeased through concessions. At the same time, the council fathers strengthened church discipline and the centralizing tendencies of the Holy See.

46   *A House Dividing*

Thus, the Council of Trent became an important milestone in the organizing of a Catholic countermovement to the Protestant advance. Another crucial impulse emanated from a new breed of activist and highly disciplined orders, exemplified most visibly by the Society of Jesus.[74] These monastic congregations were not established primarily to combat heresy, and in countries without a significant Protestant presence, they pursued and reinvigorated traditional pastoral and charitable activities. In central and northern Europe, however, the new orders formed spearheads of Catholic reassertion vis-à-vis religious dissenters. Capuchins provided spiritual support to Catholics under Protestant rule, not least among them the Irish. Jesuits established successful schools, in which the children of not always freely converted burghers and noblemen were reintegrated into the Catholic sphere, and established academies that trained missionaries for the reconverting of apostate populations all the way to Scandinavia.[75] Thousands of graduates from Jesuit institutions of learning subsequently staffed the higher echelons of the church hierarchy, successfully implanting the spirit of Tridentine Catholicism throughout Europe. At the same time, many members of the society also served the papacy in their capacity as princely confessors and confidants, with unique access to the hearts and minds of increasingly absolutist rulers.

The latter half of the sixteenth century has therefore been designated as the onset of a counterreformation. In its broader meaning, the term denotes Catholic efforts to revitalize the church and reverse the progress of Protestantism. As such, it was coined in the late 1700s and introduced into the historical debate during the subsequent century to characterize the period that followed the initial advance of reformist thought. Its semantic connotation as a mere reaction to external challenges as well as its widespread association with the suppression of dissent induced a number of Catholic scholars to take exception to the wholesale subsumption of a historical era under this term, however. They considered it more appropriate to divide the phenomenon into two complementary aspects. There existed an external and political effort, which was typically executed in cooperation with local governments. For this aspect, the term Counterreformation has also been accepted by decidedly Catholic interpreters, even if some of them originally preferred the wording of Catholic restoration. In their eyes, however, the internal process of Catholic reform was more important for understanding the eventual consolidation of the church.[76]

This renewed vigor and conviction displayed many facets. Improved education and stricter visitations improved the quality of pastoral care. The Church combated simony and pluralism, that is, the purchasing of ecclesiastical offices as well as their inappropriate accumulation. It also became more serious about enforcing clerical celibacy and putting an end to the widespread practice of priestly concubinates. As a reward, post-Tridentine clerics could expect moderately higher remunerations than their predecessors, which had the additional advantage of attracting more qualified applicants to the priesthood. A better-trained and better-paid clergy, visibly elevated above its parishioners through education, demeanor, and lifestyle, gained renewed respect and grew more naturally into its designated role as social and spiritual leader of the congregation.

Many efforts went into attracting new believers. Far from restricting themselves to combating Protestantism, the new religious orders put special emphasis on converting non-Christians, establishing an early network of global missions both within and beyond the gradually developing overseas empires of Spain and Portugal. With their diligence and zeal, the Jesuits promoted Catholic scholarship and attracted ambitious students to their academies. Notwithstanding their elitist reputation, they successfully developed their own theatrical genre, which combined popular appeal with an unmistakable spiritual message. At the same time, ecclesial institutions made skillful use of art and architecture, so that Catholic restoration and Baroque became all but synonymous in many parts of Europe.

The church also succeeded at reinvigorating popular piety. Traditional pilgrimages, shrines, and pageants were rediscovered and transformed. Dynastic cults merged with Tridentine Catholicism, not least of all in Austria and Bavaria. Marian columns shot up to celebrate the survival of pestilence and foreign attacks. Established saints' cults gained new life; new ones were added. All of the era's canonizations honored clerics, many of whom had served in reformed religious orders; their ranks included Ignatius of Loyola, who had established the Society of Jesus, as well as the founders of the Lazarists, the Piarists, and the Visitadines.[77] Yet also important reformers, mystics, bishops, and missionaries were well represented, underlining the significance ascribed to ecclesial activists.

Thus, both the Catholic Church and its Protestant counterparts defined their spiritual essence ever more sharply and demarcated themselves from the denominational Other. The ensuing formalization of creeds and doctrines finalized the division of western Christianity and is also known as the process of confessionalization. This term was introduced into the debate by the German historians Heinz Schilling and Wolfgang Reinhard, building on Ernst Walter Zeeden's postwar concept of confession-building.[78] Whereas Zeeden primarily strove to transcend the conceptual juxtaposition of Protestant Reformation and Catholic

48 A House Dividing

Counterreformation by highlighting the similarities of religious reorientation in early modern Europe, his successors broadened the comparative approach in line with a renewed German focus on social history, as expressed in the Bielefeld school and its history of society. Schilling diagnosed a continued integration of religion and politics during the confessional period. Thus, matters of church were at the same time matters of state, and the concept of confessionalization tried to join religious and societal dimensions.[79] The interpenetration of these spheres surfaced most visibly in the parallel development of confessional churches and early modern states, with confessionalization regularly serving as a precondition for the closer integration of European polities.[80] The theoretical linkage was provided by Gerhard Oestreich's concept of social discipline, in which the German historian described the absolutist state's attempt to govern all aspects of human life.[81] Social control expressed itself, *inter alia*, in an increased bureaucratization and militarization of society, as well as in more invasive legal and behavioral codes, which subjected formerly private aspects of life to public regulation. Since contemporary confessional bodies provided many of the guidelines and legitimizations of this societal transformation, in which they also participated as agents of supervision and enforcement, Wolfgang Reinhard defined confessionalization as the first step in Oestreich's process of social disciplining.[82] In a symbiotic relationship, the confessional churches drew on the resources of the government to implement their religious standardization, which in turn provided a crucial foundation of political centralization and state-building. Regardless of their doctrinal intent, Catholic restoration as well as Lutheran and Calvinist confession-building also functioned as important agents of modernization.[83]

As the concepts of Counterreformation and Catholic reform before, the paradigm of confessionalization also encountered criticism. Next to objections to its periodization and its implicit leveling of confessional differences, there also were several challenges to its fundamental approach.[84] Winfried Schulze doubted the preeminence of confessional cultures and emphasized the rise of religious tolerance and coexistence, which prepared the way for the subsequent secularization of society.[85] Other scholars pointed to the success of state-building in multidenominational and religiously tolerant polities such as the Netherlands, which questioned the linkage of confession- and state-building, and to the feasibility of confessionalization from below.[86] In general, the most severe criticism of confessionalization as an explanatory concept was directed at the central role it seemed to assign to the state. Based on his research on church discipline in the reformed Swiss canton of Berne, Heinrich Richard Schmidt ascribed the success of social control not so much to governmental institutions but to local communities.[87] Schmidt saw the fatal flaw of the paradigm in the superimposition of Oestreich's model of social-disciplining, specifically developed for matters of politics, onto Zeeden's focus on ecclesial bodies. Rather than introducing a broader social history approach to the study of early modern religious cultures, the concept of confessionalization had therefore reintroduced a state-centered history from above. Both Wolfgang Reinhard and Heinz Schilling emphatically rejected this assessment, however. In response to Schmidt, Reinhard described a one-dimensional opposition of government and populace as theoretically unproductive and cited the Swedish Reformation as an example of the symbiosis of communal and governmental confessionalization. Rather than juxtaposing micro- and macrohistorical approaches, researchers ought to combine them.[88]

These continuing controversies demonstrate that the scholarly debate about Counterreformation, Catholic reform, and confessionalization is far from exhausted. On some level, all three terms have competed for primacy in the description of the overall phenomenon.[89] Strictly speaking, however, they prioritize different aspects. In the current study, the focus lies on the political aspects, that is, on the cooperation between church and rulers in the restoration of Catholic hegemony in the territories of Catholic monarchs and thus on the Counterreformation in the narrow sense of the word. There is no doubt, however, that these political steps were paralleled by an internal rejuvenation, which tried to restore the moral spirit of the church and reaffirm its core values.

After the Habsburgs had failed in their initial attempts to bar Protestant inroads into their territories, Lutheranism expanded in a relatively quiet and inconspicuous manner. Since they faced the opposition of the dynasty, which after 1555 was able to invoke the Peace of Augsburg, Protestants had to tread lightly. They had to forego many public manifestations of their creed and wrest individual concessions from successive rulers. These concessions were frequently secured through large financial contributions; at the same time, they provoked a backlash among the Catholic hierarchy both inside the Habsburg Monarchy and beyond. Encouraged by the successful placating of Lutheran imperial princes, the promising example of the Bavarian Wittelsbachs, and the renewed vigor of international Catholicism, both clergy and dynasty became increasingly determined to stop and reverse the progress of Lutheranism in the hereditary lands.

In Inner Austria, the 1578 Pacification of Bruck marked a turning point in denominational relations. On the one hand, it represented the as

50   A House Dividing

of then most comprehensive affirmation of Protestant religious rights in this section of the Habsburg patrimony by granting at least preliminary freedom of conscience to a large part of the populace. On the other, it triggered the clandestine Munich Conference of the following year, in which Charles II of Inner Austria, Ferdinand II of Tyrol, and William V of Bavaria agreed on a program for the recatholization of Inner Austria.[90] The religious concessions of the pacification needed to be cancelled "fein tacite und per indirectum," as the German-Latin original emphasized, that is, in an inconspicuous and indirect manner.[91] The strategy was developed in greater detail in the introductory remarks, which established that these privileges should not be sustained but rescinded as soon as this seemed feasible. So ambitious an objective could be accomplished not through an official revocation but through a prudent strategy that bypassed the diet. The focus should be on actions rather than words and on gradual progress rather than on an immediate and all-out assault.[92]

The program established at Munich was symptomatic for the early phase of recatholization in the hereditary lands, and it proved highly successful. Even though Charles began to implement is principles, primarily by investing reliable Catholics with public offices and curtailing the exercise of Lutheranism in urban communities, it remained up to his successor, the later emperor Ferdinand II, to execute it fully.[93] Ferdinand, who was the son of a Wittelsbach princess and educated by Jesuit teachers in Bavarian Ingolstadt, considered it a moral duty to restore Catholic hegemony in his domains. To him, this represented more than a political necessity; he also regarded it his duty as a monarch to assure the eternal salvation of his subjects.[94] His confessor reported that Ferdinand "often asserted both in writing and orally that he would much rather and more readily renounce his provinces and kingdoms than wittingly miss an opportunity to extend the faith; that he would rather live on bread and water alone, go into exile with his wife and children equipped only with a staff, beg his bread from door to door, and be cut and torn to pieces than suffer any longer the harm done to God and the Church by the heretics in the territories under his rule."[95] No matter the rhetoric hyberbole of emperor and biographer, confessional policy in Central Europe had undoubtedly entered a new phase.

The more stringent tone in religious matters already surfaced during the negotiations that preceded Ferdinand's accession. Traditionally, these negotiations presented a window of opportunity for the estates to secure special rights and privileges from the ruler. In December 1596 the Styrian estates formulated their standpoint in petitions to the successor designate. They beseeched Ferdinand to resolve outstanding denominational

A House Dividing 51

conflicts according to the religious pacification of 1578 and argued that they were not bound to swear allegiance until the monarch had affirmed their traditional liberties.[96] The young archduke had enjoyed ample time to prepare his response, however, and steadfastly refused to confirm his predecessors' religious concessions.[97] In his view, the estates owed him unconditional homage; if they held grievances, they could subsequently appeal to him for redress. The delegates persisted, but Ferdinand had nothing more to say. In order to break the stalemate, the Styrian estates decided to interpret this silence as tacit approval. On 12 December 1596 they paid homage to their new prince; the subsequent day they informed their Carinthian and Carniolian peers and assured them that all their privileges had been upheld.[98] In early 1597 Carinthians and Carniolians followed suit.

It would not be long before the estatist interpretation proved an illusion. In September 1598 Ferdinand ordered the curial officers to abolish the church and school ministry in Graz and Judenburg as well as his other municipalities; the attached pastors were banned from the country.[99] A month later, the turn came to the Protestant teachers and ministers in Carniolian Ljubljana (Laibach).[100] A torrent of protests and supplications accomplished nothing. With undisguised sarcasm, the archduke wondered why the Protestant nobles felt violated in their freedom of conscience. Had not their preachers denied the sanctity of rites and proposed the universal priesthood of believers? If they yearned to receive the genuine sacraments, however, they could always turn to their legitimate Catholic priests.[101]

The estates did not shrink from using their sharpest weapon, the temporary withholding of revenues, but Ferdinand unwaveringly stayed the course. In June of 1600 he felt confident enough to extend his proscriptions to Carinthia, the most Protestant of his provinces. By that time, however, the removal of preachers and ministers no longer sufficed. The Inner Austrian Counterreformation reached an early climax in the campaigns of reformation commissions, whose leadership was entrusted to the Swabian-born bishop of Seckau, Martin Brenner.[102] Accompanied by a military detachment, these commissions assembled the inhabitants of towns and villages, appealed to them through sermons, and ordered them to return to Catholicism. In the course of a two-month campaign through Carinthia in the fall of 1600, four churches and their cemeteries were destroyed, 27 pastors and teachers expelled, 1500 heretical books burned, and thousands of Protestants outwardly converted.[103] The burghers in the regional centers of Villach and Klagenfurt lost their ecclesial institutions as well. Four years later, however, Bishop Brenner was forced

52   A House Dividing

to reexamine Klagenfurt, and in remote mountain districts of Styria and especially Carinthia, Protestantism was merely driven underground.

 Ferdinand's policy vindicated the careful gradualism that had been recommended to his father at the Munich Conference and impressed on the new archduke by Georg Stobäus, the sitting bishop of Lavant in Carinthia.[104] Not all of its progress can be based on the successful concealment of long-time objectives. Individual nobles in Inner Austria harbored no illusions about their monarch and predicted that he would ultimately rescind the religious privileges of the aristocracy, notwithstanding his initial focus on townspeople and peasants.[105] Nonetheless, the estates restricted their resistance to petitions, protests, and requests for support from sympathetic governments. Although the increasingly annoyed archduke repeatedly informed them that he would rather risk all his possessions than change his confessional policies, the estates did not give up hope.[106] Indeed, the Lutheran nobility was able to obstruct and delay the progress of recatholization temporarily. This may explain why a Protestant was elected mayor of Klagenfurt as late as 1622 and the governmental religious edicts did not unfold their full impact on the Carinthian peasants of Paternion as long as they were subject to Lutheran lords.[107] Such acts of defiance did not alter the fundamental course of events, however. In the end, the Khevenhüller seigniors had to emigrate und surrender Paternion to an avid proponent of the Counterreformation, and the audacious election in Klagenfurt only resulted in an annulment and a severe admonition by the archduke, who reminded the city magistrates that no one could be admitted to citizenship, not to mention public office, unless he was strongly committed to the Catholic faith. By 1630 Catholicism had been restored as the public religion of Inner Austria.

It was the dynasty that had initiated the recatholization of the Inner Austrian provinces. The local clergy was weak and needed substantial reinforcement from abroad. Of pivotal importance was the contribution of the Jesuits, whom Archduke Charles invited to his patrimony in the early 1570s.[108] In 1573 he commissioned a Jesuit college in Graz, which was regularly expanded until it finally became the basis of a newly founded university in 1585. This educational offensive was expressly directed against the flourishing grammar school of the Protestant estates. Even though its initial success was limited, the university brought forth leading protagonists of recatholization and finally achieved a monopoly on higher education after the dissolution of the Protestant church ministry in 1598.

In the archduchy, local clerics and lay activists played a much stronger role. To be sure, the accession of Maximilian's son Rudolf to the throne in 1576 also marked a caesura in the confessional policies of the Austrian heartland. The young monarch had spent the formative years of his adolescence in Spain and displayed none of the confessional ambiguities of his father. Indeed, within two years he had abolished the Lutheran center in the Estates Building and thus effectively banished Lutheran services from the confines of Vienna.[109] The government also installed a Catholic city administration, prohibited the estates from distributing Lutheran literature, and supported the revival of Corpus Christi processions. In 1585 the acquisition of citizenship in Vienna was tied to taking confession and communion in the Catholic Church, and Protestant services became illegal in municipalities throughout Lower Austria.[110] Having removed Protestant worship from the territorial towns, the government was able to concentrate on the surrounding rural estates, which had turned into attractive alternatives. By requiring ministers to bar non-members from their services, the government struck a severe blow at Lutheran church attendance among commoners.

These initial steps were skillfully coordinated between Rudolf, who had made Prague his imperial residence, and his younger brother Ernst, whom he had installed as viceregent in Vienna. The imperial siblings avoided open breaches of sworn accords, while at the same time pushing their reinterpretations of potential legal ambiguities to the limit. Protestant nobles and burghers showered them with protests, only to be sent back and forth with conflicting accounts of the origins of legislation and the appropriate venue for redress. As a consequence, the resistance exhausted itself in a futile burst of undirected activism.

In the long run, the emperor's absence and increasing seclusion diminished his personal involvement in denominational conflicts. Yet in Lower Austria, at least, Catholic restoration was not dependent on the dynasty alone. The importance of Catholic laymen is exemplified by the jurist Georg Eder.[111] Born in 1523, Eder hailed from an impeccably Catholic background in Bavaria. The Wittelsbach duchy had not only developed into a bulwark of Catholic orthodoxy in its own right, but it also provided a much-needed contingent of German-speaking activists for the early Counterreformation in the Habsburg lands. In the 1540s, Eder's studies at the University of Cologne brought him into contact with the Society of Jesus, which was just beginning to gain a foothold on German territory. Most importantly, Eder became acquainted with Peter Canisius, one of the foremost theologians of the order. The connections established in Cologne proved useful for both sides. Eder evolved into a pivotal Catholic lay activist, who could always rely on the patronage of the Jesuits, with whom he identified intensely.[112] As a doctor of law with a thorough

54   A House Dividing

understanding of theology, he was a valuable asset, above all in public positions that were closed to religious orders.

After a short period as headmaster in Passau, Eder completed his legal studies in Vienna between 1550 and 1551. Upon graduation, his career took off quickly. Eder's arrival in the Austrian capital all but coincided with the founding of the city's first Jesuit college. But the predominantly foreign brethren, without sufficient knowledge of German, were seriously impeded in their initial outreach. Not so Eder, who held increasingly prestigious posts, culminating in an appointment to the imperial aulic council in 1563. Notwithstanding its name, which evoked its origins as an advisory body, this institution also served as one of the two high courts of the Holy Roman Empire. Whereas the imperial cameral court largely remained the domain of the imperial estates, the monarch fully controlled the aulic council.[113] Yet Eder also joined the University of Vienna, over which he presided as rector for 11 terms.

Even more so than as a public official, Eder made a name for himself as an outspoken promoter of Tridentine Catholicism. He published industriously, primarily works of a catechetical or propagandistic nature, for which he garnered high praise from influential church officials. Initially, he saw himself as a true advocate of the dynasty's confessional objectives, but after the accession of Maximilian II to the throne, especially, he became disillusioned with the irenicism of the Viennese court.[114] In 1573 Eder imperiled his political career by publishing a polemic attack on not only Protestants as such but also those whom he designated as the Christians of the court and disparaged as overly erudite weathervanes and appeasers who surrendered Catholic purity and wreaked more damage on the Church than even the heretics themselves.[115] These words provoked high-ranking colleagues of Eder as well as the emperor himself, who angrily ordered his councilor to surrender all copies of the book and desist from further theological publishing.

Maximilian's sharp response sent shockwaves through Catholic Europe, which was not used to activist coreligionists being reprimanded by a Habsburg ruler. While the monarch insisted on his authority to censure imperial officials, he did not remove Eder from either the aulic council or the university. The pugnacious lawyer continued to distribute religious tracts, especially after Maximilian had been succeeded by his son, and even the contentious *Evangelische Inquisition* soon returned into circulation. Yet in spite of the unmistakable signs of Catholic restoration under Rudolf II, Eder had lost faith in the Habsburg court. He felt that too many sought religious compromise and coexistence; they proclaimed to be Catholics, but not in a Jesuit way. To Eder, the response was clear—whoever was not like a Jesuit was not a Catholic at all.[116] Although he kept his domicile in Vienna, he found a new protector in the Bavarian Wittelsbachs, who employed their compatriot as a special correspondent in the city. In this function he regularly informed the court in Munich about political events in Austria, with a distinct focus on confessional conditions.[117]

Even more important than lay supporters were forces within the church. The local Catholic hierarchy was able to provide inspiration and leadership, even if it relied on the government to subdue Protestant resistance. The leading protagonist of this new ecclesial activism was Melchior Klesl. In telling contrast to the Bavarian Eder, the Viennese Klesl was born into a Lutheran family in 1552.[118] He was raised in his parental faith and still professed it into early adulthood until he turned to Catholicism under the influence of Jesuit theologian Georg Scherer. The young convert exchanged the University of Vienna for the local Jesuit college; he subsequently finished his theological studies at the preeminent German seminary of the order in Bavarian Ingolstadt.

In more ways than one, Klesl carried on the work of Georg Eder, even if his position was different and his impact more formidable. Upon his colleague's return to his country of birth, Klesl replaced him as religious *éminence grise* at the university, where he served as chancellor and subsequently also rector, and even continued the well-established correspondence with the Bavarian court.[119] Klesl did not enter Bavarian service, to be sure, but he, too, considered it beneficial to establish good contacts to the powerful vanguard of Catholic restoration in the empire. The Wittelsbachs could not only support him at the courts of Vienna and Prague, where Protestant and irenicist councilors impeded stricter policies, but also use their authority over Bavarian exclaves in the archduchy in favor of recatholization.[120]

Like Eder before him, Klesl combined confessional zeal with personal ambition. Soon after his graduation and ordination to the priesthood, he was appointed provost of St. Stephen's Cathedral and high-ranking official of the diocese of Passau, whose ecclesial jurisdiction included the archduchy. He subsequently rose to court chaplain and bishop of both Wiener Neustadt and Vienna. At the same time, he also held expressly political offices, such as privy councilor and special emissary of the emperor in sensitive international matters.

Klesl's foremost objective, however, was the restoration of Catholic supremacy in the hereditary lands. In his eyes, the internal rejuvenation of the Catholic clergy formed a prerequisite for any successful offensive against Lutheranism. As the diocese's vicar-general for Lower Austria,

56 A House Dividing

Klesl was well positioned to initiate reforms. He encountered substantial resistance, however, not only from the clerics whose conduct he reprimanded but also from his superiors in Passau, who advised him to show patience and proceed more cautiously. Not even the concubinate could be eradicated, complained Klesl to William of Bavaria, because suitable replacements for dismissed clerics were in short supply.[121]

In 1590 Rudolf II appointed Klesl reformer general of Lower Austria, formally entrusting him with the recatholization of the territory. This promotion also marked a subtle but significant change in governmental policy. The publicly confirmed concessions to the nobility remained in force, but only in the narrowest interpretation possible; the numerous decrees against religious transgressions were strictly enforced. Klesl delineated his strategy in a memorandum to the vice regent, Archduke Ernst.[122] Since he considered it impossible to immediately rescind the religious privileges of the noble estates, he advised to target non-protected groups first. Most important was the final eradication of heterodoxy in Vienna and other municipalities by preventing the attendance of Lutheran services in surrounding communities. To accomplish this objective, Klesl not only suggested stricter punishments but also the repossession of key estates such as Vösendorf and Hernals.[123] Once the urban population had been returned to Catholicism, the nobles should be admonished to restrict their religious services to themselves and their households. If they respected these ramifications, religious conditions in Austria would improve considerably. If they refused, they would bear the blame for a revocation of the concession.[124]

These recommendations echoed the principles established at the Munich Conference and closely mirrored policies in Inner Austria. During the initial phase of recatholization, it was more promising to isolate the nobility than to challenge its confirmed privileges. Through the large-scale removal of ministers and the conversion of townspeople and peasants, Lutheranism was to lose its popular foundation. In the end, the remaining religious liberties would degenerate into an empty shell, to be pushed over at will. Even if this policy could not be implemented immediately in the archduchy, its success in neighboring Inner Austria confirms its eminent political potential.

Conclusion

The Protestant Reformation spread rapidly in the Habsburgs' hereditary lands. It was popularized by itinerant preachers, by personal contacts with the early centers of the reform movement, and not least of all by an encompassing literature, which acquainted the literate segment of the population with the new tenets. From the very beginning, it was interconnected with wider social and political issues. The peasant wars of 1525–1526 visibly displayed the interpenetration of spiritual and political impulses.

The new religious ideas touched broad segments of the Austrian populace. Only in the westernmost provinces could this development be stopped early, aided by the successful suppression of the locally strong Anabaptist movement and its joint demand for social and spiritual reform. In the remaining provinces, Lutheranism seemed destined to establish itself as the majority religion, especially among the societal elites in aristocracy and urban patriciate.

Yet religious conditions in Austria were determined by the firm adherence of the ruling dynasty to the old church. As was the case throughout much of Europe, monarchs decisively shaped confessional politics. The Peace of Augsburg epitomized a development in which the Protestant estates of the Holy Roman Empire acknowledged the emperor's religious authority over his vast patrimony in exchange for the confessional autonomy of their own lands. Thus, a religious reform movement that had reverberated throughout most of the empire was ultimately restricted to those territories in which the rulers had embraced it as well.

Church and dynasty subsequently embarked on returning the imperial hereditary lands to Catholicism. This process took time, however, because the Habsburg territories were so diverse and geographically disjunct that the authorities had to contend with divergent laws, traditions, and political systems. Moreover, Protestantism had not only taken firm roots in large segments of the populace but had made particular progress among the territorial nobles, the monarchy's main contenders for political power. Therefore, the struggle for religious authority increasingly merged with the struggle for political preeminence. The conceptual foundations of this struggle will be examined in the subsequent chapter.

Notes

1. For an introduction to late-medieval Christianity, see Francis Rapp, *L'Église et la vie religieuse en Occident à la fin du Moyen Âge* (Paris, 1980); Robert N. Swanson, *Religion and Devotion in Europe, c. 1215-c. 1515* (Cambridge, England, 1995); and John Bossy, *Christianity in the West, 1400–1700* (Oxford, 1985).

   This general religious coherence did not prevent a social and regional diversity of observance, however, as can be seen in such works as Eamon Duffy, *The Stripping of the Altars: Traditional Religion in England, c.1400-c.1580* (New Haven, CT, 1992).

58 A House Dividing

2. For an introduction to the interconnections of Humanism and religious reform, see Lewis W. Spitz, *The Religious Renaissance of the German Humanists* (Cambridge, MA, 1963), and Delio Cantimori, *Umanesimo e religione nel Rinascimento* (Torino, 1975). See also Alister McGrath, *The Intellectual Origins of the European Reformation*, 2nd ed. (Oxford, 2004).

3. For recent overviews of the reformation era, see Euan Cameron, *The European Reformation* (Oxford, 1991); James D. Tracy, *Europe's Reformations, 1450–1650* (Lanhan, MD, 1999); Diarmaid MacCullough, *Reformation: Europe's House Divided, 1490–1700* (London, 2003); and Carter Lindberg, *The European Reformations*, 2nd ed. (Malden, MA, 2010).

4. For an introduction to the diverse experiences of European reform movements, see Ronnie Po-Chia Hsia, ed., *A Companion to the Reformation World* (Oxford, 2004). For East Central Europe, see also Howard Louthan and Graeme Murdock, eds., *A Companion to the Reformation in Central Europe* (Leiden, 2015).

5. For the Croatian experience, see Joachim Bahlcke, "Außenpolitik, Konfession und kollektive Identitätsbildung: Kroatien und Innerösterreich im historischen Vergleich," in *Konfessionalisierung in Ostmitteleuropa: Wirkungen des religiösen Wandels im 16. und 17. Jahrhundert in Staat, Gesellschaft und Kultur*, ed. Joachim Bahlcke and Arno Strohmeyer (Stuttgart, 1999), 193–209.

6. The literature on the English Reformation is far too extensive to be presented in detail here. Important modern interpretations were A. G. Dickens, *The English Reformation*, 2nd ed. (London, 1989); G. R. Elton, *Reform and Reformation: England 1509–1558* (London, 1977); Christopher Haigh, *English Reformations: Religion, Politics and Society under the Tudors* (Oxford, 1993); Stanford Lehmberg, *The Reformation Parliament, 1529–1536* (Cambridge, England, 1970); David Starkey, *The Reign of Henry VIII: Personalities and Politics* (London, 1985); Diarmaid MacCullach, *The Later Reformation in England, 1547–1603*, 2nd ed. (Basingstoke, England, 2001); and idem, *Thomas Cranmer: A Life* (New Haven, CT, 1998). For a historiographical overview of major contributions in the second half of the twentieth century, see also Patrick Collinson, "The English Reformation 1945–1995," in *Companion to Historiography*, ed. Michael Bentley (London, 1997), 336–360.

7. For introductions to the history of the Protestant Reformation in Scandinavia, see Ole Peter Grell, ed., *The Scandinavian Reformation: From Evangelical Movement to Institutionalisation of Reform* (Cambridge, England, 1995); James L. Larson, *Reforming the North: The Kingdoms and Churches of Scandinavia, 1520–1545* (Cambridge, England, 2010); and Ingmar Brohed, ed., *Reformationens konsolidering i de nordiska länderna 1540–1610* (Oslo, 1990).

8. For the general affiliation of dynasty and church, see Anna Coreth, *Pietas Austriaca: Österreichische Frömmigkeit im Barock*, 2nd ed. (Vienna, 1982). For individual complexities, see Viktor Bibl, "Zur Frage der religiösen Haltung Kaiser Maximilians II," *Archiv für österreichische Geschichte* 106 (1918): 289–425.

A House Dividing 59

9. Rudolf Leeb, "Der Streit um den wahren Glauben—Reformation und Gegenreformation in Österreich," in *Geschichte des Christentums in Österreich*, ed. Rudolf Leeb et al. (Vienna, 2003), 160, 161.

10. For a significant recent investigation of the Utraquists, see Zdeněk V. David, *Finding the Middle Way: The Utraquists' Liberal Challenge to Rome and Luther* (Washington, DC, 2003).

11. For Jan Hus and Hussitism, see František Šmahel, *Husitská revoluce*, 4 vols., 2nd ed. (Prague, 1995–1996); Howard Kaminsky, *A History of the Hussite Revolution* (Berkeley, CA, 1967).

12. The text of the *Confessio Bohemica* is printed in Peter F. Barton and László Makkai, eds., *Ostmitteleuropas Bekenntnisschriften der evangelischen Kirchen A. und H.B. des Reformationszeitalters*, vol. 3:1, *1564–1576* (Budapest, 1987), 315–335. For a standard work on the original Unitas fratrum, see Rudolf Ričan, *Dějiny Jednoty bratrské* (Prague, 1957). For a classical English-language study of the Moravians, whose modern expressions are primarily based on an attempted renewal of the Brethren tradition in eighteenth-century Germany, see J. Taylor Hamilton and Kenneth G. Hamilton, *History of the Moravian Church: The Renewed Unitas Fratrum 1722–1957* (Bethlehem, PA, 1967). For a modern academic introduction, see Dietrich Meyer, *Zinzendorf und die Herrnhuter Brüdergemeine: 1700–2000* (Göttingen, 2000).

13. Thomas Winkelbauer, *Ständefreiheit und Fürstenmacht: Länder und Untertanen des Hauses Habsburg im konfessionellen Zeitalter* (Vienna, 2003), 2:165.

14. See Bernhard Raupach, *Evangelisches Oesterreich, das ist historische Nachricht von den vornehmsten Schicksahlen der Evangelisch-Lutherischen Kirchen in dem Ertz-Hertzogthum Oesterreich*, vol. 1 (Hamburg, 1732), 15–20; *Allgemeine Deutsche Biographie*, s.v. "Paul Speratus."

15. For a more detailed description of Kaspar Tauber's experience, see Bernhard Raupach, *Evangelisches Oesterreich, das ist historische Nachricht von den vornehmsten Schicksahlen der Evangelisch-Lutherischen Kirchen in dem Ertz-Hertzogthum Oesterreich*, vol. 1 (Hamburg, 1732), 11–14; *Allgemeine Deutsche Biographie*, s.v. "Kaspar Tauber"; Peter F. Barton, ed., *Die Geschichte der Evangelischen in Österreich und Südostmitteleuropa*, vol. 1, *Im Schatten der Bauernkriege: Die Frühzeit der Reformation* (Vienna, 1985), 196–206; Rudolf Leeb, "Beobachtungen zu Caspar Tauber: Zur Rezeption reformatorischen Gedankengutes beim ersten Märtyrer der österreichischen Reformation," *Jahrbuch der Gesellschaft für die Geschichte des Protestantismus in Österreich* 110/111 (1994/95): 21–45.

16. See Gustav Reingrabner, "Die kirchlichen Verhältnisse im Waldviertel im Jahre 1544," *Das Waldviertel* 49 (2000): 10.

17. Peter F. Barton, *Evangelisch in Österreich* (Vienna, 1987), 63. The *Landhaus*, which has been translated as Estates Building, was the political and administrative center of the territorial estates. It was home to the diet, but also to other estatist institutions such as archives, libraries, schools, and administrative offices. Estates Buildings were established in Vienna, Graz, Linz, Innsbruck, and Klagenfurt.

18. For an introduction to the early Reformation in Villach, see Wilhelm Neumann, "Die Reformation in Villach," in *900 Jahre Villach*, ed. Wilhelm Neumann (Villach, 1960), 411–446.

60   A House Dividing

19. Wilhelm Neumann, "Villachs Studenten an deutschen Universitäten bis 1518," in *900 Jahre Villach*, ed. Wilhelm Neumann (Villach, 1960), 246.

20. The deed is printed in Walter Fresacher, "St. Jakob in Villach: Rechtsgeschichte einer Stadtpfarre," in *900 Jahre Villach*, ed. Wilhelm Neumann (Villach, 1960), 344–346.

21. Ibid., 344f. The "chlar, lautter, an all menschlich Zuesätz" of the original corresponded to a standard formula of contemporary Protestantism.

22. Wilhelm Neumann, *Beiträge zur Geschichte Kärntens*, 2nd ed. (Klagenfurt, 1994), 464.

23. Siegfried Haider, *Geschichte Oberösterreichs* (Munich, 1987), 195.

24. For an introduction to the rise of Protestantism in Steyr, see Bernhard Raupach, *Erläutertes Evangelisches Oesterreich, oder: Dritte und Letzte Fortsetzung der historischen Nachricht von den vornehmsten Schicksalen der Evangelisch-Lutherischen Kirchen in dem Ertz-Hertzogthum Oesterreich* (Hamburg, 1740), 129–131; Caecilia Doppler, *Reformation und Gegenreformation in ihrer Auswirkung auf das Steyrer Bürgertum* (Vienna, 1977), 25–37. More broadly on the spread of the reformation in urban Upper Austria also Corina Marta Herrera, "The Ambiguous Reformation in the Territorial Cities of Upper Austria, 1520–1576: Enns, Freistadt, Gmunden, Linz, Steyr, Vöcklabruck and Wels" (Ph.D. diss., Yale University, 1980).

25. For Garsten, see Joseph F. Patrouch, *A Negotiated Settlement: The Counter-Reformation in Upper Austria under the Habsburgs* (Boston, 2000), 69.

26. See Hans Herzheimer, "Conportata Hansen Hertzhaymers ab Anno 1514 ad 1519," MS Austrian Museum of Applied Arts (Vienna), Manuscript Collection, inv. no. B.I.: 21517.

27. Their names were Johannes Evangelist and Johannes Baptist (the latter was also known as Hans Jordan). See Karl Eduard Förstemann, ed., *Album Academiae Vitebergensis*, vol. 1, *1502–1560* (Leipzig, 1841; reprint, Aalen, 1976), 41.

28. Ibid., 51, 57.

29. See Enno Bünz, "Die Heiltumssammlung des Degenhart Pfeffinger," in *Ich armer sundiger Mensch: Heiligen- und Reliquienkult am Übergang zum konfessionellen Zeitalter*, ed. Andreas Tacke (Göttingen, 2006), 167.

30. For the numbers, see Wilhelm Neumann, "Villachs Studenten an deutschen Universitäten bis 1518," in *900 Jahre Villach*, ed. Wilhelm Neumann (Villach, 1960), 243f. It should be noted that these numbers do not include the students at Italian universities and are thus most valuable for the analysis of regional shifts within the empire.

31. Karl Eder, *Glaubensspaltung und Landstände in Österreich ob der Enns 1525–1602*, vol. 2 of *Studien zur Reformationsgeschichte Oberösterreichs* (Linz, 1936), 173.

32. In 1625, Emperor Ferdinand II was finally able to make the attendance of foreign Protestant universities subject to special dispensation. See Johann Loserth, ed., *Akten und Korrespondenzen zur Geschichte der Gegenreformation in Innerösterreich unter Ferdinand II.* (Vienna, 1907), 2:756.

33. For an introduction to the Jörger family, see Heinrich Wurm, *Die Jörger von Tollet* (Linz, 1955), and *Neue deutsche Biographie*, s.v. "Jörger v. Tollet."

34. The historical German designations of these positions were *Landeshauptmann*, *Hofkammerrat*, and *Erblandhofmeister*.

A House Dividing   61

35. Franz von Thurn und Taxis, "Eine Chronik der Jörger 1497–1599," *Monatsblatt der kais. kön. heraldischen Gesellschaft Adler* 7 (1911–1916): 267f.

36. Even the Jörger family chronicle contains an obituary of Luther, which was rather unusual for a work of that nature. See Franz von Thurn und Taxis, "Eine Chronik der Jörger 1497–1599," *Monatsblatt der kais. kön. heraldischen Gesellschaft Adler* 7 (1911–1916): 267.

37. For Stiefel in Austria, see Bernhard Raupach, *Erläutertes Evangelisches Oesterreich, das ist Fortgesetzte Historische Nachricht von den Schicksahlen der Evangelisch-Lutherischen Kirchen in dem Ertz-Hertzogthum Oesterreich* (Hamburg, 1736), 35–43. See also *Allgemeine Deutsche Biographie*, s.v. "Michael Stifel." Kaiser was executed in 1527 in Schärding, in the segment of Bavaria that bordered on Upper Austria and was subsequently incorporated into the latter.

38. Franz von Thurn und Taxis, "Eine Chronik der Jörger 1497–1599," *Monatsblatt der kais. kön. heraldischen Gesellschaft Adler* 7 (1911–1916): 268, 269.

39. For the late medieval and early modern expressions of ecclesial guardianship, see Thomas Simon, *Grundherrschaft und Vogtei: Eine Strukturanalyse spätmittelalterlicher und frühneuzeitlicher Herrschaftsbildung* (Frankfurt, 1995). For a practical example of ecclesial structure on the eve of the Reformation, see also Karl Amon, *Die Steiermark vor der Glaubensspaltung: Kirchliche Zustände 1490–1520* (Graz, 1960), 164.

40. See Regina Pörtner, *The Counter-Reformation in Central Europe: Styria 1580–1630* (Oxford, 2001), 21.

41. For an introduction to the confessional age in Bavaria, see the relevant chapters in Walter Brandmüller, ed., *Handbuch der bayerischen Kirchengeschichte*, vol. 2, *Von der Glaubensspaltung bis zur Säkularisation* (St. Ottilien, Germany, 1993).

42. See, for example, Hans Sturmberger, *Aufstand in Böhmen: Der Beginn des Dreißigjährigen Krieges* (Munich and Vienna, 1959), 20.

43. Johann Loserth, ed., *Akten und Korrespondenzen zur Geschichte der Gegenreformation in Innerösterreich unter Ferdinand II.*, vol. 1 (Vienna, 1906), 563–565.

44. For a recent introduction to the history of religious reform in early-modern East Central Europe, see Howard Louthan and Graeme Murdock, eds., *A Companion to the Reformation in Central Europe* (Leiden, 2015).

45. See *Relation Der Vnter- und Oberösterreichischen Euangelischen Stände Abgesandten nach Wien: Allda Zwischen Ihrer Königlichen May. zu Hungarn etc. vnd jnen den dreyen Österreichischen Evangelischen Ständen der Frid tractiert vnd geschlossen worden* (n.p., 1610), 92.

46. For a brief introduction to the Tyrolean experience during the confessional age, see Anton Schindling and Walter Ziegler, eds., *Die Territorien des Reichs im Zeitalter der Reformation und Konfessionalisierung: Land und Konfession 1500–1650*, vol. 1, *Der Südosten* (Münster, 1989), 87–101. For the early, more tumultuous phase of reformist influence in Tyrol, see also Peter Bierbrauer, *Die unterdrückte Reformation: Der Kampf der Tiroler um eine neue Kirche 1521–1527* (Zurich, 1993).

47. See Ernst Bruckmüller, Helmut Stradal, and Michael Mitterauer, *Herrschaftsstruktur und Ständebildung: Beiträge zur Typologie der*

62 A House Dividing

österreichischen Länder aus ihren mittelalterlichen Grundlagen, vol. 3 (Munich, 1973), 14f., 179–203.

48. For the origins of Anabaptism in Tyrol and its connections to the peasant movement, see Werner Packull, *Hutterite Beginnings: Communitarian Experiments during the Reformation* (Baltimore, MD, 1995), 161–186; Astrid von Schlachta, *Die Hutterer zwischen Tirol und Amerika: Eine Reise durch die Jahrhunderte* (Innsbruck, 2006), 15–30; Gretl Köfer, "Täufertum in Tirol," in *Michael Gaismair und seine Zeit: Gaismair-Tage 1982*, ed. Christoph von Hartungen and Günther Pallaver (Bozen-Innsbruck, 1983), 112–122; and Johann Loserth, "Der Anabaptismus in Tirol: Vom Jahre 1536 bis zu seinem Erlöschen," *Archiv für österreichische Geschichte* 79 (1893): 127–276.

49. A comprehensive but very dated study of the rise and fall of Protestantism in Lower Austria is Theodor Wiedemann, *Geschichte der Reformation und Gegenreformation im Lande unter der Enns*, 5 vols. (Prague, 1879–1886). For a recent popular introduction to the history of Lower Austrian Lutheranism based on a large provincial exhibition, see Gustav Reingrabner, ed., *Evangelisch: Gestern und Heute einer Kirche* (St. Pölten, 2002).

50. For the important role of Magdeburg in the formation of Gnesio-Lutheran, that is, genuine Lutheran tendencies in the aftermath of the Augsburg Interim, see Thomas Kaufmann, *Das Ende der Reformation: Magdeburgs "Herrgotts Kanzlei" (1548–1551/2)* (Tübingen, 2003). For repercussions in Austria, see also Rudolf Leeb, "Regensburg und das evangelische Österreich," in *Die Geburt Österreichs: 850 Jahre Privilegium minus*, ed. Peter Schmid and Heinrich Wanderwitz (Regensburg, 2007), 229–247. For the Istrian-born theologian Matthias Flacius, see Oliver K. Olson, *Matthias Flacius and the Survival of Luther's Reform* (Wiesbaden, 2000), and Wilhelm Preger, *Matthias Flacius Illyricus und seine Zeit*, 2 vols. (Erlangen, 1859–1861). For Flacian tendencies in Lower Austria, see Gustav Reingrabner, "Zur Geschichte der flacianischen Bewegung im Lande unter der Enns," *Jahrbuch für Landeskunde von Niederösterreich* 54/55 (1990): 265–301. For Inner Austria, see also Oskar Sakrausky, "Der Flacianismus in Oberkärnten," *Jahrbuch der Gesellschaft für die Geschichte des Protestantismus in Österreich* 76 (1960): 83–109, and Johann Loserth, "Der Flacianismus in Steiermark und die Religionsgespräche von Schladming und Graz," *Jahrbuch der Gesellschaft für die Geschichte des Protestantismus in Österreich* 20 (1899): 1–13. For some recent analyses, see also *Jahrbuch für die Geschichte des Protestantismus in Österreich* 131 (2015), which has a special focus on Gnesio-Lutheran and Flacian tendencies.

51. See Gustav Reingrabner, "Die kirchlichen Verhältnisse im Waldviertel im Jahre 1544," *Das Waldviertel* 49 (2000): 14.

52. Anton Schindling and Walter Ziegler, eds., *Die Territorien des Reichs im Zeitalter der Reformation und Konfessionalisierung: Land und Konfession 1500–1650*, vol. 1, *Der Südosten* (Münster, 1989), 124, 126f.

53. For these schools, see Gernot Heiss, "Konfession, Politik und Erziehung: Die Landschaftsschulen in den nieder- und innerösterreichischen Ländern vor dem Dreißigjährigen Krieg," in *Bildung, Politik und Gesellschaft: Studien zur Geschichte des europäischen Bildungswesens vom 16. bis zum*

A House Dividing 63

20. Jahrhundert, ed. Grete Klingenstein, Heinrich Lutz, and Gerald Stourzh (Vienna, 1978), 13–63.

54. Siegfried Haider, *Geschichte Oberösterreichs* (Munich, 1987), 168, 169.

55. See Rudolf Leeb, "Der Streit um den wahren Glauben—Reformation und Gegenreformation in Österreich," in *Geschichte des Christentums in Österreich*, ed. Rudolf Leeb et al. (Vienna, 2003), 211; Helmut Mezler-Andelberg, *Kirche in der Steiermark: Gesammelte Aufsätze* (Vienna, 1994), 125; and Regina Pörtner, *The Counter-Reformation in Central Europe: Styria 1580–1630* (Oxford, 2001), 164f. For an older Catholic interpretation of the history of Protestantism in Styria, see Matthias Robitsch, *Geschichte des Protestantismus in der Steiermark* (Graz, 1859). For the history of a Slovenian-speaking Protestant congregation in Carinthia, see Oskar Sakrausky, *Agoritschach: Die Geschichte einer protestantischen Gemeinde im gemischtsprachigen Südkärnten* (Klagenfurt, 1960). For a brief introduction to Slovenian Protestantism in Carinthia in English, see also Tom M. S. Priestly, "Slovene Protestants in Carinthia," *Slovenian Studies Journal* 6 (1984): 177–189; the volume also contains other pertinent essays on the history of Protestantism among southern Slavs.

56. Regina Pörtner, *The Counter-Reformation in Central Europe: Styria 1580–1630* (Oxford, 2001), 35.

57. Paul Dedic, "Der Kärntner Protestantismus vom Abschluß der 'Hauptreformation' bis zur Adelsemigration 1600–1629/30," *Jahrbuch für die Geschichte des Protestantismus in Österreich* 58 (1937): 72.

58. The text of the *Confessio Carinthica* is printed in Peter F. Barton and László Makkai, eds., *Ostmitteleuropas Bekenntnisschriften der evangelischen Kirchen A. und H.B. des Reformationszeitalters*, vol. 3·1, 1564–1576 (Budapest, 1987), 39–52.

59. Ibid., 45.

60. For Maximilian II, see Paula Sutter Fichtner, *Emperor Maximilian II* (New Haven, CT, 2001); Friedrich Edelmayer and Alfred Kohler, eds., *Kaiser Maximilian II.: Kultur und Politik im 16. Jahrhundert* (Vienna, 1992); as well as Andreas Edel, *Der Kaiser und Kurpfalz: Eine Studie zu den Grundelementen politischen Handelns bei Maximilian II. (1564–1576)* (Göttingen, 1997).

61. For a detailed investigation of Maximilian's religious position, see Viktor Bibl, "Zur Frage der religiösen Haltung Kaiser Maximilians II.," *Archiv für österreichische Geschichte* 106 (1918): 289–425.

62. For Pfauser, see *Neue deutsche Biographie*, s.v. "Johann Sebastian Pfauser."

63. Paula Sutter Fichtner, *Emperor Maximilian II* (New Haven, CT, 2001), 42.

64. Ibid., 44.

65. For the prehistory of the religious concession of 1568, see Viktor Bibl, "Die Vorgeschichte der Religionskonzession Kaiser Maximilian II. (18. August 1568)," *Jahrbuch für Landeskunde von Niederösterreich*, n. s., 13/14 (1915): 400–431.

66. Ibid., 429.

67. Siegfried Haider, *Geschichte Oberösterreichs* (Munich, 1987), 170. Since Emperor Maximilian II did not want to get involved in the conflict about the political status of Upper Austria, he did not issue a separate concession

64 *A House Dividing*

but assured the Upper Austrians that they would receive the same treatment as their Lower Austrian peers.

68. Maximilian prohibited the urban curia from acting in unison with the other estates by defining the territorial towns and market towns as regalian property.

69. Johann Loserth, *Reformation und Gegenreformation in den innerösterreichischen Ländern im 16. Jahrhundert* (Stuttgart, 1898), 183f.

70. For a closer examination of the Pacification of Bruck and its prehistory, see Johann Loserth, "Die steirische Religionspazifikation und die Fälschung des Vizekanzlers Dr. Wolfgang Schranz," *Jahrbuch der Gesellschaft für die Geschichte des Protestantismus in Österreich* 48 (1927): 1–57.

71. Ibid., 23. The assurance used the then prevailing German designation Laibach for the capital of Carniola.

72. For Contarini, see Elisabeth G. Gleason, *Gasparo Contarini: Venice, Rome and Reform* (Berkeley, CA, 1993).

73. The classic study of the Council of Trent is Hubert Jedin, *Geschichte des Konzils von Trient*, 4 vols. (Freiburg, 1949–1975).

74. For the new religious orders of the period, see Richard DeMolen, ed., *Religious Orders of the Catholic Reformation* (New York, 1994). For the origins of the Society of Jesus, see John O'Malley, *The First Jesuits* (Cambridge, MA, 1993). For a history of the Jesuits in the German-speaking countries, see Bernhard Duhr, *Geschichte der Jesuiten in den Ländern deutscher Zunge*, 4 vols. (Freiburg, 1907–1928).

75. See, for example, Oskar Garstein, *Rome and the Counter-Reformation in Scandinavia*, 4 vols. (Oslo, 1963–1992).

76. For an introduction to the Counterreformation and its extensive literature, one may consult Heinrich Lutz, *Reformation und Gegenreformation*, 5th ed. (Munich, 2002); David M. Luebke, ed., *The Counter-Reformation: The Essential Readings* (Oxford, 1999); R. Po-Chia Hsia, *The World of Catholic Renewal, 1540–1770* (Cambridge, England, 1998); and Robert Bireley, *The Refashioning of Catholicism, 1450–1700* (Houndmills, England, 1999). For the terminological development, see also Albert Elkan, "Entstehung und Entwicklung des Begriffs Gegenreformation," *Historische Zeitschrift* 112 (1914): 473–493; Hubert Jedin, *Katholische Reform oder Gegenreformation? Ein Versuch der Klärung der Begriffe* (Lucerne, 1946); and John O'Malley, *Trent and All That: Renaming Catholicism in the Early Modern Era* (Cambridge, MA, 2000). For a collection of significant primary sources, see also Albrecht P. Luttenberger, *Katholische Reform und Konfessionalisierung* (Darmstadt, 2006).

77. See R. Po-Chia Hsia, *The World of Catholic Renewal, 1540–1770* (Cambridge, England, 1998), 122–125.

78. See Ernst Walter Zeeden, *Die Entstehung der Konfessionen: Grundlagen und Formen der Konfessionsbildung im Zeitalter der Glaubenskämpfe* (Munich, 1965); Wolfgang Reinhard, "Zwang zur Konfessionalisierung? Prolegomena zu einer Theorie des konfessionellen Zeitalters," *Zeitschrift für historische Forschung* 10 (1983): 257–277; Heinz Schilling, "Die Konfessionalisierung im Reich," *Historische Zeitschrift* 246 (1988): 1–45. See also Wolfgang Reinhard and Heinz Schilling, eds., *Katholische*

Konfessionalisierung (Gütersloh, 1995), and Heinrich Richard Schmidt, *Konfessionalisierung im 16. Jahrhundert* (Oldenburg, 1992).

79. Heinz Schilling, *Religion, Political Culture and the Emergence of Early Modern Society: Essays in German and Dutch History* (Leiden, 1992), 208.

80. Ibid., 209. In very similar words, Wolfgang Reinhard described confessionalization as a remarkably commonplace early phase of modern European state-building. See Wolfgang Reinhard, "Zwang zur Konfessionalisierung? Prolegemona zu einer Theorie des konfessionellen Zeitalters," *Zeitschrift für historische Forschung* 10 (1983): 257.

81. Gerhard Oestreich, "Strukturprobleme des europäischen Absolutismus," *Vierteljahrschrift für Sozial- und Wirtschaftsgeschichte* 55 (1969): 329–347.

82. Wolfgang Reinhard, "Zwang zur Konfessionalisierung? Prolegemona zu einer Theorie des konfessionellen Zeitalters," *Zeitschrift für historische Forschung* 10 (1983): 268. For the application of the concept of social discipline in the study of early modern confessional conditions, see also Ronnie Po-Chia Hsia, *Social Discipline in the Reformation: Central Europe, 1550–1750* (London, 1989), and Thomas Winkelbauer, "Sozialdisziplinierung und Konfessionaliserung durch Grundherren in den österreichischen und böhmischen Ländern im 16. und 17. Jahrhundert," *Zeitschrift für historische Forschung* 19 (1992): 317–339.

83. For the confessional differences of modernization, with a special focus on a Catholic Baroque defined as the dominance of cultural and religious aspects over economic and military ones, see also Peter Hersche, *Muße und Verschwendung: Europäische Gesellschaft und Kultur im Barockzeitalter*, 2 vols. (Freiburg im Breisgau, 2006).

84. See, for example, Harm Klueting, *Das Konfessionelle Zeitalter 1525–1648* (Stuttgart, 1989), which already displayed its divergent periodization in the title, and Anton Schindling, "Konfessionaliserung und die Grenzen von Konfessionalisierbarkeit," in *Die Territorien des Reichs im Zeitalter der Reformation und Konfessionalisierung: Land und Konfession 1500–1650*, vol. 7, *Bilanz—Forschungsperspektiven—Register*, ed. Anton Schindling and Walter Ziegler (Münster, 1997), 9–44.

85. See Winfried Schulze, "Konfessionalisierung als Paradigma zur Erforschung des konfessionellen Zeitalters," in *Drei Konfessionen in einer Region: Beiträge zur Geschichte der Konfessionalisierung im Herzogtum Berg vom 16. bis zum 18. Jahrhundert*, ed. Burkhard Dietz and Stefan Ehrenpreis (Cologne, 1999), 15–30.

86. See, for example, Olaf Mörke, "'Konfessionalisierung' als politisch-soziales Strukturprinzip: Das Verhältnis von Religion und Staatsbildung in der Republik der Vereinigten Niederlande im 16. und 17. Jahrhundert," *Tijdschrift voor Sociale Geschiedenis* 16 (1990): 31–60, and, with a somewhat different focus on parallel state-sponsored and popular confessionalizations, Ute Lotz-Heumann, *Die doppelte Konfessionalisierung in Irland: Konflikt und Koexistenz im 16. und in der ersten Hälfte des 17. Jahrhunderts* (Tübingen, 2000).

87. Heinrich Richard Schmidt, *Dorf und Religion: Reformierte Kirchenzucht in Berner Landgemeinden der Frühen Neuzeit* (Stuttgart, 1995).

88. See his comments in Anette Völker-Rasor, ed., *Oldenburg Geschichte Lehrbuch: Frühe Neuzeit* (Munich, 2000), 302f.

66 A House Dividing

89. This is expressed in a very straightforward manner by Wolfgang Reinhard, who described confessionalization as an "alternative socio-historical concept for the phenomenon that from a perspective of ecclesiastical and political history used to be called the Counterreformation." See Anette Völker-Rasor, ed., *Oldenburg Geschichte Lehrbuch: Frühe Neuzeit* (Munich, 2000), 299.

90. Archduke Ferdinand II of Tyrol was not the same person as the later Emperor Ferdinand II.

91. Johann Loserth, ed., *Acten und Correspondenzen zur Geschichte der Gegenreformation in Innerösterreich unter Erzherzog Karl II. (1578–1590)* (Vienna, 1898), 38.

92. Ibid., 36.

93. As archduke, Ferdinand was the third ruler by this name, but he is better known as Emperor Ferdinand II.

94. In a 1621 codicil to his testament he defined it as his heir's foremost task in life to "maintain his lands and his people in the genuine Apostolic Roman and only true Catholic faith, and to seriously keep out and eradicate all sects and seductive teachings, as well as everything that might cause and promote their spread." See the text printed as an appendix in Gustav Turba, *Die Grundlagen der pragmatischen Sanktion*, vol. 2, *Die Hausgesetze* (Leipzig-Vienna, 1912), 352.

95. See William Lamormaini, *Ferdinandi II. Romanorum Imperatoris Virtutes* (Antwerp, 1638), 15f. The Latin original of this often cited statement is: Sæpè voce, sæpè scripto testatus est, suis se Prouinciis Regnisque renuntiaturum citiùs ac libentiùs, quàm scienter amplificandæ Fidei occasionem neglecturum; malle solo pane & aquâ vitam trahere; malle cum Coniuge ac liberis solo scipione instructum ire in exilium; malle ostiatim panem mendicare; malle in frusta concidi ac discerpi; quàm iniuriam Deo Ecclesiæque ab Hæreticis, in subditis sibi Prouinciis hactenus illatam, diutiùs perferre.

96. See Johann Loserth, ed., *Akten und Korrespondenzen zur Geschichte der Gegenreformation in Innerösterreich unter Ferdinand II.* (Vienna, 1906), 1:213–220.

97. For some of the advice he relied on, see Johann Loserth, ed., *Akten und Korrespondenzen zur Geschichte der Gegenreformation in Innerösterreich unter Ferdinand II.* (Vienna, 1906), 1:141–149.

98. Ibid., 1:222f.

99. Ibid., 1:309f.; 1:344f.

100. Ibid., 1:376f.

101. Ibid., 1:350f.

102. For Brenner, see Franz Schmid, *Bischof Martin Brenner (1548–1616)* (Dietenheim, Germany, 1984), and Leopold Schuster, *Fürstbischof Martin Brenner: Ein Charakterbild aus der steirischen Reformations-Geschichte* (Graz, 1898). The diocese of Seckau comprised parts of Styria.

103. See Georg Loesche, *Geschichte des Protestantismus im vormaligen und heutigen Österreich* (Vienna, 1930), 249, and Rudolf Leeb, "Der Streit um den wahren Glauben—Reformation und Gegenreformation in Österreich," in *Geschichte des Christentums in Österreich*, ed. Rudolf Leeb et al. (Vienna, 2003), 261f. The most detailed contemporary source of the reformation campaign—from a highly sympathetic perspective—is Jakob (baptized

Johannes) Rosolenz, *Gründlicher Gegen Bericht Auf Den falschen Bericht vnnd vermainte Erinnerung Dauidis Rungij, Wittenbergischen Professors, Von der Tyrannischen Bäpstischen Verfolgung deß H. Evangelij, in Steyermarckt, Kärndten, vnd Crayn* . . . (Graz, 1607). This report by the Augustinian abbot of Stainz proved so controversial that it triggered a heated dispute in the Styrian diet.

104. Johann Loserth, ed., *Akten und Korrespondenzen zur Geschichte der Gegenreformation in Innerösterreich unter Ferdinand II.* (Vienna, 1906), 1:297. See also ibid, 1:140–149.

105. See the minutes of the diet in Graz of 30 April 1601 in Johann Loserth, ed., *Akten und Korrespondenzen zur Geschichte der Gegenreformation in Innerösterreich unter Ferdinand II.* (Vienna, 1907), 2:185.

106. So, for example, on 17 January 1610; see ibid., 2:560–564.

107. See ibid., 2:741f., and Alice Meir, "Der Protestantismus in der Herrschaft Paternion vom 16. Jahrhundert bis zum Toleranzpatent," *Carinthia I* 162 (1972): 311–343. For greater detail, see also the dissertation by the latter author (still published under her maiden name): Alice Csermak, "Geschichte des Protestantismus in der Herrschaft Paternion bis zum Toleranzpatent 1781" (Ph.D. diss., University of Vienna, 1969).

108. For an introduction to the role of the Jesuits in the Inner Austrian Counterreformation, see Gernot Heiss, "Die Bedeutung und die Rolle der Jesuiten im Verlauf der innerösterreichischen Gegenreformation," in *Reform und Gegenreformation in Innerösterreich 1564–1628*, ed. France M. Dolinar et al. (Graz, 1994), 63–76. For a broader examination beyond Inner Austria, see Gernot Heiss, "Die Jesuiten und die Anfänge der Katholisierung in den Ländern Ferdinands I: Glaube, Mentalität, Politik" (unpublished habilitation thesis, University of Vienna, 1986), and idem, "Princes, Jesuits and the Origins of Counter-Reformation in the Habsburg Lands," in *Crown, Church and Estates: Central European Politics in the Sixteenth and Seventeenth Centuries*, ed. R. J. W. Evans and T. V. Thomas (London, 1991), 92–109.

109. For the course of events, see Victor Bibl, "Erzherzog Ernst und die Gegenreformation in Niederösterreich (1576–1590)," *Mitteilungen des Instituts für österreichische Geschichtsforschung*, Ergänzungsband 6 (1901): 576–579.

110. Peter Csendes and Ferdinand Opll, eds., *Wien: Geschichte einer Stadt*, vol. 3, *Die frühneuzeitliche Residenz (16. bis 18. Jahrhundert)*, ed. Karl Vocelka and Anita Traninger (Vienna, 2003), 327; and Rudolf Leeb, "Der Streit um den wahren Glauben—Reformation und Gegenreformation in Österreich," in *Geschichte des Christentums in Österreich*, ed. Rudolf Leeb et al. (Vienna, 2003), 252.

111. Eder has recently received his first thorough treatment in English through Elaine Fulton's *Catholic Belief and Survival in Late Sixteenth-Century Vienna: The Case of Georg Eder (1523–87)* (Aldershot, England, 2007). For his extensive correspondence, especially with the court in Munich, see note 116 below.

112. See Elaine Fulton, *Catholic Belief and Survival in Late Sixteenth-Century Vienna: The Case of Georg Eder (1523–87)* (Aldershot, England, 2007), 68.

68   A House Dividing

113. The official German designations of these bodies were *Reichskammergericht* and *Reichshofrat*.

114. For an analysis of irenicist tendencies at the Habsburg court, see Howard Louthan, *The Quest for Compromise: Peacemakers in Counter-Reformation Vienna* (Cambridge, England, 1997), and Otto Helmut Hopfen, *Kaiser Maximilian II. und der Kompromißkatholizismus* (Munich, 1895).

115. Georg Eder, *Evangelische Inquisition Wahrer und falscher Religion* (Dillingen, Germany, 1573).

116. Victor Bibl, "Die Berichte des Reichshofrates Dr. Georg Eder an die Herzoge Albrecht und Wilhelm von Bayern über die Religionskrise in Niederösterreich (1579–1587)," *Jahrbuch für Landeskunde von Niederösterreich*, n. s., 8 (1909): 143. As Robert Bireley has documented for a later period, however, it would be overly simplistic to portray the Society of Jesus as a monolithic bloc of confessional hardliners. See Robert Bireley, *The Jesuits and the Thirty Years War: Kings, Courts and Confessors* (Cambridge, England, 2003).

117. Central parts of this correspondence are published in Victor Bibl, "Die Berichte des Reichshofrates Dr. Georg Eder an die Herzoge Albrecht und Wilhelm von Bayern über die Religionskrise in Niederösterreich (1579–1587)," *Jahrbuch für Landeskunde von Niederösterreich*, n. s., 8 (1909): 67–154, and Karl Schrauf, ed., *Der Reichshofrath Dr. Georg Eder: Eine Briefsammlung als Beitrag zur Geschichte der Gegenreformation in Niederösterreich* (Vienna, 1904).

118. For a comprehensive biography of Klesl (also spelt Khlesl), one still has to consult Joseph von Hammer-Purgstall, *Khlesls des Cardinals, Directors des geheimen Cabinetes Kaisers Mathias, Leben*, 4 vols. (Vienna, 1847–1851). See also Anton Kerschbaumer, *Kardinal Klesl: Eine Monographie*, 2nd ed. (Vienna, 1905); Johann Rainer, "Der Prozeß gegen Kardinal Klesl," *Römische Historische Mitteilungen* 5 (1961/62): 35–163; Heinz Angermeier, "Politik, Religion und Reich bei Kardinal Melchior Khlesl," *Zeitschrift der Savigny-Stiftung für Rechtsgeschichte*, Germanist. Abt. 110 (1993): 249–330; and Rona Johnston Gordon, "Melchior Khlesl und der konfessionelle Hintergrund der kaiserlichen Politik im Reich nach 1610," in *Dimensionen der europäischen Aussenpolitik zur Zeit der Wende vom 16. zum 17. Jahrhundert*, ed. Friedrich Beiderbeck, Gregor Horstkemper, and Winfried Schulze (Berlin, 2003), 199–222.

119. For this correspondence, see Victor Bibl, "Briefe Melchior Klesls an Herzog Wilhelm V. von Baiern: Ein Beitrag zur Geschichte der Gegenreformation in Oesterreich u. d. Enns," *Mitteilungen des Instituts für österreichische Geschichtsforschung* 21 (1900): 640–673.

120. Ibid., 668–670.

121. Ibid., 657. For a more general investigation of the internal reform of the Lower Austrian clergy, see also Johannes Kritzl, "'Sacerdotes incorrigibiles'? Die Disziplinierung des Sekulärklerus durch das Passauer Offizialat unter der Enns von 1580 bis 1652 im Spiegel der Passauer Offizialatsprotokolle" (Ph.D. diss., University of Vienna, 2011), and Rona Johnston, "The Implementation of Tridentine Reform: The Passau Official and the Parish Clergy in Lower Austria 1563–1637," in *The Reformation of the Parishes: The Ministry and the Reformation in Town and Country*, ed. Andrew Pettegree (Manchester, 1993), 215–237.

122. The memorandum is printed in Viktor Bibl, "Eine Denkschrift Melchior Khlesls über die Gegenreformation in Niederösterreich (c. 1590)," *Jahrbuch für Landeskunde von Niederösterreich*, n. s., 8 (1909): 164–171.

123. Ibid., 166.

124. Ibid., 168–170.

3 Last Estate Standing
Representative Government and Catholic Restoration

The religious tensions in the Habsburgs' hereditary lands gradually escalated into a power struggle between Catholic rulers and Protestant nobles. Confessional differences became ideologically charged and merged into a broader debate about the very nature of monarchy and government. This debate engaged most of contemporary Europe, regardless of religion, but it turned especially acerbic in polities with deep confessional cleavages. Religion often served as the ideological glue that held polities together, providing identity to the populace and legitimacy to the political leadership.[1] As a consequence, noncompliance with the monarch's confessional choices was seen as disobedience to his rule and majesty.

The Habsburgs had already faced the interaction of politics and religion in the Holy Roman Empire. The historical autonomy of the imperial estates had prevented the emperors from upholding their religious authority, forcing them to tolerate the establishment of heterodox polities within their perceived sphere of power. Indeed, the concepts of German liberty and freedom of religion had largely merged in Protestant discourse, where they had evolved into mutually dependent and reinforcing preconditions of the empire's political order.[2]

In response, the Habsburgs intensified their efforts to recatholize their patrimonial domains. Yet even there, the established privileges of territorial estates presented serious obstacles. Hereditary principalities were not by definition unlimited monarchies, self-assured nobles reminded their rulers. They, too, followed complex rules of power-sharing, deriving from customary law and practice as well as from individually entered accords. In the eyes of local magnates, the Habsburgs could not unilaterally control their allodial territories any more than the empire.

Who, then, were those territorial elites who considered themselves the true representatives of the commonwealth, called to govern in unison with the prince, and what was the historical basis of their lofty sense of self? This chapter places the estate system in both its Austrian and its wider European context. At the same time, it traces the implications of governmental dualism for the course of confessional politics in the hereditary lands. This examination reveals the gradual reinforcement of dynastic influence as well as the resulting radicalization of Protestant opposition.

Nature and Origin of the Estate System

"Some are devoted particularly to the service of God; others to the preservation of the State by arms; still others to the task of feeding and maintaining it by peaceful labors. These are our three orders or estates general of France, the Clergy, the Nobility, and the Third Estate."[3] With this quote from French jurist Charles Loyseau's *Traité des Ordres et Simples Dignitez* of 1610, Georges Duby introduced his much-debated study of feudal society and its constituent parts. The individual orders comprise diverse elements but remain intrinsically divided into three, reflecting the perfection of the triune, which was reanimated in medieval Europe but already present in its historical antecedents.[4] The ensuing structure relied on hierarchy and discipline, to be mitigated by Christian affection and concord.[5] As late as 1776, the royal representative defined the constituent parts of the Parisian parliament as living bodies, as links in a great chain of which the first rests in the hands of the king.[6]

Other influential interpreters put the origins of the estate system into a more pragmatic context. According to Otto Hintze, the estates acted on behalf of private interests vis-á-vis the monarch, who embodied the state.[7] The German historian saw the origins of this division of power in the monarchs' need to ensure the financial and military support of regional magnates. In return for this assistance, the notables demanded ever more substantial privileges. The desire to protect these privileges, in turn, forged previously unrelated strongmen into a new social corporation.[8] The representative system of government originated within a monarchic framework, Hintze emphasized, even though it tends to be seen as an expression of republicanism. It was conceived in medieval Western Europe and lacked direct equivalents in other contemporaneous societies.[9]

The estate system could draw on older models. With its universal councils, the medieval church provided successful examples of collective decision-making. After liberating itself from its erstwhile dependence on cooperating monarchs, the church actively promoted the limitation of secular power. It also had an intrinsic interest in substituting traditional

72 Last Estate Standing

allegiances of lineage and kinship with alternative modes of affiliation. Next to the new ecclesial councils, there also existed older Germanic traditions of popular assembly. When the two began to merge, they gave rise to separate secular and ecclesiastic curiae.[10]

Otto Brunner shared some of Hintze's interpretations but criticized a tendency to project modern concepts of sovereignty back in time. The Austrian medievalist did not see the estates as privileged corporations instated to control or limit monarchic government.[11] Such an understanding premises an originally unrestricted monarchic sovereignty, which only gradually conceded some of its power to representative institutions. It may explain the process of parliamentarization in nineteenth-century Europe but would be anachronistic in regard to medieval societies. Instead, Brunner advanced the seemingly paradoxical axiom that the estates did not represent the territory (or land, as his term tends to be rendered in literal translation) but "were" the territory.[12] Brunner anchored this aphorism in his very definition of "land," which he, at least in an Austrian context, described as a territorial community and its common law.[13]

Brunner's approach has left enduring marks on the scholarly debate, but it has also evoked criticism. Some argued that Brunner's political affinity to National Socialism had impacted his historical findings and saw his integral household of medieval society as an ideological criticism of modern individualism.[14] Yet even sympathetic historians such as Michael Mitterauer considered the equation of territory and estates most relevant for the origins of the latter, holding that it subsequently lost its real-life foundation.[15] At the same time, interest in the roots of social stratification has not been restricted to traditional historians. Focusing on the nature of feudalism, especially, sociologists and social science historians have refined our understanding of the estate system. Marxist conceptions placed economics at the center of analysis and saw medieval Europe as the home of class societies in which power derived from control over arable land and those who worked it.[16] While toning down the economic determinism of classic Marxist analysis, modern representatives such as Perry Anderson retained the theoretical focus on the primacy of materialism.[17]

Liberal and positivist functionalists, frequently drawing on Max Weber, preferred a more composite conception of social differentiation that supplemented economics with power and status.[18] Weber had paired Marx's economic concept of class with *inter alia*, the notion of status groups, which he defined as amorphous communities connected primarily by positive or negative social esteem, while acknowledging the frequent association of economic resources and social status.[19] In his attempt to modify both the dichotomic Marxian conception of class and the contractual imagery of liberal stratification theory, Frank Parkin utilized Weber's concept of closure in a manner that has special relevance for the study of Europe's medieval estates.[20] Social groups restrict access to special opportunities and benefits to a select circle of eligibles, whereby a wide variety of characteristics—ranging from race to language and social origin—can provide the basis for categorization.[21] The standards of distinction can be individualist or collectivist in nature, with individualist criteria such as education and property allowing for a larger degree of mobility than collective ones such as descent. At the same time, the monopolization of opportunities can occur in the form of outright exclusion of non-members, but also through intra-group solidarity.[22]

Drawing on established theory, Weberian as well as Marxian, W. G. Runciman affirmed the economic, ideological, and coercive dimensions of social power; this power can, in other words, express itself through access to or control of the means of production, the means of persuasion, and the means of coercion.[23] The British sociologist concretized this division with the help of the neologism "systact," which he defined as a category of people who by virtue of their social role share a similar position within the societal power structure and a common interest in preserving or improving this collective position.[24] Among such systacts, Runciman listed orders, whose location is juridically demarcated; classes, which are defined by their relation to the process of production; castes, whose membership is hereditary and based on a traditional division of labor and hierarchy of purity; and status-groups, which are distinguished by a common value system and lifestyle.[25] The fact that Runciman defined estates as systacts that are constitutionally entitled to a separate representation in government underscores the political roots of the term, whereas the full complexity of the European estate system surfaces in his discussion of international terminology.[26]

The Composition of the Estates in the Alpine Hereditary Lands

The composition of estates varied considerably, both within the borders of the Holy Roman Empire and beyond. As elaborated by Georges Duby, a division into three estates—clergy, nobility, and commoners— was most widespread, whereby the right to be represented in the third estate was regularly restricted to urban elites. This triangular structure echoed philosophical conceptions that divided society into those who prayed, those who fought, and those who worked. Due also to the French Estates-General of international renown, it is widely seen as

74 *Last Estate Standing*

normative; in fact, it was far from universal. In his attempt to develop a European typology, Otto Hintze contrasted a division into three curiae, which dominated in central and southern Europe, with a separation into two chambers, which could be found in an outer circle of northern and eastern European countries from England to Hungary.[27] Even within so circumscribed and culturally homogenous a realm as the Habsburgs' Alpine hereditary lands, representational bodies displayed considerable diversity.

In the Habsburgs' core territory of Lower Austria, the estates were divided into four curiae.[28] The first curia consisted of the prelates or ecclesiastical lords, that is, the high-ranking officeholders of the church. In spite of their honorary preeminence as clerics, however, the prelates did not form the diet's center of power. In both influence and length of representation they were overshadowed by the nobles, who were divided into two separate curiae. The second estate comprised the secular lords, corresponding to the higher and typically older nobility, in which the dynastic families of counts and lords had merged with princely ministerials.[29] As such, they formed the historical nucleus of the estate system, which they continued to dominate; the curial president (*Landmarschall*), too, was chosen from their ranks.[30] Represented in a curia of its own was the lower nobility of knights and squires. Since their social genesis lay in direct service to lords and princes, they were not originally considered worthy of independent representation, but their inclusion in the armigerous segment of the population gradually improved their social and legal status; when territorial diets emerged in the fourteenth century, they already included the lower nobility.[31] The fourth estate, finally, consisted of territorial towns and market towns. In general, market towns were poorly represented in the Lower Austrian diet, as many of them were subject to noble or municipal seigneurs. As such, they enjoyed no autonomous representation, as was also the case for urban communities that were directly subsumed in the monarch's fisc.

Conditions in Upper Austria resembled those of its larger neighbor, although influential monasteries further strengthened the representation of prelates.[32] In Inner Austria, lords and knights were united in a joint curia, even if they remained divided in social and economic status; the small number of lords explains the absence of a distinct curia.[33] Noteworthy in Carinthia was the inclusion of no fewer than four bishops in the clerical estate, among them the influential imperial prince-bishops of Salzburg and Bamberg.[34] In general, however, the similarities with the archduchy predominated.

In the Alpine core of Austria Anterior, more fundamental distinctions became visible. Noble influence was diminished. In Tyrol, the aristocracy was again represented in a unified curia. Yet in striking contrast to eastern Habsburg territories, segments of the local peasantry—organized in rural jurisdictions termed valleys and courts—enjoyed an independent representation in the diet. This created greater equality between urban and rural communities, as both were considered representatives of the territory, but it also served as a counterweight to aristocratic ambitions for power. In diminutive Vorarlberg, finally, which did not receive independent estates until 1541, towns and rural communities were the only ones to attend the diet, whereas isolated noble and clerical possessions formed enclaves of imperial immediacy.

The Advances of Catholic Restoration in Early Seventeenth-Century Austria

By the early seventeenth century, the Counterreformation had made visible progress in the Habsburgs' hereditary lands. In Inner Austria, the practice of Lutheranism was legally restricted to the indigenous nobility, even if everyday life in Carinthia and Upper Styria still deviated from the princely proscriptions. Yet also in the archduchy itself, the restoration of Catholic supremacy had advanced. The separation of urban and noble representations began to bear fruit.

The constitutional position of territorial towns had long been contested. In theory, their territorial status derived from superior autonomy. Whereas numerous comparable communities were subjected to worldly or spiritual lords, the territorial municipalities stood directly under the monarch. As a consequence, they traditionally enjoyed autonomous representation in the diet.[35] No Austrian cities lastingly rose to imperial immediacy, however. With the increase in political and confessional tensions, the Habsburgs intensified their attempts to merge the territorial municipalities into their personal fisc. Urban curiae were not dissolved, but the rulers refused to include them in many estate privileges. In particular, the monarchs challenged the right of urban representatives—as their alleged demesnial subjects—to contravene governmental policy in the diet.

Municipal councils throughout the archduchy fervently protested their demotion, but they received only halfhearted support from the aristocracy. Whereas these most Protestant segments of society upheld a confessional alliance in not only Bohemia but also Hungary, as visible in their firm stance against the monarch at the diet of Pressburg (Pozsony) in 1604, the Protestant nobles of Austria increasingly surrendered their urban coreligionists.[36] Primarily, this abandonment expressed a desire not to link their own, legally protected position to the vulnerable status of the urban populace. Yet many aristocrats were also driven by a desire to

76 *Last Estate Standing*

preserve their elevated societal standing. They sympathized with the religious aspirations of the Lutheran town councils but held little enthusiasm for enhancing their political influence.

First in Vienna and thereafter also in surrounding municipalities such as Krems and Wiener Neustadt, Protestant preachers were ordered to leave the territory. Reformation commissions replaced heterodox city councils with reliable Catholics, even if this lowered recognized standards of qualification and experience.[37] Since local notables tended to favor ecclesial reform, aspiring upstarts and newcomers enjoyed unique opportunities. Owing their social advance to the court, the new appointees diligently enforced the religious proscriptions. This also conformed to their self-image as governmental administrators rather than guardians of municipal autonomy. Popular resistance was commonplace and at times violent, but in the end, the isolated municipalities proved no match for a determined monarch. The defiant town of Waidhofen on the Ybbs was brought to its knees by a blockade of its food supply in 1590.[38] After rioting against the reformation commission in 1589, the inhabitants of Krems forfeited all municipal privileges and were administered by a princely town advocate until 1627. Many influential citizens decided to leave the city.[39]

Notable for the early spread of Lutheranism, the Upper Austrian city of Steyr also exemplified the progress of recatholization. In 1592 the court chose Hans Jakob Löbl as *Landeshauptmann*, or governor, of Upper Austria. This appointment did not only return the important post of governor to Catholic hands after decades of affiliation with the Protestant majority, but it also underlined the reorientation of the office toward the central government. With clear parallels to the newly invested town councilors, Löbl, too, saw himself as the court's representative vis-á-vis the territory, not as an intermediary between ruler and estates. In this spirit he also orchestrated the first serious effort to return those sectors of Upper Austria that were not expressly privileged by monarchic concessions to Catholicism.[40]

Following the example of Lower Austria more than a decade earlier, recatholization commenced in the territorial towns and market towns. Elections to the municipal councils came under governmental supervision; where the government held authority to make direct appointments, such as in the case of judges, confessional considerations weighed heavily. These practical measures were complemented with symbolic acts to restore Catholicism in the public sphere, such as the reintroduction of religious processions. Yet progress was modest until Protestant peasants rebelled against spiritual and economic oppression in 1594. The amalgamation of social and religious grievances gave the dynasty a unique opportunity to add confessional objectives to the restoration of law and order. A deep-seated aversion to popular unrest muted noble objections to the expanded mandate. The reopened campaign sought to reestablish Catholicism in parishes that were not protected by unassailable compacts. It added military muscle to an ecclesial visitation and secured the first more significant advances of Catholic restoration in Upper Austria.

The city fathers of Steyr were slow to grasp the full impact of the campaign.[41] Attentive observers had premonitions, to be sure. As early as 1590, Steyr witnessed preliminary steps toward the restitution of Corpus Christi processions, which had been unknown since 1557. At various points in time, the peasant rebellion also threatened to engulf the city, and as part of the ensuing Catholic restoration, the urban representatives were ordered to close Protestant churches and expel all pastors. Yet similar proscriptions had been issued in the past, and in their lengthy response the city fathers emphasized that they had built the parish church with municipal funds and freely exercised Lutheranism throughout the reign of three successive monarchs.[42] The subsequent respite in Löbl's activism seemed to confirm this optimism.

In November 1598, however, the council received a sharp reminder to discontinue Protestant services and surrender the churches. Hectic protests and petitions proved futile, and in February 1599 Catholic services were reestablished in the Steyr parish church after almost half a century's interruption. Proscriptions against attending heretical services in surrounding communities followed soon thereafter, as well as the closure of the Lutheran school. Segments of the incensed populace harassed religious commissioners and processions, but these unorganized outbursts of frustration were to no avail. On the contrary, the government used the rebellious atmosphere as justification for canceling municipal elections and keeping the city under close supervision. Following Löbl's death in 1602, the speed and intensity of restoration declined, but it took the temporary reversal of confessional policy after 1608 to restitute Lutheran services. For another decade and a half, the two confessions coexisted uneasily in the city, until Catholicism was decisively established as the sole tolerated religion during the Bavarian occupation in the 1620s.

Monarchs and Nobles: A Confrontation Long in the Making

The advances of the Counterreformation in the territorial municipalities gradually reduced the confessional dispute in the archduchy to a

78 Last Estate Standing

confrontation between monarchy and Protestant nobility. By the early 1600s, the territorial municipalities of Lower Austria had largely been converted, at least on the surface. Due to the large-scale replacement of obstinate city councils and the monarchs' refusal to tolerate urban opposition in religious matters, the urban curiae no longer formed a political counterweight in the diets. These territorial assemblies formed the central arena for the denominational confrontation, however. The final phase of the conflict witnessed the formulation of a coherent ideology of state among segments of the Protestant nobility.

It may seem peculiar that this estatist ideology flourished during a period when societal power had shifted decisively to the monarch. Yet for a long time, Austria's Protestant nobles had tried to reconcile their denominational autonomy with political loyalty to the crown. Aristocrats were not rebels by nature; they believed in and profited from a hierarchical structure that placed them below the monarch but above the bulk of society. As a consequence, Protestant officials such as Sigmund von Dietrichstein and Gotthard von Starhemberg willingly executed their princes' orders to crush peasant rebellions, even if these insurgencies had unmistakable religious undertones. It took a fundamental challenge to their inherited status and privileges to incite the well-to-do profiteers of feudal society to open resistance. Therefore, it appears only logical that the most radical formulation of estatist opposition took shape when its protagonists felt endangered politically as well as economically.

Catholic restoration required a confessional homogenization of government. The Habsburgs made a concerted effort to reinforce the Catholic aristocracy. Whereas the established nobility had largely embraced the new faith, two-fifths of the newly admitted lords between 1580 and 1620 were Catholics, and Protestants faced ever more stringent impediments in the final prewar years. The pattern of admission to the knightly estate was more changeable, with Catholics advancing most rapidly during the reign of coreligionist curial vice-presidents at the turn of the seventeenth century and Protestants temporarily reversing this trend after 1609.[43]

From a political perspective, it proved especially significant that the reinvigorated Catholic minority established its own curial faction in 1606.[44] Henceforth, there existed an organized loyalist opposition that placed its ties to the ruler above any community of interest with their Protestant peers; in view of the generous rewards through personal promotion and public service available to one confessional subgroup at the expense of the other, this community of interest had already become limited. Internal division diminished the autonomous power of the estates and prevented coordinated resistance.

Although the policy of select ennoblement and promotion achieved many of its strategic goals, it also radicalized the opposition. Karin MacHardy has emphasized the social motivations for the conflict between the monarch and heterodox nobles.[45] As the Habsburgs transformed the estates through the promotion of Catholic supporters, the old Protestant families developed an acute fear of social displacement. Service to the monarch contributed significantly to the social and economic standing of Austrian aristocrats, just as ennoblement increasingly depended on it after 1500.[46] Public employment provided a source of income for younger sons, irregular as it may have been, and invaluable access to courtly networks and benefits. Careers and fortunes were made by being present at the right place at the right time. Standing in the good graces of the monarch proved a definite advantage for ambitious nobles and commoners.

The new emphasis on denominational compliance undercut the career opportunities for Protestants at the courts of Vienna and Prague. In 1580, 35 percent of Lower Austria's Protestant nobles stood in the service of the crown and only slightly more than half focused solely on their personal estates.[47] By 1620, the share of princely servants had dropped to a mere 13 percent, with more than 80 percent of Protestant nobles attending to private affairs. Even if aristocrats enhanced their credentials through academic studies, the results of these efforts were decidedly mixed· whereas three-quarters of university-educated Catholic lords were in Habsburg service in 1620, only one-fifth of their Protestant peers enjoyed similar success.

Although these numbers fully bear out MacHardy's factual argument, one needs to be careful to place them in their right context and sequence. A fear of social decline was not the root cause of noble dissatisfaction. After all, the conscious policy of Catholic ennoblement and promotion premises the denominational conflict. The reinforcement of the Catholic minority in the noble estates formed one of the central strategies applied by the Habsburgs in their preexisting contest with the Protestant nobility. Its social implications undoubtedly exacerbated the confrontation but did not trigger it. For a nobility that already felt besieged in its religious and political status, however, the loss of economic opportunities could not but increase the willingness to resist.

Yet resistance was never the only recourse. At a time when their peers began to articulate an ideology of estatist rights, a number of prominent nobles converted to Catholicism. From the 1590s onward, Catholics regained a more solid foothold in the diets, based not only on the induction of new members but also on the conversion of established families.

80   *Last Estate Standing*

These conversions expressed a wider tendency among influential magnates throughout the Habsburg Monarchy. Living in close interaction with the court and desiring to uphold it, a small but important segment of lords in Bohemia, Moravia, Austria, and even Hungary embraced the religion of its rulers.[48]

There can be little doubt that many conversions were influenced by social and economic considerations. In an early phase, they could express a desire for a career at court, which had become difficult for Protestants. In the end, they reflected a straightforward choice between conversion and emigration. Yet at the same time, these conversions also signaled the renewed vigor and attraction of Tridentine Catholicism. Czech historian Karel Stloukal diagnosed a rationalist vitalism among Bohemian converts such as Albrecht von Wallenstein, who sensed the outcome of the political and spiritual struggle in the monarchy early on and embraced the prospective victor for both the opportunities it offered and the superior strength it exuded.[49]

Thomas Winkelbauer attempted a typology of conversions in counter-reformational Austria and Bohemia.[50] In his introductory comments, he acknowledged the difficulty of assessing personal motivations.[51] Even if he illustrated the distinct categories with examples from contemporary Habsburg society, the Austrian historian defined them as mere heuristic devices, as ideal-typical abstractions that enhance analytical understanding rather than as genuine representations of intellectual biographies.

As his first category, Winkelbauer listed conversions for exclusively secular and opportunistic reasons, which he illustrated through the rather cynical and ultimately unsuccessful negotiations between Ernst August of Hanover and the Holy See between 1677 and 1679, while considering them a rarity during the confessional age.[52] More common were conversions that were motivated primarily by external considerations, while also containing an ethical component. This component did not have to be religious; it could also derive from familial obligations or a sense of loyalty to lords and princes. For some, it constituted the only opportunity for returning from exile. Religious motivations, in turn, were not necessarily rooted in theology but often reflected the superior sensual and political attraction of Baroque Catholicism. Among representatives of this subgroup, Winkelbauer listed the Austro-Moravian magnate Karl von Liechtenstein and his confreres Franz Christoph Khevenhüller and Johann Ulrich von Eggenberg, whose conversions secured them luminous careers at the Habsburg court. The decision made by Liechtenstein, in particular, came as a surprise and was widely ascribed to political expediency. Even within the Catholic hierarchy the gain was seen as political and propagandistic rather than spiritual, and Nuncio Antonio Caetano described Liechtenstein as an eager participant in public displays of religiosity but indifferent toward genuinely Catholic concerns and objectives.[53]

The Bohemian aristocrat William Slavata serves as example for a conversion that was primarily, albeit not exclusively, spiritual.[54] Religious motives were more prevalent during the early phase of recatholization, when conversion was not yet a mandatory precondition for political acceptance at court. This was also the case for William Slavata, who joined the Catholic Church in 1597. Slavata hailed from an old and respected Bohemian family that had suffered financial setbacks in the 1500s. Like his father Adam, William belonged to the Unity of Brethren, whose origins date back to the religious turmoil of fifteenth-century Bohemia. When the Hussite mainstream developed into Utraquism, some factions stayed aloof.[55] Inspired by the religious visionary Peter Chelčický and older Waldensian and Taborite traditions, they founded independent congregations that demanded a sharper theological profile and criticized the Utraquists' concessions to the monarch and especially the Catholic Church.[56] The radicals began to call themselves *jednota bratrská*, in Latin *unitas fratrum*, that is, unity of brethren, and attracted growing support among disillusioned Utraquists and persecuted sectarians.[57] At first, the Brethren's radicalism extended to the social and political spheres, where it expressed itself in demands for communal property and pacifism. Over time, however, the congregations opened up to members of the higher estates, not least of all the nobility, and shed their most revolutionary tendencies.

The Brethren were excluded from the contractual compromises that had secured a preliminary coexistence of Catholics and Utraquists. As a consequence, they suffered repeated persecutions, whose shared experience only confirmed them in their religious convictions. Dogmatically, the new community proved to be flexible, and in the 1500s it incorporated both Lutheran and Calvinist currents. This openness reflected a prioritization of religious principles such as divine mercy over doctrinal and organizational details. In spite of recurring proscriptions and subsequent emigrations to Poland and Hungary, the Bohemian Brethren were able to expand their societal influence. Jan Blahoslav's translation of the gospel into Czech in 1564 and the subsequent Bible of Kralice, which also included the Old Testament, gave the Unity of Brethren lasting significance for the development of the modern Czech language. In 1609 the Unity was officially recognized in the Letter of Majesty, in which Emperor Rudolf II had to guarantee the fundamental rights of Bohemian

82 Last Estate Standing

Protestants. Henceforth, the Brethren shared the fate of other reformist religious communities in the Bohemian kingdom.

In 1597 the outcome of the confessional struggle was far from decided, and the overwhelming majority of the Bohemian nobility continued to adhere to various Protestant denominations. It garnered great attention, therefore, when the scion of a prominent aristocratic family discarded the Unity of Brethren in favor of Catholicism. To be sure, William Slavata had been exposed to Catholic influences throughout his life, both from his grandmother and in the service of his wealthy cousin Adam II of Neuhaus. Many suspected that the prospect of gaining the hand of Adam's daughter Lucia Ottilia in marriage gave additional impetus to Slavata's religious reorientation.[58] In the end, however, it was spiritual doubt and reflection that completed Slavata's inner journey. In prolonged discussions with Jesuit councilors, he gradually became convinced that Catholicism represented the one true faith, whereas reformist theology was both erroneous and intrinsically unstable. He defended this viewpoint in a passionate exchange of letters with his father, who strongly objected to William's conversion, and denied being driven by material or other frivolous motivations.[59]

The need for personal justification followed Slavata throughout his life, resulting in a multitude of public and private rationalizations about the nature of religion and religious conversion.[60] He strongly believed in the exclusive verity of his new faith and joined the most uncompromising wing of Bohemia's resurgent Catholic party. This radicalism earned him the intense hatred of his Protestant peers and lasting fame as a survivor of defenestration. At the same time, Slavata retained a keen awareness of the psychology of confessional reorientation and readily instrumentalized his relatives' personal misfortunes to promote their religious accommodation.[61]

These case studies illuminate the motivational diversity of conversions. Overall, however, the incorporation and promotion of Catholics altered the composition of the noble estates more substantially than did conversions, which only became prevalent after the political transformation of 1620. According to Karin MacHardy, only six to nine percent of Protestant lines in the noble curiae of Lower Austria converted between 1580 and 1620.[62] This comprised six to eight branches of Protestant knights, and ten among lords, including such luminous names as Puchheim, Liechtenstein, Losenstein, Herberstein, and Althan.[63] These conversions undoubtedly invigorated the Catholic position in the diet, but numerically they remained the exception rather than the rule.

Protestants retained a clear majority in the noble curiae of the Lower Austrian estates. Counted by individual members, they amounted to 88 percent of the total in 1580, which had declined to 74 percent by 1620.[64] The Catholic representation had historically been weakest in the lower nobility, where it expanded from a mere 10 percent in 1580 to 20 percent four decades later.[65] Among the lords, who by tradition stood in closer contact with the court, the Catholic share rose from 17 to 32 percent.[66] In spite of these advances, the dynasty had to enforce Catholic restoration in its Lower Austrian heartland against noble opposition. In Upper Austria, Protestant dominance was even more substantial.

The Tempest Before the Storm: Dynastic Dissension and Confessional Respite

The changing political climate unsettled the Protestant nobles in the archduchy of Austria. During the peasant unrests of the 1590s, they were torn between confessional sympathies and socioeconomic interests, allowing the monarch to advance his religious agenda by military means. Their insufficient solidarity with beleaguered municipal councilors, based upon social jealousy as well as juridical caution, further accelerated their political isolation. High-profile conversions showed that the tide had even turned among their closest peers. In the diet, Bishop Melchior Klesl and his associates organized an ever more effective internal opposition. The disturbing reports from neighboring Styria, where Archduke Ferdinand implemented recatholization with uncustomary rigor, provided the Austrians with an inkling of things to come.

These alarming developments caused a flurry of activities by the Protestant estates. Much publicity was generated by a mission to sympathetic German princes, which sought to alert them to the growing religious pressure in the hereditary lands and enlist their support at the imperial court. The estates assigned this task to Wolfgang von Hofkirchen, one of their most prominent leaders both in and outside the diet, who traversed the empire from April to October of 1603.[67] Hofkirchen was born in 1555 as the eldest son of a later Austrian field marshal and president of the aulic war council.[68] After years of studying in Italy and administering the family estate, the Lutheran Hofkirchen embarked on a successful career in government, until he was removed from his post as acting representative of the crown in Lower Austria in 1601. There was little doubt that Hofkirchen's religious background had undermined his position, and his Protestant peers responded by electing him officer of the Curia of Lords.

84 *Last Estate Standing*

In this capacity he visited numerous German courts and conferred personally with the electors of Saxony and Brandenburg.[69] Everywhere he submitted the supplication of the Protestant estates and described their deteriorating political and spiritual situation.[70]

The success of Hofkirchen's mission was limited. He found a sympathetic ear among his coreligionists, who tended to be well-informed about Austrian conditions. Several courts interceded in Prague and delayed requested contributions to the imperial war chest. Elector Christian of Saxony, in particular, submitted a passionate appeal to the emperor, in which he invoked the old friendship between their houses and implored Rudolf to maintain his Lutheran subjects in their established rights.[71] In the end, however, these friendly interpolations accomplished very little; the imperial court considered them annoyances rather than genuine complications and trusted its ability to assuage them with non-committal assurances.

For Hofkirchen himself, the mission had more serious consequences. Already during his journey, the emissary heard rumors about the emperor's displeasure; he, therefore, avoided places where he was bound to encounter imperial officials. Following his return, he was no longer able to elude governmental sanctions. Hofkirchen was arrested for treason and kept prisoner without facing trial. After one year, he was finally released due to the intercession of the Saxon elector, but he was not rehabilitated until 1609 and never fully recovered from the experience.[72]

The confessional conflict increasingly moved into the noble curiae of the diet, the last remaining bulwark of the Protestant aristocracy. In 1604 the emperor resolved that the leadership of these bodies had to contain at least one Catholic and selected a Catholic candidate who had remained in the minority.[73] He also reserved the right to confirm all curial officers. Rudolf was able to interject himself so forcefully into previously autonomous decisions by the estates because the formation of a distinct Catholic faction had begun to bear fruit. The Catholic lords, only too aware of their continual minority status, denied the autonomy of estatist decision-making. They suggested an intrinsic monarchic privilege to disregard and alter established practice.[74] The transformation of the estates from an independent political to a subordinate administrative body was well on its way.

For years, the constitutional situation was kept purposefully opaque. The court still hesitated to enforce its newly decreed authority over the internal administration of the estates. The Protestant nobles clung to assurances that their customary privileges remained unabridged. All sides waited for the right moment to impose their own interpretation. In the meantime, the crisis at the imperial court began to overshadow

Last Estate Standing   85

the confessional discord. It provided Austrian Protestantism with a final opportunity to reverse its seemingly inevitable decline.

Family Dissension Among the Habsburgs

Emperor Rudolf II was a man of profound talents and interests, a multilingual and widely read patron and connoisseur of the arts, who turned his self-chosen residence of Prague into a haven for artists and scientists from multiple fields and countries. He was also a withdrawn and mentally unstable personality, more beholden to his intellectual pursuits than to the duties of government, and increasingly attracted to the dark and mystical fringes of science and philosophy. His most eminent biographer consequently described him as "a remarkable, but also a remarkably unsuccessful, ruler."[75]

The emperor's eccentricities, which some have attributed to expressly medical conditions such as schizophrenia, were less pervasive during the earlier phases of his reign.[76] When they overshadowed his abilities ever more visibly by the turn of the century, the dynasty took action. For reasons that may well have been personal as much as dynastic, several archdukes began to collude against the imperial recluse. They expressed concern about his health and urged him to make arrangements for his succession; Rudolf had never married and was consequently without legitimate (albeit not without illegitimate) offspring.

Archduke Matthias, who had followed his brother Ernst as vice-regent of Austria in 1595, took Rudolf's declining abilities as a welcome opportunity to position himself as heir apparent in both dynasty and state. For this agenda he found a valuable ally in Bishop Klesl, his long-time collaborator in Lower Austria. In April 1606 a Habsburg family council assembled in Vienna and secretly agreed to elevate Matthias to effective head of dynasty. Disagreements about the appropriate policy vis-á-vis the Ottoman Empire and its Hungarian allies soon brought the intrafamilial discord into the limelight.

If Matthias openly wanted to challenge his imperial brother, he needed the support of more than just his closest relatives and advisers. It was essential to secure the cooperation of the territorial estates, which continued to be dominated by the Protestant nobility. It was not without irony that Matthias set out to enlist these nobles against Rudolf, whom he had regularly accused of insufficient dedication to Catholic restoration. Under the impact of reignited hostilities in eastern Hungary, he reached an agreement with the Austrian, Hungarian, and Moravian estates. Although Bohemian opposition precluded an outright overthrow

86 *Last Estate Standing*

of Rudolf, the emperor felt pressured to cede the rebellious provinces—as well as the prospect of future succession in Bohemia—to his brother in the Treaty of Lieben (Libeň) in June 1608.

The Protestant nobles had demanded substantial religious concessions for their assistance. Having learned from previous experiences, the Austrian representatives, in particular, insisted that Matthias officially confirm these assurances prior to his accession to the throne. A majority of Upper and Lower Austrian nobles, together with the urban curia of the former, resolved not to pay homage until Matthias had reverted religious conditions in their territories to the state in which they had been at the death of Maximilian II.[77] When the pretender refused, the bulk of Lower Austria's Protestant estates moved to the safe haven of Horn, demesnial property of the Lutheran barons of Puchheim. From this modest town in the vicinity of Upper Austria and Moravia, they negotiated the modalities of Matthias's succession, leaving behind only a small delegation to represent them in the capital. In Horn they also concluded an alliance, which was signed by 166 Protestant nobles and designed to secure their religious and political privileges; corresponding steps had already been taken in Upper Austria. Whereas the Catholic minority and two lone Protestants followed Matthias's order to swear allegiance unconditionally, a solid majority insisted on prior confirmation of its liberties.

Horn turned into a symbol of Protestant resistance. The dramatic confrontation within the dynasty had offered Austria's Protestant aristocracy an unexpected opportunity to reassert its interpretation of customary law and practice, which Habsburg princes had increasingly felt at liberty to disregard. To the Protestant estates, a change in rulership had never been an objective in itself, but leverage for a lasting affirmation of their constitutional privileges. Even if Matthias fully shared the dynastic view of hereditary succession and feudal obedience, his fragile military position did not allow him to enforce it. When negotiations with the pretender reached a standstill, the noble opposition even contemplated a return to the imperial camp, which had signaled a new willingness to accommodate them.[78] The nobles also reminded Matthias of his recent concessions in Hungary when they demanded the reversal of counterreformational restrictions.

Following protracted negotiations and Matthias's enthronement in both Moravia and Hungary, the parties finally reached an agreement in March of 1609. In a decree generally known as capitulation resolution, Matthias had to confirm the concessions granted by his father Maximilian and add critical modifications and clarifications.[79] Most important among the latter was the assurance that nobles no longer had to bar

Last Estate Standing 87

non-parishioners from attending services in their privileged churches, which gave the inhabitants of Catholic towns and parishes a renewed opportunity to practice their faith. Customary law and practice should be reaffirmed in municipal elections and public appointments, reestablishing Protestant access to these positions. The decree also provided for the institution of impartial courts for the adjudication of ecclesial disputes.

As always, the treatment of urban communities posed the greatest difficulties. In spite of urgent pressure from the estates, Matthias declined to include them in the concession. Tempers flew high, also within the Protestant camp. A moderate wing advised to accept the confirmation of established liberties and declare victory rather than try to force the future monarch to extend the concessions to the urban populace.[80] The majority remained firm, however, and refused to simply abandon the towns. In the end, the parties agreed on a compromise. The written resolution only addressed the nobles. Yet in a separate oral declaration, Matthias assured the urban communities that his government would place no undue burden or pressure on them, which was subsequently clarified as entailing individual freedom of religion and the right to attend Lutheran services elsewhere.[81] In Upper Austria, select urban communities even secured the public exercise of Lutheranism. The Protestant estates made sure to record these oral assurances in writing and include them in subsequent publications.[82]

Having achieved most of their objectives, the Protestant nobles paid homage to Matthias. Their victory seemed almost complete. Moreover, Emperor Rudolf had to assuage the Bohemian and Silesian opposition with similar concessions. The Bohemian Letter of Majesty, or *majestát*, granted full freedom of worship to noble and urban adherents of the Bohemian Confession of 1575, as well as freedom of conscience to subject peasants.[83] It also confirmed the independent administration of important cultural and political institutions. As the Bohemian Confession was conceived as a unifying charter for religious heterodoxy rather than a strict doctrinal guideline, a broad coalition of Lutherans, Utraquists, and Brethren shared in the benefits of the concession as well as the accompanying accommodation between Catholic and non-Catholic estates.[84]

Reaffirmed in their rights by the Bohemian Letter of Majesty and the Austrian capitulation resolution, Protestants in both territories appeared to have rebuffed the advance of the Counterreformation. It soon became clear, however, that the religious conflict had not come to an end. The Bohemian high chancellor Zdeněk Lobkowicz refused to countersign the *majestát*, and other Catholic stalwarts shared his sentiments. Even

88   *Last Estate Standing*

more ominous was the reaction by the emperor, who not only retained Lobkowicz in office but made no secret of the fact that he himself considered the charter a temporary concession made under duress. In Lower Austria, the Catholic estates simply ignored the monarch's resolution.[85] Since they had not been included in the negotiations, they informed their Protestant peers, no agreement could bind them. In this manner, they echoed earlier Protestant attempts to disregard monarchic resolutions that lacked their explicit acceptance.

Nonetheless, the subsequent years were characterized by greater equality between the religious factions than the decades before. In the Lower Austrian diet, the opposing parties grudgingly accepted a temporary compromise that added an additional officer to each of the noble curiae and supplemented the two Protestant deputies with one Catholic; together with the two prelates, the Catholic nobles had thus reached numerical parity with their Protestant peers.[86] At the same time, the admission of Protestants to the Estate of Knights (albeit not the Lords) increased noticeably again after a period of Catholic favoritism.[87] In Bohemia, Rudolf's desperate attempt to reverse his demotion ended in abject failure; Matthias succeeded him in Bohemia and—following Rudolf's death in 1612—in the empire. Thus, the reign over the Austrian archduchy and the Bohemian lands was again united in one person. The dispute about his succession was to ignite the Thirty Years' War.

Tschernembl

During these decisive years of confessional confrontation, Protestant strategy and ideology in Austria was increasingly shaped by one personality. It appears futile to speculate if he supplied Austrian Protestantism with the leadership it so desperately needed in an hour of existential danger or if, as others have argued, it was the very radicalism of his conceptions that led to the destruction of all he held dear. There is some truth to both of these suppositions. With the succession of Archduke Ferdinand of Inner Austria in the Austro-Bohemian lands and the empire, at the latest, a peaceable survival of domestic Protestantism had become all but impossible. By attaching itself to the ensuing rebellion in Bohemia, a central segment of Austria's Protestant aristocracy hesitatingly embraced the one political movement that still held the promise of averting an otherwise inevitable decline. The utter defeat of this challenge, on the other hand, freed Ferdinand from any further need to delay and compromise.

Aristocratic leadership also required consent, however. No single noble was in a position to coerce or seduce his peers. Activists found resonance when they verbalized common sentiments, and the growing willingness to receive radical prescriptions also reflected the perceived menace and lack of alternatives. The core of Austria's hereditary aristocracy was too individualistic and headstrong to be pushed down a path it did not want. Not by their prince and emperor, if at all avoidable; much less by one of their own. No ten emperors could alienate him from his religion, Sigmund Ludwig von Polheim declared self-assuredly in 1598, because emperors also owe their position to the estates.[88]

The controversial leader of the Protestant estates was a country baron from Upper Austria. Georg Erasmus von Tschernembl was born on 26 January 1567 in Schwertberg, not far from the historic town of Enns. He was the fifth child and second son of Hans von Tschernembl, scion of an old and renowned Carniolian family that had filled prestigious posts in the administration of this duchy and acquired the honorary title of hereditary cupbearers in Carniola and the Wendish March. The family derived its name from the castle and market town of Tschernembl, Črnomelj in Slovenian, where they had started their ascent in the service of the influential comital dynasty of the Counts of Görz (Gorizia). In the 1500s individual family members expanded their holdings to other territories. Following his marriage to Margarethe von Scherffenberg, Christoph von Tschernembl purchased the estate of Windegg from his Upper Austrian in-laws.[89] When his son Hans acquired neighboring Schwertberg castle in 1563 and relinquished his Carniolian possessions soon thereafter, the line had fully established itself in its new homeland.[90]

Whereas Georg Erasmus's paternal lineage pointed to the southeastern tip of the empire, he was planted firmly in the center of Upper Austria's aristocracy on his mother's side. When Hans von Tschernembl took Barbara von Starhemberg as his wife in 1561, he not only established familial ties with this eminent Austrian house but also with the regional magnates with whom they had intermarried. After the death of his first wife, Hans entered into two further marriages, which also affiliated his line with the houses of Strein von Schwarzenau and Schönkirchen. His son was therefore a close relative and associate of numerous noble contemporaries, not least of all his cousins and political allies Erasmus and Reichard von Starhemberg.

If the new masters of Schwertberg and Windegg were well-positioned within their country's social and political elite, they were not predestined to leadership from a purely economic perspective. Even though Georg Erasmus succeeded his father in both estates, he was not to be counted among the most affluent landowners of the region. It was his personality and his intellect, combined with a profound education and erudition,

90 *Last Estate Standing*

that formed the basis for his steep political ascent, and not an inherited preeminence in status and wealth.

Education was to influence the course of Tschernembl's life in more ways than one. At the age of thirteen, he entered the future university at Altdorf together with his older brother Hans Christoph.[91] Altdorf in Franconia was developing into a significant place of study for Protestants from the German southeast, and at the turn of the seventeenth century, especially, many noble families from Habsburg territories sent their children there.[92] Even though they already arrived in 1580, the brothers Tschernembl were accompanied by their compatriots Georg Rupert and Johannes from the prominent Welzer family, whose brother Bernhard, in turn, commenced his studies together with Heinrich Tschernembl two years later.[93] The young Tschernembls left a positive impression at their alma mater, and Hans Christoph was honored with the rectorship in 1582.[94]

Yet Tschernembl also seems to have received first impulses for a gradual religious reorientation, which eventually led him away from the orthodox Lutheranism of his father's Upper Austrian environment. To be sure, Altdorf was a creation of the solidly Lutheran free imperial city of Nuremberg and considered a loyal representative of its confessional orientation, but Calvinist leanings were not uncommon among individual faculty members. Even more important was the impact of Tschernembl's private tutor Paulus Melissus, a celebrated poet and Humanist who had embraced Calvinism during his extensive travels in Switzerland and France.[95] Melissus not only influenced his noble pupils through his own works and ideas but also through his suggestions for the customary grand tour on which he accompanied them. As a consequence, the educational journey took Georg Erasmus to France and England and ultimately Geneva. His well-connected tutor had arranged this sojourn at the very center of the contemporary Calvinist world prior to his own departure for Heidelberg, where he took charge of the renowned library. Although Tschernembl continued his journey to Italy and concluded it at the imperial cameral court in Speyer, his extensive contacts with the Reformed milieus of Western Europe distinguished his experience from the Austrian norm. Tschernembl returned to the empire a convinced Calvinist, albeit in a spirit of Protestant unity that enabled him to cooperate efficiently with his Lutheran friends and associates.

After over a decade on the move, Tschernembl finally reestablished himself in Upper Austria in the early 1590s. The sophisticated young noble soon caught the attention of his peers, who began to entrust him with sensitive political missions. Following the renewed outbreak of hostilities with the Ottoman Empire in 1593, the Upper Austrian estates

Last Estate Standing   91

dispatched Tschernembl to the courts in Vienna, Innsbruck, and Munich. Before long, the costs of warfare triggered domestic disturbance, as the peasantry revolted against the increased burdens imposed on them. Since the rebellion also had religious overtones, rooted in the increasing pressure to revert the region to Catholicism, the nobility initially vacillated, but in the end, it prioritized the preservation of the established social order.

Even Tschernembl, who in an earlier memorandum had expressed considerable understanding for the rural discontent, ultimately joined the aristocratic consensus.[96] In the meantime, he had personally assumed his place among the landowning elite of the territory. Upon his father's death in 1595, he inherited Windegg and Schwertberg through an amicable settlement within the family; the year after, he entered his first marriage and established a proper household. As a seignior, too, Tschernembl remained bound to tradition; he proved receptive to complaints that demonstrated violations of established practice, but insisted on the fulfillment of customary obligations, heavy as they may be. In this spirit, he also presented the estatist view of the rural unrest to the emperor in 1597. Tschernembl matured into a skillful negotiator, who quickly adapted to the backroom dealings that prevailed at the court in Prague. The Habsburg administration found itself in the favorable position of umpire between discordant heretics and took ample time to restore order. After the peasants had been subdued in unison with the nobles, the latter soon appreciated the questionable nature of their success, as the court eagerly availed itself of the opportunity to implement its confessional program among the commoners.

The main imperial resolution of 18 October 1598 formed the basis for the recatholization of Upper Austria, and unlike many of his predecessors, Governor Hans Jakob Löbl was determined to enforce this policy.[97] The territorial nobles were not yet endangered directly, but the emperor threatened to counter any resistance with a cancellation of existing privileges. Faced with this open challenge to the religious equilibrium, Tschernembl moved to the forefront of estatist politics. In 1599 he succeeded his ally Hans Wilhelm Zelking as officer in the baronial curia of the Upper Austrian estates. Throughout his tenure, he experienced the bitter confessional strife in the territory and the resulting tensions between the governor and the estatist majority. In this conflict, Tschernembl increasingly distinguished himself as the most eloquent spokesman of the Protestant nobility, highly visible to friend and foe alike. Again he received an audience with the emperor, whom he implored to suspend the divisive religious campaign in Upper Austria. Yet Rudolf remained unmovable. In

92 Last Estate Standing

fact, the defiant resumption of Lutheran services in the Estates Building in Linz earned Tschernembl and his closest allies a citation to the court of Archduke Matthias, where they had to submit to governmental policy. Only the death of Governor Löbl in 1602 provided the Protestant estates with a temporary respite, and a perceptive Tschernembl advocated a moderate and cooperative course toward his less activist successor.

After four years of service, Tschernembl withdrew from his public position in 1603. He initially applied his newly won spare time to consolidating his landholdings, but it did not take long until the country baron reentered the political limelight. The emerging confrontation within the dynasty reignited Protestant activism, with Tschernembl among the foremost protagonists. In 1606 he represented the Upper Austrian estates during the peace negotiations with Hungary. Even though the urgency of the Hungarian crisis undercut his attempts to add the Austrian religious question to the agenda, Tschernembl recognized the value of international coordination. In the following years, his contacts to the Protestant estates of other Habsburg territories became of paramount importance. Beginning within the archduchy, but gradually extending to the lands of the Bohemian and Hungarian crowns, the Upper Austrians joined a network of ideological confreres. Through Christian of Anhalt and his circle, the lines of communication extended to the activist party in the empire.[98]

Tschernembl played a central role in the triangular conflict between Rudolph II, Archduke Mathias, and the Protestant opposition in 1609, developing the juridical line of argument and presenting it in grand speeches to the monarch and the confederated estates.[99] The successful outcome of the negotiations allowed him to resume a more private life. The loss of his first wife in 1611, the ensuing urgency to watch over his household and the upbringing of his children, and his remarriage in 1615 all kept him fully engaged with domestic matters. Under any circumstances, there was little he could have accomplished at the court in Vienna, where his name had become anathema; Matthias deeply resented Tschernembl for the concessions wrung from him during his tumultuous path to accession.[100] Yet at the same time, the Protestant leader harbored no illusions about the durability of the compromise. Behind the scenes, he continued to advise his Upper Austrian peers and cultivate his contacts with international Protestantism.

When the declining health of the childless Matthias and the prospect of Ferdinand of Inner Austria at the helm of the dynasty reopened the thinly veiled fault lines within Habsburg society, it was, therefore, only natural that Tschernembl would resurface on the political stage. Who among his peers could match his contacts in the world of international

Protestantism, his juridical and diplomatic experience, and his familiarity with Ferdinand's record in his hereditary domains? As soon as the crisis began to unfold in 1617, Tschernembl found himself in its midst. This time the Bohemians led the charge, and in a memorandum to Matthias, Tschernembl advised a peaceful solution to their grievances.[101] The emperor had much to lose and nothing to gain in a war against his own subjects, explained the baron. A military conquest of Bohemia would only confirm his possession of a territory that already belonged to him, and in the process diminish its value through the ravages of warfare. The outcome of military conflict was unpredictable, furthermore, and foreign powers might take an interest in the matter. Matthias should avoid military escalation and seek a negotiated settlement.

Notwithstanding the politically suspect background of its author, the emperor did not simply dismiss the memorandum. In an interesting twist, his old counselor Melchior Klesl, who could take more credit for the regeneration of Catholicism in Matthias's domains than anyone else, had come out in favor of moderation and thereby gained the lasting wrath of a new generation of Catholic militants. Klesl's violent removal from influence and the subsequent death of the emperor squashed any remaining hopes for reconciliation, however. The designated successor Ferdinand counted as the leader of these militants and had amply demonstrated his resolve to confront defiant subjects. At the same time, the ensuing interregnum rekindled memories of 1609 and provided Protestant activists such as Tschernembl with an opportunity to reaffirm the estates' role in the transfer of power.

Prelude to War

The appropriate course of succession was disputed. Ferdinand owed his elevation to heir apparent solely to the dynasty; its factual implementation faced a variety of constitutional challenges in the individual crown lands. Resistance could be most effective in the lands of the Bohemian and Hungarians crowns, where no inherited claim to succession was universally recognized; as a consequence, Matthias had his Styrian cousin elected or acknowledged in these kingdoms during his own lifetime.[102] In Hungary, Habsburg authority was always restricted to parts of the kingdom, whose core remained under Ottoman control. In this period of crisis, only Ferdinand's military successes in the empire sustained this modest power base against the challenge from Bethlen Gábor, the Calvinist ruler of Transylvania.[103] In Bohemia, the initially outwitted estatist opposition regained momentum when Catholic hardliners began to

94 *Last Estate Standing*

enforce their own interpretation of contested legal matters. Even moderate Protestants perceived these unilateral acts as ominous violations of the Letter of Majesty. Their more radical coreligionists responded with the historically evocative act of defenestrating royal councilors.[104] Henceforth, activist leaders such as Heinrich Matthias von Thurn charted the course of the Bohemian estates, which mobilized in defense of divided government and religious freedom.[105] In the beginning, this freedom surmised genuine confessional pluralism, which also explains the support of individual Catholic nobles. Over time, the dynastic sympathies of mainstream Catholicism triggered a more restrictive policy.[106]

While an undeclared war began to wreak havoc on the Bohemian countryside, a new societal model took shape. A confederation of the Bohemian lands placed the estates at the center of government, overshadowing a narrowly circumscribed elective kingship that presaged the constitutional monarchy of subsequent centuries.[107] Ferdinand, in turn, saw the destruction of estatist codominion as a prerequisite of rulership. The consequences of this philosophical chasm were predictable. The Bohemian general diet found Ferdinand guilty of having acceded to power by deceit and coercion and having violated his oath of coronation; it removed him from office on 19 August 1619. The following week the assembly chose Frederick V, the Calvinist Elector Palatine, as successor to the throne.[108] To Ferdinand and his supporters, this was blatant rebellion.

The constitutional situation in Austria was different. As the Habsburgs' central hereditary land, the archduchy had no tradition of lifetime succession. Dynastic continuity appeared secured and required no elections. Yet there was the seemingly small complication that the existing rules of inheritance designated Matthias's last surviving brother Albert as legitimate successor. Under normal circumstances, this juridical hitch would not have given much reason for concern. The childless Albert ruled the Habsburg Netherlands and had agreed to cede his claim to Ferdinand in exchange for financial compensation. To this end, he had already entrusted his cousin with plenipotentiary powers to assume the governance of Austria in Albert's name. But in 1619, circumstances were anything but normal. The dynasty's candidate was feared and mistrusted. The neighboring Bohemians were in the process of dethroning him. The military conflict had already touched the archduchy.

In this situation, the Protestant majority moved to secure its power base. Since the Lower Austrian estates contained a sizable Catholic faction, they were plagued by internal divisions, which eventually split the Protestant nobility as well. Their more cohesive neighbors to the west pushed ahead, with Tschernembl back at the helm. Shortly after the

Last Estate Standing 95

demise of Matthias, the Upper Austrian estates took control of the castle in Linz. The following month they assumed the administration of the territory and appointed Sigmund Ludwig von Polheim governor. They based these unilateral acts on an interpretation of dynastic succession that gave the estates a decisive role during a monarchic interregnum. In this case, the estates deduced the existence of an interregnum from the personal absence of the legitimate successor, Archduke Albert, whose power of attorney for Ferdinand they rejected on formal grounds.[109] In an extensive treatise, the estates claimed to be historically entitled to administer the archduchy until the new monarch had personally arrived in the territory and received their oath of loyalty.[110] This interpretation was immediately rejected by Ferdinand, resulting in an acrimonious juridical exchange between the parties.

Ferdinand was fully aware of Tschernembl's influence and invited him to Vienna. The estatist leader pointed to the dangerous military situation and chose to submit his advice in written form. In yet another lengthy memorandum, he tried to convince the monarch that they differed only in means, not in aims. The estates wished their territory in the hands of a powerful and internationally respected ruler. Therefore, they not only desired Ferdinand's succession in the archduchy, but also in Bohemia, Hungary, and the empire. If the monarch's advisors had focused less on dynastic reputation and more on the welfare of the territories, the current crisis could have been averted. Even now, Ferdinand could easily win the Austrians over by accepting their customary privileges and granting them freedom of religion. In the meantime, he should not press for a hasty transfer of power but gain the trust of the estates, which would be the most successful path to a felicitous succession in all his domains.[111]

Although Ferdinand was not inclined to take Tschernembl's advice, which would have required a fundamental reorientation of his political program, the lines of communication between monarchy and estates remained open. At the same time, however, both sides were busy recruiting allies. Ferdinand successfully negotiated with Bavaria, Spain, and Saxony to increase both his resources and his international legitimacy. For the latter, the support of Lutheran Saxony proved especially valuable, together with Ferdinand's election to Holy Roman Emperor in August 1619. The Upper Austrian estates, for their part, signed an act of confederation with the Bohemians, which affiliated them in an outer circle with the already established Bohemian Confederation in defense of estatist rights and religious freedom.[112]

The Protestant estates of Lower Austria concluded a similar accord with their powerful neighbors to the north.[113] Their legitimacy to speak

96 Last Estate Standing

for the whole territory was more dubious, however. The strong Catholic minority had not only charted a completely different course vis-á-vis the dynasty, but in September 1619 the Catholic representatives of the prelates, towns, and nobles paid homage to the absent Albert, in whose place his nephew Leopold, the bishop of Passau and Strassburg (Strasbourg), accepted the pledge.[114] It was of limited significance that a handful of Protestant nobles also took the oath; comparable deviations had occurred a decade earlier. More ominous were signs of disagreement within the Protestant core.

In a symbolic evocation of past triumphs, the Protestant estates had again withdrawn to the small northern stronghold of Horn. There they received Ferdinand's increasingly sterner admonitions to pay homage. During the ensuing negotiations, Ferdinand finally agreed to confirm all historical privileges prior to receiving the oath of fealty if the estates withdrew from their confederation with the Bohemian estates. This well-timed offer drove a wedge into the opposition. Whereas the greater part of the Protestant nobles, whom the military situation by then had driven to Retz at the Moravian border, refused to surrender their Bohemian alliance, a sizable minority began to waver. Pressured by the international situation, Ferdinand had made important concessions. At the same time, he threatened to prosecute all recalcitrants as rebels. In spite of continued misgivings about his ominous record in Inner Austria, an estimated 80 Protestant lords and knights paid homage to Ferdinand on 13 July 1620.[115] Including the Catholics, approximately half of the nobles had joined the prelates and towns on this momentous day. In turn, a contemporary listing of Lower Austrian nobles who had not sworn contains 110 names.[116]

The newly confirmed monarch granted the absentees a final fortnight to relent and avoid punishment. Indeed, a steady trickle of belated homages continued to drain the opposition at Retz. The future of the remaining holdouts had become inseparably tied to the fate of Bohemia. On 3 August 1620, 29 lords and 33 knights affirmed the confederation with their northern neighbors, and all but a handful subsequently supported negotiations about a transfer of power to King Frederick.[117] In their instructions, the beleaguered aristocrats not only motivated their rejection of Ferdinand and endorsement of Frederick but once again presented their view of shared government and religious tolerance.[118] By then, most of them were outlawed by the emperor and subject to immediate arrest.

In Upper Austria, Ferdinand faced a more cohesive estatist opposition, where only the Catholic prelates served as a moderating counterweight.

Since the emperor had no military presence in the territory, he drew on his international connections. While he was still negotiating with the Upper Austrians, he concluded an agreement with Duke Maximilian of Bavaria, who had successfully reorganized the Catholic League under his leadership.[119] Maximilian placed heavy conditions on his intervention. In the Munich Accord of October 1619, he secured a Bavarian directorate over the non-Habsburg forces of German Catholicism, insured himself against unilateral peace negotiations by the emperor, and was promised full compensation for military expenditures and potential territorial losses.[120] Informally, the duke gained the prospect of even more enticing remunerations. In a legally and politically contentious move, the emperor indicated his willingness to fulfill a long-standing desire of the Bavarian Wittelsbachs, namely, their elevation to the rank of imperial electors. If the Elector Palatine were to be outlawed due to his acceptance of the Bohemian crown, the emperor promised Maximilian both the succession to the vacated seat and the possession of Palatine territories he may have conquered.[121]

On 30 June 1620 Ferdinand formally entrusted his Bavarian cousin with the submission of the noncompliant Upper Austrian estates.[122] The conquered territory was to remain under Bavarian administration until Maximilian had been fully compensated for his efforts. Before he executed the imperial mandate, Maximilian achieved yet another diplomatic victory. In order to protect his territory from attacks by imperial Protestants, the cautious duke approached the Evangelical Union. Aided by the intervention of a French delegation, which laid considerable pressure on politically vulnerable Union leaders, the two sides reached an agreement in early July. In the Treaty of Ulm, Maximilian of Bavaria and Joachim Ernst of Brandenburg-Ansbach obligated their respective alliances to refrain from mutual confrontations on imperial soil. Although this accord allowed Union troops to counter Spanish attacks upon the Palatine without fear of Bavarian interference, it proved most valuable for Maximilian, who could concentrate his military resources on a full-scale invasion of Upper Austria and Bohemia.[123] News of the agreement was met with anger and disbelief by King Frederick and his supporters. Its ultimate results also disappointed the French, who had hoped for a diffusion of the Bohemian conflict that would uphold the Catholic position in the empire without strengthening the Habsburgs.[124]

On 24 July 1620 the powerful army of the Catholic League crossed into Upper Austria.[125] Its more than 20,000 soldiers stood under the leadership of Johann Tserclaes, Count of Tilly, whose exploits were to dominate the early phase of the Thirty Years' War. Any resistance by

98   *Last Estate Standing*

their own forces, barely 5000 in number, was hopeless, so the estates desperately tried to halt the invasion through further negotiations. Yet Maximilian relentlessly advanced to Linz, which fell on August 4, and demanded instant recognition as interim sovereign. The estates tried to introduce their privileges. Maximilian pointed to the exceptional nature of his administration and refused brusquely. Lacking real alternatives, the majority of the estates took the required oath. Several dozen members had excused themselves, however, and the most incriminated leaders such as Andreas Ungnad and Tschernembl had fled the country. With its homelands in the hands of Catholic armies, the future of Austrian Protestantism was decided on the battlefields of Bohemia.

Conclusion

At the turn of the seventeenth century, the confrontation over religion and government in the Habsburgs' hereditary lands intensified. Following decades of covert struggle and subterfuge, both sides increasingly accepted the inevitability of open conflict. Buoyed by the advances of recatholization in Inner Austria, the dynasty expanded its gradualist strategy to the archduchy. By separating townspeople and nobles, the Habsburgs hoped to replicate their Styrian triumph. Afraid of muddling their own privileged status with the exposed position of the commoners, the bulk of Styria's Protestant aristocracy had acquiesced to the religious transformation of the territory. It found itself isolated and vulnerable in the end.

Yet the Styrian experience also informed the estatist opposition in the archduchy. The fate of Inner Austrian Protestantism became an ominous manifestation of the dynasty's religious agenda. At the same time, it demonstrated the dangers of accepting a new monarch without an unassailable confirmation of existing privileges. In the eyes of his noble detractors, Archduke Ferdinand came to personify the dynasty's intention to deprive them of their liberties. His elevation to heir apparent moved the long-smoldering conflict to a new level.

The gradual escalation into European war was neither linear nor inevitable. As demonstrated during the conflict between the imperial brothers Rudolf and Matthias, peaceful accommodation between the confessional parties was not impossible. Yet the inner logic of confessionalization and state-building pointed toward a violent solution. In spite of mutual attempts to preserve an appearance of commonality, the constitutional visions of the Catholic dynasty and its Protestant nobility could not be reconciled. In the end, the numerous concessions the nobility had wrought from successive monarchs proved to be temporary respites. Whereas the nobles viewed them as hard-won victories that had established lasting

Last Estate Standing 99

precedent, the Habsburgs defined them as personal favors by individual rulers, with no inherent obligation to their successors.

The conflict came to a head in Bohemia, the richest and most independent of the Habsburgs' imperial possessions.[126] Yet the developments in individual territories were closely intertwined. The progress of recatholization in Styria informed the political decisions of Austrian and Bohemian Protestants. Their insistence on constitutional guarantees prior to the acceptance of a new ruler was a logical response to Ferdinand's Styrian strategy. Aristocratic solidarity with the urban communities of Bohemia formed a counterpoint to their substantive surrender in Inner Austria. The noble estates looked beyond their immediate domains and interconnected in an ever tighter web of mutual information and cooperation. As will be seen in the subsequent chapter, this expansion of horizons also expressed itself in the intellectual arena.

Notes

1. For the importance of coercion and legitimization in general and of religion in particular for the coherence of political entities, see also Anthony H. Richmond, "Ethnic Nationalism and Postindustrialism," *Ethnic and Racial Studies* 7 (1984): 4–18.
2. The concept of German liberty, or "teutsche Libertät", formed an important element of political discourse in early modern Germany. It emphasized the decentralized nature of the Holy Roman Empire and the autonomy of the imperial estates.
3. Georges Duby, *The Three Orders: Feudal Society Imagined* (Chicago, 1980), 1. See also Charles Loyseau, *A Treatise of Orders and Plain Dignities*, ed. by Howell A. Lloyd (Cambridge, England, 1994). For Duby's broader view of feudal society, see also Georges Duby, *Qu'est que la société féodale?* (Paris, 2002).
4. Georges Duby, *The Three Orders: Feudal Society Imagined* (Chicago, 1980), 3, 5. For older precedents, see also Georges Dumézil, *Mythe et Épopées*, 3 vols. (Paris, 1968–1973).
5. Georges Duby, *The Three Orders: Feudal Society Imagined* (Chicago, 1980), 66–75.
6. A. R. Myers, *Parliaments and Estates in Europe to 1789* (London, 1975), 9. Myers also provides a useful overview of the development of representative government in different parts of Europe. For such an overview within a narrower German framework, see also Francis L. Carsten, *Princes and Parliaments in Germany from the Fifteenth to the Eighteenth Century* (Oxford, 1963).
7. Felix Gilbert, ed., *The Historical Essays of Otto Hintze* (New York, 1975), 304.
8. Ibid., 312.
9. See also A. R. Myers, *Parliaments and Estates in Europe to 1789* (London, 1975), 34–47. For a divergent view on the existence of representative government outside Western Europe, based on the Russian zemski sobor,

100   *Last Estate Standing*

see M. N. Tikhomirov, "Soslovno-predstavitel'nye uchrezhdenia (zemskie sobory) v Rossii XVI veka," *Voprosy istorii* (1958:5): 3–22. For a concise critique of the equation of the zemski sobor with western parliamentary institutions, see Peter B. Brown, "The *Zemskii Sobor* in Recent Soviet Historiography," *Russian History* 10 (1983): 77–90.

10. Felix Gilbert, ed., *The Historical Essays of Otto Hintze* (New York, 1975), 319.

11. For the following, see Otto Brunner, *Land und Herrschaft: Grundfragen der territorialen Verfassungsgeschichte Österreichs im Mittelalter*, 5th ed. (Vienna, 1965), 414f.

12. For the following, see ibid., 422f.

13. For Brunner's discussion of the concept of territory, see ibid., 180–196, especially 194f.

14. See, for example, James Van Horn Melton, "From Folk History to Structural History: Otto Brunner (1898–1982) and the Radical-Conservative Roots of German Social History," in *Paths of Continuity: Central European Historiography from the 1930s to the 1950s*, ed. Hartmut Lehmann and James Van Horn Melton (Cambridge, England, 1994), 263–292, and Peter N. Miller, "Nazis and Neo-Stoics: Otto Brunner and Gerhard Oestreich before and after the Second World War," *Past and Present* 176 (2002): 144–186.

15. Ernst Bruckmüller, Michael Mitterauer, and Helmuth Stradal, *Herrschaftsstruktur und Ständebildung 3: Beiträge zur Typologie der österreichischen Länder aus ihren mittelalterlichen Grundlagen* (Munich, 1973), 115f.

16. For examples of Marxist analyses of the feudal period, see E. A. Kosminsky, *Studies in the Agrarian History of England in the Thirteenth Century* (Oxford, 1956); Robert Brenner, "Agrarian Class Structure and Economic Development in Pre-Industrial Europe," *Past and Present* 70 (1976): 30–74; or Christopher Dyer, *Standards of Living in the Later Middle Ages: Social Change in England c. 1200–1520* (Cambridge, England, 1989). For a discussion of Marx's focus on productive forces, see Stephen H. Rigby, *Marxism and History: A Critical Introduction* (Manchester, 1987).

17. See especially Perry Anderson, *Passages from Antiquity to Feudalism* (London, 1974), but also idem, *Lineages of the Absolutist State* (London, 1974). For a discussion of the challenges feudalism poses to classic Marxist theory, see Rodney Hilton, "Feudalism in Europe: Problems for Historical Materialism," *New Left Review* 147 (1984): 84–93. For another aspect of this scholarly controversy, see T. H. Aston and C. H. E. Philpin, eds., *The Brenner Debate: Agrarian Class Structure and Economic Development in Pre-Industrial Europe* (Cambridge, England, 1993).

18. For a pronounced expression of classical stratification theory, see Robert Nisbet, "The Decline and Fall of the Concept of Social Class," *Pacific Sociological Review* 2 (1959): 11–17, as well as idem, *The Sociological Tradition* (New York, 1966). For additional examples, see Kingsley Davis and Wilbert E. Moore, "Some Principles of Stratification," *American Sociological Review* 10 (1945): 242–249, and Kaare Svalastoga, *Social Differentiation* (New York, 1965). For a practical application in modern settings, see also Kaare Svalastoga and Preben Wolf, *Social rang og mobilitet*, 2nd ed. (Copenhagen, 1972).

Last Estate Standing 101

19. See especially his essay "Klasse, Stand, Parteien," published posthumously as a chapter of *Wirtschaft und Gesellschaft*. See Max Weber, *Wirtschaft und Gesellschaft*, 2nd ed. (Tübingen, 1925), 631–640. Weber's German colleague Ferdinand Tönnies, too, saw estates, and especially ruling estates, as distinguished by pride of status. At the same time, he set them apart from classes by their organic interconnection, which not only contains economic but also political and ideological dimensions. See especially Ferdinand Tönnies, "Stände und Klassen," in *Handwörterbuch der Soziologie*, ed. Alfred Vierkandt (Stuttgart, 1931), 617–638.

20. For a recent overview of the conflicting interpretations of social differentiation, consult also the useful collection of central texts in David Grusky, ed., *Social Stratification: Class, Race, and Gender in Sociological Perspective*, 4th ed. (Boulder, CO, 2014).

21. Frank Parkin, "Strategies of Social Closure in Class Analysis," in *The Social Analysis of Class Structure*, ed. Frank Parkin (London, 1974), 3. Randall Collins argued that education can serve the same purpose, especially where it provides cultural and technicist socialization rather than concrete job preparation. See, for example, Randall Collins, "Functional and Conflict Theories of Educational Stratification," *American Sociological Review* 36 (1971): 1002–1019, and idem, *The Credential Society: An Historical Sociology of Education and Stratification* (New York, 1979).

22. Frank Parkin, "Strategies of Social Closure in Class Analysis," in *The Social Analysis of Class Structure*, ed. Frank Parkin (London, 1974), 4.

23. W. G. Runciman, *A Treatise on Social Theory*, vol. 2 (Cambridge, England, 1989), 12. For a summarization of his approach, see also W. G. Runciman, "Toward a Theory of Social Stratification," in *The Social Analysis of Class Structure*, ed. Frank Parkin (London, 1974), 55–101.

24. W. G. Runciman, *A Treatise on Social Theory*, vol. 2 (Cambridge, England, 1989), 20.

25. Ibid., 23f.

26. Ibid., 24n.

27. Otto Hintze, "Typologie der ständischen Verfassungen des Abendlands," *Historische Zeitschrift* 141 (1930): 229–248.

28. For the following, see especially Michael Mitterauer, "Ständegliederung und Ländertypen," in *Herrschaftsstruktur und Ständebildung 3: Beiträge zur Typologie der österreichischen Länder aus ihren mittelalterlichen Grundlagen*, by Ernst Bruckmüller, Michael Mitterauer, and Helmuth Stradal (Munich, 1973), 115–203.

29. Otto Brunner, *Land und Herrschaft: Grundfragen der territorialen Verfassungsgeschichte Österreichs im Mittelalter*, 5th ed. (Vienna, 1965), 405. In contemporary German terminology, the lords or barons, in other words, the upper nobility, were known as the *Herrenstand*, whereas the lower nobility, or knights, formed the *Ritterstand*.

30. The curial vice-president (*Landuntermarschall*), in turn, was taken from the knightly curia, further underlining the central role of the nobility.

31. Otto Brunner, *Land und Herrschaft: Grundfragen der territorialen Verfassungsgeschichte Österreichs im Mittelalter*, 5th ed. (Vienna, 1965), 407f.

102   Last Estate Standing

32. Ernst Bruckmüller, Michael Mitterauer, and Helmuth Stradal, *Herrschaftsstruktur und Ständebildung 3: Beiträge zur Typologie der österreichischen Länder aus ihren mittelalterlichen Grundlagen* (Munich, 1973), 145–147.

33. Herbert Hassinger, "Die Landstände der österreichischen Länder: Zusammensetzung, Organisation und Leistung im 16. bis 18. Jahrhundert," *Jahrbuch für Landeskunde von Niederösterreich*, n. s., 36 (1964): 995.

34. In practice, the bishops were represented by their local vicedomes.

35. Not all urban communities availed themselves of this opportunity, however. In order to avoid the associated expenses, cities whose incorporation into Lower Austria occurred relatively late, such as Wiener Neustadt and St. Pölten, never joined the urban curia. See Silvia Petrin, *Die Stände des Landes Niederösterreich* (St. Pölten, 1982), 17.

36. For an introduction to the history of Hungary during the period of confessional strife in one of the more widely read languages, see Márta Fata, *Ungarn, das Land der Stephanskrone, im Zeitalter der Reformation und Konfessionalisierung: Multiethnizität, Land und Konfession 1500 bis 1700* (Münster, 2000). For a history of Hungarian Protestantism, see also Mihály Bucsay, *Der Protestantismus in Ungarn 1521–1978: Ungarns Reformationskirchen in Geschichte und Gegenwart*, 2 vols. (Vienna, 1977–1979).

37. For the experience of Bruck an der Leitha, where the commissioners for lack of alternatives even had to install an aging and reluctant Protestant instead of the dismissed major, see the contemporary report by the former town clerk Georg Khirmair in Laurenz Pröll, *Die Gegenreformation in der l.-f. Stadt Bruck a. d. L.: Ein typisches Bild, nach den Aufzeichnungen des Stadtschreibers Georg Khirmair* (Vienna, 1897).

38. See Friedrich Schragl, *Glaubensspaltung in Niederösterreich: Beiträge zur niederösterreichischen Kirchengeschichte* (Vienna, 1973), 113–116.

39. The city lost its privileges after a lengthy trial in 1593 and subsequently pleaded every year for their reinstitution, which was finally granted in 1615; the town advocate (*Stadtanwalt*) remained in office even longer. See Rudolf Wolkan, "Die Ächtung der Horner Konföderierten und die Konfiskation ihrer Güter" (Ph.D. diss., University of Vienna, 1913), 13f.; Andrea Pühringer, *Contributionale, Oeconomicum und Politicum: Die Finanzen der landesfürstlichen Städte Nieder- und Oberösterreichs in der Frühneuzeit* (Vienna, 2002), 129; and idem, "'Topographie der Gegenreformation' oder 'Austrian Urban Renaissance',," in *Staatsmacht und Seelenheil: Gegenreformation und Geheimprotestantismus in der Habsburgermonarchie*, ed. Rudolf Leeb, Susanne Claudine Pils, and Thomas Winkelbauer (Vienna and Munich, 2007), 295–297. For a more detailed examination of Krems in the confessional era, see also Franz Schönfellner, *Krems zwischen Reformation und Gegenreformation* (Vienna, 1985).

40. For Hans Jakob Löbl, baron of Greinburg, and the initial phase of the Counterreformation in Upper Austria, see Karl Eder, *Glaubensspaltung und Landstände in Österreich ob der Enns 1525–1602*, vol. 2 of *Studien zur Reformationsgeschichte Oberösterreichs* (Linz, 1936), 249–416.

41. For the confessional period in Steyr, see Caecilia Doppler, *Reformation und Gegenreformation in ihrer Auswirkung auf das Steyrer Bürgertum* (Vienna, 1977). See also Karl Eder, *Glaubensspaltung und Landstände in Österreich*

ob der Enns 1525–1602, vol. 2 of *Studien zur Reformationsgeschichte Oberösterreichs* (Linz, 1936), 348–351.

42. Caecilia Doppler, *Reformation und Gegenreformation in ihrer Auswirkung auf das Steyrer Bürgertum* (Vienna, 1977), 55n8.

43. See Karin MacHardy, *War, Religion and Court Patronage in Habsburg Austria: The Social and Cultural Dimensions of Political Interaction, 1521–1622* (Houndmills, England, 2003), 142f.

44. Victor Bibl, "Die katholischen und protestantischen Stände Niederösterreichs im XVII. Jahrhundert: Ein Beitrag zur Geschichte der ständischen Verfassung," *Jahrbuch für Landeskunde von Niederösterreich*, n. s., 2 (1903): 197f.

45. Karin MacHardy, *War, Religion and Court Patronage in Habsburg Austria: The Social and Cultural Dimensions of Political Interaction, 1521–1622* (Houndmills, England, 2003), 125f.

46. Otto Brunner, "Bürgertum und Adel in Nieder- und Oberösterreich," chap. in *Neue Wege der Verfassungs- und Sozialgeschichte*, 2nd enlarged ed. (Göttingen, 1968), 266–280.

47. These and the following numbers are taken from Karin MacHardy, *War, Religion and Court Patronage in Habsburg Austria: The Social and Cultural Dimensions of Political Interaction, 1521–1622* (Houndmills, England, 2003), 197, 198.

48. It should be noted, however, that the opposite could still occur in late sixteenth-century Bohemia, as evidenced by the conversion of Stefan Georg von Sternberg from Catholicism to Utraquism around 1600. See Petr Maťa, "Vorkonfessionelles, überkonfessionelles, transkonfessionelles Christentum· Prolegomena zu einer Untersuchung der Konfessionalität des böhmischen und mährischen Hochadels zwischen Hussitismus und Zwangskatholisierung," in *Konfessionelle Pluralität als Herausforderung: Koexistenz und Konflikt in Spätmittelalter und Früher Neuzeit*, ed. Joachim Bahlcke, Karen Lambrecht, and Hans-Christian Maner (Leipzig, 2006), 310.

The need for religious reorientation could also arise among individuals who remained within their church, as has recently been demonstrated for the influential imperial councilor Leonhard von Harrach, who gradually exchanged his pragmatic irenicism for the rising Catholic activism. See Michael Haberer, *Ohnmacht und Chance: Leonhard von Harrach (1514–1590) und die erbländische Machtelite* (Vienna, 2011). For the fluidity of confessional identities in the Bohemian aristocracy, see also Petr Maťa, "Constructing and Crossing Confessional Boundaries: The High Nobility and the Reformation of Bohemia," in *Diversity and Dissent: Negotiating Religious Difference in Central Europe, 1500–1800*, ed. Howard Louthan, Gary B. Cohen, and Franz A. J. Szabo (New York, 2011), 10–29.

49. See Karel Stloukal-Zlinský, *Karel z Lichtenštejna a jeho účast ve vládě Rudolfa II. (1569–1607)* (Prague, 1912). For a recent English-language biography of Wallenstein, see Geoff Mortimer, *Wallenstein: The Enigma of the Thirty Years War* (Houndmills, England, 2010).

50. For the following section, see Thomas Winkelbauer, *Fürst und Fürstendiener: Gundaker von Liechtenstein, ein österreichischer Aristokrat des konfessionellen Zeitalters* (Vienna-Munich, 1999), 85–158.

104 *Last Estate Standing*

51. For additional challenges, see Ronald G. Asch, "Religiöse Selbstinszenierung im Zeitalter der Glaubenskriege: Adel und Konfession in Westeuropa," *Historisches Jahrbuch* 125 (2005): 67–100.

52. For a more detailed examination of these negotiations, which did not result in a change of faith, see also Hans Schmidt, "Konversion und Säkularisation als politische Waffe am Ausgang des konfessionellen Zeitalters: Neue Quellen zur Politik des Herzogs Ernst August von Hannover am Vorabend des Friedens von Nymwegen," *Francia* 5 (1977–78): 183–230. For an actual conversion with comparable motives, Winkelbauer could also have pointed to Augustus the Strong of Saxony and Poland.

53. Thomas Winkelbauer, *Fürst und Fürstendiener: Gundaker von Liechtenstein, ein österreichischer Aristokrat des konfessionellen Zeitalters* (Vienna-Munich, 1999), 92. For a more detailed analysis of Karl von Liechtenstein, see also Karel Stloukal-Zlinský, *Karel z Lichtenštejna a jeho účast ve vládě Rudolfa II. (1569–1607)* (Prague, 1912).

54. For the following discussion of Slavata's motives for conversion, see Thomas Winkelbauer, *Fürst und Fürstendiener: Gundaker von Liechtenstein, ein österreichischer Aristokrat des konfessionellen Zeitalters* (Vienna-Munich, 1999), 111–119; Petr Mat'a, "Von der Selbstapologie zur Apologie der Gegenreformation: Konversion und Glaubensvorstellungen des Oberstkanzlers Wilhelm Slawata (1572–1652)," in *Konversion und Konfession in der Frühen Neuzeit*, ed. Ute Lotz-Heumann, Jan-Friedrich Mißfelder, and Matthias Pohlig (Gütersloh, 2007), 287–322; Josef Jireček, *Leben des Obersten Hofkanzlers von Böhmen Wilhelm Grafen Slavata* (Prague, 1876); and as a source for Slavata's own interpretation, Josef Jireček, ed., *Paměti nejvyššího kancléře království českého Viléma hraběte Slavaty z Chlumu a z Košmberka*, 2 vols. (Prague, 1866–1868).

55. For this development, see the discussion in Chapter 2.

56. For Chelčický, see Murray L. Wagner, *Petr Chelčický: A Radical Separatist in Hussite Bohemia* (Scottsdale, PA, 1983).

57. For the development of the Unity of Brethren and its teachings, see Rudolf Ričan, *Dějiny Jednoty bratrské* (Prague, 1957); C. Daniel Crews, *Faith, Love, Hope: A History of the Unitas Fratrum* (Winston Salem, NC, 2008); and Craig D. Atwood, *The Theology of the Czech Brethren from Hus to Comenius* (University Park, PA, 2009). For the modern Moravian Church that sees itself in the tradition of the historical Unity of Brethren, see also J. Taylor Hamilton and Kenneth G. Hamilton, *History of the Moravian Church: The Renewed Unitas Fratrum 1722–1957*, 2 vols. (Bethlehem, PA, 1967).

58. See Thomas Winkelbauer, *Fürst und Fürstendiener: Gundaker von Liechtenstein, ein österreichischer Aristokrat des konfessionellen Zeitalters* (Vienna-Munich, 1999), 109.

59. The arguments can be followed in detail in František Teplý, ed., "Proč se stal Vilém Slavata z Chlumu a Košumberka z českého bratra katolíkem," *Sborník Historického kroužku* 13 (1912): 205–221, and 14 (1913): 25–41, 171–181.

60. Among the general works was an apology of the Jesuits and a religious history of Bohemia. See Josef Salaba, "Slavatova apologie Jesuitů," *Český*

časopis historický 4 (1898): 324–332, and Hanuš Opočenský, ed., *Vilém Slavata z Chlumu a Košumberka: Přehled náboženských dějin českých* (Prague, 1912).

61. See Petr Maťa, "Von der Selbstapologie zur Apologie der Gegenreformation: Konversion und Glaubensvorstellungen des Oberstkanzlers Wilhelm Slawata (1572–1652)," in *Konversion und Konfession in der Frühen Neuzeit*, ed. Ute Lotz-Heumann, Jan-Friedrich Mißfelder, and Matthias Pohlig (Gütersloh, 2007), 298–307.

62. Karin MacHardy, *War, Religion and Court Patronage in Habsburg Austria: The Social and Cultural Dimensions of Political Interaction, 1521–1622* (Houndmills, England, 2003), 146.

63. Ibid., 258n.58.

64. All the numbers are taken or computed from ibid., 147, 144, 146. Counted by families, the Protestant share had been reduced from 87 to 69 percent within the combined curiae, with a Catholic increase from 10 to 26 percent among knights and from 25 to 39 percent among lords. Since MacHardy could not establish the confession of a sizable minority, especially in 1580, the percentages are indicative rather than final. For the religious composition of the contemporary Lower Austrian nobility, see also Gustav Reingrabner, *Adel und Reformation: Beiträge zur Geschichte des protestantischen Adels im Lande unter der Enns während des 16. und 17. Jahrhunderts* (St. Pölten, 1976), 11–20.

65. Karin MacHardy, *War, Religion and Court Patronage in Habsburg Austria: The Social and Cultural Dimensions of Political Interaction, 1521–1622* (Houndmills, England, 2003), 144.

66. Ibid., 146.

67. For Hofkirchen, see Gustav Reingrabner, "Wolfgang (II.) von Hofkirchen (1555–1611): Schlossherr in Drösiedl und protestantischer Ständepolitiker," in *Waldviertler Biographien*, ed. Harald Hitz et al., vol. 1 (Horn, Austria, 2001), 23–40.

68. For the father Wilhelm von Hofkirchen, see his entry in *Allgemeine Deutsche Biographie*, vol. 12 (Leipzig, 1880), 621–622.

69. Hofkirchen's personal description of his journey is printed in Johann Loserth, ed., *Akten und Korrespondenzen zur Geschichte der Gegenreformation in Innerösterreich unter Ferdinand II.*, vol. 2, *Fontes rerum Austriacarum* 60 (Vienna, 1907), 318–323.

70. The text of the supplication is printed in Bernhard Raupach, *Erläutertes Evangelisches Oesterreich, Oder: Dritte und Letzte Fortsetzung der Historischen Nachricht von den vornehmsten Schicksahlen der Evangelisch-Lutherischen Kirchen in dem Ertz-Hertzogthum Oesterreich* (Hamburg, 1740), 152f.

71. See ibid., 156–158.

72. Bernhard Raupach, *Kleine Nachlese einiger zu den Evangelischen Kirchen-Geschichten des Ertz-Herzogthums Oesterreich annoch gehörigen und zum theil bisher ungedruckten Urkunden und Nachrichten* (Hamburg, 1741), 27f. The estates expressly promoted Hofkirchen's rehabilitation in his negotiations with Archduke Matthias, as can also be seen in *Relation Der Vnter- und Oberösterreichischen Euangelischen Stände Abgesandten nach*

106   *Last Estate Standing*

Wien: Allda Zwischen Ihrer Königlichen May. zu Hungarn etc. vnd jnen den dreyen Österreichischen Evangelischen Ständen der Frid tractiert vnd geschlossen worden (n.p., 1610), 82.

73. See Victor Bibl, "Die katholischen und protestantischen Stände Niederösterreichs im XVII. Jahrhundert: Ein Beitrag zur Geschichte der ständischen Verfassung," *Jahrbuch für Landeskunde von Niederösterreich*, n. s., 2 (1903): 188f.

74. Ibid., 180.

75. R. J. W. Evans, *The Making of the Habsburg Monarchy 1550–1700: An Interpretation* (Oxford, 1979), 59. For a more detailed look at the emperor, see idem, *Rudolf II and His World: A Study in Intellectual History, 1576–1612* (Oxford, 1973). For Rudolf's political role, see also Josef Janáĉek, *Rudolf II. a jeho doba* (Prague, 1987).

76. For an in-depth examination of the later years of Rudolf's reign, see Anton Gindely, *Rudolf II. und seine Zeit: 1600 bis 1612*, 2 vols. (Prague, 1863–1868). For medical interpretations, see also Felix Stieve's entry on the emperor in *Allgemeine Deutsche Biographie*, s.v. "Rudolf II.".

77. "Vereinigungs-Articul/ auf welche die drey politischen Stände des Ertz-Hertzogthums Oesterreich von Herren Ritterschafft und Städten ob der Enß sich gegen einander verbunden/Anno 1608," in *Das Teutsche Reichs-Archiv*, vol. 5, ed. Johann Christian Lünig (Leipzig, 1713), 52–54.

78. Victor Bibl, "Die katholischen und protestantischen Stände Niederösterreichs im XVII. Jahrhundert: Ein Beitrag zur Geschichte der ständischen Verfassung," *Jahrbuch für Landeskunde von Niederösterreich*, n. s., 2 (1903): 215.

79. For the content of the resolution, see *Relation Der Vnter- und Oberösterreichischen Euangelischen Stände Abgesandten nach Wien: Allda Zwischen Ihrer Königlichen May. zu Hungarn etc. vnd jnen den dreyen Österreichischen Evangelischen Ständen der Frid tractiert vnd geschlossen worden* (n.p., 1610), 129–132, and Victor Bibl, "Die katholischen und protestantischen Stände Niederösterreichs im XVII. Jahrhundert: Ein Beitrag zur Geschichte der ständischen Verfassung," *Jahrbuch für Landeskunde von Niederösterreich*, n. s., 2 (1903): 219f. Matthias himself distinctly rejected the term capitulation resolution due to its conceptual proximity to election capitulations, which he considered inappropriate in a hereditary principality.

80. See Arno Strohmeyer, *Konfessionskonflikt und Herrschaftsordnung: Widerstandsrecht bei den österreichischen Ständen (1550–1650)* (Mainz, 2006), 160f.

81. See *Relation Der Vnter- und Oberösterreichischen Euangelischen Stände Abgesandten nach Wien: Allda Zwischen Ihrer Königlichen May. zu Hungarn etc. vnd jnen den dreyen Österreichischen Evangelischen Ständen der Frid tractiert vnd geschlossen worden* (n.p., 1610), 65, 66, 81, 105, 122f.; and Victor Bibl, "Die katholischen und protestantischen Stände Niederösterreichs im XVII. Jahrhundert: Ein Beitrag zur Geschichte der ständischen Verfassung," *Jahrbuch für Landeskunde von Niederösterreich*, n. s., 2 (1903): 218.

82. As in the *Relation Der Vnter- und Oberösterreichischen Euangelischen Stände Abgesandten nach Wien: Allda Zwischen Ihrer Königlichen May. zu*

Last Estate Standing   107

Hungarn etc. vnd jnen den dreyen Österreichischen Evangelischen Ständen der Frid tractiert vnd geschlossen worden (n.p., 1610), cited above.

83. For the text of the Bohemian Letter of Majesty, see "Kaysers Rudolphi II. Majestät-Brief/ welchen er denen Ständen des Königreichs Böheim sub utraque ertheilet/ das freye Exercitium Religionis betreffend/ de An. 1609," in *Das Teutsche Reichs-Archiv*, vol. 5, ed. Johann Christian Lünig (Leipzig, 1713), 55–58. For analysis see also Kamil Krofta, *Majestát Rudolfa II.* (Prague, 1909), and Anton Gindely, *Geschichte der Ertheilung des böhmischen Majestätsbriefes von 1609* (Prague, 1858).

   For a recent analysis, see also Jaroslava Hausenblasová, Jiří Mikulec, and Martina Thomsen, eds., *Religion und Politik im frühneuzeitlichen Böhmen: Der Majestätsbrief Kaiser Rudolfs II. von 1609* (Stuttgart, 2014).

84. For an analysis of the relationship between the three denominations sub utraque of contemporary Bohemian usage, that is, the Utraquists, Lutherans, and Brethren, in the early seventeenth century, see Zdeněk V. David, "A Cohabitation of Convenience: The Utraquists and the Lutherans Under the Letter of Majesty, 1609–1620," in *The Bohemian Reformation and Religious Practice 3*, ed. Zdeněk V. David and David R. Holeton (Prague, 2000), 173–214.

85. See Victor Bibl, "Die katholischen und protestantischen Stände Niederösterreichs im XVII. Jahrhundert: Ein Beitrag zur Geschichte der ständischen Verfassung," *Jahrbuch für Landeskunde von Niederösterreich*, n. s., 2 (1903): 221f.

86. See ibid., 237.

87. See the chart in Karin MacHardy, *War, Religion and Court Patronage in Habsburg Austria: The Social and Cultural Dimensions of Political Interaction, 1521–1622* (Houndmills, England, 2003), 143.

88. Siegfried Haider, *Geschichte Oberösterreichs* (Munich, 1987), 176f.

89. Even if the name of the castle is sometimes also spelled Windeck, this study will consistently use the now prevailing spelling Windegg.

90. For the general biography of Georg Erasmus von Tschernembl, see especially Hans Sturmberger, *Georg Erasmus Tschernembl: Religion, Libertät und Widerstand* (Graz, 1953); as well as Helmuth Feigl, "Beiträge zur Biographie des Freiherrn Georg Erasmus von Tschernembl" (Ph.D. diss., University of Vienna, 1949); Jodok Stülz, "Zur Charakteristik des Freiherrn Georg Erasmus von Tschernembl und zur Geschichte Oesterreichs in den Jahren 1608 bis 1610," *Archiv für Kunde österreichischer Geschichts-Quellen* 9 (1853): 169–226; and the entry on Tschernembl in *Allgemeine Deutsche Biographie* by Austrian historian Franz von Krones.

91. Elias von Steinmeyer, ed., *Die Matrikel der Universität Altdorf*, vol. 1 (Würzburg, 1912), 13.

92. Alfred Kohler emphasized the special attraction of Altdorf for the Protestant aristocracy of the Habsburg lands; see Alfred Kohler, "Bildung und Konfession," in *Bildung, Politik und Gesellschaft: Studien zur Geschichte des europäischen Bildungswesens vom 16. bis zum 20. Jahrhundert*, ed. Grete Klingenstein, Heinrich Lutz, and Gerald Stourzh (Vienna, 1978), 76.

93. Elias von Steinmeyer, ed., *Die Matrikel der Universität Altdorf*, vol. 1 (Würzburg, 1912), 13, 19.

108   *Last Estate Standing*

94. Ibid., 17, 21.
95. For Melissus, see *Neue Deutsche Biographie*, s.v. "Melissus, Paulus."
96. For his arguments during the discussion in the diet, see Grete Mecenseffy, "Evangelisches Glaubensgut in Oberösterreich: Ein Beitrag zur Erschließung des religiösen Gehaltes der Reformation im Lande ob der Enns," *Mitteilungen des Oberösterreichischen Landesarchivs* 2 (1952): 143–147.
97. For the resolution, see Karl Eder, *Glaubensspaltung und Landstände in Österreich ob der Enns 1525–1602*, vol. 2 of *Studien zur Reformationsgeschichte Oberösterreichs* (Linz, 1936), 317.
98. For Tschernembl's contacts to Calvinist activists, see Aart A. Van Scheelven, "Der Generalstab des politischen Calvinismus in Zentraleuropa zu Beginn des Dreißigjährigen Krieges," *Archiv für Reformationsgeschichte* 36 (1939): 117–141. For recent introductions to Christian von Anhalt, see Ernst-Joachim Westerburg, *Fürst Christian I. von Anhalt-Bernburg und der politische Calvinismus* (Thalhofen, Germany, 2003), and Hartmut Ross, *Für ein anderes Europa: Fürst Christian I. von Anhalt-Bernburg* (Oranienbaum, Germany, 2003).
99. These events are explored in greater detail in Chapter 4.
100. Imre Lukinich, "Geschichte Siebenbürgens, von Baron Georg Erasmus Tschernembl," *Jahrbuch des Wiener ungarischen historischen Instituts* 1 (1931): 135.
101. Already Franz Christoph Khevenhüller identified Tschernembl as the author of this anonymous memorandum, which he also printed in his *Annales Ferdinandei, oder Wahrhaffte Beschreibung Kaysers Ferdinandi des Andern . . .*, 2nd ed., vol. 9 (Leipzig, 1723), 294–310.
102. For the nature of Ferdinand's acceptance in Bohemia in 1617, see Jan P. Kučera, "Stavovská opozice v Čechách a volba Ferdinanda Štýrského českým králem," *Studia Comeniana et Historica* 14 (1984): 5–42.
103. For Bethlen Gábor, see Lajos Demény, *Bethlen Gábor és kora* (Bukarest, 1982), and László Nagy, *Sok dolog próbála Bethlen Gábor* (Budapest, 1981). Bethlen's first name is frequently rendered in its international form of Gabriel.
104. For one of the victims, see the segment on William Slavata earlier in this chapter. The historic precedent of 1419 has been described in Chapter 2.
105. As an integral part of the history of the Thirty Years' War, the outbreak of the Bohemian conflict has been treated in countless analyses of this conflict. Particularly interesting for their focus on specifically Bohemian aspects are volume 1 of Anton Gindely, *Geschichte des dreißigjährigen Krieges*, 3 vols. (Leipzig, 1882–1883), and the relevant chapters of J. V. Polišenský, *The Thirty Years War* (London, 1971).
106. See J. V. Polišenský, *The Thirty Years War* (London, 1971), 101, 104.
107. For the text of the Bohemian Confederation, see Gottfried Lorenz, ed., *Quellen zur Vorgeschichte und zu den Anfängen des Dreißigjährigen Krieges* (Darmstadt, 1991), 332–358. For analysis, see also Joachim Bahlcke, "Modernization and State-Building in an East-Central European Estates' System: The Example of the Confoederatio Bohemica of 1619," *Parliaments, Estates and Representation* 17 (1997): 61–73, and Karolina

Last Estate Standing   109

Adamová, "K politickému programu městského stavu v českém státě v roce 1619," *Právněhistorické studie* 31 (1990): 169–175.

108. For a recent English-language biography of Frederick of the Palatinate and Bohemia, see Brennan C. Pursell, *The Winter King: Frederick V of the Palatinate and the Coming of the Thirty Years' War* (Aldershot, England, 2003).

109. A detailed summarization of the estatist objections to Albert's power of attorney can be found in *Räthliches Bedencken Eines vornemen Oesterreichischen Freyherrn ob der Ens, Was massen die im Königreich Böhmen, und benachbarten Landen entstandene Unruhen, mit des Hochlöblichen Hauses Oesterreich Reputation, Nutz und Ehren zu accommodiren . . .* (n.p., 1619), where Tschernembl emphasized, *inter alia*, that the document was written in Latin, was too dated to ascertain Albert's current wishes, and had been composed without consultation of the estates.

110. *Gegründter Nothwendiger Bericht was biszhero nach Absterben des Allerdurchleuchtigsten Großmächtigsten Fürsten unnd Herrn, Herrn Matthiae Röm. Kay. auch zu Hungern und Böhemb Kön. Mtt. Ertzhertzogens . . . Alberti als nägsten Successorn des Ertzhertzogthumben Oesterreich unter und ob der Ens wegen der Landtadministration biß auff künfftige Huldigung dem uralten Oesterreichischen Herkommen nach fürgenommen unnd gehandelt worden* (Linz, 1619).

111. This memorandum was printed as *Räthliches Bedencken Eines vornemen Oesterreichischen Freyherrn ob der Ens, Was massen die im Königreich Böhmen, und benachbarten Landen entstandene Unruhen, mit des Hochlöblichen Hauses Oesterreich Reputation, Nutz und Ehren zu accommodiren . . .* (n.p., 1619).

112. For the text of the confederation, see *Historische Aktenstücke über das Ständewesen in Oesterreich*, vol. 5 (Leipzig, 1848), 30–36.

113. Printed in ibid., 26–30.

114. See Victor Bibl, "Die katholischen und protestantischen Stände Niederösterreichs im XVII. Jahrhundert: Ein Beitrag zur Geschichte der ständischen Verfassung," *Jahrbuch für Landeskunde von Niederösterreich*, n. s., 2 (1903): 292, and Arno Strohmeyer, *Konfessionskonflikt und Herrschaftsordnung: Widerstandsrecht bei den österreichischen Ständen (1550–1650)* (Mainz, 2006), 238.

115. Estimates range from numbers in the sixties to numbers in the eighties, as can be seen in Arno Strohmeyer, *Konfessionskonflikt und Herrschaftsordnung: Widerstandsrecht bei den österreichischen Ständen (1550–1650)* (Mainz, 2006), 271f.

116. Rudolf Wolkan, "Die Ächtung der Horner Konföderierten und die Konfiskation ihrer Güter" (Ph.D. dissertation, University of Vienna, 1913), 32.

117. Ibid., 35.

118. See ibid., 35f., and Arno Strohmeyer, *Konfessionskonflikt und Herrschaftsordnung: Widerstandsrecht bei den österreichischen Ständen (1550–1650)* (Mainz, 2006), 273–275.

119. The Catholic League and the Evangelical Union were the empire's foremost confessional alliances in the period leading up to the Thirty Years' War. For a recent investigation of their role, see Ernst Albrecht and Anton Schindling,

110   *Last Estate Standing*

eds., *Union und Liga 1608/09: Konfessionelle Bündnisse im Reich—Weichenstellung zum Religionskrieg?* (Stuttgart, 2010).

120. For the full text of the accord, see Gottfried Lorenz, ed., *Quellen zur Vorgeschichte und zu den Anfängen des Dreißigjährigen Krieges* (Darmstadt, 1991), 398–407.

121. The exact nature of these promises caused considerable controversy after Frederick subsequently was put under the imperial ban. See Anton Gindely, *Geschichte des dreißigjährigen Krieges*, vol. 1 (Leipzig, 1882), 164.

122. Printed in *Auff der Röm. Kayserl. auch zu Hungarn und Böheim Kön. May. Herrn, Herrn Ferdinanden II., Ertzhertzogen zu Oesterreich unter und ob der Enß etc., Unsers Allergnädigisten Herrn beschwerliche Commissions-Resolution, oder Declaration cum Mandato, an gemeine Stände und Inwohner deß Ertzherzogthumbs Oesterreich ob der Enß, vom Dato 30. Junii 1620, derselben Ersamen Landschafft notwendige, gegründte und allergehorsamiste Kurtze Verantwortung wegen ihres allzu langwirigen stillschweigens* (n.p., 1621), which also contains a careful response to the accusations from an estatist perspective.

123. For the text of the Treaty of Ulm, see Rainer A. Müller, ed., *Deutsche Geschichte in Quellen und Darstellungen*, vol. 4, *Gegenreformation und Dreißigjähriger Krieg, 1555–1648*, ed. by Bernd Roeck (Stuttgart, 1996), 213–216.

124. Dieter Albrecht, *Maximilian I. von Bayern 1573–1651* (Munich, 1998), 521f.

125. An additional smaller contingent of approximately 7,000 soldiers was deployed closer to Bohemia and Saxony to allow quicker cooperation with the latter. See Anton Gindely, *Geschichte des dreißigjährigen Krieges*, vol. 1 (Leipzig, 1882), 201.

126. For two expressions of the conflicting concepts of state in Bohemia, see Melchior Goldast von Heiminsfeld, *De Bohemiae regni, incorporatarumque provinciarum, iuribus ac privilegiis, necnon de hereditaria Regiae Bohemorum familiae successione, commentarii* . . . (Frankfurt, 1627), by an adviser to Ferdinand II, and Pavel Stránský, *Respublica Bohemiae* (Leiden, 1634), by a Bohemian exile.

4 The Thinker

Georg Erasmus von Tschernembl and the Ideology of Resistance

The early modern era brought a significant shift in European politics. In the preceding centuries, government had displayed a genuine dualism of monarchy and estates, just as society in general had been shaped by the not always congruent influences of monarchy and church. It would be misleading to propose an intrinsic antagonism between these societal forces that shared so many fundamental interests, not least of all the preservation of a social order that benefitted them all. Yet in spite of those commonalities of interest, both the estates, largely represented by the nobility, and the church had also served as counterweights to princely power.

In the sixteenth century, the independent position of the church suffered serious setbacks. The Protestant Reformation broke the factual monopoly of the Catholic Church on religious propagation. In many newly Protestantized polities the princes established themselves as supreme heads of the church, effectively precluding any future challenge to the monarchy from the dominant religious body. Yet even in the remaining Catholic realms, the relationship between monarchy and church was transformed. Not only had the papacy forfeited any remnant of universally acknowledged authority over western Christendom, but it had been up to princes to restore the predominance of Catholicism in much of Europe. Even before Enlightenment, revolution, and modernization fundamentally changed the position of Christianity in European societies, the autonomous political influence of religious bodies had receded markedly from its medieval apex.[1]

The church was not the only societal force under duress. The representative assemblies of shared government also felt the pressure emanating from self-assured princes. In response, they refined their own ideology of estatist codominion, which distinctly challenged a monarchic monopoly on power. Thus, the emergence of new modes of governance in France

112 *The Thinker*

or the Habsburg Monarchy was accompanied by protracted conflict, in which the monarchs could not impose their conceptions until the estatist opposition had been defeated militarily. The suppression of the Fronde by Louis XIV between 1648 and 1653 and of the Bohemian rebellion by Ferdinand II in 1620 became important milestones in the resolution of constitutional disputes in favor of the crown.[2]

Yet also the very nature of governance and politics changed. Early modern Europe experienced an expansion of both governmental institutions and the responsibilities they assumed.[3] New philosophies of state redefined the content and legitimation of monarchic rule, while advances in civic, military, and not least of all fiscal administration increased its impact on everyday life. A growing number of formerly private conditions became subject to regulation, and the pressure to adhere to public ordinances increased.[4] Collectively, these developments contributed to the emergence of modern statehood and thus reformed the nature of human organization.[5] They also faced protracted resistance.

This chapter traces the ideology of Austria's estatist opposition during the early decades of the seventeenth century. In the writings of Georg Erasmus von Tschernembl, especially, an alternative vision of state and governance took shape, whose implementation would have transformed the history of Central Europe. It took a continental war to resolve this fundamental ideological discord in favor of the dynasty.

The Theory of Legitimate Resistance

The princes' determination to expand their role in government provoked diverse reactions among the estates. Whereas most of their protagonists initially expressed opposition, many soon relented, and some groups, such as the Catholic minority in the Lower Austrian diet, grasped the opportunities offered by an outright alliance with the sovereign against estatist recalcitrants.[6] While the advocates of princely sovereignty developed concepts of absolute monarchy, proponents of estatism refined their own philosophy of state, which emphasized the importance of their institutions as representatives of the land and its established customs.[7]

An important element of estatist opposition was the notion of legitimate resistance against unjust rulers. The origins of this concept can be traced to diverse sources. Both Greek and Roman tradition were familiar with it, as was early Christianity with its inherent tension between Paul's much-quoted demand in Romans 13:1 that everyone must submit himself to the governing authorities, for there is no authority except that which

The Thinker 113

God has established, and Peter's insistence in Acts 5:29 that one must obey God rather than men.[8] Most important for the early-modern debate, however, were the more immediate antecedents of resistance theory in medieval Europe. Christian traditions retained significance, not least of all for the crucial relationship between secular rulers and the pope.[9] Medieval Christianity also refined older concepts of tyranny, according to which a ruler forfeited his lawful status by violating the fundamental principles of divine and natural law. Resistance against such a ruler did not constitute rebellion, as long as it did not cause more damage to the common good than tyranny itself.[10]

An important medieval innovation derived from the reciprocal nature of vassalage.[11] Homage and fealty connected lord and vassal through mutual obligations, which both sides were bound to uphold. A lord's neglect of these obligations gave the vassal the right to renounce his obedience through the act of diffidatio. Estatist ideology also transferred this contractual imagery from the individual to the societal level. Monarchic rule was anchored in a mutually binding set of obligations, whereby the estates participated in government as representatives of the territory. The monarchs customarily affirmed their obligations in charters and election capitulations. If a ruler subsequently violated them, the estates reserved the right to disobey or even renounce him.

In the sixteenth century, these historical traditions merged into an ongoing debate about the religious authority of princes. The Reformation had transformed this debate by creating large-scale defections from the established church and its dynastic supporters. Suppression of heresy was no longer simply law enforcement against individuals; it had moved to the center of politics and touched the very nature of government. Both the Catholic Church and the emerging Protestant denominations searched for legally and theologically viable responses, which were especially important for the proponents of the religious reform movements, as it was they who needed to claim their place within a juridical framework that did not include them. Thus, Protestant leaders also sought to legitimize resistance against rulers who tried to suppress their teachings.

Early twentieth-century historiography tended to derive modern theories of resistance from Calvinist roots, distinguishing a protodemocratic Western European Reformed tradition from a more subservient German Lutheran one. These arguments were formulated by German theologian Ernst Troeltsch and his followers at the turn of the century and subsequently popularized by refugees from the Third Reich such as Hans Baron, who put them into a context of contemporary politics.[12] A Lutheran

114 *The Thinker*

insistence on suffering obedience had prepared the ground for Prussian authoritarianism and subsequently National Socialism, whereas Calvinist teachings had inspired successful rebellions in countries reaching from the Netherlands to the United States.

As far as Luther's own theology was concerned, these interpretations found plenty of arguments upon which to rely. In his famous publication, "On Secular Authority," Luther had taken Paul's admonition to respect authority as a guiding principle.[13] The world was divided into spiritual and secular spheres, each with their respective governments. Whereas the former existed for the few true Christians, the latter constrained the wicked and thus protected the just. Secular authority was indispensable until all of mankind genuinely followed Christ's teaching, which Luther did not consider a realistic prospect, no matter how many outwardly confessed to be Christians. Therefore, both governments were necessary complements of each other. The spiritual authorities guided the secular toward justice. The secular authorities ensured safety and peace for believers and non-believers alike. This positive view of secular government made disobedience difficult. In a central passage, Luther consequently emphasized that authorities were not to be resisted by force but only by professing the truth. If authorities were to ignore a subject's testimony, he would bear no responsibility for their actions and suffer injustice for the sake of God.[14]

In spite of its fundamental insistence on obedience toward lawful authority, one can trace some reservations even in this early formulation of Luther's political philosophy. Subjects were not bound to follow a prince who was clearly in the wrong, because no one has a duty to act against what is right and all must obey God rather than men.[15] Even then, however, permissible disobedience was largely confined to emigration. Over time, Luther had to reconsider this passive response to political injustice. Faced with the emperor's consistent attempts at suppressing the religious reform movement, Luther reluctantly opened up a window for legitimate resistance in 1530. In a strictly juridical interpretation that fully preserved the abstract obligation to respect authority, Luther deduced that imperial law had permitted resistance in select situations and thus adopted it into the framework of positive law.[16] Nine years later he went one step further and allowed all forms of resistance against a destructive power such as the pope, even if the latter had gathered the support of lawful rulers.[17] While continuing to uphold a duty to obey secular government, Luther had thus created a loophole for cases of extreme emergency in which external forces misused legitimate institutions to subvert society.

Calvin shared Luther's aversion to rebellion. The chapter on civil government in his *Institutio Christianae Religionis* is permeated with respect for lawful authority.[18] After all, Calvin as well as other mainstream reformers felt a strong need to distance themselves from the theological as well as social radicalism of the Anabaptists, with whom they were widely identified in Catholic literature.[19] Calvin warned against misinterpretations of biblical passages that promise a liberty without kings and masters, describing them as allusions to the kingdom of God. In the world of humans, by contrast, civil order represents an essential precondition of successful association; any thought of abolishing it must be seen as a monstrous barbarism.[20] Calvin stressed the necessity of order and authority and drew special attention to the office of the magistrate, whose instructions were not to be resisted. Since these magistrates held a commission from God, their rejection amounted to a rejection of God himself.[21] Next to the magistrates came the laws, which he defined as the sinews of the commonwealth and, citing Cicero, the soul without which the magistrates cannot survive, whereas they in turn remain powerless without the latter.[22]

Mere subjects were to hold the authorities in the highest possible regard and show them obedience.[23] This required little explanation in regard to just rulers. Yet even cruel or incapable rulers owed their office to God, who invested them in order to punish the iniquity of the people.[24] Therefore, they were to be shown the same reverence as excellent kings. In comparison with these forceful invocations, references to legitimate resistance remained subtle. Calvin saw parallels between the modern estates and historical correctives of power such as the Spartan ephors and the Athenian demarchs; the estates functioned as popular tribunes to guard the community against royal transgressions.[25] In this definition, their disobedience was not true resistance at all, as long as it occurred within the legally determined responsibilities of their public authority. Even though Calvin subsequently broadened his concept of legitimate resistance, it tended to remain within a framework of positive law.[26]

It was the British intellectual historian Quentin Skinner, especially, who modified perceptions of denominational politics.[27] Skinner argued that Calvinism initially was quite unprepared to confront governmental coercion.[28] Faced with imperial proscriptions against their theology, German Lutheran thinkers, on the other hand, soon felt the need to legitimize their disobedience. As early as 1529, Luther's associate Johann Bugenhagen distinguished between a divinely ordained authority and a tyrannical, which he ascribed to the devil. The imperial princes, in turn, were not to be seen as the emperor's subjects but as subordinate leaders who owe

116   *The Thinker*

only proper, not unconditional, obedience.[29] Thus arose early Lutheran justifications of resistance, which either followed the constitutionalist approach of Hessian or the private-law approach of Saxon jurists.[30] The former based the right of German Protestant rulers to defy the emperor on their status as territorial princes. The latter saw it as permissible self-defense against unjust force, especially in matters over which the emperor was said to lack legitimate jurisdiction, such as religion. Skinner conceded that Luther only reluctantly agreed to such concepts in a time of crisis, but invoked subsequent refinements as evidence for the continuity of Lutheran resistance theory.

In 1550 the reignited confrontation between the Catholic Habsburgs and their imperial opposition triggered one of Lutheranism's most explicit calls for defiance. The free imperial city of Magdeburg, long a bulwark of the new faith, had turned into a hotbed of opposition to the Augsburg Interim of 1548. Through this imposed compromise, Emperor Charles V had attempted to lead German Lutherans back into the Catholic fold. Protestant holdouts such as Magdeburg needed to justify their disregard of imperial law. Under the leadership of Luther's old friend and confederate Nikolaus von Amsdorf, a group of local theologians formulated a fundamental defense of resistance. The memorandum known as the Magdeburg Confession summarized its core message in the introduction: if higher authorities not only persecute their subjects violently and unjustly, but also deprive them of their innate right to hear and practice true religion, lower authorities are duty-bound to resist.[31] A distinct subsection of the publication discusses the preconditions of legitimate resistance. While acknowledging the divine origins of authority, it simultaneously ties it to the fulfillment of God's mandates. Authority is put in place to honor the good and punish the wicked; if it does the opposite, it is no longer ordained by God but by the devil and must therefore be defied.[32]

Not everyone is entitled to resistance, however, and not every infraction justifies it. Resistance should occur according to status and vocation, and it must be commensurate with the violation.[33] Unjust force is, therefore, divided into four categories.[34] In matters of limited significance, lower authorities were to implore the ruler to abstain, but otherwise patiently suffer such injustices. Even a more serious type of violation, such as an emperor's illegitimate warfare against a territorial prince, should not necessarily provoke a violent response, understandable as it may be. As the third degree of injustice, the confession lists superior authorities' attempt to coerce lower magistrates into sinful conduct, which the latter may resist within the confines of divine law. Most attention is devoted to the fourth category, however. If supreme authorities degrade beyond mere tyranny and not only persecute their subordinates and subjects but also violate supreme law and its divine promulgator, resistance is not only legitimate but obligatory.

The Magdeburg Confession formulated a radical Lutheran theory of resistance. While retaining a fundamental respect for authority as ordained by God, its proponents devised a model by which this authority loses and ultimately inverts its divine status. Resistance, then, is not directed against a legitimate authority but follows the rules of self-defense against any unjust force. Not every dereliction of duties entails such a loss of divine ordination; only the ruler's continual and deliberate attempt to destroy the good works of the community does. By comparing resistance to a mad tyrant to a family's refusal to receive the housefather's criminal companions, the Confession also placed this resistance in a context of individual self-defense, drawing on older Saxon arguments as well as more recent publications such as Justus Menius's *Von der Notwehr unterricht*, arguably the most far-reaching expression of contemporary Lutheran resistance theory.[35] In its central passage, Menius derived a universal right to resistance from legitimate self-defense, comparing it to a father's prerogative to protect his family.[36]

Eventually, these conceptions resonated among Calvinists as well. Transmitted through the Magdeburg Confession or taken directly from the earlier writings it relied upon, they influenced leading Huguenot theorists. The constitutional elevation of lower magistrates, largely identified with the noble estates, established their entitlement and outright obligation to resist injustice. The axiom spread throughout the Calvinist world, not least of all to Scotland, where John Knox called on the aristocracy to support religious reform and defend the law of God against blasphemous kings.[37] Even Calvin himself began to abandon his original hesitance toward political resistance in view of the increasing pressure on his followers in France and the Low Countries, entitling lower authorities to hold the prince within the limits of godly government.[38]

Neither Calvinist nor Lutheran thinking intrinsically supported concepts of resistance. Each radical statement could be countered by calls for restraint and submission. To a large extent, the choice of philosophy was guided by political circumstances rather than abstract theology. In times of duress, proponents of all major denominations could be attracted to theories of resistance. Safely in power, they gravitated toward obedience and orthodoxy. As a consequence, the clergy of thoroughly Lutheranized imperial territories tended to lose interest in the language of defiance

118 *The Thinker*

following the Peace of Augsburg, whereas more endangered Calvinists took up the torch, especially in France. The denominational linkage was not inherent, however, as can be seen in the case of Austrian Lutheranism.

Monarchomachs

The rejection of monarchic sovereignty became especially pronounced when the competition for power and influence was reinforced by confessional conflict. As a result, the confrontations between France's Catholic monarchs and their Calvinist subjects inspired some of the most expressive manifests of estatist opposition. Among the radical proponents of limited monarchy and legitimate resistance was a small group of thinkers who were subsequently designated as Monarchomachs. The term consists of Greek elements meaning those who fight the ruler and is widely attributed to Scottish-born Catholic William Barclay, who applied it disparagingly to the largely Huguenot opponents of absolute monarchy whose works he had encountered as professor of civil law in France.[39] Under the impact of state-sponsored violence against their religious community, Huguenot Monarchomachs promoted notions of popular sovereignty and legitimate resistance. They proposed a contractual view of rulership, in which the monarch had to negotiate his power with the magistrates of the people. Those magistrates, largely identified with the estates, could legitimately resort to resistance against tyranny.

It would be misleading to associate Monarchomachism solely with Calvinism. Not altogether surprising, such concepts held particular appeal among religious minorities. In polities ruled by Catholic princes, theories of resistance were more popular among Protestants, and refugees from the Catholic restoration under Mary Tudor figured prominently among their early proponents. Following the Protestant turn in England as well as Scotland, Catholics promoted similar conceptions, and few more energetically than the Jesuits. The denominational frontlines did not have to be as clear-cut as in those examples. In France, Monarchomach concepts spread from Huguenots to radical Catholics, who decried the temporary political accommodation of Catholic dynasty and Calvinist minority.[40] On the British Isles, Puritans confronted the, in their eyes, insufficiently Protestant policies of the Stuart kings.

French Huguenots made a special contribution to Monarchomach thought, however. Following the challenge to their very survival on St. Bartholomew's Night of 1572, especially, Huguenot intellectuals condensed and transformed existing concepts of resistance, be they of historical or recent Protestant origin. Their fundamental challenge to monarchic omnipotence found its classic expression in the writings of François Hotman, Theodore Beza, and the only pseudonymously known Stephanus Junius Brutus. While it was catalyzed by the existential crisis of their community, its basic contentions reverberated far beyond the times and circumstances of their creation.

François Hotman counted among the leading French scholars of his era.[41] Born into a family of lawyers in 1524, he entered a promising academic career in his early twenties. Due to his contemporaneous embrace of Calvinism, however, Hotman's further advancement depended on the fortunes of this religious community. Repeatedly changing workplace and residence, he finally left France after a narrow escape from the anti-Huguenot excesses in 1572. In his exile at Geneva, he also completed his most famous work, *Francogallia*, which he had started during the growing denominational tensions of the preceding decade. First published in 1573 in Latin, the treatise evoked great interest due to its grand historical design and its immediate relevance for contemporary politics; it was soon reissued in French and revised Latin editions.[42]

In his *Francogallia*, Hotman strove to vindicate his support of divided government through a historical analysis of French institutions and governance. Reaching back as far as pre-Roman Gaul, Hotman diagnosed a tradition of popular liberty that formed a precondition of the country's prosperity. In recent centuries, the estates had served as the guarantors of these ancient liberties, which had survived in customary law. Therefore, he decried the increasing emphasis on monarchic sovereignty and Roman law as a harmful deviation from the due course of French constitutional history.

Hotman largely anchored his argument in a notion of popular sovereignty. The people never surrendered their original claim to all public authority to the king but only delegated some aspects of it, and under specific conditions. In particular, they reserved their right to invest the king, as well as to remove him from office in case of abuse.[43] In practice, popular sovereignty was to be exercised by the estates, which ensured that decision-making did not rest with the unreasonable masses.[44] Hotman went to great lengths to document the significance of popular assemblies and representative bodies in French history. The assemblies had to be consulted in all important matters of state. Kings held an important place, to be sure; they were like fathers to a family or captains to a ship. This elevated position was to serve the commonwealth, however, and not the monarch himself. Just as the captain was appointed for the sake of the ship, kings were selected for the benefit of the people. A people without a king was feasible; a king without a people was beyond imagination.[45] As

120 *The Thinker*

a consequence, Hotman saw kingship as conditional upon performance and public consent. Royal subjects were not slaves, and obedience to a monarch did not equal servitude. Kings had been instituted as defenders of liberty, not as tyrants.[46] A prince was to respect the country's customs and laws. If he failed to do so, he could be removed, argued Hotman with reference to French history.[47]

The *Francogallia* stirred public attention, but its reception was mixed. While the study was widely discussed and influenced Protestant leaders in France and abroad, the general reaction was negative. Even a number of Huguenots felt a genuine or tactical need to disavow its controversial theses, which Catholic opponents quickly countered in a series of rebuttals.[48] In view of these highly charged responses it may seem surprising that the study did not yet contain an explicit theory of resistance. The core of the argument expounded the historical limitations of monarchy rather than the legal basis for disobedience. Moreover, Hotman argued as a constitutional historian, not as a theologian or philosopher. In keen awareness of demographic realities, he avoided tying his analysis of French government to contemporary denominational conflicts. Whereas he cited historical examples of antimonarchic resistance, he did not integrate them into a coherent doctrine. This task was subsequently assumed by his Genevan associate Theodore Beza under the immediate impact of St. Bartholomew's Night.

Theodore de Bèze, widely known as Beza, was born in 1519 to a noble Burgundian family.[49] The talented youth studied law at Orleans and Bourges and entered a legal career, but his true interests lay elsewhere. He impressed his contemporaries with Latin poetry and taught Greek at the Lausanne academy, where he had moved after his conversion to Protestantism. His spiritual journey, instigated by the German humanist Melchior Volmar who served as his tutor, was completed by the time Calvin received him in Geneva in 1548.[50] His life and work were increasingly dedicated to his faith, both through his writings and through his support for the Reformed Church in France. For a long time, he favored cooperation with the royal court and advised more activist coreligionists to find solace in prayer and patience.[51] Following the attacks of 1572, however, his position hardened. Having assumed the leadership of the Genevan church after Calvin's death in 1564, Beza needed to chart a course for beleaguered French Calvinism. For this purpose, he anonymously published his treatise *On the Rights of Magistrates* in 1574.[52]

Beza felt an urgent need to provide his coreligionists with a legal and moral basis for defying the monarch in matters of faith. Not only Christian theology in general, but also Calvin in particular had emphasized the subjects' obligation to respect authority. Therefore, Beza introduced his study

The Thinker 121

with biblical references to popular disobedience that had been justified by God. By way of philosophical explanation, he added that the power of secular authorities is limited by faith and love. Where they transgress these limitations and issue orders that violate divine law, their subjects are to remember the biblical admonition to obey God rather than men.[53]

Beza added nine more investigations into the nature of authority, the subjects' duty to obey, and their legitimate reasons to refuse. In his central arguments, Beza echoed Hotman's notion of popular sovereignty and the priority of popular over monarchic interests. People selected rulers to create order and advance the general good.[54] They placed explicit conditions on the transfer of power, which royal claimants had to affirm and subsequently adhere to. By no means did monarchs stand above the law. On the contrary, those who swore to defend and uphold all laws were bound by each and every one of them.[55] They were only entitled to govern as long as they respected these principles.[56]

Having established the constitutional framework, Beza proceeded to its practical implementation. How should subjects respond to a monarch's violation of societal ground rules? To answer this question, Beza divided transgressors and potential respondents into categories. Tyrants who usurp power that does not legally belong to them can and must be opposed by everyone.[57] More complex was the treatment of initially legitimate rulers who so grossly abused their authority as to turn into tyrants.[58] In this case, Beza did not grant mere subjects the right to resist because he feared the commotion and lawlessness it would trigger. Once a monarch has been properly accepted by the people, no subject can individually annul this act.

Yet Beza did not conclude his argument with a resigned call for suffering obedience. Whereas he rejected an individual right to resistance against kings turned tyrants, he referred this task to the mediated authorities he called lower magistrates. This intermediate societal power did not consist of the king's personal servants, but of public officials who served the realm rather than the ruler. As such, they were not simply subjects but legitimate authorities in their own right, with an express obligation to protect the commonwealth. Beza described it as self-evident that lower magistrates, having sworn to ensure the rule of law, were entitled to confront a tyrannical ruler who had violated the terms of his investiture.[59] In fact, private individuals, lacking the legal basis to defy the ruler on their own, could always urge the lower magistrates to protect the commonwealth from tyranny.[60]

In his final proposition, Beza examined the subjects' right to an armed defense of their faith.[61] The question posed considerable difficulties to

122 *The Thinker*

Beza, who assigned government an important role in the upholding of true religion. He even defended the suppression of blasphemy and heresy. As a consequence, he was unable to base the religious rights of his coreligionists on a generic freedom of conscience. With implicit reference to France, however, he invoked existing statutes that guaranteed the true believers the exercise of their faith. Were a prince to violate the legal order in so fundamental a question as religion, he could undoubtedly be resisted as a tyrant.[62]

On the Rights of Magistrates was so contentious that Genevan authorities initially refused publication in 1573. When it subsequently appeared in France, its immediate impact was reduced by the anonymity of its illustrious author. Yet the study advanced Monarchomach thinking in more ways than one. Beza went beyond Hotman, to whom he was otherwise clearly indebted, in providing an explicit theory of resistance. In this theory, he fused long-established doctrines on confronting tyranny with more recent arguments for the constitutional significance of subordinate authorities. In practical politics, Beza's elaborations on lower magistrates assumed the most immediate significance. Resistance to obvious usurpers was not a very controversial or politically relevant aspect of sixteenth-century philosophy of state; defiance of legitimate rulers accused of exceeding their powers was. By instituting a body of authorities to curb such transgressions, Beza provided a formal counterweight to monarchic sovereignty. His arguments remained to a large extent theological, however; they served to assuage a Christian conscience concerned about neglecting proper obedience. The call for political action was issued soon thereafter by an author assuming the pseudonym Stephanus Junius Brutus, the Celt.

Who was this author, whose true identity even eluded the king of France in spite of his reported efforts at establishing it?[63] This question has been discussed for centuries, without resulting in a universally accepted answer. The most serious contenders are Hubert Languet and Philippe Duplessis-Mornay, even though alternative suggestions continue to arise.[64] Since both candidates intimately knew and appreciated each other, their thinking intertwined, making it difficult to determine their respective roles in the production process and generating suggestions of a collaborative effort. Hubert Languet was a writer and diplomat, who spent much of his life in the service of Protestant princes, most notably Elector Augustus I of Saxony.[65] Duplessis-Mornay descended from a distinguished noble family and made a career as a soldier, diplomat, and political advisor, not least of all to Henry of Navarre.[66] Both were highly educated and devoted Huguenots who spent considerable parts of their

The Thinker 123

lives outside France. Whereas Languet already passed away in Antwerp in 1581, Duplessis-Mornay lived to see the temporary consolidation of Huguenot influence following the accession of Henry IV to the French throne. The implicit price paid for this political respite, Henry's conversion to Catholicism, so alienated him from his former idol that he withdrew into the countryside, where he also died on his estate in 1623.

The *Vindiciae, contra tyrannos* appeared pseudonymously in 1579 at Basel, even if the front page lists the place of publication as Edinburgh.[67] Its subtitle stated that the study examines the legitimate power of a prince over the people and of the people over the prince, highlighting the contractual imagery of political rule that permeated the study. The author postulated the existence of two fundamental covenants. A covenant between God and kings, concluded under participation of the people, obligated kings to rule in accordance with divine law.[68] In a separate covenant between king and people, the former obligated himself to rule justly, whereas the latter pledged obedience to a just ruler.[69] Through the first compact, the king promised piety; through the second, he promised justice.[70]

Vindiciae, contra tyrannos is no abstract treatise on the nature of rulership, however. Three core questions structure the analysis. Are subjects bound to obey princes if their commands violate divine law? Who, if anyone, is allowed to resist such a prince and by what means? And is such resistance also permissible against a prince who oppresses or ruins a commonwealth?[71] The fundamental legitimacy of resistance derives from the nature of monarchy. Kings are instituted by and thus derivative of God, who also entrusted the people with the authority to select and approve them.[72] Kings were created for the benefit of the commonwealth; the people would not have surrendered their innate freedom but for an expectation of superior benefits. Foremost among those benefits was the enforcement of law and justice.[73]

The people exercised their rights through their representatives, who may be officers of the kingdom or estatist assemblies. Amidst these popular representatives, a king was merely the first among equals. Although he was superior to them as individuals, he ranked below them as a collective entity.[74] It was, therefore, up to those popular representatives to uphold the constitutional order and resist princely transgressions. To be sure, tyrannical usurpers could be defied by anyone. Resistance to legitimate rulers was a more delicate matter. As humans, princes were bound to be fallible; their commonplace foibles did not render their tenure illegitimate.[75] Yet a king who openly broke his compacts with God and the people also absolved the latter from any obligations toward him.[76]

124   *The Thinker*

Tyrants committed the worst crime imaginable because their debasement of the commonwealth harmed many and all together rather than just individuals. They were guilty of high treason against the supreme majesty, the kingdom itself.[77]

Yet who was called to stop and restrain a once legitimate ruler who had turned into a tyrant? The author emphatically rejected a universal right to resistance.[78] No private individual was entitled to rouse the subjects to arms. The commonwealth was not entrusted to individuals; those who could not even protect themselves were not called to protect the commonwealth. If they resorted to violence, even in pursuit of a seemingly just cause, they were seditious. It was up to the officers of the realm, with their superior insight into the nature of monarchic duties and privileges, to defend the commonwealth against a tyrant by conduct.[79] They were bound by their office to judge him according to the law and rein him in if he failed to comply. Federal officeholders were entitled to restrain a tyrant collectively or individually. Local officeholders could bar him from entering their districts. Without such privileges, individuals needed an explicit injunction by legitimate authorities to put up resistance.

Vindiciae, contra tyrannos completed the formulation of classic Huguenot Monarchomachism. It integrated most preceding arguments, while at the same time deepening and extending them. Hotman's insistence on the conditional and utilitarian nature of kingship permeates the study, as does Beza's promotion of lower authorities to guardians of the realm and its constitutional order. In the *Vindiciae*, however, resistance has moved to the center of the argument. There are remnants of Luther's and Calvin's insistence on suffering obedience, but they are largely reserved for commoners without magisterial support. The rights of officeholders are reinforced, by contrast. Even though they are only defined as the monarch's superiors as a collective body, the author does not tie the legitimacy of resistance to majority consent. Individual magistrates can be called to restrain a tyrannical ruler, just as regional officials are entitled to ward off illegitimate royal encroachments. Thus, Huguenot resistance theory formulated a radical rejection of unlimited monarchy, while accentuating the divine boundaries of rulership, as well as the crucial position of representative institutions as guardians of public interest. This emphasis appealed to estatist activists far beyond France.

Georg Erasmus von Tschernembl and the Austrian Ideology of Estatism

The international debate about the rights of rulers and estates, including the discussion about legitimate resistance, reverberated in Austria as well.

Even though theological or philosophical conceptions were not unknown to them, however, the Austrian estates primarily operated within a framework of historical tradition and affirmed privileges. A positivist approach was not only more in line with their own thinking but also promised to carry weight with the monarch. Contemporary Habsburg rulers continued to pay attention to the legality of governmental acts, at least on a formal basis. It is in this light that we can understand the otherwise inexplicable evasiveness and subterfuge that characterized political negotiations, especially around a new monarch's accession to power. Prospective rulers offered oral assurances, more open to interpretation and denial, while balking at written confirmations. Where formal guarantees proved unavoidable, they would subsequently be depleted of content rather than expressly retracted. Activist rulers such as Ferdinand II felt little obligation toward a Protestant nobility they considered rebellious almost by definition, but they valued their own appearance of legality and respectability.[80]

As a consequence, the Austrian debate frequently took its starting point in constitutional history. The estates regularly reminded claimants to the throne of the privileges granted by their predecessors and demanded their confirmation. When the Upper Austrian estates submitted a memorandum to Ferdinand at the height of the ideological conflict in 1619, they traced their rights to the very arrival of the Habsburgs in Austria and in some facets even beyond.[81] In their eyes, historical precedent entrusted territorial administration to the estates until a new ruler had personally received their oath of loyalty. This strong position of the estates during an interregnum was anchored in the claim that they had initiated the dynastic transfer from the Přemyslids to the Habsburgs. Their complaints against the Bohemian king Přemysl Otakar II had triggered imperial intervention, confirming the elevated position of the estates in times of crisis. This authority to administer the realm in the absence of confirmed rulers had been retained through the centuries.

Regardless of the factual correctness of these arguments, which was immediately challenged by the monarch, the focus on customary law is apparent.[82] The estates did not merely address the immediate point of contention, which centered on the dynasty's intent to transfer the succession to the sitting emperor and archduke Matthias from his brother Albert to his cousin Ferdinand. More urgent was their desire to secure a central role in the delineation of constitutional ground rules. Habsburg princes had repeatedly reminded the Austrian greats that they, unlike their Hungarian and arguably also their Bohemian peers, were subjects of a hereditary ruler. Concessions made in neighboring territories should therefore not be seen as natural examples to be followed. By

126   *The Thinker*

emphasizing the primacy of their own role in government, estatist leaders defended their right to negotiate the terms of governance with a prince whose succession was preordained.

Georg Erasmus von Tschernembl sat on the committee that composed the memorandum, indicating that he, too, believed in the power of constitutional arguments.[83] Tschernembl, however, was among the few who also developed theoretical conceptions. His wide intellectual horizon is visible in the size and composition of his library. Personal misfortune deprived him of this book collection during the final years of his life, but it also made it possible to reconstruct much of its content. When Schwertberg and Windegg were confiscated as rebel property and sold to Count Leonhard Helfried von Meggau, the library was excluded from the transfer. The Society of Jesus had requested the collection and composed a preliminary inventory upon its acceptance in 1623. This catalogue contains approximately 1,800 entries, which, due to imprecisions and repetitions, does not correspond directly to the number of books.[84] In the past decades, researchers have attributed 579 volumes still available in the provincial library of Upper Austria, which incorporated the remnants of the former Jesuit and other relevant libraries, to Tschernembl's collection.[85] In combination, these materials provide valuable insight into Tschernembl's personal interests and occupations.

The composition of aristocratic libraries in early modern Austria exhibits many similarities that reflect the intellectual trends and conventions of the era.[86] Whereas the book collections of fifteenth-century Austria were still dominated by the essentials of religion, jurisprudence, popular literature, and daily life, largely published in German, their nature changed considerably in the subsequent centuries.[87] Humanism and the expansion of university education added both classical and contemporary works in Latin and the Romance languages. This expansion mirrored the new expectations placed upon a court nobility in an era of incipient bureaucratization, professionalization, and state-building.

Tschernembl's library also displayed distinct characteristics, however. One of them was its sheer size, which appreciably exceeded contemporary averages, even if it fell short of such exceptionally comprehensive collections as the historian and genealogist Job Hartmann von Enenkel's.[88] Most noticeable in regard to content was the abundance of historical and theological literature, reflecting Tschernembl's pervasive interest in these fields. Philosophical and juridical works held an important place as well, as did classical literature, philology, and the natural sciences. Yet almost every other field of knowledge was represented by occasional volumes; noteworthy, perhaps, was the comparatively modest share of economic and agricultural literature. Linguistically, works in Latin predominated, but also publications in German, Greek, and various Romance languages contributed sizable shares.[89]

The theological literature, which holds special interest in view of Tschernembl's denominational idiosyncrasy, displayed surprising breadth. The collection contained major works of both the Lutheran and the Calvinist tradition, as well as many Catholic contributions. The latter included not only classics from the church's ecumenical past but also the writings of contemporary activists. Among Calvinist militants, in turn, leading protagonists of resistance theory such as Philippe Duplessis-Mornay and François Hotman were well represented and confirm Tschernembl's exposure to their ideas.

These varied influences already surface in a 1600 treatise titled "De resistentia subditorum adversus principem legitima."[90] The lengthy manuscript, which shows all the marks of an unfinished draft, is written by Tschernembl's hand while lacking any direct confirmation of his authorship.[91] It is, therefore, more definitive for Tschernembl's avid interest in the ideas it espouses than for his personal contribution. As the study's core arguments are derivative rather than original, the distinction is minor. In line with the tenor of Protestant resistance theory, the author focuses on the *provinciales*, to be understood as the territorial estates, as the only legitimate carriers of resistance. The study explores under which circumstances the estates are entitled to defy a monarch and by what means. Among legitimate reasons for resistance, it emphasizes infractions on religious freedoms but also on positive law and established custom. The legality of resistance, however, depends on the confirmation of customary privileges at the monarch's accession. As a consequence, the negotiations preceding the subjects' oath of loyalty hold crucial significance. They establish the contractual relationship between ruler and subjects, which subsequently can be invoked.

The manner in which resistance expresses itself has to be commensurate with the infringement. It needs to be moderate at first, relying on petitions and appeals to the prince's clemency. Gifts may be an appropriate measure to further one's case. Only if these camouflaged forms of resistance prove futile, more overt acts such as threats, tax strikes, as well as outright disobedience or defensive armaments are justified. Even though the author also touches on the debate about tyrannicide, his focus remains on persuading and reforming a wayward prince.

Thus, at the turn of the seventeenth century, Tschernembl already displayed his familiarity with diverse strands of resistance theory. Almost a decade later, during the conflict between the dynastic brothers Rudolf

128　*The Thinker*

and Matthias, the estatist leader interjected his personal view of legitimate governance into the public debate. On 4 March 1609 he addressed a Moravian delegation that was sent to Vienna to advance negotiations between Archduke Matthias and Austria's Protestant nobles. The speech served a dual purpose. It was to inform and persuade the Moravian allies, who had embarked on a more conciliatory course. Yet at least implicitly, it was also directed at Matthias, whom the Moravians were sure to inform about the general tenor of Tschernembl's presentation.[92]

In the early, programmatic part of the speech, Tschernembl presaged many of the arguments that the estates were to present to the court in 1619.[93] Drawing on historical examples dating back to the demise of the Babenberg dynasty in 1246, he postulated the estates' customary right to administer Austria in the absence of legitimate rulers. This absence could be understood literally, as in the case of confirmed rulers whose international obligations had diverted them from domestic duties. More commonly, however, it would occur during an interregnum between the departure of a sitting monarch and the official affirmation of his successor. Even a hereditary principality such as Austria enjoyed extensive liberties and privileges.[94] Among these privileges, he listed the estates' right to request a new ruler from the imperial authorities and dismiss an incapable one, to temporarily administer the territory in the absence of a confirmed ruler, to decide in which manner a new prince was to govern, and to negotiate and secure the preservation of customary practice.[95] Therefore, the estates were only exercising their established rights when they insisted on prior confirmation of their privileges. To do otherwise would constitute a grave neglect of their duties, as could be seen from the fate of their Inner Austrian peers.[96]

In this manner, Tschernembl had drawn a line from his guiding principles of government to the conflict at hand. In two oral presentations to Matthias directly, he described the compatibility of these principles with the monarch's own conviction and reputation.[97] The estates merely requested freedom of conscience, to be defined not as individualist arbitrariness but as protection from coercive conversion.[98] The monarch's reputation, in turn, was not endangered by religious concessions. The estates had a personal stake in the international standing of their monarch, as it also reflected on their own status as his subjects. Yet the measure of a prince's greatness was not his rule over numerous serfs and slaves but his recognition by an illustrious free nobility. The greater the privileges of a territory and its estates, the greater the reputation of its ruler.[99]

The *Consultationes*: Tschernembl and the Early Thirty Years' War

Another decade later, Tschernembl stood at the crossroads of triumph and annihilation. The impending elevation of Archduke Ferdinand of Inner Austria to new head of dynasty had diminished the prospects for a compromise solution. Ferdinand's ominous record in his Alpine realm energized his detractors and provided them with palpable arguments against a conventional transfer of power. If Ferdinand could not be bound by iron-clad guarantees to respect religious freedom and estatist codominion, it was preferable to choose another ruler. Even though this line of reasoning was most widespread in Bohemia, where constitutional conditions seemed more conducive, estatist activists increasingly related it to the archduchy as well.

When the Bohemian opposition searched for allies in surrounding territories, Tschernembl's name stood high on the list. Having returned to public life as an officer of the Upper Austrian diet in 1617, he quickly emerged as a natural leader of the Protestant estates not only in his immediate homeland but also in neighboring Lower Austria.[100] Building on his wide-ranging contacts, Tschernembl served as a crucial liaison between Austrian, Hungarian, Bohemian, and imperial activists. Although he initially offered his services to the dynasty as well, particularly under Matthias, whom he tried to convince of a peaceful approach to the Bohemian crisis, the court increasingly viewed the Upper Austrian as the *spiritus rector* of aristocratic disobedience. After the Bavarian takeover of his home territory, Tschernembl consequently had to take refuge in Bohemia.

In Prague, Tschernembl engaged passionately in the defense of the Protestant monarchy created by the dramatic replacement of King Ferdinand with the Calvinist Elector Palatine Frederick V in 1619. His domestic experience as a Calvinist among overwhelmingly Lutheran peers and his distinct emphasis on Protestant unity gave him a natural advantage within the denominational diversity of Frederick's Bohemia, in which the differences between Utraquists, Calvinists, Lutherans, and Bohemian Brethren could not always be kept out of the political sphere. Tschernembl had promoted the candidacy of the Elector and consistently supported the cooperation between the Austrian and the Bohemian estates. After his arrival in the Bohemian capital, he headed a war council, which also counted compatriots such as Lower Austrian Lorenz von Hofkirchen and Upper Austrians Andreas von Ungnad and Gotthard von Starhemberg among its members.[101] Tschernembl fully appreciated the seriousness of the situation. He proposed reducing frivolous expenditures and

130   *The Thinker*

introducing new taxes and levies, imposing obligatory war loans and selling off ecclesial property, debasing coinage and donating jewelry and silverware. As an ultimate measure, Tschernembl even suggested lifting servitude in order to rally the commoners to the Bohemian cause.[102] Yet most of these proposals remained unheard, and time was running out.

In an ironic twist, the scope of Tschernembl's efforts has been preserved most comprehensively by his critics. When Leaguist troops occupied the Palatinate capital of Heidelberg in 1622, they also took possession of valuable documents. This was not the first time that sensitive information about Palatine strategy had fallen into enemy hands. During King Frederick's hasty retreat from Prague, numerous papers remained behind in his chancellery. The following year, Emperor Ferdinand encouraged his Bavarian allies to publish the most incriminating ones as evidence of Frederick's disloyalty toward sovereign and empire.[103] Although the Palatinate side tried to deflate the issue through swiftly distributed refutations and counterattacks, much of the damage had been done.[104] The documents were to haunt the Elector for years to come and helped justify the imperial ban against him.[105]

In 1622 the Bavarian conquerors were primarily interested in official documents from the Palatine chancellery that could further embarrass the Elector in the courts of law and public opinion. When they discovered several chests with political papers that Tschernembl had stored in his former quarters, they found them particularly useful.[106] The president of the Jesuit College at Munich, Jakob Keller, selected and arranged central passages of a lengthy manuscript written by Tschernembl's hand and published them, accompanied by a running commentary, as the minutes of the Elector's privy council.[107] The following year, the Palatine side responded with a rebuttal that documented the true origins of the manuscript and criticized its misrepresentation and rearrangement.[108] In the process, the refutation decisively established Tschernembl's authorship.

A discursive analysis of the *Consultationes* poses challenges. Even though the authenticity of the actual text was not even disputed in the contemporary rebuttal, the publication itself is the work of Jakob Keller.[109] It was he who decided to employ the private notes of a political opponent for political effect. The original manuscript was not composed for publication. In addition, the editor only selected those sections that suited his purpose; a contemporary Bavarian letter indicates that fewer than half of Tschernembl's original chapters were included in the published version.[110] The editor also restructured the text into the "consultations," or pieces of advice, that gave the work its name. In reality, they were fragments of the political debate since the outbreak of the Bohemian conflict, which may often have started as preparatory drafts of internal presentations and memoranda, interspersed with personal renditions of treaties and other public documents.

These complications do not detract from the study's unique value for the understanding of Tschernembl's thinking during the final and most dramatic period of his life. Its internal nature may even provide superior insight into the aging dissident's philosophy of state, less mitigated by concerns about political prudence and strategy. To be sure, its content was selected and arranged to emphasize its radicalism; the author's efforts for peace and other sections considered propagandistically unhelpful were carefully omitted.[111] Yet the body of arguments displays sufficient similarities with Tschernembl's previous writings to render it a legitimate representation of his response to the crisis that engulfed him.

The *Consultationes* center on the Bohemian War, which they accompany, attempt to influence, and subsequently evaluate. They are divided into 38 recommendations, of which 21 belong to a period when Tschernembl still played a leading role in his Upper Austrian homeland, nine to his time as political adviser in Bohemia, and eight to his exile following the defeat at White Mountain.[112] Thus, they include both phases in which the author found himself in the midst of political controversy and phases of retrospective analysis. This diversity is also reflected in the character of the entries. A considerable part of the text consists of public documents such as the confederation between Upper Austria and Bohemia. Other sections contain practical advice that addresses immediate political challenges and more fundamental reflections about the nature of state and governance.

Tschernembl's contemplations quickly reveal the crucial importance of the Habsburgs' decision to designate Archduke Ferdinand as successor to his childless cousin Matthias. The elevation of the Styrian ruler brings the long-smoldering conflict between Catholic dynasty and Protestant nobles to a head. In spite of intermittent attempts to negotiate with the prince, Protestant leaders such as Tschernembl fundamentally distrust him. The Upper Austrian baron regularly invokes Ferdinand's record in his ancestral domains to illustrate the dangers of rashly entrusting him with power. This warning goes out to the Bohemians, in particular, whose constitutional status provides them greater liberty to stand firm.[113] Ferdinand will not keep his assurances, as he has amply demonstrated in Inner Austria. Tschernembl even relates a rumor that Ferdinand had received the pope's permission to keep his promises to the Bohemians for five years, only to rescind them thereafter. For his decision-making, the monarch only relies on Catholic confidants such as the papal nuncio, the

132   *The Thinker*

Spanish ambassador, and domestic hardliners, while ignoring the recommendations of his Protestant nobility.

Whereas Tschernembl substantively advises the Bohemians to reject Ferdinand, his initial counsel to the Austrians remains more cautious. Tschernembl has to concede the constitutional differences between elective and hereditary principalities. As one of the latter, Austria is tied more intimately to its ruling dynasty than is Bohemia. Therefore, Tschernembl focuses on securing the sworn concessions that would prevent Ferdinand from extending his counterreformational policies from Styria to the archduchy. It would be dishonorable to enslave oneself voluntarily, he implores his Protestant peers.[114] Before they accept a ruler, he must promise not to ruin the territory, to retain its liberties, and to protect it from clerical interference.[115] To assuage the concerns of less rebellious natures, Tschernembl lists numerous rulers who had only received their homage after they had affirmed estatist privileges.[116]

The limitations Tschernembl wants to impose on Ferdinand's rule reflect his distrust.[117] They center on confessional conditions. The designated successor is expected to guarantee religious freedom to all adherents of the Augsburg Confession, under which Tschernembl subsumes Calvinists such as himself. As a consequence, he also has to confirm Matthias' concessions of 1609 and clarify its disputed stipulations. Church buildings seized in recent drives for recatholization should be returned, and Catholic priests lose their proceeds from rites performed by Protestant pastors.

Yet the stipulated concessions are not restricted to the religious sphere. The representative bodies are to participate in the governing of the realm, with the prince selecting his political and juridical advisers in consultation with the estates and without regard to religion. The monarch must not engage in wars or station foreign troops without seeking the estates' advice. Even the disposal of his demesne goods is not exempt from public scrutiny. Most significant, though, is the envisioned duration of these concessions. No longer should such constitutional ground rules be renegotiated during each succession; instead, they are to be binding on future monarchs as well.

At heart, however, Tschernembl does not believe in a peaceful arrangement with Ferdinand. The archduke has made promises before and not kept them, he warns the Lower Austrians who are gathered at Retz.[118] He is a tyrant in the midst of subjugating Upper Austria with Bavarian help.[119] Paying homage would not afford the estates the peace they desire. In fact, Tschernembl no longer considers it possible to escape a potentially devastating confrontation. If the Protestant nobles resist Ferdinand, he will ruin them; if they submit to him, they will have to join his

The Thinker 133

battle against their natural associates in Hungary and Bohemia. Yet even then, he will treat them as rebels if they do not follow his every whim, and there will be no allies left to support them.[120]

The longer the conflict draws out, the more clearly Tschernembl formulates his opposition to the dynastic claimant. Ferdinand cannot accede to the throne in Austria after all the damage he has wreaked, both spiritually in his Styrian domains and physically in his campaign against the Austrian and Bohemian opposition. Yet how can a hereditary principality reject its designated ruler? To preempt predictable objections, Tschernembl has to develop a constitutional counternarrative.[121] Whereas his open-ended premise that a territory's status depends on divine providence may have constituted a truism in the eyes of contemporaries, Tschernembl's *sequitur* proved more controversial. Although God entrusts rulers with territories, he does so through the people, and whoever creates a hereditary ruler can also depose him. A territory only selects hereditary rulers to enhance its own status and security. If a ruler subsequently puts personal and dynastic interests above territorial ones, he provides grounds for removal. No dynasty has retained power forever, so there are numerous examples of hereditary rulers who have lost their crown.

With the waning of Protestant resistance in Austria, Tschernembl put ever greater hopes on Bohemia. He counted among the early supporters of the Elector Palatine's elevation to the throne, discussing and dismissing potential alternatives such as the Duke of Savoy, the King of Denmark, and the Saxon Elector.[122] He personally encouraged Frederick to accept the crown, appealing to his sense of honor, his political ingenuity, and his obligation to further the Protestant cause.[123] At the same time, he implored recalcitrant nobles such as Karel the Elder of Žerotín to join the anti-Habsburg opposition. In political matters one is obligated to support good governance and resist evil, he advises the influential Moravian magnate.[124] God invests and divests princes, and Ferdinand owed his acceptance as king of Bohemia to trickery. The consolidation of Frederick's rule not only secures the Bohemians a monarch of their own choosing but also promises tangible political benefits. The loss of Bohemia could not but weaken the House of Austria, which is deeply entangled with the Pope and Catholic Spain. A Calvinist prince, by contrast, enhances the status of this confession among his subjects. At the same time, so dramatic an upheaval cautions future rulers to better respect their estates and reminds the Habsburgs that there are many in their estates who are their equals.

During the subsequent war, Tschernembl advises the king to draw into battle himself, to have his son confirmed as successor, and not to surrender capital and kingdom following the rout at White Mountain.[125] In the

134 *The Thinker*

end, however, he can only join his monarch's hasty retreat and ponder its causes and implications. He defines the Bohemian conflict as rooted in both region and religion, involving estatist self-determination as well as Protestant religious freedom.[126] To him, the last two concepts are intrinsically linked; any suppression of the one also undermines the other. As a consequence, Saxony's support for the emperor effectively promoted the suppression of Protestantism, regardless of the Elector's assurances to the contrary. Throughout the Austrian and Bohemian provinces, the disastrous consequences have become visible. In the long run, the imperial victories are bound to advance the restitution of Catholicism not only in the hereditary lands but also in the remainder of the empire. In particular, the emperor will return ecclesial properties that have been secularized in Protestant territories to their former owners.[127]

Beyond military defeat, Tschernembl clings to a program of Protestant restoration. On the one hand, he retains hope that Frederick and his allies may be able to retake the kingdom by force.[128] On the other, he strives to convince Ferdinand to achieve peace through surrendering the Bohemian crown voluntarily.[129] An emperor is to place the common good above his own and make the sacrifices necessary to pacify his realm. Since a drawn-out conflict puts all his domains and even the imperial crown at risk, such magnanimity would also serve Ferdinand's personal interests.

In less optimistic moments, Tschernembl concedes that Bohemia may be lost for good, at least to Frederick himself.[130] Even then, however, his expectations of a tolerable settlement appear hard to fulfill. While Frederick may be forced to surrender the factual control of Bohemia, he must retain the royal title. In this manner, he would not only save face but, even more importantly, uphold his line's claim to succession. A general peace must include all imperial parties while excluding Spain, and be accompanied by the dissolution of the Catholic League as the sole remaining confessional alliance. Again, Tschernembl also demands the inclusion of the reformed confession in any final accord to secure the harmonious coexistence of different religious groups.

Even these more modest aspirations lacked any chance of forming the basis of a compromise between Ferdinand and his domestic opposition. In real life, the victorious emperor had initiated the transformation of his territories into monoconfessional dynastic allods with a politically domesticated court nobility. Confronted with this fundamental threat to all he held dear, Tschernembl's own conceptions radicalize as well. He increasingly sees the conflict in the Habsburgs' own domains in a larger imperial and even continental context. In his view, the emperor intends to suppress German liberty and supplant it with a hereditary

The Thinker 135

monarchy allied to Spain and other Catholic powers.[131] The Catholic Church would reestablish full control over Germany, aided not least of all by the Jesuits.

Against this menacing imagery, Tschernembl formulates his alternative vision of Protestant internationalism.[132] He implores the (Protestant) German princes and estates to intervene in the conflict, not in the interest of the Elector Palatine but in the interest of all German territories that suffer from the misrule of the emperor and his supporters. The princes should act out of love and concern for Germany and unite against the threat to its very nature and existence. To secure political and religious liberty, Tschernembl envisions a comprehensive reorganization of the empire. Most revolutionary are his designs for the Habsburgs' own domains. He demands not only the full restitution of Frederick in the Palatinate and in Bohemia, the expulsion of the Spaniards from Germany, and the surrender of Hungary to Bethlen Gábor. Even the Habsburgs' imperial core territories, the Austrian archduchy and Inner Austria, should receive new, Protestant rulers. Under these circumstances, of course, the Bohemian and Austrian refugees were to be fully restituted.

Yet also the remainder of the empire was to undergo fundamental change. The princes should seize both spiritual electorships and other ecclesial principalities, as well as the possessions of the Jesuits and the Teutonic Order. The incomes from secularized ecclesial principalities could subsequently provide the emperor with a regular endowment, diminishing his dependence on patrimonial domains. A new electoral college was to be created, consisting of eight secular princes. Various hostile rulers were to be curtailed, not least of all the duke of Bavaria, who was to suffer the territorial expansion of the Imperial City of Regensburg. These measures were to secure peace, liberty, and prosperity for both the Protestant community and the German nation. This renewed freedom and prosperity would also draw other Protestant countries such as Denmark, Sweden, and the Netherlands toward the empire, further increasing its international standing and influence.

This grand antithesis to universal monarchy stood in glaring contrast to Tschernembl's personal experience. The disastrous outcome at White Mountain, in which a significant Austrian contingent participated on the Bohemian side, forced Tschernembl to move on once again.[133] After he had vainly pleaded with Frederick to defend the capital, he had no choice but to join the general flight.[134] The fate of close associates such as Gotthard von Starhemberg, who perished in imperial confinement, and of the Bohemian leaders executed in the Old Town Square of Prague leaves little doubt about the prospects awaiting Tschernembl in case of

136 *The Thinker*

capture.[135] The sharp-tongued commentator of the *Consultationes* sardonically observed that his escape may have saved the author's life but not his honor. If he had stayed behind, someone would assuredly have grabbed him as well.[136]

The Austrian émigré initially took refuge in the Upper Palatinate, but rumors of an impending invasion pushed him on to the Lutheran duchy of Württemberg.[137] Hiding under the somewhat transparent pseudonym of Georg von Windegg in the small town of Vaihingen northwest of Stuttgart, he had ample time to ponder the dramatic events that had transformed his life.[138] His Austrian properties had been confiscated; his son was increasingly estranged, resenting the financial repercussions of his father's political activism. Only the arrival of his wife, who joined her ailing husband in exile, promised to alleviate some of his hardships. He even engaged in politics again, advising the returned Elector Palatine at Heidelberg until Tilly and his Spanish allies also drove Frederick from his last remaining stronghold.

The fall of Heidelberg endangered the Habsburgian refugees throughout the German southwest, forcing Tschernembl on his final move. In the autumn of 1622 he set out for Geneva, hoping to find safety in the spiritual capital of Calvinism, which he had last visited during his student years. The city council also welcomed its illustrious coreligionist, enabling him to spend his final years in modest but secure circumstances.[139] He retained occasional contact with former political associates such as the Elector Palatine but lived for the most part a rather quiet and isolated life in the Francophone city far removed from his native Austrian and imperial environment. He continued to submit memoranda on a possible reversal of fortunes, but the international balance of power only tilted further toward his adversaries. When the exiled baron died in Geneva on 18 November 1626, the troops of Christian IV of Denmark had recently been defeated in the Battle of Lutter and the Protestant peasants of Upper Austria devastated by the Bavarian army. There was little left of the world for which Tschernembl had fought.

Conclusion

The Habsburgs' increasing determination to enforce religious conformity fundamentally challenged the societal position of Austria's Protestant nobility. Some chose accommodation and joined the gradually expanding ranks of converts and newcomers that had reestablished a significant Catholic presence in the Austrian aristocracy. Others became disillusioned with the dynasty and determined to secure their established privileges. Their actions and conceptions formed part of a larger European current, as the new emphasis on monarchic sovereignty simultaneously reinvigorated historic notions of legitimate resistance. This dialectic unfolded in a variety of regional settings, not least of all in the Holy Roman Empire, where Lutherans had to secure their existence in the face of a hostile emperor. Following the gradual consolidation of a Lutheran political sphere within the empire, theoretical refinement shifted to more exposed communities. The harsh suppression of the vigorous Calvinist minority in France proved especially significant for the radical strain of resistance theory termed Monarchomachism, which combined a focus on divided government with a theologically and juridically supported case for legitimate resistance.

The Austrian estates relied primarily on historical and legal arguments. Yet among the intellectual leaders of the Protestant aristocracy, the theoretical debate had not gone unnoticed. Activists such as Georg Erasmus von Tschernembl placed their domestic conflict with the dynasty in an international context. They were convinced that Archduke Ferdinand and his allies in the papal curia and the new orders only viewed concessions to heretics as temporary arrangements necessitated by *force majeure*, to be vacated as soon as more favorable circumstances allowed for it. Ultimately, even the Peace of Augsburg was designed as a temporary truce rather than as the final settlement its commonplace designation implies. During the decades that followed these imperial and territorial compromises, the dynasty had substantially reinforced its position in its hereditary domains. If this development was to be stopped, it had to be sooner rather than later.

Tschernembl was willing to take up this fight. His untiring organization of resistance has focused attention on him and his personal confessional leanings. To both his adversaries and later observers it seemed natural to associate Tschernembl's passionate defiance with his Calvinist beliefs. Yet the question of whether or not Tschernembl followed the ideology of Calvinist Monarchomachs requires a more nuanced response. There is no doubt that the Austrian nobleman was familiar with some of their writings. His library, his personal acquaintance with Hotman, and his sojourn at Geneva provide ample evidence of his exposure to their ideas. An implicit assumption, however, that Tschernembl's Calvinism introduced an alien Huguenot radicalism to the pacific world of Austrian Lutheranism overlooks the intense cross-fertilization of various strands of resistance thinking. Monarchomach writers received impulses from the Magdeburg Confession and older Lutheran approaches, and they in

138   *The Thinker*

turn inspired imperial activists. In the Austrian discussion, these diverse theoretical traditions refined the dominant estatist discourse of customary law and practice, without fundamentally altering it.

Tschernembl came to personify the Protestant nobility of the archduchy, but he simultaneously transcended it in both time and space. At his ablest, he proved prescient of future tendencies and developments. When he warned the Protestant princes of Ferdinand's plans to return secularized ecclesial properties to the Catholic Church, he correctly predicted the emperor's Edict of Restitution of 1629. By promoting the lifting of servitude in Bohemia, he outgrew the confines of aristocratic self-interest and foreshadowed the future realignment of loyalties toward modern mass societies. In his regular invocation of multiconfessional tolerance and coexistence, he conceptually distinguished himself from many of his peers. At the same time, his biting attacks on the Jesuits, whom he not only desired removed from German soil but mowed down in a Hungarian attack on Inner Austria, demonstrated the practical limits of this proclaimed tolerance.[140] Ultimately, Tschernembl viewed the world from a highly confessional perspective, which was rooted in a concept of Protestant unity versus an all-encompassing threat of Catholic restoration.

In the final analysis, Georg Erasmus von Tschernembl was both a radical reformer predating societal transformations of a later age and a conservative defender of an estate system under siege. This challenging duality was shared by many contemporaneous proponents of estatist resistance. Yet even though his political program ended in utter defeat, it would be simplistic to ascribe its failure to historical anachronism. The course of Habsburg history was not decided by innate social and intellectual trends but by international politics and military superiority. To Tschernembl, the difference may have seemed academic. For him and a substantial segment of the old aristocracy, there was no future in the Austrian and Bohemian lands.

Notes

1. To what extent this changing status of Christian churches and beliefs can best be defined as secularization has been the focus of a protracted debate, not least of all among sociologists. See a summarization of this debate in Philip S. Gorski, "Historicizing the Secularization Debate: Church, State, and Society in Late Medieval and Early Modern Europe, ca. 1300 to 1700," *American Sociological Review* 65 (2000): 138–167, and William H. Swatos, Jr. and Kevin J. Christiano, "Secularization Theory: The Course of a Concept," *Sociology of Religion* 60 (1999): 209–228. For an outspoken challenge to the secularization paradigm, see also Rodney Stark, "Secularization, R.I.P.," *Sociology of Religion*

60 (1999): 249–273. For the redefinition of monarchy in rational rather than sacral terms, see also Paul Kléber Monod, *The Power of Kings: Monarchy and Religion in Europe 1589–1715* (New Haven, CT, 1999).

2. For a history of the Fronde, see Orest A. Ranum, *The Fronde: A French Revolution (1648–1652)* (New York, 1993).

3. For the history of public authority in Europe, see Wolfgang Reinhard, *Geschichte der Staatsgewalt: Eine vergleichende Verfassungsgeschichte Europas von den Anfängen bis zur Gegenwart* (Munich, 1999).

4. For the role of public ordinances in early modern Europe, see Karl Härter, ed., *Policey und frühneuzeitliche Gesellschaft* (Frankfurt, 2000), Achim Landwehr, *Policey im Alltag: Die Implementation frühneuzeitlicher Policeyordnungen in Leonberg* (Frankfurt, 2000), and Thomas Simon, "Gute Policey"— *Ordnungsleitbilder und Zielvorstellungen politischen Handelns in der Frühen Neuzeit* (Frankfurt, 2004), but also Jürgen Schlumbohm, "Gesetze, die nicht durchgesetzt werden—ein Strukturmerkmal des frühneuzeitlichen Staates?" *Geschichte und Gesellschaft* 23 (1997): 647–663. For a stronger focus on the Habsburg territories, see also Michael Hochedlinger and Thomas Winkelbauer, eds., *Herrschaftsverdichtung, Staatsbildung, Bürokratisierung: Verfassungs-, Verwaltungs- und Behördengeschichte der Frühen Neuzeit* (Vienna, 2010).

5. This transformation was the subject of a large cooperative research project under the auspices of the European Science Foundation, published as Wim Blockmans, ed., *The Origins of the Modern State in Europe, 1300–1800*, 7 vols. (Oxford, 1995–2000).

6. See the detailed portrayal of the Lower Austrian developments in Victor Bibl, "Die katholischen und protestantischen Stände Niederösterreichs im XVII. Jahrhundert: Ein Beitrag zur Geschichte der ständischen Verfassung," *Jahrbuch für Landeskunde von Niederösterreich*, n. s., 2 (1903): 165–323.

7. For some important contributions to the debate triggered by recent challenges to the concept of absolutism, with a special focus on Central Europe, see Nicholas Henshall, *The Myth of Absolutism: Change and Continuity in Early Modern European Monarchy* (London, 1992); Heinz Duchhardt, "Absolutismus: Abschied von einem Epochenbegriff?" *Historische Zeitschrift* 258 (1994): 113–122; Ronald G. Asch and Heinz Duchhardt, eds., *Der Absolutismus—ein Mythos? Strukturwandel monarchischer Herrschaft in West- und Mitteleuropa (ca. 1550–1700)* (Cologne, 1996); Olaf Mörke, "Die Diskussion um den Absolutismusbegriff als Epochenbegriff: Ein Beitrag über den Platz Katharinas II. in der europäischen Politikgeschichte," in *Rußland zur Zeit Katharinas II.: Absolutismus—Aufklärung—Pragmatismus*, ed. Eckhard Hübner et al. (Cologne, 1998), 9–32; Johannes Kunisch, *Absolutismus: Europäische Geschichte vom Westfälischen Frieden bis zur Krise des Ancien Régime*, 2nd, rev. ed. (Göttingen, 1999); Ernst Hinrichs, *Fürsten und Mächte: Zum Problem des europäischen Absolutismus* (Göttingen, 2000); Peter Baumgart, "Absolutismus ein Mythos? Aufgeklärter Absolutismus ein Widerspruch? Reflexionen zu einem kontroversen Thema gegenwärtiger Frühneuzeitforschung," *Zeitschrift für Historische Forschung* 27 (2000): 573–589; Peter H. Wilson, *Absolutism in Central Europe* (London, 2000); Hans-Wolfgang Bergerhausen, "Die Verneuerte Landesordnung in Böhmen

140 *The Thinker*

1627: Ein Grunddokument des habsburgischen Absolutismus," *Historische Zeitschrift* 272 (2001): 327–351; Fanny Cosandey and Robert Descimon, *L'absolutisme en France: Histoire et historiographie* (Paris, 2002); and Reinhard Blänkner, *"Absolutismus": Eine begriffsgeschichtliche Studie zur politischen Theorie und zur Geschichtswissenschaft in Deutschland, 1830–1870* (Frankfurt, 2011).

Engaging and analytically fruitful as it may have been, the debate about the conceptual validity of subsuming a crucial period of early modern history under the term absolutism only touches the current study peripherally. In this examination, the focus lies on the transformation of shared governance and on the ideological debate that preceded it. This angle is narrower in both time and space than the periodization of European history. Its findings do not mesh with interpretations that reject any relevant change in the early-modern practice of mixed government, however. At least in the Habsburgian core territories of Austria and Bohemia, monarchy and nobility developed conflicting views of political powersharing, which came to a head in the initial decades of the seventeenth century. The outcome of this conflict also altered the existing balance of power.

8. For a brief introduction, see Josef Anton Stütler, "Das Widerstandsrecht und seine Rechtfertigungsversuche im Altertum und im frühen Christentum," in *Widerstandsrecht*, ed. Arthur Kaufmann (Darmstadt, 1972), 1–58.

9. See, for example, Rudolf Schieffer, "Von Mailand nach Canossa: Ein Beitrag zur Geschichte der christlichen Herrscherbuße von Theodosius dem Großen bis zu Heinrich IV," *Deutsches Archiv für Erforschung des Mittelalters* 28 (1972): 333–370.

10. For the medieval definition of tyranny, see, for example, Friedrich Schoenstedt, *Der Tyrannenmord im Spätmittelalter: Studien zur Geschichte des Tyrannenbegriffs und der Tyrannenmordtheorie, insbesondere in Frankreich* (Berlin, 1938), and Jeannine Quillet, "Tyrannie et tyrannicide dans la pensée politique médiévale tardive (XIV-XVe siècles)," in *Actes du Colloque La Tyrannie, mai 1984*, ed. Centre de publications de l'Université de Caen (Caen, 1984), 61–73. For a broader examination of the concept, see also Mario Turchetti, *Tyrannie et tyrannicide de l'Antiquité à nos jours* (Paris, 2001).

11. For the following, see Eike Wolgast, *Die Religionsfrage als Problem des Widerstandsrechts im 16. Jahrhundert* (Heidelberg, 1980), 10–12.

12. See Ernst Troeltsch, *Die Soziallehren der Christlichen Kirchen und Gruppen* (Tübingen, 1912), and Hans Baron, "Calvinist Republicanism and its Historical Roots," *Church History* 8 (1939): 30–42.

13. For the following, see Martin Luther, "Von welltlicher Uberkeytt, wie weyt man yhr gehorsam schuldig sey," in *D. Martin Luthers Werke: Kritische Gesamtausgabe*, vol. 11 (Weimar, 1900), 245–281. For a modern English translation, see also Harro Höpfl, ed., *Luther and Calvin on Secular Authority* (Cambridge, England, 1991), 3–43. For the development of Lutheran political philosophy, see also Eike Wolgast, *Die Wittenberger Theologie und die Politik der evangelischen Stände* (Gütersloh, 1977); Tilman Peter Koops, *Die Lehre vom Widerstandsrecht des Volkes gegen die weltliche Obrigkeit in der lutherischen Theologie des 16. und 17. Jahrhunderts* (Kiel,

The Thinker 141

1969); and Karl Dietrich Erdmann, "Luther über Obrigkeit, Gehorsam und Widerstand," in *Luther und die Folgen: Beiträge zur sozialgeschichtlichen Bedeutung der lutherischen Reformation*, ed. Hartmut Löwe and Claus-Jürgen Roepke (Munich, 1983), 28–59.

14. Martin Luther, "Von welltlicher Uberkeytt, wie weyt man yhr gehorsam schuldig sey," in *D. Martin Luthers Werke: Kritische Gesamtausgabe*, vol. 11 (Weimar, 1900), 277.

15. Ibid., 277.

16. Eike Wolgast, *Die Religionsfrage als Problem des Widerstandsrechts im 16. Jahrhundert* (Heidelberg, 1980), 20.

17. See Martin Luther, "Die Zirkulardisputation über das Recht des Widerstands gegen den Kaiser," in *D. Martin Luthers Werke: Kritische Gesamtausgabe*, vol. 39:2 (Weimar, 1932), 39–51.

18. For the French version, see Jean Calvin, *Joannis Calvini opera quae supersunt omnia*, ed. Johann Wilhelm Baum et al., vol. 4 (Braunschweig, 1866), 1125–1162. The following references follow the English translation in Harro Höpfl, ed., *Luther and Calvin on Secular Authority* (Cambridge, England, 1991), 47–86.

19. Even the generally more moderate Luther was regularly associated with social radicalism, as visible in Hieronymus Emser, "Wie Luther in seinen Büchern zum Aufruhr getrieben hat," and Johannes Cochläus, "Antwort auf Luthers Schrift 'Wider die räuberischen und mörderischen Rotten der Bauern': Ein kurzer Begriff vom Aufruhr der Bauern," in *Flugschriften der Bauernkriegszeit*, ed. Adolf Laube and Hans Werner Seiffert, 2nd ed. (Cologne, 1978), 356–412.

20. Harro Höpfl, ed., *Luther and Calvin on Secular Authority* (Cambridge, England, 1991), 50.

21. Ibid., 55.

22. Ibid., 65f.

23. Ibid., 74.

24. Ibid., 76f.

25. Ibid., 82f.

26. See also Ernst Wolf, "Das Problem des Widerstandsrechts bei Calvin," in *Widerstandsrecht*, ed. Arthur Kaufmann (Darmstadt, 1972), 152–169.

27. For the following, see Quentin Skinner, *The Foundations of Modern Political Thought*, vol. 2 (Cambridge, England, 1978), 189–224.

28. See also Marc-Édouard Cheneviere, *La pensée politique de Calvin* (Geneva, 1937).

29. With these basic contentions Bugenhagen connected medieval antecedents with the central arguments of subsequent, more elaborate justifications of resistance. See Diethelm Böttcher, *Ungehorsam oder Widerstand? Zum Fortleben des mittelalterlichen Widerstandsrechtes in der Reformationszeit (1529–1530)* (Berlin, 1991), 24.

30. Skinner preferred the term private-law, while others also anchored the Saxon approach in natural law.

31. Nicolaus von Amsdorff et al., *Bekentnis Vnterricht vnd vermanung, der Pfarrhern vnd Prediger, der Christlichen Kirchen zu Magdeburgk* (Magdeburg, 1550), 1. Since the volume lacks explicit pagination, page

142 *The Thinker*

references are added, starting after the title page with the "kurtzer begriff oder inhalt dieses Buchs" as page 1 and subsequently new page starts at the beginning of individual sections.

32. Nicolaus von Amsdorff et al., *Bekentnis Vnterricht vnd vermanung, der Pfarrhern vnd Prediger, der Christlichen Kirchen zu Magdeburgk* (Magdeburg, 1550), part 2, p. 16.

33. Ibid., part 2, p. 16.

34. For the following, see ibid., part 2, pp. 18–23.

35. Justus Menius, *Von der Nothwehr unterricht* (Wittenberg, 1547). For the strong influence of Melanchton on the wording of Menius's treatise, see Luther D. Peterson, "Justus Menius, Philipp Melanchton, and the 1547 Treatise, *Von der Notwehr Unterricht*," *Archiv für Reformationsgeschichte* 81 (1990): 138–157. See also Curt Christmann, *Melanchtons Haltung im schmalkaldischen Kriege* (Berlin, 1902).

36. Justus Menius, *Von der Nothwehr unterricht* (Wittenberg, 1547), 42f. Since the original lacks pagination, page numbers have been added, starting with the prologue following the title page as page 1.

37. See his *The Appellation* from 1558, printed in David Laing, ed., *The Works of John Knox*, vol. 4 (Edinburgh, 1855), 461–520, here especially page 496. For the influence of German precedents on the theory of resistance and self-defense on the British Isles, see also Robert von Friedeburg, *Self-Defence and Religious Strife in Early Modern Europe: England and Germany, 1530–1680* (Aldershot, England, 2002).

38. See his twenty-ninth homily on the First Book of Samuel, printed in Jean Calvin, *Joannis Calvini opera quae supersunt omnia*, ed. Johann Wilhelm Baum et al., vol. 29 (Braunschweig, 1885), 551–563. See also Max Engammare, "Calvin monarchomaque? Du soupçon à l'argument," *Archiv für Reformationsgeschichte* 89 (1998): 207–225.

39. William Barclay, *De regno et regali potestate* (Paris, 1600). Barclay took not only exception from French Calvinist writers but also included the Scottish Presbyterian George Buchanan and radical Catholic supporters of the Catholic League in France among his adversaries.

40. Some Catholic radicals explicitly referred to Calvinist Monarchomachs, as visible in Louis Dorléans, *Advertissement des Catholiqves Anglois avx François Catholiques* ([Paris], 1586).

41. For Hotman's life, see Donald R. Kelley, *François Hotman: A Revolutionary's Ordeal* (Princeton, NJ, 1983), and Rodolphe Dareste, *Essai sur François Hotman* (Paris, 1850).

42. François Hotman, *Francogallia* (Geneva, 1573). For modern translations, see also François Hotman, *Francogallia*, Latin text by Ralph E. Giesey, translated by J. H. M. Salmon (Cambridge, England, 1972), and Jürgen Dennert, ed., *Beza, Brutus, Hotman: Calvinistische Monarchomachen* (Cologne, 1968), 203–327.

43. See, for example, Jürgen Dennert, ed., *Beza, Brutus, Hotman: Calvinistische Monarchomachen* (Cologne, 1968), 236 and 251.

44. Ibid., 257f.

45. Ibid., 284f.

46. Ibid., 227.

47. Ibid., 235–237.
48. Examples of Huguenot skepticism surface in Hotman's correspondence, printed in Rodolphe Dareste, "François Hotman, sa vie et sa correspondance," *Revue Historique* 2 (1876): 367–435. For a rebuttal, see Antoine Matharel, *Ad Franc. Hotomani Franco-Galliam . . . responsio* (Paris, 1575).
49. For an introduction to Beza's life and personality, see Alain Dufour, *Théodore de Bèze, poète et théologien* (Paris, 2006), Paul F. Geisendorf, *Théodore de Bèze* (Geneva, 1949), and Violaine Weben, ed., *Théodore de Bèze: Un grand de l'Europe* (Paris 2000).
50. The name is frequently spelled Wolmar.
51. See his letter to the Swiss reformer Heinrich Bullinger of 12 September 1559, where he still maintained that "precibus et patientia superandum esse tempestatum . . . ." See Theodore Beza, *Correspondance de Théodore de Bèze*, ed. Alain Dufour et al., vol. 3, *1559–1561*, ed. Henri Meylan and Alain Dufour (Geneva, 1963), 21.
52. [Theodore Beza], *Du droit des magistrats sur leurs suiets* (n.p., 1574). For modern translations, see idem, *Concerning the Rights of Rulers over their Subjects and the Duty of Subjects towards their Rulers*, ed. A. H. Murray (Cape Town, 1956); idem, *De iure magistratuum*, ed. Klaus Sturm (Neukirchen, Germany, 1967); idem, *Du droit des Magistrats*, ed. Robert M. Kingdon (Geneva, 1970); as well as Jürgen Dennert, ed., *Beza, Brutus, Hotman: Calvinistische Monarchomachen* (Cologne, 1968), 1–60. For a discussion of place and date of publication, see Aart A. Van Scheelven, "Beza's De Iure Magistratuum in Subditos," *Archiv für Reformationsgeschichte* 45 (1954): 62–83.
53. Jürgen Dennert, ed., *Beza, Brutus, Hotman: Calvinistische Monarchomachen* (Cologne, 1968), 2f.
54. Ibid., 7.
55. Ibid., 17.
56. Ibid., 37.
57. Ibid., 6–12.
58. For the following, see ibid., 12–53.
59. Ibid., 16.
60. Ibid., 45f.
61. See ibid., 55–60.
62. Ibid., 58.
63. See the story in Pierre Bayle, "Dissertation sur le livre de Junius Brutus," in *Dictionnaire historique et critique*, 4th ed., vol. 4 (Basel, 1730), 569–577.
64. For a selection of differing viewpoints on Languet and Duplessis-Mornay, see Albert Elkan, *Die Publizistik der Bartholomäusnacht und Mornays "Vindiciae contra tyrannos"* (Heidelberg, 1905); Ernest Baker, "The Authorship of the Vindiciae Contra Tyrannos," *Cambridge Historical Journal* 3 (1930): 164–181; G. T. van Ysselsteyn, "L'auteur del'ouvrage 'Vindiciae contra tyrannos' public sous le nom de Stephanus Junius Brutus," *Revue historique* 167 (1931): 46–59; Graham Jagger, "On the Authorship of the Vindiciae contra tyrannos," *Durham University Journal* 60 (1968): 73–80; and Martin N. Raitière, "Hubert Languet's Authorship of the Vindiciae contra Tyrannos," *Il pensiero politico* 14 (1986): 395–420. For

144   *The Thinker*

a controversial argument in favor of Johan Junius de Jonghe, see Derek Visser, "Junius: The Author of Vindiciae contra Tyrannos?" *Tijdschrift voor Geschiedenis* 84 (1971): 510–525. For a more recent general discussion, see also George Garnett's introduction in Stephanus Julius Brutus, *Vindiciae contra tyrannos: Or, Concerning the Legitimate Power of a Prince over the People, and of the People over a Prince*, ed. George Garnett (Cambridge, England, 1994), lv–lxxvi.

65. For Languet's life, see Béatrice Nicollier-de Weck, *Hubert Languet (1518–1519): Un réseau politique international de Melanchthon à Guillaume d'Orange* (Geneva, 1995), and Henri Chevreul, *Hubert Languet* (Paris, 1852). See also Oscar Scholz, *Hubert Languet als kursächsischer Berichterstatter und Gesandter in Frankreich während der Jahre 1560–1572* (Halle, 1875).

66. For Duplessis-Mornay, see Hugues Daussy, *Les huguenots et le roi: Le combat politique de Philippe Duplessis-Mornay (1572–1600)* (Geneva, 2002); Raoul Patry, *Philippe Duplessis-Mornay: Un huguenot homme d'État* (Paris, 1933); as well as the extensive collection of original sources in Philippe Duplessis Mornay, *Mémoires et correspondance*, 12 vols. (Paris, 1824–1825).

67. Stephanus Julius Brutus [pseud. for Philippe Duplessis-Mornay or Hubert Languet], *Vindiciae, contra tyrannos* (Edinburgh, 1579). For modern translations, see Stephanus Julius Brutus [pseud. for Philippe Duplessis-Mornay or Hubert Languet], *Vindiciae contra tyrannos: Or, Concerning the Legitimate Power of a Prince over the People, and of the People over a Prince*, ed. George Garnett (Cambridge, England, 1994), and Jürgen Dennert, ed., *Beza, Brutus, Hotman: Calvinistische Monarchomachen* (Cologne, 1968), 61–202.

68. For this covenant, see Stephanus Julius Brutus [pseud. for Philippe Duplessis-Mornay or Hubert Languet], *Vindiciae contra tyrannos: Or, Concerning the Legitimate Power of a Prince over the People, and of the People over a Prince*, ed. George Garnett (Cambridge, England, 1994), 22–34.

69. Ibid., 21.

70. Ibid., 131.

71. The exact wording of these questions can be seen in ibid., 14, 35, and 67. A final section examined the more immediate and pragmatic question as to which foreign potentates may intervene in favor of suppressed populations.

72. Ibid., 68.

73. See ibid., 92–96.

74. Ibid., 78.

75. Ibid., 154.

76. Ibid., 158.

77. Ibid., 156.

78. For the following, see ibid., 168f.

79. For the following, see ibid., 172.

80. For the association of Protestantism and disloyalty, see Karin MacHardy, *War, Religion and Court Patronage in Habsburg Austria: The Social and Cultural Dimensions of Political Interaction, 1521–1622* (Houndmills, England, 2003), 109.

81. For the following, see *Gegründter Nothwendiger Bericht was biszhero nach Absterben des Allerdurchleuchtigsten Großmächtigsten Fürsten unnd*

Herrn, Herrn Matthiae Röm. Kay. auch zu Hungern und Böhemb Kön. Mtt. Ertzhertzogens . . . Alberti als nägsten Successorn des Ertzhertzogthumben Oesterreich unter und ob der Ens wegen der Landtadministration biß auff künfftige Huldigung dem uralten Oesterreichischen Herkommen nach fürgenommen unnd gehandelt worden (Linz, 1619). The initial estatist arguments are presented in "Wie es von Uraltem her auff Absterben und Veränderung der Landtsfürsten und Ertzherzogen zu Oesterreich etc. Biß zu würklicher Antretung volgender Erbherrn und gelaister Huldigung mit Adminstration deß Landts gehalten worden." In a subsequent exchange between court and estates, the respective arguments were developed further. The estates subsequently published the exchange in the *Gegründter Nothwendiger Bericht*.

82. Ferdinand's counterarguments can be seen in "Gründtlicher Gegenbericht auff ainen unlangst eingelangten Bericht als solte die Admininstration der Oesterreichschen Erblandt nach ableiben der Landtsfürsten biß zu gelaister newen Huldigung nit der Erbherrschafft sondern den Landständen gebühren," which was also printed in the *Gegründter Nothwendiger Bericht*.

83. Older assessments ascribing sole authorship to Tschernembl have been corrected. See Helmuth Feigl, "Beiträge zur Biographie des Freiherrn Georg Erasmus von Tschernembl" (Ph.D. diss., University of Vienna, 1949), 187f.

84. Hans Sturmberger, *Georg Erasmus Tschernembl: Religion, Libertät und Widerstand* (Graz, 1953), 254. A copy of the catalogue titled "Catalogus Librorum Dni. Georgii Erasmi L. B. à Tschernembl ad Bibliothecam RR:PP: Soc: Jesus in Lynnz perlatorum" is added as appendix to Günther Sachsenhofer, *Die Bibliothek des Freiherrn Georg Erasmus von Tschernembl: Fine Rekonstruktion* (Linz, 1992)

85. See Heidelinde Jung, "Die Bibliothek des Georg Erasmus von Tschernembl," in *Der oberösterreichische Bauernkrieg 1626: Ausstellung des Landes Oberösterreich, Linzer Schloß, Schloß zu Scharnstein im Almtal, 14. Mai bis 31. Oktober 1976*, ed. Dietmar Straub (Linz, 1976), I/138; and Günther Sachsenhofer, *Die Bibliothek des Freiherrn Georg Erasmus von Tschernembl: Eine Rekonstruktion* (Linz, 1992), 31. The library used to be known as Linzer Studienbibliothek.

86. For an introduction to the nature of these libraries, see Otto Brunner, "Österreichische Adelsbibliotheken des 15. bis 17. Jahrhunderts," *Anzeiger der Österreichischen Akademie der Wissenschaften, philosophisch-historische Klasse* 86 (1949): 109–126, and Alfred Kohler, "Umfang und Bedeutung historisch-geographischer Werke in oberösterreichischen Adelsbibliotheken des 17. Jahrhunderts," *Mitteilungen des Oberösterreichischen Landesarchivs* 13 (1981): 230–233.

87. See Otto Brunner, "Österreichische Adelsbibliotheken des 15. bis 17. Jahrhunderts," *Anzeiger der Österreichischen Akademie der Wissenschaften, philosophisch-historische Klasse* 86 (1949): 115.

88. Differing estimates put Enenkel's library at between 6000 and 8000 volumes. Yet also the collection of Heinrich Wilhelm von Starhemberg comprised 3472 titles. The library of Wolf von Oedt at Helfenberg, by contrast, contained a more modest 370 titles. For these numbers, see Andreas Brandtner, "Habeant sua fata libelli: Bausteine zur Erforschung der Enenkel Bibliothek," *Jahrbuch des Oberösterreichischen Musealvereins*

146   *The Thinker*

145 (2000): 145, and Alfred Kohler, "Umfang und Bedeutung historisch-geographischer Werke in oberösterreichischen Adelsbibliotheken des 17. Jahrhunderts," *Mitteilungen des Oberösterreichischen Landesarchivs* 13 (1981): 230–233.

89. For the composition of the library based on varying sources and parameters, see Günther Sachsenhofer, *Die Bibliothek des Freiherrn Georg Erasmus von Tschernembl: Eine Rekonstruktion* (Linz, 1992), especially pages 193–195 and the catalogue in the appendix, as well as Hans Sturmberger, *Georg Erasmus Tschernembl: Religion, Libertät und Widerstand* (Graz, 1953), 255–259.

90. For the following, see "De resistentia subditorum adversus principem legitima," Österreichisches Staatsarchiv, Haus-, Hof- und Staatsarchiv, HS Blau 381, fol. 442r–469v.

91. For a discussion of the authorship, see Hans Sturmberger, *Georg Erasmus Tschernembl: Religion, Libertät und Widerstand* (Graz, 1953), 95–97.

92. About the contemporary function of courtly speeches, with a chapter on Tschernembl, see Georg Braungart, *Hofberedsamkeit: Studien zur Praxis höfisch-politischer Rede im deutschen Territorialabsolutismus* (Tübingen, 1988).

93. The speech is printed in *Relation Der Vnter- und Oberösterreichischen Euangelischen Stände Abgesandten nach Wien: Allda Zwischen Ihrer Königlichen May. zu Hungarn etc. vnd jnen den dreyen Österreichischen Evangelischen Ständen der Frid tractiert vnd geschlossen worden* (n.p., 1610), 26–45.

94. Ibid., 27.

95. These and other proposed privileges are discussed in ibid., 37–39.

96. Ibid., 32f.

97. See *Relation Der Vnter- und Oberösterreichischen Euangelischen Stände Abgesandten nach Wien: Allda Zwischen Ihrer Königlichen May. zu Hungarn etc. vnd jnen den dreyen Österreichischen Evangelischen Ständen der Frid tractiert vnd geschlossen worden* (n.p., 1610), 48–51 and 91–96.

98. Ibid., 49.

99. Ibid., 95.

100. The *Verordnete*, or officers, of the individual curiae formed the executive leadership of the diet. Tschernembl was elected officer of the Curia of Lords.

101. See Anton Gindely, *Geschichte des dreißigjährigen Krieges*, vol. 1 (Leipzig, 1882), 206, and Helmuth Feigl, "Beiträge zur Biographie des Freiherrn Georg Erasmus von Tschernembl" (Ph.D. diss., University of Vienna, 1949), 261.

102. For these suggestions, see recommendations 5 and 6 in [Georg Erasmus von Tschernembl], *Consultationes Oder Underschidliche Rathschläg/ Der maisten und wichtigisten sachen/ welche von Anfang der Böhemischen/ und andern folgenden Auffständ fürgangen/ unnd zu Werck gericht worden/ oder werden sollen: Von wort zu wort auß dem Original Protocoll, so in der Haidelbergischen Cantzley gefunden worden/ gezogen. Mit nohtwendigen Glossis erklärt*, [ed. Jakob Keller] (n.p., 1624), 57–71.

103. See *Fürstlich Anhaltische gehaimbe Cantzley, das ist begründte Anzaig der verdeckten, unteutschen, nachtheiligen Consilien, Anschläg und Practicken, welche der Correspondierenden Union Häupter und Directores,*

in der Böhmischen Unruhe zu derselben Cron, auch deß H. Römischen Reichs höchste gefahr geführt, und auß sonderbarer verordnung Gottes durch die den 8. Novemb. jüngst fürgangne ernstliche nambhaffte Böhaimische Niederlag vor Prag in der anhaltischen gehaimen Cantzley in Originali gefunden und der Welt kundthar worden: allen so wol auß- als jnnländischen Potentaten, Chur-Fürsten, Ständen und Herrschafften auch sonst menniglich zu beständiger nachricht trewhertziger warnung und wahrhaffter information, 3rd ed. (n.p., 1621).

104. For a direct response, see [Ludwig Camerarius], *Bericht und Antwort/ Uff die vornembste Capita, Päß/ und Puncten der Bayer-Anhaltischen geheimen Cantzeley: Sampt Etlichen Beylagen* (n.p., 1623). For a broader counterattack, which strove to establish Ferdinand's long-term strategy to curtail German Protestantism in collusion with Spain, see [Ludwig Camerarius, ed.], *Prodromus, Oder Vortrab/ Nothwendiger Rettung vornehmer Evangelischer Hohen und niedern Standts/ betrangten und verleumbden Personen unschuldt/ durch gründliche entdeckung der Papistischen schädlichen Intention unnd Vorhabens. Das ist: Wahrhaffter unnd glaubwirdiger Abdruck etzlicher intercipirten sehr weit außsehenden gefährlichen Schreiben unnd Schrifften/ welche auß den Originalien, mit fleiß abcopirt/ und theils auß denen Sprachen/ darinnen sie geschrieben/ trewlich verteutschet sein/ mit angehengter kurtzer Information unnd Anleitung: Allen Evangelischen/ so wol in: als außlendischen Potentaten/ Chur: Fürsten/ Ständen/ und Herrschafften . . . wider die verfälschte also genante geheimbte Anhaltische Cantzley* (n.p., 1622).

105. For the impact of the original publication, see Reinhold Koser, *Der Kanzleienstreit, ein Beitrag zur Quellenkunde der Geschichte des dreissigjährigen Krieges* (Halle, 1874), 12–16.

106. See *Kurtze/ und Gegründete anzeig/ Was es für eine beschaffenheit habe/ mit der Schrifft/ welche die Bayerischen erstlich unter dem Titul Consultationes, oder unterschiedliche Rahtschläge /et/c. Und bald hernacher unter dem Titul Böhmische geheime Cantzley/ /et/c. Das ist/ Consultationes, Oder underschiedliche Rathschläge und Vota /et/c. und unterm schein eines in der Heidelbergischen Cantzley gefundenen Protocols/ im Jahr 1624 in offenen Truck gegeben/ und ausgesprenget haben* (n.p., 1625), 4.

107. [Georg Erasmus von Tschernembl], *Consultationes Oder Underschidliche Rathschläg/ Der maisten und wichtigisten sachen/ welche von Anfang der Böhemischen/ und andern folgenden Auffständ fürgangen/ unnd zu Werck gericht worden/ oder werden sollen: Von wort zu wort auß dem Original Protocoll, so in der Haidelbergischen Cantzley gefunden worden/ gezogen. Mit nohtwendigen Glossis erklärt,* [ed. Jakob Keller] (n.p., 1624). For the identity of the unnamed editor, see Reinhold Koser, *Der Kanzleienstreit, ein Beitrag zur Quellenkunde der Geschichte des dreissigjährigen Krieges* (Halle, 1874), 63.

108. *Kurtze/ und Gegründete anzeig/ Was es für eine beschaffenheit habe/ mit der Schrifft/ welche die Bayerischen erstlich unter dem Titul Consultationes, oder unterschiedliche Rahtschläge /et/c. Und bald hernacher unter dem Titul Böhmische geheime Cantzley/ /et/c. Das ist/ Consultationes, Oder underschiedliche Rathschläge und Vota /et/c. und unterm schein eines in der*

148　*The Thinker*

Heidelbergischen Cantzley gefundenen Protocols/ im Jahr 1624 in offenen Truck gegeben/ und ausgesprenget haben (n.p., 1625). The editor defined them in the preface as the record of statements that the author (whom he does not name, but describes in a manner that fits Tschernembl) had taken down or made in the meetings of the Elector's privy council in Heidelberg.

109. See the discussion of the manuscript's background in Hans Sturmberger, *Georg Erasmus Tschernembl: Religion, Libertät und Widerstand* (Graz, 1953), 337–342.

110. Ibid., 339f.

111. Ibid., 341.

112. This categorization concurs with Hans Sturmberger, *Georg Erasmus Tschernembl: Religion, Libertät und Widerstand* (Graz, 1953), 341f., rather than Reinhold Koser, *Der Kanzleienstreit, ein Beitrag zur Quellenkunde der Geschichte des dreissigjährigen Krieges* (Halle, 1874), 61.

113. For the following, see recommendation 9 in [Georg Erasmus von Tschernembl], *Consultationes Oder Underschidliche Rathschläg/ Der maisten und wichtigisten sachen/ welche von Anfang der Böhemischen/ und andern folgenden Auffständ fürgangen/ unnd zu Werck gericht worden/ oder werden sollen: Von wort zu wort auß dem Original Protocoll, so in der Haidelbergischen Cantzley gefunden worden/ gezogen. Mit nohtwendigen Glossis erklärt*, [ed. Jakob Keller] (n.p., 1624), 82–106.

114. Ibid., 104.

115. Ibid., 106. This rejection of clerical influence on politics also expresses itself in other places, not least of all in Tschernembl's recommendation to remove the prelates from the estates because they lack proper attachment to the territory and owe their primary allegiance to external religious authorities. See recommendation 33 in ibid., 304–310.

116. Ibid., 113–115.

117. For the following, see the 11th recommendation in ibid., 117–123.

118. Ibid., 109.

119. Ibid., 111.

120. Ibid., 102f.

121. For the following, see the 8th recommendation in ibid., 75–82.

122. See recommendations 12, 13, 14 and 15 in ibid., 123–144.

123. See the 16th recommendation in ibid., 144–162.

124. For the following, see the 4th recommendation in ibid., 26–57.

125. See recommendations 18, 19, 20 and 21 in ibid., 171–188.

126. For his retroactive contemplations, see the 23rd recommendation in ibid., 200–212.

127. See the 32nd recommendation in ibid., 298–304.

128. Ibid., 288.

129. For the following, see the 29th recommendation in ibid., 266–274.

130. For the following, see the 28th recommendation in ibid., 252–266.

131. For the following, see the 25th recommendation in ibid., 214–224.

132. For the following, see the 27th recommendation in ibid., 228–252.

133. For the Austrian contingent in the Bohemian forces, see Anton Gindely, ed., *Die Berichte über die Schlacht auf dem Weissen Berge bei Prag* (Vienna, 1877), 125.

The Thinker   149

134. His arguments for continuing the fight can be seen in recommendations 20 and 21 in [Georg Erasmus von Tschernembl], *Consultationes Oder Underschidliche Rathschläg/ Der maisten und wichtigisten sachen/ welche von Anfang der Böhemischen/ und andern folgenden Auffständ fürgangen/ unnd zu Werck gericht worden/ oder werden sollen: Von wort zu wort auß dem Original Protocoll, so in der Haidelbergischen Cantzley gefunden worden/ gezogen. Mit nohtwendigen Glossis erklärt,* [ed. Jakob Keller] (n.p., 1624), 177–184.

135. See Constant von Wurzbach, *Biographisches Lexikon des Kaiserthums Oesterreich,* vol. 37 (Vienna, 1878), 177f.; Anton Gindely, *Geschichte des dreißigjährigen Krieges,* vol. 1 (Leipzig, 1882), 237–245.

136. [Georg Erasmus von Tschernembl], *Consultationes Oder Underschidliche Rathschläg/ Der maisten und wichtigisten sachen/ welche von Anfang der Böhemischen/ und andern folgenden Auffständ fürgangen/ unnd zu Werck gericht worden/ oder werden sollen: Von wort zu wort auß dem Original Protocoll, so in der Haidelbergischen Cantzley gefunden worden/ gezogen. Mit nohtwendigen Glossis erklärt,* [ed. by Jakob Keller] (n.p., 1624), 179, 181.

137. He "did not trust the Bavarian air" in the Upper Palatinate, mocked Jakob Keller in *Siebender Theil Anhaldischer geheimber Cancelley/ Das ist: Gründtliche Widerlegung/ nicht allein der ohnelangst von D. Ludovico Camerario wider die Litura oder Strich/ durch die Spanische Cancelley/ außgesprengter Apologia, sondern auch der vornembsten/ biß dahero/ wider die Catholische publicirter Schmehecarten/ als Synceratio Syncerationum, Catholicon, und anderer mehr/ beständige refutation* (n.p., 1626), 5.

138. Windegg, of course, was one of his Upper Austrian estates.

139. For Tschernembl's final years in Geneva, see also Jean-Antoine Gautier, *Histoire de Genève des origines a l'année 1691,* vol. 7 (Geneva, 1909), 150f.

140. See [Georg Erasmus von Tschernembl], *Consultationes Oder Underschidliche Rathschläg/ Der maisten und wichtigisten sachen/ welche von Anfang der Böhemischen/ und andern folgenden Auffständ fürgangen/ unnd zu Werck gericht worden/ oder werden sollen: Von wort zu wort auß dem Original Protocoll, so in der Haidelbergischen Cantzley gefunden worden/ gezogen. Mit nohtwendigen Glossis erklärt,* [ed. by Jakob Keller] (n.p., 1624), 73.

5 The Noble Warriors
Austrian Protestants in Swedish Services

In the early seventeenth century Georg Erasmus von Tschernembl developed an alternative vision of Austrian society, which fundamentally challenged the status of the dynasty. Yet few Austrian noblemen shared the radicalism and intellectual depth of Tschernembl. Loyalty toward the monarch was deeply ingrained in aristocratic thinking, as it formed a central pillar of hierarchic society. Obstinacy and rebellion, in turn, entailed grave risks to life and property. Moreover, the Habsburg aristocracy had long lived with the divergence of princely prescriptions and pragmatic realities. Although the dynasty had promoted Catholic conformity from the very inception of the religious reform movement, the nobles had successfully carved out their own religious sphere. In the early 1600s they could look back on almost a century of denominational accommodation.

In the Inner Austrian territories of Carinthia and Styria, especially, Protestant aristocrats kept their heads down when the conflict between crown and estates shook the monarchy's core. They struggled to preserve their status and lifestyle while steadfastly clinging to their religious convictions. Only when the policies of Emperor Ferdinand II made it all but impossible to uphold this established way of life, even the pragmatists could no longer eschew painful choices. By the turn of the 1620s, at the latest, the era of aristocratic latitude was coming to a close.

This chapter investigates the reaction of Protestant nobles to the final abrogation of confessional privileges. Boosted by years of military success, Ferdinand eyed an opportunity to end the denominational conflict in his patrimony. The time for indulgence was over. Neither status nor conduct would any longer exempt from confessional compliance. The indigenous nobility followed the path of peasants and townspeople. The conciliatory Inner Austrians received similar terms as the one-time rebels in the archduchy. Only the loyalist minority of Lower Austria was shielded by the emperor's personal guarantee of 1620.

The Noble Warriors   151

When these mandates achieved their full impact, the international situation had changed again. After a decade of triumphs, the Habsburgs finally faced a serious challenge. The Swedish intervention in the imperial conflict did not only alter the military balance; it also returned the war to the vicinity of the hereditary lands. When the army of Gustavus Adolphus arrived in the imperial cities of southern Germany, it encountered the refugees from Habsburg religious policy. Formerly powerless exiles lived through a historical sea change. For a moment, Habsburg history and Swedish history intertwined.

Austrian Protestants and the Kingdom of Sweden

In the decades leading up to the Thirty Years' War, the religious future of Austria was still open. Although Protestantism was commonplace in both the general population and the nobility, the Counterreformation had made visible progress. Increasingly pressured by their Habsburg rulers, the Protestant estates appealed for external support. Initially, they primarily mobilized princes of the empire.[1] The impact of their intercessions was limited, however. Even the most Protestant princes felt allegiance to the emperor. They also feared the consequences of antagonizing him. Not least of all, they subscribed to the constitutional foundation of Habsburg religious regimentation, the Peace of Augsburg. The Habsburgs regularly reminded them that emperors could not have fewer prerogatives in their own patrimony than did minor potentates.

Due to these limitations, Austrian Protestants began to look beyond the empire. Sweden was only beginning to become a relevant political factor. Under the leadership of Gustav Vasa, the country had left the Danish-dominated Union of Calmar in 1523. The new king had not only fought for political independence but also promoted the Lutheran reformation, which he had pushed through at the 1527 diet at Västerås.[2]

The dynasty profited from the seizure of church property and the eventual confirmation of hereditary succession. Before long, however, it began to undermine itself. Gustav's oldest son, Erik XIV, was deposed by his half-brothers John and Charles in 1568. The former subsequently ruled the country as John III until his death in 1592, whereupon he was succeeded by his son Sigismund. As the nephew of the last Jagiellonian king, Sigismund had already been elected to the throne of Poland in 1587.[3] To prepare him for this opportunity, he had been familiarized with Catholicism from childhood, resulting in his open embrace of his mother's church as a teenager.[4]

Sweden was thrown into a serious crisis. The very dynasty that had fought for independence and religious reform now linked the country to

152   *The Noble Warriors*

a powerful Catholic neighbor. Since the Polish magnates refused to be ruled from Stockholm, Sigismund had to control his Swedish patrimony from afar. His uncle Charles was installed as regent in 1594 and cast himself as the guardian of specifically Swedish and Protestant interests.[5] Sigismund's influence waned so rapidly that he chose to invade his own kingdom. Defeated on the battlefield, he withdrew to Poland in 1598 and was deposed the year after. The victor assumed the throne as Charles IX in 1607, but his embittered nephew never truly surrendered his dream of return.

When Charles' eldest son with Christina of Holstein-Gottorp succeeded his father in 1611, he thus inherited a dynastic mission together with a series of international conflicts.[6] By mastering these conflicts, Gustavus II Adolphus transformed Sweden into a Protestant regional power. In this role, the country also took an interest in neighboring Central Europe. Habsburg support of Poland and the advance of the Counterreformation to northern Germany were seen as threats to realm and dynasty.[7]

German Protestants, divided into Lutherans and Calvinists and seldom in agreement on imperial politics, were perennially in need of assistance. When the newly founded Evangelical Union looked for international allies in 1608, however, Sweden was not yet highest on its list. Due to his superior resources and his role as a prince of the empire, the king of Denmark was more coveted.[8] There were hopes for a broader Protestant coalition, to be sure, but it proved impossible to reconcile the interests of Denmark and Sweden, as well as those of England and the Netherlands.[9] Instead, Sweden entered into a defensive alliance with The Hague in 1614. Stockholm also tried to impress on the Dutch that Danish intransigence was preventing the Swedish army from bringing its struggle against Poland and thus the Counterreformation to a successful conclusion.[10]

The onset of the Thirty Years' War prompted renewed attempts to intensify cooperation between the Union and the Scandinavian kingdoms. The assembled alliance members at Heilbronn and Ulm sent urgent calls to Stockholm.[11] The Union was so ridden by crisis, however, that it inspired no trust among potential allies. Gustavus Adolphus listed his drawn-out conflict with Poland as sufficient contribution to the strengthening of international Protestantism.[12]

By that time, Habsburg Protestants had begun to pay attention to Sweden as well. Representatives of the Bohemian estates and their Palatine allies stressed the parallels between their own resistance to the dynasty's religious pressure and the opposition of Gustavus's father to a Catholic ruler.[13] By deposing a king who had endangered their religious freedom, the Bohemians argued, they had merely emulated the Swedish example. With the defeat at White Mountain, calls for support became more urgent, and the appeals by the Protestant estates of Lower Austria in August 1620 betrayed their growing desperation.[14]

The internal disunity of German Protestantism, which had again been revealed in the Bohemian conflict, continued to deter Gustavus Adolphus from intervening militarily. The war with Poland remained a priority, although its spread to Prussia moved it closer to the German battlegrounds. The rivalry between the two Scandinavian kingdoms, in turn, also extended to their role as potential patrons of German Protestantism. When England and the Netherlands proffered an alliance against the Catholic advance in 1624, Gustavus demanded so many prerogatives and guarantees that the maritime powers reached an agreement with Christian IV instead.[15] Following its resounding victory at Lutter in August 1626, however, the imperial army advanced so far north that Swedish intervention again became a possibility.

Emigrants Prior to the Thirty Years' War

Even before Gustavus Adolphus assumed the throne, the increasing religious pressure in their home country had driven individual Austrian Protestants into Swedish services. As early as 1603 the Carinthian Jakob Zenegg surfaced as ensign of a regiment of German mercenaries.[16] For this purpose he had recruited six horsemen, including his cousin Augustin Paul as well as two additional countrymen, Bartholomäus Amlacher and Gabriel Langenmantel. Zenegg advanced to captain but subsequently returned to Carinthia, where he administered Khevenhüller estates in Wernberg and Paternion until the increased religious pressure in the late 1620s forced him to emigrate to Regensburg.[17]

For Zenegg's relatives in Malborghet, Sweden received more lasting significance. The protoindustrialist Paul family belonged to the patriciate of this southern Carinthian market town.[18] The financial upswing of the early 1500s provided them with the means to acquire the estate of Nagerschigg near Villach, whereupon they began to call themselves Paul von Nagerschigg. In 1598 Emperor Rudolf II ennobled several members of the family.[19] Their social ascendancy was soon endangered, however. Most Pauls were Lutherans, and the advance of Catholic restoration drove them into exile.

The cadet branch of the family left in the early seventeenth century. Its patriarch Wolfgang Paul died soon after his arrival in Nuremberg and was buried alongside many countrymen in St. John's Cemetery.[20] His sons

154 *The Noble Warriors*

were scattered throughout Protestant Europe. Matthias tried his fortune in different parts of Germany; in 1658 his daughter Elisabeth married the Nördlingen councilman and subsequent mayor Johann Konrad Gundelfinger.[21] The turmoil of the war years repeatedly uprooted Michael Paul as well; in the end, he settled in Regensburg.[22] Hans initially tried to retain the family seat at Nagerschigg. The court records of Rosegg show, however, that he was ordered to leave the country for religious reasons in 1628.[23] Between 1629 and 1631 he was registered in Regensburg, and in the summer of 1637 he finally sold Nagerschigg.[24] Although the senior branch of the family largely acquiesced to the confessional transformation and remained in Carinthia, individual members chose emigration as well.[25]

Many of the exiles eventually joined the Swedish military. Matthias Paul rose to major and served as Swedish commander of Mannheim in 1632.[26] Michael made a name for himself as a cavalry officer under General Åke Tott.[27] As late as 1635 he was dispatched to Sweden to raise a new regiment. Neither Michael nor Matthias permanently relocated to the country, however.

Four other brothers tried a fresh start in the Scandinavian kingdom. Andreas, Thomas, Augustin, and Zacharias Paul arrived in Sweden in 1608. Whereas the two middle brothers soon disappeared from the sources, Andreas and Zacharias left a more lasting impression. Following his arrival in Sweden, Andreas, increasingly known as Anders Pauli, joined the cavalry. In May 1616 he emerged as captain in Helsinki; a few months later he camped outside Narva.[28] In 1618 he commanded a Finnish cavalry unit.[29] In the following decade he served in the war against Poland. Under General Gustaf Horn he fought in the Battle of Wallhof (Valle) outside Riga, which confirmed Swedish dominion over the Baltic provinces.[30] Two years later he traversed royal Prussia, until his unit returned to Finland following the Truce of Altmark. After 1630 he led his Finnish horsemen against the emperor, among others in the battle of Lützen. In 1633, advancing age and deteriorating health forced him to retire from active duty. Over the years he had received substantial land grants in southern Finland, which formed an integral part of the Swedish monarchy. The Swedish peerage calendar could therefore report in 1633 that Anders Pauli had taken residence on his Finnish estate and that his foreign title had been given proper recognition.[31]

Anders Pauli died in Finland in 1645. His eldest son Anders, born in 1611, followed his father into the cavalry in 1635, rising to major at the end of many years of battle in Germany, Russia, and Poland.[32] Their perennial wartime service kept the Finnish Paulis away from their estates and hampered their economic advance. Since his marriage remained childless and his half brother Axel had fallen as lieutenant in Wilhelm Üxküll's company in Prussia in 1656, the Finnish branch of the family already died out with Anders's passing in 1671.

Thus, all the modern-day members of the Swedish Pauli family descend from the youngest brother Zacharias, who was born in Carinthia in 1586. His funeral sermon has survived, leaving an abundance of personal information.[33] His parents repeatedly sent him abroad to gain international experience. After several years in Italy he took an initial soujourn to Sweden in 1603. Yet he also fought against the Ottomans under Gotthard von Starhemberg.[34]

Soon after his permanent departure for Sweden in 1608, Zacharias gained employment at the court of Charles IX. He subsequently served both the king's widow and his younger son Karl Philipp, in whose personal regiment he quickly rose through the ranks. His military career led him to the many battlegrounds of the era. In 1622 he was stationed outside Riga, where he held responsibility for Gustavus Adolphus's personal horses.[35] The second half of the decade he spent primarily as commander of the Södermanland cavalry in royal Prussia.[36] In preparation for transfer to Stralsund, Pauli was entrusted with recruiting reinforcements in Sweden.[37] Awaiting departure for Pomerania, he succumbed to the plague in Stockholm in August 1630. Almost a year later he was buried in the family church of Lista north of Lake Hjälmaren.[38]

Zacharias Pauli was generously rewarded for his efforts. In 1615 he received land grants in central Sweden and combined them into the estate of Vingsleör.[39] During the same year he also married Brita Hård af Segerstad, lady in waiting to the royal widow.[40] Through this union, Pauli became affiliated with a prominent Swedish family; Brita's father Olof served as governor in Jönköping.[41] It was no surprise, therefore, that Zacharias was subsequently inducted into the House of Knights and joined the core of the Swedish aristocracy in 1625. The still existing noble family of Pauli was established.

Protestant Exiles After the Battle at White Mountain

Not by coincidence, these early examples of Austrians in Swedish services were common or recently ennobled Carinthians. In his hereditary domain of Inner Austria, the later emperor Ferdinand II had been able to implement his confessional policies earlier than in the remainder of Austria. It was only consistent, therefore, that the next wave of Austrian émigrés originated from the archduchy. Ferdinand's accession to power

156   *The Noble Warriors*

in the Danubian and Bohemian provinces and his subsequent defeat of the Protestant opposition drove many into exile.[42] Among them was Melchior Wurmbrand, baron of Steyersberg and Stuppach, born in Lower Austria in 1586.[43] Wurmbrand hailed from old noble stock; his father Hieronymus had served in the executive committee of the territorial estates.[44] Melchior was well-educated and well-travelled; in a different era he might have embarked on a successful career in his native country.[45] Any such prospects ended in 1620, however, when Wurmbrand was outlawed for joining the Protestant resistance and failing to pay homage to Ferdinand II; he lost his estates and took refuge abroad.[46] In 1621–1622 he served Protestant warlord Ernst von Mansfeld.[47] Johan Skytte, royal tutor and member of Sweden's council of the realm, established contact with Wurmbrand in Germany and recommended him to Chancellor Axel Oxenstierna.[48] In 1625 Wurmbrand entered Swedish services as colonel and commander of Seaton's new infantry regiment, which was stationed in Riga and engaged in the war against Poland.[49]

Wurmbrand was not just another foreign officer in Swedish uniform, however. He came to the king's attention when he offered to construct a so-called leather gun. This light cannon was designed to increase the mobility and thus enhance the battlefield use of artillery. Its exact construction varied, but typically consisted of a sheet-thin copper barrel, reinforced with iron rails and rings, wound with rope, and encased in leather.[50] Wurmbrand may have encountered this innovation in Zurich, where the Swiss craftsmen Philip Eberhard and Alexander Bierbrüyer had already presented such cannons in 1623.[51] The presence of a Colonel Wurmbrand is documented in Zurich in 1622, which supports the proposition that the two inventions were connected.[52] There is no definite proof of the matter, however. Nor can it be established who influenced whom, although the Swiss constructors can claim priority of completion. For his part, Wurmbrand was no stranger to metallurgy; as early as 1615 he had applied for a copper mining privilege.[53] His inscription on a gun carriage indicates that he at least implicitly laid claim to intellectual ownership.[54]

Gustavus Adolphus showed great interest in the invention, and Wurmbrand was ready to share his technical know-how.[55] He agreed to both manufacture such cannons and train Swedish experts in building them independently. As a reward as well as a means to launch production, the Austrian baron obtained the royal estate of Julita in the central Swedish province of Södermanland. This imposing manor dates back to the Middle Ages, where it had also functioned as a monastery, and was closely linked to the king's immediate family. His half brother Karl Karlsson

The Noble Warriors   157

Gyllenhielm grew up on Julita, which subsequently also served as the dower residence of Gustavus's mother Christina.[56]

Wurmbrand's leather cannons were employed in the Polish war and during the earliest phase of the Swedish intervention in Germany.[57] Their mobility emerged most impressively near Weichselmünde in 1628, where they were transported through swampy marshland to surprise and cripple a Polish naval unit.[58] Overall, however, the price for this mobility proved too high. The guns could only deliver a small charge and developed a disturbing tendency toward overheating. After the Battle of Breitenfeld they were taken out of use again.

In spite of their brief service, Wurmbrand's cannons inspired a modernization of the Swedish artillery. Their creator also learned from the drawbacks of the leather guns and shifted production to more traditional iron pieces. When industrialist Louis de Geer complained about illegal competition in 1630, the council of the realm emphasized Wurmbrand's crucial refinement of artillery production.[59] Wurmbrand himself departed from Sweden soon thereafter to participate directly in the war in Germany. In 1632 he served as Swedish governor of Donauwörth and Lauingen.[60] Subsequently, he fought under Duke Bernhard of Weimar in Alsace, where he was taken prisoner by imperial Croats in June 1636. The exact details of his further fate are unknown, but he did not survive beyond 1638.[61] On 16 June of that year Queen Christina noted that Julita had reverted to the crown upon the death of Colonel Wurmbrand.[62]

Whereas Melchior Wurmbrand entered the Swedish history books as military inventor, one of his countrymen excelled as military commander. Maximilian Teufel, baron of Guntersdorf, was born in Lower Austria in the late sixteenth century.[63] His family was renowned for its military tradition—Georg Teufel even served as president of the court council of war from 1566 to 1578—and its avid Protestantism.[64] Maximilian upheld this legacy on both counts. Following his education, which also included studies at the universities of Padua and Siena, he initially served the emperor.[65] The advances of the Counterreformation increasingly strained relations between the Protestant nobles and their Catholic sovereign, however. In 1608 Teufel supported the Protestant Federation of Horn, and in the early phases of the Thirty Years' War he was again to be found among the aristocratic opposition to the Habsburgs.[66] Whereas many of his peers subsequently made their peace with the emperor, Maximilian Teufel chose emigration.

In 1624 Teufel joined the regiment Hans Georg von Arnim was recruiting for Gustavus Adolphus. The following year he was promoted

158   *The Noble Warriors*

to regimental commander and well on his way to becoming one of the most visible officers in Swedish services.[67] In October 1627 he was put in charge of the court regiment, also known by the color of its uniform as the yellow regiment.[68] In this post he succeeded a fellow Protestant émigré, the Bohemian count Franz Bernhard von Thurn, who had been promoted to commander of the infantry and subsequently major general under Field Marshal Hermann von Wrangel. Franz Bernhard's father was Heinrich Matthias von Thurn, one of the central leaders of the Protestant opposition to Habsburg rule in Bohemia.[69] Following the defeat of the Bohemians at White Mountain, Heinrich Matthias continued to resist the Habsburgs in the service of ever-changing adversaries. In 1627 he joined his son in Sweden and concluded his life as a Livonian nobleman in 1640. Franz Bernhard von Thurn had already died during the Polish war in 1628, whereupon Teufel also succeeded him as sergeant major general of the army. Under Teufel's leadership, the yellow regiment gained its stature as Swedish elite unit and royal guard.[70]

Teufel participated in all the Swedish military engagements of the period. He fought in Livonia, leading a regiment in the critical Battle of Wallhof in 1626. Thereafter he joined the offensive against Poland in royal Prussia. Defeated by Hetman Stanisław Koniecpolski at Hammerstein, Teufel fell into enemy hands in April 1627.[71] Following his release in a prisoner exchange, Teufel contributed significantly to the Swedish victory at Gorzno in February 1629.[72] His regiment was indispensable for the Swedish intervention in the Thirty Years' War. It was shipped from Elbing to Usedom at the beginning of July 1630, whereupon Teufel was quickly ordered to the king's side at Stettin.[73]

During the following months Teufel traversed northeastern Germany at Gustavus Adolphus's side.[74] The yellow regiment blocked imperial relief to the beleaguered fortress of Kolberg. It also spearheaded the storming of Greifenhagen on Christmas Day of 1630. Following a raid into Mecklenburg, Teufel returned to Pomerania and confronted the vanguard of General Tilly's Leaguist and imperial forces. On reconnaissance with the king during the siege of Frankfurt on the Oder, the colonel was hit by a bullet. He recovered quickly, however, and rejoined the storming of the city. The capture of Frankfurt put the Oder River under Swedish control and provided direct access to Habsburg Silesia.

The king had planned to raise an army in eastern Pomerania, which Teufel would lead as field marshal, but the war took a different turn.[75] Tilly's attack on Magdeburg shifted the conflict toward the center of Germany. Teufel provided crucial support for the king at Werben, where Tilly unsuccessfully attempted to dislodge the Swedish encampment.[76]

The Noble Warriors   159

Yet the real measure of the two armies followed in September 1631 near the Saxon village of Breitenfeld.[77] Gustavus Adolphus spent the eve of the battle sleeping in an open wagon alongside his most trusted officers, the generals Gustaf Horn and Johan Banér and Colonel Teufel. The next day Teufel commanded the first division of the Swedish center. The battle commenced unevenly. Whereas the Swedish left flank came under severe pressure, the right, where also the king had taken position, successfully beat back all attacks by Gottfried Heinrich zu Pappenheim's imperial cavalry. Trying to restore communication between disconnected units, Teufel was fatally wounded by a musket shot.[78] He did not live to see the Swedish victory, which marked a turning point in the war. Having inflicted the first significant defeat on the Catholic armies, Gustavus Adolphus established himself as a tactical innovator and as a serious military and political challenger to the emperor. At the same time, his success in central Germany opened gateways to the southern bastions of imperial Catholicism.

Maximilian Teufel had excelled as one of the king's most capable military leaders. He was especially renowned for courage and speed: referring to the complementary temperaments of two of his foremost officers, Gustavus Adolphus is quoted as calling Teufel his hammer and Knyphausen his anvil, while pitying the unlucky adversary who ends up between them.[79] In spite of their elation over the victory, king and chancellor did not overlook the price paid for it and expressly deplored the loss of their skillful commander.[80]

Yet there was more to Teufel than his military exploits. The Austrian refugee was not one of the crude mercenaries associated with the era. He was a well-educated man, who had attended university and mastered several languages. The king could therefore employ him in multiple capacities, not least of all as a recruiter of foreign troops.[81] His financial situation was often precarious, but he saw his service in the Swedish military as more than an arbitrary engagement. Appealing to Chancellor Oxenstierna for overdue reimbursements in 1629, Teufel emphasized "how he had valued His Majesty's service so highly that he had not hesitated to put the prospect of his moderate inheritance at risk, to reject the pardon offered to him, together with generous propositions, because he had hoped to have found a new fatherland, which would sustain him."[82] As one of the early recruits to the Swedish cause, Teufel turned into a natural point of contact for later refugees from Habsburg lands. When the exiled baron Paul Khevenhüller was approached by a fellow Carinthian nobleman intent on going into Swedish service, he matter-of-factly referred him to Colonel Teufel.[83]

160   *The Noble Warriors*

Teufel did not overlook the terrible consequences of the war for the civilian population.[84] In the spring of 1631 he criticized the Swedish cavalry for losing discipline and indulging in plunder.[85] He cited the laments of the peasants and predicted lasting consequences for Sweden's reputation. In a revealing glimpse of his religious disposition, he also expressed his fear of divine retribution. In tune with these sentiments, Teufel repeatedly tried to alleviate individual predicaments. In 1627 he intervened on behalf of Polish prisoners.[86] In the spring of 1631 he personally wrote to Oxenstierna and informed him that "my old landlady in Elbing beseeches your excellency to grant her house *salva guardia*. Your excellency would thereby commit an act of compassion, and I would consider it a big favor."[87] He also employed his influence on behalf of fellow exiles.[88]

Maximilian Teufel was not long survived by any offspring; a daughter Appolonia is reported to have followed him in death within a month.[89] He bequeathed 5000 taler to his sister Margaretha, who was married to another Protestant refugee, Johann Georg Streun von Schwarzenau.[90] The Streuns took residence in Dresden, where Johann Georg served as an officer in the Saxon army. Another branch of the family remained as Protestants in Lower Austria, in accordance with the personal toleration guaranteed them in the Peace of Westphalia. Like many of their peers, however, the Teufels eventually preferred emigration to societal marginalization. In 1688 Otto Christoph Teufel relocated to Dresden, where he was buried in St. Sophia's Church two years later.[91] Dresden thus became the foremost place of refuge of the Teufel family, and their grave markers, including Maximilian von Teufel's coat of arms, long remained visible on the walls of St. Sophia.[92]

These individual affiliations with Sweden were complemented by more ambitious proposals for an integration of embattled Protestants from the Holy Roman Empire. In the mid 1620s Gustavus Adolphus offered refuge in the recently conquered province of Ingria.[93] Austrian magnate Hans Ludwig von Kuefstein was intrigued enough to contact the king and discuss the idea with close friends. In the end, the allure of the remote northern Baltic was still limited and the uncertainty of the project too daunting. It took the arrival of Swedish troops in Germany to familiarize more Austrians with the opportunities in the Swedish Empire.

Protestant Exiles Following the Swedish Intervention

The most visible wave of Austrians in Swedish services followed the large-scale emigration of the Protestant nobility in 1628–1629. This exodus hit the Inner Austrian provinces of Styria and Carinthia particularly hard. As his inherited domains, they had been the testing grounds of Ferdinand's confessional strategy. By the turn of the seventeenth century, townspeople and peasants had lost all religious privileges. With his general mandate of March 1601, the archduke had ordered the remaining Protestant pastors and teachers out of his patrimony.[94] Only the territorial nobility was still exempt.

The legal framework cannot tell the whole story, however. The conversion of Protestant Upper Styria and Carinthia posed many challenges. Whenever possible, Protestant landowners shielded their subjects from the most far-reaching consequences of religious regimentation.[95] The aristocracy chose to undercut confessional mandates through quiet insubordination rather than open confrontation.[96] Individual hardliners such as Ernreich von Saurau suggested a more combative approach and promoted closer cooperation with Protestant princes.[97] Inspired by their peers in the archduchy, wider circles flirted with the language of resistance in 1609.[98] In the long run, however, the majority preferred restraint.[99] At the same time, Catholics began to gain a foothold in the aristocracy and demand greater influence on estatist politics.[100]

When Archduke Ferdinand succeeded his cousin Matthias as head of the dynasty, he faced more urgent challenges than the persistence of Alpine heterodoxy. Following his many battlefield victories, however, the emperor felt emboldened to intensify his efforts. Throughout the 1620s, remaining religious liberties continued to dwindle. In 1625 the reformation commission was officially reinstated. The attendance of heterodox universities was subjected to monarchic control.[101] In October 1627 the reformation commission ordered territorial officers to convert or emigrate; an exception was still made for members of the established nobility.[102] It was a last respite. Following a similar decree in Upper Austria the year before, the emperor finally turned to the Inner Austrian nobility in August 1628. In a general decree, Ferdinand listed his efforts to guide his subjects to religious orthodoxy.[103] His ever more comprehensive measures against heresy had not been in vain, but his hope that patience and clemency would sway the remaining holdouts had proven illusory. His paternal responsibility therefore forced him to extend the existing religious mandates to the territorial nobility. It would pain him to see the departure of so many established families, which had faithfully served his dynasty for generations. They had also refrained from disobedience and rebellion. Yet there was no better way to recompense them for their loyalty than to show them the path to true salvation. As a consequence, he gave them one last year to accept the Catholic religion or leave the country. In recognition of their loyalty and as an expression of

162   *The Noble Warriors*

his clemency, he was willing to wave the customary emigration tax. The core of the resolution was unequivocal, however. Following the expiration of the deadline on 30 July 1629, no Protestant could legally reside in Inner Austria.

A substantial share of the Inner Austrian nobility chose emigration. Exact numbers are difficult to establish. Contemporary compilations list approximately 800 aristocratic émigrés from the Austrian lands. The inclusion of recently ennobled raises the total to over 1000. These compilations are neither complete nor free of mistakes, however. For Carinthia, two surviving registers contain 114 and 160 names, respectively, which do not always include family members. Paul Dedic and Werner Wilhelm Schnabel, in particular, have complemented the historical compilations with an abundance of additional materials. The resulting totals must be held up to the overall size of the contemporary nobility. The Upper Austrian diet contained around 150 lords and knights. The territorial nobility of Carniola comprised approximately 100 families. A Carinthian peerage registry of 1611 included 107 families with 222 individuals, again without full representation of all family members. Even though the diversity of the sources makes them difficult to compare, the magnitude of the exodus is unmistakable.[104]

During the subsequent years, the Austrian lands witnessed a peculiar spectacle. Representatives of their most illustrious families returned on short-term permits to sell off their estates. During his visit in 1630, Hans Khevenhüller alone attempted to find buyers for his ancestral seats of Landskron and Velden as well as the imposing Hollenburg castle of his father-in-law, Bartholomäus von Dietrichstein. The resulting problems were to be expected. The market was swamped. Few had the means to provide adequate compensation for the most valuable properties. And those who did exploited the émigrés' calamity to drive down the price and delay payment. The bitterness of the exiles ran deep.

In the free imperial cities of southern Germany, where many had taken refuge, they had to reevaluate their lives. In this situation they encountered the emissaries of the Swedish king, who urged them to join his campaign to save German liberty and the embattled Protestant religion.[105] But could these appeals be trusted? The discussion about the underlying motives of the Swedish intervention in Germany has been as intense as enduring. In 1992 Swedish historian Sverker Oredsson published a metastudy of 166 pertinent works in seven languages, which stretched from Bogislaff Chemnitz's contemporary assessment from 1648 all the way to Konrad Repgen's edited volume *Krieg und Politik 1618–1648* from 1988.[106] Oredsson found 11 interpretative categories. According to the respective accounts, Gustavus Adolphus went to war for the narrowly subscribed reasons of the war manifesto, in defense of German Protestantism, in support of freedom of conscience and religion, as an instrument of God or history, in defense of German liberty, to restore the international balance of power, in defense of the king himself and his lineage, to protect Sweden from hostile imperial designs, for lust of conquest, to improve Sweden's economic position, or in the interest of the Swedish feudal lords.[107]

If one disregards the infrequent economic explanations, most of which originated during the heydays of historical materialism, the remaining interpretations can be subsumed under two encompassing headings: religion and politics. Their respective preeminence has provoked passionate disagreements, but a straightforward juxtaposition is misleading. The recurrent debate of military options in the council of the realm shows an amalgamation of political and religious aspects.[108] Since council meetings also served a propagandistic purpose, they should be supplemented with the king's personal communications.[109] In a letter sent to Axel Oxenstierna on 8 October 1630, Gustavus Adolphus made the case for intervention: "We are certain that you agree with us that the House of Austria intends to subjugate all of Germany and change its status. Furthermore, that the House of Austria wishes to completely uproot the Protestant religion in Germany and implant the erroneous popish creed instead. And I am well aware that you have carefully considered the dangers this entails for us, our country, and the whole region."[110] Therefore, the king was skeptical toward peace offers that in essence surrendered Germany to the emperor. Gustavus argued that no peace should be contemplated "unless the whole of Germany is religiously pacified and all of our neighbors are restored to their previous status so that we, through their security, would be secure in our own country."[111]

In Gustavus's confessionalized world view, the emperor's attempt at Catholic restoration in Germany represented both a religious and a political challenge. The two aspects were intertwined further by the Vasas' intradynastic conflict. Supported by a reinvigorated Catholic monarchy in the empire, the Polish branch could regain control of Sweden and supplant both Gustavus Adolphus and the Lutheran creed. Religion and politics were two sides of the same coin.

With the continuing advance of Habsburg and Leaguist forces, calls for a confessional counterweight and security zone in the Holy Roman Empire began to resonate among German Protestants. To be sure, a number of later allies from Pomerania to Brandenburg and Saxony hesitated to back the Swedish intervention. In view of the uncertainty about Sweden's political designs and military capabilities, their caution was

164   *The Noble Warriors*

well-founded. Yet contrary to a widespread perception, Gustavus could also draw on instant support.[112] Prominent examples were the recently deposed leaders of the Palatinate, Mecklenburg, and Bohemia.[113] Since they had by no means recognized the loss of their positions and to some extent regained them, they cannot be excluded from the political landscape.[114] In Stralsund, calls for Swedish intervention had been desperate. Following the Swedish consolidation, additional princes flocked to Gustavus, among them the landgrave of Hesse. And last, but by no means least, one will also have to include the enormous echo of the Swedish position in the Protestant public.[115]

The royal chancellery was expanded with German-speaking staff.[116] A network of political agents informed king and chancellor about attitudes and developments in individual German territories. It also promoted Stockholm's view of the war in the German public. The specifically Swedish effort is difficult to quantify, however. Much of the propagandistic offensive was carried out by German Protestants who genuinely identified with Gustavus's intervention. Key representatives of Swedish interests in the empire were natives. Among them were the former Palatine privy councilor Ludwig Camerarius, who also served as Swedish ambassador at so pivotal a location as The Hague, and the Bohemian émigré leader Heinrich Matthias von Thurn, who represented Sweden at the court in Berlin.

Swedish sympathies were especially pronounced among the most imperiled elements of imperial Protestantism. No one had more reason to feel imperiled than the Austrian refugees. Yet far from all of them put their hopes on Sweden. A large segment simply wanted to rebuild their lives.[117] A few even joined the imperial forces, among them Andre Ludwig von Windischgrätz, who had reluctantly left Carinthia for Nuremberg in 1630. For most of them, this represented a step toward return and conversion, and also Windischgrätz publicly embraced Catholicism in 1639. He ended his career as military commander of Carinthia.[118]

The appeal of Gustavus Adolphus was unmistakable, however. The contribution of Austrians to the Swedish intervention was too large and diverse to be fully reconstructed. Its protagonists included members of the country's leading families, such as Jörgers, Herbersteins, Stubenbergs, and Starhembergs. Andre von Bernardin was lieutenant general in the Schlammersdorf regiment. Friedrich von Egg served as captain in the Solms regiment; Gottfried von Egg ended his career as colonel. Maximillian Gienger von Grünbühel held the rank of major in the white regiment. Christoph Amann von Ammansegg as well as his brother Georg Sigmund fell as Swedish officers, as did Paul and Adam von Hallegg, Melchior

Leopold von Hohberg, Hans Hermann von Hohenwart, Hans Christoph von Kronegg, Hans Georg Prunner von Vasoldsberg, Georg Ehrenreich von Rottal, Franz Ludwig von Teuffenbach, and numerous others.[119]

Support for Sweden was not restricted to military contributions. Bartholomäus von Dietrichstein held the coveted title of hereditary cup bearer of Carinthia, where he was also one of the leading landowners.[120] By the time of his emigration to Nuremberg he had passed fifty. Unlike several of his sons and sons-in-law, he no longer saw his place on the battlefield. Instead, he focused on politics and introduced Upper Austrian insurgents to the Swedish leadership in 1632.[121] Ferdinand accused Dietrichstein of treason and summoned him to Vienna.[122] The unreconstructed exile relocated to more secure Hanau, where he died in 1635.

A particularly visible example of émigré activism followed during the Swedish occupation of Regensburg.[123] Duke Bernhard of Weimar put the Styrian exile Johann Friedrich von Teuffenbach in charge of the city and adjacent Bavarian possessions in 1633. Encouraged by Swedish plans to advance into the Habsburg heartland, Austrian refugees played an important role in Teuffenbach's administration. In the eyes of concerned natives, the Swedish faction in the city even seemed to be dominated by exiles. As a consequence, many of them left Regensburg together with the Swedish forces in 1634. Teuffenbach himself continued his support for Sweden and struggle for restitution until his death in 1647.

Among those who decided to throw in their lot with Gustavus Adolphus were the brothers Khevenhüller. Paul and Hans Khevenhüller belonged to the cream of the Carinthian nobility.[124] Paul served as head of the territorial estates until his resignation in 1629. His half-brother sat on the executive committee and counted among the biggest landowners. Whereas Paul had managed to dispose of his more modest possessions, Hans found no buyers for his grand manors. He already experienced the atmosphere during his 1630 return visit as hostile and wrote to his wife in Nuremberg that God may forgive the emperor for all the pain he had caused.[125]

It could not come as a surprise that the brothers put their hopes on Gustavus Adolphus. Their sympathies already emerged in the choice of godfathers for Paul's children, who included the later Swedish Lord High Constable Lars Kagg and the prominent exile and military commander Johann Jakob von Thurn.[126] More important was their financial contribution to the Swedish campaign. In 1631 they loaned 70,000 taler to the king. In return, Gustavus signed a promissory note that not only guaranteed repayment but also assured the brothers of his special protection all the way to an eventual peace settlement.[127] In the following spring

166 *The Noble Warriors*

the Khevenhüllers raised a mounted regiment for the Swedish army. The emperor was not amused and confiscated their remaining properties.[128]

By the middle of 1632 the Khevenhüller regiment comprised 11 companies. The leading officers of the unit—Colonel Paul Khevenhüller, his brother, Lieutenant Colonel Hans Khevenhüller, and their brother-in-law, Major Rudolf von Dietrichstein—were all Carinthian refugees, as were many of their subordinates. Among the officers, one finds Dietrichstein's brother Cornet Christian von Dietrichstein, Cornet Klement von Welz, Lieutenant Hans Ulrich von Ernau, Wolf Friedrich von Metnitz, as well as Bartholomäus and Carl Putz.[129] Yet also the enlisted soldiers included many Carinthians, especially from the Khevenhüllers' core domains around Villach and Paternion. Finally, the military chaplain Johann Schwäger was the son of a Protestant refugee from Villach as well.[130]

The regiment crisscrossed southern Germany in 1632. During the summer it fought primarily in Franconia and the Upper Palatinate.[131] On 30 July it participated in the storming of Freystadt. In the heat of the battle, Hans Khevenhüller was shot by his own troops while trying to open the city gates from inside.[132] He was buried at St. John's cemetery at Nuremberg; the male line of the family extinguished two generations later in the same city.[133]

The battlefield death of Gustavus Adolphus in November 1632 brought the brief exuberance of Protestant Central Europe to an end. The loss of a leader who almost single-handedly had shaken the entrenched supremacy of emperor and League deprived the Swedish campaign of its special mystique. Moreover, the war had again retreated from the vicinity of the hereditary lands, diminishing hopes for impending restitution. The allure of Swedish service faded. Many exiles of the first generation had already paid the ultimate price. Of the nine officers of the Khevenhüller regiment listed above, Hans Khevenhüller, Wolf Friedrich von Metnitz, and both brothers Putz were no longer alive by the end of 1632; Hans Ulrich von Ernau followed within the decade.[134]

Paul Khevenhüller also withdrew from military life, but his ties to Sweden remained close. In 1636 he headed for Stockholm to expedite repayment of his loan. Since he had contributed 50,000 of the 70,000 taler, he acted as loan-holder but promised to pass on his brother's share.[135] For his military efforts, Gustavus Adolphus had invested him with German feoffs, including the Swabian town of Riedlingen.[136] These wartime donations to Swedish officers received no lasting validity, however.[137]

In view of the unrelenting war, Paul Khevenhüller secured no immediate settlement of the loan. In the long run, however, his compensation proved even more profitable. In a mortgage deed dated 26 June 1638, Queen Christina emphasized the invaluable services Khevenhüller had delivered to her father.[138] She also thanked him for accepting a deferral of repayment and gave him the royal estate of Julita as security and erstwhile residence. In an intriguing twist, Julita was the very property formerly granted to Khevenhüller's Austrian compatriot Melchior Wurmbrand. It had recently reverted to the crown following Wurmbrand's death in captivity.[139]

Paul Khevenhüller's household became the center of a German-Swedish family circle. German ties remained strong. In 1637 Paul's six surviving sons Georg Christoph, Bernhard, Andreas, Bartholomäus, Paul, and Augustin had entered Altdorf in Franconia, a popular university among Habsburg Protestants.[140] They regularly returned to the empire later, so that Bernhard died during a sojourn at Vienna and Bartholomäus at Nuremberg.[141] All children found German-speaking spouses, ranging from Styrian émigrés to Livonian barons.[142] Paul's wife Regina deplored in a letter to her sister-in-law that their estates were located in Sweden proper rather than Pomerania.[143] Sweden was no Germany, she commented as late as 1652, even though one could also lead a good life there.[144]

The family also retained close relations to its exiled relatives in Nuremberg. The wives of Paul and Hans corresponded extensively, and the latter's son, yet another Bartholomäus, spent many years at Julita.[145] Together with Paul's children he engaged in the customary activities of Swedish noble youths and subsequently served the queen as courtier, officer, and diplomat. He did not write as diligently as his aunt, but in December 1645 he reported to his mother that he kept busy hunting with his cousin Bernhard and shared the hope of many that the devastating war might be over by Easter.[146]

There even was contact to the now Catholic relations in the hereditary lands. Following the Peace of Westphalia, the well-connected Franz Christoph Khevenhüller offered to promote the restitution of his relatives. In 1649 he informed them that he had personally submitted their supplications to the emperor.[147] Even though Franz Christoph's death the following year cut his efforts short, communication between the different branches of the family did not end altogether.[148]

The growing integration into Swedish society was just as visible, however. In 1644 the council of the realm discussed Paul Khevenhüller's request for naturalization.[149] In view of his great merits, Khevenhüller's induction into the Swedish nobility seemed unproblematic to both the chancellor and the marshal of the realm. He was of prominent birth and a faithful servant to the crown; no less than four of his sons currently

168   *The Noble Warriors*

served in the war.[150] When Queen Christina subsequently invested him with Julita in 1645, Khevenhüller had become a major Swedish land-holder.[151] Two years later he was introduced into the House of Knights and joined the inner circle of the Swedish aristocracy.[152] The same year he was appointed lord chamberlain of the queen dowager Maria Eleonora and governor of her Pomeranian domains.[153]

This elevated position aided the family's attempts at regaining its confiscated Austrian properties. During their initial contacts with Gustavus Adolphus, the Khevenhüllers had been assured of Swedish protection against the emperor's foreseeable reprisals.[154] After peace negotiations had commenced at Osnabrück, Paul Khevenhüller could finally have these promises redeemed. In June 1645 the council of the realm debated his case.[155] In April 1646 the emperor's chief representative Maximilian von Trauttmansdorff informed his monarch that the Swedish delegate Johan Adler Salvius had praised Khevenhüller's qualities and interceded on his behalf.[156] Queen Christina repeatedly expressed her interest in the matter. As late as September 1647 she reminded her envoys of previous interpolations and urged them to write Khevenhüller's restitution explicitly into the treaty.[157] Finally, Chancellor Oxenstierna intervened so vigorously that the Swedish chief negotiator—his own son Johan—had little choice but to comply.[158]

Due to these powerful advocates Paul Khevenhüller was personally included in the Peace of Westphalia. Sweden had fought for a general rehabilitation of Habsburg Protestants. The country's peace proposal of June 1645 did not only seek compensation for individual sympathizers but also called for a return to prewar conditions in all parts of the empire, including the Kingdom of Bohemia.[159] The Swedish delegates regularly reiterated these demands.[160] The imperial side rejected them just as consistently, however, and Count Trauttmansdorff retorted that his monarch would rather risk his life and worldly possessions.[161] These disagreements seriously imperiled a settlement. In 1645 the landgravine Amalie Elisabeth of Hesse-Kassel even saw them as the main reason for Sweden's advance into the hereditary lands.[162]

Neither France nor even all of its German allies shared Sweden's interest in Habsburg Protestantism. Vienna eagerly seized the opportunity. Court chancellor Matthias Prickelmayr suggested mobilizing the French against Swedish calls for a general amnesty.[163] Indeed, Paris repeatedly intervened on behalf of Catholic confessional interests.[164] Among Protestant princes, the Saxon elector yet again sympathized with the emperor's position. His negotiator Johannes Leuber was quoted as saying that it would not be right to prolong the terrible war in Germany for the sake of the Bohemian rebels.[165] Saxony did not stand alone with this assessment, and Swedish delegates complained in 1647 that moderates had accused them of needlessly delaying a settlement.[166] At the same time, close allies such as Brunswick-Lüneburg and Hesse-Kassel urged Stockholm to secure the interests of German Protestantism.[167]

The secret instructions to Count Trauttmansdorff reveal that a tacit toleration of personal heterodoxy might have been achievable for nobles outside of Lower Austria as well. If it was unavoidable, the emperor delineated on 16 October 1645, Protestants restituted in his patrimony by a general amnesty could return and receive lenient treatment, if they kept quiet and only attended heterodox services abroad.[168] In view of its vagueness, however, such a concession would hardly have had long-term consequences. It is also doubtful if it was still realistic in 1648, after Vienna had observed Sweden's growing isolation in this question. Faced with the exhaustion of its allies, Stockholm accepted more limited concessions.[169]

The strong and active Bohemian émigré community felt especially betrayed. Philosopher and theologian John Amos Comenius complained bitterly to his long-term protector Axel Oxenstierna in October 1648, but subsequently acknowledged the limits of Sweden's possibilities.[170] An analysis of the peace negotiations shows that Stockholm was the foremost guardian of Habsburg Protestantism, but that it ultimately prioritized its own financial and territorial compensation and the safety of Protestant northern Germany.[171] At the eleventh hour Queen Christina urged her negotiators to use recent military advances to at least secure better conditions for the exiles. It had not been possible to promote their case sufficiently in the past, the queen conceded in October 1648, but now God had "bestowed victory and success upon our arms in those places and given us the opportunity to speak for them."[172] It was too late. In Habsburg territories, Sweden primarily gained symbolic concessions. The remaining heterodox nobles in Lower Austria secured an international confirmation of their modest privileges.[173] A more substantive protection of territorial Protestantism was only instituted in Silesia, where Saxony was engaged as well.[174]

This backdrop makes it all the more noteworthy that article IV, paragraph 45 of the Peace Treaty of Osnabrück stipulated that "baro Paulus Khevenhüller cum nepotibus ex fratre . . . quisque in omnia sibi per confiscationem adempta plenarie restituti sunto", in other words, that Baron Paul Khevenhüller and his brother's sons should regain all their confiscated possessions.[175] Queen Christina praised the provision and admonished her delegates to secure its implementation.[176] The emperor's

170 *The Noble Warriors*

plenipotentiaries, for their part, saw it as a bearable price for averting genuine constitutional revisions. Since any return would have required conversion to Catholicism, the restitution could only have taken the form of financial compensation. After the withdrawal of Swedish troops, Habsburg bureaucrats easily obstructed this sole concession to Inner Austrian Protestantism. No compensation was ever paid.[177]

Paul Khevenhüller lived out his remaining years as a prominent Swedish aristocrat. In 1653 he was even appointed to the council of the realm, which assisted the monarch in the governing of the country.[178] It was to be a brief honor. Khevenhüller died in 1655 at Stockholm Castle while attending the baptism of the later King Charles XI.[179] Thus, his life ended very symbolically at the political center of the country that had allowed him a new start. The respect he had earned speaks from the council's minutes almost a decade earlier. He recommends Khevenhüller as lord chamberlain to the queen dowager, Chancellor Oxenstierna informed his fellow members, because he is "a good economist and a good Swede."[180]

Khevenhüller's children, too, put themselves at the disposal of their host society. No fewer than five sons served in the armed forces, as did their Nuremberg cousin Bartholomäus. They paid a heavy price. Georg Christoph fell in 1645 during the Battle of Jankau (Jankov) in Bohemia.[181] Andreas was killed in the final months of the war at Bremervörde.[182] Paul the Younger was mortally wounded by a cannon ball during the siege of Copenhagen in 1658.[183] Of the two remaining sons, Bernhard died in Vienna in 1660 and Bartholomäus in Nuremberg in 1662.[184] After only 15 years, the Swedish baronial family of Khevenhüller was extinguished.

Yet although some of Paul's daughters died without progeny as well, the Khevenhüllers did not disappear completely from Swedish history. The descendants of two daughters largely merged into the Baltic-German and Prussian aristocracies.[185] Paul's eldest daughter Anna Regina, however, married the Pomeranian-born nobleman Mathias Palbitzki, who served Queen Christina as diplomat and art expert.[186] In the 1660s Palbitzki's diplomatic missions also brought him to Vienna, where he promoted both the restitution of the Khevenhüller family and the general interests of Austrian Protestantism.[187] Whereas he accomplished little in Austria, the family flourished in Sweden and kept possession of Julita until its extinction in the nineteenth century.[188]

As a member of the council of the realm and leading landowner, Paul Khevenhüller had entered the inner circle of Sweden's social and political elite. Due to the premature death of his sons, however, the Swedish Khevenhüllers remained a brief episode. The experience of other Austrian newcomers to the Swedish aristocracy may have been less spectacular, but proved to be more enduring. Over the centuries, the Pauli family gave its new homeland an abundance of military and cultural leaders.[189] The Styrian noble Hans Christoph Frölich served as colonel in Gustavus Adolphus's army.[190] His descendants largely followed in his military footsteps; they were naturalized in 1682 and subsequently elevated to barons and counts. As a commoner, the Lutheran furrier Matthias Vult already left his Styrian homeland in the early phases of recatholization. He found refuge in Silesia, but his son Elias considered it safer to move on to Sweden. Grandson Johannes Vultejus studied theology and became court chaplain in Stockholm.[191] Great-grandson Johan Julius crowned a long public career with the position of auditor-general of public finances, having been ennobled under the name of Vult von Steijern along the way. All of these families continue to flourish today.

Conclusion

In the initial decade of the Thirty Years' War, the Counterreformation finally engulfed the Austrian nobility. Bishop Klesl's prediction had come true.[192] Deprived of its popular base, aristocratic Protestantism had turned into an empty shell, which only survived at the mercy of the monarch. The Austrian nobility had chosen to guard its prerogatives rather than take a stand with the commoners. Yet a privileged minority formed no challenge to a determined ruler. By the early 1630s, hundreds of noble exiles populated the Protestant havens of southern Germany. The Austrian aristocracy was fundamentally transformed.

During the same period, the kingdom of Sweden evolved into a European power. With his triumphant establishment in Germany, Gustavus Adolphus ended a sheer endless series of Habsburg victories. At long last, the emperor had met his equal. Although the fortunes of war fluctuated after Gustavus's death at Lützen, Sweden remained a significant force in German politics. The era of unilateral Habsburg supremacy was over.

At first sight, these two developments seem unrelated. Gustavus Adolphus cared about Habsburg Protestantism, but he did not enter the war to save it. Exiles from the Habsburg lands played a significant role in the Swedish military, but they did not determine the outcome of the struggle. In the end, Sweden's intervention barely altered the fate of Protestantism in the Austrian and Bohemian lands.

Yet the interconnections between Sweden and Habsburg Protestantism illuminate the confessional overtones of seventeenth-century foreign policy.[193] Heinz Schilling divided the imperial process of confessionalization into four stages.[194] The period between the 1540s and the early 1560s

172   *The Noble Warriors*

formed a preparatory phase, in which Tridentine Catholicism and Calvinism made their modest entry into German society. The second phase, which commenced in the 1570s, witnessed the differentiation of two Protestant confessions and a reinvigoration of Catholicism, foreshadowing the more conflictual relationship to follow. The generation that had successfully negotiated the denominational compromise of Augsburg was succeeded by a more belligerent one, setting the stage for phase three, the apogee of confessionalization. This period contained both a so-called second reformation in originally Lutheran territories, whose princes reoriented themselves toward the more activist Calvinism, and the decisive breakthrough of Tridentine doctrines in Catholic polities.[195] The willingness to use violence for political goals resulted in an all-encompassing war. Its dire consequences, in a fourth and final phase, triggered a return of irenicism and a weakening of militant confessionalization, at least on the imperial level. Based on this model, Ingun Montgomery saw the religious policies of Charles IX as an attempt to implement a second reformation within a Lutheran framework.[196]

Few aspects of the Thirty Years' Wars have been discussed as passionately as the motives of Swedish intervention. Their explanatory value, however, is limited. Since they were hidden to contemporaries, these motives cannot explain the success of Swedish policy. It is of eminent theoretical importance, in contrast, how a peripheral and economically underdeveloped polity such as Sweden turned into a great power. This phenomenon has received a number of functional explanations, which include Gustavus Adolphus's military innovations, the temporary power vacuum in the Baltic, the national recruiting system, and the reliance on French subsidies as well as levies on occupied populations.[197] In recent years the literature has received new facets. Mats Hallenberg examined the financing of military expansion through a privatization of tax collection.[198] Jan Glete ascribed Sweden's advances to superior administration and the successful integration of sociopolitical interest groups, which allowed the monarchy to establish military security within the realm and subsequently export it to adjacent regions.[199] Erik Ringmar, in turn, saw Swedish expansion as the result of a military intervention that advanced not only national security but also national identity.[200]

All these interpretations fall short, however, if they ignore Sweden's status in Protestant Central Europe. The confessional division of the Holy Roman Empire had created an imbalance, in which a Catholic emperor and Electoral College faced a Protestant popular majority. With the promulgation of the Edict of Restitution in 1629, Emperor Ferdinand II had removed any remaining doubts about his ultimate goal of marginalizing Protestantism throughout the empire.[201] At that juncture, no German prince was able to challenge dynasty and League. Moreover, the traditional Protestant hegemon of Saxony had isolated itself through collaboration with the emperor.

An apprehensive Protestant community experienced ever more painful setbacks. Further retreat endangered its very survival, but resistance seemed futile. The successful Swedish invasion resolved this dilemma. For an important segment of German Protestantism, which exploded in a burst of sermons and pamphlets, Gustavus Adolphus and his army were no foreign occupants. Instead, the most confessionally engaged put great hopes on them, as can be seen by the response of Habsburg émigrés. Their often enthusiastic embrace of the Swedish king betrayed his deep impact on the Protestant public.

The confessional and cultural aspects of this identification surface in comparative perspective. Even though France repeatedly aided German Protestantism, it never triggered the emotional response evoked by Gustavus Adolphus. Unlike their French allies, the Swedes were seen as credible religious protectors. Cultural considerations should not be ignored, either. Gustavus Adolphus was the son and husband of German princesses and spoke the language fluently. Chancellor Axel Oxenstierna and other Swedish leaders were also familiar with country and culture; a substantial portion hailed from the Baltic-German nobility.[202] This did not only improve communication with the general public but also alleviated the integration of local personal.

The biographies of Habsburg refugees show the openness of the Swedish elite to Protestant newcomers. Paul Khevenhüller's ascent to the council of the realm only formed the most visible expression of a process, in which German, Scottish, and Dutch immigrants gained influential positions in the Swedish administration.[203] The Swedish Empire did not only benefit from the financial resources of Protestant Central Europe, but also from its human capital. At the height of its great power status, one cannot measure Sweden by its domestic resources alone but has to include those of its natural allies. Prussia's subsequent replacement of Sweden underscored how much the ascendancy of both powers owed to the political weakness of northern Germany.

As protector of embattled coreligionists in the Holy Roman Empire, Sweden reassured Protestant Germany of both its military prowess and its religious foundation. As international advocate and place of refuge,

174   *The Noble Warriors*

the country became an integral part of German politics. Two histories were so interwoven that any disentanglement seems illusory. In their midst we find the noble exiles from the Habsburg Monarchy.

Notes

1. See the mission by Wolfgang von Hofkirchen described in Chapter 3.
2. For an introduction to Gustav Vasa and the early history of his dynasty, see Michael Roberts, *The Early Vasas: A History of Sweden, 1523–1611* (Cambridge, England, 1968); Ivan Svalenius, *Gustav Vasa* (Stockholm, 1950); Lars-Olof Larsson, *Gustav Vasa—landsfader eller tyrann?* (Stockholm, 2002), and idem, *Arvet efter Gustav Vasa: En berättelse om fyra kungar och ett rike* (Stockholm, 2005). For English-language introductions to the history of the Protestant reformation in Sweden and the remainder of Scandinavia, see Ole Peter Grell, ed., *The Scandinavian Reformation: From Evangelical Movement to Institutionalisation of Reform* (Cambridge, England, 1995); James L. Larson, *Reforming the North: The Kingdoms and Churches of Scandinavia, 1520–1545* (Cambridge, England, 2010); and Lars Anton Anjou, *The History of the Reformation in Sweden*, translated by Henry M. Mason (New York, 1859). For a classic Swedish work, see also Hjalmar Holmquist and Hilding Pleijel, eds., *Svenska kyrkans historia*, vol. 3, *Reformationstidevarvet 1523–1611*, by Hjalmar Holmquist (Stockholm, 1933).
3. For Sigismund, see Henryk Wisner, *Zygmunt III Waza*, 2nd ed. (Warszawa, 2006), and Stefan Östergren, *Sigismund: en biografi över den svensk-polske monarken* (Ängelholm, Sweden, 2005)
4. For interpretations of this step, see Lars-Olof Larsson, *Arvet efter Gustav Vasa: En berättelse om fyra kungar och ett rike* (Stockholm, 2005), 250–253, and Stefan Östergren, *Sigismund: en biografi över den svensk-polske monarken* (Ängelholm, Sweden, 2005), 24–26.
5. For a recent biography of Charles IX, see Erik Petersson, *Den skoningslöse: en biografi över Karl IX* (Stockholm, 2009).
6. There are far too many works on Gustavus II Adolphus to list them here; a useful metahistory of this literature is Sverker Oredsson, *Gustav Adolf, Sverige og Trettioåriga kriget: Historieskrivning och kult* (Lund, 1992). As a concise and well-informed introduction in English one can still use Michael Roberts, *Gustavus Adolphus*, 2nd ed. (London, 1992). A more critical newer perspective was presented in Sverker Oredsson, *Gustav II Adolf* (Stockholm, 2007).
7. Even the Spanish branch of the Habsburgs developed concrete plans for an anti-Swedish alliance with Poland, as has been documented in Ryszard Skowron, *Olivares, Wazowie i Bałtyk: Polska w polityce zagranicznej Hiszpanii w latach 1621–1632* (Kraków, 2002).
8. American historian Paul Lockhart has repeatedly shown the close involvement of the Danish composite monarchy in the politics of the empire. See Paul Douglas Lockhart, "Denmark and the Empire: A Reassessment of Danish Foreign Policy under King Christian IV," *Scandinavian Studies* 64 (1992): 390–416; idem, "Religion and Princely Liberties: Denmark's Intervention

The Noble Warriors 175

in the Thirty Years' War, 1618–1625," *The International History Review* 17 (1995): 1–22; idem, *Denmark in the Thirty Years War, 1618–1648: King Christian IV and the Decline of the Oldenburg State* (Selinsgrove, PA, 1996); idem, "Dansk propaganda under Kejserkrigen 1625–29," *Historie* (1998): 222–248; and idem, *Frederik II and the Protestant Cause: Denmark's Role in the Wars of Religion, 1559–1596* (Leiden, 2004). For Denmark's interest in the Peace of Westphalia, see also Michael Bregnsbo, "Denmark and the Westphalian Peace," in *Der Westfälische Friede: Diplomatie—politische Zäsur—kulturelles Umfeld—Rezeptionsgeschichte*, ed. Heinz Duchhardt (Munich, 1998), 361–367. For the role of Schleswig and Holstein as links between Denmark and Germany, see also Peter Thaler, *Of Mind and Matter: The Duality of National Identity in the German-Danish Borderlands* (West Lafayette, IN, 2009).

9. For the English approach to these efforts, see Simon Adams, "The Protestant Cause: Religious Alliance with the West European Calvinist Communities as a Political Issue in England, 1585–1630" (Ph.D. diss., Oxford University, 1973).

10. Bertil Thyresson, *Sverige och det protestantiska Europa från Knäredfreden till Rigas erövring* (Uppsala, 1928), 45.

11. See Sven Fromhold Hammarstrand, *Försök till en historisk framställning af förhandlingarne om Sveriges deltagande i trettioåriga kriget, till fördraget i Beerwalde, d. 13 Januari 1631* (Uppsala, 1855), 152.

12. See ibid., 188.

13. See Bertil Thyresson, *Sverige och det protestantiska Europa från Knäredfreden till Rigas erövring* (Uppsala, 1928), 205f.

14. "Dem Durchleüchtigen, Durchleüchtigsten und Großmechtigen Fürsten und Herren, Herren Gustavo Adolpho . . . .", übergeben den 15. August 1620, Riksarkivet, Germanica A:III, no. 248, Evangeliska Unionens och andra evang. ständers bref till kongl. majt. 1614, 1619–1621.

15. Wilhelm Tham, *Den svenska utrikespolitikens historia*, vol. 1:2, 1560–1648 (Stockholm, 1960), 137–143.

16. Emerich Zenegg-Scharffenstein, "Schloss Weildegg zu Würmlach im Gailtale," Kärntner Landesarchiv, Topographische Sammlung Zenegg, box 4, no. 2.

17. Emerich Zenegg-Scharffenstein, "Schloss Weildegg zu Würmlach im Gailtale," Kärntner Landesarchiv, Topographische Sammlung Zenegg, box 4, no. 2; James Pauli, *Adliga Ätten Pauli: En släkts öden under fyra århundraden, 1500–1920* (Stockholm, 1920), 76; Paul Dedic, "Kärntner Exulanten des 17. Jahrhunderts," *Carinthia I* 150 (1960): 314f.

18. Malborgeth is now Malborghetto in Italy.

19. Facsimile of the patent of nobility in James Pauli, *Adliga Ätten Pauli: En släkts öden under fyra århundraden, 1500–1920* (Stockholm, 1920), 16.

20. See Johann Martin Trechsel, *Verneuertes Gedächtnis Des Nürnbergischen Johannis-Kirch-Hofs* (Frankfurt-Leipzig, 1736), 480; Walther Fresacher, "Ansitze und Hammerwerke im Süden von Villach: Gödersdorf, Neufinkenstein, der Nagerschigg-Hof und das Gut Müllnern," *Neues aus Alt-Villach* 12 (1975): 41; Franz Xaver Kohla, Gustav Adolf von Metnitz, and Gotbert Moro, *Kärntner Burgenkunde: Ergebnisse und Hinweise in Übersicht* (Klagenfurt, 1973), part 2, *Quellen- und Literaturhinweise zur*

176   *The Noble Warriors*

> *geschichtlichen und rechtlichen Stellung der Burgen, Schlösser und Ansitze in Kärnten sowie ihrer Besitzer,* by Gustaf Adolf von Metnitz, 109; and James Pauli, *Adliga Ätten Pauli: En släkts öden under fyra århundraden, 1500–1920* (Stockholm, 1920), 261.

21. See Daniel Eberhard Beyschlag, continued by Johannes Müller, *Beyträge zur Nördlingischen Geschlechtshistorie,* vol. 2 (Nördlingen, 1803), 158 and 160.

22. James Pauli, *Adliga Ätten Pauli: En släkts öden under fyra århundraden, 1500–1920* (Stockholm, 1920), 92.

23. Walther Fresacher, "Ansitze und Hammerwerke im Süden von Villach: Gödersdorf, Neufinkenstein, der Nagerschigg-Hof und das Gut Müllnern," *Neues aus Alt-Villach* 12 (1975): 41ff.

24. Since Hans Paul was a relatively frequent name, there has been considerable confusion about his fate. See "Copia Khauffbriefs . . .," 22 July 1637, Kärntner Landesarchiv, Portia Herrschaftsarchiv, box 367; Jürgen Sydow, "Die innerösterreichische Zuwanderung nach Regensburg im 16. und 17. Jahrhundert," *Blätter für Heimatkunde* 29 (1955): 65; Werner Wilhelm Schnabel, *Österreichische Exulanten in oberdeutschen Reichsstädten* (Munich, 1992), 103; Conradin Bonorand, "Adam Seenuß: Ein Villacher Exulant und seine Beziehungen zu evangelischen Pfarrern der Ostschweiz," *Neues aus Alt-Villach* 1 (1964): 245; and "Emerich Zenegg an Knut Pauli," 5 May 1922, Pauli Archives, Sweden.

25. See the genealogy table in the annex of James Pauli, *Adliga Ätten Pauli: En släkts öden under fyra århundraden, 1500–1920* (Stockholm, 1920), as well as Emerich Zenegg's version in Kärntner Landesarchiv, Genealogische Sammlung Zenegg, box 20/5 (Paul von Nagerschigg), fol. 293.

26. See, for example, Kungliga Vitterhets-, Historie- och Antiquitets-Akademien, ed., *Rikskansleren Axel Oxenstiernas skrifter och brefvexling,* vol. 1:7 (Stockholm, 1926), 348f., 358f., and 440f.

27. See Gustaf Droysen, *Gustaf Adolf,* vol. 2 (Leipzig, 1870), 358; Kungliga Vitterhets-, Historie- och Antiquitets-Akademien, ed., *Rikskansleren Axel Oxenstiernas Skrifter och brefvexling,* vol. 2:9 (Stockholm, 1898), 718; James Pauli, *Adliga Ätten Pauli: En släkts öden under fyra århundraden, 1500–1920* (Stockholm, 1920), 283.

28. Kungliga Vitterhets-, Historie- och Antiquitets-Akademien, ed., *Rikskansleren Axel Oxenstiernas skrifter och brefvexling,* vol. 1:2 (Stockholm, 1896), 273; James Pauli, *Adliga Ätten Pauli: En släkts öden under fyra århundraden, 1500–1920* (Stockholm, 1920), 285.

29. James Pauli, *Adliga Ätten Pauli: En släkts öden under fyra århundraden, 1500–1920* (Stockholm, 1920), 82.

30. Ibid., 85.

31. Ibid., 87.

32. For the elder Anders Pauli's offspring, see ibid., 88–91.

33. Laurentius Benedict, "En Christeligh Lijk-Predikan Utöffwer then Edle och Wälborne Öffwersten Zacharias Paul til Winxla . . . " (Strengnäs, 1632), printed in James Pauli, *Adliga Ätten Pauli: En släkts öden under fyra århundraden, 1500–1920* (Stockholm, 1920), 109–125. For a critical use of funeral sermons as historical sources, see Rudolf Lenz, *De mortuis nil nisi bene? Leichenpredigten als multidisziplinäre Quelle unter*

besonderer Berücksichtigung der Historischen Familienforschung, der Bildungsgeschichte und der Literaturgeschichte (Sigmaringen 1990). For the introduction of printed funeral sermons in Sweden, see also Otfried Czaika, "Die Anfänge der gedruckten Leichenpredigt im schwedischen Reich," in *Kommunikationsstrukturen im europäischen Luthertum der Frühen Neuzeit*, ed. Wolfgang Sommer (Gütersloh, 2005), 135–152.

34. The funeral sermon described him as cornet under "Göddart von Starenbergh". See James Pauli, *Adliga Ätten Pauli: En släkts öden under fyra århundraden, 1500–1920* (Stockholm, 1920), 120.

35. Kungliga Vitterhets-, Historie- och Antiquitets-Akademien, ed., *Rikskansleren Axel Oxenstiernas Skrifter och brefvexling*, vol. 1:2 (Stockholm, 1896), 482, 485, and 487.

36. Royal Prussia was the contemporary designation for the section of the former territory of the Teutonic Knights that had been assigned to Poland by the Second Peace of Thorn in 1466. It largely corresponded to the later German province of West Prussia and the region of Warmia in East Prussia.

    For some of Pauli's tasks in Prussia, see Riksarkivet, Riksregistratur, "Memorial för Öffwerste Leutnantten, Edell och Wellbördigh Zacharias Paulj til Wingzlö på de ährender H. K. Mtt: honom i befallning gifuitt hafwer," 1 July 1626; and Riksarkivet, Riksregistratur, "Swar til Zacharias Paulj opå Felttmarschalckzens tilsch:ne Bref af Zacharias Paulj anlangandes en mechta här medh Styken at belägra them, 4 August 1626."

37. Kungliga Vitterhets-, Historie- och Antiquitets-Akademien, ed., *Rikskansleren Axel Oxenstiernas skrifter och brefvexling*, vol. 2:1 (Stockholm, 1888), 471.

38. Gustaf Elgenstierna, *Den introducerade svenska adelns ättartavlor*, vol. 5 (Stockholm, 1930), 662.

39. For Vingsleör, see James Pauli, *Adliga Ätten Pauli: En släkts öden under fyra århundraden, 1500–1920* (Stockholm, 1920), 357–367.

40. Gustaf Elgenstierna, *Den introducerade svenska adelns ättartavlor*, vol. 5 (Stockholm, 1930), 662.

41. The genealogy of the Hård af Segerstad kan be followed in their entry in Riddarhusdirektionen, ed., *Riddarhusets stamtavlor*, CD-Rom (Stockholm, 2002).

42. For Bohemian equivalents, see Jiří Mikulec, "Die staatlichen Behörden und das Problem der konfessionellen Emigration aus Böhmen nach dem Jahr 1620," in *Glaubensflüchtlinge: Ursachen, Formen und Auswirkungen frühneuzeitlicher Konfessionsmigration in Europa*, ed. Joachim Bahlcke (Berlin, 2008), 165–186.

43. For the biography of Wurmbrand, see Gertrud Buttlar-Elberberg, "Melchior Freiherr von Wurmbrand zu Stuppach (1586-ca. 1637)—Ein niederösterreichischer Edelmann im Dienste König Gustav II. Adolf von Schweden und der Königin Christine," in *Festschrift Heide Dienst zum 65. Geburtstag*, ed. Anton Eggendorfer, Christian Lackner, and Willibald Rosner (St. Pölten, 2004), 1–18; and *Biografiskt lexicon öfver namnkunnige svenske män*, vol. 21 (Örebro, 1855), 213–215.

44. For the history of the Wurmbrand family, see Josef von Hormann and Alois von Mednyánszky, eds., *Taschenbuch für die vaterländische Geschichte* 8 (Vienna, 1827), 7–24, and Constant von Wurzbach, *Biographisches*

178 *The Noble Warriors*

Lexikon des Kaiserthums Oesterreich, vol. 58 (Vienna, 1889), 289–314. For information on the sources available in the Wurmbrand family archives, see also Hans von Zwiedineck, "Das reichsgräflich Wurmbrand'sche Haus- und Familien-Archiv zu Steyersberg," *Beiträge zur Kunde steiermärkischer Geschichtsquellen* 27 (1896): 103–212.

45. For his studies at Italian universities, see Arnold Luschin von Ebengreuth, "Oesterreicher an italienischen Universitäten zur Zeit der Reception des römischen Rechts," *Blätter des Vereines für Landeskunde von Niederösterreich* 15 (1881): 262.

46. Ignaz Hübel, "Die 1620 in Nieder- und Oberösterreich politisch kompromittierten Protestanten," *Jahrbuch für die Geschichte des Protestantismus in Österreich* 60 (1939): 125. Wurmbrand was also included in a list of 27 obstinate rebels from Lower Austria, which Ferdinand II explicitly brought to the attention of his general Charles Bonaventure de Longueval, Count of Bucquoy, in September 1620. See Josef Kočí, Josef Polišenský, and Gabriela Čechová, eds., *Documenta Bohemica bellum tricennale illustrantia,* vol. 2 (Prague, 1972), 249. For a broader description of the confiscations, see Rudolf Wolkan, "Die Ächtung der Horner Konföderierten und die Konfiskation ihrer Güter" (Ph.D. diss., University of Vienna, 1913), and Gustav Reingrabner, "Die Beschlagnahme adeliger Güter in der Gegenreformation," *Österreich in Geschichte und Literatur mit Geographie* 45 (2001): 259–280.

47. Walter Krüssmann, *Ernst von Mansfeld (1580–1626): Grafensohn, Söldnerführer, Kriegsunternehmer gegen Habsburg im Dreißigjährigen Krieg* (Berlin, 2010), 272.

48. Olof Granberg, *Allart van Everdingen och hans "norska" landskap: Det gamla Julita och Wurmbrandts kanoner* (Stockholm, 1902), 67.

49. See Bertil C. Barkman and Sven Lundkvist, *Kungl. Svea Livgardes historia,* vol. 3:1 (Stockholm, 1963), 446; and *Nordisk familjebok,* 2nd ed., vol. 32 (Stockholm, 1921), 1220.

50. See Henning Hamilton, *Afhandling om krigsmaktens och krigskonstens tillstånd i Sverige under Konung Gustaf II Adolfs regering* (Stockholm, 1846), 246f. For general discussions of the era's leather cannons by Wurmbrand and others, see also Åke Meyerson, *Läderkanonen från Tidö i livrustkammaren* (Stockholm, 1938); Eduard A. Gessler, "Die sogen. Lederkanonen aus dem Zeughausbestand der Stadt Zürich," *Anzeiger für schweizerische Altertumskunde* 26 (1924): 51–66 and 154–166; David Stevenson and David H. Caldwell, "Leather Guns and Other Light Artillery in Mid-17th-Century Scotland," *Proceedings of the Society of Antiquaries of Scotland* 108 (1976–1977): 300–317; Olof Blom, *Smaa bidrag til artilleriets historie under Kristian IV* (Copenhagen, 1901); and Wilhelm Gohlke, "Versuche zur Erleichterung der Feldgeschütze im 17. und 18. Jahrhundert," *Zeitschrift für Historische Waffenkunde* 4 (1906–1908): 387–395.

51. Eduard A. Gessler, "Die sogen. Lederkanonen aus dem Zeughausbestand der Stadt Zürich," *Anzeiger für schweizerische Altertumskunde* 26 (1924): 161.

52. Ibid., 166.

53. Arnold Luschin von Ebengreuth, "Oesterreicher an italienischen Universitäten zur Zeit der Reception des römischen Rechts," *Blätter des Vereines für Landeskunde von Niederösterreich* 15 (1881): 262.

The Noble Warriors   179

54. According to Åke Meyerson, *Läderkanonen från Tidö i livrustkammaren* (Stockholm, 1938), 15, the German inscription reads as follows:

> Leicht bin ich und wenig geacht/Thue so viel, als Manch'r nicht gedacht/ Meins Gleichen von Metall gemacht/Kan ich bestehn mit meiner Macht/ Durch Gottes Gnad bin ich erfunden/Mein'm Herren zu glücklichen Stunden/Der mich erdacht, helt sich vor schlecht/bleibt doch sein's Herren treuer knecht.

This can be loosely translated as:

> I am light and in low regard/but I can accomplish more than people thought/My metal peers/I can match with my power/By the grace of God I was conceived/by my master in blessed hours/He who has invented me considers himself wretched/but remains a true servant to his Lord.

The inscription was signed with Baron Melchior Wurmbrandt, Julita, 22 August 1627.

55. See the king's letters from March and April 1627 cited in Åke Meyerson, *Läderkanonen från Tidö i livrustkammaren* (Stockholm, 1938), 13f.
56. For the history of the estate, see Marshall Lagerquist, "Julita gård i Södermanland," *Fataburen* (1957): 29–56, and Bengt G. Söderberg, *Slott och herresäten i Sverige: Södermanland*, vol. 1 (Malmö, 1968), 323–331.
57. See Åke Meyerson, *Läderkanonen från Tidö i livrustkammaren* (Stockholm, 1938), 25–34.
58. See also Johannes Philipp Abelin, *Theatrum Europæum*, 3rd ed., vol. 1 (Frankfurt, 1662), 1140.
59. Olof Granberg, *Allart van Everdingen och hans "norska" landskap: Det gamla Julita och Wurmbrandts kanoner* (Stockholm, 1902), 78.
60. Generalstaben, ed., *Sveriges krig*, bilagsband 2 (Stockholm, 1938), 180.
61. Whereas some authors described a relatively quick execution of Wurmbrand at the hand of his Croat captors, others have uncovered correspondence by him until late 1637. Compare Joseph Philipp Brunemayr, *Geschichte der Königl. Baierischen Stadt und Herrschaft Mindelheim* (Mindelheim, Germany, 1821), 400–401; *Nordisk familjebok*, 2nd ed., vol. 32 (Stockholm, 1921), 1220; Ignaz Hübel, "Die 1620 in Nieder- und Oberösterreich politisch kompromittierten Protestanten," *Jahrbuch für die Geschichte des Protestantismus in Österreich* 60 (1939): 125; on the one hand with Gertrud Buttlar-Elberberg, "Melchior Freiherr von Wurmbrand zu Stuppach (1586-ca. 1637)—Ein niederösterreichischer Edelmann im Dienste König Gustav II. Adolf von Schweden und der Königin Christine," in *Festschrift Heide Dienst zum 65. Geburtstag*, ed. Anton Eggendorfer, Christian Lackner, and Willibald Rosner (St. Pölten, 2004), 17f.; on the other.
62. Queen Christina noted in her mortgage deed for Paul Khevenhüller in June 1638 that Julita had reverted to the crown with the passing of Colonel Melchior Wurmbrand. See "Pantebref," 26 June 1638, Julita Gårdsarkiv, F1:1 Handlingar rörande familjen Khevenhüller 1631–1747.
63. For Maximilian Teufel, see *Nordisk familjebok*, 2nd ed., vol. 28 (Stockholm, 1919), 1013–1014; Richard Schmertosch von Riesenthal, *Adelige Exulanten*

180   *The Noble Warriors*

in Kursachsen nach Urkunden des Dresdner Hauptstaatsarchivs (Dresden, 1902), 146; and the relevant passages in the general works on the Teufel family listed in the subsequent note. Both Teufel and Guntersdorf have been spelled in several different ways, among them especially Teuffel and Gundersdorf.

64. The court council of war in essence constituted an early ministry of defense. For the Teufel family, see Matthias Glatzl, "Die Freiherrn von Teufel in ihrer staats- und kirchenpolitischen Stellung zur Zeit der Reformation und Restauration" (Ph.D. diss., Univ. of Vienna, 1950); Franz Karl Wissgrill, "Teüfel von Krottendorf Freyh: zu Gunderstorf, Eckhartsau etc.," *Berichte und Mittheilungen des Alterthums-Vereines zu Wien* 23 (1886): 131–136; Anton Widter, "Die Teufel zu Winzendorf," *Berichte und Mittheilungen des Alterthums-Vereines zu Wien* 23 (1886): 104–114; and Karl Schrauf, *Das Gedenkbuch der Teufel zu Gundersdorf* (Vienna, 1892). For the opportunities opened up by conversion, see the career of a different Georg Teufel in Erich von Kielmansegg, *Beiträge zur Geschichte der niederösterreichischen Statthalterei: Die Landeschefs und Räthe dieser Behörde von 1501 bis 1896* (Vienna, 1897), 242–246.

65. Ingrid Matschinegg, "Österreicher als Universitätsbesucher in Italien (1500–1630)" (Ph.D. diss., University of Graz, 1999), 280.

66. Adalbert Mainhart Boehm, "Der Bundbrief der evangelischen Stände Österreichs ddo. Horn 3. October 1608 nach dem Originale im Archive der n. östr. Landschaft mit genealogisch-biographischen Anmerkungen," *Notitzenblatt* 4 (1854): 324.

67. See *Nordisk familjebok*, 2nd ed., vol. 28 (Stockholm, 1919), 1013.

68. For Teufel and the early history of the court regiment, see Julius Mankell, *Anteckningar rörande svenska regimentars historia*, 2nd ed. (Örebro, 1866), 3–6. For a detailed history of the regiment in the period 1611–1632, see Bertil C. Barkman and Sven Lundkvist, *Kungl. Svea Livgardes historia*, vol. 3:1 (Stockholm, 1963). For individual biographies, see also Wilhelm Ridderstad, *Gula Gardet, 1526–1903* (Stockholm, 1903).

69. For Heinrich Matthias von Thurn and his family, see Miloš Pojar, *Jindřich Matyáš Thurn—muž činu* (Prague, 1998), and Friedrich Conrad Gadebusch, *Versuche in der livländischen Geschichtskunde und Rechtsgelehrsamkeit*, vol. 1, piece 2, *Von dem Grafen Heinrich Matthias von Thurn und seinen Nachkommen* (Riga, 1779). See also Gustaf Elgenstierna, *Den introducerade svenska adelns ättartavlor*, vol. 8 (Stockholm, 1934), 274f.

70. Julius Mankell, *Anteckningar rörande svenska regimentars historia*, 2nd ed. (Örebro, 1866), 7.

71. Kungliga Vitterhets-, Historie- och Antiquitets-Akademien, ed., *Rikskansleren Axel Oxenstiernas Skrifter och brefvexling*, vol. 1:3 (Stockholm, 1900), 528–531; Johannes Micraelius, *Fünfftes Buch der Pommerschen Jahr-Geschichten, Vom 1627. Jahr, Biß auff den Todt Bogislai XIV. des letzten Hertzogen in Pommern* (Stettin, 1639), 177f.

72. Julius Mankell, *Anteckningar rörande svenska regementernas historia* (Örebro, 1866), 4, and Wilhelm Ridderstad, *Gula Gardet, 1526–1903* (Stockholm, 1903), 7.

73. Kungliga Vitterhets-, Historie- och Antiquitets-Akademien, ed., *Rikskansleren Axel Oxenstiernas Skrifter och brefvexling*, vol. 2:9 (Stockholm, 1896), 550.

The Noble Warriors   181

74. His movements during this period, which are treated in the following paragraphs, can be traced in his correspondence with chancellor Oxenstierna, printed in Kungliga Vitterhets-, Historie- och Antiquitets-Akademien, ed., *Rikskansleren Axel Oxenstiernas Skrifter och brefvexling*, vol. 2:9 (Stockholm, 1896), 551–570.

75. Ibid., vol. 2:1 (Stockholm, 1888), 649.

76. See *Nordisk familjebok*, 2nd ed., vol. 28 (Stockholm, 1919), 1013.

77. For the Battle of Breitenfeld, see Walter Opitz, *Die Schlacht bei Breitenfeld am 17. September 1631* (Leipzig, 1892), and the contemporary description in *Gründlicher vnd außführlicher Bericht, Wie die König. Schwedische, vnd Churf. Sächs. Armee, mit der Ligistischen oder Tyllischen Armee den 7. Sept. Anno 1631. bey dem Gut Breitenfeld, eine Meile von Leipzig gelegen, getroffen, wie es allenthalben damit zugangen, Auch wie die Schwedische vnd Sächs. Armee die Victoriam erhalten* (Dresden, 1631).

78. See William Watts, *The Swedish Discipline*, vol. 3 (London, 1632), 23.

79. Anders Frydell, *Berättelser ur svenska historien*, part 7, *Gustaf II Adolf*, 4th ed. (Stockholm, 1847), 172. The East Frisian nobleman Dodo von Knyphausen also put his hopes on Gustavus Adolphus following the many Protestant defeats during the early years of the Thirty Years' War. He rose to the rank of Swedish field marshal in 1633 but fell in the Battle of Haselünne in 1636.

80. See Kungliga Vitterhets-, Historie- och Antiquitets-Akademien, ed., *Rikskansleren Axel Oxenstiernas Skrifter och brefvexling*, vol. 2:1 (Stockholm, 1888), 742; ibid., vol. 1:6 (Stockholm, 1918), 495.

81. So in 1626, as visible in ibid., vol. 2:9 (Stockholm, 1896), 538f.

82. Letter dated 27 May 1629 in ibid., vol. 2:9 (Stockholm, 1896), 545. The personal pronoun in the translation was changed from first to third person.

83. Paul Khevenhüller to Hans Khevenhüller, 24 February 1631, "Correspondenz zwischen Herrn Paul und Herrn Hans Khevenhüller . . .," Kärntner Landesarchiv, Khevenhüller Archiv, box 13/21.

84. These consequences have recently been highlighted again in Hans Medick, *Der Dreißigjährige Krieg: Zeugnisse vom Leben mit der Gewalt* (Göttingen, 2018).

85. Kungliga Vitterhets-, Historie- och Antiquitets-Akademien, ed., *Rikskansleren Axel Oxenstiernas Skrifter och brefvexling*, vol. 2:9 (Stockholm, 1896), 568.

86. Ibid., 529.

87. Ibid., 563.

88. See ibid., 548f.

89. See Sächsisches Hauptstaatsarchiv Dresden, Sammlung Bergmann, volume 2, page 542. See also Adalbert Mainhart Boehm, "Der Bundbrief der evangelischen Stände Österreichs ddo. Horn 3. October 1608 nach dem Originale im Archive der n. östr. Landschaft mit genealogisch-biographischen Anmerkungen," *Notitzenblatt* 4 (1854): 351.

90. Richard Schmertosch von Riesenthal, *Adelige Exulanten in Kursachsen nach Urkunden des Dresdner Hauptstaatsarchivs* (Dresden, 1902), 140f.

91. For Otto Christoph Teufel, see Matthias Glatzl, "Die Freiherrn von Teufel in ihrer staats- und kirchenpolitischen Stellung zur Zeit der Reformation

182 *The Noble Warriors*

und Restauration" (Ph.D. diss., Univ. of Vienna, 1950), 94–104, and Sächsisches Hauptstaatsarchiv Dresden, Sammlung Bergmann, volume 2, pages 539–541.

92. Richard Schmertosch von Riesenthal, *Adelige Exulanten in Kursachsen nach Urkunden des Dresdner Hauptstaatsarchivs* (Dresden, 1902), 146.

93. For the following, see Bernhard Raupach, *Erläutertes Evangelisches Oesterreich, oder: Dritte und Letzte Fortsetzung der historischen Nachricht von den vornehmsten Schicksalen der Evangelisch-Lutherischen Kirchen in dem Ertz-Hertzogthum Oesterreich* (Hamburg, 1740), 435–437.

94. Johann Loserth, ed., *Akten und Korrespondenzen zur Geschichte der Gegenreformation in Innerösterreich unter Ferdinand II.* (Vienna, 1907), 2:154–157. This mandate largely repeated previous directives.

95. See the examples in Johann Loserth, ed., *Akten und Korrespondenzen zur Geschichte der Gegenreformation in Innerösterreich unter Ferdinand II.* (Vienna, 1907), 2:627–629, and Alice Meir, "Der Protestantismus in der Herrschaft Paternion vom 16. Jahrhundert bis zum Toleranzpatent," *Carinthia I* 162 (1972): 311–343.

96. Rudolf Leeb suggested the expression "suffering disobedience" as an alternative to the established imagery of "suffering obedience". See Rudolf Leeb, "Widerstand und leidender Ungehorsam gegen die katholische Konfessionalisierung," in *Staatsmacht und Seelenheil: Gegenreformation und Geheimprotestantismus in der Habsburgermonarchie*, ed. Rudolf Leeb, Susanne Claudine Pils, and Thomas Winkelbauer (Vienna-Munich, 2007), 183–201.

97. Regina Pörtner, *The Counter-Reformation in Central Europe: Styria 1580–1630* (Oxford, 2001), 125f. As a consequence, Saurau emigrated to Brandenburg-Ansbach in 1601, where he continued to function as a link between Austrian and imperial Protestantism.

98. See Arno Strohmeyer, "Konfessionszugehörigkeit und Widerstandsbereitschaft: Der 'leidende Gehorsam' des innerösterreichischen Adels in den religionspolitischen Auseinandersetzungen mit den Habsburgern (ca. 1570–1630)," in *Konfessionelle Pluralität als Herausforderung: Koexistenz und Konflikt in Spätmittelalter und Früher Neuzeit*, ed. Joachim Bahlcke, Karen Lambrecht, and Hans-Christian Maner (Leipzig, 2006), 333–354, and idem, "Zwischen Widerstand und Gehorsam: Zur Religionspolitik der Kärntner Landstände im konfessionellen Zeitalter," in *Glaubwürdig bleiben: 500 Jahre protestantisches Abenteuer*, ed. Wilhelm Wadl (Klagenfurt, 2011), 106–122. See also Robert Leidenfrost, "Religionsbeschwerden der evangelischen Stände von Steiermark, Kärnten und Krain," *Jahrbuch der Gesellschaft für die Geschichte des Protestantismus in Österreich* 4 (1883): 26–30.

99. For a complex assessment that shows the diversity of estatist thinking in Inner Austria, see Regina Pörtner, "Gegenreformation und ständischer Legalismus in Innerösterreich, 1564–1628," *Zeitschrift für Historische Forschung* 27 (2000): 499–542.

100. See Paul Dedic, "Der Kärntner Protestantismus vom Abschluß der 'Hauptreformation' bis zur Adelsemigration (1600–1629/30)," *Jahrbuch der Gesellschaft für die Geschichte des Protestantismus in Österreich* 58 (1937): 72–74.

The Noble Warriors   183

101. Johann Loserth, ed., *Akten und Korrespondenzen zur Geschichte der Gegenreformation in Innerösterreich unter Ferdinand II.* (Vienna, 1907), 2:756.
102. Ibid., 2:792f.
103. The text of the decree is printed in ibid., 2:814–821.
104. Although the nobles had the highest ratio of emigration, they only constituted a small minority of all emigrants. For the contemporary compilations, see Paul Dedic, *Kärntner Exulanten des 17. Jahrhunderts* (Klagenfurt, 1979), 117ff.; Franz Scheichl, "Glaubensflüchtlinge aus den österreichischen Gebieten in den letzten vier Jahrhunderten," *Jahrbuch für die Geschichte des Protestantismus in Österreich* 14 (1893): 140; Hermann Clauss, "Ein Nürnberger Verzeichnis österreich. Emigranten vom Jahre 1643," *Beiträge zur Bayrischen Kirchengeschichte* 13 (1907): 226–253; and "Zur Statistik der Religionsbewegung in Steiermark im 16. und 17. Jahrh.," *Steiermärkische Geschichtsblätter* 2 (1881): 72–108. For Carinthia, see also Claudia Fräss-Ehrfeld, *Geschichte Kärntens*, vol. 2, *Die ständische Periode* (Klagenfurt, 1994), 692; and Paul Dedic, "Der Kärntner Protestantismus vom Abschluß der 'Hauptreformation' bis zur Adelsemigration (1600–1629/30)," *Jahrbuch für die Geschichte des Protestantismus in Österreich* 58 (1937): 70–108. For the overall size of the nobility, see Herbert Hassinger, "Die Landstände der österreichischen Länder," *Jahrbuch für Landeskunde von Niederösterreich*, n. s., 36 (1964): 1005–1007. For a wide selection of additional sources, see also Werner Wilhelm Schnabel, *Österreichische Exulanten in oberdeutschen Reichsstädten* (Munich, 1992).
105. This is how Gustavus Adolphus defined his mission in "Schuldurkunde Gustav Adolphs König der Schweden für die Brüder Johann und Paul Khevenhüller . . .," 23 December 1631, Kärntner Landesarchiv, Khevenhüller-Archiv, box 6/109.
106. Sverker Oredsson, *Gustav Adolf, Sverige og Trettioåriga kriget: Historieskrivning och kult* (Lund, 1992). The works examined were written in Swedish, Danish, English, German, French, Russian, and Latin. A few peripheral works exceed the time frame delineated by Bogislaff Philip von Chemnitz, *Königlich Schwedischen in Teutschland geführten Krieg* (Stettin, 1648) and Konrad Repgen, ed., *Krieg und Politik 1618–1648: Europäische Probleme und Perspektiven* (Munich, 1988).
107. Sverker Oredsson, *Gustav Adolf, Sverige og Trettioåriga kriget: Historieskrivning och kult* (Lund, 1992), 12f.
108. These debates from the prelude and the early stages of the war can be followed in Riksarkivet, ed., *Svenska Riksrådets Protokoll*, vol. 1 (Stockholm, 1878), and vol. 2 (Stockholm, 1880). See also Nils Ahnlund, "Öfverläggningarna i riksrådet om tyska kriget 1628–1630," *Historisk Tidskrift* 34 (1914): 108–123.
109. See also Sverker Arnoldsson, *Krigspropagandan i Sverige före trettioåriga kriget* (Göteborg, 1941).
110. Kungliga Vitterhets-, Historie- och Antiquitets-Akademien, ed., *Rikskansleren Axel Oxenstiernas Skrifter och brefvexling*, vol. 2:1 (Stockholm, 1888), 654.
111. Ibid.
112. For those alternative views see, for example, Sverker Oredsson, *Gustav II Adolf* (Stockholm, 2007), 198.

184   *The Noble Warriors*

113. As Palatine ambassador, Ludwig Camerarius already tried to motivate Gustavus Adolphus to enter the war in 1623. See Friedrich Hermann Schubert, *Ludwig Camerarius, 1573–1651* (Kallmünz, Germany, 1955), 248–256.

114. For the much-debated Palatine question, which formed a major obstacle to peace, see Jürgen Steiner, *Die pfälzische Kurwürde während des Dreißigjährigen Krieges (1618–1648)* (Speyer, 1985). For the role of the dukes of Mecklenburg, see Otto Schulenburg, *Die Vertreibung der mecklenburgischen Herzöge Adolf Friedrich und Johann Albrecht durch Wallenstein und ihre Restitution: Ein Beitrag zur Geschichte Mecklenburgs im dreissigjährigen Kriege* (Rostock, 1892). Only the leaders of the Bohemian opposition failed to regain lasting influence in their homeland.

115. For examples of the mass appeal of Gustavus Adolphus in Protestant Germany, see Silvia Serena Tschopp, *Heilsgeschichtliche Deutungsmuster in der Publizistik des Dreißigjährigen Krieges: Pro- und antischwedische Propaganda in Deutschland 1628 bis 1635* (Frankfurt, 1991), and Thomas Kaufmann, *Dreißigjähriger Krieg und Westfälischer Friede: Kirchengeschichtliche Studien zur lutherischen Konfessionskultur* (Tübingen, 1998), 56–65. For the significance of contemporary newspapers, see also Holger Böning, *Dreißigjähriger Krieg und Öffentlichkeit: Zeitungsberichte als Rohfassung der Geschichtsschreibung* (Bremen, 2018).

116. For the following, see also Pekka Suvanto, *Die deutsche Politik Oxenstiernas und Wallenstein* (Helsinki, 1979), especially 10–12.

117. For the differences in contemporary émigré conduct, see Tomáš Knoz, "Die mährische Emigration nach 1620," in *Staatsmacht und Seelenheil: Gegenreformation und Geheimprotestantismus in der Habsburgermonarchie*, ed. Rudolf Leeb, Susanne Claudine Pils, and Thomas Winkelbauer (Vienna-Munich, 2007), 247–262.

118. Paul Dedic, "Kärntner Exulanten des 17. Jahrhunderts," *Carinthia I* 150 (1960): 308.

119. For these and other names, see Werner Wilhelm Schnabel, *Österreichische Exulanten in oberdeutschen Reichsstädten* (Munich, 1992), 303–305. See also Paul Dedic, *Kärntner Exulanten des 17. Jahrhunderts* (Klagenfurt, 1979), and Johannes Johansson, *Österrikes martyrkyrka* (Linköping, 1930), 235–246.

120. For Dietrichstein, see Paul Dedic, "Kärntner Exulanten des 17. Jahrhunderts," *Carinthia I* 136/137 (1948): 130f.; and Felix Anton von Benedikt, *Die Fürsten von Dietrichstein*, Schriften des historischen Vereins für Innerösterreich 1 (Graz, 1848), 160f.

121. See Franz Kurz, *Beyträge zur Geschichte des Landes Oesterreich ob der Enns*, vol. 2 (Linz, 1808), 55, 59; Paul Dedic, "Kärntner Exulanten des 17. Jahrhunderts," *Carinthia I* 136/137 (1948): 130f.; and Kungliga Vitterhets-, Historie- och Antiquitets-Akademien, ed., *Rikskansleren Axel Oxenstiernas Skrifter och brefvexling*, vol. 1:7 (Stockholm, 1926), 559–561.

122. The summons is printed in Franz Kurz, *Beyträge zur Geschichte des Landes Oesterreich ob der Enns*, vol. 2 (Linz, 1808), 380–382.

123. For the following, see Werner Wilhelm Schnabel, *Österreichische Exulanten in oberdeutschen Reichsstädten* (Munich, 1992), 309–317, 622f.

The Noble Warriors 185

124. For the Khevenhüller family, see Bernhard Czerwenka, *Die Khevenhüller* (Vienna, 1867), and Karl Dinklage, *Kärnten um 1620: Die Bilder der Khevenhüller-Chronik* (Vienna, 1980).

125. Johannes Falke, ed., "Briefe des Herrn Hans von Khevenhüller an seine Gemahlin Maria Elisabeth geb. von Dietrichstein (1630–1632)," *Zeitschrift für deutsche Kulturgeschichte* (1857): 279 and 282.

126. Werner Wilhelm Schnabel, *Österreichische Exulanten in oberdeutschen Reichsstädten* (Munich, 1992), 300.

127. "Schuldurkunde Gustav Adolphs König der Schweden für die Brüder Johann und Paul Khevenhüller . . .," 23 December 1631, Kärntner Landesarchiv, Khevenhüller-Archiv, box 6/109. Additional copies are preserved in Julita Gårdsarkiv, F1:1 Handlingar rörande familjen Khevenhüller 1631–1747. There one can also find the original promissory note of 9 October 1631 for 50,000 imperial taler, which is subsequently vacated in the new note of 23 December 1631.

    Some authors refer to an additional sum of 60,000 taler, which the Khevenhüllers had provided to Gustavus Adolphus. See Paul Dedic, "Kärntner Exulanten des 17. Jahrhunderts," *Carinthia I* 142 (1952): 353, and Gustaf Elgenstierna, *Den introducerade svenska adelns ättartavlor*, vol. 4 (Stockholm, 1928), 123. Since Paul Khevenhüller only lists 70,000 taler plus interest in his debt registry of 1638 and Queen Christina refers to the same amount in her mortgage deed for Julita, the additional loan seems unlikely. See "Die königliche Obligation . . . "; and "Pantebref," 26 June 1638; both in Julita Gårdsarkiv, F1:1 Handlingar rörande familjen Khevenhüller 1631–1747.

128. See Bernhard Czerwenka, *Die Khevenhüller* (Vienna, 1867), 494–499.

129. For Dietrichstein, see Rullor—1723, Register, Kungliga Krigsarkivet Stockholm, Referenskod SE/SVAR/KrA-141010003/ R. For Welz, see Rullor 1632:26, fol. 150, Kungliga Krigsarkivet Stockholm, Referenskod SE/SVAR/ KrA-141010003/ D1, Svarnummer KO1556. For Ernau, see Rullor 1632:26, fol. 152, Kungliga Krigsarkivet Stockholm, Referenskod SE/SVAR/KrA-141010003/ D1, Svarnummer KO1556. For Metnitz (misspelled Mecknitz), see Franz von Soden, *Gustav Adolph und sein Heer in Süddeutschland*, vol. 1 (Erlangen, 1865), 514; for Carl and Bartholomäus Putz, see Rullor 1632:26, fol. 150, Kungliga Krigsarkivet Stockholm, Referenskod SE/ SVAR/KrA-141010003/ D1, Svarnummer KO1556.

130. Paul Dedic, "Der Kärntner Protestantismus vom Abschluß der 'Hauptreformation' bis zur Adelsemigration 1600–1629/30," *Jahrbuch für die Geschichte des Protestantismus in Österreich* 58 (1937): 71.

131. See, for example, Samuel von Pufendorf, *Herrn Samuel von Pufendorf Sechs und Zwantzig Bücher der Schwedisch- und Deutschen Kriegs-Geschichte . . .* (Frankfurt and Leipzig, 1688), 91.

132. See "Beschreibung Ihr Gnaden Herrn Hans Khevenhüllers Geschlecht, Herkommen, Geburth, Leben, Wandel und seligen Abschieds," 1632, Kärntner Landesarchiv, Khevenhüller-Archiv, box 2/12; and Franz von Soden, *Gustav Adolph und sein Heer in Süddeutschland*, vol. 1 (Erlangen, 1865), 347. This incidence gained wide attention and was included in the

186   *The Noble Warriors*

well-known contemporary report by Robert Monro, a Scottish officer in Swedish services. See William S. Brockington, ed., *Monro, His Expedition with the Worthy Scots Regiment Called Mac-Keys* (Westport, CT, 1999), 275.

133. See Paul Dedic, "Kärntner Exulanten des 17. Jahrhunderts," *Carinthia I* 142 (1952): 361–363.

134. See Paul Dedic, "Kärntner Exulanten des 17. Jahrhunderts," *Carinthia I* 142 (1952): 353, 374; *Carinthia I* 139 (1949): 398f.; and *Carinthia I* 145 (1955): 583.

135. "Recognition" Paul Khevenhüller of 27 October 1632, Julita Gårdsarkiv, F1:1 Handlingar rörande familjen Khevenhüller 1631–1747.

136. Kungliga Vitterhets-, Historie- och Antiquitets-Akademien, ed., *Rikskansleren Axel Oxenstiernas Skrifter och brefvexling*, vol. 1:9 (Stockholm, 1926), 514.

137. For Swedish donations in Germany, see Hans Landberg, Lars Ekholm, Roland Nordlund, and Sven A. Nilsson, *Det kontinentala krigets ekonomi: Studier i krigsfinansiering under svensk stormaktstid* (Kristianstad, 1971), 346–410.

138. "Pantebref," 26 June 1638, Julita Gårdsarkiv, F1:1 Handlingar rörande familjen Khevenhüller 1631–1747.

139. See "Pantebref," 26 June 1638, Julita Gårdsarkiv, F1:1 Handlingar rörande familjen Khevenhüller 1631–1747.

140. Elias von Steinmeyer, ed., *Die Matrikel der Universität Altdorf*, vol. 1 (Würzburg, 1912), 233–238.

141. Gustaf Elgenstierna, *Den introducerade svenska adelns ättartavlor*, vol. 4 (Stockholm, 1928), 123f.

142. Ibid.

143. Bernhard Czerwenka, *Die Khevenhüller* (Vienna, 1867), 502.

144. "Regina, geb. Windischgrätz an Maria Elisabeth, geb. Dietrichstein," 10 April 1652, Kärntner Landesarchiv, Khevenhüller-Archiv, box 19/89, "Briefverkehr von Regina, geb. Windischgrätz und Maria Elisabeth Khevenhüller," fol. 138–139.

145. See Kärntner Landesarchiv, Khevenhüller-Archiv, box 19/89, "Briefverkehr von Regina, geb. Windischgrätz und Maria Elisabeth Khevenhüller."

146. Khevenhüller, Bartholme, Freiherr, "Schreiben an seine Frau Mutter," Kärntner Landesarchiv, Khevenhüller-Archiv, box 3/34.

147. "Franz Christoph Khevenhüller an Maria Elisabeth, geb. Dietrichstein," 18 May 1649, Kärntner Landesarchiv, Khevenhüller Archiv, box 3/33 (1641–1657). See also Bernhard Czerwenka, *Die Khevenhüller* (Vienna, 1867), 388–390.

148. See Bernhard Czerwenka, *Die Khevenhüller* (Vienna, 1867), 504.

149. For an earlier discussion in 1642, see also Riksarkivet, ed., *Svenska Riksrådets Protokoll*, vol. 9 (Stockholm, 1902), 241.

150. Ibid., vol. 10 (Stockholm, 1905), 570f.

151. "Wij Christina medh Gudz nådhe . . .," 20 June 1645, Julita Gårdsarkiv, F1:1 Handlingar rörande familjen Khevenhüller 1631–1747. See also Marshall Lagerquist, "Khevenhüller i dikt och verklighet," *Fataburen* (1960): 59.

152. Riksarkivet, ed., *Svenska Riksrådets Protokoll*, vol. 12 (Stockholm, 1909), 75. Sweden had both an introduced and a non-introduced nobility.

The Noble Warriors 187

153. Riksarkivet, ed., *Svenska Riksrådets Protokoll*, vol. 12 (Stockholm, 1909), 119, 185; Gustaf Elgenstierna, *Den introducerade svenska adelns ättartavlor*, vol. 4 (Stockholm, 1928), 123f.

154. This was also guaranteed to him in the king's promissory note. See "Schuldurkunde Gustav Adolphs König der Schweden für die Brüder Johann und Paul Khevenhüller . . .," 23 December 1631, Kärntner Landesarchiv, Khevenhüller-Archiv, box 6/109.

155. Riksarkivet, ed., *Svenska Riksrådets Protokoll*, vol. 11 (Stockholm, 1906), 93.

156. "Trauttmansdorff to Ferdinand III.," Osnabrück, 30 April 1646, *Acta Pacis Westphalicae*, series II, sec. A, *Die kaiserlichen Korrespondenzen*, vol. 4, ed. Nordrhein-Westfälische Akademie der Wissenschaften in Verbindung mit der Vereinigung zur Erforschung der Neueren Geschichte durch Konrad Repgen (Münster, 2001), 116.

157. Nordrhein-Westfälische Akademie der Wissenschaften in Verbindung mit der Vereinigung zur Erforschung der Neueren Geschichte durch Konrad Repgen, ed., *Acta Pacis Westphalicae*, series II, sec. C, *Die schwedischen Korrespondenzen*, vol. 4:1 (Münster, 1994), 3f.

158. Ibid., 92f.

159. See especially articles 1 and 8 of the Swedish proposition, printed in Johann Gottfried von Meiern, *Acta Pacis Westphalicae publica oder Westphälische Friedens-Handlungen und Geschichte*, part 1 (Hannover, 1734), 440f.

160. See Helge Almquist, "Königin Christina und die österreichische Protestantenfrage um die Zeit des Westfälischen Friedens," *Archiv für Reformationsgeschichte* 36 (1939): 1–24.

161. Nordrhein-Westfälische Akademie der Wissenschaften in Verbindung mit der Vereinigung zur Erforschung der Neueren Geschichte durch Konrad Repgen, ed., *Acta Pacis Westphalicae*, series II, sec. A, *Die kaiserlichen Korrespondenzen*, vol. 4 (Münster, 2001), 254. See also ibid., 137. The wording reminds strikingly of the formulations used by his father, Ferdinand II. Trauttmansdorff had already stated several months earlier that the emperor would rather see everything go to ruin than overturn the conditions his father had established in the hereditary lands. See Nordrhein-Westfälische Akademie der Wissenschaften in Verbindung mit der Vereinigung zur Erforschung der Neueren Geschichte durch Konrad Repgen, ed., *Acta Pacis Westphalicae*, series II, sec. C, *Die schwedischen Korrespondenzen*, vol. 2 (Münster, 1971), 316.

162. Nordrhein-Westfälische Akademie der Wissenschaften in Verbindung mit der Vereinigung zur Erforschung der Neueren Geschichte durch Konrad Repgen, ed., *Acta Pacis Westphalicae*, series III, sec. A, *Die Beratungen der kurfürstlichen Kurie*, vol. 1 (Münster, 1975), 34.

163. Ibid., series I, *Instruktionen*, vol. 1 (Münster, 1962), 442.

164. See Försvarsstabens Krigshistoriska Avdelning, ed., *Från Femern och Jankow til Westfaliska Freden* (Stockholm, 1948), 214f.; Clas Theodor Odhner, *Die Politik Schwedens im Westphälischen Friedenscongress und die Gründung der schwedischen Herrschaft in Deutschland* (Gotha, 1877), 160 and 207–209.

165. Nordrhein-Westfälische Akademie der Wissenschaften in Verbindung mit der Vereinigung zur Erforschung der Neueren Geschichte durch Konrad

188   *The Noble Warriors*

Repgen, ed., *Acta Pacis Westphalicae*, series III, sec. C, *Diarien*, vol. 2:2 (Münster, 1984), 1056.

166. Clas Theodor Odhner, *Die Politik Schwedens im Westphälischen Friedenscongress und die Gründung der schwedischen Herrschaft in Deutschland* (Gotha, 1877), 206.

167. Ibid.

168. See Nordrhein-Westfälische Akademie der Wissenschaften in Verbindung mit der Vereinigung zur Erforschung der Neueren Geschichte durch Konrad Repgen, ed., *Acta Pacis Westphalicae*, series I, *Instruktionen*, vol. 1 (Münster, 1962), 441.

169. For the divergent positions and Sweden's growing isolation in this question, see Bedřich Šindelář, "Comenius und der Westfälische Friedenskongreß," *Historica 5* (1963): 71–107.

170. For the wording of the two letters, see Veit-Jakobus Dieterich and Hans Hecker, eds., *Comenius der Politiker* (Baltmannsweiler, Germany, 2004), 45f., and Gerhard Michel and Jürgen Beer, eds., *Johann Amos Comenius—Leben, Werk und Wirken* (Sankt Augustin, Germany, 1992), 113ff. For Comenius' relations to Sweden, see also Sven Göransson, "Comenius och Sverige 1642–1648," *Lychnos* 1957/58 (1958): 102–137, and Emil Schieche, *J. A. Comenius und Schweden* (Stockholm, 1968).

171. These priorities surface in the instructions to the Swedish negotiators in Nordrhein-Westfälische Akademie der Wissenschaften in Verbindung mit der Vereinigung zur Erforschung der Neueren Geschichte durch Konrad Repgen, ed., *Acta Pacis Westphalicae*, series I, *Instruktionen*, vol. 1 (Münster, 1962), 193–266. These instructions only cover the period from 1636 to 1641, however, which was generally not very advantageous for Sweden. See also Clas Theodor Odhner, *Die Politik Schwedens im Westphälischen Friedenscongress und die Gründung der schwedischen Herrschaft in Deutschland* (Gotha, 1877), and Jenny Öhman, *Der Kampf um den Frieden: Schweden und der Kaiser im Dreißigjährigen Krieg* (Vienna, 2005).

172. See the queen's letter to her plenipotentiaries Oxenstierna and Salvius printed in Nordrhein-Westfälische Akademie der Wissenschaften in Verbindung mit der Vereinigung zur Erforschung der Neueren Geschichte durch Konrad Repgen, ed., *Acta Pacis Westphalicae*, series II, sec. C, *Die schwedischen Korrespondenzen*, vol. 4:2 (Münster, 1994), 746f.

173. See Konrad Müller, ed., *Instrumenta Pacis Westphalicae*, 3rd ed. (Bern, 1975), 127.

174. See especially article V, paragraphs 38–41 of the Peace Treaty of Osnabrück. For the negotations about Silesia, see also Bedřich Šindelář, "Slezská otázka na mírovém kongresu vestfálském 1643–1648," *Sborník prací Filozofické fakulty brněnské univerzity*, C, Řada historická, vol. 10:8 (1961): 266–295.

175. Konrad Müller, ed., *Instrumenta Pacis Westphalicae*, 3rd ed. (Bern, 1975), 22.

176. Nordrhein-Westfälische Akademie der Wissenschaften in Verbindung mit der Vereinigung zur Erforschung der Neueren Geschichte durch Konrad Repgen, ed., *Acta Pacis Westphalicae*, series II, sec. C, *Die schwedischen Korrespondenzen*, vol. 4:1 (Münster, 1994), 808.

177. For the untiring attempts of Khevenhüller descendants to receive compensation, see Bernhard Czerwenka, *Die Khevenhüller* (Vienna, 1867), 508–516; 528–533; 550–557.

The Noble Warriors 189

178. Riksarkivet, ed., *Svenska Riksrådets Protokoll*, vol. 15 (Stockholm, 1920), 480.
179. Gustaf Elgenstierna, *Den introducerade svenska adelns ättartavlor*, vol. 4 (Stockholm, 1928), 123.
180. Riksarkivet, ed., *Svenska Riksrådets Protokoll*, vol. 12 (Stockholm, 1909), 130. Oxenstierna used the word economist in the historical sense, referring to an economical person.
181. Gustaf Elgenstierna, *Den introducerade svenska adelns ättartavlor*, vol. 4 (Stockholm, 1928), 123; Försvarsstabens Krigshistoriska Avdelning, ed., *Slaget vid Jankow* (Stockholm, 1945), 92ff. Khevenhüllers participated in the battle on both sides. They paid a high price. Whereas Georg Christoph fell in Swedish uniform, a letter from Swedish headquarters at Iglau (Jihlava) reported to Chancellor Oxenstierna on 5 March 1645 that the wounded lieutenant colonel Count Khevenhüller had been permitted to receive medical treatment behind Austrian lines and return to Swedish captivity thereafter. See ibid., 148.
182. Gustaf Elgenstierna, *Den introducerade svenska adelns ättartavlor*, vol. 4 (Stockholm, 1928), 123.
183. See the epitaph of Paul Khevenhüller the Younger in Österåker Church and Gustaf Elgenstierna, *Den introducerade svenska adelns ättartavlor*, vol. 4 (Stockholm, 1928), 123.
184. For Paul's children, see also Detlev Schwennicke, ed., *Europäische Stammtafeln: Stammtafeln zur Geschichte der europäischen Staaten*, n. s., vol. 5 (Marburg, 1988), table 41.
185. See *Genealogisches Handbuch der baltischen Ritterschaften*, part 1, vol. 2, *Livland*, ed. Astaf von Transehe-Roseneck (Görlitz, 1929), 1112; and Ian Fettes and Leo van de Pas, *Plantagenet Cousins: Selected Descendants of Geoffrey V, Count of Anjou, in Australia, America, Africa, Europe and Asia* (Erindale, Australia, 2007), 2f.
186. For Anna Regina Khevenhüller, see Andreas Lindblom, "Anna Regina Khevenhüller till Julita," *Fataburen* (1949): 61–72. For Mathias Palbitzki see Wilhelm Nisser, *Mathias Palbitzki som connoisseur och tecknare* (Uppsala, 1934).
187. See Wilhelm Nisser, *Mathias Palbitzki som connoisseur och tecknare* (Uppsala, 1934), 24f., and Paul Dedic, "Der Kärntner Protestantismus von der Adelsemigration bis zum Ende des siebzehnten Jahrhunderts," *Jahrbuch für die Geschichte des Protestantismus in Österreich* 59 (1938): 138, 141.
188. For the later generations of Palbitzkis, see Sigurd Wallin, "Palbitzki i vapenlunden," *Fataburen* (1962): 97–108, and the family's entry in Riddarhusdirektionen, ed., *Riddarhusets stamtavlor*, CD-Rom (Stockholm, 2002.
189. See the discussion of the Pauli experience earlier in this chapter and in James Pauli, *Adliga Ätten Pauli: En släkts öden under fyra århundraden, 1500–1920* (Stockholm, 1920).
190. For the Frölichs, see their entry in Riddarhusdirektionen, ed., *Riddarhusets stamtavlor*, CD-Rom (Stockholm, 2002), and *Nordisk familjebok*, 2nd ed., vol. 9 (Stockholm, 1908), 63ff. For additional details especially about Hans Christoph's daughter Eva Margaretha, who developed into a religious visionary and unsuccessfully tried to convince King Charles XI of his mission

190   *The Noble Warriors*

as biblically ordained savior of Christendom, see Johannes Kirschfeld, "Eva Margaretha Frölich," *Theologische Studien und Kritiken* 101 (1929): 205–252; Bo Andersson, "Eva Margaretha Frölich: Nationell eskatologi och profetisk auktoritet," *Kyrkohistorisk årsskrift 1991* (1991): 57–81; and idem, "Eva Margaretha Frölich und ihre Schriften: Ein aufgefundener Sammelband," *Wolfenbütteler Barock-Nachrichten* 14 (1987): 71–76.

191. His brother Gabriel chose a military career and was ennobled in 1689 under the name Lilliesvärd. For more information on the descendants of the Vult family, see the entries on Vult von Steijern and Lilliesvärd in Riddarhusdirektionen, ed., *Riddarhusets stamtavlor*, CD-Rom (Stockholm, 2002), as well as *Nordisk familjebok*, 2nd ed., vol. 32 (Stockholm, 1921), 1209f.

192. See Viktor Bibl, "Eine Denkschrift Melchior Khlesls über die Gegenreformation in Niederösterreich (c. 1590)," *Jahrbuch für Landeskunde von Niederösterreich*, n. s., 8 (1909): 157–171.

193. The significance of confessionalization for the early-modern state-building not least of all in Sweden has recently been examined in Heinz Schilling, *Konfessionalisierung und Staatsinteressen: Internationale Beziehungen 1559–1660* (Paderborn, 2007).

194. For the following, see Heinz Schilling, "Confessionalization in the Empire: Religious and Societal Change in Germany between 1555 and 1620," chapt. in *Religion, Political Culture and the Emergence of Early Modern Society: Essays in German and Dutch History* (Leiden, 1992), 205–245, here especially 216–232.

195. For the concept of a second reformation, see also Heinz Schilling, ed., *Die reformierte Konfessionalisierung in Deutschland—Das Problem der "Zweiten Reformation"* (Gütersloh, 1986).

196. Ingun Montgomery, "Die cura religionis als Aufgabe des Fürsten: Perspektiven der Zweiten Reformation in Schweden," in *Die reformierte Konfessionalisierung in Deutschland—Das Problem der "Zweiten Reformation"*, ed. Heinz Schilling (Gütersloh, 1986), 266–290.

197. See especially Hans Landberg, Lars Ekholm, Roland Nordlund, and Sven A. Nilsson, *Det kontinentala krigets ekonomi: Studier i krigsfinansiering under svensk stormaktstid* (Kristianstad, 1971); Sven A. Nilsson, *De stora krigens tid: Sverige som militärstat och bondesamhälle* (Uppsala, 1990); Jan Lindegren, "The Swedish 'Military State' 1560–1720," *Scandinavian Journal of History* 10:4 (1985): 305–336; Jan Lindegren, *Maktstatens resurser: Danmark och Sverige under 1600-tallet* (Uppsala, 2001); Sven Lundquist, "Svensk krigsfinansiering 1630–1635," *Historisk Tidskrift* 86 (1966): 377–421; Bertil C. Barkman, *Gustaf II Adolfs regementsorganisation vid det inhemska infanteriet* (Stockholm, 1931); Nils Erik Villstrand, *Sveriges historia 1600–1721* (Stockholm, 2011); and central essays in Michael Roberts, *Essays in Swedish History* (London, 1967). In a recent analysis of the concluding years of the Thirty Years' War, Lothar Höbelt also emphasized the operational superiority of the Swedish army and its successful employment of limited resources. See Lothar Höbelt, *Von Nördlingen bis Jankau: Kaiserliche Strategie und Kriegführung 1634–1645* (Vienna, 2016), especially the conclusion on pages 438–452.

The Noble Warriors 191

198. See Mats Hallenberg, *Statsmakt till salu: Arrendesystemet och privatiseringen av skatteuppbörden i det svenska riket 1618–1635* (Lund, 2008). For the preceding period, see also Mats Hallenberg, *Kungen, fogdarna och riket: Lokalförvaltning och statsbyggande under tidig Vasatid* (Stockholm, 2001).

199. Jan Glete, *War and the State in Early Modern Europe: Spain, the Dutch Republic and Sweden as Fiscal-Military States, 1500–1660* (London, 2002).

200. Erik Ringmar, *Identity, Interest and Action: A Cultural Explanation of Sweden's Intervention in the Thirty Years War* (Cambridge, England, 1996).

201. For text and interpretation of the Edict of Restitution, see Michael Frisch, *Das Restitutionsedikt Kaiser Ferdinands II. vom 6. März 1629: Eine rechtsgeschichtliche Untersuchung* (Tübingen, 1993).

202. Oxenstierna's crosscultural abilities can be seen in the correspondence published in *Rikskansleren Axel Oxenstiernas skrifter och brefvexling* and in Lotte Kurras, ed., *Axel Oxenstiernas Album amicorum und seine eigenen Stammbucheinträge* (Stockholm, 2004). For a newer biography of the chancellor, see Gunnar Wetterberg, *Kanslern: Axel Oxenstierna i sin tid,* 2 vols. (Stockholm, 2002).

203. Their importance for the era's diplomatic corps, to take one example, has recently been described in Heiko Droste, *Im Dienste der Krone: Schwedische Diplomaten im 17. Jahrhundert* (Berlin, 2006). For Scotsmen in Swedish services, see also Mary Elizabeth Ailes, *Military Migration and State Formation: The British Military Community in Seventeenth-Century Sweden* (Lincoln, Nebr., 2002); Alexia Grosjean, *An Unofficial Alliance: Scotland and Sweden 1569–1654* (Leiden, 2003); and Steve Murdoch and Alexia Grosjean, *Alexander Leslie and the Scottish Generals of the Thirty Years' War, 1618–1648* (London, 2014).

6 The Peasants
When Humble Subjects Mar the Mighty's Sleep

The preceding chapters focused on the confessional politics of nobles and townspeople. This emphasis has not been coincidental. In a predemocratic era, the upper echelons of society left a stronger imprint on political life, as well as on the historical source material available to modern researchers. Yet aristocratic and urban segments only constituted a minority of the overall population. To get the full picture, it is essential to integrate the rural core into the analysis. In early modern Europe, agriculture continued to form the backbone of economic production and employ the largest segment of the workforce.

For the early 1600s, the population of the Habsburg Monarchy is estimated at 7 to 7.5 million, a substantial part of which lived in the lands of the Bohemian crown.[1] Royal Hungary contained one-and-a-half to two million inhabitants, which equaled the numbers under Ottoman or Transylvanian governance. This left approximately two million Habsburg subjects in the Alpine hereditary lands. Their social composition reflected the Central European norm. Aristocrats and clerics held positions of great influence but constituted only one percent of the overall population.[2] Urban communities were home to one-fifth of the populace, if one includes small farming and mining towns; settlements with more than 2,000 inhabitants accounted for less than half that number.[3] Vienna formed the sole great city of lasting significance, reaching around 30,000 inhabitants in 1600.[4] The population of mining communities such as Schwaz could temporarily swell to almost comparable figures but collapsed just as rapidly again in times of economic downturn.[5] Gradually expanding municipalities such as the regional centers of Innsbruck and Klagenfurt barely surpassed 5,000 inhabitants in the early 1600s; only the important administrative seat of Graz approached the 15,000 mark.[6] The bulk of the Alpine population therefore consisted of agrarian cultivators in the broadest sense of the word, with a regionally significant segment of miners and salters.

The Peasants 193

This rural majority had undergone substantial changes in its social and economic position. By the High Middle Ages, the armigerous tribal entities, which had unified large segments of Central Europe's free populations in their dual roles as cultivators and warriors, had transformed into feudal societies with permanently differentiated socioeconomic functions. Medieval peasants were, therefore, not simply an economic category defined by their occupation in agriculture but also a social group with distinct functions and obligations.[7] Most of them cultivated land that legally belonged to others. The specific terms of this arrangement varied, ranging from outright serfdom to diverse forms of land tenure such as annual, lifetime, and inheritable leases.[8] In all cases, however, dependents owed their landlords regular payments and/or labor services. Disagreements about the nature and extent of these services, as well as the reciprocal societal function of lords, formed a regular feature of peasant unrest.

Yet economic matters were not the only points of contention. Religious diversification had introduced a new set of societal frictions. In the Habsburg domains, the dynasty's resolve to uphold or subsequently reestablish the old faith antagonized large sectors of the populace. Confessional cleavages did not inevitably line up peasants against monarchs because their social distance was too great to define them as natural counterparts. More often than not, remote rulers were seen as protectors against the transgressions of local landlords. At times, however, the Habsburgs' religious policy brought them into direct conflict with segments of the peasantry. This occurred in the early phase of the Reformation, when a broad diversity of reformist thought influenced peasant activism. Yet it also returned at a later stage of Austrian confessionalization, when a reinvigorated church and dynasty had begun to roll back the advances of the new creed. During its final period in the midst of the Thirty Years' War, Austrian peasants even sympathized with the Habsburgs' international adversaries, personified above all by Sweden's King Gustavus II Adolphus. These confrontations between monarchy and commoners form the centerpiece of this chapter.

Peasant Spirituality Between Landlords and Monarchs

The early reformation was a popular movement whose impact was social and political as much as religious. Regardless of the intention of major reformers, the rural masses often received their teachings as a message of social liberation.[9] Less than a decade after the inception of religious reform, the societal order of Central Europe consequently faced a challenge of its own. The Great Peasants' War of 1525 formed the apex of

194   *The Peasants*

rural rebellion in early modern Germany.[10] As in other parts of the empire, social and spiritual grievances also triggered unrest in Alpine regions. In the western territory of Tyrol, rebel leader Michael Gaismair even formulated an alternative societal vision, which would have transformed his home country into a reformist Christian peasant republic.[11] Following the defeat of this activism in the 1520s, however, the Central European peasantry seemed to fade into the background again. Few of its political demands had been met. Sporadic concessions tended to be retracted once the old order was reestablished. In the religious sphere, too, the often enthusiastic adoption of reformist teachings gave way to more mundane forms of propagation and practice. The confessional future of the rural majority was shaped by landlords and monarchs.

In the Austrian lands, different layers of authority exercised conflicting influences on the subject populace. In many other principalities, the political elites soon converged on a unified confessional stance, which was subsequently imposed on society at large. In Habsburg territories, by contrast, the rise of separate denominational bodies tended to divide court and aristocracy. Confessional policies collided, with Protestant nobles finding ways to contravene the stringently Catholic directives of their monarchs.

In a 1584 letter to his well-connected confrere, the imperial high steward Adam von Dietrichstein, Melchior Klesl drew a dire picture of ecclesial conditions in rural Lower Austria.[12] While Catholic priests kept their heads down, the territorial nobles promoted the spread of Protestantism. They opened their patrimonial churches to the local peasantry and encouraged it to redeploy its tithes from the legitimate parish priest to the local Lutheran preacher. They even erected new synagogues, as the visibly agitated vicar general designated these houses of worship, and pressured villeins into attending their services. The Catholic clergy lost its congregations and not least of all its income.

Although Klesl was hardly a disinterested observer, his description sheds light on the social instruments available to the Protestant aristocracy. In spite of the dynasty's unwavering support for the Catholic Church, alternative societal forces retained influence over the religious landscape. Not just the princes, but also the nobles felt called to secure the spiritual salvation of their subjects, based on feudal notions of lordly protection and guidance.[13] On this fundamental question, counterreformational hardliners such as Ferdinand II and his most diehard opponents found themselves in rare agreement.

The impact of lordship and church patronage helps us understand the social differentiation of contemporary religious observance. Relative to

The Peasants 195

the aristocracy of the eastern Austrian territories, which had overwhelmingly embraced Protestantism by the middle of the sixteenth century, the rural majority remained more divided. The spiritual preferences of early-modern commoners escape easy quantifications. Protestant ecclesiastical historians such as Georg Loesche defined Lutheranism as the natural majority religion of sixteenth-century Austria, only subjugated by governmental coercion; conservative Catholics such as Emil Franzel associated it primarily with the higher echelons of society.[14] Whereas the preponderance of Lutheranism in the peasantries of late sixteenth-century Carinthia and Upper Austria appears well-established today, estimates for Lower Austria and Styria continue to differ.[15] There is fundamental agreement, however, that Catholicism retained stronger support among peasants than among nobles and townspeople.

Much of this divergence can be attributed to the persistence of Catholic lordship. It needs to be remembered that the increasingly Protestantized nobles only dominated one segment of rural society. The dynasty held extensive demesnial properties; imperial princes and corporations retained enclaves of political and ecclesial jurisdiction. That a number of urban municipalities also controlled their rural environs may have proven less divisive, since Protestantism initially stood strong in these communities as well. Absolutely crucial, however, was the position of the Catholic Church. The extent of ecclesial landownership varied with time and place, but Tyrolean calculations assigning it one-quarter of all agricultural parcels provide an instant appreciation of its significance.[16] Upper Austrian surveys back up these computations. Georg Grüll's careful analysis of subject hearths in the crucial period of 1620/25 found the following distribution:

Table 6.1 Subject Hearths according to Category of Landlord in Upper Austria 1620–1625 (Property Registry)

Category	Absolute Number of Hearths	Percentage
Upper Nobility	12,861	29.1
Princely Seignieuries	10,754	24.3
Prelates	10,337	23.4
Lower Nobility	7,093	16.1
Territorial Cities	2,609	5.9
Parishes	535	1.2
Total	44,189	100

Source: Georg Grüll, *Der Bauer im Lande ob der Enns am Ausgang des 16. Jahrhunderts: Abgaben und Leistungen im Lichte der Beschwerden und Verträge von 1597–1598* (Linz, 1969), 60.

196   The Peasants

From a formalistic perspective, these conditions subjected a narrow majority of villeins to Catholic seigneurs, to whom belonged all dynastic and ecclesial holdings plus a minority of noble ones; the not very extensive municipal lordships were most liable to confessional discontinuity. As Hermann Rebel has pointed out, however, legal ownership did not necessarily correspond to factual exercise of authority. Tax rolls from the middle of the eighteenth century provide a more accurate account of the latter:

Table 6.2 Subject Hearths according to Category of Landlord in Upper Austria 1750 (Tax Rolls)

Category	Number of Subjects	Percentage
Upper Nobility	32,348	50.2
Prelates	20,136	31.3
Lower Nobility	3,522	5.5
Princely Seigneuries	1,288	2.0
Territorial Cities	2,891	4.5
Parishes	1,853	2.9
Pious Endowments	1,399	2.2
Other	1,078	1.7
Total	64,413	100

Source: Georg Grüll, "Die Herrschaftsschichtung in Österreich ob der Enns 1750," *Mitteilungen des Oberösterreichischen Landesarchivs 5* (1957): 314, 317. Individual percentages have been rounded up or down to the closest digit. The numbers for the cities include 2,572 urban hearths.

The tax rolls indicate that the upper nobility controlled a larger segment of subjects than is discernible in property surveys. This expansion occurred primarily at the expense of the dynasty, which mortgaged demesnial holdings in exchange for debts incurred. The position of the prelates, in contrast, remained undiminished. Corresponding statistics from the first half of the sixteenth century substantiate that the extent of ecclesial landownership in 1750 was not the result of recent transformations. From 1527 to 1544, the prelates controlled 37 percent of the villeins subject to the higher estates and the dynasty, whereas the nobility held lordship over more than 60 percent and the dynasty over less than 2 percent.[17] In select regions, ecclesial lordship appreciably surpassed these numbers. A 1613 tax collection act assigned 58 percent of upper estates' subject hearths to the prelates in the southeastern quadrant of Upper Austria known as Traunviertel, 48 percent in the northwestern Mühlviertel quadrant, 16 percent in the southwestern Hausruckviertel, and another 16 percent in the northeastern Machlandviertel.[18] At the same time, landownership did not necessarily coincide with parish guardianship, so that many ecclesial lords had to negotiate confessional authority with heterodox nobles.[19]

Within their domains, Protestant and Catholic seigneurs successfully promoted their religious agenda.[20] Yet peasants were not mere objects of confessionalization. Ecclesial landlords, in particular, regularly complained about heterodox villeins under their jurisdiction. Recurrent decrees against church attendance in outside parishes underscore the extent of the phenomenon. The complicated web of lordship, patronage, and guardianship left room for peasant autonomy as well. If subject to multiple authorities, villeins sought protection from sympathetic coreligionists; this constellation commonly entailed the influence of secular guardians on ecclesial properties.[21] Within their economic limits, some peasants exchanged confessionally exposed holdings for more secure ones, as has been documented for the Schröffl family of Upper Styria.[22] When his inherited homestead passed to Catholic landlords in the midst of the Styrian counterreformation, Lutheran Ruep Schröffl traded it for a smaller farm under a confirmed Protestant seigneur. For a while at least, this strategic relocation spared Schröffl the most severe sanctions of contemporary confessional policy.

Peasant agency also expressed itself in the initial response to the recatholization of rural parishes. Resistance to the investiture of Catholic priests was widespread, leading to public unrest, harassment of clergy, and even violence.[23] In Carinthia's Gegend valley and other Protestant strongholds, the threat of armed resistance kept Bishop Brenner's reformation commission at bay.[24] In the Upper Austrian community of Windhag, parishioners protested the removal of their Lutheran pastor by refraining temporarily from such ecclesial acts as weddings and baptisms.[25] Other congregations disrupted mass with communal singing or stoned their unwanted priest out of the village.[26] Dramatic as they were, however, these undirected outbursts of exasperation also revealed the limits of popular autonomy. Rural and urban commoners rarely progressed beyond turbulent flare-ups of mass activism, which only temporarily deterred local clergy and officeholders. Following the restoration of public order and the prosecution of resistance leaders, church and government resumed their program of Catholic restoration.

Ultimately, the boundaries of religious self-determination were set by ecclesiastical law. Subject peasants typically lacked the right to erect churches and appoint clergy.[27] To exercise heterodoxy in a communal setting, they depended on autonomous ecclesial structures under noble or urban patronage. As a consequence, the right to attend Lutheran services in surrounding communities moved to the center of Austrian

198   *The Peasants*

confessional politics. Nobles and burghers saw any obligation to bar coreligionists from their churches as a fundamental challenge to their freedom of conscience.[28] Catholic activists, in turn, considered such decrees indispensable for the success of confessional mandates. As long as recalcitrant commoners had access to the religious infrastructure of privileged nobles, parish recatholization remained ineffective. Once they felt powerful enough, therefore, the monarchs narrowly restricted aristocratic liberties to the nobles themselves. The subsequent advance of Catholicism among commoners confirmed their dependence on aristocratic protection.

Restoration and Rebellion

A full restitution of religious orthodoxy took time, however, and a concerted effort by church and government. The ensuing sense of spiritual oppression spread discontent, and by the end of the sixteenth century, popular unrest regained religious overtones. To be sure, the peasants continued to complain about excessive economic burdens. The lopsided social profile of individual uprisings preempts purely religious explanations as well, and Protestant nobles repeatedly spearheaded their suppression. Yet in Upper Austria, especially, confessional disagreements contributed so consistently to the outbreak of hostilities that it is difficult to disregard their impact.

While initial demonstrations against undesirable clergymen remained localized, the turbulences plaguing the Traunviertel community of Sierning in 1588 showed the growing potential for larger disruptions.[29] A new parish priest's determination to implement Tridentine practice galvanized the locals in defense of established heterodoxy. Peasant assemblies petitioned for religious freedom and implored aristocratic coreligionists for assistance. The conflict escalated when incensed protesters insulted a governmental fact-finding commission. Confessional tempers flared in the Upper Austrian diet. In the end, estatist intervention secured a compromise that temporarily suspended Catholic restoration without settling the fundamental disagreement about the confessional future of rural Upper Austria.

The subsequent decades witnessed a succession of greater or lesser disturbances. The series of clashes in the years 1594 to 1597 that are frequently designated as the Second Upper Austrian Peasant Uprising followed the rigorous execution of confessional mandates by Governor Hans Jakob Löbl.[30] Local protests against Catholic priests once again expanded into a wider confrontation. The unrest erupted in the Mühlviertel region to the north of the river Danube, dominated by ecclesial landlords, whom

The insurgents encountered as both spiritual and economic adversaries. As a consequence, Protestant landowners initially sympathized with some of the peasant demands and actively backed the resumption of heterodox services. After the rebellion had grown in strength and spread to other parts of the territory, economic disagreements moved to the forefront. At that point, the nobles fell more wholeheartedly in line behind the government. Nonetheless, the military situation ebbed back and forth until estatist mercenaries decisively crushed any remaining resistance in the fall of 1597. Earlier that year, Emperor Rudolph II had passed an interim resolution that disregarded the insurgents' religious demands, ordering them instead to return all churches to their rightful owners and remove their Protestant preachers. In regard to economics, the resolution contained moderate concessions to the villeins, most importantly the restriction of labor services to 14 days per year.[31]

The insurgency of 1594–1597 was characterized by shifting foci and alliances. The initial spotlight on confessional disagreements left the princely governor to face the insurgents on his own because the Protestant nobility showed little inclination to sustain his confessional agenda. The subsequent expansion of the conflict all but reversed the constellation. Once the focus had shifted to socioeconomic questions, the emperor returned to the enviable position of elevated arbiter, beseeched and courted by all parties. As a result, interpretations of the conflict have varied. Based on grievances submitted to an imperial arbitration commission, Georg Grüll defined the uprising as economic.[32] Josef Löffler, in contrast, drew attention to the religious demands of earlier peasant manifestos.[33]

Regardless of the primary origins of the insurgency, its suppression reverberated immediately in the field of confessional policy. Court and church did not miss the opportunity to advance the Counterreformation among commoners.[34] Dissatisfied with the military and political focus of the initial campaign, led by Protestant noble Gotthard von Starhemberg, Governor Löbl appended a drive for parish recatholization. Urged by the bishop of Passau, Urban von Trennbach, the emperor subsequently extended this policy to the remainder of Upper Austria. Recatholization was dissociated from pacification and defined as a policy objective in its own right. The Protestant nobles had to recognize that their pursuit of socioeconomic interests had advanced the recovery of Catholicism.

Whereas economic and confessional motives were deeply intertwined in the Upper Austrian uprising of 1594–1597, they expressed themselves more independently in two comparable cases. The depth of social discontent surfaced in the almost simultaneous unrest in neighboring Lower Austria.[35] Next to general complaints about their deteriorating economic

200 *The Peasants*

situation as well as transgressions by lords and officials, the peasants particularly decried the increased financial and military obligations brought on by the Ottoman wars. Confessional grievances only surfaced sporadically, since Protestants dominated among both the insurgents and their landowning adversaries. Religious tensions had undermined the relationship between Catholic landlords and Protestant peasants, however, adding to the socioeconomic tensions and lowering the threshold for violence.[36]

In the socially distinctive salt-mining region of Salzkammergut at the intersection of Upper Austria, Salzburg, and Styria, by contrast, confessional policy stood at the center of the conflict. The district contributed heavily to the imperial treasury and formed a separate administrative entity under the Lower Austrian court chamber in Vienna, with a resident chief administrator called *Salzamtmann*.[37] At the outbreak of the Thirty Years' War, the yearly output of the salt mines in Hallstatt, Ebensee, and Ischl amounted to 16,300 tons, and as late as 1770, the national salt monopoly accrued 14 percent of the monarchy's public revenue.[38] The local salt workers and entrepreneurs had almost universally embraced Lutheranism and saw their economic significance as a guarantee against heavy-handed confessional interventions. As soon as rumors of an impending examination by reformation commissioners arrived in the Salzkammergut in 1598, local administrators, therefore, tried to dissuade the governor.[39] They warned of dire financial consequences if confessional pressure were to alienate the salters. Strategic production withholdings served to underscore the admonition.

After some hesitation the government persisted and replaced heterodox administrators and pastors in 1600. The population initially responded with passive resistance. Congregations boycotted the imposed clergy and its services; conspiratorial meetings reassured the participants of impending policy reversals. Yet in the following year the new chief administrator dismissed additional officeholders and ordered the population to adopt Catholicism or leave the country within three months. Sullen defiance turned into open rebellion. Incensed locals detained unpopular officials and expelled recently appointed parish priests. They established defense units and armed themselves for the predictable military retribution. The longer the conflict dragged on, however, the more the initial unity of the community dwindled. Whereas the wealthier burghers were intimidated by the ominous decrees announced by governmental heralds, peasants and salters refused to turn in their weapons.

In the meantime, Archduke Matthias and his local administrators devised their counterstrategy. The government rejected all complaints and demanded an unconditional cessation of hostilities. The archduke also requested the assistance of nearby princes, alerting them to potential reverberations of

The Peasants 201

the unrest in their own territories. In the end, it was the archbishop of Salzburg, Wolf Dietrich von Raitenau, who came to the dynasty's rescue. In February 1602 a mixed detachment of 1,200 territorial and mercenary troops easily dispersed the inadequately armed rebels. The local communities quickly surrendered, and the princely commissioners began to execute the governmental mandates. A number of ringleaders paid with their lives. Insurgent communities temporarily lost their communal liberties. Catholic parish priests were reinstated. The bulk of the populace was let off with a public declaration of contrition, loyalty, and adherence to the Catholic religion. Below the surface, however, the Salzkammergut remained a bastion of Protestantism.[40]

The Upper Austrian Peasants' War of 1626

The recurrent flare-ups of violence at the turn of the seventeenth century warned of the depth of rural discontent. Compared to the eruption that followed a few decades later, however, they paled in significance. The Upper Austrian Peasants' War of 1626 formed the most dramatic expression of popular resistance in early modern Austria.[41] Following the diet's support for the Bohemian insurgency, Upper Austria had been subjugated by Ferdinand II's Bavarian allies in 1620. The territory was to remain under Bavarian lien administration until the emperor recompensed Duke Maximilian for his military intervention. The duke viewed this arrangement as invaluable security for his central foreign policy objective: to take the place of the Elector Palatine in both the Upper Palatinate and the imperial electoral college. This wider political context, in turn, ensured Maximilian's adherence to the emperor's confessional directives. Any occupation by foreign troops was liable to create tensions, but its conflation with religious repression brought matters to a head. On Ferdinand's insistence, the Bavarian administrators advanced the recatholization of the Lutheran peasantry, even if the duke was apprehensive about its timing and potential repercussions.[42] In 1624 the emperor ordered the expulsion of Protestant clergy and teachers.[43] A general reformation decree followed the year after, requiring all but the members of the territorial nobility to accept Catholicism or leave Upper Austria by Easter 1626.[44] Implementation was entrusted to the Bavarian governor Count Adam Herberstorff, himself a Styrian-born convert, and an adjoined reformation commission.[45] To ensure the desired political and financial effects, emigrants were subsequently burdened with heavy fees and taxes.[46]

The new vigor behind confessional mandates aggravated an already tense political climate. In 1625 the installation of an Italian priest in the market town of Frankenburg triggered a short-lived revolt.[47] Initially

202 *The Peasants*

gathering more than 5,000 protesters, the commotion quickly dissolved after promises of clemency. Herberstorff decided to set an example, however. Since the instigators of the upheaval had escaped, he assembled the local populace and ordered parish leaders to roll dice for their lives. They had all deserved to be broken on the wheel, the governor informed the unfortunate victims, but because he had promised them mercy he would merely have them hanged. Sparing half of them just amplified his generosity. In the end, seventeen hapless notables swung from the gallows.[48]

Popular resentment about this widely publicized event, the approaching deadline for conversion or emigration, and pent-up frustration with spiritual and economic powerlessness all prepared the ground for the massive insurrection of the following year. Unlike many similar endeavors, the Upper Austrian rising followed a period of careful planning, even if a coincidental brawl with Bavarian soldiers triggered its outbreak prematurely. Under the leadership of the Protestant tenant farmer Stefan Fadinger and his brother-in-law, the innkeeper Christoph Zeller, tens of thousands eventually took up arms.[49] From its origins in the Mühlviertel and Hausruckviertel, the insurgency swiftly engulfed Upper Austria. In their mobilization, the peasants successfully availed themselves of the existing militia system; recalcitrants were threatened into at least providing money and supplies.[50] Although rural commoners and their households formed the core, townsmen and individual nobles joined the struggle, with Wolf Madlseder and Lazarus Holzmüller from the city of Steyr and the aristocrat Achaz von Wiellinger holding important positions of influence.[51] Madlseder and Holzmüller served as negotiators and spokesmen for the insurgents and formulated many of their grievances; Wiellinger functioned as a military leader during the later phase of the hostilities. Notwithstanding occasional signs of covert support, however, the bulk of the Protestant nobility kept out of the struggle.[52]

In spite of episodic excesses in the heat of the moment, the insurgents strove to maintain a functioning, lawful society.[53] They avoided conflicts at the borders with adjacent territories and even showed consideration for the emperor's economic interests, especially in the salt-mining regions of the south, where they exempted key regalian personnel from military service.[54] Notwithstanding widespread hostility to the Catholic Church and the removal of newly installed or particularly hated clergymen, many priests were able to continue their office; ecclesial property formed a prime target of looting, however.

Interdenominational cooperation formed a sensitive issue. Not without success, resistance leaders tried to integrate the confessional minority.[55] They even appointed Catholic regional commanders to reassure local coreligionists.[56] Yet rank and file insurgents harbored deep reservations about their Catholic neighbors, whom they suspected of lukewarm support at best, potential duplicity and subversion at worst. Whereas hostility against the lien administration unified the peasants, confessional agendas divided them. As a consequence, Catholics did not melt easily into the rebel forces, and in some districts they stood altogether aloof. Inhabitants of select mountain communities south of Steyr objected to the draft, and following the arrival of imperial troops, Catholic peasants in the Traunviertel withdrew from the insurgency.[57]

The motives of the uprising have been debated controversially. At the time of the conflict, already, Bavarian representatives were inclined to blame the insurgency on recatholization, decreed by the emperor, whereas Habsburg officials pointed to Bavarian misrule.[58] Originally, these disagreements were rooted in palpable political interests, such as the assignment of military expenses, but rival dynastic and ideological sympathies continued to color scholarly interpretation until at least the nineteenth century.[59] In more recent literature, the underlying economic discontent has come into focus, with Georg Grüll pointing to the continuity of socioeconomic conflicts and Hermann Rebel documenting the contribution of inflation and coin debasement to the indebtedness of tenant farmers.[60]

There can be little doubt that religious, political, and economic considerations all contributed to the outbreak of hostilities. Important information about these motives can be extracted from the peasants' own petitions and manifestos. In summer 1626 the United Lutheran Community of Upper Austria, as the insurgents tellingly defined themselves, submitted a detailed list of grievances to the emperor.[61] The petition took its starting point in the reformation patent but further elaborated on its multiple implications. Not only did the decree deprive them of their long-standing religious liberties, but it also subjected them to maltreatment and exploitation by foreign occupants. If they availed themselves of the right to emigrate, they were burdened with additional charges and restrictions. Although they repeatedly requested freedom of religion, the peasants assured the emperor of their loyalty and restricted their criticism to the occupation regime.

These goals were confirmed by the peasant articles distributed in various closely related versions during the conflict. A 1626 broadsheet arranged in 12 stipulations called for the propagation of God's word, the restoration of the emperor instead of the Bavarian duke, the removal of Herberstorff and the investiture of a domestic governor, the appointment of Lutheran officials in the cities, the substitution of the prelates with the peasants in the diet, the replacement of foreign troops with a popular militia and the

204   *The Peasants*

abolishment of urban garrisons, the expulsion of all Jesuits except for the prelates, a general amnesty, the implementation of Emperor Matthias's religious concession that permitted territorial lords to install Protestant preachers on their estates, and the full restitution of those who had been dispossessed and driven into exile.[62] An otherwise similar text, presented during the siege of Steyr, specified that all Catholic clergy other than the prelates were to leave the country and distinctly mentioned the restitution of prosecuted nobles. It also added articles on the removal of Bavarian counselors, the restitution of recently alienated Lutheran churches, and the abolishment of select inheritance fees.[63] Subtle differences can be explained by the fact that most of the anticlerical animus was directed at the counterreformational priests imposed on Protestant congregations, whereas there was little interest in depriving genuine Catholics of pastoral care.

Most far-reaching among those demands were the lifting of Bavarian occupation, the full restoration of Protestant freedom of religion, and the representation of the peasant majority in the diet. Corresponding priorities also surfaced in the insurgents' martial symbolism. "Because we've staked both land and soul/we'll stake our life and blood as whole/ dear Lord, make us like heroes bold," proclaimed a central rallying call of the peasant army, together with "From Bavaria's yoke and tyranny/ and its enormous slavery/dear Lord, please set us free."[64] The insurgents expressed that their whole existence was on the line, both spiritually and materially, leaving them no choice but to resist. Not by coincidence, "It has to be!" was the third and last of their emblematic slogans.[65]

In spite of promising victories in the early phase of the rising, the peasants of Upper Austria eventually joined their regional and imperial predecessors in defeat. Yet while the God to whom they had appealed could not fulfill their political aspirations, he did make them "like heroes bold." Unlike many contemporary peasant militias, the Upper Austrians did not disperse at the sight of professional soldiers. They routed the overconfident governor in the first serious encounter at Peuerbach and brought much of the territory under their control. Both Herberstorff and the emperor pushed for negotiations, biding time to prepare their military response. The insurgents embraced the hope of compromise and urged the noble estates to back their struggle for spiritual concessions through interpolations in Vienna and Munich.[66] They even offered the emperor to redeem his debts to Maximilian and thereby end the lien administration, if they gained religious freedom in exchange.[67] Following the successful advance of imperial troops into the territory, the peasants substantially moderated their expectations, and a peaceful resolution seemed within

The Peasants   205

reach. Yet the Bavarians preferred a military approach and ignored the agreements reached between peasants and emperor.

The unexpected Bavarian attack reignited peasant morale, and initial inroads suffered embarrassing defeats. Maximilian further raised the stakes and detached Gottfried Heinrich zu Pappenheim, one of the subsequently most famous generals of the Thirty Years' War, to the unruly province.[68] After the combined Bavarian and imperial forces had grown to more than 8,000 men, they met the not much stronger peasant armies in several bloody and decisive battles. The insurgents had become desperate and radicalized, having lost their foremost leaders to battle wounds and capture and whole sections of the province to despair and resignation. Among their final organizers was a mysterious student of theology by the name of Casparus, who reinforced them with rousing sermons until he, too, met his fate at the hands of enemy soldiers.[69]

In the end, the peasants were defeated by inferior armament and strategy, but it was no easy victory for their professional opponents.[70] None less than their conqueror Pappenheim, a veteran of many wars, praised the insurgents' bravery and resilience. In a letter dispatched to his stepfather Herberstorff right after the first major battle at Emling, Pappenheim reported that the peasants had fearlessly defended themselves with clubs, to which they had attached metal blades, so that the attacking cavalry encountered a wall of rocks. The peasants fought not like human beings, but like furies from the netherworld, and put up miraculous resistance. When they were finally pushed back, they did not drop their clubs and run but retreated step by step until they were mowed down in droves.[71] And following the equally bitter encounter at Pinsdorf near Gmunden, the experienced officer confessed that he "had been in many a battle, but had never seen more stubborn, defiant, and terrible fighting."[72]

Decimated by their superior opponents, the insurgents finally lay down their weapons in November 1626. Now it was time to pay the price for their defiance. Surviving leaders such as Wiellinger and Madlsperger were put to death the following spring. Not even the fallen escaped the victors' vengeance, and the bodies of Fadinger and Zeller were dug up from their graves and reburied by the executioner in a nearby swamp.[73] Next to their own losses in life and property, the peasants also had to shoulder the invaders' military expenses. The religious reformation continued undiminished and soon included the nobility as well. The rising had brought no confessional, political, or economic relief.

In the Upper Austrian Peasants' War of 1626, popular resistance to the Counterreformation reached a dramatic zenith. Yet although frustration with the heavy-handed recatholization of their communities formed a

206   *The Peasants*

decisive catalyst of resistance, the struggle was not directed primarily against the Habsburgs. The increasingly desperate peasants even projected their hopes for redress and salvation onto a remote dynasty, which might lead the country back to the established liberties of the past. Not all of them realized that in the field of confessional policy, especially, Herberstorff was largely executing imperial mandates. At the same time, however, one must not overlook that the insurgents battled imperial mercenaries as determinedly as Bavarian ones and inundated Ferdinand's emissaries with appeals for policy reorientation. Their pleas for a return to Habsburg administration reflected a sober awareness that this represented the only realistic alternative to an intolerable present. In the end, the restitution of the emperor did not much resemble their hopeful projections. Having expelled the Elector Palatine from his last remaining strongholds along the Rhine, the emperor was finally able to compensate his Bavarian ally and redeem his patrimony in 1628. Ferdinand quickly dispersed any illusions about potential differences with Herberstorff by taking him into his own service after the Bavarian withdrawal in 1628. The Bavarian conqueror of Upper Austrian resistance ended his life as the emperor's trusted governor.

Peasants and Swedes: The Making of a Habsburg Nightmare

With the defeat of the Upper Austrian uprising, serious internal opposition to Ferdinand's religious policies had all but dissipated. Townsmen, nobles, and peasants had been subjugated one by one, sometimes by persuasion and the mere threat of sanctions, other times by undisguised coercion and victory on the battlefield. Whereas the pacification of the higher estates seemed complete, however, segments of the peasantry remained suspect. This unreliability became worrisome in an international context. As long as the Habsburgs fought an unrelenting continental war with denominational overtones, the fear of internal opposition never subsided.

Most acute was the concern about cross-border alliances. Much of the Habsburgs' military success rested on isolating their opponents. Time after time, confreres and associates kept their heads down while the armies of the dynasty crushed local resistance, if they did not fall in line behind the government altogether. All the more ominous seemed a potential intertwining of domestic and international opposition. By driving thousands of recalcitrant Protestants into exile, however, the Habsburgs themselves prepared the ground for such cooperation. Embittered by the loss of their homeland, free from Habsburg supervision, and desperate to make a living in a strange environment, uprooted Austrians sought refuge in the mercenary units of the Thirty Years' War. Since common soldiers are more difficult to trace than noble officers, most of them have remained nameless. There are exceptions, however. In the enlistment rolls of the Swedish Khevenhüller regiment, to take one example, one encounters numerous non-aristocratic Carinthians, among them Hans Altenhauser from Paternion, Kaspar Altziebler from Paternion, Michael Stegger from Paternion, and Melchior Haibacher from Villach.[74] Additional names can be found in the publications of Protestant church historian Paul Dedic.[75]

Few were as fortunate as Georg Derfflinger, whose service in the Swedish cavalry catalyzed his ascent from Austrian farm boy to Brandenburg general and nobleman.[76] Derfflinger was born to Upper Austrian peasants and innkeepers in 1606.[77] Since the family was strongly Lutheran—Derfflinger's sister Regina even married Christoph Crinesius, subsequently professor of theology at Altdorf University—it was driven into exile in 1624. Georg soon attached himself to varying anti-Habsburg forces. Following the arrival of Gustavus Adolphus in Germany, he entered the king's service and rose to colonel in the Swedish cavalry. His military career opened new social venues and enabled him to marry a Brandenburg baroness, whereupon he purchased her indebted ancestral estate Gusow and turned it into his own family seat.[78]

His establishment in Brandenburg benefitted Derfflinger at the end of the war, when Sweden's mercenaries lost both their livelihood and their erstwhile land donations in Germany. After a peaceful interlude as country squire he entered the Brandenburg military, where he rose to field marshal and trusted adviser to Elector Frederick William I. Derfflinger reformed the Brandenburg cavalry but also promoted the transformation of military leaders from hired technicians of warfare to patriotic servants of the state, making him one of the founding fathers of the modern Prussian army. He also served his monarch in diplomatic missions and as governor in Pomerania and East Prussia.

In 1674 Emperor Leopold I awarded Derfflinger an imperial baronage. Toward the end of his career the Protestant émigré gave the Habsburgs ample reason for gratitude.[79] As Brandenburg field marshal he supported the emperor against both France and the Ottoman Empire; his younger son Karl remained on the battlefield in Hungary in 1686. Derfflinger himself passed away peacefully on his estate at the age of 88, uncommon at that time not only for members of his own perilous profession. Whereas the male line of the family already died out in the subsequent generation, the female descendancy intermarried extensively with the Prussian aristocracy. As a consequence, eminent Prussian families such as the Stolbergs, Haugwitzes, Marwitzes, and Zietens prided themselves on

208 *The Peasants*

their descent from the scion of Upper Austrian peasants, as did no other than the Habsburgs' nineteenth-century nemesis Otto von Bismarck.[80]

The Unrest of 1632 and the Hope for a Savior

Overall, however, the emperor's advisers were less concerned about individual Protestants in foreign services than about the alignment of domestic rebellions and international campaigns. During the uprising of 1626, already, the Upper Austrians stood in contact with a reputed emissary of Denmark's King Christian IV, who had become sufficiently concerned about the Habsburgs' expansion toward the north to enter the war in his role as prince of the empire.[81] The genuineness of the Danish mission to the insurgents has been questioned, and it never moved beyond vague promises.[82] Yet Christian had a well-established interest in the area, having encouraged Bethlen Gábor of Transylvania to distract the emperor through inroads into the hereditary lands.[83] The increasingly desperate peasants took the overture seriously enough to compose an appeal to the king in August 1626, in which they described the tribulations they had experienced for the sake of their shared religion and implored the monarch for help.[84] Local authorities were concerned as well and feared especially that an incursion of condottiere Ernst von Mansfeld would find the support of religiously oppressed natives.[85] As soon as Christian had been defeated at Lutter and Mansfeld intercepted in Moravia, any chance of international assistance to the insurgents had dissipated.

It was the Swedish intervention in the war that created more tangible opportunities for defiant commoners from the Habsburg lands. Some of the exiles quickly answered the call of Swedish recruitment agents.[86] More dangerous, however, were submerged strains of resistance in the hereditary lands. The terrible defeat of their insurgency had subdued the peasants, but the unrelenting progress of religious homogenization kept discontent alive. With the steep increase in refugees following the virtual eradication of legal Protestantism in the late 1620s, exiles and domestic holdouts began to interact. In 1632 the long-held fears of the Habsburg authorities seemed to materialize. Not by coincidence, it was Upper Austria that again formed the center of unrest.

The initial linkage between internal and external opposition was created by a lay preacher from the Mühlviertel region named Jakob Greimbl, who had already accompanied the peasant armies in 1626 and had subsequently been arrested for heterodox religious activity in 1630.[87] After his release from confinement, Greimbl relocated to Prague, where he experienced the Saxon occupation in 1631 and established contact with

Austrian émigré officers. The Bohemia of late 1631 was a most peculiar place, where for a short while it seemed possible to turn back the wheel of history. Numerous exiles prepared to reclaim their confiscated possessions. Even the newly appointed commander of the capital, Lorenz von Hofkirchen, was a Protestant from Lower Austria.[88] Jakob Greimbl, too, was infected by the ebullience of his fellow émigrés and their belief in a miraculous new hero from the north.

In 1632 Greimbl reappeared in Upper Austria. He traveled from village to village, preached Lutheranism, and informed the locals about the advance of Gustavus Adolphus's armies.[89] He assured them of the king's support if they were to cooperate. Throughout the year he convened growing numbers of peasants, administering communion and encouraging them to rise against spiritual oppression.[90] Rumors of his activity soon reached Governor Hans Ludwig von Kuefstein, but the authorities proved unable to detain or deter Greimbl. During the summer, thousands again flocked to the historical assembly place in the Weiberau commons and selected Stephan Nimmervoll and Abraham Luegmayer as their leaders. By August, the region was in open rebellion.

Haunted by the memories of 1626, Catholic priests and administrators fled in panic.[91] Yet in spite of outside similarities, the rising of 1632 did not match its predecessor. Differences already surfaced in the general political setting, where the demise of the Protestant nobility had removed the possibility of estatist mediation. The insurrection itself was largely restricted to the Hausruck quarter; even there, only parts of the population supported it.[92] As a consequence, the rebels never amassed the number of troops required for a serious challenge to the government. Yet also the latter failed to gather sufficient backing among the peasants. Although Catholic lords such as Kremsmünster Abbey and Franz Christoph Khevenhüller were able to mobilize their subjects, a still Protestant majority refused to fight its coreligionists, and in the Mühlviertel district to the north, the mood seemed so hostile that imperial representatives feared outright collusion with the rebels.[93] Once again, the authorities had to rely on professional soldiers.

Any lasting success of the rising depended on outside support. All parties understood this—the Habsburgs, the insurgents, and even the Swedes. From the very beginning, local authorities strove to dissuade the agitated peasants from revolting by depicting their hopes for Swedish assistance as illusory. They reminded them of the terrible fate of previous rebels and the devastation in store for the country.[94] The impact of these arguments revealed itself not only in the reluctance of so many openly discontented communities to join the rising but also in the anxiety of the insurgents

210 *The Peasants*

themselves. The authenticity of Swedish promises recurred as a central question posed to Greimbl, so important that the preacher called divine punishment upon himself if he had misrepresented his mission.[95]

Those who were not reassured by magical invocations demanded evidence. Emissaries made their way to the Swedish vanguard, which had already advanced into neighboring Bavaria. After initial contacts in the preparatory phase, a formal delegation requested written assurances.[96] Thanks to the intercession of exiled Austrian nobles such as Bartholomäus von Dietrichstein and Gottfried von Egg and the almost mythic status of the 1626 rebellion, they gained unprecedented access to the royal entourage.[97] Gustavus Adolphus and his advisers paid close attention to the brewing discontent in the emperor's patrimony.

The first central decisionmaker the Upper Austrians encountered was Chancellor Axel Oxenstierna. Oxenstierna had already learned of the unrest from enemy interlopers.[98] In September 1632 he informed the king of a meeting at Nuremberg.[99] The emissaries had reported that while one-quarter of the province had taken up arms, the remainder still feared a repetition of 1626, where promised Danish assistance had not materialized. The insurgents pleaded for military support and affirmed that the arrival of Swedish troops would spread the rising throughout the territory.

The chancellor had the delegates escorted to royal headquarters at Donauwörth, where they obtained the requested confirmation.[100] Yet Gustavus and Oxenstierna also entered into a principal discussion of strategic options. The chancellor described the urgency of the matter.[101] If help did not arrive within a month, the rising might collapse, which put great pressure on an army still separated from Upper Austria by much of Bavaria and the Upper Palatinate. Successful cooperation with insurgent peasants and the speedy transfer of so many troops posed great challenges. The prospects, however, were even greater. Oxenstierna expected the territory to be religiously and politically sympathetic to the king and deeply alienated from the current regime. Its control would encircle Bavaria and provide access to both Bohemia and the Alpine provinces; it would move the war right into the emperor's core domains.

The king agreed wholeheartedly.[102] Although he needed to reinforce his volatile Saxon ally against Wallenstein, he preferred to retain the bulk of his troops in the south. This would allow him to invade the hereditary lands, assisting the Upper Austrian peasants in the process and creating so much commotion that Wallenstein would be withdrawn from Saxony. Oxenstierna's vision went even further. If Gustavus could fight his way down the Danube into Upper Austria, both the duke of Bavaria and the emperor would be lost.[103]

King and chancellor took the Upper Austrians very seriously and hoped for at least a significant distraction of the imperial troops, if not a decisive breakthrough into the Habsburg heartland. We will never know what the arrival of a triumphant Protestant army in an only partially subdued heterodox province would have resulted in. Military reversals in the north forced Gustavus Adolphus to postpone his Austrian plans and head toward Saxony.[104] The moment never returned. On the battlefield of Lützen, Sweden lost more than a king. It also lost a symbol that had rekindled hope among the vanquished of southern Protestantism.[105]

By the time of the king's death in November, events in Upper Austria had run their course. Upon the return of their emissaries, peasant leaders quickly heralded the royal decree. Wherever they came, they styled themselves as representatives of the king of Sweden. Yet words alone proved insufficient to win over reluctant populations. The opposite was the case: as long as the promised Swedish help failed to arrive, a steady trickle of departures further drained the already inadequate rebel forces.[106] Even though the insurgents achieved sporadic victories, they lacked the military equipment and leadership to withstand the imperial troops and their local allies. By October, the insurgency had collapsed. Within months, the ringleaders who had not managed to escape were executed.[107]

The Tragedy of 1636 and the Afterglow of Rebellion

In spite of the apparent futility of resistance, the rebellion of 1632 did not mark the final flare-up of peasant defiance. Only a few years later, the region was again gripped by socioreligious unrest. At first sight, there were considerable similarities between the events of 1632 and 1635 – 1636. In both cases, itinerant preachers gathered a following. They invoked connections to the Swedish army, the era's prime symbol of Protestant power. Their actions were disconcerting enough to require governmental intervention and resulted in substantial bloodshed. In the end, however, the movement assembling around the Machlandviertel peasant Martin Aichinger, generally known by the name of his farmstead as Laimbauer, represented yet another stage in the decline of a both socially and ideologically complex mass phenomenon to a colorful but isolated fringe spectacle.[108]

Laimbauer had already been arrested for heterodox religious activities in 1632 but had not been taken seriously by the authorities. After his release he covertly resumed his preaching, and by 1635 he had begun

212 *The Peasants*

to assemble hundreds of followers. He saw himself as a Lutheran and beseeched his compatriots to uphold their established faith rather than defect to Catholicism. There is no doubt, indeed, that the trauma of coercive conversion fueled his movement, and many of his earliest disciples had been driven from their homes for refusing to comply.[109] Yet in both content and form, Laimbauer's deportment eluded confessional orthodoxy. The itinerant preacher who dressed in flamboyant outfits and claimed to have conversed with God while sitting on a cloud would have provoked more conventional clergy of any mainstream denomination.[110]

Following minor skirmishes, Laimbauer's entourage dissolved again, but their leader enjoyed sufficient support in the population to evade capture. In the spring of 1636, he resumed his campaign through the Machland quarter.[111] From small beginnings, Laimbauer's following rapidly expanded again, owing more to his powers of persuasion than to feeble attempts at forced conscription.[112] The administration mobilized local militias, but initial confrontations betrayed their inadequacy. Following a proven approach, the authorities tried to gain time for military reinforcement by offering negotiations. Due to Laimbauer's deep distrust of government, however, the strategy failed. Government emissaries found themselves surrounded by agitated peasants, from whose fury they did not always escape unscathed. Indeed, there was little to negotiate about, since Laimbauer's societal designs far exceeded the jurisdiction of local authorities.

Governor Kuefstein called up additional troops, and on 12 May 1636 the pilgrimage of the peasant revivalists came to an end. A numerically superior detachment confronted them on the Frankenberg heights east of Linz.[113] The dissidents dug in around the local church and defended themselves valiantly, until the attackers set fire to the surrounding farmsteads, from where it quickly engulfed the church. Deprived of protective cover, the ragtag army of men, women, and children could no longer resist; few of them survived the ensuing massacre. Martin Laimbauer himself was found wounded but alive and spared for a more lurid spectacle.[114] Already the next day the captives were triumphantly displayed at Linz. Within a month, they were interrogated, tortured, and sentenced.

Within a decade, Upper Austria had experienced no less than three peasant rebellions. In the eyes of many observers, the obstinacy of the locals seemed to have survived defeat and retribution. Yet in spite of outside similarities, each successive rising was a mere shadow of its predecessor. The insurgents of 1626 levied tens of thousands throughout the territory; from a modern perspective, they appear as the true representatives of the country. The rebels assembled in 1632 still counted in the

The Peasants   213

thousands, and even if their impact was restricted to select districts, they succeeded at calling up dozens of parishes. The supporters of Laimbauer no longer represented any wholesale communities—they were individuals who followed a charismatic leader, consisting primarily of women, minors, and non-proprietors. In its final battle, the group comprised but 400 members, a minority of whom were able-bodied men.

Yet numbers were not the only difference. Notwithstanding an abstract desire to keep the region Protestant, Laimbauer never formulated a concrete political program.[115] In spite of frequent invocations, the movement also lacked substantive Swedish connections, diminishing the threat of outside intervention that had given the unrest of 1632 its distinct quality. Most damaging, however, was the absence of a long-term strategy. Laimbauer did not envision a military resolution, although his band was armed and willing to defend itself. When the representatives of Steyregg refused him entry, Laimbauer responded that he did not wish to "inconvenience or coerce anyone, but merely to carry out what God had instructed him to do. And since they did not want to receive the word of God and the holy cross from him, he would bypass the town and move on."[116] If anything, his concept foreshadowed the mass demonstrations of modern societies, attempting to influence policy through an ever-growing mobilization of public support. In the strictly hierarchic society of early modern Austria, this invocation of popular will was destined for disaster. It had no realistic chance of challenging the authorities and reversing the progress of Catholic restoration.

In reality, a mystic component had begun to overshadow the political. Among a people in deep spiritual turmoil, millennial and magical concepts found open ears. Laimbauer was a prophet and a seer rather than a rebel leader. He proclaimed supernatural visions and powers, promising his followers invulnerability and the legendary support of Emperor Frederick Barbarossa's sleeping army.[117] He sprinkled his followers with magical water and invoked divine mandates. The slaughter at Frankenberg did not annihilate a rebel army but a forlorn assembly of religious dreamers.

The tragedy's final act on the town square of Linz has been immortalized in William Crowne's diary of the Earl of Arundel's embassy to Germany.[118] When the English delegates arrived in the city in June 1636, they observed the beheading of Laimbauer and his close associates. Crowne described how the executioners seized the ringleader, who had persuaded himself that no bullet had the power to harm him, "firmly by the chest with a massive pair of red-hot pincers and, nailing his right hand to the block, chopped it off."[119] Then the executioner "cut off the wretched

214 *The Peasants*

fellow's head which an assistant raised, shouting into the ears of the dead man: 'Jesus, Jesus.'"[120] Following the execution of Laimbauer, six more insurgents, including a young boy, were beheaded and quartered.[121]

Thus ended the last substantive peasant rebellion of Upper Austria's age of confessionalization. There was still opposition, to be sure, but the time for armed conflict had passed.[122] Many more peasants now joined the exodus of burghers and nobles. Others withdrew into the secrecy of spiritual dissent. A majority merely sought to reestablish their lives. Following a century of religious and social turbulence, quiet again fell over the land.

Conclusion

In the still largely agrarian society of early modern Austria, the peasantry was essential for the consolidation of religious reform. A spiritual movement that was restricted to the privileged estates was doomed to fail. Yet at the same time, the rural majority was strongly dependent on its lords and superiors, whose control extended deeply into the social and religious sphere. As a consequence, political elites tended to dismiss the peasants as autonomous political subjects or cast themselves in the role of their natural leaders and spokespersons. This understanding united princes and nobles, Catholics and Protestants. Absolute monarchs such as Ferdinand II assumed paternal responsibility for the spiritual welfare of their subjects.[123] Aristocratic landlords ascribed themselves a similar role, and even radical theorists such as the French Monarchomachs shrank from extending an independent right of resistance to commoners.[124]

Yet peasants were no mere objects of princes and magnates; they consistently emerged as historical actors. Depending on time and place, they resorted to different means of retaining influence over their lives. In remote mountain regions of the Austrian interior, many opted to lie low, hoping for the armies of religious regimentation to pass by and return to the centers of wealth and power. They outwardly lived as Catholics and practiced their true faith in concealment. For some communities, this life of spiritual duplicity lasted for generations.

In other regions, resistance took more dramatic forms. The Tyrolean rebellion of 1525 gave an early indication of the explosive new combination of social and spiritual discontent, but nowhere did its implications surface more persistently than in Upper Austria. The chain of rural revolts with confessional overtones that began in the late 1500s and culminated in the terrible bloodshed of 1626 put this small territory on the international map. To friend and foe alike, Upper Austria seemed a bastion of untamable peasants and Protestants, long after the spirit of mass resistance had been broken.

The rural insurgents of the Habsburg lands held diverse attitudes toward their monarchs. They regularly put their hopes on an idealized prince and emperor who would protect them from their more immediate superiors. Sometimes the court did intervene as arbiter in social conflicts between landlords and villeins, as in the case of Rudolph II's interim resolution of 1597.[125] Other times the peasants' expectations proved illusionary, as in the case of Upper Austrians who hoped to regain the privileges canceled under Maximilian of Bavaria from the very emperor who had orchestrated their abolition.[126] At select crossroads, however, insurgents turned more decisively against the dynasty and called upon international assistance, gaining themselves the lasting disapproval of domestic historical commentators. One may ascribe Franz Kurz's characterization of the 1632 commotion as a despicable rebellion against the sovereign to the societal context of the nineteenth-century monarchy, but the same event was still described as inexcusable treason as late as 1976.[127]

If one moves beyond contemporary juridical terminology, however, the moral picture becomes more complex. The Upper Austrian rebels of 1632 sought help from religious oppression from whoever seemed willing and able to provide it. They did not understand their resistance as deliberate aid to Gustavus Adolphus or as a call for Swedish sovereignty. If anyone, Ferdinand himself risked alienating the territory by surrendering it to Bavarian lien administration. Among the major peasant leaders of the era, only Michael Gaismair developed a full-fledged plan to depose the Habsburgs. It highlights the subsequent identification of land and dynasty that he, too, has been accused of betraying his country.[128] Yet Gaismair was deeply steeped in Tyrolean patriotism. He did not want to surrender his homeland to foreign conquerors; he tried to transform it into an independent peasant republic.

While Tyrol had only briefly followed the clarion call of popular reform and Swiss liberty, Upper Austria formed a more enduring challenge to the dynasty. As late as 1645, Emperor Ferdinand III was haunted by the fear that local peasants might collude with their one-time compatriot Georg Derfflinger.[129] His suspicions were shared by the Swedes, who expected an invasion to rekindle the fire of 1626 and restore the opportunity lost six years later.[130] Yet by the 1640s, in the final phase of the Thirty Years' War, the rebel soul of Upper Austria had entered the realm of legend. Its protagonists had been decimated by emigration and death. Rural bureaucratization had consolidated governmental control of the countryside.[131] The bulk of the population had resigned itself to the futility of

216   *The Peasants*

resistance, and new generations had been raised in the triumphant imagery of Baroque Catholicism. In Upper Austria, too, the future belonged to the Habsburg dynasty and its state church.

Notes

1. For the regional population numbers cited in this paragraph, consult Kurt Klein, "Die Bevölkerung Österreichs vom Beginn des 16. bis zur Mitte des 18. Jahrhunderts," in *Beiträge zur Bevölkerungs- und Sozialgeschichte Österreichs*, ed. Heimold Helczmanovszki (Munich, 1973), 47–112; Thomas Winkelbauer, *Ständefreiheit und Fürstenmacht: Länder und Untertanen des Hauses Habsburg im konfessionellen Zeitalter*, vol. 1 (Vienna, 2003), 13–24; Charles W. Ingrao, *The Habsburg Monarchy, 1618–1815*, 2nd ed. (Cambridge, England, 2000), 6–16; Ernst Wolfgang Buchholz, *Vom Mittelalter zur Neuzeit*, vol. 2 of *Raum und Bevölkerung in der Weltgeschichte: Bevölkerungs-Ploetz*, by Ernst Kirsten, Ernst Wolfgang Buchholz, and Wolfgang Köllmann, 3rd ed. (Würzburg, 1966), 57; Carlo M. Cipolla and Knut Borchardt, eds., *Bevölkerungsgeschichte Europas: Mittelalter bis Neuzeit* (Munich, 1971), 81; Robert A. Kann and Zdeněk V. David, *The Peoples of the Eastern Habsburg Lands, 1526–1918* (Seattle, WA, 1984), 117; Hugh Agnew, *The Czechs and the Lands of the Bohemian Crown* (Stanford, CA, 2004), 72; Ludwig Petry and Josef Joachim Menzel, eds., *Geschichte Schlesiens*, vol. 2, 2nd ed. (Stuttgart, 2000), 102; Jaroslav Miller, *Urban Societies of East Central Europe: 1500– 1700* (Aldershot, England, 2008), 21; and Eric Fügedi, "The Demographic Landscape of East-Central Europe," in *East-Central Europe in Transition*, ed. Antoni Mączak, Henryk Samsonowicz, and Peter Burke (Cambridge, England, 1985), 47–58. It needs to be stressed that these are estimates and thus subject to uncertainty and differing assessments. Thus, a combination of individual regional estimates can result in totals reaching from below seven to almost eight million.

2. For the clergy, see Andreas Weigl, *Bevölkerungsgeschichte Europas* (Vienna, 2012), 78. For a comparative overview of the clergy's size in different countries and periods, see also Peter Hersche, *Muße und Verschwendung: Europäische Gesellschaft und Kultur im Barockzeitalter*, vol. 1 (Freiburg im Breisgau, 2006), 247–257. For the nobility, see Thomas Winkelbauer, "Krise der Aristokratie? Zum Strukturwandel des Adels in den böhmischen und niederösterreichischen Ländern im 16. und 17. Jahrhundert," *Mitteilungen des Instituts für Österreichische Geschichtsforschung* 100 (1992): 331. Rudolf Endres estimated that the average aristocratic share of Germany's population amounted to approximately 1.5 percent of the overall population in 1500, declining to approximately 1 percent in 1800, whereas the numbers for the Bohemian lands were considerably lower. The census numbers for 1837 subsequently indicate an average aristocratic percentage of noticeably less than 0.5 percent in the Austrian Alps. See Rudolf Endres, *Adel in der Frühen Neuzeit* (Munich, 1993), 3, and Siegfried Becher, *Statistische Übersicht der Bevölkerung der österreichischen*

Monarchie nach den Ergebnissen der Jahre 1834–1840 (Stuttgart, 1841), 358–361.

3. See Ernst Bruckmüller, *Sozialgeschichte Österreichs* (Vienna, 1985), 136, and Roman Sandgruber, *Ökonomie und Politik: Österreichische Wirtschaftsgeschichte vom Mittelalter bis zur Gegenwart* (Vienna, 1995), 107.

4. Thomas Winkelbauer, *Ständefreiheit und Fürstenmacht: Länder und Untertanen des Hauses Habsburg im konfessionellen Zeitalter*, vol. 1 (Vienna, 2003), 21.

5. For the early 1500s, the population of Schwaz has been estimated to have reached up to 20,000 inhabitants. See Heimold Helczmanovszki, ed., *Beiträge zur Bevölkerungs- und Sozialgeschichte Österreichs* (Munich, 1973), 105.

6. See ibid., 87, 63 and 79. For a brief overview of Austria's urban demographics, see also Roman Sandgruber, *Ökonomie und Politik: Österreichische Wirtschaftsgeschichte vom Mittelalter bis zur Gegenwart* (Vienna, 1995), 107.

7. For the societal role of the European peasantry, see Werner Rösener, *The Peasantry of Europe* (Oxford, 1994), and Eric C. Wolf, *Peasants* (Englewood Cliffs, NJ, 1966).

8. In an Austrian context, these categories largely correspond to the designations *Freistift, Leibgedinge* and *Erbleihe*, but both terminology and legal content could vary.

9. For the highly divergent views on rebellion and peasant resistance held by Martin Luther and his one-time confrere Thomas Müntzer, see Martin Luther, *Wider die Mordischen und Reubischen Rotten der Bawren* ([Landshut], 1525), also printed in idem, *D. Martin Luthers Werke: Kritische Gesamtausgabe*, vol. 18 (Weimar, 1908), 344–361, and Thomas Müntzer, *Hoch verursachte Schutzrede* ([Nuremberg], 1524). For scholarly interpretations of this divergence, see Carl Hinrichs, *Luther und Müntzer: Ihre Auseinandersetzung über Obrigkeit und Widerstandsrecht*, 2nd ed. (Berlin, 1962); Gordon Rupp, "'True History': Martin Luther and Thomas Müntzer," in *History, Society and the Churches: Essays in Honour of Owen Chadwick*, ed. Derek Beales and Geoffrey Best (Cambridge, England, 1985), 77–87; and Harry Loewen, *Luther and the Radicals: Another Look at Some Aspects of the Struggle between Luther and Radical Reformers* (Waterloo, ON, 1974). For a general discussion of Luther's role during the Peasants' War, see also Paul Althaus, *Luthers Haltung im Bauernkrieg* (Tübingen, 1952); Robert N. Crossley, *Luther and the Peasants War: Luther's Actions and Reactions* (New York, 1974); and Martin Greschat, "Luthers Haltung im Bauernkrieg," *Archiv für Reformationsgeschichte* 65 (1965): 31–47.

10. Strictly speaking, the Great Peasants' War culminated during the first half of 1525 but included both a southwestern prelude in 1524 and an Alpine aftermath extending into 1526. It has been the subject of numerous scholarly investigations. Among still widely used studies, one may list Günther Franz, *Der deutsche Bauernkrieg*, 12th ed. (Darmstadt, 1984); Horst Buszello, Peter Blickle, and Rudolf Endres, eds., *Der deutsche Bauernkrieg* 3rd ed. (Paderborn, 1995); Peter Blickle, *Der Bauernkrieg: Die Revolution des Gemeinen Mannes*, 4th ed. (Munich, 2012); and idem, *Die Revolution von 1525*, 4th ed. (Munich, 2004); an earlier edition was translated into

218   The Peasants

English as *The Revolution of 1525: The German Peasants' War from a New Perspective* (Baltimore, 1981). For an introduction to diverse interpretations in English, see also Bob Scribner and Gerhard Benecke, eds., *The German Peasant War of 1525: New Viewpoints* (Boston, 1979).

11. For the charismatic leader of Tyrolean resistance, see Josef Macek, *Tyrolská selská válka a Michal Gaismair* (Prague, 1960); Jürgen Bücking, *Michael Gaismair: Reformer—Sozialrebell—Revolutionär* (Stuttgart, 1978); Walter Klaassen, *Michael Gaismair: Revolutionary and Reformer* (Hague, 1978); Angelika Bischoff-Urack, *Michael Gaismair: Ein Beitrag zur Sozialgeschichte des Bauernkrieges* (Innsbruck, 1983); Giorgio Politi, *Gli statuti impossibili: La rivoluzione tirolese del 1525 e il programma di Michael Gaismair* (Torino, 1995); and Aldo Stella, *Il 'Bauernführer' Michael Gaismair e l'utopia di un repubblicanesimo popolare* (Bologna, 1999).

12. The letter is printed in Victor Bibl, "Klesls Briefe an Kaiser Rudolfs II. Obersthofmeister Adam Freiherrn von Dietrichstein (1583–1589): Ein Beitrag zur Geschichte Klesls und der Gegenreformation in Niederösterreich," *Archiv für österreichische Geschichte* 88 (1900): 524–529.

13. See Otto Brunner, *Land und Herrschaft: Grundfragen der territorialen Verfassungsgeschichte Österreichs im Mittelalter*, 5th ed. (Vienna, 1965), 258–271.

14. See Georg Loesche, *Geschichte des Protestantismus im vormaligen und neuen Österreich* (Vienna, 1930), 33, and Emil Franzel, *Geschichte des deutschen Volkes: Von den Germanen bis zur Teilung nach dem Zweiten Weltkrieg* (Gütersloh, 1985), 255. Yet also a deeply Catholic historian such as Friedrich Heer defined late sixteenth-century Austria as a Protestant society. See Friedrich Heer, *Der Kampf um die österreichische Identität*, 2nd ed. (Vienna, 1996), 65.

15. See Rudolf Leeb, "Der Streit um den wahren Glauben—Reformation und Gegenreformation in Österreich," in *Geschichte des Christentums in Österreich*, ed. Rudolf Leeb et al. (Vienna, 2003), 211; Thomas Winkelbauer, *Ständefreiheit und Fürstenmacht: Länder und Untertanen des Hauses Habsburg im konfessionellen Zeitalter* (Vienna, 2003), 1:68; Anton Schindling and Walter Ziegler, eds., *Die Territorien des Reichs im Zeitalter der Reformation und Konfessionalisierung: Land und Konfession 1500–1650*, vol. 1, *Der Südosten* (Münster, 1992), 126f.; Helmut Mezler-Andelberg, *Kirche in der Steiermark: Gesammelte Aufsätze* (Vienna, 1994), 186f.; and France M. Dolinar et al., eds., *Katholische Reform und Gegenreformation in Innerösterreich 1564–1628* (Klagenfurt, 1994), 15. In regard to at least parts of the Carinthian peasantry one may also want to consider the assessment of the Catholic governor Christoph David Urschenbeck. As late as 1616, Urschenbeck called it deplorable to find only a handful of Catholics among so many thousands of souls. See Johann Loserth, ed., *Akten und Korrespondenzen zur Geschichte der Gegenreformation in Innerösterreich unter Ferdinand II.* (Vienna, 1907), 2: 690.

16. See Hermann Wopfner, *Die Lage Tirols zu Ausgang des Mittelalters und die Ursachen des Bauernkriegs* (Berlin-Leipzig, 1908), 3, and idem, "Bäuerliches Besitzrecht und Besitzverteilung in Tirol," *Forschungen und Mitteilungen zur Geschichte Tirols und Vorarlbergs* 4 (1907): 405.

The Peasants 219

17. The percentages are calculated from the numbers listed in Georg Grüll, "Die Herrschaftsschichtung in Österreich ob der Enns 1750," *Mitteilungen des Oberösterreichischen Landesarchivs* 5 (1957): 317.

18. Wendelin Hujber, "Der Prälatenstand des Landes ob der Enns 1600–1620: Beiträge zu seiner und der Geschichte der Landschaft im Zeitalter der Gegenreformation" (Ph.D. diss., University of Vienna, 1972), 32f.

19. Joseph F. Patrouch, *A Negotiated Settlement: The Counter-Reformation in Upper Austria under the Habsburgs* (Boston, 2000), 30f. The relationship between different forms of authority varied considerably, however. The Bishop of Passau, for example, also served as guardian for many of his own parishes in the northern Mühlviertel region of Upper Austria. See Josef Löffler, *Der zweite oberösterreichische Bauernaufstand 1594–1597 im Mühlviertel: Versuch einer systematischen Darstellung* (Saarbrücken, 2009), 28–30. For the broader relationship between lordship and guardianship, see also Thomas Simon, *Grundherrschaft und Vogtei: Eine Strukturanalyse spätmittelalterlicher und frühneuzeitlicher Herrschaftsbildung* (Frankfurt, 1995).

20. For the influence of landlords on the conduct and attitudes of their subjects, see Gustav Reingrabner, "Adelige Grundherrschaft und Reformation," *Heimatkundliches Jahrbuch des Waldviertler Heimatbundes* 2 (1978/79): 43–64, and Thomas Winkelbauer, "Sozialdisziplinierung und Konfessionalisierung durch Grundherren in den österreichischen und böhmischen Ländern im 16. und 17. Jahrhundert," *Zeitschrift für historische Forschung* 19 (1992): 317–339.

21. For an example from Upper Austria, see Joseph F. Patrouch, *A Negotiated Settlement: The Counter-Reformation in Upper Austria under the Habsburgs* (Boston, 2000), 31f.

22. For Ruep Schröffl, see Wolfgang Sittig, "Die Schröffl in der Pfarre Gröbming," *Zeitschrift des Historischen Vereines für Steiermark* 46 (1955): 177–180.

23. See Rudolf Leeb, "Der Streit um den wahren Glauben—Reformation und Gegenreformation in Österreich," in *Geschichte des Christentums in Österreich*, ed. Rudolf Leeb et al. (Vienna, 2003), 256.

24. See Georg Loesche, *Geschichte des Protestantismus im vormaligen und neuen Österreich* (Vienna, 1930), 250f., and Rudolf Leeb, "Der Streit um den wahren Glauben—Reformation und Gegenreformation in Österreich," in *Geschichte des Christentums in Österreich*, ed. Rudolf Leeb et al. (Vienna, 2003), 262.

25. This 1624 incident is recorded in Georg Grüll, "Geschichte des Schlosses und der Herrschaft Windhag bei Perg," *Jahrbuch des Oberösterreichischen Musealvereines* 87 (1937): 214. The exact spelling of the community, which is currently known as Windhaag bei Perg, has changed over time.

26. See Karl Eder, *Glaubensspaltung und Landstände in Österreich ob der Enns 1525–1602*, vol. 2 of *Studien zur Reformationsgeschichte Oberösterreichs* (Linz, 1936), 237.

27. See Rudolf Leeb, "Die protestantischen Kirchenbauten des 16. Jahrhunderts in Österreich und ihre Bedeutung für die Sicht der Anfänge des evangelischen Kirchenbaues," in *Geschichte des protestantischen Kirchenbaues: Festschrift Peter Poscharsky zum 60. Geburtstag*, ed. Klaus Raschzok and Reiner Sörries (Erlangen, 1994), 149f.

220 *The Peasants*

28. See, for example, the appeal submitted to Archduke Ernst in 1585 that is related in Bernhard Raupach, *Evangelisches Oesterreich: das ist historische Nachricht, von den vornehmsten Schicksahlen der evangelisch-lutherischen Kirchen in dem Ertz-Hertzogthum Oesterreich*, vol. 1 (Hamburg, 1732), 157–159.

29. The events are described in Bernhard Raupach, *Evangelisches Oesterreich: das ist historische Nachricht, von den vornehmsten Schicksahlen der evangelisch-lutherischen Kirchen in dem Ertz-Hertzogthum Oesterreich*, vol. 5, *Zwiefache Zugabe zu dem Evangelischen Oesterreich* (Hamburg, 1744), 157–159. See also Karl Eder, *Glaubensspaltung und Landstände in Österreich ob der Enns 1525–1602*, vol. 2 of *Studien zur Reformationsgeschichte Oberösterreichs* (Linz, 1936), 237–245.

30. For the Second Upper Austrian Peasant Insurgency, see especially Albin Czerny, *Der zweite Bauernaufstand in Oberösterreich 1595–1597* (Linz, 1890), and Josef Löffler, *Der zweite oberösterreichische Bauernaufstand 1594–1597 im Mühlviertel: Versuch einer systematischen Darstellung* (Saarbrücken, 2009). Useful for the socioeconomic aspects is Georg Grüll, *Der Bauer im Lande ob der Enns am Ausgang des 16. Jahrhunderts: Abgaben und Leistungen im Lichte der Beschwerden und Verträge von 1597–1598* (Linz, 1969).

31. The full text of the interim resolution, which also included further moderate concessions to the peasants, is printed in Georg Grüll, *Der Bauer im Lande ob der Enns am Ausgang des 16. Jahrhunderts: Abgaben und Leistungen im Lichte der Beschwerden und Verträge von 1597–1598* (Linz, 1969), 240–244.

32. See ibid., 12f.

33. See Josef Löffler, *Der zweite oberösterreichische Bauernaufstand 1594–1597 im Mühlviertel: Versuch einer systematischen Darstellung* (Saarbrücken, 2009), 170–189.

34. See Karl Eder, *Glaubensspaltung und Landstände in Österreich ob der Enns 1525–1602*, vol. 2 of *Studien zur Reformationsgeschichte Oberösterreichs* (Linz, 1936), 277–302.

35. For the insurgency in Lower Austria, see Otto Kainz, "Das Kriegsgerichtsprotokoll im niederösterreichischen Bauernaufstand aus dem Jahre 1597" (Ph.D. diss., University of Vienna, 2008), subsequently also published as idem, *Das Kriegsgerichtsprotokoll zum Niederösterreichischen Bauernaufstand von 1596/97: Analyse und Edition* (St. Pölten, 2010); Helmut Feigl, *Der niederösterreichische Bauernaufstand 1596/97* (Vienna, 1972); and idem, "Die Ursachen der niederösterreichischen Bauernkriege des 16. Jahrhunderts und die Ziele der Aufständischen," in *Die Bauernkriege und Michael Gaismair*, ed. Fridolin Dörrer (Innsbruck, 1982), 197–209.

36. See Otto Kainz, "Das Kriegsgerichtsprotokoll im niederösterreichischen Bauernaufstand aus dem Jahre 1597" (Ph.D. diss., University of Vienna, 2008), 273f. For a specific discussion of the rebellion's religious aspects, see also Gustav Reingrabner, "Religiöse Aspekte des niederösterreichischen Bauernaufstandes," in *Sozialrevolution und Reformation*, ed. Peter F. Barton (Vienna, 1975), 73–84.

37. For an administrative history of the Salzkammergut, see Franz Hufnagl, *Die Maut zu Gmunden: Die Entwicklungsgeschichte des Salzkammergutes*

The Peasants 221

(Vienna, 2008), a moderately abbreviated version of the author's 1999 dissertation "Die landesfürstliche Stadt Gmunden als Sitz der Kammergutsverwaltung: Die Stadt im Spannungsfeld mit den Habsburgern und den Salzamtmännern" at the University of Salzburg. See also Friedrich Satzinger, *Vöcklabruck Stadtgeschichte: Von den Anfängen bis 1850* (Vöcklabruck, Austria, 2006), 123f.

38. See Julia Zangerl, "Die Bedeutung des Salzamts Wien für die landesfürstlichen Finanzen," in *Finanzen und Herrschaft: Materielle Grundlagen fürstlicher Politik in den habsburgischen Ländern und im Heiligen Römischen Reich im 16. Jahrhundert*, ed. Friedrich Edelmayer, Maximilian Lanzinner, and Peter Rauscher (Vienna, 2003), 215–233, here especially p. 218, and Ernst Bruckmüller, *Sozialgeschichte Österreichs* (Vienna, 1985), 255. The percentage listed for 1770 refers to the salt monopoly in the whole monarchy. For the broader history of the era's Upper Austrian salt production, see Carl Schraml, *Das oberösterreichische Salinenwesen vom Beginne des 16. bis zur Mitte des 18. Jahrhunderts* (Vienna, 1932).

39. For the following, see especially Franz Christoph Khevenhiller, *Annales Ferdinandei, oder Wahrhaffte Beschreibung Kaysers Ferdinandi des Andern*, vol. 5, 2nd ed. (Leipzig, 1722), 2388–2397, 2497–2507; and Franz Scheichl, *Aufstand der protestantischen Salzarbeiter und Bauern im Salzkammergute 1601 und 1602* (Linz, 1885).

40. For the continuing importance of Protestantism in the region, see Franz Hufnagl, *Die Maut zu Gmunden: Die Entwicklungsgeschichte des Salzkammergutes* (Vienna, 2008), 428–441, 461, 489f., 508–519.

41. For the Upper Austrian uprising, see Felix Stieve, *Der oberösterreichische Bauernaufstand des Jahres 1626*, 2 vols. (Munich, 1891); Julius Strnadt, *Der Bauernkrieg in Oberösterreich* (Wels, 1924); Georg Heilingsetzer, *Der oberösterreichische Bauernkrieg 1626* (Vienna, 1976); and Karl Eichmeyer, Helmuth Feigl, and Rudolf Walter Litschel, *Weiß gilt die Seel und auch das Guet: Oberösterreichische Bauernaufstände und Bauernkriege im 16. und 17. Jahrhundert* (Linz, 1976).

42. See Hans Sturmberger, *Adam Graf Herberstorff: Herrschaft und Freiheit im konfessionellen Zeitalter* (Munich, 1976), 202, and Felix Stieve, *Der oberösterreichische Bauernaufstand des Jahres 1626*, vol. 1 (Munich, 1891), 34.

43. Christoph Khevenhiller, *Annales Ferdinandei, oder Wahrhaffte Beschreibung Kaysers Ferdinandi des Andern . . .*, vol. 10, 2nd ed. (Leipzig, 1724), 496–498.

44. The decree is printed in Bernhard Raupach, *Nützliche Beylagen zum Dritten und letzten Theil des Erläuterten Evangelischen Oesterreichs* (Hamburg, 1740), 237–246.

45. For a comprehensive biography of Herberstorff, see Hans Sturmberger, *Adam Graf Herberstorff: Herrschaft und Freiheit im konfessionellen Zeitalter* (Munich, 1976). In official terminology, he served as Bavarian *Statthalter*, whereas the Upper Austrian office was called *Landeshauptmann*. Both titles are traditionally translated as governor, however.

46. See Felix Stieve, *Der oberösterreichische Bauernaufstand des Jahres 1626*, vol. 1 (Munich, 1891), 43f.

222 The Peasants

47. For a concise examination, see Georg Grüll, "Das Frankenburger Würfelspiel," *Oberösterreich* 9 (1959): 4–9. The event subsequently entered regional lore under the name of Frankenburg Dice Game. Repeatedly instrumentalized for varying political agendas, it continues to be commemorated in large-scale amateur performances.

48. The draft of Herberstorff's report to Maximilian of Bavaria is printed in Georg Grüll, "Das Frankenburger Würfelspiel," *Oberösterreich* 9, no. 3/4 (1959): 4–7. Two of the losers at dice were pardoned. Strictly speaking, the victims were hung from trees and church steeples.

49. Felix Stieve's rough estimate that the peasants never had more than 40,000 men under arms has established this number in many later accounts. See Felix Stieve, *Der oberösterreichische Bauernaufstand des Jahres 1626*, vol. 1 (Munich, 1891), 98. For Fadinger, see Hans Fattinger, "Stefan Fadinger und Christoph Zeller: Ihre Familien und ihre Heimat," *Oberösterreichische Heimatblätter* 19 (1965): 49–60, and *Neue deutsche Biographie*, s.v. "Stefan Fadinger."

50. Felix Stieve, *Der oberösterreichische Bauernaufstand des Jahres 1626*, vol. 1 (Munich, 1891), 92.

51. For the role of Steyr and individual citizens such as Madlseder in 1626, see Caecilia Doppler, *Reformation und Gegenreformation in ihrer Auswirkung auf das Steyrer Bürgertum* (Vienna, 1977), 127–135.

52. See Felix Stieve, *Der oberösterreichische Bauernaufstand des Jahres 1626*, vol. 1 (Munich, 1891), 68–71.

53. For the following, see ibid., 90–97.

54. A certificate of exemption from military service, issued by Stefan Fadinger, is printed in Albin Czerny, "Einige Blätter aus der Zeit der Gegenreformation in Oberösterreich," *Jahrbuch des Oberösterreichischen Musealvereines* 42 (1884): 171f.

55. For the mixed picture of Catholic peasant response, see Wendelin Hujber, "Der Prälatenstand im Jahre 1626," in *Der oberösterreichische Bauernkrieg 1626: Ausstellung des Landes Oberösterreich, Linzer Schloß, Schloß zu Scharnstein im Almtal, 14. Mai bis 31. Oktober 1976*, ed. Dietmar Straub (Linz 1976), 136.

56. The most visible Catholic among the insurgents was the district commander Andreas Hamel. See Felix Stieve, *Der oberösterreichische Bauernaufstand des Jahres 1626*, vol. 1 (Munich, 1891), 154.

57. For the Catholic mountain communities south of Steyr, see Helmuth Feigl, "Die befreiten Ämter der Herrschaft Steyr in den Bauernkriegen des 16. und 17. Jahrhunderts," *Mitteilungen des Oberösterreichischen Landesarchivs* 6 (1959): 252f. For the Traunviertel, see "Kurtze und aigentliche Beschreibung Deß Grausamen auffstands der Paurn im Landt Österreich Ob der Enß, so sich im Monath May deß 1616 Jars, wegen Der scharffen undt starkhen Reformation in Religion undt glaubenssachen, angefangen, Undt Biß in Monath Nouember dißes Jahr gewehret hat," *Taschenbuch für die vaterländische Geschichte* 42 (1856): 33.

58. See, for example, the letter written by Gerhard von Questenberg to fellow imperial official Franz Christoph Khevenhüller on 3 June 1626, printed in Walter Goetz, ed., *Die Politik Maximilians I. von Baiern und seiner Verbündeten 1618–1651*, part 1, vol. 3, *1626, 1627* (Leipzig, 1942), 208f.

The Peasants 223

59. For the contemporary interests, see Felix Stieve, *Der oberösterreichische Bauernaufstand des Jahres 1626*, vol. 1 (Munich, 1891), 218 and 220. For the differences between Catholic Habsburgian and liberal Bavarian historiographies in the 1800s one may compare the assessments in Franz Kurz, *Versuch einer Geschichte des Bauernkrieges in Oberösterreich unter der Anführung des Stephan Fadinger und Achatz Wiellinger* (Leipzig, 1805), and Felix Stieve, *Der oberösterreichische Bauernaufstand des Jahres 1626*, 2 vols. (Munich, 1891).

60. See Georg Grüll, *Der Bauer im Lande ob der Enns am Ausgang des 16. Jahrhunderts: Abgaben und Leistungen im Lichte der Beschwerden und Verträge von 1597–1598* (Linz, 1969), 219–223, 239; Hermann Rebel, *Peasant Classes: The Bureaucratization of Property and Family Relations under Early Habsburg Absolutism, 1511–1636* (Princeton, NJ, 1983), 239–245. In his economic history of Upper Austria, in contrast, Alfred Hoffmann concluded that the socioeconomic position of the Upper Austrian peasants was better than in surrounding territories, so that economic oppression could not explain the high number of peasant insurgencies in the territory. See Alfred Hoffmann, *Wirtschaftsgeschichte des Landes Oberösterreich*, vol. 1, *Werden, Wachsen, Reifen von der Frühzeit bis zum Jahre 1848* (Salzburg, 1952), 96.

61. Printed in Felix Stieve, *Der oberösterreichische Bauernaufstand des Jahres 1626*, vol. 2 (Munich, 1891), 244–260.

62. See "Gedechtnis des Bauren Kriegs im Jahr 1626," 1626, Oberösterreichisches Landesarchiv, Neuerwerbungen, Inventarnummer: Aktenband 102, no. 7.

63. This version comprising 15 articles is already presented in Franz Christoph Khevenhiller, *Annales Ferdinandei, oder Wahrhaffte Beschreibung Kaysers Ferdinandi des Andern*, vol. 10, 2nd ed. (Leipzig, 1724), 1129f., but reprinted based on an original source in Albin Czerny, "Einige Blätter aus der Zeit der Gegenreformation in Oberösterreich," *Jahrbuch des Oberösterreichischen Musealvereines* 42 (1884): 171f.

64. The English translation in the main text strives to retain some of the original's poetic nature. The rhymed early modern German "Weiß gilt die Seel vnd auch das guet, so gilts auch vnsser leib vnd bluet, Gott geb vnnss einen Hölten mueth," printed in Georg Grüll, *Bauer, Herr und Landesfürst: Sozialrevolutionäre Bestrebungen der oberösterreichischen Bauern von 1650 bis 1848* (Linz, 1963), 7, literally translates as "Because our soul and our belongings are on the line, so are our body and blood; may God instill heroic courage in us." The original of the anti-occupation verse, cited the same place, was "Vom Bayrischen Joch vnd Tyranney vnd seiner großen Schinderey, Mach vnnß O lieber Herr Gott frey."

65. Georg Grüll, *Bauer, Herr und Landesfürst: Sozialrevolutionäre Bestrebungen der oberösterreichischen Bauern von 1650 bis 1848* (Linz, 1963), 7.

66. See Felix Stieve, *Der oberösterreichische Bauernaufstand des Jahres 1626*, vol. 1 (Munich, 1891), 166.

67. Georg Heilingsetzer, *Der oberösterreichische Bauernkrieg 1626* (Vienna, 1976), 15.

68. For Pappenheim, see Barbara Stadler, *Pappenheim und die Zeit des Dreißigjährigen Krieges* (Winterthur, 1991), and Johann Eduard Heß, *Gottfried Heinrich, Graf zu Pappenheim* (Leipzig, 1855).

224 *The Peasants*

69. For this student, see "Kurtze und aigentliche Beschreibung Deß Grausamen auffstands der Paurn im Landt Österreich Ob der Enß, so sich im Monath May deß 1616 Jars, wegen Der scharffen undt starkhen Reformation in Religion undt glaubenssachen, angefangen, Undt Biß in Monath Nouember dißes Jahr gewehret hat," *Taschenbuch für die vaterländische Geschichte* 42 (1856): 20; as well as Felix Stieve, *Der oberösterreichische Bauernaufstand des Jahres 1626*, vol. 1 (Munich, 1891), 276f., 299, and 303; and Albin Czerny, *Bilder aus der Zeit der Bauernunruhen in Oberösterreich* (Linz, 1876), 51.

70. According to Albin Czerny, only one-tenth of the insurgents who lay siege to the city of Gmunden in one of the final major confrontations of the war owned a firearm, while most had to rely on clubs and spears. See Albin Czerny, *Bilder aus der Zeit der Bauernunruhen in Oberösterreich* (Linz, 1876), 51n1.

71. The letter is printed in Franz Kurz, *Beyträge zur Geschichte des Landes Oesterreich ob der Enns*, vol. 2 (Linz, 1808), 287–291.

72. Felix Stieve, *Der oberösterreichische Bauernaufstand des Jahres 1626*, vol. 1 (Munich, 1891), 301.

73. See Hans Fattinger, "Stefan Fadinger und Christoph Zeller: Ihre Familien und ihre Heimat," *Oberösterreichische Heimatblätter* 19 (1965): 53.

74. See Rullor 1632:26, fol. 152, 153a, 157, Kungliga Krigsarkivet Stockholm, Referenskod SE/SVAR/KrA-141010003/ D1, Svarnummer KO1556. Ennobled men could be found among common cavallerymen as well, as can be seen in the case of Mathias Nitsch in Rullor 1632:26, fol. 154b, Kungliga Krigsarkivet Stockholm, Referenskod SE/SVAR/KrA-141010003/ D1, Svarnummer KO1556.

75. See, for example, Paul Dedic, "Kärntner Exulanten des 17. Jahrhunderts," *Carinthia I* 140 (1950): 802.

76. For a modern-day introduction to Derfflinger, see Gerd-Ulrich Herrmann, *Georg Freiherr von Derfflinger* (Berlin, 1997).

77. For Derfflinger's family background, see Hans Hülber, "Georg Derfflinger—seine Vorfahren und der Lebensraum seiner frühen Jugend," *Oberösterreichische Heimatblätter* 37 (1983): 23–33.

78. The nineteenth-century novelist Theodor Fontane dealt extensively with Gusow und Derfflinger in his well-known *Wanderungen durch die Mark Brandenburg*. See Theodor Fontane, *Sämtliche Werke*, vol. 10, *Das Oderland* (Munich, 1960), 172–191.

79. As late as the final years of the Thirty Years' War, the Habsburgs appreciated the officer considerably less. At that time, Derfflinger led his Swedish army through Bohemia and Moravia and took up residence in the palace of the emperor's brother Leopold Wilhelm, bishop of Olomouc/Olmütz. See Lothar Höbelt, *Ferdinand III.(1608–1657): Friedenskaiser wider Willen* (Graz, 2008), 212.

80. *Allgemeine deutsche Biographie*, vol. 5 (Leipzig, 1877), 63.

81. Christian was duke of Holstein and commander of the empire's Lower Saxon Circle. For his role in the Thirty Years' War, see Paul Douglas Lockhart, *Denmark in the Thirty Years' War, 1618–1648: King Christian IV and the Decline of the Oldenburg State* (Selinsgrove, PA, 1996). A

The Peasants   225

standard biography of the king is Steffen Heiberg, *Christian 4: Monarken, Mennesket og Myten*, new and rev. ed. (Copenhagen, 2006).

82. See the assessments in "Kurtze und aigentliche Beschreibung Deß Grausamen auffstands der Paurn im Landt Österreich Ob der Enß, so sich im Monath May deß 1616 Jars, wegen Der scharffen undt starkhen Reformation in Religion undt glaubenssachen, angefangen, Undt Biß in Monath Nouember dißes Jahr gewehret hat," *Taschenbuch für die vaterländische Geschichte* 42 (1856): 65f.; Franz Kurz, *Versuch einer Geschichte des Bauernkrieges in Oberösterreich unter der Anführung des Stephan Fadinger und Achatz Wiellinger* (Leipzig, 1805), 270–272; and Felix Stieve, *Der oberösterreichische Bauernaufstand des Jahres 1626*, vol. 1 (Munich, 1891), 172.

83. Much of the correspondence between Bethlen and Christian is published in Vilmos Fraknói, "Bethlen Gábor és IV. Keresztély dán király (1625–1628): Közlemények a koppenhágai kir. levéltárból," *Magyar Történelmi Tár*, series 3, vol. 4 (1881): 98–113. The contacts between Bethlen and various European courts are also examined in Gábor Kármán and Kees Teszelszky, eds., *Bethlen Gábor és Európa* (Budapest, 2013).

84. The letter is printed in Franz Kurz, *Versuch einer Geschichte des Bauernkrieges in Oberösterreich unter der Anführung des Stephan Fadinger und Achatz Wiellinger* (Leipzig, 1805), 368–371.

85. Felix Stieve, *Der oberösterreichische Bauernaufstand des Jahres 1626*, vol. 1 (Munich, 1891), 206. Christian IV of Denmark and Gustavus Adolphus of Sweden paid close attention to these military endeavors as well and discussed possible contributions. See Carl Frederik Bricka and Julius Albert Fridericia, eds., *Kong Christian den Fjerdes egenhændige Breve*, vol. 2 (Copenhagen, 1889–1891), 33–40.

86. See the examples above and in the preceding chapter.

87. For Jakob Greimbl and the Upper Austrian uprising of 1632, see especially Franz Kurz, *Beyträge zur Geschichte des Landes Oesterreich ob der Enns*, vol. 2 (Linz, 1808), 1–390; Albin Czerny, *Bilder aus der Zeit der Bauernunruhen in Oberösterreich* (Linz, 1876), 159–270; and Friedrich Schober, "Zur Geschichte des Bauernaufstandes 1632," *Mitteilungen des Oberösterreichischen Landesarchivs* 2 (1950): 77–174. Franz Christoph Khevenhüller, who personally participated in the suppression of the rebellion, provided a contemporary description in his *Annales Ferdinandei, oder Wahrhaffte Beschreibung Kaysers Ferdinandi des Andern . . .*, 2nd ed., vol. 12 (Leipzig, 1727), 261–301.

88. See Renatus Karl von Senkenberg, *Versuch einer Geschichte des Teutschen Reichs im siebenzehnten Jahrhundert*, vol. 5 (Halle, 1795), 344, and Franz Karl Wißgrill, *Schauplatz des landsässigen Niederoesterreichischen Adels vom Herren- und Ritterstande von dem XI. Jahrhundert an bis auf jetzige Zeiten*, vol. 4 (Vienna, 1800), 362. Hofkirchen's first name is also rendered as Laurenz, Wolf Lorenz, and Wolf Laurenz.

89. If not referenced otherwise, the following is based on the criminal interrogation, held under the threat of torture, of the peasant deputy Thomas Ecklehner. It is printed in Franz Kurz, *Beyträge zur Geschichte des Landes Oesterreich ob der Enns*, vol. 2 (Linz, 1808), 51–64.

226 *The Peasants*

90. Albin Czerny, *Bilder aus der Zeit der Bauernunruhen in Oberösterreich* (Linz, 1876), 168.
91. Franz Kurz, *Beyträge zur Geschichte des Landes Oesterreich ob der Enns*, vol. 2 (Linz, 1808), 74.
92. Ibid., 79–81
93. Ibid., 112f.
94. Ibid., 71.
95. Ecklehner reported that Greimbl had publically called for a drink of wine to turn into poison if he had not been sent by Sweden and Saxony. See Franz Kurz, *Beyträge zur Geschichte des Landes Oesterreich ob der Enns*, vol. 2 (Linz, 1808), 51f.
96. Ibid., 55.
97. See ibid., 55, 59; Paul Dedic, *Kärntner Exulanten des 17. Jahrhunderts* (Klagenfurt, 1979), 392. For the initial contact, also Hans Khevenhüller played an important role.
98. Kungliga Vitterhets-, Historie- och Antiquitets-Akademien, ed., *Rikskansleren Axel Oxenstiernas skrifter och brefvexling*, vol. 1:7 (Stockholm, 1926), 547f.
99. For the following, see ibid., vol. 1:7 (Stockholm, 1926), 559–563.
100. Ibid., vol. 1:7 (Stockholm, 1926), 579; Franz Kurz, *Beyträge zur Geschichte des Landes Oesterreich ob der Enns*, vol. 2 (Linz, 1808), 54.
101. For the following, see ibid., vol. 1:7 (Stockholm, 1926), 559–561.
102. For the following, see ibid., vol. 2:1 (Stockholm, 1888), 840–842.
103. Ibid., vol. 1:7 (Stockholm, 1926), 569.
104. See ibid., vol. 1:7 (Stockholm, 1926), 614, and ibid., vol. 2:1 (Stockholm, 1888), 857.
105. For a Marxist perspective that both emphasized the hopes placed on Gustavus Adolphus by the imperial peasantry and the reluctance of the king to fulfill them, see B. F. Porshnev, *Muscovy and Sweden in the Thirty Years' War, 1630–1635* (Cambridge, England, 1995), 165–207. Porshnev's conclusions about Gustavus' disinterest in the Upper Austrians are not confirmed by the king's letters to Oxenstierna, however. For the near-mythical expectations to Gustavus Adolphus among Bohemian Protestants at home and in exile, see Per Magnus Hebbe, *Svenskarna i Böhmen och Mähren: Studier i tjeckisk folktradition och litteratur* (Uppsala, 1932), 1–31; for the exiles, see also Alfred Jensen, *Svenska minnen från Böhmen och Mähren: Kulturhistoriska skisser från trettioåriga kriget* (Lund, 1910), 74–80.
106. Both Swedish and Bavarian sources refer to the detachment of a small Swedish vanguard to Upper Austria, but there are no signs of its engagement in the conflict. See Kungliga Vitterhets-, Historie- och Antiquitets-Akademien, ed., *Rikskansleren Axel Oxenstiernas skrifter och brefvexling*, vol. 1:7 (Stockholm, 1926), 576, and Albin Czerny, *Bilder aus der Zeit der Bauernunruhen in Oberösterreich* (Linz, 1876), 171.
107. Greimbl was cruelly beheaded and displayed in Linz on 19 February 1633. Nimmervoll and Luegmayer escaped to the Swedes, however. See Franz Christoph Khevenhüller, *Annales Ferdinandei, oder Wahrhaffte Beschreibung Kaysers Ferdinandi des Andern . . .*, 2nd ed., vol. 12 (Leipzig, 1727), 499; Friedrich Schober, "Zur Geschichte des Bauernaufstandes

The Peasants 227

1632," *Mitteilungen des Oberösterreichischen Landesarchivs* 2 (1950): 185; and Wenzel Kopal, *Geschichte der Stadt Eferding* (Linz, 1875), 115f.

108. For Laimbauer and his rebellion, see Franz Wilflingseder, "Martin Laimbauer und die Unruhen im Machlandviertel, 1632–1636," *Mitteilungen des Oberösterreichischen Landesarchivs* 6 (1959): 136–202; Franz Christoph Khevenhüller, *Annales Ferdinandei, oder Wahrhaffte Beschreibung Kaysers Ferdinandi des Andern . . .*, 2nd ed., vol. 12 (Leipzig, 1727), 1955–1957; and with a special focus on spiritual and anthropological aspects Ernst Burgstaller, "Martin Laimbauer und seine Machländische Bauernbewegung: Versuch einer volkskundlichen Durchleuchtung," *Kunstjahrbuch der Stadt Linz 1973* (1974): 3–30.

109. Franz Wilflingseder, "Martin Laimbauer und die Unruhen im Machlandviertel, 1632–1636," *Mitteilungen des Oberösterreichischen Landesarchivs* 6 (1959): 141.

110. See ibid., 196, 198.

111. The Machland no longer forms one of Upper Austria's four quarters today. Following the acquisition of the Innviertel region from Bavaria in the late 1700s, the formerly distinct Machlandviertel merged into an enlarged Mühlviertel region.

112. See Ernst Burgstaller, "Martin Laimbauer und seine Machländische Bauernbewegung: Versuch einer volkskundlichen Durchleuchtung," *Kunstjahrbuch der Stadt Linz 1973* (1974): 6f. Laimbauer admitted in his interrogation that he had also resorted to coercive drafts, but their success seems to have been limited. See Franz Wilflingseder, "Martin Laimbauer und die Unruhen im Machlandviertel, 1632–1636," *Mitteilungen des Oberösterreichischen Landesarchivs* 6 (1959): 205.

113. For details of the battle, see Franz Wilflingseder, "Martin Laimbauer und die Unruhen im Machlandviertel, 1632–1636," *Mitteilungen des Oberösterreichischen Landesarchivs* 6 (1959): 173–176. Kuefstein was himself a recent convert to Catholicism. For his biography, see Madeleine Welsersheimb, "Hans Ludwig von Kuefstein (1582–1656)" (Ph.D. diss., University of Vienna, 1970).

114. For a description of the arrest from a hostile perspective, see Albin Czerny, *Ein Tourist in Österreich während der Schwedenzeit: Aus den Papieren des Pater Reginbald Möhner, Benedictiners von St. Ulrich in Augsburg* (Linz, 1874), 53f.

115. In the beginning, this absence of explicit political goals actually protected him, as officials and landlords struggled to assess his relevance.

116. Franz Christoph Khevenhüller, *Annales Ferdinandei, oder Wahrhaffte Beschreibung Kaysers Ferdinandi des Andern . . .*, 2nd ed., vol. 12 (Leipzig, 1727), 1955.

117. For this characterization, see the excerpts from Laimbauer's criminal interrogation, partially produced by torture, printed in Franz Wilflingseder, "Martin Laimbauer und die Unruhen im Machlandviertel, 1632–1636," *Mitteilungen des Oberösterreichischen Landesarchivs* 6 (1959): 204–206. German mythology has assigned Emperor Frederick Barbarossa several mountains, in which he lies asleep with his army until he returns to restitute the medieval empire. For a recent examination of the Barbarossa legend

228   *The Peasants*

in modern national symbolism, see Camilla G. Kaul, *Friedrich Barbarossa im Kyffhäuser: Bilder eines nationalen Mythos im 19. Jahrhundert*, 2 vols. (Cologne, 2007).

118. William Crowne, *A True Relation of All the Remarkable Places and Passages Observed in the Travels of the Right Honourable Thomas Lord Hovvard, Earle of Arundell and Surrey, Primer Earle, and Earle Marshall of England, Ambassadour Extraordinary to His Sacred Majesty Ferdinando the Second, Emperour of Germanie, Anno Domini 1636* (London, 1637). The subsequent citations are based on the modernized version of Francis C. Springell, ed., *Connoisseur and Diplomat: The Earl of Arundel's Embassy to Germany in 1636 as Recounted in William Crowne's Diary, the Earl's Letters and Other Contemporary Sources, with a Catalogue of the Topographical Drawings Made on the Journey by Wenceslaus Hollar* (London, 1963).

119. Francis C. Springell, ed., *Connoisseur and Diplomat: The Earl of Arundel's Embassy to Germany in 1636 as Recounted in William Crowne's Diary, the Earl's Letters and Other Contemporary Sources, with a Catalogue of the Topographical Drawings Made on the Journey by Wenceslaus Hollar* (London, 1963), 65.

120. Ibid.

121. It is assumed that the boy in question was Laimbauer's four-year-old son. See Ernst Burgstaller, "Martin Laimbauer und seine Machländische Bauernbewegung: Versuch einer volkskundlichen Durchleuchtung," *Kunstjahrbuch der Stadt Linz 1973* (1974): 4; Karl Eichmeyer, Helmuth Feigl, and Rudolf Walter Litschel, *Weiß gilt die Seel und auch das Guet: Oberösterreichische Bauernaufstände und Bauernkriege im 16. und 17. Jahrhundert* (Linz, 1976), 166.

122. For the sporadic signs of unrest, see Albin Czerny, *Bilder aus der Zeit der Bauernunruhen in Oberösterreich* (Linz, 1876), 273–298.

123. See, for example, the codicil to his 1621 testament, printed in Gustav Turba, *Die Grundlagen der pragmatischen Sanktion*, vol. 2, *Die Hausgesetze* (Leipzig-Vienna, 1912), 351–355.

124. See, for example, Stephanus Julius Brutus [pseud. for Philippe Duplessis-Mornay or Hubert Languet], *Vindiciae contra tyrannos: Or, Concerning the Legitimate Power of a Prince over the People, and of the People over a Prince*, ed. George Garnett (Cambridge, England, 1994), 168f.

125. For the text of the resolution, see Georg Grüll, *Der Bauer im Lande ob der Enns am Ausgang des 16. Jahrhunderts: Abgaben und Leistungen im Lichte der Beschwerden und Verträge von 1597–1598* (Linz, 1969), 240–244. For the context, see also Josef Löffler, *Der zweite oberösterreichische Bauernaufstand 1594–1597 im Mühlviertel: Versuch einer systematischen Darstellung* (Saarbrücken, 2009), and Albin Czerny, *Der zweite Bauernaufstand in Oberösterreich 1595–1597* (Linz, 1890).

126. See Hans Sturmberger, *Adam Graf Herberstorff: Herrschaft und Freiheit im konfessionellen Zeitalter* (Munich, 1976), 201.

127. Franz Kurz, *Beyträge zur Geschichte des Landes Oesterreich ob der Enns*, vol. 2 (Linz, 1808), 171f.; Karl Eichmeyer, Helmuth Feigl, and Rudolf Walter Litschel, *Weiß gilt die Seel und auch das Guet: Oberösterreichische Bauernaufstände und Bauernkriege im 16. und 17. Jahrhundert* (Linz, 1976), 163.

The Peasants   229

128. See Michael Forcher, *Michael Gaismair: Um Freiheit und Gerechtigkeit* (Innsbruck, 1982), 147.

129. Lothar Höbelt, *Ferdinand III. (1609–1657): Friedenskaiser wider Willen* (Graz, 2008), 227. See also the continuing concerns until the very end of the war that are discernible in Samuel von Pufendorf, *Herrn Samuel von Pufendorf Sechs und Zwantzig Bücher der Schwedisch- und Deutschen Kriegs-Geschichte* . . . (Frankfurt and Leipzig, 1688), 520.

130. See Albin Czerny, *Bilder aus der Zeit der Bauernunruhen in Oberösterreich* (Linz, 1876), 278f.

131. See Hermann Rebel, *Peasant Classes: The Bureaucratization of Property and Family Relations under Early Habsburg Absolutism, 1511–1636* (Princeton, NJ, 1983), 201.

7 Beyond Habsburg
A Conclusion

Monarchy Triumphant

The first half of the seventeenth century formed a turning point in Habsburg history. The future of the dynasty was at stake. Depending on the fortunes of war, it could have lost its core patrimony or established a powerful monarchy for all of Germany. In the end, three decades of fighting resulted in a dichotomous solution. The Habsburgs lost further ground in the Holy Roman Empire but established full control over their hereditary lands.

This outcome was not preordained. The politics of Austria's Protestant estates proved particularly controversial. Some called them rebellious.[1] Others called them overly accommodating.[2] And many argued that Inner Austrian passivity, especially, had saved the dynasty.[3] Yet in an era of mercenary warfare, it was financial solvency rather than popular support that decided military conflicts. Local resources only constituted one element of political and military power. Even though the Habsburgs were domestically outmatched in the Bohemian and Danubian lands in 1620, their superior international standing brought them victory. The Spanish branch of the family reinforced the emperor's political and military position. The curia provided subsidies and diplomatic backing. The intervention of Maximilian of Bavaria and the Catholic League decided central battles. Even the powerful Bohemian estates collapsed in the face of this coalition. It is difficult to see how their much weaker Danubian and Alpine peers would have fared better.

The lack of solidarity among the Protestant opposition played an important role, however. Internationally, German Protestantism was too divided to challenge the House of Habsburg. The Evangelical Union proved no match for its Catholic counterpart. Deep divisions between Lutherans and Calvinists prevented comprehensive alliances. The 1550 switch from the Albertine to the Ernestine branch of the Wettin dynasty in Lutheranism's initial bastion, the Electorate of Saxony, had left a lasting mark on imperial politics. It placed the former cadet branch in deep obligation to the Habsburgs, who had made this transfer possible, and fundamentally changed the principality's role in German politics. From being stalwarts of the Reformation and protectors of Luther and his disciples, the Saxon electors become centrist mediators between a Catholic emperorship and its loyal Lutheran subjects.[4] The final step was taken when Augustus the Strong converted to Catholicism to become king of Poland in 1697.[5]

Domestically, the Habsburgs were able to take down heterodox challengers one by one, often aided by external military and, not least of all, financial support. Once more, the peasants mustered the strongest military challenge. Held up to the gruesome fighting that devastated Upper Austria in 1626, the estates' timid attempts at resistance in 1618–1620 paled in significance. Yet standing alone against cooperating princes, the rural insurgents went down in defeat as well. In defense of the existing monarchic order, otherwise rivaling domestic and international elites found common ground. This social aspect also underscores the limits of the confessionalization paradigm. Identification with the emerging denominational bodies strongly influenced early modern Austrians, but it did not overshadow all other allegiances. The upper echelons of society, in particular, saw religion as a pillar of their status and habitus, not as an alternative to it. The Protestant nobles may have interceded in favor of suppressed coreligionists at court, but they were not ready to join the rebellion of commoners. Only in times of acute crisis, such as the collapse of the estatist regime in Bohemia in 1620, were there calls for social transformation in the name of confessional mobilization.[6] Protestant resistance in the Habsburgs' hereditary lands never evolved into an all-embracing mass movement comparable to its Hussite antecedent.

One could also argue that the peasants failed because they were insufficiently radical. With few exceptions, the rural insurgents did not attempt to imitate the Swiss, as their opponents so consistently insinuated. After their initial successes they reverted to dialogue, since most of them only sought to modify the existing societal structure. The peasants surrendered the strategic advantage of being entrenched in the territory. The princes gained time to recruit and deploy mercenaries. It became standard procedure for a besieged government to disrupt the insurgents' advance by calling for negotiations. These negotiations brought few results, while allowing the government to divide moderates and radicals and gather strength for a decisive military intervention.

The only domestic alternative would have been a popular front against an oppressive dynasty. The Upper Austrian peasants also appealed to

232 Beyond Habsburg

their aristocratic coreligionists in 1626, but the nobles remained evasive.[7] Plans to liberate serfs and tenants only surfaced when all had been lost on the battlefield. With few exceptions, these suggestions came too early for Austria's aristocracy. In the end, most nobles found it easier to relinquish their faith than their status. It was mere battle lore when friend and foe reported to have seen the exiled Baron of Tschernembl fighting with his Protestant brethren in the peasant army.[8]

The struggle for the confessional future of the Habsburg Monarchy was interwoven with the conflict between monarchy and estates. As a consequence, Habsburg history also advances the analysis of absolutism. It directs the focus toward content rather than form, toward practice rather than theory. The history of the Habsburg estates combines formal continuity with functional transformation. Throughout the core territories of the monarchy, the estates never disappeared from the public limelight in the seventeenth and eighteenth century.[9] On the surface, they also retained substantial political rights, especially in regard to taxation. Even in Bohemia, where the attempt to depose the dynasty resulted in the military defeat of 1620 and the Renewed Land Ordinance of 1627, the outward appearance of estatist institutions changed remarkably little.

It would nonetheless be misleading to conclude that the Austrian or Bohemian estates effectively upheld their political influence beyond the Thirty Years' War and therefore demonstrate the extension of mixed government into a correspondingly mislabeled era of absolutism. To be sure, the Habsburg experience highlights the survival of the estatist nobility as a corporation with customary legal, social, and economic privileges. Nobles also remained important for the financial and military administration of the monarchy. The political role of the estates was fundamentally altered in the early 1600s, however. The Austrian and Bohemian estates never regained the status of autonomous complements to monarchic power, which they had so vehemently claimed at the turn of the seventeenth century. The history of the Habsburg lands shows that it is not sufficient to examine the existence or nonexistence of estatist institutions or even their formal constitutional status. In order to provide a full picture of governmental practice in early modern Europe, the legal framework needs to be seen in combination with its ideological foundation and its political implementation.

Interpretation and Harmonization

This study does not restrict itself to the history of power in early modern Austria. It also examines two interrelated but distinct conceptual

Beyond Habsburg   233

questions. It explores the visions of seventeenth-century Austrians who dared to imagine alternatives to the ruling dynasty. Some developed these thoughts in peacetime, while they were still integrated in their native society. Many only embraced them after their involuntary emigration. Some were explicit: they challenged the right of monarchs to impose their religious convictions on their subjects and defined the territorial estates as the true representatives of the *res publica*, who could also reject a sovereign who did not adhere to customary law and practice. Others never arrived at an equally coherent ideology of state. They merely yearned for relief from spiritual and social oppression and put their hopes on a foreign monarch, whom much of the empire's Protestant public had adopted as one of their own.

Yet the study also explores the commemorative afterlife of these events. It questions the fixation of Austrian public memory on a governmental perspective that only constituted one understanding of contemporary Austrian politics; if one contrasts the societal forces that were engaged in the conflict, arguably not even the most representative one. This unilateral dependence on one historical tradition has diverse origins. It reflects the educational efforts of Habsburg state-building, which elevated the dynastic polity of Baroque Catholicism into a symbol of collective identity. At the same time, it underlines the retrospective vision of historical interpretation. When modern-day Austrians think of domestic Protestantism, they do not visualize the vibrant mass movement of the Reformation era that had stirred and transformed contemporary society. Instead, they envision the marginal Lutheran Church of their personal experience, no less orthodox and institutionalized than its Catholic counterpart but much less enshrined in the everyday lives of most citizens. This makes it easier to understand why so many identify with a government that their ancestors experienced as oppressive.

Yet the adoption of select perspectives is only one of many mechanisms that transform historical recollection. Even those who moved beyond the limitations of dynastic or confessional historiography, be it Catholic or Protestant, frequently remained caught in the intransigent web that connects past and present. Some downplayed the repercussions of public policy. In defense of Ferdinand II, they emphasized his legalist approach, intimating that the Protestant estates had forfeited their religious privileges as rightful punishment for obstinacy and rebellion.[10] Yet the ostensible legalism of Ferdinand and his secular and ecclesial supporters had a distinctive character. Its roots lay in political realism, not in an abstract respect for the law. As far back as the 1570s, allies and councilors had advised the Habsburg princes to forego open breaches of

234 Beyond Habsburg

sworn concessions in favor of their gradual erosion. The Munich Conference of 1579 suggested an inconspicuous and indirect approach, and Rudolf II received the same advice from the courts in Munich, Innsbruck, and Graz.[11] The rationale of this advice was formulated clearly: any premature provocation of a still solid Protestant majority held unforeseeable consequences. Since the monarchs defined confessional liberties as personal concessions tied to the regency of individual rulers, it was preferable to dilute the position of Protestantism in society and confine it to an increasingly isolated aristocratic sphere. In time, new rulers would be better positioned to curtail the remaining privileges of the nobility.

This remarkably successful policy followed political expediency, not legal positivism. Their spiritual advisers had repeatedly assured the princes that they were not bound by concessions to Protestants. These privileges were the result of insubordination and blackmail; God did not condone an oath that was given under duress.[12] Thus, the increasingly restrictive redefinitions of denominational liberties did not so much reflect a change in ideology or interpretation but the steady reinforcement of Catholic political power, which made such redefinitions enforceable. The failed rebellion of Bohemian and Austrian Protestants provided Ferdinand with a unique opportunity to reorganize state and religion in his own image. Yet the fate of Inner Austrian Protestantism demonstrates that formal loyalty did not protect from involuntary recatholization. Ultimately, Ferdinand saw himself as both entitled and obligated to determine the religious orientation of his subjects, which made the continued adherence to Protestantism disloyal in itself.

Yet legal positivism is quite generally a blunt instrument of historical analysis. The law owns the present, where it always seems to prevail, since its interpretations tend to echo the existing distribution of power. As a consequence, the defeated nobles were sentenced for rebellion and high treason. If estatist interpretations had won out, the dynasty would have paid the price. For modern observers, in contrast, the fine points of seventeenth-century jurisprudence are of minor significance. Virtually all political systems define fundamental opposition as treasonous. Their judgments are not binding on subsequent regimes, however. Monarchic absolutism was a fleeting phase of societal development. It was not instituted by popular consent or subject to democratic challenge. It would strike most readers as peculiar if today's works of history were to judge the burning of Christians by the legal conventions of ancient Rome. To be sure, historical writing rarely profits from imposing anachronistic moral standards. Yet neither should it be beholden to the reverse anachronism of contemporaneous jurisprudence. Historians need to understand why early modern monarchs felt entitled to prescribe the religious orientation of their subjects, but they do not have to validate their judicial justifications.

By the same token, the recurring imagery of Protestant devotion to the dynasty cannot reflect a more composite reality. This *topos* characterized a post-toleration consensus historiography that strove to reintegrate the remaining Protestants into Austrian public life. It appealed both to Protestants intent on underscoring their patriotic credentials and to a more accommodating wing of governmental conservatism, which was willing to offer a societal niche to a Protestant minority that did not challenge the dynastic legacy.[13] Yet unconditional loyalty was no unshakable guidepost of Austrian Protestantism. To be sure, the nobility of Inner Austria refrained from armed resistance. It was confirmed in this position by spiritual advisers such as Jakob Andreæ, who justified monarchic prerogative through a sacralization of Luther's much more situational concept of suffering obedience.[14] These theologians from Protestant territorial churches and universities reflected the institutionalization of Lutheranism. They lived in polities in which the new creed had established itself as theology of state. Gone was the spirit of rebellion. Lutheranism was the new orthodoxy, and local rulers were heads of church. It was not surprising that these authorities emphasized respect for positive law and government.

Yet Austrian Lutherans did not universally follow their advice. From the very beginning, burghers and nobles in both Inner Austria and the archduchy resorted to protests and supplications; they engaged in drawn-out legal arguments and appealed for support from foreign coreligionists. They refused taxes and contributions or tied them to religious counter-claims. In the archduchy, a substantial segment of the Protestant aristocracy eventually supported the Bohemian resistance. Even those who shrank from this ultimate step were guided by caution as much as loyalty. As repeatedly demonstrated by Habsburg history, open rebellion carried grave risks.

The oppositional facets of Protestant estatism have long been known. Austrian historiography largely ascribed them to the central role of Calvinists such as Georg Erasmus von Tschernembl. This interpretation built on Ernst Troeltsch's influential thesis distinguishing between obedient Lutheranism and rebellious, freedom-seeking Calvinism.[15] Troeltsch's interpretation was widely adopted, not least of all because it seemed to explain the societal differences between modern Germany and the English-speaking world. In Austria, it informed Hans Sturmberger's pathbreaking biography of Georg Erasmus von Tschernembl, which emphasized the Calvinist foundations of the resistance leader.

236 Beyond Habsburg

In recent decades, the dichotomy of docile Lutheranism and defiant Calvinism has been questioned. In detailed studies, historians such as Robert von Friedeburg and Arno Strohmeyer have shown the interconnections and situational adaptations of both traditions.[16] In regard to Austria, any unilateral focus on Calvinist intellectual traditions faces additional challenges. It is difficult to see why the overwhelmingly Lutheran nobles of Upper and Lower Austria would have yielded to a miniscule minority. At the turn of the seventeenth century, the Upper Austrian nobility contained a mere handful of Calvinists and a small but growing Catholic element, whereas the great majority adhered to Lutheranism.[17] Since the followers of the Augsburg Confession were the only tolerated heterodox Christians, local Calvinists included themselves in this definition and downplayed doctrinal differences within Protestantism. As a consequence, the denominational tensions impeding Protestant solidarity among the princes of the empire did not prevent Georg Erasmus von Tschernembl's rise to regional influence. The close relationship with Bohemian and Hungarian allies, who frequently held Calvinist or yet other reformist views, also precluded a narrow focus on Lutheran orthodoxy.[18] Only in the final phase of estatist resistance did subtle disagreements become more visible.[19]

The biographies of Austria's Calvinist nobles reflect Protestant universalism. Time proved too short for intergenerational continuity; the leading representatives of reformed thought in Austria were all raised as Lutherans and personally attracted to its Genevan alternative in adulthood. Calvinist spiritual and political leaders had established a reputation for activism both within the Holy Roman Empire and outside. This reputation derived primarily from their resistance to Catholic rulers and their confessional mandates. The reorientation of individual Austrian Lutherans toward Calvinism also expressed an embrace of this image and its call to arms. In other words: Tschernembl and his confreres were not radicalized by Calvinist socialization, but their opposition to recatholization attracted them to a more activist theology. Since both interpretations premise the greater militancy of Calvinism, the distinction may seem subtle. Its implications are significant nonetheless. Faced with a determined attempt to return their territories to Catholicism, a majority of Austrian Protestant nobles initially took a stand. Most of them remained Lutherans. A few became Calvinists. Their fundamental spiritual and political socialization was the same.

In contrast to their Danubian peers, the nobles in Inner Austria refrained from armed resistance. They have, therefore, served to exemplify suffering obedience. Yet even the more accommodating stance of the Inner Austrian aristocracy concealed a more multifaceted reality. There always existed a strain of resistance in Styria and Carinthia.[20] At the height of the early Thirty Years' War in the Bohemian and Danubian lands, rumors of Inner Austrian restlessness reached friend and foe alike.[21] The Venetian ambassador to Vienna described the religious grumblings he had encountered throughout Inner Austria and the threats to join the Bohemians.[22] The estates once again chose a cautious approach that minimized the danger of military expenses and devastations, but it was a decision guided by pragmatism rather than theological constraints. The Inner Austrian nobles kept quiet in 1618 because they clung to status and possessions, not because they chafed under the spiritual yoke of suffering obedience.

Drawing their lessons from Ferdinand's recatholization of his hereditary domains, which the local estates had not been able to prevent by peaceful means, the nobles of the archduchy decided to take a stand. Their peers in Inner Austria kept calm. It made little difference. In the end, both communities were put before the choice between conversion and emigration. In fact, the only ones to escape this fate were those Lower Austrian nobles who relented while Ferdinand still felt besieged enough to make concessions. In some sense, they were the indirect profiteers of Protestant resistance, whereas their equally pacific Inner Austrian peers had no rebellion from which they could be compensated to abstain. Just like their Catholic counterparts, Austria's Protestants subjected their ideological programs to considerations of feasibility and *realpolitik*.

Neither Phoenix Nor Mere Ashes

With the end of the Thirty Years' War, Catholic restoration was secured. Even such territories as Upper Austria and Carinthia, where a substantial majority of not only the political elites but also the general population had embraced the new faith, were returned to the fold. After most peasants and townspeople had faced this agonizing decision several decades earlier, also the Protestant aristocracy was forced to choose between conversion and emigration in the late 1620s. The dynasty had prevailed both politically and confessionally. The era of open resistance was over.

The turnaround was most complete in the formerly most Protestant segments of society, burghers and nobles. Urban Protestantism was depleted by repeated waves of voluntary and involuntary emigrations. This exodus did not only weaken the heterodox community numerically but also deprived it of its most activist element. The replacement of Protestant officials with confessionally reliable newcomers further accelerated the

238 Beyond Habsburg

restoration of the old faith. In public appearance, Austria's towns and cities soon reflected an image of Catholic orthodoxy.

Below this surface, the process took longer. The gradual dissipation of now universally prohibited heterodoxy proceeded largely unseen. In spite of more than 200 emigrants and the seeming conversion of the remaining Protestants, a confessional registry from Upper Austrian Steyr still listed 22 Lutherans in 1652.[23] In Carinthian Klagenfurt, the burghers still elected a Protestant mayor in the 1620s, two decades after the official return of the city to Catholicism.[24] The municipal priest ascribed this to the persisting confessional deviance of influential citizens. Also thereafter, the Catholic parish registry continued to identify heretics. Many of them were the wives of townsmen who had converted to escape deportation. In the narrow confines of urban society, without access to communal practice with pastors and coreligionists, the increasingly isolated dissenters proved unable to pass on their beliefs. Their children were socialized into the encompassing world of Baroque Catholicism.

The conversion of the nobles began later but proceeded more rapidly. Regular interaction with the court put the aristocracy under even closer scrutiny. The dramatic exodus that followed the revocation of confessional privileges transformed the estate. Not all Protestants left immediately, to be sure. Individual pragmatists hoped to weather the turmoil through public accommodation and private dissent. Such attitudes rarely survived into the next generation. The public life that was so important for the nobility had no place for confessional evasion.

This bitter truth was soon to be learned by Austria's only heterodox Christians who still enjoyed religious privileges. Timely homage to Ferdinand II during the crisis of 1620 had secured a substantial segment of Lower Austria's Protestant aristocracy a promise of confessional latitude. Unlike their peers in Upper and Inner Austria, they did not have to leave the country at the end of the decade. Their dispensation to exercise the Augsburg Confession was interpreted increasingly more narrowly, however. The expulsion of all Protestant pastors and teachers in 1627 effectively reduced tolerated heterodoxy to freedom of conscience; its formal practice was only permissible abroad.[25] The Protestant nobles had to appoint Catholic priests in the churches for which they still held the right of presentation. Catholics also secured a permanent majority among estatist officers, effectively ending Protestant influence in the diet.[26] Administrative positions became just as elusive, and by 1652 only three estatist clerks were still listed as heterodox.[27]

Even this narrow toleration was endangered by monarchic succession. Ferdinand III had not explicitly confirmed his father's confessional dispensations. As a consequence, peace negotiations in Westphalia formed the final opportunity for securing constitutional safeguards. The gravity of the situation was not lost on the remaining dissidents. In a remarkable step, domestic and exiled Lower Austrian Protestants jointly approached sympathetic delegations.[28] Their memoranda and documents largely echoed the estatist arguments of earlier decades, supporting the demand for religious freedom with the historical development and constitutional status of the archduchy. Yet in spite of persistent attempts by the Swedish delegation, especially, the restoration of prewar conditions proved impossible. The emperor staunchly refused to reopen the confessional question in his patrimony. As a minimal concession, the Treaty of Osnabrück protected the Lutheran nobles still residing in Lower Austria from forced emigration and allowed them to attend Lutheran services beyond the border.[29] Thus, the toleration of noble Protestantism in Lower Austria had been elevated from princely favor to international treaty provision.

In the long run, its constitutional protection failed to save Lower Austrian Protestantism. In 1650 approximately 150 of 420 territorial nobles still adhered to Lutheranism, but growing social isolation eroded their position.[30] The renewed drive for confessional homogenization in the aftermath of the war finally put an end to peasant heterodoxy, turning Protestant landlords into tolerated outsiders on their own estates. Public office was increasingly closed to them. The resulting withdrawal into private life triggered a late cultural bloom, which has survived in the writings of Wolf Helmhard von Hohberg, Hans Wilhelm von Stubenberg, and Catharina Regina von Greiffenberg.[31] It was the afterglow of Protestant intellectual life in early modern Austria.

Over the subsequent decades, conversion and emigration continually depleted the Protestant nobility. The prospect of reintegration into courtly society with its promise of wealth and status was seductive to many. Yet there was more at play than the desire for personal and familial ascent. Lutheranism had lost the allure of its founding period, both theologically and as a cultural milieu. Even descendants of emigrants turned back and embraced the religion of the dynasty. David von Ungnad, son of Tschernembl's fellow activist and exile Andreas von Ungnad, advanced to president of the state treasury.[32] Johann Quintin Jörger, scion of a family instrumental in the establishment and defense of Austrian Lutheranism, returned to a spectacular career in public service.[33] Gundaker von Dietrichstein, whose father Bartholomäus died in unreconstructed opposition to the dynasty at Hanau, converted around 1650 and rose to princehood, while his brother Christian remained in Lutheran exile.[34] And Ernreich

240 *Beyond Habsburg*

Khevenhüller, whose father Sigmund had left Carinthia in 1629, returned in the 1660s to secure his ancestral estate of Hochosterwitz.[35]

The unconverted holdouts increasingly looked for alternatives abroad. Recurring affronts, such as the prohibition to be buried in now Catholic family tombs and the surrender of Lutheran orphans to Catholic guardians, reminded them of their tenuous position.[36] Many established second domiciles in Protestant Germany and began to administer their estates from afar. Over time, this geographical and emotional ambiguity proved too burdensome, and subsequent generations saw their future in the more accommodating settings of the new country. By the eighteenth century, the number of Protestants had dwindled to insignificance, and in the 1760s the last remaining families sold their Lower Austrian possessions or converted.[37]

Peasants

Thus it was the peasantry, originally less thoroughly converted to the new creed than other segments of society, in which the final remnants of Lutheranism survived. Legally, the remaining sanctuaries of peasant heterodoxy had been abolished by the 1620s. The termination of noble privileges also closed loopholes for their subjects. Rural emigration picked up. Its impact was not as immediate as the noble exodus, even if it numerically exceeded it by far. During the war, emigration was still limited. Adverse moving conditions reduced its appeal and the government's military priorities its urgency. As soon as the peace accord had confirmed the confessional status of the hereditary lands, however, the authorities started a determined effort to bring Catholization to a successful end.

The preparatory mandates and instructions for the reinstituted reformation commissions in Lower Austria illustrate the process. At first, local priests identified potential heretics.[38] Thereafter, the commissions summoned the suspects and gave them six weeks to decide between conversion and emigration.[39] During that period, they received obligatory religious counseling. To discourage departures, the commissioners elaborated their dire economic and personal consequences. Village leaders were offered special privileges if they converted but were separated from the community if they refused. Careful reports and controls were to ensure the lasting success of the effort.

The commission reports also showed the extent of the problem. Decades after its legal prohibition, Protestantism still had a hold in the general population. This was especially true for the northwestern quarter of the territory known as Waldviertel. This region bordering Upper Austria and the Bohemian lands had long been a Protestant bastion. Even after the confiscations of 1620, it was equally divided between Catholic and Protestant landlords.[40] Although the latter had lost the right to appoint Lutheran pastors, they had mitigated the impact of confessional mandates. Not surprisingly, the regional commission still found twenty percent Lutherans in a population of approximately 100,000.

The renewed drive for confessional homogeneity made significant progress, even if its practical outcome deviated appreciably from the published reports. According to the official résumé, 22,224 newly converted had joined the Catholic majority, whereas only a few hundred had chosen emigration.[41] The sincerity of many conversions remained doubtful, however, so that the commissions revisited problem areas.[42] More important was the divergence between factual and reported emigration. A substantial portion of the summoned had only relented to gain time. Some hoped to outlast yet another commission. Others saw conversion as an opportunity to alleviate their inevitable departure, securing more favorable conditions for the transfer of property. As a consequence, many newly converted subsequently showed up as immigrants in the Protestant territories of southern Germany.[43] Overall, around 7,000 left the Waldviertel between 1620 and 1660.[44]

Corresponding developments throughout the hereditary lands coalesced into a substantial relocation movement. The heavily devastated districts of central Franconia proved especially attractive because they combined confessional safety with economic opportunity. More than 30,000 left the archduchy for this region in the 1600s, but also Swabia and other south German territories experienced a significant influx.[45] Together with the inner acceptance of the religious turnaround among those who stayed, this final exodus marked the end of territorial Protestantism in the Danubian provinces.

Crypto-Protestantism

Austrian Lutheranism went underground. With the successful renewal of confessional homogenization in the 1650s, at the latest, clandestine perseverance had become the only option for remaining holdouts. Although the term crypto-Protestantism may overemphasize the concealment of the phenomenon, whose collective presence often formed an open secret, it has established itself firmly in scholarly discourse.[46] It could be defined as the individual or collective insistence on Protestant heterodoxy in the

242   *Beyond Habsburg*

face of public prohibitions and sanctions.[47] In its Austrian context, it produced a distinctive Lutheran lay Christianity that persisted within and coexisted with public Catholicism.

The covert retention of heterodox beliefs relied on multiple factors. It was facilitated by the geographical seclusion and familial self-sufficiency of Alpine communities, even if the long-perpetuated imagery of isolated mountain farms simplified a more complex reality. In other communities, seasonal trading and working sojourns provided access to Protestant ecclesial life. Crypto-Protestants could draw on the support of émigrés such as the Salzburg lay preacher Josef Schaitberger, whose missives from exile provided spiritual comfort and guidance; they were widely distributed among underground Protestants and combined into books.[48] At times, sympathetic coreligionists in the empire provided spiritual and political assistance.[49] Carefully hidden religious texts were handed down through generations and supplemented with contraband from Protestant territories. The authorities did not miss the importance of this literature, and book raids regularly challenged the coexistence of public conformity and covert heterodoxy. The detection of Protestant writings called for official action. The loss of their beloved texts, in turn, provoked previously silent dissidents into openly demanding religious concessions or free emigration.

The delicate balance of conformity and dissent also depended on official pragmatism. As long as authorities contented themselves with formal adherence to secular and ecclesial regulations, the submerged continuation of theological divergence formed no challenge to church and monarchy. Any replacement of local priests or administrators could unravel the existing accommodation, however, and trigger an investigation of genuine convictions. The church had prepared instructions for the uprooting of camouflaged dissent.[50] Among the signs of secret Protestantism, they listed insufficient generosity toward the clergy, lax use of Catholic symbols such as holy water and rosary, absence from public vigils and processions, and nonadherence to holidays and obligatory fasts. The possession of banned books formed another crucial criterion. Interrogations were to check for any hesitance in affirming distinctly Catholic doctrines and test children for exposure to Lutheran theology. Even an ability to discuss scripture was seen as suspicious.[51]

Crypto-Protestants, in turn, relied on secretly circulated guidebooks on permissible strategies of disguise and evasion.[52] They should outwardly follow Catholic practice, but think Lutheran in the process. Religious topics should not be discussed in public or in front of Catholic domestics. The Protestant instruction of children should not begin until they had finished their schooling. If interrogated by authorities, the guidelines advised evasion and the appearance of ignorance. The employment of these strategies is visible in the governmental reports; their success differed in tune with official attitudes and expectations. They also came at a psychological price. Committed Protestants such as Schaitberger experienced their outward adherence to Catholicism as sinful weakness, for which they could only seek divine forgiveness.[53]

Relations between the local confessional groups varied. In many settings, familial and economic bonds tied small communities together.[54] Denunciations were frowned upon and incurred the risk of social reprisals. In other environments, generous rewards for reporting suspicious conduct and the strategic settlement of reliable Catholics from other regions furthered division and mutual suspicion.[55] Overall, however, the confessional conflict primarily involved dissenters and authorities rather than resident Catholics.

Although islands of clandestine heterodoxy persisted throughout the hereditary lands, the Alpine heartland of the Austrian interior formed its nucleus. From a solid core in Upper Carinthia, where the authorities in the 1730s still estimated the heterodox population at 20,000, it stretched northwards into westernmost Styria and southern Upper Austria.[56] Exact numbers are elusive, however, due not only to the very nature of the phenomenon but also its fluidity. Researchers found surprising fluctuation in the adherence to heterodoxy.[57] Next to long-term dissenter families, the authorities also discovered recent converts. Some were farmhands drawn into the spiritual world of Lutheran households. Others were influenced by spouses and relatives. In spite of public pressure, conversion was no one-way street.

The human and geographical nexus between the centers of underground Protestantism was Alpine Salzburg. Without Salzburg, the retreat areas of Austrian heterodoxy formed dispersed patches; with it, they fused into a more coherent subdivision of the central Alps. The Lutheran element in the mountainous south of the prince-bishopric was strongly connected with adjacent coreligionists.[58] As a consequence, developments in Salzburg regularly reverberated in Habsburg provinces. Although the legal status of Protestantism had generally been weaker in the prince-bishopric than in the eastern Austrian lands, pragmatic necessities long sustained a more lenient practice. The economic importance of heterodox miners, especially, advised against a strict implementation of confessional mandates.

From the late 1600s, however, the ruling prince-bishops toughened their policies. Expulsions from the Defereggen Valley and the salt-mining

244   *Beyond Habsburg*

area around Hallein warned of things to come. In the Tyrolean Defereggen Valley, which was partially under Salzburg jurisdiction, more than
600 Protestants were ordered out of the country in the winter of 1684.[59]
In the Hallein district, outright expulsions primarily affected suspected
leaders such as the later famous Schaitberger, but several hundred followed them into exile to escape the oppressive conditions. In both cases,
minor children were withheld and placed into Catholic care, until the
intervention of the Protestant imperial estates contributed to a partial
reunification of Defereggen families.[60]

These localized events were overshadowed by the great expulsion of
1731–1732.[61] Unlike its precursors, it encompassed a large part of the
principality and fundamentally changed its religious composition. The
reinvigorated confessional policies of Archbishop Leopold Anton von
Firmian triggered a protest movement among Salzburg Lutherans, who
now publicly affirmed their heterodoxy and appealed for assistance by
imperial Protestantism. The regent dispatched a commission to the mountain districts, which found over 20,000 dissidents. On 31 October 1731
Firmian responded with a decree of emigration.[62] All Protestants were to
leave the territory: non-proprietors within eight days; proprietors within
one to three months.

The decree created an international uproar. Since its terms diverged
from the Peace of Westphalia, the prince-bishop tried to deny the treaty's
applicability and define the heterodox as rebels and sectarians. Protestant rulers protested and threatened reprisals. Reinforced by the albeit
reluctant support of the emperor, Firmian stayed the course. In the winter
of 1731, the first of over 5,000 non-proprietors arrived in neighboring
territories. The removal of the more numerous proprietors was destined
to exacerbate the international controversy, until King Frederick William I of Prussia offered refuge in his northeastern borderlands.[63] This
proposition completely changed the situation. The prospect of an assisted
transfer to acceptable conditions in a Protestant German state diminished resistance among both the emigrants and the imperial princes. The
emigrants' march to East Prussia and other destinations turned into a
spiritual affirmation.[64] And the prince-bishop had successfully purged his
country of heretics.

The Salzburg expulsions marked a turning point in confessional relations. They stirred the international public and triggered an outburst of
polemical literature.[65] They also reverberated in the Habsburg lands.[66]
Clandestine Protestants in adjacent territories were both frightened
and inspired. Authorities heightened their vigilance. The status quo had
been broken. Yet the departure of 20,000 inhabitants, amounting to

15 percent of the territory's overall population and appreciably more in the most affected districts, had never been the desired outcome. It did not call for repetition in the Habsburgs' patrimony. At the same time, the confessional homogeneity of the hereditary lands remained dogma. The emperor's councilors devised a seemingly ingenious solution.

In an era of mercantilist theory, human capital was to be increased rather than decreased. Surrendering it to potential rivals such as the rising regional power of Prussia held little appeal. In one of the many inconsistencies of confessional politics, however, the Habsburgs had grudgingly accepted heterodoxy in parts of their empire. Territories in which princely conscience and political philosophy precluded confessional tolerance coexisted with territories that required a more pragmatic approach. Among the latter was the Principality of Transylvania, whose confessional tolerance and diversity had been guaranteed upon incorporation into the Habsburg Monarchy.[67] Since German-speaking Lutherans known as Saxons formed one of the protected communities, Habsburg administrators eyed an opportunity to rid the hereditary lands of obstinate heretics without losing them to foreign powers. The concept of transmigration was born.

During the following decades, thousands of Alpine heterodox were deported to Transylvania.[68] The measures began as early as 1734 under the regency of Charles VI and were continued under his daughter Maria Theresa until the 1770s.[69] They struck at the centers of crypto-Protestantism. Soldiers and missionaries were dispatched to the problem areas in Upper Austria, Carinthia, and northwestern Styria. Reported dissenters who were found guilty faced assorted punishments, including incarceration, confiscations, and induction into the military. These coercive measures were regularly complemented with religious instruction. The desired outcome was the acceptance of Catholicism, usually expressed by a confessional oath. These oaths had accompanied the reformation commissions from their very beginnings in the sixteenth century. They were designed as challenges and tests but varied in content. Some sought detailed concurrence with the most distinctive aspects of Catholic theology.[70] Others emphasized the drastic rejection of past error.[71] Yet others contained a clear element of personal humiliation.[72]

Recalcitrants faced deportation. Approximately 4,500 were brought out of the country.[73] Their further destiny strongly depended on the circumstances of their relocation. Intact family units that were given solid economic opportunities in their new domiciles had a fair chance of survival. Deportees who were deprived of spouses and children and treated as common criminals perished in great numbers. The overall success of

246   Beyond Habsburg

the project was questionable. A handful of Transylvanian communities were rejuvenated by the arrivals, who developed into a distinctive new element known as *Landler*.[74] Mortality numbers were staggering, however, so that deportation frequently turned into a death sentence.[75] In 1735 the city fathers of Hermannstadt (Sibiu) informed the federal administration that "the unfortunate emigrants in general, but especially the destitute Carinthians, catch the local fevers and largely die with longing for their withheld children and from lack of food."[76] In the old country, smaller islands of heterodoxy such as the uppermost Mur Valley were wiped out. Coherent strongholds in Upper Carinthia and the Salzkammergut survived almost unshaken.

The passing of Maria Theresa in 1780 also marked the end of an era.[77] Her successor Joseph II had long objected to his mother's confessional policies. Toward the end of his titular co-regency he had even threatened to resign rather than bear responsibility for a continued harassment of religious minorities.[78] Among the major reforms of his personal reign was therefore the Patent of Toleration of 1781, which granted limited toleration to Lutheran, Calvinist, and Greek-Orthodox Christians.[79] Similar legislation was subsequently passed for Jews.[80] Joseph was not motivated by sympathy for spiritual dissenters. He wished they would see the truth in Catholicism.[81] Yet he subscribed to a new philosophy of state that no longer considered religious coercion a tolerable expression of monarchic governance.[82] Even under the new regulations, many aspects of heterodox life remained burdensome. Those who benefitted still experienced them as a liberation.

Altogether, 100,000 Protestants professed their faith throughout the Austro-Bohemian lands within the first few years.[83] Almost 30 Austrian communities gathered the necessary minimum of 100 families or 500 individuals and were permitted to found congregations. Of these so-called tolerance congregations, 13 were situated in Carinthia, followed by nine congregations in Upper Austria, two in Styria and Vienna, and one in rural Lower Austria.[84] These communities soon developed a distinct cultural milieu, but only in Carinthia did it become vigorous enough to influence provincial politics and identity.[85] With the integration of Hungary's German-speaking rim as the new province of Burgenland in 1921, the Austrian republic subsequently gained a second nucleus of Protestantism.[86]

Austrian Protestantism did not rise like a phoenix, but more had remained than just ashes. To secular and ecclesial authorities, the numbers came as a shock. After a century and a half in the underground, Protestantism had resurfaced in Austrian public life. Compared to its zenith in the reformation era, in contrast, the reborn community was a mere shadow. Toleration liberated the remnants of Austria's once powerful Lutheran movement, but it did not turn back the wheel of history. In the time that had past, Catholicism had reestablished itself as the popular faith of the country. It no longer needed the government for protection.

Habsburg Recatholization and International Politics

The confessional pacification of the Habsburg Monarchy formed an important element of political consolidation. The Catholic Church became a crucial pillar of the culturally and constitutionally diverse conglomerate state. The victorious wars against the Ottoman Empire complemented the restoration of religious orthodoxy and finalized the monarchy's rise to European power. In the eyes of their supporters, the Habsburgs had fulfilled their historic mission.[87]

Confessional stringency also posed a challenge to Habsburg foreign policy, however. The decline of imperial authority in the Thirty Years' War was not the last setback for the dynasty. Imperial Protestantism and its international allies continued to resist the emperors' confessional policies. As compensation for their failure to secure freedom of religion in the hereditary lands, Sweden and the Protestant imperial estates had inserted a right of diplomatic intercession into the Treaty of Osnabrück.[88] These intercessions became a recurrent feature of imperial politics and stemmed primarily from the *corpus evangelicorum*, the assembly of Protestant estates within the imperial diet.[89]

Confessional caucuses had already formed in the 1500s. Confronted with a Catholic majority in the plenum, the Protestant estates tried to prevent unilateral decisions in matters of religion. Although Catholics insisted on the indivisibility of the diet, Protestant concertation necessitated corresponding countermeasures. By the seventeenth century, corporate negotiations of confessional grievances had become a common if informal feature of imperial politics. During the peace talks in Westphalia, these corporations gained special significance and were implicitly inscribed in the final accord. Article V, paragraph 52, of the Treaty of Osnabrück established that controversial matters in which Catholic and Protestant estates separated into distinct parties were to be decided by amicable agreement rather than majority vote. Although not specified by name, the *corpus evangelicorum* and the *corpus catholicorum* had become integrated into the constitutional order.

In the following century, the *corpus evangelicorum* repeatedly intervened in favor of its coreligionists in Austria as well as Salzburg.[90] In

248 Beyond Habsburg

connection with expulsions and deportations, especially, the caucus pleaded for clemency and the adherence to imperial law. The intercessions primarily functioned as an irritant. They rarely changed the fate of Alpine dissenters, but they highlighted the emperors' partisanship. Their futility drove a wedge between the dynasty and sectors of the empire and prepared the ground for later challenges to Habsburg dominance.

Concrete results required military and political strength. The new regional power of Sweden tried to uphold its wartime stature.[91] At first, it exerted its stipulatory right of intercession. At the Diet of Regensburg in 1653-1654, the Swedish plenipotentiary Matthias Biörnklou energetically promoted the cause of Alpine Protestantism and criticized the confessional homogenization of Lower Austria.[92] Similar interventions followed. Stockholm had to recognize, however, that its military withdrawal had diminished the Habsburgs' readiness for concessions.

Yet Sweden's interest in its Habsburg coreligionists persisted. Due to the virtual disappearance of public heterodoxy in the Alpine provinces, this interest increasingly focused on Silesia, where Protestantism enjoyed treaty privileges.[93] Nonetheless, recatholization resumed soon after the departure of Swedish troops. In the 1650s it still centered on the Habsburgs' patrimonial domains. Following the extinction of the Silesian Piasts in 1675, it was extended to the principalities of Liegnitz, Brieg, and Wohlau, whose Lutheran practice had been guaranteed at Osnabrück. The protests of Stockholm and other Protestant courts accomplished little.

At the turn of the eighteenth century, however, one more Swedish monarch at the height of his power shook up the world of Habsburg Protestantism. In 1700, Denmark, Russia, and the newly united Poland-Saxony had joined forces against Swedish supremacy in the Baltic. Yet in the early phase of the war, Sweden's new king Charles XII dominated the battlefield.[94] After the surrender of Augustus of Poland and Saxony, a powerful Swedish army threatened Habsburg borders. Charles strongly identified with the legacy of Gustavus Adolphus. During his military transversal of Silesia, local Protestants had sought his support. In his negotiations with the imperial ambassador Johann Wenzel Wratislaw von Mitrowitz, the king increasingly focused on confessional politics.[95]

Emperor Joseph I faced a dilemma. His troops fought the arduous War of the Spanish Succession in the southern and western outskirts of the continent, as well as domestic Hungarian opposition. A revival of the Franco-Swedish alliance had to be avoided at all costs. To underline his demands, Charles deployed several regiments to Silesia. The emperor relented. In the Convention of Altranstädt of September 1707, many infringements on the Westphalian accord were rescinded.[96] Silesia's biconfessional character was confirmed once more.

Two years later, the annihilation of the Swedish army at Poltava effectively ended the country's stature as an international power.[97] In time, Sweden lost not only its Baltic provinces but also its significance for German politics. This decline also reduced Stockholm's efficacy as religious protector. The resulting power vacuum in Protestant northern Germany was progressively filled by the new kingdom of Prussia.[98] The invitation of the Salzburg refugees in 1732 underlined the country's claim to Protestant leadership. With the conquest of Silesia in the 1740s, for which continued discrimination of local Protestants provided valuable propagandistic cover, Prussia added military force to this claim.[99] The Habsburgs never regained full control over the Holy Roman Empire.

When the German question moved to the center of European politics in the nineteenth century, religion no longer formed the heart of collective identity. The new spirit of nationalism dominated the intellectual debate.[100] Religion was increasingly assigned to the private sphere. Yet below the surface, confessional divisions continued to influence public sentiment.[101] With the dissolution of the Holy Roman Empire and its spiritual principalities, Catholics had lost their grip on German politics. Long past were dreams of restoring Catholic supremacy throughout Central Europe. In an era of incipient mass politics, devout Catholics began to feel outnumbered by Protestants and the growing phenomenon of liberal secularists.

These changes did not bode well for Habsburg leadership in Central Europe.[102] The dynastic foundations of their empire seemed outdated in an era of popular sovereignty. Its cultural diversity contradicted the creed of national unity. Yet also religiously, the Habsburg Monarchy began to deviate from the German mainstream. Purely Catholic polities had largely disappeared with the territorial restructuring of the Napoleonic era. In the first decade of the nineteenth century, the formerly more than 300 imperial entities were consolidated into fewer than 40.[103] Most significantly, the Catholic ecclesial principalities, once the guarantors of Catholic and Habsburg dominance, were secularized and merged into territorial states. Even surviving Catholic strongholds such as Bavaria had incorporated substantial Protestant populations, which forced them to moderate their denominational policies. As emperors, the Habsburgs had frequently cast themselves as a more accommodating expression of German Catholicism, towering above the confessional parties of the empire. After 1815, they were perceived as relics of confessional stringency.

250 *Beyond Habsburg*

In 1837 the Austrian government gave new fuel to these perceptions. In the western crown land of Tyrol, open heterodoxy had already disappeared in the 1500s, following the suppression of early Lutheran and especially Anabaptist tendencies.[104] Not even the tolerance legislation of Joseph II had led to the establishment of Protestant congregations. In the early 1800s it became visible, however, that reformist traditions had survived in the Zillertal region. This remote mountain valley had been politically affiliated with Salzburg, which may account for the persistence of heterodoxy. Local petitions for the introduction of Lutheran practice surprised provincial leaders and triggered an acerbic debate. At its center stood the religious unity of Tyrol, which was to be preserved at all costs.[105]

The impetus did not come from the dynasty but from Catholic traditionalists in the Tyrolean diet. With reference to the valley's historical affiliation with Salzburg and the province's temporary annexation by Bavaria, they questioned the validity of the Patent of Toleration in Tyrol or at least the Zillertal. Following historical precedent, they also redefined underground Protestants as unlawful sectarians. After some hesitation, the emperor sided with the diet. In January 1837 dissenters were given two weeks to renounce Catholicism. If they took this step, they had to resettle in provinces with existing Lutheran congregations or leave the country. If not, they had to remain in the Catholic Church.

More than 400 Zillertalers chose emigration. In a symbolic reenactment of the Salzburg narrative, they sought and received refuge in Prussia. The terms of their transfer to a Silesian mountain district differed favorably from previous displacements. Nonetheless, the episode shocked German public opinion and confirmed long-held prejudices about the Habsburgs.[106] The past caught up with the present, and centuries of confessional history merged into an imagery of intolerance. Secularization had not diminished the impact of this imagery. To the contrary, the experience of religious expulsions offended liberals no less than devout Protestants, and even many Catholics found it difficult to defend. A minor incident grew beyond its local significance because it interjected past conflicts into the ongoing debate about the German future. When the Zillertalers arrived in Prussia, the Habsburgs had lost yet another skirmish in their struggle for leadership in Germany.

History Shared and Memory Divided

Over time, Austrian history became synonymous with Habsburg history. An important ideological tradition defined the Protestant estates as dangerous detractors from the country's innate mission. As a true representative of this historical perspective, Ernst Tomek did not hesitate to declare that the Battle at White Mountain had saved Austria—not the Catholic Church in Central Europe or the Habsburg dynasty, but nothing less than the country itself. The accomplished ecclesial historian was fully aware of the Protestantization of Austrian society. He knew that crucial segments of the population had supported the Bohemian cause. To many conservatives, however, Austria was simply unimaginable without Catholicism and the Habsburg legacy. Austria was saved from itself at White Mountain. The identification of country, church, and dynasty was complete.[107]

Yet if one examines the religious and societal schism of the confessional era, the dynastic legacy does not naturally lead up to a modern republic. Protestantism had taken deep roots in the Austrian populace, and the restoration of Catholic homogeneity had required a concerted effort of church and monarchy. Moreover, the religious conflict of the epoch was interwoven with the struggle between the estates' insistence on divided governance and the dynasty's claim to unilateral authority. When Archduke Ferdinand of Inner Austria tried to delegitimize the Protestant estates by linking them to Dutch and Swiss republicanism, he may have swayed his princely contemporaries more easily than twentieth-century democrats.[108] And if one observes the desperate hopes that Upper Austrian peasants placed on the Swedish king in 1632, it appears too one-dimensional to equate Austria's historical legacy with the legacy of its government.[109]

It has long been argued that the Thirty Years' War also was a civil war. This designation has commonly been applied in an imperial context. Yet the conflict was not only a German or imperial civil war. It also constituted a civil war within the nascent Habsburg Monarchy. In the Austrian and Bohemian lands, central societal forces took different sides. As a consequence, this Habsburgian civil war was not resolved domestically. The Habsburgs proved unable to subjugate the Protestant nobles of Bohemia and Austria until they received external support, especially from Duke Maximilian of Bavaria. The future of the Austro-Bohemian lands was determined by international politics. The Catholic monarchy kept the upper hand, but its domestic opponents were no less representative of contemporary Austrian society and no less legitimate a part of Austrian historical tradition.

Why has Austrian public memory rarely reflected this fundamental truism?[110] As long as the Austrian political system was defined along dynastic lines, it was difficult to reevaluate popular uprisings against

252 Beyond Habsburg

previous representatives of the ruling family. If the dynasty constituted the polity, any opposition to it had to be illegitimate. More surprising than its historical dominance was the substantial retention of this dynastic perspective in republican Austria. Whereas Czech and Hungarian historians subjected Habsburg historiography to comprehensive revision, their Austrian colleagues have been more hesitant to do so.[111] The history of the small Germanophone republic merged with that of its imperial predecessor, whereas the contemporaneous histories of Bohemia, Slovenia, or Hungary depicted the interrelationship of local populations and that empire. The implicit premise transformed Habsburg sovereignty into the rule of Styrian farmers and Tyrolean mineworkers over Bohemian counts and Hungarian magnates. Only by assigning a distinctly German mission to the Habsburgs, however, can one distinguish between their rule over Carinthia and Moravia, not to mention over those crown lands' individual nationalities. Heinrich von Srbik may have been among the last leading scholars to interpret the history of the dynasty from this perspective.[112]

Yet the Habsburg Monarchy was never the realm of modern-day Austrians. The peripheral status of the Alpine and Danubian provinces changed when they became the hereditary domains of an imperial dynasty. Located at the intersection between the old European core and its more volatile eastern margins, their rise to prominence was not altogether coincidental. The Habsburg Monarchy was not simply the result of Austrian political and military prowess, however. Its rulers relied on the resources of the Holy Roman Empire and the security interests of their exposed neighbors to the east. The emerging realm was rooted in a dynasty and not a people. The Habsburg Monarchy was not ruled by its Alpine Germanophones, but by a supranational monarchic elite. During much of its history, German functioned as the lingua franca of the empire, and one should not overlook the practical and emotional advantages this provided to native speakers. Yet Germans held no monopoly of power in this conglomerate state, and at crucial historical junctions such as the Thirty Years' War, significant sectors of the Austro-German population could be found among the opponents of the dynasty.

For an aristocratic and bureaucratic elite, the transition from the Habsburg Monarchy to the Republic of Austria may indeed have resembled a mere change in size and governance. They were the truly vanquished who were left behind without a fatherland in 1919, as Joseph Roth has described so grippingly in his literary masterpieces.[113] For Austrian society in general, however, the transition was reminiscent of, rather than distinct from, that of other successor states. As pivotal a figure as the first state chancellor even recommended burying the historical name together with the dismantled empire.[114]

It can be argued that the persistence of dynastic perspectives reflected historical realities. Habsburg absolutism and the Catholic Church prevailed and shaped Alpine Austria for centuries. The Protestant estates disappeared from historical consciousness because they did not tie in with the society that succeeded them. This argument only sounds plausible within a purely Austrian context, however. The victory of the Habsburgs was equally decisive in Bohemia. Yet as soon as modern Czech historiography took root, it integrated the estatist opposition to the Habsburgs into its own image of Czech tradition. For many historians, the Battle of White Mountain initiated the decline of their society into centuries of *temno*, darkness, and those who disagreed only sought to reconcile the legacy of Protestant estatism with that of its dynastic conqueror.[115] Modern Czechs do not judge their seventeenth-century history based on who had proven more influential for their subsequent development, and even devout Catholics do not automatically assume the Habsburg legacy.[116]

It would be misleading, however, to interpret the early Thirty Years' War as a conflict between Austrians and Bohemians.[117] In reality, both were divided in their loyalties, although their politically active segments predominantly flocked to the Habsburgs' adversaries. At White Mountain, Austrians contributed five companies of infantry and eight— albeit incomplete—companies of cavalry to the Bohemian army.[118] They encountered a highly international imperial and Leaguist force, in which native Austrians only formed a small minority.[119] Both sides were convinced they were fighting for a just cause. The outcome of the battle, in turn, changed Bohemia as well as Austria.

Like their Bohemian counterparts, the Protestant nobles of the archduchy conceived of themselves as deeply patriotic, but their vision of patriotism did not correspond to the dynasty's. Whereas the latter developed the ultimately prevailing image of Austria as the Catholic, absolutist Habsburg Empire, in other words, as a political entity rooted in a princely family, the Protestant nobles anchored their patriotism in the individual territories and their customary laws and privileges. The seceding Protestant estates in Horn turned to their Catholic peers in 1620 and implored them, as good patriots, to collaborate on the securing of estatist rights.[120] This corresponded to the understanding of Bohemian Heinrich Mathias von Thurn, who even in Swedish exile continued to define himself as a patriot who had only served his native land.[121]

Georg Erasmus von Tschernembl developed this alternative sense of identity most explicitly.[122] At the center of his loyalty stood the territory, the land, which was personified by the estates. It was the duty of the estates to uphold the interests of the land, also against the monarch. In particular, this responsibility included the obligation to preserve customary

254 *Beyond Habsburg*

law and practice. Estates that failed to ensure the preservation of territorial liberties and privileges, such as the Styrians who swore allegiance to Archduke Ferdinand without having secured unassailable constitutional guarantees, neglected their duty and caused irreparable damage to their territory. Territorial representatives may entrust a dynasty with a hereditary claim to the throne. In doing so, however, they do not transfer their loyalty from the commonwealth to the ruler. The selection of hereditary princes occurs exclusively for the benefit of the territory, providing it with increased status and security. If the dynasty neglects the common good in favor of its own, it forfeits its claim to the throne.

Tschernembl's vision was Austrian rather than Habsburgian. His view of the dynasty turned increasingly negative. The Habsburgs prioritized dynastic aggrandizement and were beholden to papal and Spanish interests. International marriages further removed them from their indigenous roots, which also expressed itself in a haughty self-elevation over the native nobility. It was therefore the obligation of the estates to curb the dynasty's ambition and restore the primacy of territorial interests. The requisite patriotism could only be expected from truly indigenous corporations such as the nobility and the towns, whereas the clergy owed allegiance to foreign potentates and deserved no influence on domestic politics.

In this manner, Tschernembl constructed a polity around the land and its people rather than a ruling family. It was a vision that differed fundamentally from the reality of Habsburgian Austria for centuries to come. Yet in many ways, its foundation in popular representation and the local tradition of Alpine territories might be expected to hold a stronger appeal for the democratic Austrian republic than the multinational absolutism of the Habsburg Monarchy.[123] It is therefore intriguing from the viewpoint of historical imagery and elite continuity that the Habsburgian tradition has retained and even expanded its hold on republican self-representation. Postwar Austria identified with the legacy of a dynastic conglomerate state even at those historical junctures, at which many Austrians, be they peasants, townsmen, or nobles, had fought this legacy. It shows the power of historical tradition-making that the Austrian populace has largely internalized this sense of self.

Collective memory consists of facets of the past that bind and legitimize a community. It shapes the identity of its members through the deliberate commemoration of a real or imaginary past; Barry Schwartz aptly defined it as part of a culture's meaning-making apparatus.[124] As social beings, humans are exposed to the selected invocations of a communal past. Not only politicians and scholars, but also teachers, bureaucrats,

Beyond Habsburg 255

and journalists presort the heroes and villains whom society commemorates or forgets. Our individual understanding of the past owes more to the society in which we live than to the historical experience of our ancestors. If most contemporary Austrians remember the seventeenth century through the eyes of a former dynasty, and many Czechs through the eyes of its opponents, the original experience only plays a peripheral role. To a much greater degree, this divergence echoes the subsequent commemoration and historical representation of a common past.

If Austrians truly want to come to terms with their historical legacy, they have to recognize that the Habsburg Monarchy was not their empire, but a dynasty's. The Austrian experience was deeply intertwined with this polity, of course, as was the experience of Czechs, Hungarians, and many others. Yet Austrians need not look at the past through the eyes of their one-time rulers. Their true history is the history of the people who inhabited and built their land, not the history of a monarchic family and its ever-changing conglomerate state. To fully understand themselves, Austrians will have to think beyond Habsburg.

Notes

1. See, for example, Ernst Tomek, *Kirchengeschichte Österreichs*, vol. 2 (Innsbruck, 1949), 521.
2. Johann Loserth, *Reformation und Gegenreformation in den innerösterreichischen Ländern im 16. Jahrhundert* (Stuttgart, 1898), 363.
3. See, for example, Helmut Mezler-Andelberg, *Kirche in der Steiermark: Gesammelte Aufsätze* (Vienna, 1994), 133.
4. For Saxon foreign policy in the early 1600s, see Axel Gotthard, "'Politice seint wir Bäpstisch': Kursachsen und der deutsche Protestantismus im frühen 17. Jahrhundert," *Zeitschrift für historische Forschung* 20 (1993): 275–319.
5. For newer biographies of Augustus, see Karl Czok, *August der Starke und seine Zeit: Kurfürst von Sachsen, König in Polen* (Munich, 2006), and Jacek Staszewski, *August II Mocny* (Wrocław, 1998).
6. See [Georg Erasmus von Tschernembl], *Consultationes Oder Underschidliche Rathschläg/ Der maisten und wichtigisten sachen/ welche von Anfang der Böhemischen/ und andern folgenden Auffständ fürgangen/ unnd zu Werck gericht worden/ oder werden sollen: Von wort zu wort auß dem Original Protocoll, so in der Haidelbergischen Cantzley gefunden worden/ gezogen. Mit nohtwendigen Glossis erklärt*, [ed. Jakob Keller] (n.p., 1624), 69f.
7. See Felix Stieve, *Der oberösterreichische Bauernaufstand des Jahres 1626*, vol. 1 (Munich, 1891), 166, 68–71, and Arndt Schreiber, *Adeliger Habitus und konfessionelle Identität: Die protestantischen Herren und Ritter in den österreichischen Erblanden nach 1620* (Vienna, 2013), 265–267.
8. See Hans Sturmberger, *Georg Erasmus Tschernembl: Religion, Libertät und Widerstand* (Graz, 1953), 395.

256 Beyond Habsburg

9. William D. Godsey has examined diverse aspects of noble influence and power relations in the Habsburg Monarchy after 1648. See, for example, William D. Godsey, *The Sinews of Habsburg Power: Lower Austria in a Fiscal-Military State 1650–1820* (Oxford, 2018); idem, "Adelsautonomie, Konfession und Nation im österreichischen Absolutismus ca. 1648–1848," *Zeitschrift für Historische Forschung* 33 (2006) 197–239; idem, "Österreichische Landschaftsverwaltung und Stehendes Heer im Barockzeitalter: Niederösterreich und Krain im Vergleich," in *Kriegführung und Staatsfinanzen: Die Habsburgermonarchie und das Heilige Römische Reich vom Dreißigjährigen Krieg bis zum Ende des habsburgischen Kaisertums 1740*, ed. Peter Rauscher (Münster, 2010), 313–354; and idem, "Herrschaft und politische Kultur im Habsburgerreich: Die niederösterreichische Erbhuldigung (ca. 1648–1848)," in *Aufbrüche in die Moderne: Frühparlamentarismus zwischen altständischer Ordnung und modernem Konstitutionalismus 1750–1850: Schlesien—Deutschland— Mitteleuropa*, ed. Roland Gehrke (Cologne, 2005), 141–177. See also Shuichi Iwasaki, *Stände und Staatsbildung in der frühneuzeitlichen Habsburgermonarchie in Österreich unter der Enns 1683–1748* (St. Pölten, 2014).

   For a broader examination of the relationship between monarchy and estates in the Habsburg Monarchy, see also Gerhard Ammerer et al., eds., *Bündnispartner und Konkurrenten der Landesfürsten: Die Stände in der Habsburgermonarchie* (Vienna, 2007).

10. Very explicit in this emphasis was the Austrian church historian Ernst Tomek; see, for example, pages 482 and 520f. in his *Kirchengeschichte Österreichs*, vol. 2 (Innsbruck, 1949). Yet also international researchers such as Peter H. Wilson argued that Ferdinand had "remained within his albeit narrow interpretation of the law" during his initial recatholization of Inner Austria. See Peter H. Wilson, *Europe's Tragedy: A History of the Thirty Years War* (London, 2009), 71. For similar approaches, see also Hugo Hantsch, *Geschichte Österreichs*, 4th ed., vol. 1 (Graz, 1959), 333, 344, and Karl Eichmeyer, Helmuth Feigl, and Rudolf Walter Litschel, *Weiß gilt die Seel und auch das Guet: Oberösterreichische Bauernaufstände und Bauernkriege im 16. und 17. Jahrhundert* (Linz, 1976), 163.

11. See Victor Bibl, "Erzherzog Ernst und die Gegenreformation in Niederösterreich (1576–1590)," *Mitteilungen des Instituts für österreichische Geschichtsforschung*, Ergänzungsband 6 (1901): 577, and Johann Loserth, ed., *Acten und Correspondenzen zur Geschichte der Gegenreformation in Innerösterreich unter Erzherzog Karl II. (1578–1590)* (Vienna, 1898), 38.

12. Johann Loserth, ed., *Akten und Korrespondenzen zur Geschichte der Gegenreformation in Innerösterreich unter Ferdinand II.* (Vienna, 1906), 1:147.

13. See, for example, Helmut Mezler-Andelberg, *Kirche in der Steiermark: Gesammelte Aufsätze* (Vienna, 1994), 183f.

14. One of Andreæ's central advisory opinions is printed in Helmut Mezler-Andelberg, *Kirche in der Steiermark: Gesammelte Aufsätze* (Vienna, 1994), 225–230. For further discussion of Andreæ's viewpoint and its reception, see also Hans Sturmberger, "Jakob Andreæ und Achaz von Hohenfeld: Eine Diskussion über das Gehorsamsproblem zur Zeit der Rudolfinischen Gegenreformation in Österreich," in *Festschrift Karl Eder zum siebzigsten Geburtstag*, ed. Helmut Mezler-Andelberg (Graz, 1959), 381–394.

Beyond Habsburg 257

15. See especially Ernst Troeltsch, *Die Soziallehren der Christlichen Kirchen und Gruppen* (Tübingen, 1912).

16. See, for example, Arno Strohmeyer, *Konfessionskonflikt und Herrschaftsordnung: Widerstandsrecht bei den österreichischen Ständen (1550–1650)* (Mainz, 2006); Robert von Friedeburg, *Self-Defence and Religious Strife in Early Modern Europe: England and Germany, 1530–1680* (Aldershot, England, 2002); and Robert von Friedeburg, ed., *Widerstandsrecht in der frühen Neuzeit: Erträge und Perspektiven der Forschung im deutsch-britischen Vergleich* (Berlin, 2001).

17. For the religious composition of the Upper Austrian nobility around 1600, see Siegfried Haider, *Geschichte Oberösterreichs* (Munich, 1987), 173, and Hans Sturmberger, *Georg Erasmus Tschernembl: Religion, Libertät und Widerstand* (Graz, 1953), 47.

18. For the early modern significance of Calvinism in the region, see R. J. W. Evans, "Calvinism in East Central Europe: Hungary and her Neighbours, 1540–1700," in *International Calvinism, 1541–1715*, ed. Menna Prestwich (Oxford, 1985), 167–196.

19. The Lutheran theologian Johann Valentin Andreae, who visited Upper Austria from his native Württemberg in 1619, reported such tensions in his autobiography. For this travel report, see Johann Valentin Andreae, *Vita, ab ipso conscripto*, edited by F. H. Rheinwald (Berlin, 1849), 82–94.

20. See Winfried Schulze, "Zur politischen Theorie des steirischen Ständetums der Gegenreformationszeit," *Zeitschrift des historischen Vereins für Steiermark* 62 (1971): 33–48, and the example from the 1580s printed in Johann Loserth, "Miscellen zur steiermärkischen Religionsgeschichte," *Jahrbuch der Gesellschaft für die Geschichte des Protestantismus in Österreich* 20 (1899): 188–192.

21. See Hans von Zwiedineck-Südenhorst, *Fürst Christian der Andere von Anhalt und seine Beziehungen zu Innerösterreich* (Graz, 1874), 52–84. Ferdinand's supporters, in turn, accused the Bohemian leaders of inveigling the Inner Austrians against the emperor. See "Relation des Fürsten von Liechtenstein am 29. April 1621," printed in Christian d' Elvert, *Die Bestrafung der böhmischen Rebellion, insbesondere die Correspondenz Ferdinand II. mit dem Fürsten Liechtenstein* (Brünn, 1868), 55–58.

22. See the report by secretary Valerio Antelmi from 25 January 1620 printed in Hans von Zwiedineck-Südenhorst, *Venetianische Gesandtschaftsberichte über die böhmische Rebellion (1618–1620)* (Graz, 1880), 62–64.

23. See Caecilia Doppler, *Reformation und Gegenreformation in ihrer Auswirkung auf das Steyrer Bürgertum* (Vienna, 1977), 163 and 169.

24. For the following, see Helmut Rumpler, "Sozialer Wandel in Klagenfurt," in *Katholische Reform und Gegenreformation in Innerösterreich 1564–1628*, ed. France M. Dolinar et al. (Klagenfurt, 1994), 573–587, here especially 580.

25. The decree is printed in Bernhard Raupach, *Nützliche Beylagen zum Dritten und Letzten Theil des Erläuterten Evangelischen Österreichs* (Hamburg, 1740), 254–258.

26. See Victor Bibl, "Die katholischen und protestantischen Stände Niederösterreichs im XVII. Jahrhundert: Ein Beitrag zur Geschichte der ständischen Verfassung," *Jahrbuch für Landeskunde von Niederösterreich*, n. s., 2 (1903): 319f.

258   Beyond Habsburg

27. Ibid., 323.

28. For the following, see Arno Strohmeyer, "Konfessionsmigration und religionspolitische Handlungsspielräume: Eine Initiative niederösterreichischer Glaubensflüchtlinge bei den Verhandlungen zum Westfälischen Frieden," in *Glaubensflüchtlinge: Ursachen, Formen und Auswirkungen frühneuzeitlicher Konfessionsmigration in Europa*, ed. Joachim Bahlcke (Berlin, 2008), 187–206.

29. See Konrad Müller, ed., *Instrumenta Pacis Westphalicae*, 3rd ed. (Berne, 1975), 127. The permission to attend Lutheran services referred to territories outside Lower Austria where Lutheran services were legal. In practice, this tended to be Hungarian cities such as Pressburg/Poszony and Ödenburg/Sopron.

30. Gustav Reingrabner, *Adel und Reformation: Beiträge zur Geschichte des protestantischen Adels im Lande unter der Enns während des 16. und 17. Jahrhunderts* (St. Pölten, 1976), 19. See also the lists published in Hermann Clauss, "Zur Geschichte der Gegenreformation in Niederösterreich," *Jahrbuch der Gesellschaft für die Geschichte des Protestantismus in Österreich* 28 (1907): 10–13. For a comprehensive examination of Lower Austria's Protestant nobility after 1620, see Arndt Schreiber, *Adeliger Habitus und konfessionelle Identität: Die protestantischen Herren und Ritter in den österreichischen Erblanden nach 1620* (Vienna, 2013).

31. Hohberg has been the subject of Otto Brunner's influential study *Adeliges Landleben und europäischer Geist: Leben und Werk Wolf Helmhards von Hohberg 1612–1688* (Salzburg, 1949). For Stubenberg and his circle, see Martin Bircher, *Johann Wilhelm von Stubenberg (1619–1663) und sein Freundeskreis: Studien zur österreichischen Barockkultur protestantischer Edelleute* (Berlin, 1968). For the biography of Greiffenberg, who is frequently described as the leading female poet of the German Baroque, see Horst-Joachim Frank, *Catharina Regina von Greiffenberg: Untersuchungen zu ihrer Persönlichkeit und Sonettdichtung* (Göttingen, 1967), and Heimo Czerny, *Catharina Regina von Greiffenberg, geb. Freiherrin von Seisenegg (1633–1694): Herkunft, Leben und Werk der größten deutschen Barockdichterin* (Amstetten, Austria, 1983).

32. See Thomas Winkelbauer, *Fürst und Fürstendiener: Gundaker von Liechtenstein, ein österreichischer Aristokrat des konfessionellen Zeitalters* (Vienna-Munich, 1999), 100.

33. See Heinrich Wurm, *Die Jörger von Tollet* (Linz, 1955), 167 and 205.

34. See Thomas Winkelbauer, *Fürst und Fürstendiener: Gundaker von Liechtenstein, ein österreichischer Aristokrat des konfessionellen Zeitalters* (Vienna-Munich, 1999), 144f.

35. See Paul Dedic, "Kärntner Exulanten des 17. Jahrhunderts," *Carinthia I* 142 (1952): 358. The descendants of Ernreich Khevenhüller still own the imposing castle north of Klagenfurt. See also Georg Khevenhüller-Metsch, *Die Burg Hochosterwitz in Kärnten und ihre Geschichte* (Klagenfurt, 1953), and idem, "Vierhundert Jahre Hochosterwitz," *Carinthia I* 131 (1941): 172–181.

36. See Gustav Reingrabner, "Wo ist der evangelische Adel Österreichs geblieben?" in *Kirche im Wandel*, ed. Peter Barton (Vienna, 1993), 79.

Beyond Habsburg 259

37. For the circumstances of the departure of the Stockhorner family, see Otto Stockhorner von Starein, *Die Stockhorner von Starein: Versuch der Darstellung der Geschichte dieses Geschlechtes* (Vienna, 1896), 79. Around the same time the last remaining Protestants of the Auersperg family converted or passed away. See Miha Preinfalk, *Auersperg: Geschichte einer europäischen Familie* (Graz, 2006), 379f., 384f.; and idem, "Evangelische, Lutheraner, Accatholici: Die Familie Auersperg und der Protestantismus in Niederösterreich," *Jahrbuch für die Geschichte des Protestantismus in Österreich* 123 (2007): 227f.

38. Kurt Piringer, "Ferdinands III. katholische Restauration" (Ph.D. diss., University of Vienna, 1950), 124.

39. For the following, see the instructions to the commissions in Gustav Reingrabner, "Gegenreformation in Niederösterreich—das Protokoll der Reformationskommission für das Viertel ober dem Wienerwald von 1657–1660," *Jahrbuch für die Geschichte des Protestantismus in Österreich* 113 (1997): 33–38.

40. Kurt Piringer, "Ferdinands III. katholische Restauration" (Ph.D. diss., University of Vienna, 1950), 5f.

41. Their names were collected in 1654 in an inventory of all newly converted in the region between 1652 and 1654. This "Nomenclatur oder Namen der Neübekherte im Viertl Ober Manhardtsberg vnnder Ferdinandi III. Röm: Kay: etc: hailsammen Religions Reformation im Erzherzogthumb Österreich vnnder des Enns . . .," which is invaluable for not just the confessional history of the region, has been published in Georg Kuhr and Gerhard Bauer, eds., *Verzeichnis der Neubekehrten im Waldviertel 1652–1654: Codex Vindobonensis 7757 der Nationalbibliothek Wien* (Nuremberg, 1992), 69–428.

42. Hans Krawarik, *Exul austriacus: Konfessionelle Migrationen aus Österreich in der Frühen Neuzeit* (Vienna, 2010), 90f.

43. Georg Kuhr and Gerhard Bauer, eds., *Verzeichnis der Neubekehrten im Waldviertel 1652–1654: Codex Vindobonensis 7757 der Nationalbibliothek Wien* (Nuremberg, 1992), 65.

44. Manfred Enzner, *Exulanten aus dem südlichen Waldviertel in Franken (ca. 1627–1670)* (Nuremberg, 2001), 7. The author presents many details about almost 1000 migrants from the southern Waldviertel region he examined.

45. Hans Krawarik, *Exul austriacus: Konfessionelle Migrationen aus Österreich in der Frühen Neuzeit* (Vienna, 2010), 192f.

46. For a discussion of the term, see Rudolf Leeb, Martin Scheutz, and Dietmar Weikl, eds., *Geheimprotestantismus und evangelische Kirchen in der Habsburgermonarchie und im Erzstift Salzburg (17./18. Jahrhundert)* (Vienna, 2008), 7–11. For a critical assessment favoring its replacement by underground-Protestantism, see Stephan Steiner, *Reisen ohne Wiederkehr: Die Deportationen von Protestanten aus Kärnten 1734–1736* (Vienna—Munich, 2007), 26f.

47. This definition is an adaptation of the definition proffered in Peter G. Tropper, *Staatliche Kirchenpolitik, Geheimprotestantismus und katholische Mission in Kärnten (1752–1780)* (Klagenfurt, 1989), 13.

48. For Schaitberger and his so-called *Sendbrief*, see the introductory biography in Joseph Schaitberger, *Neu-vermehrter evangelischer Send-Brief*

260 Beyond Habsburg

(Reutlingen, Germany, 1799); Hermann Langer, *Joseph Schaitberger: Ein evangelischer Glaubenskämpfer des 17. Jahrhunderts* (Salzburg, 1985); Hermann Clauss, "Josef Schaitberger und sein Sendbrief," *Beiträge zur Bayrischen Kirchengeschichte* 15 (1909): 105–123, 153–166; and James Van Horn Melton, "Pietism, Print Culture, and Salzburg Protantism on the Eve of Expulsion," in *Pietism in Germany and North America 1680–1820*, ed. Jonathan Strom, Hartmut Lehmann, and James Van Horn Melton (Farnham, England, 2009), 229–249. The *Sendbrief* was printed in numerous collected editions from the late 1600s onward. For other examples of emigrant support, see Rudolf Weiss, *Das Bistum Passau unter Kardinal Joseph Dominikus von Lamberg (1723–1761): Zugleich ein Beitrag zur Geschichte des Kryptoprotestantismus in Oberösterreich* (St. Ottilien, Germany, 1979), 315–318.

49. For the role of the Protestant imperial estates, see Friedrich Reissenberger, "Das Corpus evangelicorum und die österreichischen Protestanten (1685–1764)," *Jahrbuch der Gesellschaft für die Geschichte des Protestantismus in Österreich* 17 (1896): 207–222.

50. For the following, see the *Instructio pastoralis ad usum missionariorum in Austria superiore expositorum* (Passau, 1752), especially paragraphs 4 and 5. These instructions were issued by the bishop of Passau, Joseph Dominikus von Lamberg, and are only listed in short excerpts here.

51. At times, even the ability to read raised suspicions, as can be seen in a Carinthian visitation report of 1734–1735. See the report printed in Christine Tropper, *Glut unter der Asche und offene Flamme: Der Kärntner Geheimprotestantismus und seine Bekämpfung 1731–1738* (Vienna, 2011), 296–361, here specially pages 333 and 334.

52. For the following, see Regina Pörtner, "Die Kunst des Lügens: Ketzerverfolgung und geheimprotestantische Überlebensstrategien im theresianischen Österreich," in *Kommunikation und Medien in der Frühen Neuzeit*, ed. Johannes Burkhardt and Christine Werkstetter (Munich, 2005), 402–405.

53. See Joseph Schaitberger, *Neu-vermehrter evangelischer Send-Brief* (Reutlingen, Germany, 1799), 17, 24, 46.

54. For the following, see Rudolf Leeb, "Zwei Konfessionen in einem Tal: Vom Zusammenleben der Konfessionen im Alpenraum in der Zeit des 'Geheimprotestantismus' und zum Verständnis der Konfessionalisierung," in *Impulse für eine religiöse Alltagsgeschichte des Donau-Alpen-Adria-Raumes*, ed. Rupert Klieber and Hermann Hold (Vienna, 2005), 129–150.

55. See "Methodus extirpandi haeresin Lutheranam in parochia Azbacensi usurpatam" from 1740, printed in Rudolf Weiss, *Das Bistum Passau unter Kardinal Joseph Dominikus von Lamberg (1723–1761): Zugleich ein Beitrag zur Geschichte des Kryptoprotestantismus in Oberösterreich* (St. Ottilien, Germany, 1979), 457–460, here 458, and Rudolf Leeb, Martin Scheutz, and Dietmar Weikl, eds., *Geheimprotestantismus und evangelische Kirchen in der Habsburgermonarchie und im Erzstift Salzburg (17./18. Jahrhundert)* (Vienna, 2008), 75.

56. See Paul Dedic, *Der Geheimprotestantismus in Kärnten während der Regierung Karls VI. (1711–1740)* (Klagenfurt, 1940), 87.

Beyond Habsburg 261

57. See Rudolf Leeb, "Zwei Konfessionen in einem Tal: Vom Zusammenleben der Konfessionen im Alpenraum in der Zeit des 'Geheimprotestantismus' und zum Verständnis der Konfessionalisierung," in *Impulse für eine religiöse Alltagsgeschichte des Donau-Alpen-Adria-Raumes*, ed. Rupert Klieber and Hermann Hold (Vienna, 2005), 145f.

58. The official designation prince-archbishopric is substituted with the more common and manageable shortened version.

59. For a more detailed analysis, see Alois Dissertori, *Die Auswanderung der Defregger Protestanten 1666–1725* (Innsbruck, 2001).

60. When a change in legal practice gave exiles the opportunity to reclaim removed children, a number of the latter barely remembered their parents and decided to remain in their home valley. For a detailed investigation of the Defereggen children, see Ute Küppers-Braun, "Zerrissene Familien und entführte Kinder: Staatlich verordnete Protestantenverfolgung im Osttiroler Defereggental (1684–1691)," *Jahrbuch für die Geschichte des Protestantismus in Österreich* 121 (2005): 91–168.

61. For the emigration of 1731–1732, see especially Mack Walker, *The Salzburg Transaction: Expulsion and Redemption in Eighteenth-Century Germany* (Ithaca, NY, 1992), and Gerhard Florey, *Geschichte der Salzburger Protestanten und ihrer Emigration 1731/32* (Vienna, 1977).

62. See *Hochfürstl. Saltzburgisches Emigrations-Patent, De dato 31. Octobris 1731* (Stadt am Hoff, 1731).

63. For the place of the Salzburgers in the king's colonization projects, see Max Beheim-Schwarzbach, *Friedrich Wilhelm's I. Colonisationswerk in Lithauen, vornehmlich die Salzburger Colonie* (Königsberg, 1879).

64. Notwithstanding the support given to the emigrants, hundreds still succumbed to the exertions of the long march. See Gerhard Florey, *Geschichte der Salzburger Protestanten und ihrer Emigration 1731/32* (Vienna, 1977), 107. Not all the exiles went to East Prussia. Next to other German territories, also the Netherlands and even colonial America received Salzburg immigrants. For the settlement in Georgia, see George Fenwick Jones, *The Salzburger Saga: Religious Exiles and Other Germans along the Savannah* (Athens, GA, 1984).

65. See Arthur Ehmer, *Das Schrifttum zur Salzburger Emigration 1731/33* (Hamburg, 1975), and also Angelika Marsch, *Die Salzburger Emigration in Bildern*, 3rd ed. (Weissenhorn, Germany, 1986).

66. See Stephan Steiner, *Reisen ohne Wiederkehr: Die Deportationen von Protestanten aus Kärnten 1734–1736* (Vienna—Munich, 2007), 99–118, 131. Instructive sources on the conditions in neighboring Carinthia can be found in Christine Tropper, *Glut unter der Asche und offene Flamme: Der Kärntner Geheimprotestantismus und seine Bekämpfung 1731–1738* (Vienna, 2011).

67. For religious conditions in early modern Transylvania, see Volker Leppin and Ulrich A. Wien, eds., *Konfessionsbildung und Konfessionskultur in Siebenbürgen in der frühen Neuzeit* (Stuttgart, 2005), and Ludwig Binder, *Grundlagen und Formen der Toleranz in Siebenbürgen bis zur Mitte des 17. Jahrhunderts* (Cologne-Vienna, 1976).

68. For an introduction to the history of these deportations, see especially Erich Buchinger, *Die "Landler" in Siebenbürgen: Vorgeschichte, Durchführung*

262   Beyond Habsburg

und Ergebnis einer Zwangsumsiedlung im 18. Jahrhundert (Munich, 1980); Stephan Steiner, *Reisen ohne Wiederkehr: Die Deportationen von Protestanten aus Kärnten 1734–1736* (Vienna—Munich, 2007); Dieter Knall, *Aus der Heimat gedrängt: Letzte Zwangsumsiedlungen steirischer Protestanten nach Siebenbürgen unter Maria Theresia* (Graz, 2002); and Martin Bottesch, Franz Grieshofer, and Wilfried Schabus, eds., *Die Siebenbürgischen Landler: Eine Spurensicherung* (Cologne, 2002).

69. In the Bohemian lands, a not altogether comparable procedure still continued into the 1780s.

70. See the lengthy example printed in note 186 of Dieter Knall, *Aus der Heimat gedrängt: Letzte Zwangsumsiedlungen steirischer Protestanten nach Siebenbürgen unter Maria Theresia* (Graz, 2002), 85f.

71. The following oath was required in Upper Austrian Atzbach in the mid-1700s: "I curse and reject the arch-heretic Luther and his false, heretical teachings and swear by the almighty God that I henceforth will live and die in the only true Catholic faith, that I will not acquire any heretical books and that I will also raise and instruct my children and housemates in the true Catholic faith. So help me God and the holy gospel." See the "Methodus extirpandi haeresin Lutheranam in parochia Azbacensi usurpatam" from 1740, printed in Rudolf Weiss, *Das Bistum Passau unter Kardinal Joseph Dominikus von Lamberg (1723–1761): Zugleich ein Beitrag zur Geschichte des Kryptoprotestantismus in Oberösterreich* (St. Ottilien, Germany, 1979), 457–460, here 459.

72. A clear example can be seen in the affirmation demanded by Carinthian peasants in 1601: "As a wretched sinner I confess to you, honorable priest, as a representative of God and the dear Virgin Mary and all dear saints, that I have followed the seductive, damnable, and godless sectarian teachings for [insert number] years and have been trapped in their terrible error. During their abhorrent sacrament I have received nothing but bad baker's bread, and from the chalice nothing but bad wine from the wood. I renounce this awful error and damnable creed and promise never to follow it again. So help me God and all saints." See David Rungius, *Bericht und Erinnerung, von der Tyrannischen Bäpstischen verfolgung deß H. Evangelii, in Steyermarckt, Kärndten und Krain . . .* (Wittenberg, 1601), 8f.

73. Stephan Steiner, *Rückkehr unerwünscht: Deportationen in der Habsburgermonarchie in der Frühen Neuzeit und ihr europäischer Kontext* (Vienna, 2014), 292.

74. Some Carinthian deportees affiliated with the Hutterite community in Transylvania and joined its subsequent migration to Wallachia, the Ukraine, and ultimately North America. See Erich Buchinger, "Die Geschichte der Kärntner Hutterischen Brüder in Siebenbürgen und in der Walachei (1755–1770), in Rußland und Amerika: Ein Beitrag zum Schicksal von Kärntner Transmigranten und zur Geschichte der heutigen Hutterischen Bruderhöfe in den USA und Kanada," *Carinthia I* 172 (1982): 145–303.

For the Hutterites, see also Werner Packull, *Hutterite Beginnings: Communitarian Experiments during the Reformation* (Baltimore, MD, 1995); Rod Janzen and Max Stanton, *The Hutterites in North America* (Baltimore, MD, 2010); John A. Hostetler, *Hutterite Society* (Baltimore,

MD, 1974); and Astrid von Schlachta, *Die Hutterer zwischen Tirol und Amerika: Eine Reise durch die Jahrhunderte* (Innsbruck, 2006).

75. See Erich Buchinger, *Die "Landler" in Siebenbürgen: Vorgeschichte, Durchführung und Ergebnis einer Zwangsumsiedlung im 18. Jahrhundert* (Munich, 1980), 369f., 261.

76. Cited in Liliana Popa, "Urkunden im Hermannstädter Staatsarchiv zur Transmigration österreichischer Protestanten nach Siebenbürgen 1733–1737," in *Die Siebenbürger Landler*, ed. Martin Bottesch, Franz Grieshofer, and Wilfried Schabus, vol. 1 (Vienna, 2002), 89f.

77. For a massive new bibliography of this important ruler, see Barbara Stollberg-Rilinger, *Maria Theresia: Die Kaiserin in ihrer Zeit* (Munich, 2017).

78. Derek Beales, *Joseph II*, vol. 1 (Cambridge, England, 1987), 469f. For Joseph's role as co-regent with limited authority, see ibid., 134–241.

79. Strictly speaking, the emperor issued not one but multiple regionally adjusted edicts for individual crown lands in 1781 and 1782. For text and discussion of the edict(s), see Peter F. Barton, ed., *Im Zeichen der Toleranz* (Vienna, 1981), 152–202, and Harm Klueting, ed., *Der Josephinismus: Ausgewählte Quellen zur Geschichte der theresianisch-josephinischen Reformen* (Darmstadt, 1995), 252–255.

80. See Joseph Karniel, *The Toleranzpolitik Kaiser Josephs II.* (Gerlingen, Germany, 1986). For the complicated status of Jews in Habsburg lands and the discrepancy between positive law and social practice, see also William O. McCagg, *A History of Habsburg Jews, 1670–1918* (Bloomington, IN, 1992).

81. See the letter to his mother of 20 July 1777 cited in Derek Beales, *Joseph II*, vol. 2 (Cambridge, England, 2009), 209.

82. See, for example, the letters to his mother from the late 1770s presented in Derek Beales, *Joseph II*, vol. 1 (Cambridge, England, 1987), 467f. and 469.

83. See Peter F. Barton, *Evangelisch in Österreich* (Vienna, 1987), 130. Less than half of this number was in today's Austria. On the other hand, the number does not include the later province of Burgenland, which still belonged to Hungary. For Austrian numbers, see Peter F. Barton, ed., *Im Zeichen der Toleranz* (Vienna, 1981), 348.

84. See Peter F. Barton, *Evangelisch in Österreich* (Vienna, 1987), 129. The distinction between Lower Austria and Vienna reflects current conditions.

85. For some aspects of this milieu, see Alfred Elste and Dirk Hänisch, *Kärnten von der Ersten zur Zweiten Republik: Kontinuität oder Wandel?* (Klagenfurt, 1998), 217–223.

86. Due to a different legal and political history, almost 20 Protestant congregations in formerly Hungarian Burgenland date back to the era of toleration. In today's Austria, the province has the highest share of Protestants, amounting to approximately 13 percent of the population. Carinthia lies in second place as the only historically Austrian province with a Protestant share of around 10 percent; this number is increasingly challenged by immigration and religious non-affiliation, however.

87. See Josef Wodka, *Kirche in Österreich: Wegweiser durch ihre Geschichte* (Vienna, 1959), 245–249.

88. See Article V, paragraph 41 of the Treaty of Osnabrück.

89. For origin and function of the *corpus evangelicorum* and its Catholic counterpart, see Fritz Wolff, *Corpus Evangelicorum und Corpus*

264 Beyond Habsburg

Catholicorum auf dem westfälischen Friedenskongreß: Die Einfügung der konfessionellen Ständeverbindungen in die Reichsverfassung (Münster, 1966); Ulrich Belstler, *Die Stellung des Corpus Evangelicorum in der Reichsverfassung* (Bamberg, 1968); and Klaus Schlaich, "Corpus evangelicorum und Corpus catholicorum: Aspekte eines Parteienwesens im Hlg. Römischen Reich Deutscher Nation," *Der Staat* 11 (1972): 218–230. That international attention was not restricted to the Austrian lands can be seen in Graeme Murdock, "Responses to Habsburg Persecution of Protestants in Seventeenth-Century Hungary," *Austrian History Yearbook* 40 (2009): 37–52.

90. See Friedrich Reissenberger, "Das Corpus evangelicorum und die österreichischen Protestanten (1685–1764)," *Jahrbuch der Gesellschaft für die Geschichte des Protestantismus in Österreich* 17 (1896): 207–222.

91. The strong involvement of Sweden in the *corpus evangelicorum* during the second half of the seventeenth century can be seen in the collection of its actions and resolutions published as Eberhard Christian Wilhelm von Schauroth, *Vollständige Sammlung Aller Conclusorum, Schreiben Und anderer übrigen Verhandlungen Des Hochpreißlichen Corporis Evangelicorum*, 3 vols. (Regenburg, 1751–1752).

92. See also Helge Almquist, "Königin Christina und die österreichische Protestantenfrage um die Zeit des Westfälischen Friedens," *Archiv für Reformationsgeschichte* 36 (1939): 1–24.

93. See Article V, paragraphs 38–40 of the Treaty of Osnabrück.

94. Charles XII is arguably Sweden's most controversial monarch. For divergent interpretations of his reign, see Frans G. Bengtsson, *Karl XII:s levnad*, 2 vols. (Stockholm, 1935–1936); Ragnhild Marie Hatton, *Charles XII of Sweden* (London, 1968); Sverker Oredsson, ed., *Tsar Peter och Kung Karl: Två härskare och deras folk* (Stockholm, 1998); Bengt Liljegren, *Karl XII: En biografi* (Lund, 2000); and Axel Svensson, ed., *Karl XII som fältherre* (Luleå, 2001).

95. For the negotiations of Altranstädt and the subsequent implementation of the agreement, see Kurt Engelbert, "Die Konvention von Altranstädt 1707," *Archiv für schlesische Kirchengeschichte* 16 (1958): 243–264, and Norbert Conrads, *Die Durchführung der Altranstädter Konvention in Schlesien 1707–1709* (Cologne, 1971).

96. For the text of the convention, see Frank Metasch, *300 Jahre Altranstädter Konvention—300 Jahre Schlesische Toleranz* (Dresden, 2007), 83–89.

97. See Peter Englund, *Poltava: Berättelsen om en armés undergång* (Stockholm, 1988).

98. See also Gabriele Haug-Moritz, "Corpus Evangelicorum und deutscher Dualismus," in *Alternativen zur Reichsverfassung in der Frühen Neuzeit*, ed. Volker Press (Munich, 1995), 189–207.

99. For the religious implications of Silesia's passage from Habsburg to Prussian sovereignty, see Peter Baumgart, ed., *Kontinuität und Wandel: Schlesien zwischen Österreich und Preußen* (Sigmaringen, Germany, 1990), 239–256, 287–306. See also Joachim Bahlcke, "Religion und Politik in Schlesien: Konfessionspolitische Strukturen unter habsburgischer und preußischer Herrschaft (1650–1800)," *Blätter für deutsche Landesgeschichte* 134

Beyond Habsburg 265

(1998): 33–57. For the petitions of Silesian Protestants to the Prussian King Frederick II, see also Reinhold Schaefer, ed., *Bittgesuche evangelischer Schlesier an Friedrich den Großen* (Görlitz, 1941). For Frederick's subsequent pragmatic policy toward Silesian Protestantism, see also Josef Joachim Menzel, ed., *Geschichte Schlesiens*, vol. 3, *Preußisch-Schlesien 1740–1945; Österreichisch-Schlesien 1740–1918/45* (Stuttgart, 1999), 252–259.

100. For an English-language introduction to the German unification movement, see Hagen Schulze, *The Course of German Nationalism: From Frederick the Great to Bismarck, 1763–1867* (Cambridge, England, 1991).

101. For an investigation of the relationship between religion and nationhood with a special focus on Germany, see Michael Geyer and Hartmut Lehmann, eds., *Religion und Nation, Nation und Religion: Beiträge zu einer unbewältigten Geschichte* (Göttingen, 2004).

102. For a recent analysis of the public debate about German unification and its Austrian aspects, see Mark Hewitson, *Nationalism in Germany, 1848–1866: Revolutionary Nation* (Basingstoke, England, 2010).

103. For the most important act of mediatization and territorial reorganization, the so-called Final Recess of the Imperial Deputation of 1803, see Harm Klueting, ed., *200 Jahre Reichsdeputationshauptschluss: Säkularisation, Mediatisierung und Modernisierung zwischen Altem Reich und neuer Staatlichkeit* (Münster, 2005), and Ulrich Hufeld, ed., *Der Reichsdeputationshauptschluss von 1803: Eine Dokumentation zum Untergang des Alten Reiches* (Cologne, 2003).

104. For the early suppression of religious reform in Tyrol, see Peter Bierbrauer, *Die unterdrückte Reformation: Der Kampf der Tiroler um eine neue Kirche 1521–1527* (Zurich, 1993).

105. For detailed examinations of the Zillertal emigration, one still needs to consult relatively old and/or politically engaged publications. See especially Ekkart Sauser, *Die Zillertaler Inklinanten und ihre Ausweisung im Jahre 1837* (Innsbruck, 1959); Gustav von Gasteiger, *Die Zillerthaler Protestanten und ihre Ausweisung aus Tirol* (Meran, 1892); and Georg Friedrich Heinrich Rheinwald, *Die Evangelischen Zillerthaler in Schlesien* (Berlin, 1838).

For some more recent but shorter analyses, see Sebastian Hölzl, "Die Zillertaler Protestanten vor 150 Jahren: Dargestellt am Beispiel Brandbergs," *Tiroler Heimat* 50 (1986): 149–173; Werner Maleczek, "Glaube und Heimat: Zur Vertreibung der Zillertaler Inklinanten vor 150 Jahren," *Das Fenster* 42 (1987): 4152–4158; and Florian Huber, "Konfessionelle Identitätsbildung in Tirol: Antiprotestantismus ohne Protestanten (1830–1848)," *Geschichte und Region/Storia e regione* 19 (2010): 28–52.

106. This event also undermined Habsburg attempts at creating a more tolerant image among the international public, which have been described somewhat generously in Scott Berg, "'The Lord Has Done Great Things for Us': The 1817 Reformation Celebrations and the End of the Counter-Reformation in the Habsburg Lands," *Central European History* 49 (2016): 69–92.

107. Ernst Tomek, *Kirchengeschichte Österreichs*, vol. 2 (Innsbruck, 1949), 520.

108. See Adam Wolf, *Geschichtliche Bilder aus Österreich*, vol. 1 (Vienna, 1878), 24.

266 Beyond Habsburg

109. See Kungliga Vitterhets-, Historie- och Antiquitets-Akademien, ed., *Rikskansleren Axel Oxenstiernas skrifter och brefvexling*, vol. 1:7 (Stockholm, 1926), 559–563.

110. For some regional exceptions primarily in earlier historical periods, see Philipp Tolloi, *Aspekte der Rezeptionsgeschichte des Tiroler Bauernkrieges und Michael Gaismairs von 1525 bis 1945* (Master's thesis, University of Vienna, 2006), and the relevant chapters in Peter Rauscher and Martin Scheutz, eds., *Die Stimme der ewigen Verlierer? Aufstände, Revolten und Revolutionen in den österreichischen Ländern (ca. 1450–1815)* (Vienna, 2013).

111. For an introduction to pertinent Czech historiography, see Victor S. Mamatey, "The Battle of the White Mountain as Myth in Czech History," *East European Quarterly* 15 (1981): 335–345; Josef Petráň, "Na téma mýtu Bílé hory," in *Traditio et Cultus: Miscellanea historica Bohemica Miloslao Vlk archiepiscopo Pragensi ab eius collegis amicisque ad annum sexagesimum dedicata*, ed. Zdeňka Hledíková (Prague, 1993), 141–162; as well as Josef Petráň and Lydia Petráňova, "The White Mountain as a Symbol in Modern Czech History," in *Bohemia in History*, ed. Mikuláš Teich (Cambridge, England, 1998), 143–163; Jiří Rak, *Bývali Čechové: české historické mýty a stereotypy* (Jinočany, Czech Republic, 1994); Frederick G. Heymann, "Das Temno in der neuen tschechischen Geschichtsauffassung," *Bohemia* 9 (1968): 323–339; Richard Georg Plaschka, *Von Palacký bis Pekař: Geschichtswissenschaft und Nationalbewußtsein bei den Tschechen* (Graz, 1955); and also František Kavka, *Bílá hora a české dějiny* (Prague, 1962). For the contentious relationship between the Czech national movement and the Catholic tradition, see also Martin Schulze Wessel, "Tschechische Nation und katholische Konfession vor und nach der Gründung des tschechoslowakischen Nationalstaates," *Bohemia* 39 (1997): 311–337.

For an introduction to Hungarian equivalents, see Ignác Romsics, "Ungarische Geschichtsschreibung im 20. Jahrhundert—Tendenzen, Autoren, Werke," in *Nationale Geschichtskulturen—Bilanz, Ausstrahlung, Europabezogenheit*, ed. Heinz Duchhardt (Stuttgart, 2006), 195–219, and Géza Pálffy, *The Kingdom of Hungary and the Habsburg Monarchy in the Sixteenth Century* (New York, 2009), 1–6. For general overviews of Hungarian historiography, see also Péter Gunst, *A magyar történetírás története* (Debrecen, 2000), and Steven Béla Vardy, *Modern Hungarian Historiography* (Boulder, CO, 1976).

112. See especially Heinrich von Srbik, *Deutsche Einheit: Idee und Wirklichkeit vom Heiligen Reich bis Königgrätz*, 4 vols. (Munich, 1935–1942).

113. See Joseph Roth, *Radetzkymarsch* (Berlin, 1932).

114. Karl Renner suggested Southeast-Germany as a possible alternative. See Ruth Wodak et al., eds. *The Discursive Construction of National Identity*, 2nd ed. (Edinburgh, 2009), 51.

115. For alternative nineteenth- and early twentieth-century interpretations of Czech history in general and the impact of the Thirty Years' War in particular, see František Palacký, *Dějiny národu českého v Čechách a v Moravě*, 5 vols. (Prague, 1848); Tomáš G. Masaryk, *Česká otázka: Snahy a tužby národního obrození* (Prague, 1895); Kamil Krofta, *Bílá hora* (Prague,

Beyond Habsburg   267

1913); and Josef Pekař, *Bílá hora: Její příčiny i následky* (Prague, 1921). For an introduction to Masaryk's perspective in English, see Tomáš G. Masaryk, *The Meaning of Czech History*, ed. René Wellek (Chapel Hill, NC, 1974). This founding father of the Czechoslovak republic also stated that "our rebellion against the throne was accompanied by our aversion to the church that served the dynasty." See Karel Čapek, *Gespräche mit T.G. Masaryk* (Munich, 1969), 263. For the treatment of the topic in fictional literature, see also Miloslav Hýsek, "Bílá hora v české literatuře," in *Na Bílé hoře*, ed. Josef Teige et al. (Prague, 1921), 107–145.

116. For the confessional aspects of Czech identity, see also Marie-Élizabeth Ducreux, "Entre catholicisme et protestantisme: l'identité tchèque," *Le Débat* 59 (1990): 103–125.

117. For the multifaceted relationship between the three core components of the Habsburg Monarchy, that is, the Austrian, the Bohemian, and the Hungarian lands, see R. J. W. Evans, *The Making of the Habsburg Monarchy 1550–1700: An Interpretation* (Oxford, 1979), and idem, *Austria, Hungary, and the Habsburgs: Essays on Central Europe, c.1683–1867* (Oxford, 2006). For differing historiographical traditions, see also idem, "Historians and the State in the Habsburg Lands," in *Visions sur le développement des États européens*, ed. Wim Blockmans and Jean-Philippe Genet (Rome, 1993), 203–218.

118. See Christian von Anhalt's battle report in Anton Gindely, ed., *Die Berichte über die Schlacht auf dem Weissen Berge bei Prag* (Vienna, 1877), 125–128.

119. Ibid.

120. See Victor Bibl, "Die katholischen und protestantischen Stände Niederösterreichs im XVII. Jahrhundert: Ein Beitrag zur Geschichte der ständischen Verfassung," *Jahrbuch für Landeskunde von Niederösterreich*, n. s., 2 (1903): 297.

121. See his *Abgenötigte doch rechtmäßige und warhaffte Beanttwortung und Ablahnung der Calumnien und Iniurien . . .* (Stockholm, 1636), printed in Hermann Hallwich, ed., *Heinrich Matthias Thurn als Zeuge im Process Wallenstein: Ein Denkblatt zur dritten Säcularfeier Wallensteins* (Leipzig, 1883), 1–26, here 22. For the self-image of Upper Austrian rebel Erasmus von Starhemberg, see also Georg Heilingsetzer, "Ständischer Widerstand und Unterwerfung: Erasmus von Starhemberg und seine Rechtfertigungsschrift (1621)," *Mitteilungen des oberösterreichischen Landesarchivs* 14 (1984): 269–289.

For conflicting discourses in Bohemia, see also Petr Mat'a, "Patres Patriae or Proditores Patriae? Legitimizing and De-Legitimizing the Authority of the Provincial Estates in Seventeenth-Century Bohemia", in *Whose Love of Which Country? Composite States, National Histories and Patriotic Discourses in Early Modern East Central Europe*, ed. Balázs Trencsényi and Márton Zászkaliczky (Leiden—Boston, 2010), 405–444.

122. For the following, see [Georg Erasmus von Tschernembl], *Consultationes Oder Underschidliche Rathschläg/ Der maisten und wichtigisten sachen/ welche von Anfang der Böhemischen/ und andern folgenden Auffständ fürgangen/ unnd zu Werck gericht worden/ oder werden sollen: Von wort*

268 *Beyond Habsburg*

> *zu wort auß dem Original Protocoll, so in der Haidelbergischen Cantzley gefunden worden/ gezogen. Mit nohtwendigen Glossis erklärt,* [ed. Jakob Keller] (n.p., 1624), especially recommendations 8, 25, and 33.

123. The estatist variety of representative government differed substantially from its modern democratic expression, of course. Yet this is equally true in England, without diminishing historical identification.

124. Barry Schwartz, *Abraham Lincoln and the Forge of National Memory* (Chicago, 2000), 17.

8 Historiographical Essay

An Introduction to Historical Writing on Austria's Confessional Age

The literature on Reformation and Counterreformation in the Habsburgs' Alpine patrimony is too encompassing to be discussed in detail within the framework of this review. The focus of an introductory overview must lie on studies that hold particular relevance for the history of Austrian Protestantism during the confessional era, with an emphasis on newer works in English and German, which will be most accessible for the bulk of the readership. Such an overview does not strive for completeness, but places the current study in the existing scholarly debate and directs to supplementary readings. With few exceptions, it will concentrate on works that examine distinctly Austrian or at least Habsburgian conditions. Thus, the extensive literature on the Holy Roman Empire during the same period falls outside the scope of this literature review, whereas it remains eminently valuable for a better understanding of broader political and theoretical ramifications and consequently for the current study as well.[1] The same holds true for analyses of Swedish policy.

Due to the period's deep impact on the subsequent development of the Habsburg Monarchy and its political system, it figures prominently in the major surveys of Austrian history, such as Robert Kann's *A History of the Habsburg Empire, 1526–1918* and Erich Zöllner's *Geschichte Österreichs*, but also in studies that examine the origins of the Habsburg empire, such as R. J. W. Evans' *The Making of the Habsburg Monarchy, 1550–1700*.[2] After all, the outcome of the denominational conflict not only determined the religious future of the hereditary lands but also formed the basis of the absolutist monarchy that developed into the pre-eminent polity of the European southeast. Since this transformation was equally consequential for individual crown lands, it has also been treated competently in regional overviews such as Siegfried Haider's history of Upper Austria or Claudia Fräss-Ehrfeld's history of Carinthia.[3]

270   Historiographical Essay

By the same token, the era of Reformation and Counterreformation holds a significant place in surveys of Austrian ecclesiastical history. The monumental history of Austria that came out under the editorship of Herwig Wolfram between 1994 and 2006 forms a passage between the subfields of general and church history, as it includes a volume dedicated solely to the history of Christianity in Austria, which allows the Viennese ecclesiastical historian Rudolf Leeb to devote almost 150 pages to the confessional era.[4] The volume is representative of a contemporary form of ecclesiastical history that strives to transcend the denominational cleavages of older historiography. Classical works such as Ernst Tomek's *Kirchengeschichte Österreichs* and Cölestin Wolfsgruber's *Kirchengeschichte Österreich-Ungarns* grew out of the research tradition of Catholic schools of theology.[5] At the same time, the history of the evangelical churches in Austria largely remained the domain of Protestant scholars. The authors of the principal academic overviews of the subject, such as Georg Loesche, Grete Mecenseffy, and Peter Barton, were all affiliated with the evangelical theological faculty at the University of Vienna.[6]

The relationship between estates and monarchy, which is almost inseparably connected with the denominational conflict in Austria, has formed another important topic of investigation. As early as 1903, Victor Bibl analyzed the complications of estatist politics in the Lower Austrian diet, and numerous studies have followed.[7] Michael Mitterauer developed a genealogy and typology of representative assemblies in the Austrian provinces.[8] Günther Burkert traced the political conflict to the very beginning of the religious schism and the accessions of Charles V and Ferdinand I to the throne.[9] In several essays, Winfried Schulze examined status and ideology of Austrian nobles at the transition from estatist to absolutist conceptions of state, whereas Petr Maťa and Thomas Winkelbauer presented the ongoing debate about the nature of governance following the defeat of estatist opposition in the Habsburg patrimony.[10] Within the framework of Wolfram's history of Austria, Winkelbauer also provided a comprehensive synthesis of the era.[11] Not least of all, a promising wave of comparative studies, spearheaded by R. J. W. Evans in Britain and Joachim Bahlcke in Germany, placed the governmental structure of the Habsburg lands in a wider Central European context.[12]

Next to such broader works, there exists a wealth of more narrowly circumscribed analyses. Due to their pivotal role in the confessional conflict, the biographies of Habsburg rulers form an integral part of this literature. The Central European significance of Charles V surfaces most clearly in the classic study by Karl Brandi as well as the more recent

Historiographical Essay 271

biography by Alfred Kohler.[13] Paula Sutter Fichtner examined Ferdinand I through the prism of dynastic politics, which was so fundamental for this founding father of the Danubian Habsburg Monarchy of subsequent centuries; Alfred Kohler supplemented this picture with the monarch's pan-European dimension.[14] Fichtner can also take credit for the foremost biography of Ferdinand's son Maximilian II, in which she emphasized the emperor's failure to realize his chief goals of defeating the Ottoman Empire and easing confessional tensions in Germany, not to mention the more elusive ambition of reuniting Western Christianity.[15]

In general, Maximilian's two sons on the imperial throne have not been judged more kindly. In his not unsympathetic assessment of Rudolf II, R. J. W. Evans captured the anachronistic mood of a Renaissance court past its time, with a melancholy monarch beholden to philosophy and mysticism rather than the everyday routine of practical politics.[16] Whereas his brother and successor Matthias still awaits an equally thought-provoking treatment, Ferdinand II has received his in Robert Bireley's *Religion and Politics in the Age of the Counter Reformation*, as well as in the same author's subsequent biography of the ruler.[17] Unlike his predecessors, Ferdinand has never been accused of lacking a political program or the determination to pursue it, and Bireley succeeds at bringing this program to light in his portrayal of the emperor's relationship with his Jesuit confessor William Lamormaini.[18] Finally, Lothar Höbelt toned down the popular image of Ferdinand III as inherently more compromising and peace-loving than his father by highlighting the military and geopolitical pressures that finally convinced the emperor to make the necessary concessions.[19]

The rise and fall of Protestantism in early modern Austria constitutes another centerpiece of the period's historiography.[20] As far back as 1732, the Lutheran theologian Bernhard Raupach commenced the publication of his multi-volume opus on the fate of his Alpine coreligionists, and in spite of its inherent shortcomings as a work of history, it continues to be valuable source material.[21] In the twentieth century, evangelical ecclesiastic historians stood in the forefront of this research, above all in regard to the internal politics of Protestant communities. Scholars and theologians such as Gustav Reingrabner and Paul Dedic painstakingly documented the Protestant experience in the Austrian lands, with Reingrabner focusing especially on the Danubian region and Dedic on the southern provinces of Styria and Carinthia.[22] In recent years, Protestant church historians have increasingly participated in large comparative and interdenominational research projects. Rudolf Leeb contributed to significant collaborative publications on Reformation, Counterreformation,

272   Historiographical Essay

and crypto-Protestantism in Austria.[23] Through their affiliation with the Institute of Ecclesiastical History of the Danubian and Carpathian Lands, Peter Barton and Karl Schwarz, in turn, put the history of Austrian Protestantism into a broader East Central European context.[24] At the same time, scholars affiliated with Catholic institutions of learning in Austria have also begun to participate more actively in the exploration of the country's Protestant tradition.[25]

Due to its long-term repercussions, the restoration of Catholic supremacy is treated in most works on the period. Among specific studies of the Counterreformation, Joseph von Hammer-Purgstall's detailed biography of Cardinal Melchior Klesl, its foremost proponent in the archduchy, is still informative, not least of all for its extensive source material.[26] Among older works on Inner Austria, the *oeuvre* of Graz historian Johann Loserth carries the same distinction, again for its abundance of sources.[27] In other respects, of course, recent works are more pertinent today. Arno Herzig's wider Central European study of recatholization, which emphasizes the role of the state and its insistence on loyalty and conformity, pays special attention to the Habsburg Monarchy.[28] Ronnie Po-Chia Hsia's global overview of the Catholic renewal between 1540 and 1770 provides a deeper understanding of the social, political, and intellectual framework within which the reestablishment of Catholic supremacy in the Habsburg lands became possible.[29] Howard Louthan's analysis of Bohemia, whose conditions differed little from those in the Alpine hereditary lands, complements established images of governmental coercion with a stronger emphasis on the mass appeal of Baroque Catholicism.[30] By the same token, Jörg Deventer's study of recatholization in the Silesian cities of Glogau and Schweidnitz gains special relevance for Austria by demonstrating that the Habsburgs were capable of nuancing their confessional policies, if overriding considerations of foreign policy so required.[31]

Most important, however, are those new studies that focus distinctly on the Austrian lands. The trilingual conference volume on Catholic Reform and Counterreformation in Inner Austria published by France Dolinar et al. in 1994 stressed the spiritual depth of recatholization at this intersection of German, Slovenian, and Italian influences.[32] Based on her careful examination of Styrian conditions, Regina Pörtner concluded that the Counterreformation in the Habsburg Monarchy relied heavily on the government and formed a crucial part of state-building by strengthening the power of the monarch and providing an ideology of state.[33] By examining the everyday interchange of Catholic reformers and local populace in the Traunviertel district of Upper Austria, Joseph Patrouch investigated recatholization from the bottom up and concluded that the process was not unilaterally steered by authorities but consistently negotiated between rulers and ruled.[34]

The intellectual climate of the Counterreformation also formed the background of two closely related phenomena that represented the most commonplace responses to the new political realities. On the one hand, there was the option of embracing Catholicism. In several important contributions, culminating in his thematic biography of the Austro-Moravian aristocrat Gundaker von Liechtenstein, Thomas Winkelbauer brought out the motivational diversity of noble conversions in an environment of increasing pressure to conform.[35] Karin MacHardy documented the impact of confessionalized court patronage for the resurgence of Catholicism within the Austrian nobility.[36] Taking his starting point in the minutes of the reformation commission that returned Lower Austrian holdouts to Catholicism in the 1650s, Gustav Reingrabner expanded the prevalent focus on the aristocracy to include the peasantry.[37] Through their investigations of broader Central European developments, Peter Schimert and Jörg Deventer shed light on Austrian conditions as well.[38]

On the other hand, there was the option of seeking freedom of worship abroad. The experience of religious refugees from the Habsburgs' Alpine patrimony evoked interest in both Austria and the south German territories in which most of them settled. Whereas local historians and pastors such as Hermann Clauss prepared the ground with meticulous archival searches, Paul Dedic converted his extensive source material into a multifaceted account of the religious emigration from Carinthia.[39] From the perspective of their primary places of refuge, Georg Rusam examined the impact of Austrian immigrants in Franconia and Swabia.[40] In the 1990s the research on Austria's confessional migration was raised to a new level by Werner Wilhelm Schnabel, whose detailed investigation of Austrian exiles in the free imperial cities of southern Germany dramatically expanded the existing knowledge base.[41] In recent years, comparative approaches have also enriched the study of confessional refugees, with contributions on exiles from the Habsburg lands prominently represented.[42] Based on this extensive research, Hans Krawarik was able to provide a broad overview of Austria's confessional emigration in 2010.[43]

The literature on the Thirty Years' War transcends this historiographical overview in both volume and scope, even if its major works are indispensable for the assessment of Austrian developments. Some studies hold particular relevance, however. Anton Gindely's classic investigation from the 1880s is unavoidably dated, but its detailed coverage of the Habsburg Monarchy still provides a wealth of pertinent facets that elude more contemporary international publications.[44] Similar observations could be

274 *Historiographical Essay*

made about Hans Sturmberger's analysis of the war's outbreak, whereas Josef Polišenský's comprehensive synthesis remains relevant not only for its Bohemian focus but also for its argument, which views the conflict as a contest between universalist monarchy and nascent civil society.[45] Habsburg developments play an important role in Winfried Schulze's collected volume on the preconditions of war, which diagnosed a widespread sense of vulnerability among leading protagonists on both sides.[46] Looking at the final phase of the conflict, Karsten Ruppert, in turn, analyzed the imperial negotiation strategies at the peace conference.[47] Jenny Öhman's Viennese dissertation *Der Kampf um den Frieden* from 2005 provided at least an introduction to the multifaceted interplay of Swedish and Habsburgian politics during the war and especially the peace talks in Osnabrück, whereas Pekka Suvanto illuminated this interplay through the negotiations between Chancellor Axel Oxenstierna and Albrecht von Wallenstein.[48]

The more recent investigations of the war support this study in a different manner. Whereas they do not regularly add new source material on the religious dualism of early modern Austria, they reinterpret the fundamental outlines of the larger conflict in light of current scholarship. Most influential has been Johannes Burkhardt, who ascribed the war to competing concepts of state-building; its outcome determined the size and nature of statehood in early-modern Europe. Conceptions of universal monarchy had to be moderated; the future belonged to the coexistence of sovereign states.[49] Günter Barudio's study triggered debate for its insistence on the essentially German character of the war and its favorable assessment of the political polycentricity of the empire that followed in its wake, but it is also relevant for its thorough treatment of Swedish aspects.[50] Similarly, Geoffrey Parker's edited volume deserves mention not only for its stature as regularly republished English standard work but also for its knowledgeable contributors on conditions Scandinavian as well as Austrian.[51] Including the war in the wider framework of international relations between 1559 and 1660, Heinz Schilling highlighted the confessionalization of foreign policy during this period.[52] Peter H. Wilson, by contrast, sees religion as the driving force of a militant minority only, whereas the larger war was shaped by traditional politics—and eminently avoidable.[53]

Whereas analyses of Reformation and Counterreformation are abundant, studies on Protestant resistance remain the exception. For a long time, the literature on Austrian Protestantism adhered to the paradigm of Lutheran suffering obedience. This axiom already predominated with Johann Loserth over a century ago but is still faintly discernible in recent

Historiographical Essay 275

works such as Regina Pörtner's.[54] There are solid arguments to support it, particularly in regard to the Inner Austria estates that stood at the center of these authors' investigations.[55] The nobles of Styria and Carinthia did not resort to arms to prevent the recatholization campaigns against peasants and townspeople, and they ultimately bowed to their archduke's command to convert or emigrate.

Yet the absence of armed resistance against recatholization among the estates of Inner Austria does not establish the unconditional acceptance of monarchic authority among Austrian Lutherans. As Arno Strohmeyer has shown, contemporary notions of resistance encompassed much more than outright rebellion.[56] More often, the estates resorted to written interpolations such as memoranda and supplications to promote their interpretation of established law, custom, and agreement. These intercessions were not empty gestures, but part of an elaborate system of mutual obligations that were understood by monarch and vassal alike. Even seemingly defeatist demonstrations such as collective genuflections contained a tangible element of defiance, as they invoked the ruler's sense of justice and clemency to achieve a fulfilment of political aspirations. While international influences were not absent, Strohmeyer ascribed the core of this ideology of resistance to native traditions. Winfried Schulze uncovered corresponding tendencies among the nobles of Inner Austria as well.[57]

Almost absent is the scholarly analysis of the more radical strain of Protestant opposition. There exists an increasingly dated literature on the peasant uprising in Upper Austria, but its focus is wider, which is legitimate in regard to so complex an event as mass rebellion.[58] With his groundbreaking study of Georg Erasmus von Tschernembl, Hans Sturmberger has at least assured this pivotal representative of Protestant estatism a thorough scholarly treatment, even if the author's emphasis on the Calvinist origins of resistance thinking has subsequently been challenged.[59] Nothing similarly informative has been written on other aspects of fundamental opposition, particularly the cooperation with Protestant Sweden during the Thirty Years' War. The topic surfaced sketchily in confessional Catholic literature, where it tended to be represented as an expression of Protestant treachery that vindicated the coercive features of recatholization, but has otherwise largely escaped scholarly attention.[60] It has been one of the foremost purposes of the current study to fill this gap.

Notes

1. For some influential newer interpretations of this polity, see Georg Schmidt, *Geschichte des Alten Reiches: Staat und Nation in der Frühen Neuzeit*

276 Historiographical Essay

1495–1806 (Munich, 1999); Joachim Whaley, *Germany and the Holy Roman Empire*, 2 vols. (Oxford, 2012); and Barbara Stollberg-Rilinger, *Des Kaisers alte Kleider: Verfassungsgeschichte und Symbolsprache des Alten Reiches*, 2nd ed. (Munich, 2013).

2. Robert A. Kann, *A History of the Habsburg Monarchy, 1526–1918* (Berkeley, CA, 1974); Erich Zöllner, *Geschichte Österreichs: Von den Anfängen bis zur Gegenwart* (Vienna, 1990); R. J. W. Evans, *The Making of the Habsburg Monarchy, 1550–1700* (Oxford, 1979).

3. Siegfried Haider, *Geschichte Oberösterreichs* (Munich, 1987); Claudia Fräss-Ehrfeld, *Geschichte Kärntens*, vol. 2, *Die ständische Periode* (Klagenfurt, 1994).

4. Rudolf Leeb, Maximilian Liebmann, Georg Scheibelreiter, and Peter G. Tropper, *Geschichte des Christentums in Österreich: Von der Spätantike bis zur Gegenwart* (Vienna, 2003).

5. Ernst Tomek, *Kirchengeschichte Österreichs*, 3 vols. (Innsbruck et al., 1935–1959); Cölestin Wolfsgruber, *Kirchengeschichte Österreich-Ungarns* (Vienna, 1909).

6. Among their central works are Georg Loesche, *Geschichte des Protestantismus im vormaligen und neuen Österreich* (Vienna, 1930); Grete Mecenseffy, *Geschichte des Protestantismus in Österreich* (Graz, 1956); Peter F. Barton, *Die Geschichte der Evangelischen in Österreich und Südostmitteleuropa*, vol. 1, *Im Schatten der Bauernkriege: Die Frühzeit der Reformation* (Vienna, 1985), and idem, *Evangelisch in Österreich* (Vienna, 1987).

7. Victor Bibl, "Die katholischen und protestantischen Stände Niederösterreichs im XVII. Jahrhundert: Ein Beitrag zur Geschichte der ständischen Verfassung," *Jahrbuch für Landeskunde von Niederösterreich*, n. s., 2 (1903): 165–323.

8. Michael Mitterauer, "Ständegliederung und Ländertypen," in *Herrschaftsstruktur und Ständebildung 3*, ed. Ernst Bruckmüller, Michael Mitterauer, and Helmuth Stradal (Munich, 1973), 115–203.

9. Günther R. Burkert, *Landesfürst und Stände: Karl V., Ferdinand I. und die österreichischen Erbländer im Ringen um Gesamtstaat und Landesinteressen* (Graz, 1987).

10. See, for example, Winfried Schulze, "Das Ständewesen in den Erblanden der Habsburgermonarchie bis 1740: Vom dualistischen Ständestaat zum organisch-föderativen Absolutismus," in *Ständetum und Staatsbildung in Brandenburg-Preußen*, ed. Peter Baumgart and Jürgen Schmädeke (Berlin, 1983), 263–279; and idem, "Estates and the Problem of Resistance in Theory and Practice in the Sixteenth and Seventeenth Centuries," in *Crown, Church and Estates: Central European Politics in the Sixteenth and Seventeenth Centuries*, ed. R. J. W. Evans and T. V. Thomas (London, 1991), 158–175. For an examination of the military aspects of contemporary state-building by the same author, see idem, *Landesdefension und Staatsbildung: Studien zum Kriegswesen des innerösterreichischen Territorialstaates (1564–1619)* (Vienna, 1973). For the discussion of Habsburg absolutism, see Petr Maťa and Thomas Winkelbauer, eds., *Die Habsburgermonarchie 1620 bis 1740: Leistungen und Grenzen des Absolutismusparadigmas* (Stuttgart, 2006). For another reappraisal that emphasizes the continuing significance of the

Historiographical Essay   277

estates beyond the caesura of the 1620s, see also Gerhard Ammerer et al., eds., *Bündnispartner und Konkurrenten der Landesfürsten: Die Stände in der Habsburgermonarchie* (Vienna, 2007).

11. Thomas Winkelbauer, *Ständefreiheit und Fürstenmacht: Länder und Untertanen des Hauses Habsburg im konfessionellen Zeitalter*, 2 vols. (Vienna, 2003).

12. See, for example, Joachim, Bahlcke, Hans-Jürgen Bömelburg, and Norbert Kersken, eds., *Ständefreiheit und Staatsgestaltung in Ostmitteleuropa: Übernationale Gemeinsamkeiten in der politischen Kultur vom 16.—18. Jahrhundert* (Leipzig 1996); Joachim Bahlcke and Arno Strohmeyer, eds., *Konfessionalisierung in Ostmitteleuropa: Wirkungen des religiösen Wandels im 16. und 17. Jahrhundert in Staat, Gesellschaft und Kultur* (Stuttgart, 1999); and R. J. W. Evans and T. V. Thomas, eds., *Crown, Church and Estates: Central European Politics in the Sixteenth and Seventeenth Centuries* (London, 1991).

13. Karl Brandi, *Karl V.: Werden und Schicksal einer Persönlichkeit und eines Weltreichs*, 2 vols. (Munich, 1937–1941); Alfred Kohler, *Karl V. 1500–1558* (Munich, 2001).

14. Paula Sutter Fichtner, *Ferdinand I of Austria: The Politics of Dynasticism in the Age of the Reformation* (Boulder, CO, 1982); Alfred Kohler, *Ferdinand I. 1503–1564: Fürst, König und Kaiser* (Munich, 2003). See also Ernst Laubach, *Ferdinand I. als Kaiser: Politik und Herrschaftsauffassung des Nachfolgers Karls V.* (Münster, 2001), and Martina Fuchs and Alfred Kohler, eds., *Kaiser Ferdinand I.: Aspekte eines Herrscherlebens* (Münster, 2003).

15. Paula Sutter Fichtner, *Emperor Maximilian II* (New Haven, CO, 2001). A more positive assessment of Maximilian's regency and personality emerges from Viktor Bibl's studies of the emperor; see Viktor Bibl, *Maximilian II.: Der rätselhafte Kaiser* (Hellerau, Germany, 1929), and idem, "Zur Frage der religiösen Haltung Kaiser Maximilians II.," *Archiv für österreichische Geschichte* 106 (1918): 289–425.

16. R. J. W. Evans, *Rudolf II and His World: A Study in Intellectual History, 1576–1612* (Oxford, 1973). For Rudolf's political role, see also Josef Janáček, *Rudolf II. a jeho doba* (Prague, 1987).

17. See Robert Bireley, *Religion and Politics in the Age of the Counterreformation: Emperor Ferdinand II, William Lamormaini, S.J., and the Formation of Imperial Policy* (Chapel Hill, NC, 1981), and idem, *Ferdinand II: Counter-Reformation Emperor, 1578–1637* (New York, 2014). See also Hans Sturmberger, *Ferdinand II. und das Problem des Absolutismus* (Munich, 1957). In view of Ferdinand's historical significance and popularity in older confessional literature, the scarcity of comprehensive scholarly biographies in recent decades is noticeable, however. Among the famous older works, on can cite Franz Christoph Khevenhiller, *Annales Ferdinandei, oder Wahrhaffte Beschreibung Kaysers Ferdinandi des Andern . . .*, 2nd ed., 12 vols. (Leipzig, 1721–1726) as well as Friedrich von Hurter, *Geschichte Kaiser Ferdinands II.*, 11 vols. (Schaffhausen, 1850–1864); see also the reference to William Lamormaini in the subsequent note. For Matthias, one can resort to Bernd Rill, *Kaiser Matthias: Bruderzwist und Glaubenskampf* (Graz 1999).

18. Besides serving as his confessor, Lamormaini (also known as Guillaume Germe De Lamormain) authored an early biography extolling the emperor

278 Historiographical Essay

the year after the latter's death. See William Lamormaini, *Ferdinandi II Romanorum Imperatoris Virtutes* (Vienna, 1638).

19. Lothar Höbelt, *Ferdinand III. (1609–1657): Friedenskaiser wider Willen* (Graz, 2008). Mark Hengerer largely confirmed this assessment in his own biography, which showed the dilemmas of Ferdinand's peace efforts and the lack of clear and realistic political goals. See Mark Hengerer, *Kaiser Ferdinand III.* (Vienna, 2012).

20. For an introduction, see Rudolf Leeb, "Das Erbe der Protestantengeschichtsschreibung in Österreich: Die Fragen der Vergangenheit und die Perspektiven für die zukünftige Forschung," *Carinthia I* 189 (1999): 711–723.

21. Bernhard Raupach, *Evangelisches Oesterreich: das ist historische Nachricht, von den vornehmsten Schicksahlen der evangelisch-lutherischen Kirchen in dem Ertz-Hertzogthum Oesterreich*, 6 vols. (Hamburg, 1732–1744).

22. Gustav Reingrabner's *Adel und Reformation: Beiträge zur Geschichte des protestantischen Adels im Lande unter der Enns während des 16. und 17. Jahrhunderts* (St. Pölten, 1976); and "Gegenreformation in Niederösterreich: Das Protokoll der Reformationskommission für das Viertel ober dem Wienerwald von 1657–1660," *Jahrbuch der Gesellschaft für die Geschichte des Protestantismus in Österreich* 113 (1997): 9–115; as well as Paul Dedic's *Der Protestantismus in Steiermark im Zeitalter der Reformation und Gegenreformation* (Leipzig, 1930); "Der Kärntner Protestantismus vom Abschluß der 'Hauptreformation' bis zur Adelsemigration (1600–1629/30)," *Jahrbuch der Gesellschaft für die Geschichte des Protestantismus in Österreich* 58 (1937): 70–108; and "Der Kärntner Protestantismus von der Adelsemigration bis zum Ende des siebzehnten Jahrhunderts," *Jahrbuch der Gesellschaft für die Geschichte des Protestantismus in Österreich* 59 (1938): 63–165; are important examples of these regional analyses of Austrian Protestantism.

23. See Rudolf Leeb, Susanne Claudine Pils, and Thomas Winkelbauer, eds., *Staatsmacht und Seelenheil: Gegenreformation und Geheimprotestantismus in der Habsburgermonarchie* (Vienna, 2007), and Rudolf Leeb, Martin Scheutz, and Dietmar Weikl, eds., *Geheimprotestantismus und evangelische Kirchen in der Habsburgermonarchie und im Erzstift Salzburg (17./18. Jahrhundert)* (Vienna, 2008).

24. See, for example, Peter F. Barton, *Die Geschichte der Evangelischen in Österreich und Südostmitteleuropa*, vol. 1, *Im Schatten der Bauernkriege: Die Frühzeit der Reformation* (Vienna, 1985); idem, "Reformatorische Bekenntnisse im österreichisch-südosteuropäischen Raum," *Jahrbuch der Gesellschaft für die Geschichte des Protestantismus in Österreich* 92 (1976): 3–41, and 93 (1977): 59–68; Peter F. Barton, ed., *Religion oder Rebellion* (Budapest, 1977); Karl Schwarz and Peter Švorc, eds., *Die Reformation und ihre Wirkungsgeschichte in der Slowakei* (Vienna, 1996). These works are, of course, only thematically selected excerpts of these authors' broader research agenda.

25. See, for example, Peter G. Tropper, *Staatliche Kirchenpolitik, Geheimprotestantismus und katholische Mission in Kärnten (1752–1780)* (Klagenfurt, 1989), and idem, "Emigriert—missioniert—deportiert: Protestanten und Geheimprotestantismus in Österreich und Salzburg zwischen Gegenreformation und Toleranz," *Rottenburger Jahrbuch für Kirchengeschichte* 13 (1994): 179–189. The fact that the most comprehensive analysis of the

Historiographical Essay 279

Reformation in Upper Austria was written by a Catholic historian and theologian in the 1930s shows, moreover, that there were early precursors of this development. See Karl Eder, *Studien zur Reformationsgeschichte Oberösterreichs*, 2 vols. (Linz, 1932–1936).

26. Joseph von Hammer-Purgstall, *Khlesls des Cardinals, Directors des geheimen Cabinetes Kaisers Mathias, Leben*, 4 vols. (Vienna, 1847–1851).

27. See especially Johann Loserth, *Reformation und Gegenreformation in den innerösterreichischen Ländern im 16. Jahrhundert* (Stuttgart, 1898); Johann Loserth, ed., *Acten und Correspondenzen zur Geschichte der Gegenreformation in Innerösterreich unter Erzherzog Karl II. (1578–1590)* (Vienna, 1898); and idem, *Akten und Korrespondenzen zur Geschichte der Gegenreformation in Innerösterreich unter Ferdinand II.*, 2 vols. (Vienna, 1906–1907).

28. Arno Herzig, *Der Zwang zum wahren Glauben: Rekatholisierung vom 16. bis zum 18. Jahrhundert* (Göttingen, 2000).

29. R. Po-Chia Hsia, *The World of Catholic Renewal, 1540–1770* (Cambridge, England, 1998).

30. Howard Louthan, *Converting Bohemia: Force and Persuasion in the Catholic Reformation* (Cambridge, England, 2009). The author had already demonstrated his detailed knowledge of Austrian conditions with his dissertation, published in 1997, in which he traced the rise and fall of Catholic irenicism at the Viennese court. See Howard Louthan, *The Quest for Compromise: Peacemakers in Counter-Reformation Vienna* (Cambridge, England, 1997).

31. Jörg Deventer, *Gegenreformation in Schlesien: Die habsburgische Rekatholisierungspolitik in Glogau und Schweidnitz 1526–1707* (Cologne, 2003).

32. France Martin Dolinar et al., eds., *Katholische Reform und Gegenreformation in Innerösterreich 1564–1628* (Klagenfurt, 1994).

33. Regina Pörtner, *The Counter-Reformation in Central Europe: Styria 1580–1630* (Oxford, 2001).

34. Joseph F. Patrouch, *A Negotiated Settlement: The Counter-Reformation in Upper Austria under the Habsburgs* (Boston, 2000).

35. See Ernst Winkelbauer, *Fürst und Fürstendiener: Gundaker von Liechtenstein, ein österreichischer Aristokrat des konfessionellen Zeitalters* (Vienna-Munich, 1999).

36. Karin MacHardy, *War, Religion and Court Patronage in Habsburg Austria: The Social and Cultural Dimensions of Political Interaction, 1521–1622* (Houndmills, England, 2003). See also idem, "The Rise of Absolutism and Noble Rebellion in Early Modern Habsburg Austria, 1570–1620," *Comparative Studies in Society and History* 34 (1992): 407–438.

37. Gustav Reingrabner, "Gegenreformation in Niederösterreich: Das Protokoll der Reformationskommission für das Viertel ober dem Wienerwald von 1657–1660," *Jahrbuch der Gesellschaft für die Geschichte des Protestantismus in Österreich* 113 (1997): 9–115. For the confessionalization of the Lower Austrian Weinviertel region, see also Arthur Stögmann, *Die Konfessionalisierung im niederösterreichischen Weinviertel: Methoden, Erfolge, Widerstände* (Saarbrücken, 2010).

38. See Peter George Schimert, "Péter Pázmány and the Reconstitution of the Catholic Aristocracy in Habsburg Hungary, 1600–1650" (Ph.D. diss., University of North Carolina, 1990); Jörg Deventer, "'Zu Rom übergehen':

280 *Historiographical Essay*

Konversion als Entscheidungshandlung und Handlungsstrategie—Ein Versuch," in *Staatsmacht und Seelenheil: Gegenreformation und Geheimprotestantismus in der Habsburgermonarchie,* ed. Rudolf Leeb, Susanne Claudine Pils, and Thomas Winkelbauer (Vienna-Munich, 2007), 168–180; Jörg Deventer, "Konversionen zwischen den christlichen Konfessionen im frühneuzeitlichen Europa," in *Glaubenswechsel,* ed. Marlene Kurz and Thomas Winkelbauer (Innsbruck, 2007)), 8–24; Maria Crăciun, Jörg Deventer, and Martin Elbel, "Confession and Conversion: Transcending Religious Boundaries in Central and Eastern Europe, 1560–1700," *Bohemia* 48:1 (2008): 192–202.

39. For Clauss, see, for example, "Ein Nürnberger Verzeichnis österreich. Emigranten vom Jahre 1643," *Beiträge zur Bayrischen Kirchengeschichte* 13 (1907): 226–253. For Dedic, see *Kärntner Exulanten des 17. Jahrhunderts* (Klagenfurt, 1979).

40. Georg Rusam, *Österreichische Exulanten in Franken und Schwaben* (Munich, 1952).

41. Werner Wilhelm Schnabel, *Österreichische Exulanten in oberdeutschen Reichsstädten: Zur Migration von Führungsschichten im 17. Jahrhundert* (Munich, 1992).

42. See, for example, Joachim Bahlcke, ed., *Glaubensflüchtlinge: Ursachen, Formen und Auswirkungen frühneuzeitlicher Konfessionsmigration im neuzeitlichen Europa* (Berlin, 2008).

43. Hans Krawarik, *Exul austriacus: Konfessionelle Migrationen aus Österreich in der Frühen Neuzeit* (Vienna, 2010).

44. Anton Gindely, *Geschichte des dreißigjährigen Krieges,* 3 vols. (Leipzig, 1882–1883).

45. Hans Sturmberger, *Aufstand in Böhmen: Der Beginn des Dreißigjährigen Krieges* (Munich-Vienna, 1959); Josef V. Polišenský, *The Thirty Years War* (London, 1971).

46. Winfried, Schulze, ed., *Friedliche Intentionen—kriegerische Effekte: War der Ausbruch des Dreißigjährigen Krieges unvermeidlich?* (St. Katharinen, Germany, 2002).

47. Karsten Ruppert, *Die kaiserliche Politik auf dem Westfälischen Friedenskongreß (1643–1648)* (Münster, 1979).

48. Jenny Öhman, *Der Kampf um den Frieden: Schweden und der Kaiser im Dreißigjährigen Krieg* (Vienna, 2005); Pekka Suvanto, *Die deutsche Politik Oxenstiernas und Wallensteins* (Helsinki, 1979).

49. Johannes Burkhardt, *Der Dreißigjährige Krieg* (Frankfurt, 1992), and *Der Krieg der Kriege: Eine neue Geschichte des Dreißigjährigen Krieges* (Stuttgart, 2018).

50. Günter Barudio, *Der teutsche Krieg, 1618–1648* (Frankfurt, 1985).

51. Geoffrey Parker, ed., *The Thirty Years' War,* 2nd ed. (London, 1997).

52. Heinz Schilling, *Konfessionalisierung und Staatsinteressen: Internationale Beziehungen 1559–1660* (Paderborn, 2007). A broader international focus also characterizes R. J. W. Evans and Peter H. Wilson, eds., *The Holy Roman Empire, 1495–1806* (Leiden, 2012), whereas Georg Schmidt, *Die Reiter der Apokalypse: Geschichte des Dreißigjährigen Krieges* (Munich, 2018) shares Schilling's focus on confessional aspects. For comparisons

Historiographical Essay 281

with modern conflicts, see also Herfried Münkler, *Der Dreißigjährige Krieg: Europäische Katastrophe, deutsches Trauma 1618–1648* (Berlin, 2017).

53. Peter H. Wilson, *Europe's Tragedy: A History of the Thirty Years War* (London, 2009).

54. See Johann Loserth, *Reformation und Gegenreformation in den innerösterreichischen Ländern im 16. Jahrhundert* (Stuttgart, 1898), and Regina Pörtner, *The Counter-Reformation in Central Europe: Styria 1580–1630* (Oxford, 2001).

55. For a recent challenge to the axiom, see Rudolf Leeb, "Widerstand und leidender Ungehorsam gegen die katholische Konfessionalisierung," in *Staatsmacht und Seelenheil: Gegenreformation und Geheimprotestantismus in der Habsburgermonarchie,* ed. Rudolf Leeb, Susanne Claudine Pils, and Thomas Winkelbauer (Vienna-Munich, 2007), 183–201. To underscore his point, the Austrian ecclesial historian introduces the alternative designation of "suffering disobedience."

56. Arno Strohmeyer, *Konfessionskonflikt und Herrschaftsordnung: Widerstandsrecht bei den österreichischen Ständen (1550–1650* (Mainz, 2006).

57. See Winfried Schulze, "Zur politischen Theorie des steirischen Ständetums der Gegenreformationszeit," *Zeitschrift des historischen Vereins für Steiermark* 62 (1971): 33–48.

58. For the older literature, see Felix Stieve, *Der oberösterreichische Bauernaufstand des Jahres 1626,* 2 vols. (Munich, 1891), and Julius Strnadt, *Der Bauernkrieg in Oberösterreich* (Wels, 1924). Somewhat newer, but less detailed are Georg Heilingsetzer, *Der oberösterreichische Bauernkrieg 1626* (Vienna, 1976), and Karl Eichmeyer, Helmuth Feigl, and Rudolf Walter Litschel, *Weiß gilt die Seel und auch das Guet: Oberösterreichische Bauernaufstände und Bauernkriege im 16. und 17. Jahrhundert* (Linz, 1976).

59. Hans Sturmberger, *Georg Erasmus Tschernembl: Religion, Libertät und Widerstand* (Graz, 1953).

60. See, for example, Franz Kurz, *Beiträge zur Geschichte des Landes ob der Enns,* vol. 2 (Linz, 1808).

Bibliography

Manuscript Sources

Kärntner Landesarchiv (Klagenfurt)

Khevenhüller-Archiv

Box 2 and 3, "Korrespondenzen Khevenhüller." Parts 1 and 2.
Box 6/109, "Schuldurkunde Gustav Adolphs König der Schweden für die Brüder Johann und Paul Khevenhüller . . . "
Box 13/21, "Correspondenz zwischen Herrn Paul und Herrn Hans Khevenhüller . . . "
Box 19/89, "Briefverkehr von Regina, geb. Windischgrätz und Maria Elisabeth Khevenhüller."

Genealogische Sammlung Zenegg

Box 20/5 (Paul von Nagerschigg).

Topographische Sammlung Zenegg

Box 4/2.

Herrschaftsarchiv Porcia

Box 367.

Österreichisches Staatsarchiv (Vienna)

Haus-, Hof- und Staatsarchiv

HS Blau 381.

Bibliography 283

Oberösterreichisches Landesarchiv (Linz)

Neuerwerbungen

Inventarnummer: Aktenband 102, no. 7.

Österreichisches Museum für Angewandte Kunst (Vienna)

Handschriftensammlung

Inventarnummer: B. I.: 21517.

Sächsisches Hauptstaatsarchiv (Dresden)

Sammlung Bergmann

Volume 2.

Riksarkivet (Stockholm)

Riksregistratur

"Memorial för Öffwerste Leutnantten, Edell och Wellbördigh Zacharias Paulj til Wingzlö på de ährender H. K. Mtt: honom i befallning gifuitt hafwer," 1 July 1626.
"Swar til Zacharias Paulj opå Felttmarschalckzens tilsch:ne Bref af Zacharias Paulj anlangandes en mechta här medh Styken at belägra them," 4 August 1626.

Germanica

A:III no. 248. Evangeliska Unionens och andra evang. ständers bref till kungl. majt. 1614, 1619–1621.

Krigsarkivet (Stockholm)

Rullor -1723 Referenskod SE/SVAR/KrA-141010003.
Register Referenskod SE/SVAR/KrA-141010003/ R.
1632:26 Referenskod SE/SVAR/KrA-141010003/ D1, Svarnummer KO1556.
1632:27 Referenskod SE/SVAR/KrA-141010003/ D1, Svarnummer KO1557.

Julita Gårdsarkiv (Julita)

F1:1 Handlingar rörande familjen Khevenhüller 1631–1747.

284   *Bibliography*

Pauli Släktsarkiv (Sweden; private)

"Emerich Zenegg to Knut Pauli," 5 May 1922.

Printed Sources and Reference Works

Abelin, Johannes Philipp. *Theatrum Europæum*. 3rd ed. Vol. 1. Frankfurt, 1662.

Amsdorff, Nicolaus von, et al. *Bekentnis Vnterricht vnd vermanung, der Pfarrhern vnd Prediger, der Christlichen Kirchen zu Magdeburgk*. Magdeburg, 1550.

Andreae, Johann Valentin. *Vita, ab ipso conscripto*. Edited by F. H. Rheinwald. Berlin, 1849.

Auff der Röm. Kayserl. auch zu Hungarn und Böheim Kön. May. Herrn, Herrn Ferdinanden II., Ertzhertzogen zu Oesterreich unter und ob der Enß etc., Unsers Allergnädigisten Herrn beschwerliche Commissions-Resolution, oder Declaration cum Mandato, an gemeine Stände und Inwohner deß Ertzherzogthumbs Oesterreich ob der Enß, vom Dato 30. Junii 1620, derselben Ersamen Landschafft notwendige, gegründte und allergehorsamiste Kurtze Verantwortung wegen ihres allzu langwirigen stillschweigens. N.p., 1621.

Barclay, William. *De regno et regali potestate*. Paris, 1600.

Barton, Peter F., and László Makkai, eds. *Ostmitteleuropas Bekenntnisschriften der evangelischen Kirchen A. und H.B. des Reformationszeitalters*. Vol. 3:1, 1564–1576. Budapest, 1987.

Bayle, Pierre. *Dictionnaire historique et critique*. 5th ed. Vol. 4. Amsterdam, 1730.

Baylor, Michael G., ed. *The Radical Reformation*. Cambridge, England, 1991.

Becher, Siegfried. *Statistische Übersicht der Bevölkerung der österreichischen Monarchie nach den Ergebnissen der Jahre 1834–1840*. Stuttgart, 1841.

Beyschlag, Daniel Eberhard. *Beyträge zur Nördlingischen Geschlechtshistorie die Nördlingischen Familien und Epitaphien enthaltend . . . .* Vol. 2, continued by Johannes Müller. Nördlingen, 1803.

[Beza, Theodore]. *Du droit des magistrats sur leurs suiets*. N.p., 1574.

Beza, Theodore. *Concerning the Rights of Rulers over Their Subjects and the Duty of Subjects towards their Rulers*. Edited by A. H. Murray. Cape Town, 1956.

―――. *Correspondance de Théodore de Bèze*. Edited by Alain Dufour et al. 36 vols. to date. Geneva, 1960–.

―――. *De iure magistratuum*. Edited by Klaus Sturm. Neukirchen, Germany, 1967.

―――. *Du droit des Magistrats*. Edited by Robert M. Kingdon. Geneva, 1970.

Bibl, Victor. "Briefe Melchior Klesls an Herzog Wilhelm V. von Baiern: Ein Beitrag zur Geschichte der Gegenreformation in Oesterreich u. d. Enns." *Mitteilungen des Instituts für österreichische Geschichtsforschung* 21 (1900): 640–673.

―――. "Klesls Briefe an Kaiser Rudolfs II. Obersthofmeister Adam Freiherrn von Dietrichstein (1583–1589): Ein Beitrag zur Geschichte Klesls und der Gegenreformation in Niederösterreich." *Archiv für österreichische Geschichte* 88 (1900): 475–580.

Bibliography 285

————. "Die Berichte des Reichshofrates Dr. Georg Eder an die Herzoge Albrecht und Wilhelm von Bayern über die Religionskrise in Niederösterreich (1579–1587)." *Jahrbuch für Landeskunde von Niederösterreich*, n. s. 8 (1909): 67–154.

Biografiskt lexicon öfver namnkunnige svenske män. 23 vols. Uppsala and Örebro, 1835–1857.

Boehm, Adalbert Mainhart, ed. "Der Bundbrief der evangelischen Stände Österreichs ddo. Horn 3. October 1608 nach dem Originale im Archive der n. östr. Landschaft mit genealogisch-biographischen Anmerkungen." *Notizenblatt* 4 (1854): 321–328; 345–352; 371–376; 390–395.

Böhm, Wilhelm. "Oesterreich." *Wiener Zeitung,* Beilage der Wiener Zeitung, 30 October 1946, 3.

Bohman, Nils, ed. *Svenska män och kvinnor.* 8 vols. Stockholm, 1942–1955.

Brandi, Karl, ed. *Der Augsburger Religionsfriede vom 25. September 1555: Kritische Ausgabe mit den Entwürfen und der königlichen Deklaration.* 2nd ed. Leipzig, 1927.

Bricka, Carl Frederik, Julius Albert Fridericia, and Johanne Skovgaard, eds. *Kong Christian den Fjerdes egenhændige Breve.* 8 vols. Copenhagen, 1887–1947.

Brockington, William S., ed. *Monro, His Expedition with the Worthy Scots Regiment Called Mac-Keys.* Westport, CT, 1999.

Brutus, Stephanus Julius [pseud. for Philippe Duplessis-Mornay or Hubert Languet]. *Vindiciae contra tyrannos: sive, de principis in populum, populique in principem, legitima potestate.* Edinburgh, 1579.

————. *Vindiciae contra tyrannos: Or, Concerning the Legitimate Power of a Prince over the People, and of the People over a Prince.* Edited by George Garnett. Cambridge, England, 1994.

Bundesministerium für Unterricht, ed. *Österreichische Zeitgeschichte im Geschichtsunterricht.* Vienna, 1961.

Calvin, Jean. *Joannis Calvini opera quae supersunt omnia.* Edited by Johann Wilhelm Baum et al. 59 vols. Braunschweig, 1863–1900.

[Camerarius, Ludwig]. *Bericht und Antwort/ Uff die vornembste Capita, Päß/ und Puncten der Bayer-Anhaltischen geheimen Cantzeley: Sampt Etlichen Beylagen.* N. p., 1623.

————, ed. *Prodromus, Oder Vortrab/ Nothwendiger Rettung vornehmer Evangelischer Hohen und niedern Standts/ betrangten und verleumbden Personen unschuldt/ durch gründliche entdeckung der Papistischen schädlichen Intention unnd Vorhabens. Das ist: Wahrhaffter unnd glaubwirdiger Abdruck etzlicher intercipirten sehr weit außsehenden gefährlichen Schreiben unnd Schrifften/ welche auß den Originalien, mit fleiß abcopirt/ und theils auß denen Sprachen/ darinnen sie geschrieben/ trewlich verteutschet sein/ mit angehengter kurtzer Information unnd Anleitung: Allen Evangelischen/ so wol in: als außlendischen Potentaten/ Chur: Fürsten/ Ständen/ und Herrschafften . . . wider die verfälschte also genante geheimbte Anhaltische Cantzley.* N. p., 1622.

Čapek, Karel. *Gespräche mit T.G.Masaryk.* Munich, 1969.

Chemnitz, Bogislaff Philip von. *Königlich Schwedischen in Teutschland geführten Krieg.* Stettin, 1648.

286 Bibliography

Clauss, Hermann. "Ein Nürnberger Verzeichnis österreich. Emigranten vom Jahre 1643." *Beiträge zur Bayrischen Kirchengeschichte* 13 (1907): 226–253.

———. "Zur Geschichte der Gegenreformation in Niederösterreich." *Jahrbuch der Gesellschaft für die Geschichte des Protestantismus in Österreich* 28 (1907): 1–16.

Crowne, William. *A True Relation of All the Remarkable Places and Passages Observed in the Travels of the Right Honourable Thomas Lord Hovvard, Earle of Arundell and Surrey, Primer Earle, and Earle Marshall of England, Ambassadour Extraordinary to his Sacred Majesty Ferdinando the Second, Emperour of Germanie, Anno Domini 1636.* London, 1637.

Czerny, Albin. *Ein Tourist in Österreich während der Schwedenzeit: Aus den Papieren des Pater Reginbald Möhner, Benedictiners von St. Ulrich in Augsburg.* Linz, 1874.

Dareste, Rodolphe. "François Hotman, sa vie et sa correspondance." *Revue Historique* 2 (1876): 1–59 and 367–435.

Dennert, Jürgen, ed. *Beza, Brutus, Hotman: Calvinistische Monarchomachen.* Cologne, 1968.

Dingel, Irene, ed. *Reaktionen auf das Augsburger Interim: Der Interimistsiche Streit (1548–1549).* Göttingen, 2010.

Dorléans, Louis. *Advertissement des Catholiqves Anglois avx François Catholiques: du danger où ils sont de perdre leur religion et d'experimenter, comme en Angleterre, la cruauté des ministres s'ils reçoiuent à la couronne vn roy qui soit heretique.* Paris, 1586.

Duplessis Mornay, Philippe. *Mémoires et correspondance.* 12 vols. Paris, 1824–1825.

Eder, Georg. *Evangelische Inquisition Wahrer und falscher Religion.* Dillingen, Germany, 1573.

Elgenstierna, Gustaf. *Den introducerade svenska adelns ättartavlor.* 9 vols. Stockholm, 1925–1936.

Elvert, Christian d'. *Die Bestrafung der böhmischen Rebellion, insbesondere die Correspondenz Ferdinand II. mit dem Fürsten Liechtenstein.* Brünn, Moravia, 1868.

Falke, Johannes, ed. "Briefe des Herrn Hans von Khevenhüller an seine Gemahlin Maria Elisabeth, geb. von Dietrichstein, 1630–1632)." *Zeitschrift für deutsche Kulturgeschichte* 1:2 (1857): 276–289.

Fettes, Ian, and Leo van de Pas. *Plantagenet Cousins: Selected Descendants of Geoffrey V, Count of Anjou, in Australia, America, Africa, Europe and Asia.* Erindale, Australia, 2007.

Fischer, Ernst. *Die Entstehung des österreichischen Volks-Charakters.* London, 1944.

Flégl, Oldřich. "Relace kardinála Harracha o stavu pražské arcidiecése do Říma." *Věstník České Akademie pro Vědy, Slovesnost a Umění* 23 (1914): 185–197; 227–243.

Förstemann, Karl Eduard, ed. *Album Academiae Vitebergensis.* Vol. 1, *1502–1560.* Leipzig, 1841; reprint, Aalen, 1976.

Bibliography 287

Fraknói, Vilmos. "Bethlen Gábor és IV. Keresztély dán király (1625–1628): Közlemények a koppenhágai kir. levéltárból." *Magyar Történelmi Tár*, series 3, 4 (1881): 98–113.

Franklin, Julian H., ed. *Constitutionalism and Resistance in the Sixteenth Century: Three Treatises by Hotman, Beza and Mornay.* New York, 1969.

Franz, Georg, ed. *Die Politik Maximilians I. von Bayern und seiner Verbündeten 1618–1651.* Part 1, vol. 1, *Januar 1618-Dezember 1620.* Munich, 1966.

Fürstlich Anhaltische gehaimbe Cantzley, das ist begründte Anzaig der verdeckten, unteutschen, nachtheiligen Consilien, Anschläg und Practicken, welche der Correspondierenden Union Häupter und Directores, in der Böhmischen Unruhe zu derselben Cron, auch deß H. Römischen Reichs höchste gefahr geführt, und auß sonderbarer verordnung Gottes durch die den 8. Novemb. jüngst fürgangne ernstliche nambhaffte Böhaimische Niederlag vor Prag in der anhaltischen gehaimen Cantzley in Originali gefunden und der Welt kundthar worden: allen so wol auß- als jnnländischen Potentaten, Chur-Fürsten, Ständen und Herrschafften auch sonst menniglich zu beständiger nachricht trewhertziger warnung und wahrhaffter information. 3rd ed. N. p., 1621.

Gegründter Nothwendiger Bericht was biszhero nach Absterben des Allerdurchleuchtigsten Großmächtigsten Fürsten unnd Herrn, Herrn Matthiae Röm. Kay. auch zu Hungern und Böhemb Kön. Mtt. Ertzhertzogens . . . Alberti als nägsten Successorn des Ertzhertzogthumben Oesterreich unter und ob der Ens wegen der Landtadministration biß auff künfftige Huldigung dem uralten Oesterreichischen Herkommen nach fürgenommen unnd gehandelt worden. Linz, 1619.

Genealogisches Handbuch der baltischen Ritterschaften. Part 1, vol. 2, *Livland,* edited by Astaf von Transehe-Roseneck. Görlitz, 1929.

Gindely, Anton, ed. *Die Berichte über die Schlacht auf dem Weissen Berge bei Prag.* Vienna, 1877.

Goetz, Walter, ed. *Die Politik Maximilians I. von Baiern und seiner Verbündeten 1618–1651.* Part 1, vol. 3, *1626, 1627.* Leipzig, 1942.

Goldast von Heiminsfeld, Melchior. *De Bohemiae regni, incorporatarumque provinciarum, iuribus ac privilegiis, necnon de hereditaria Regiae Bohemorum familiae successione, commentarii . . . .* Frankfurt, 1627.

Görlich, Ernst Joseph. *Das Handbuch des Österreichers.* Salzburg, 1949.

Gründlicher vnd außführlicher Bericht, Wie die König. Schwedische, vnd Churf. Sächs. Armee, mit der Ligistischen oder Tyllischen Armee den 7. Sept. Anno 1631. bey dem Gut Breitenfeld, eine Meile von Leipzig gelegen, getroffen, wie es allenthalben damit zugangen. Auch wie die Schwedische vnd Sächs. Armee die Victoriam erhalten. Dresden, 1631.

Hallwich, Hermann, ed. *Heinrich Matthias Thurn als Zeuge im Process Wallenstein: Ein Denkblatt zur dritten Säcularfeier Wallensteins.* Leipzig, 1883.

Historische Aktenstücke über das Ständewesen in Oesterreich. 6 vols. Leipzig, 1847–1848.

288 Bibliography

Historische Commission bei der Königlichen Akademie der Wissenschaften, ed. *Allgemeine deutsche Biographie*. 56 vols. Munich-Leipzig, 1875–1912.

Historische Kommission bei der Bayerischen Akademie der Wissenschaften, ed. *Neue deutsche Biographie*. 24 volumes to date. Berlin, 1953–.

Hochfürstl. Saltzburgisches Emigrations-Patent, De dato 31. Octobris 1731. Stadt am Hoff, 1731.

Höpfl, Harro, ed. *Luther and Calvin on Secular Authority*. Cambridge, England, 1991.

Hotman, François. *Francogallia*. Geneva, 1573.

———. *Francogallia*. Latin text by Ralph E. Giesey. Translated by J. H. M. Salmon. Cambridge, England, 1972.

Hufeld, Ulrich, ed. *Der Reichsdeputationshauptschluss von 1803: Eine Dokumentation zum Untergang des Alten Reiches*. Cologne, 2003.

Instructio pastoralis ad usum missionariorum in Austria superiore expositorum. Passau, 1752.

Jireček, Josef, ed. *Paměti nejvyššího kancléře království českého Viléma hraběte Slavaty z Chlumu a z Košmberka*. 2 vols. Prague, 1866–1868.

[Keller, Jakob]. *Siebender Theil Anhaldischer geheimber Cancelley/ Das ist: Gründtliche Widerlegung/ nicht allein der ohnelangst von D. Ludovico Camerario wider die Litura oder Strich/ durch die Spanische Cancelley/ außgesprengter Apologia, sondern auch der vornembsten/ biß dahero/ wider die Catholische publicirter Schmehecarten/ als Synceratio Syncerationum, Catholicon, und anderer mehr/ beständige refutation*. N. p., 1626.

Khevenhiller, Franz Christoph. *Annales Ferdinandei, oder Wahrhaffte Beschreibung Kaysers Ferdinandi des Andern*. 2nd ed. 12 vols. Leipzig, 1721–1726.

Klueting, Harm, ed. *Der Josephinismus: Ausgewählte Quellen zur Geschichte der theresianisch-josephinischen Reformen*. Darmstadt, 1995.

Knoll, August, Alfred Missong, Wilhelm Schmid, Ernst Karl Winter, and H. K. Zeßner-Spitzenberg. *Die Österreichische Aktion*. Vienna, 1927.

Kočí, Josef, Josef Polišenský, and Gabriela Čechová, eds. *Documenta Bohemica bellum tricennale illustrantia*. 7 vols. Prague, 1971–1981.

Kohler, Alfred, ed. *Quellen zur Geschichte Karls V*. Darmstadt, 1990.

Kuhr, Georg, and Gerhard Bauer, eds. *Verzeichnis der Neubekehrten im Waldviertel 1652–1654: Codex Vindobonensis 7757 der Nationalbibliothek Wien*. Nuremberg, 1992.

Kungliga Vitterhets-, Historie- och Antiquitets-Akademien, ed. *Rikskansleren Axel Oxenstiernas skrifter och brefvexling*. 31 vols. to date. Stockholm, 1888–.

Kurras, Lotte, ed. *Axel Oxenstiernas Album amicorum und seine eigenen Stammbucheinträge*. Stockholm, 2004.

"Kurtze und aigentliche Beschreibung Deß Grausamen auffstands der Paurn im Landt Österreich Ob der Enß, so sich im Monath May deß 1616 Jars, wegen Der scharffen undt starkhen Reformation in Religion undt glaubenssachen, angefangen, Undt Biß in Monath Nouember dißes Jahr gewehret hat." *Taschenbuch für die vaterländische Geschichte* 42 (1856): 4–68.

Kurtze/ und Gegründete anzeig/ Was es für eine beschaffenheit habe/ mit der Schrifft/ welche die Bayerischen erstlich unter dem Titul Consultationes, oder unterschiedliche Rahtschläge /et/c. Und bald hernacher unter dem Titul Böhmische geheime Cantzley/ /et/c. Das ist/ Consultationes, Oder underschiedliche Rathschläge und Vota /et/c. und unterm schein eines in der Heidelbergischen Cantzley gefundenen Protocols/ im Jahr 1624 in offenen Truck gegeben/ und ausgesprenget haben. N.p., 1625.

Laing, David, ed. *The Works of John Knox.* 6 vols. Edinburgh, 1846–1864.

Lamormaini, William. *Ferdinandi II. Romanorum Imperatoris Virtutes.* Antwerp, 1638.

Laube, Adolf, and Hans Werner Seiffert, eds. *Flugschriften der Bauernkriegszeit.* 2nd ed. Cologne, 1978.

Lenz, Wilhelm, ed. *Deutschbaltisches biographisches Lexikon 1710–1960.* Cologne, 1970.

Lorenz, Gottfried, ed. *Quellen zur Vorgeschichte und zu den Anfängen des Dreißigjährigen Krieges.* Darmstadt, 1991.

Loserth, Johann, ed. *Acten und Correspondenzen zur Geschichte der Gegenreformation in Innerösterreich unter Erzherzog Karl II. (1578–1590). Fontes rerum Austriacarum* 50. Vienna, 1898.

———. "Miscellen zur steiermärkischen Religionsgeschichte." *Jahrbuch der Gesellschaft für die Geschichte des Protestantismus in Österreich* 20 (1899): 185–192.

———. *Akten und Korrespondenzen zur Geschichte der Gegenreformation in Innerösterreich unter Ferdinand II.* 2 vols. *Fontes rerum Austriacarum* 58–60. Vienna, 1906–1907.

Loyseau, Charles. *A Treatise of Orders and Plain Dignities.* Edited by Howell A. Lloyd. Cambridge, England, 1994.

Lünig, Johann Christian. *Das Teutsche Reichs-Archiv.* Vol. 5. Leipzig, 1713.

Luschin von Ebengreuth, Arnold. "Oesterreicher an italienischen Universitäten zur Zeit der Reception des römischen Rechts." *Blätter des Vereines für Landeskunde von Niederösterreich* 15 (1991): 262.

Luther, Martin. *Eyn brieff an die Fürsten von Sachsen von dem auffrurischen geyst.* Wittenberg, 1524.

———. *Wider die Mordischen und Reubischen Rotten der Bawren.* Landshut, 1525.

———. *D. Martin Luthers Werke: Kritische Gesamtausgabe.* 120 vols. Weimar, 1883–2009.

Luttenberger, Albrecht P., ed. *Katholische Reform und Konfessionalisierung.* Darmstadt, 2006.

Marsch, Angelika. *Die Salzburger Emigration in Bildern.* 3rd ed. Weissenhorn, Germany, 1986.

Matharel, Antoine. *Ad Franc. Hotomani Franco-Galliam . . . responsio.* Paris, 1575.

Mehlhausen, Joachim, ed. *Das Augsburger Interim von 1548.* 2nd ed. Neukirchen-Vluyn, Germany, 1996.

290   Bibliography

Meiern, Johann Gottfried von. *Acta Pacis Westphalicae publica oder Westphälische Friedens-Handlungen und Geschichte*. 6 parts. Hannover, 1734–1736.

Menius, Justus. *Von der Nothwehr unterricht*. Wittenberg, 1547.

Michel, Gerhard, and Jürgen Beer, eds. *Johannes Amos Comenius—Leben, Werk und Wirken: Autobiographische Texte und Notizen*. Sankt Augustin, Germany, 1992.

Micraelius, Johannes. *Fünfftes Buch der Pommerschen Jahr-Geschichten, Vom 1627. Jahr, Biß auff den Todt Bogislai XIV. des letzten Hertzogen in Pommern*. Stettin, 1639.

Miller, Jaroslav. *Urban Societies of East Central Europe: 1500–1700*. Aldershot, England, 2008.

Müller, Konrad, ed. *Instrumenta Pacis Westphalicae*. 3rd ed. Bern, 1975.

Müller, Rainer A., ed. *Deutsche Geschichte in Quellen und Darstellung*. Vol. 4, *Gegenreformation und Dreißigjähriger Krieg 1555–1648*, edited by Bernd Roeck. Stuttgart, 1996.

Müntzer, Thomas. *Hoch verursachte Schutzrede*. Nuremberg, 1524.

Nordisk familjebok. 2nd ed. 38 vols. Stockholm, 1904–1926.

Nordrhein-Westfälische Akademie der Wissenschaften in Verbindung mit der Vereinigung zur Erforschung der Neueren Geschichte durch Konrad Repgen, ed. *Acta Pacis Westphalicae*. Münster, 1962–.

Opočenský, Hanuš, ed. *Vilém Slavata z Chlumu a Košumberka: Přehled náboženských dějin českých*. Prague, 1912.

"Proklamation über die Selbständigkeit Österreich." *Staatsgesetzblatt für die Republik Österreich Nr. 1/1945*.

Pröll, Laurenz. *Die Gegenreformation in der l.-f. Stadt Bruck a. d. L.: Ein typisches Bild, nach den Aufzeichnungen des Stadtschreibers Georg Khirmair*. Vienna, 1897.

Pufendorf, Samuel von. *Herrn Samuel von Pufendorf Sechs und Zwantzig Bücher der Schwedisch- und Deutschen Kriegs-Geschichte von König Gustav Adolfs Feldzuge in Deutschland an biss zur Abdanckung der Königin Christina: Darinn zugleich beschrieben wird, was die Cron Schweden selbige Zeit über mit andern Staaten von Europa zu thun gehabt; nebst dem Osnabrügischen und Münsterischen Friedens-Schlusse; wie auch einem doppelten Register der Sachen und Nahmen tapferer Leute und Familien, so in dieser Historie vorkommen*. Frankfurt and Leipzig, 1688.

Raupach, Bernhard. *Evangelisches Oesterreich: das ist historische Nachricht, von den vornehmsten Schicksahlen der evangelisch-lutherischen Kirchen in dem Ertz-Hertzogthum Oesterreich*. 6 vols. Hamburg, 1732–1744.

Reiter, Ludwig. *Österreichische Staats-und Kulturgeschichte*. Klagenfurt, 1947.

Relation Der Vnter- und Oberösterreichischen Euangelischen Stände Abgesandten nach Wien: Allda Zwischen Ihrer Königlichen May. zu Hungarn etc. vnd jnen den dreyen Österreichischen Evangelischen Ständen der Frid tractiert vnd geschlossen worden. N.p., 1610.

Riddarhusdirektionen, ed. *Riddarhusets stamtavlor*. CD-Rom. Stockholm, 2002.

Bibliography 291

Riksarkivet, ed. *Svenska riksrädets protokoll.* 18 vols. to date. Stockholm, 1878–.

Rosolenz, Jakob. *Gründlicher Gegen Bericht Auf Den falschen Bericht vnnd vermainte Erinnerung Dauidis Rungij, Wittenbergischen Professors, Von der Tyrannischen Bäpstischen Verfolgung deß H. Evangelij, in Steyermarckt, Kärndten, vnd Crayn . . . .* Graz, 1607.

Roth, Joseph. *Radetzkymarsch.* Berlin, 1932.

Rungius, David. *Bericht und Erinnerung, von der Tyrannischen Bäpstischen verfolgung deß H. Evangelii, in Steyermarckt, Kärndten und Krain . . . .* Wittenberg, 1601.

Schaefer, Reinhold, ed. *Bittgesuche evangelischer Schlesier an Friedrich den Großen.* Görlitz, Germany, 1941.

Schaitberger, Joseph. *Neu-vermehrter evangelischer Send-Brief.* Reutlingen, Germany, 1799.

Schauroth, Eberhard Christian Wilhelm von. *Vollständige Sammlung Aller Conclusorum, Schreiben Und anderer übrigen Verhandlungen Des Hochpreißlichen Corporis Evangelicorum.* 3 vols. Regenburg, 1751–1752.

Schmertosch von Riesenthal, Richard. *Adelige Exulanten in Kursachsen nach Urkunden des Dresdner Hauptstaatsarchivs.* Dresden, 1902.

Schmitz, Oscar. *Der österreichische Mensch.* Vienna, 1924.

Schrauf, Karl. *Das Gedenkbuch der Teufel zu Gundersdorf.* Vienna, 1892.

Schrauf, Karl, ed. *Der Reichshofrath Dr. Georg Eder: Eine Briefsammlung als Beitrag zur Geschichte der Gegenreformation in Niederösterreich.* Vienna, 1904.

Schwennicke, Detlev. *Europäische Stammtafeln: Stammtafeln zur Geschichte der europäischen Staaten.* New series. Vol. 5. Marburg, 1988.

Springell, Francis C., ed. *Connoisseur and Diplomat: The Earl of Arundel's Embassy to Germany in 1636 as Recounted in William Crowne's Diary, the Earl's Letters and Other Contemporary Sources, with a Catalogue of the Topographical Drawings Made on the Journey by Wenceslaus Hollar.* London, 1963.

Steinmeyer, Elias von. *Die Matrikel der Universität Altdorf.* 2 vols. Würzburg, 1912.

Stránský, Pavel. *Respublica Bohemiae.* Leiden, 1634.

Sydow, Jürgen. "Die innerösterreichische Zuwanderung nach Regensburg im 16. und 17. Jahrhundert." *Blätter für Heimatkunde* 29 (1955): 63–66.

Teplý, František, ed. "Proč se stal Vilém Slavata z Chlumu a Košumberka z českého bratra katolíkem." *Sborník Historického kroužku* 13 (1912): 205–221, and 14 (1913): 25–41, 171–181.

Thurn und Taxis, Franz von. "Eine Chronik der Jörger 1497–1599." *Monatsblatt der kais. kön. heraldischen Gesellschaft Adler* 7 (1911–1916): 258–260, 267–269, 273–275, 282–284, 292–297.

Trechsel, Johann Martin. *Erneuertes Gedächtnis Des Nürnbergschen Johannes-Kirch-Hofs.* Frankfurt-Leipzig, 1735.

[Tschernembl, Georg Erasmus von]. *Räthliches Bedencken Eines vornemen Oesterreichischen Freyherrn ob der Ens, Was massen die im Königreich Böhmen, und benachbarten Landen entstandene Unruhen, mit des Hochlöblichen*

292   Bibliography

Hauses Oesterreich Reputation, Nutz und Ehren zu accommodiren . . . . N.p., 1619.

————. *Consultationes Oder Underschidliche Rathschläg/ Der maisten und wichtigisten sachen/ welche von Anfang der Böhemischen/ und andern folgenden Auffständ fürgangen/ unnd zu Werck gericht worden/ oder werden sollen: Von wort zu wort auß dem Original Protocoll, so in der Haidelbergischen Cantzley gefunden worden/ gezogen. Mit nohtwendigen Glossis erklärt.* [Edited by Jakob Keller.] N.p., 1624.

Turba, Gustav. *Die Grundlagen der pragmatischen Sanktion.* 2 vols. Leipzig-Vienna, 1911–1912.

Walder, Ernst, ed. *Religionsvergleiche des 16. Jahrhunderts.* Vol 1. 2nd ed. Bern, 1960.

Watts, William. *The Swedish Discipline.* London, 1632.

Winter, Ernst Florian, ed. *Ernst Karl Winter: Bahnbrecher des Dialogs.* Vienna, 1969.

Wissgrill, Franz Karl. *Schauplatz des landsässigen Niederoesterreichischen Adels vom Herren- und Ritterstande von dem XI. Jahrhundert an bis auf jetzige Zeiten.* 5 vols. Vienna, 1794–1804.

"Würdevolle Feier in Mariazell." *Wiener Zeitung,* 8 July 1935, 2.

Wurzbach, Constant von. *Biographisches Lexikon des Kaiserthums Oesterreich.* 60 vols. Vienna, 1856–1891.

"Zur Statistik der Religionsbewegung in Steiermark im 16. und 17. Jahrh." *Steiermärkische Geschichtsblätter* 2 (1881): 72–108.

Zwiedineck, Hans von. "Das reichsgräflich Wurmbrand'sche Haus- und Familien-Archiv zu Steyersberg." *Beiträge zur Kunde steiermärkischer Geschichtsquellen* 27 (1896): 103–212.

Literature

Adamová, Karolina. "K politickému programu městského stavu v českém státě v roce 1619." *Právněhistorické studie* 31 (1990): 169–175.

Adams, Simon L. "The Protestant Cause: Religious Alliance with the West European Calvinist Communities as a Political Issue in England, 1585–1630." Ph.D. dissertation, Oxford University, 1973.

Agnew, Hugh. *The Czechs and the Lands of the Bohemian Crown.* Stanford, CA, 2004.

Ahnlund, Nils. "Öfverläggningarna i riksrådet om tyska kriget 1628–1630." *Historisk Tidskrift* 34 (1914): 108–123.

Ailes, Mary Elizabeth. *Military Migration and State Formation: The British Military Community in Seventeenth-Century Sweden.* Lincoln, NE, 2002.

Albrecht, Dieter. *Maximilian I. von Bayern 1573–1651.* Munich, 1998.

Albrecht, Ernst, and Anton Schindling, eds. *Union und Liga 1608/09: Konfessionelle Bündnisse im Reich—Weichenstellung zum Religionskrieg?* Stuttgart, 2010.

Almquist, Helge. "Königin Christina und die österreichische Protestantenfrage um die Zeit des Westfälischen Friedens." *Archiv für Reformationsgeschichte* 36 (1939): 1–24.

Bibliography 293

Althaus, Paul. *Luthers Haltung im Bauernkrieg.* Tübingen, 1952.

Ammerer, Gerhard, et al., eds. *Bündnispartner und Konkurrenten der Landesfürsten: Die Stände in der Habsburgermonarchie.* Vienna, 2007.

Amon, Karl. *Die Steiermark vor der Glaubensspaltung: Kirchliche Zustände 1490–1520.* Graz, 1960.

———, ed. *Die Bischöfe von Graz-Seckau 1218–1968.* Graz, 1969.

Anderson, Perry. *Lineages of the Absolutist State.* London, 1974.

———. *Passages from Antiquity to Feudalism.* London, 1974.

Andersson, Bo. "Eva Margaretha Frölich und ihre Schriften: Ein aufgefundener Sammelband." *Wolfenbütteler Barock-Nachrichten* 14 (1987): 71–76.

———. "Eva Margaretha Frölich: Nationell eskatologi och profetisk auktoritet." *Kyrkohistorisk årsskrift* (1991): 57–81.

Angermeier, Heinz. "Politik, Religion und Reich bei Kardinal Melchior Khlesl." *Zeitschrift der Savigny-Stiftung für Rechtsgeschichte,* Germanist. Abt. 110 (1993): 249–330.

Anjou, Lars Anton. *The History of the Reformation in Sweden.* Translated by Henry M. Mason. New York, 1859.

Arnoldsson, Sverker. *Krigspropagandan i Sverige före trettioåriga kriget.* Göteborg, 1941.

Asch, Ronald G. "Religiöse Selbstinszenierung im Zeitalter der Glaubenskriege: Adel und Konfession in Westeuropa." *Historisches Jahrbuch* 125 (2005): 67–100.

Asch, Ronald G., and Heinz Durchhardt, eds. *Der Absolutismus—ein Mythos? Strukturwandel monarchischer Herrschaft in West- und Mitteleuropa (ca. 1550–1700).* Cologne, 1996.

Assmann, Aleida. *Erinnerungsräume: Formen und Wandlungen des kulturellen Gedächtnisses.* Munich, 1999.

Assmann, Jan. *Das kulturelle Gedächtnis: Schrift, Erinnerung und politische Identität in frühen Hochkulturen.* Munich, 1992.

Aston, Trevor H., and Charles H. E. Philpin, eds. *The Brenner Debate: Agrarian Class Structure and Economic Development in Pre-Industrial Europe.* Cambridge, England, 1993.

Atwood, Craig D. *The Theology of the Czech Brethren from Hus to Comenius.* University Park, PA, 2009.

Bahlcke, Joachim. *Regionalismus und Staatsintegration im Widerstreit: Die Länder der Böhmischen Krone im ersten Jahrhundert der Habsburgerherrschaft (1526–1619).* Munich, 1994.

———. "Modernization and State-Building in an East-Central European Estates' System: The Example of the Confoederatio Bohemica of 1619." *Parliaments, Estates and Representation* 17 (1997): 61–73.

———. "Religion und Politik in Schlesien: Konfessionspolitische Strukturen unter habsburgischer und preußischer Herrschaft (1650–1800)." *Blätter für deutsche Landesgeschichte* 134 (1998): 33–57.

———, ed. *Glaubensflüchtlinge: Ursachen, Formen und Auswirkungen frühneuzeitlicher Konfessionsmigration im neuzeitlichen Europa.* Berlin, 2008.

294 Bibliography

Bahlcke, Joachim, and Arno Strohmeyer, eds. *Konfessionalisierung in Ostmitteleuropa: Wirkungen des religiösen Wandels im 16. und 17. Jahrhundert in Staat, Gesellschaft und Kultur*. Stuttgart, 1999.

Bahlcke, Joachim, Hans-Jürgen Bömelburg, and Norbert Kersken, eds. *Ständefreiheit und Staatsgestaltung in Ostmitteleuropa: Übernationale Gemeinsamkeiten in der politischen Kultur vom 16.—18. Jahrhundert*. Leipzig, 1996.

Bahlcke, Joachim, Karen Lambrecht, and Hans-Christian Maner, eds. *Konfessionelle Pluralität als Herausforderung: Koexistenz und Konflikt in Spätmittelalter und Früher Neuzeit*. Leipzig, 2006.

Baker, Ernest. "The Authorship of the *Vindiciae Contra Tyrannos*." *Cambridge Historical Journal* 3 (1930): 164–181.

Barkman, Bertil C. *Gustaf II Adolfs regementsorganisation vid det inhemska infanteriet*. Stockholm, 1931.

Barkman, Bertil C., and Sven Lundkvist. *Kungl. Svea Livgardes historia*. Vol. 3:1. Stockholm, 1963.

Baron, Hans. "Calvinist Republicanism and its Historical Roots." *Church History* 8 (1939): 30–42.

Barton, Peter F. "Reformatorische Bekenntnisse im österreichisch-südosteuropäischen Raum." *Jahrbuch der Gesellschaft für die Geschichte des Protestantismus in Österreich* 92 (1976): 3–41, and 93 (1977): 59–68.

———. *Die Geschichte der Evangelischen in Österreich und Südostmitteleuropa*. Vol. 1, *Im Schatten der Bauernkriege: Die Frühzeit der Reformation*. Vienna, 1985.

———. *Evangelisch in Österreich*. Vienna, 1987.

———, ed. *Sozialrevolution und Reformation*. Vienna, 1975.

———. *Religion oder Rebellion*. Budapest, 1977.

———. *Im Zeichen der Toleranz*. Vienna, 1981.

———. *Kirche im Wandel: Festschrift Bischof Oskar Sakrausky zum 80. Geburtstag*. Vienna, 1993.

Barudio, Günter. *Der teutsche Krieg, 1618–1648*. Frankfurt, 1985.

Baumgart, Peter. "Absolutismus ein Mythos? Aufgeklärter Absolutismus ein Widerspruch? Reflexionen zu einem kontroversen Thema gegenwärtiger Frühneuzeitforschung." *Zeitschrift für Historische Forschung* 27 (2000): 573–589.

———, ed. *Kontinuität und Wandel: Schlesien zwischen Österreich und Preußen*. Sigmaringen, Germany, 1990.

Baumgart, Peter, and Jürgen Schmädeke, eds. *Ständetum und Staatsbildung in Brandenburg-Preußen*. Berlin, 1983.

Beales, Derek. *Joseph II*. 2 vols. Cambridge, England, 1987–2009.

Beales, Derek, and Geoffrey Best, eds. *History, Society and the Churches: Essays in Honour of Owen Chadwick*. Cambridge, England, 1985.

Beheim-Schwarzbach, Max. *Friedrich Wilhelm's I. Colonisationswerk in Lithauen, vornehmlich die Salzburger Colonie*. Königsberg, 1879.

Beiderbeck, Friedrich, Gregor Horstkemper, and Winfried Schulze, eds. *Dimensionen der europäischen Aussenpolitik zur Zeit der Wende vom 16. zum 17. Jahrhundert*. Berlin, 2003.

Bibliography 295

Belstler, Ulrich. *Die Stellung des Corpus Evangelicorum in der Reichsverfassung.* Bamberg, 1968.

Benedikt, Felix Anton von. *Die Fürsten von Dietrichstein.* Schriften des historischen Vereins für Innerösterreich 1. Graz, 1848.

Benedikt, Heinrich, ed. *Geschichte der Republik Österreich.* Munich, 1954.

Bengtsson, Frans G. *Karl XII:s levnad.* 2 vols. Stockholm, 1935–1936.

Bentley, Michael, ed. *Companion to Historiography.* London, 1997.

Berg, Scott. "'The Lord Has Done Great Things for Us': The 1817 Reformation Celebrations and the End of the Counter-Reformation in the Habsburg Lands." *Central European History* 49 (2016): 69–92.

Berger, Stefan. "On the Role of Myths and History in the Construction of National Identity in Modern Europe." *European History Quarterly* 39 (2009): 490–502.

Berger, Stefan, Mark Donovan, and Kevin Passmore, eds. *Writing National Histories: Western Europe since 1800.* London, 1999.

Bergerhausen, Hans-Wolfgang. "Die 'Verneuerte Landesordnung' in Böhmen 1627: Ein Grunddokument des habsburgischen Absolutismus." *Historische Zeitschrift* 272 (2001): 327–351.

Bibl, Victor. "Erzherzog Ernst und die Gegenreformation in Niederösterreich (1576–1590)." *Mitteilungen des Instituts für österreichische Geschichtsforschung,* Ergänzungsband 6 (1901): 575–596.

———. "Die katholischen und protestantischen Stände Niederösterreichs im XVII. Jahrhundert: Ein Beitrag zur Geschichte der ständischen Verfassung." *Jahrbuch für Landeskunde von Niederösterreich,* n. s., 2 (1903): 165–323.

———. "Eine Denkschrift Melchior Khlesls über die Gegenreformation in Niederösterreich (c. 1590)." *Jahrbuch für Landeskunde von Niederösterreich,* n. s., 8 (1909): 157–171.

———. "Die Vorgeschichte der Religionskonzession Kaiser Maximilians II. (18. August 1568)." *Jahrbuch für Landeskunde von Niederösterreich,* n. s., 13/14 (1915): 400–431.

———. "Zur Frage der religiösen Haltung Kaiser Maximilians II." *Archiv für österreichische Geschichte* 106 (1918): 289–425.

———. *Maximilian II.: Der rätselhafte Kaiser.* Hellerau, Germany, 1929.

Bierbrauer, Peter. *Die unterdrückte Reformation: Der Kampf der Tiroler um eine neue Kirche 1521–1527.* Zurich, 1993.

Binder, Ludwig. *Grundlagen und Formen der Toleranz in Siebenbürgen bis zur Mitte des 17. Jahrhunderts.* Cologne-Vienna, 1976.

Bircher, Martin. *Johann Wilhelm von Stubenberg (1619–1663) und sein Freundeskreis: Studien zur österreichischen Barockkultur protestantischer Edelleute.* Berlin, 1968.

Bireley, Robert. *Religion and Politics in the Age of the Counterreformation: Emperor Ferdinand II, William Lamormaini, S.J., and the Formation of Imperial Policy.* Chapel Hill, NC,1981.

———. *The Refashioning of Catholicism, 1450–1700.* Houndmills, England, 1999.

296 Bibliography

———. *The Jesuits and the Thirty Years War: Kings, Courts and Confessors.* Cambridge, England, 2003.

———. *Ferdinand II: Counter-Reformation Emperor, 1578–1637.* New York, 2014.

Bischoff-Urack, Angelika. *Michael Gaismair: Ein Beitrag zur Sozialgeschichte des Bauernkrieges.* Innsbruck, 1983.

Blänkner, Reinhard. "'Der Absolutismus war ein Glück, der doch nicht zu den Absolutisten gehört': Eduard Gans und die Ursprünge der Absolutismusforschung in Deutschland." *Historische Zeitschrift* 256 (1993): 31–66.

———. *"Absolutismus": Eine begriffsgeschichtliche Studie zur politischen Theorie und zur Geschichtswissenschaft in Deutschland, 1830–1870.* Frankfurt, 2011.

Blickle, Peter. *The Revolution of 1525: The German Peasants' War from a New Perspective.* Baltimore, MD, 1981.

———. *Die Revolution von 1525.* 4th ed. Munich, 2004.

———. *Der Bauernkrieg: Die Revolution des Gemeinen Mannes.* 4th ed. Munich, 2012.

Blockmans, Wim. *Emperor Charles V: 1500–1558.* London, 2002.

———, ed. *The Origins of the Modern State in Europe, 1300–1800.* 7 vols. Oxford, England, 1995–2000.

Blockmans, Wim, and Jean-Philippe Genet, eds. *Visions sur le développement des États européens.* Rome, 1993.

Blom, Olof. *Smaa bidrag til artilleriets historie under Kristian IV.* Copenhagen, 1901.

Böning, Holger. *Dreißigjähriger Krieg und Öffentlichkeit: Zeitungsberichte als Rohfassung der Geschichtsschreibung.* Bremen, 2018.

Bonorand, Conradin. "Adam Seenuß: Ein Villacher Exulant und seine Beziehungen zu evangelischen Pfarrern der Ostschweiz." *Neues aus Alt Villach* 1 (1964): 243–252.

Bossy, John. *Christianity in the West, 1400–1700.* Oxford, England, 1985.

Böttcher, Diethelm. *Ungehorsam oder Widerstand? Zum Fortleben des mittelalterlichen Widerstandsrechtes in der Reformationszeit (1529–1530).* Berlin, 1991.

Bottesch, Martin, Franz Grieshofer, and Wilfried Schabus, eds. *Die Siebenbürgischen Landler: Eine Spurensicherung.* Cologne, 2002.

Brandi, Karl. *Karl V.: Werden und Schicksal einer Persönlichkeit und eines Weltreichs.* 2 vols. Munich, 1937–1941.

Brandmüller, Walter, ed. *Handbuch der bayerischen Kirchengeschichte.* Vol. 2, *Von der Glaubensspaltung bis zur Säkularisation.* St. Ottilien, Germany, 1993.

Brandtner, Andreas. "Habeant sua fata libelli: Bausteine zur Erforschung der Enenkel Bibliothek." *Jahrbuch des Oberösterreichischen Musealvereins* 145 (2000): 145–152.

Braungart, Georg. *Hofberedsamkeit: Studien zur Praxis höfisch-politischer Rede im deutschen Territorialabsolutismus.* Tübingen, 1988.

Brenner, Robert. "Agrarian Class Structure and Economic Development in Pre-Industrial Europe." *Past and Present* 70 (1976): 30–74.

Bibliography 297

Brohed, Ingmar, ed. *Reformationens konsolidering i de nordiska länderna 1540–1610.* Oslo, 1990.

Brown, Peter B. "The *Zemskii Sobor* in Recent Soviet Historiography." *Russian History* 10 (1983): 77–90.

Bruckmüller, Ernst. *Nation Österreich: Sozialhistorische Aspekte ihrer Entwicklung.* Vienna, 1984; 2nd enlarged ed. Vienna, 1996.

———. *Sozialgeschichte Österreichs.* Vienna, 1985.

Bruckmüller, Ernst, Michael Mitterauer, and Helmuth Stradal. *Herrschaftsstruktur und Ständebildung 3: Beiträge zur Typologie der österreichischen Länder aus ihren mittelalterlichen Grundlagen.* Munich, 1973.

Brunemayr, Joseph Philipp. *Geschichte der Königl. Baierischen Stadt und Herrschaft Mindelheim.* Mindelheim, Germany, 1821.

Brunner, Otto. *Adeliges Landleben und europäischer Geist: Leben und Werk Wolf Helmhards von Hohberg 1612–1688.* Salzburg, 1949.

———. "Österreichische Adelsbibliotheken des 15. bis 17. Jahrhunderts." *Anzeiger der Österreichischen Akademie der Wissenschaften, philosophisch. historische Klasse* 86 (1949): 109–126.

———. *Land und Herrschaft: Grundfragen der territorialen Verfassungsgeschichte Österreichs im Mittelalter.* 5th ed. Vienna, 1965.

———. *Neue Wege der Verfassungs- und Sozialgeschichte.* 2nd enlarged ed. Göttingen, 1968.

Buchinger, Erich. *Die "Landler" in Siebenbürgen: Vorgeschichte, Durchführung und Ergebnis einer Zwangsumsiedlung im 18. Jahrhundert.* Munich, 1980.

———. "Die Geschichte der Kärntner Hutterischen Brüder in Siebenbürgen und in der Walachei (1755–1770), in Rußland und Amerika: Ein Beitrag zum Schicksal von Kärntner Transmigranten und zur Geschichte der heutigen Hutterischen Bruderhöfe in den USA und Kanada." *Carinthia I* 172 (1982): 145–303.

Bücking, Jürgen. *Michael Gaismair: Reformer—Sozialrebell—Revolutionär.* Stuttgart, 1978.

Bucsay, Mihály. *Der Protestantismus in Ungarn 1521–1978: Ungarns Reformationskirchen in Geschichte und Gegenwart.* 2 vols. Vienna, 1977–1979.

Burgstaller, Ernst. "Martin Laimbauer und seine Machländische Bauernbewegung: Versuch einer volkskundlichen Durchleuchtung." *Kunstjahrbuch der Stadt Linz 1973* (1974): 3–30.

Burkert, Günther R. *Landesfürst und Stände: Karl V., Ferdinand I. und die österreichischen Erbländer im Ringen um Gesamtstaat und Landesinteressen.* Graz, 1987.

Burkhardt, Johannes. *Der Dreißigjährige Krieg.* Frankfurt, 1992.

———. "Der Dreißigjährige Krieg als frühmoderner Staatsbildungskrieg." *Geschichte in Wissenschaft und Unterricht* 45 (1994): 487–499.

———. *Der Krieg der Kriege: Eine neue Geschichte des Dreißigjährigen Krieges.* Stuttgart, 2018.

Burkhardt, Johannes, and Christine Werkstetter, eds. *Kommunikation und Medien in der Frühen Neuzeit.* Munich, 2005.

298   Bibliography

Buszello, Horst, Peter Blickle, and Rudolf Endres, eds. *Der deutsche Bauernkrieg.* 3rd ed. Paderborn, 1995.

Cameron, Euan. *The European Reformation.* Oxford, England, 1991.

Cantimori, Delio. *Umanesimo e religione nel Rinascimento.* Torino, 1975.

Carsten, Francis L. *Princes and Parliaments in Germany from the Fifteenth to the Eighteenth Century.* Oxford, England, 1963.

Cheneviere, Marc-Édouard, *La pensée politique de Calvin.* Geneva, 1937.

Chevreul, Henri. *Hubert Languet.* Paris, 1852.

Christmann, Curt. *Melanchtons Haltung im schmalkaldischen Kriege.* Berlin, 1902.

Cipolla, Carlo M., and Knut Borchardt, eds. *Bevölkerungsgeschichte Europas: Mittelalter bis Neuzeit.* Munich, 1971.

Clauss, Hermann. "Ein Nürnberger Verzeichnis österreich. Emigranten vom Jahre 1643." *Beiträge zur Bayrischen Kirchengeschichte* 13 (1907): 226–253.

———. "Josef Schaitberger und sein Sendbrief." *Beiträge zur Bayrischen Kirchengeschichte* 15 (1909): 105–123; 153–166.

Collins, Randall. "Functional and Conflict Theories of Educational Stratification." *American Sociological Review* 36 (1971): 1002–1019.

———. *The Credential Society: An Historical Sociology of Education and Stratification.* New York, 1979.

Conermann, Klaus. *Die Mitglieder der Fruchtbringenden Gesellschaft 1617–1650.* Weinheim, 1985.

Connerton, Paul. *How Societies Remember.* Cambridge, England, 1989.

Conrads, Norbert. *Die Durchführung der Altranstädter Konvention in Schlesien 1707–1709.* Cologne, 1971.

Coreth, Anna. *Pietas Austriaca: Österreichische Frömmigkeit im Barock.* 2nd ed. Vienna, 1982.

Cosandey, Fanny, and Robert Descimon. *L'absolutisme en France: Histoire et historiographie.* Paris, 2002.

Crăciun, Maria, Jörg Deventer, and Martin Elbel. "Confession and Conversion: Transcending Religious Boundaries in Central and Eastern Europe, 1560–1700." *Bohemia* 48:1 (2008): 192–202.

Crews, C. Daniel. *Faith, Love, Hope: A History of the Unitas Fratrum.* Winston Salem, NC, 2008.

Crossley, Robert N. *Luther and the Peasants War: Luther's Actions and Reactions.* New York, 1974.

Csendes, Peter, and Ferdinand Opll, eds. *Wien: Geschichte einer Stadt.* 3 vols. Vienna, 2001–2006.

Csermak, Alice. "Geschichte des Protestantismus in der Herrschaft Paternion bis zum Toleranzpatent 1781." Ph.D. dissertation, University of Vienna, 1969.

Curtis, Benjamin. *The Habsburgs: The History of a Dynasty.* London, 2013.

Czerny, Albin. *Bilder aus der Zeit der Bauernunruhen in Oberösterreich.* Linz, 1876.

———. *Der zweite Bauernaufstand in Oberösterreich 1595–1597.* Linz, 1890.

———. "Einige Blätter aus der Zeit der Gegenreformation in Oberösterreich." *Jahrbuch des Oberösterreichischen Musealvereines* 42 (1884): 1–196.

Bibliography 299

Czerny, Heimo. *Catharina Regina von Greiffenberg, geb. Freiherrin von Seisenegg (1633–1694): Herkunft, Leben und Werk der größten deutschen Barockdichterin.* Amstetten, Austria, 1983.

Czerwenka, Bernhard. *Die Khevenhüller: Geschichte des Geschlechts mit besonderer Berücksichtigung des XVII. Jahrhunderts.* Vienna, 1867.

Czok, Karl. *August der Starke und seine Zeit: Kurfürst von Sachsen, König in Polen.* Munich, 2006.

Dareste, Rodolphe. *Essai sur François Hotman.* Paris, 1850.

Daussy, Hugues. *Les huguenots et le roi: Le combat politique de Philippe Duplessis-Mornay (1572–1600).* Geneva, 2002.

Dávid, Géza, and Pál Fodor, eds. *Ottomans, Hungarians, and Habsburgs in Central Europe: The Military Confines in the Era of Ottoman Conquest.* Leiden, 2000.

David, Zdeněk V. *Finding the Middle Way: The Utraquists' Liberal Challenge to Rome and Luther.* Washington, DC, 2003.

David, Zdeněk V., and David R. Holeton, eds. *The Bohemian Reformation and Religious Practice 3.* Prague, 2000.

Davis, Kingsley, and Wilbert E. Moore. "Some Principles of Stratification." *American Sociological Review* 10 (1945): 242–249.

Dedic, Paul. *Der Protestantismus in Steiermark im Zeitalter der Reformation und Gegenreformation.* Leipzig, 1930.

———. "Der Kärntner Protestantismus vom Abschluß der 'Hauptreformation' bis zur Adelsemigration (1600–1629/30)." *Jahrbuch der Gesellschaft für die Geschichte des Protestantismus in Österreich* 58 (1937): 70–108.

———. "Der Kärntner Protestantismus von der Adelsemigration bis zum Ende des siebzehnten Jahrunderts." *Jahrbuch der Gesellschaft für die Geschichte des Protestantismus in Österreich* 59 (1938): 63–165.

———. *Der Geheimprotestantismus in Kärnten während der Regierung Karls VI. (1711–1740).* Klagenfurt, 1940.

———. *Kärntner Exulanten des 17. Jahrhunderts.* Klagenfurt, 1979.

Demény, Lajos. *Bethlen Gábor és kora.* Bukarest, 1982.

DeMolen, Richard L., ed. *Religious Orders of the Catholic Reformation.* New York, 1994.

Deventer, Jörg. *Gegenreformation in Schlesien: Die habsburgische Rekatholisierungspolitik in Glogau und Schweidnitz 1526–1707.* Cologne, 2003.

Dickens, Arthur Geoffrey. *The English Reformation.* 2nd ed. London, 1989.

Dieterich, Veit-Jakobus, and Hans Hecker, eds. *Comenius der Politiker.* Baltmannsweiler, Germany, 2004.

Dietz, Burkhard, and Stefan Ehrenpreis, eds. *Drei Konfessionen in einer Region: Beiträge zur Geschichte der Konfessionalisierung im Herzogtum Berg vom 16. bis zum 18. Jahrhundert.* Cologne, 1999.

Dillon, Kenneth J. *King and Estates in the Bohemian Lands, 1526–1564.* Brussels, 1976.

Dinklage, Karl. *Kärnten um 1600: Die Bilder der Khevenhüller-Chronik.* Vienna, 1980.

300 Bibliography

Dissertori, Alois. *Die Auswanderung der Defregger Protestanten 1666–1725*. Innsbruck, 2001.

Dolinar, France Martin, et al., eds. *Katholische Reform und Gegenreformation in Innerösterreich 1564–1628*. Klagenfurt, 1994.

Doppler, Caecilia. "Reformation und Gegenreformation in ihrer Auswirkung auf das Steyrer Bürgertum." Dissertationen der Universität Wien 135. Vienna, 1977.

Dörrer, Fridolin, ed. *Die Bauernkriege und Michael Gaismair*. Innsbruck, 1982.

Droste, Heiko. *Im Dienste der Krone: Schwedische Diplomaten im 17. Jahrhundert*. Berlin, 2006.

Droysen, Gustaf. *Gustaf Adolf*. 2 vols. Leipzig, 1870.

Duby, Georges. *L'économie rurale et la vie des campagnes dans l'Occident médiéval*. 2 vols. Paris, 1962.

———. *The Three Orders: Feudal Society Imagined*. Chicago, 1980.

———. *Qu'est que la société féodale?* Paris, 2002.

Duchhardt, Heinz. "Absolutismus: Abschied von einem Epochenbegriff?" *Historische Zeitschrift* 258 (1994): 113–122.

———, ed. *Der Westfälische Friede: Diplomatie—politische Zäsur—kulturelles Umfeld—Rezeptionsgeschichte*. Munich, 1998.

———. *Nationale Geschichtskulturen—Bilanz, Ausstrahlung, Europabezogenheit*. Stuttgart, 2006.

Ducreux, Marie-Élizabeth. "Entre catholicisme et protestantisme: l'identité tchèque." *Le Débat* 59 (1990): 103–125.

Duffy, Eamon. *The Stripping of the Altars: Traditional Religion in England, c.1400–c.1580*. New Haven, CT, 1992.

Dufour, Alain. *Théodore de Bèze, poète et théologien*. Paris, 2006.

Duhr, Bernhard. *Geschichte der Jesuiten in den Ländern deutscher Zunge*. 4 vols. Freiburg, 1907–1928.

Dumézil, Georges. *Mythe et Épopées*. 3 vols. Paris, 1968–1973.

Dyer, Christopher. *Standards of Living in the Later Middle Ages: Social Change in England c. 1200–1520*. Cambridge, England, 1989.

Edel, Andreas. *Der Kaiser und Kurpfalz: Eine Studie zu den Grundelementen politischen Handelns bei Maximilian II. (1564–1576)*. Göttingen, 1997.

Edelmayer, Friedrich, and Alfred Kohler, eds. *Kaiser Maximilian II.: Kultur und Politik im 16. Jahrhundert*. Vienna, 1992.

Edelmayer, Friedrich, Maximilian Lanzinner, and Peter Rauscher, eds. *Finanzen und Herrschaft: Materielle Grundlagen fürstlicher Politik in den habsburgischen Ländern und im Heiligen Römischen Reich im 16. Jahrhundert*. Vienna, 2003.

Eder, Karl. *Studien zur Reformationsgeschichte Oberösterreichs*. 2 vols. Linz 1932–1936.

Eggendorfer, Anton, Christian Lackner, and Willibald Rosner, eds. *Festschrift Heide Dienst zum 65. Geburtstag*. St. Pölten, 2004.

Ehmer, Arthur. *Das Schrifttum zur Salzburger Emigration 1731/33*. Hamburg, 1975.

Bibliography 301

Eichmeyer, Karl, Helmuth Feigl, and Rudolf Walter Litschel. *Weiß gilt die Seel und auch das Guet: Oberösterreichische Bauernaufstände und Bauernkriege im 16. und 17. Jahrhundert.* Linz, 1976.

Elkan, Albert. *Die Publizistik der Bartholomäusnacht und Mornays "Vindiciae contra tyrannos".* Heidelberg, 1905.

———. "Entstehung und Entwicklung des Begriffs Gegenreformation." *Historische Zeitschrift* 112 (1914): 473–493.

Elste, Alfred, and Dirk Hänisch. *Kärnten von der Ersten zur Zweiten Republik: Kontinuität oder Wandel?* Klagenfurt, 1998.

Elton, Geoffrey Rudolph. *Reform and Reformation: England 1509–1558.* London, 1977.

Emkens, Franz-Reiner, and Hartmut Wolff, eds. *Von Sacerdotium und Regnum: Geistliche und weltliche Gewalt im frühen und hohen Mittelalter.* Cologne, 2002.

Endres, Rudolf. *Adel in der Frühen Neuzeit.* Munich, 1993.

Engammare, Max. "Calvin monarchomaque? Du soupçon à l'argument." *Archiv für Reformationsgeschichte* 89 (1998): 207–225.

Engelbert, Kurt. "Die Konvention von Altranstädt 1707." *Archiv für schlesische Kirchengeschichte* 16 (1958): 243–264.

Englund, Peter. *Poltava: Berättelsen om en armés undergång.* Stockholm, 1988.

Enzner, Manfred. *Exulanten aus dem südlichen Waldviertel in Franken (ca. 1627– 1670).* Nuremberg, 2001.

Evans, Robert J. W. *Rudolf II and His World: A Study in Intellectual History, 1576–1612.* Oxford, England, 1973.

———. *The Making of the Habsburg Monarchy 1550–1700: An Interpretation.* Oxford, England, 1979.

———. *Austria, Hungary, and the Habsburgs: Essays on Central Europe, c.1683– 1867.* Oxford, England, 2006.

Evans, Robert J. W., and Trevor V. Thomas, eds. *Crown, Church and Estates: Central European Politics in the Sixteenth and Seventeenth Centuries.* London, 1991.

Evans, Robert J. W., and Peter H. Wilson, eds. *The Holy Roman Empire, 1495– 1806.* Leiden, 2012.

Fata, Márta. *Ungarn, das Land der Stephanskrone, im Zeitalter der Reformation und Konfessionalisierung: Multiethnizität, Land und Konfession 1500 bis 1700.* Münster, 2000.

Fattinger, Hans. "Stefan Fadinger und Christoph Zeller: Ihre Familien und ihre Heimat." *Oberösterreichische Heimatblätter* 19 (1965): 49–60.

Feigl, Helmuth. "Beiträge zur Biographie des Freiherrn Georg Erasmus von Tschernembl." Ph.D. dissertation, University of Vienna, 1949.

———. "Die befreiten Ämter der Herrschaft Steyr in den Bauernkriegen des 16. und 17. Jahrhunderts." *Mitteilungen des Oberösterreichischen Landesarchivs* 6 (1959): 209–262.

Fernández Álvarez, Manuel. *Carlos V: El césar y el hombre.* Madrid, 1999.

302 Bibliography

Fichtner, Paula Sutter. *Ferdinand I of Austria: The Politics of Dynasticism in the Age of the Reformation*. Boulder, CO, 1982.

———. *Emperor Maximilian II*. New Haven, CT, 2001.

———. *The Habsburgs: Dynasty, Culture and Politics*. London, 2014.

Flacke, Monika, ed. *Mythen der Nationen: 1945—Arena der Erinnerungen*. Mainz, 2004.

Florey, Gerhard. *Geschichte der Salzburger Protestanten und ihrer Emigration 1731/32*. Vienna, 1977.

Fontane, Theodor. *Sämtliche Werke*. Vol. 10, *Das Oderland*. Munich, 1960.

Forcher, Michael. *Michael Gaismair: Um Freiheit und Gerechtigkeit. Leben und Programm des Tiroler Bauernführers und Sozialrevolutionärs 1490–1532*. Innsbruck, 1982.

Försvarstabens Krigshistoriska Avdelning, ed. *Slaget vid Jankow*. Stockholm, 1945.

———. *Från Femern och Jankow til Westfaliska Freden*. Stockholm, 1948.

Frank, Horst-Joachim. *Catharina Regina von Greiffenberg: Untersuchungen zu ihrer Persönlichkeit und Sonettdichtung*. Göttingen, 1967.

Franz, Günther. *Der deutsche Bauernkrieg*. 10th ed. Darmstadt, Germany, 1975.

Franzel, Emil. *Geschichte des deutschen Volkes: Von den Germanen bis zur Teilung nach dem Zweiten Weltkrieg*. Gütersloh, Germany, 1985.

Fräss-Ehrfeld, Claudia. *Geschichte Kärntens*. Vol. 2, *Die ständische Periode*. Klagenfurt, 1994.

Fresacher, Walther. "Ansitze der Hammerwerke im Süden von Villach: Gödersdorf, Neufinkenstein, der Nagerschigg-Hof und das Gut Müllnern." *Neues aus Alt-Villach* 12 (1975): 19–94.

Friedeburg, Robert von. *Self-Defence and Religious Strife in Early Modern Europe: England and Germany, 1530–1680*. Aldershot, England, 2002.

———, ed. *Widerstandsrecht in der frühen Neuzeit: Erträge und Perspektiven der Forschung im deutsch-britischen Vergleich*. Berlin, 2001.

Friesen, Abraham. *Thomas Müntzer, a Destroyer of the Godless: The Making of a Sixteenth-Century Revolutionary*. Berkeley, CA, 1990.

Frisch, Michael. *Das Restitutionsedikt Kaiser Ferdinands II. vom 6. März 1629: Eine rechtsgeschichtliche Untersuchung*. Tübingen, 1993.

Frydell, Anders. *Berättelser ur svenska historien*. Part 7, *Gustaf II Adolf*. 4th ed. Stockholm, 1847.

Fuchs, Ralf-Peter. *Ein 'Medium zum Frieden': Die Normaljahrsregel und die Beendigung des Dreißigjährigen Krieges*. Munich, 2010.

Fulton, Elaine. *Catholic Belief and Survival in Late Sixteenth-Century Vienna: The Case of Georg Eder (1523–87)*. Aldershot, England, 2007.

Funkenstein, Amos. "Collective Memory and Historical Consciousness." *History and Memory* 1 (1989): 5–26.

Gadebusch, Friedrich Conrad. *Versuche in der livländischen Geschichtskunde und Rechtsgelehrsamkeit*. Vol. 1, piece 2, *Von dem Grafen Heinrich Matthias von Thurn und seinen Nachkommen*. Riga, 1779.

Garstein, Oskar. *Rome and the Counter-Reformation in Scandinavia*. 4 vols. Oslo, 1963–1992.

Gasteiger, Gustav von. *Die Zillerthaler Protestanten und ihre Ausweisung aus Tirol.* Meran, 1892.

Gautier, Jean-Antoine. *Histoire de Genève des origines a l'année 1691.* Vol. 7. Geneva, 1909.

Gehrke, Roland, ed. *Aufbrüche in die Moderne: Frühparlamentarismus zwischen altständischer Ordnung und modernem Konstitutionalismus 1750–1850: Schlesien—Deutschland—Mitteleuropa.* Cologne, 2005.

Geisendorf, Paul F. *Théodore de Bèze.* Geneva, 1949.

Generalstaben, ed. *Sveriges krig 1611–1632.* 8 vols. Stockholm, 1936–39.

Gessler, Eduard A. "Die sogen. Lederkanonen aus dem Zeughausbestand der Stadt Zürich." *Anzeiger für schweizerische Altertumskunde* 26 (1924): 51–66 and 154–166.

Geyer, Michael, and Hartmut Lehmann, eds. *Religion und Nation, Nation und Religion: Beiträge zu einer unbewältigten Geschichte.* Göttingen, 2004.

Gilbert, Felix, ed. *The Historical Essays of Otto Hintze.* New York, 1975.

Gindely, Anton. *Geschichte der Ertheilung des böhmischen Majestätsbriefes von 1609.* Prague, 1858.

———. *Beiträge zur Geschichte des Dreißigjährigen Krieges.* Wiener Akademieschriften 20. Vienna, 1859.

———. *Rudolf II. und seine Zeit: 1600 bis 1612.* 2 vols. Prague, 1863–1868.

———. *Geschichte des dreißigjährigen Krieges.* 3 vols. Leipzig, 1882–1883.

Glatzl, Matthias. "Die Freiherrn von Teufel in ihrer staats- und kirchenpolitischen Stellung zur Zeit der Reformation und Restauration." Ph.D. dissertation, University of Vienna, 1950.

Gleason, Elisabeth G. *Gasparo Contarini: Venice, Rome and Reform.* Berkeley, CA, 1993.

Glete, Jan. *War and the State in Early Modern Europe: Spain, the Dutch Republic and Sweden as Fiscal-Military States, 1500–1660.* London, 2002.

Godsey, William D. "Adelsautonomie, Konfession und Nation im österreichischen Absolutismus ca. 1620–1848." *Zeitschrift für historische Forschung* 33 (2006): 197–239.

———. *The Sinews of Habsburg Power: Lower Austria in a Fiscal-Military State 1650–1820.* Oxford, England, 2018.

Goertz, Hans-Jürgen. *Thomas Müntzer: Apocalyptic, Mystic and Revolutionary.* Edinburgh, 1993.

Gohlke, Wilhelm. "Versuche zur Erleichterung der Feldgeschütze im 17. und 18. Jahrhundert." *Zeitschrift für Historische Waffenkunde* 4 (1906–1908): 387–395.

Göransson, Sven. "Comenius och Sverige 1642–1648." *Lychnos* 1957/58 (1958): 102–137.

Gorski, Philip S. "Historicizing the Secularization Debate: Church, State, and Society in Late Medieval and Early Modern Europe, ca. 1300 to 1700." *American Sociological Review* 65 (2000): 138–167.

Gotthard, Axel. "'Politice seint wir Bäpstisch': Kursachsen und der deutsche Protestantismus im frühen 17. Jahrhundert." *Zeitschrift für historische Forschung* 20 (1993): 275–319.

304 Bibliography

————. *Der Augsburger Religionsfrieden*. Münster, 2004.

Granberg, Olof. *Allart van Everdingen och hans "norska" landskap*. Stockholm, 1902.

Grell, Ole Peter, ed. *The Scandinavian Reformation: From Evangelical Movement to Institutionalisation of Reform*. Cambridge, England, 1995.

Greschat, Martin. "Luthers Haltung im Bauernkrieg." *Archiv für Reformationsgeschichte* 65 (1965): 31–47.

Gritsch, Eric W. *Thomas Müntzer: A Tragedy of Errors*. Minneapolis, 1989.

Grosjean, Alexia. *An Unofficial Alliance: Scotland and Sweden 1569–1654*. Leiden, 2003.

Grossmann, Walter. "Toleration: Exercitium Religionis Privatum." *Journal of the History of Ideas* 40:1 (1979): 129–134.

Grüll, Georg. "Geschichte des Schlosses und der Herrschaft Windhag bei Perg." *Jahrbuch des Oberösterreichischen Musealvereines* 87 (1937): 185–311.

————. "Die Herrschaftsschichtung in Österreich ob der Enns 1750." *Mitteilungen des Oberösterreichischen Landesarchivs* 5 (1957): 311–339.

————. "Das Frankenburger Würfelspiel." *Oberösterreich* 9:3/4 (1959): 4–9.

————. *Bauer, Herr und Landesfürst: Sozialrevolutionäre Bestrebungen der oberösterreichischen Bauern von 1650 bis 1848*. Linz, 1963.

————. *Der Bauer im Lande ob der Enns am Ausgang des 16. Jahrhunderts: Abgaben und Leistungen im Lichte der Beschwerden und Verträge von 1597–1598*. Linz, 1969.

Grusky, David, ed. *Social Stratification: Class, Race, and Gender in Sociological Perspective*. 4th ed. Boulder, CO, 2014.

Gunst, Péter. *A magyar történetírás története*. Debrecen, 2000.

Haberer, Michael. *Ohnmacht und Chance: Leonhard von Harrach (1514–1590) und die erbländische Machtelite*. Vienna, 2011.

Haider, Siegfried. *Geschichte Oberösterreichs*. Munich, 1987.

Haigh, Christopher. *English Reformations: Religion, Politics and Society under the Tudors*. Oxford, England, 1993.

Halbwachs, Maurice. *Les cadres sociaux de la mémoire*. Paris, 1925.

————. *La Topographie légendaire des Évangiles en Terre Sainte: Étude de mémoire collective*. Paris, 1941.

————. *La mémoire collective*. Paris, 1950.

————. *On Collective Memory*. Edited and translated by Lewis A. Coser. Chicago, 1992.

Hallenberg, Mats. *Kungen, fogdarna och riket: Lokalförvaltning och statsbyggande under tidig Vasatid*. Stockholm, 2001.

————. *Statsmakt till salu: Arrendesystemet och privatiseringen av skatteuppbörden i det svenska riket 1618–1635*. Lund, 2008.

Hamilton, Henning. *Afhandling om krigsmaktens och krigskonstens tillstånd i Sverige under Konung Gustaf II Adolfs regering*. Stockholm, 1846.

Hamilton, J. Taylor, and Kenneth G. Hamilton. *History of the Moravian Church: The Renewed Unitas Fratrum 1722–1957*. 2 vols. Bethlehem, PA, 1967.

Bibliography 305

Hammarstrand, Sven Fromhold. *Försök til en historisk framställning af förhandlingarne om Sveriges deltagende i trettioåriga kriget.* Uppsala, 1855.

Hammer-Purgstall, Joseph von. *Khlesls des Cardinals, Directors des geheimen Cabinetes Kaisers Mathias, Leben.* 4 vols. Vienna, 1847–1851.

Hantsch, Hugo. *Geschichte Österreichs.* Vol. 2. 4th ed. Graz, 1959.

Härter, Karl, ed. *Policey und frühneuzeitliche Gesellschaft.* Frankfurt, 2000.

Hartungen, Christoph von, and Günther Pallaver, eds. *Michael Gaismair und seine Zeit: Gaismair-Tage 1982.* Bozen-Innsbruck, 1983.

Hassinger, Herbert. "Die Landstände der österreichischen Länder: Zusammensetzung, Organisation und Leistung im 16. bis 18. Jahrhundert." *Jahrbuch für Landeskunde von Niederösterreich,* n. s., 36 (1964): 989–1035.

Hatton, Ragnhild Marie. *Charles XII of Sweden.* London, 1968.

Haug-Moritz, Gabriele. *Der Schmalkaldische Bund 1530–1541/42: Eine Studie zu den genossenschaftlichen Strukturelementen der politischen Ordnung des Heiligen Römischen Reiches Deutscher Nation.* Leinfelden-Echterdingen, Germany, 2002.

Hausenblasová, Jaroslava, Jiří Mikulec, and Martina Thomsen, eds. *Religion und Politik im frühneuzeitlichen Böhmen: Der Majestätsbrief Kaiser Rudolfs II. von 1609.* Stuttgart, 2014.

Hebbe, Per Magnus. *Svenskarna i Böhmen och Mähren: Studier i tjeckisk folktradition och litteratur.* Uppsala, 1932.

Heer, Friedrich. *Der Kampf um die österreichische Identität.* 2nd ed. Vienna, 1996.

Heiberg, Steffen. *Christian 4: Monarken, Mennesket og Myten.* Copenhagen, 1988; new and rev. ed., 2006.

Heilingsetzer, Georg. *Der oberösterreichische Bauernkrieg 1626.* Vienna, 1976.

———. "Ständischer Widerstand und Unterwerfung: Erasmus von Starhemberg und seine Rechtfertigungsschrift (1621)." *Mitteilungen des oberösterreichischen Landesarchivs* 14 (1984): 269–289.

Heiss, Gernot. "Die Jesuiten und die Anfänge der Katholisierung in den Ländern Ferdinands I.: Glaube, Mentalität, Politik." Unpublished habilitation thesis, University of Vienna, 1986.

Helczmanovski, Heimold, ed. *Beiträge zur Bevölkerungs- und Sozialgeschichte Österreichs.* Munich, 1973.

Hengerer, Mark. *Kaiser Ferdinand III.* Vienna, 2012.

Henshall, Nicholas. *The Myth of Absolutism: Change and Continuity in Early Modern European Monarchy.* London, 1992.

Herrera, Corina Marta. "The Ambiguous Reformation in the Territorial Cities of Upper Austria, 1520–1576: Enns, Freistadt, Gmunden, Linz, Steyr, Vöcklabruck and Wels." Ph.D. dissertation, Yale University, 1980.

Herrmann, Gerd-Ulrich. *Freiherr von Derfflinger.* Berlin, 1997.

Hersche, Peter. *Muße und Verschwendung: Europäische Gesellschaft und Kultur im Barockzeitalter.* 2 vols. Freiburg im Breisgau, 2006.

Herzig, Arno. *Der Zwang zum wahren Glauben: Rekatholisierung vom 16. bis zum 18. Jahrhundert.* Göttingen, 2000.

306 Bibliography

Heß, Johann Eduard. *Gottfried Heinrich, Graf zu Pappenheim*. Leipzig, 1855.

Hewitson, Mark. *Nationalism in Germany, 1848–1866: Revolutionary Nation*. Basingstoke, England, 2010.

Heymann, Frederick G. "Das Temno in der neuen tschechischen Geschichtsauffassung." *Bohemia* 9 (1968): 323–339.

Hilton, Rodney H. "Feudalism in Europe: Problems for Historical Materialism." *New Left Review* 147 (1984): 84–93.

Hinrichs, Carl. *Luther und Müntzer: Ihre Auseinandersetzung über Obrigkeit und Widerstandsrecht*. 2d ed. Berlin, 1962.

Hinrichs, Ernst. *Fürsten und Mächte: Zum Problem des europäischen Absolutismus*. Göttingen, 2000.

Hintze, Otto. "Typologie der ständischen Verfassungen des Abendlands." *Historische Zeitschrift* 141 (1930): 229–248.

Hitz, Harald, et al., eds. *Waldviertler Biographien*. Vol. 1. Horn, Austria, 2001.

Hledíková, Zdeňka, ed. *Traditio et Cultus: Miscellanea historica Bohemica Miloslao Vlk archiepiscopo Pragensi ab eius collegis amicisque ad annum sexagesimum dedicata*. Prague, 1993.

Höbelt, Lothar. *Ferdinand III. (1609–1657): Friedenskaiser wider Willen*. Graz, 2008.

———. *Von Nördlingen bis Jankau: Kaiserliche Strategie und Kriegführung 1634–1645*. Vienna, 2016.

Hobsbawm, Eric. *Nations and Nationalism since 1780*. Cambridge, England, 1990.

Hobsbawm, Eric, and Terence Ranger, eds. *The Invention of Tradition*. Cambridge, England, 1983.

Hochedlinger, Michael, and Thomas Winkelbauer, eds. *Herrschaftsverdichtung, Staatsbildung, Bürokratisierung: Verfassungs-, Verwaltungs- und Behördengeschichte der Frühen Neuzeit*. Vienna, 2010.

Hoffmann, Alfred, and Erich Maria Meixner. *Wirtschaftsgeschichte des Landes Oberösterreich*. 2 vols. Salzburg, 1952.

Holmquist, Hjalmar, and Hilding Pleijel, eds. *Svenska kyrkans historia*. Vol. 3, *Reformationstidevarvet 1523–1611*, edited by Hjalmar Holmquist. Stockholm, 1933.

Hölzl, Sebastian. "Die Zillertaler Protestanten vor 150 Jahren: Dargestellt am Beispiel Brandbergs." *Tiroler Heimat* 50 (1986): 149–173.

Hopfen, Otto Helmut. *Kaiser Maximilian II. und der Kompromißkatholizismus*. Munich, 1895.

Hormann, Josef von, and Alois von Mednyánszky, eds. *Taschenbuch für die vaterländische Geschichte 8*. Vienna, 1827.

Hostetler, John A. *Hutterite Society*. Baltimore, MD, 1974.

Hsia, Ronnie Po-Chia. *Social Discipline in the Reformation: Central Europe, 1550–1750*. London, 1989.

———. *The World of Catholic Renewal, 1540–1770*. Cambridge, England, 1998.

———, ed. *A Companion to the Reformation World*. Oxford, England, 2004.

Bibliography 307

Hübel, Ignaz. "Die 1620 in Nieder- und Oberösterreich politisch kompromittierten Protestanten." *Jahrbuch der Gesellschaft für die Geschichte des Protestantismus im ehemaligen Österreich* 59 (1938): 45–62, and 60 (1939): 105–125.

Huber, Florian. "Konfessionelle Identitätsbildung in Tirol: Antiprotestantismus ohne Protestanten (1830–1848)." *Geschichte und Region/Storia e regione* 19 (2010): 28–52.

Hübner, Eckhard, et al., eds. *Rußland zur Zeit Katharinas II: Absolutismus—Aufklärung—Pragmatismus*. Cologne, 1998.

Hufnagl, Franz. "Die landesfürstliche Stadt Gmunden als Sitz der Kammergutsverwaltung: Die Stadt im Spannungsfeld mit den Habsburgern und den Salzamtmännern." Ph.D. dissertation, University of Salzburg, 1999.

———. *Die Maut zu Gmunden: Die Entwicklungsgeschichte des Salzkammergutes*. Vienna, 2008.

Hujber, Wendelin. "Der Prälatenstand des Landes ob der Enns 1600–1620: Beiträge zu seiner und der Geschichte der Landschaft im Zeitalter der Gegenreformation." Ph.D. dissertation, University of Vienna, 1972.

Hülber, Hans. "Georg Derfflinger—seine Vorfahren und der Lebensraum seiner frühen Jugend." *Oberösterreichische Heimatblätter* 37 (1983): 23–33.

Hurter, Friedrich von. *Geschichte Kaiser Ferdinands II*. 11 vols. Schaffhausen, 1850–1864.

Hutton, Patrick. *History as an Art of Memory*. Hanover, NH, 1993.

———. "Recent Scholarship on Memory and History." *The History Teacher* 33 (2000): 533–548.

Ingrao, Charles W. *State and Society in Early Modern Austria*. West Lafayette, Ind., 1994.

———. *The Habsburg Monarchy, 1618–1815*. 2nd ed. Cambridge, England, 2000.

Iwasaki, Shuichi. *Stände und Staatsbildung in der frühneuzeitlichen Habsburgermonarchie in Österreich unter der Enns 1683–1748*. St. Pölten, 2014.

Jagger, Graham. "On the Authorship of the Vindiciae contra tyrannos." *Durham University Journal* 60 (1968): 73–80.

Janáček, Josef. *Rudolf II. a jeho doba*. Prague, 1987.

Janzen, Rod, and Max Stanton. *The Hutterites in North America*. Baltimore, MD, 2010.

Jedin, Hubert. *Katholische Reform oder Gegenreformation? Ein Versuch der Klärung der Begriffe*. Lucerne, 1946.

———. *Geschichte des Konzils von Trient*. 4 vols. Freiburg im Breisgau, 1949–1975.

Jensen, Alfred. *Svenska minnen fran Böhmen och Mähren: Kulturhistoriska skisser från trettioåriga kriget*. Lund, 1910.

Jireček, Josef. *Leben des Obersten Hofkanzlers von Böhmen Wilhelm Grafen Slavata*. Prague, 1876.

Johansson, Johannes. *Österrikes martyrkyrka*. Linköping, 1930.

Jones, George Fenwick. *The Salzburger Saga: Religious Exiles and Other Germans along the Savannah*. Athens, GA, 1984.

Kainz, Otto. "Das Kriegsgerichtsprotokoll im niederösterreichischen Bauernaufstand aus dem Jahre 1597." Ph.D. dissertation, University of Vienna, 2008.

308   Bibliography

———. *Das Kriegsgerichtsprotokoll zum Niederösterreichischen Bauernaufstand von 1596/97: Analyse und Edition*. St. Pölten, 2010.

Kaminsky, Howard. *A History of the Hussite Revolution*. Berkeley, CA, 1967.

Kann, Robert A. *A History of the Habsburg Monarchy, 1526–1918*. Berkeley, CA, 1974.

Kann, Robert A., and Zdeněk V. David. *The Peoples of the Eastern Habsburg Lands, 1526–1918*. Seattle, WA, 1984.

Kármán, Gábor, and Kees Teszelszky, eds. *Bethlen Gábor és Európa*. Budapest, 2013.

Karniel, Joseph. *The Toleranzpolitik Kaiser Josephs II*. Gerlingen, Germany, 1986.

Kaufmann, Arthur, ed. *Widerstandsrecht*. Darmstadt, 1972.

Kaufmann, Thomas. *Dreißigjähriger Krieg und Westfälischer Friede: Kirchengeschichtliche Studien zur lutherischen Konfessionskultur*. Tübingen, 1998.

———. *Das Ende der Reformation: Magdeburgs "Herrgotts Kanzlei" (1548–1551/2)*. Tübingen, 2003.

Kaul, Camilla G. *Friedrich Barbarossa im Kyffhäuser: Bilder eines nationalen Mythos im 19. Jahrhundert*. 2 vols. Cologne, 2007.

Kavka, František. *Bílá hora a české dějiny*. Prague, 1962.

Kelley, Donald R. *François Hotman: A Revolutionary's Ordeal*. Princeton, NJ, 1983.

Kerschbaumer, Anton. *Kardinal Klesl: Eine Monographie*. 2nd ed. Vienna, 1905.

Khevenhüller-Metsch, Georg. "Vierhundert Jahre Hochosterwitz." *Carinthia I* 131 (1941): 172–181.

———. *Die Burg Hochosterwitz in Kärnten und ihre Geschichte*. Klagenfurt, 1953.

Kielmansegg, Erich von. *Beiträge zur Geschichte der niederösterreichischen Statthalterei: Die Landeschefs und Räthe dieser Behörde von 1501 bis 1896*. Vienna, 1897.

Kirschfeld, Johannes. "Eva Margaretha Frölich." *Theologische Studien und Kritiken* 101 (1929): 205–252.

Kirsten, Ernst, Ernst Wolfgang Buchholz, and Wolfgang Köllmann. *Raum und Bevölkerung in der Weltgeschichte: Bevölkerungs-Ploetz*. 3rd ed. 4 vols. Würzburg, 1966.

Klaassen, Walter. *Michael Gaismair: Revolutionary and Reformer*. Hague, 1978.

Kleinheyer, Gerd. *Die kaiserlichen Wahlkapitulationen: Geschichte, Wesen und Funktion*. Karlsruhe, 1968.

Klieber, Rupert, and Hermann Hold, eds. *Impulse für eine religiöse Alltagsgeschichte des Donau-Alpen-Adria-Raumes*. Vienna, 2005.

Klingenstein, Grete, Heinrich Lutz, and Gerald Stourzh, eds. *Bildung, Politik und Gesellschaft: Studien zur Geschichte des europäischen Bildungswesens vom 16. bis zum 20. Jahrhundert*. Vienna, 1978.

Klueting, Harm. *Das Konfessionelle Zeitalter 1525–1648*. Stuttgart, 1989.

———, ed. *200 Jahre Reichsdeputationshauptschluss: Säkularisation, Mediatisierung und Modernisierung zwischen Altem Reich und neuer Staatlichkeit*. Münster, 2005.

Bibliography 309

Knall, Dieter. *Aus der Heimat gedrängt: Letzte Zwangsumsiedlungen steirischer Protestanten nach Siebenbürgen unter Maria Theresia.* Graz, 2002.

Kohla, Franz Xaver, Gustav Adolf von Metnitz, and Gotbert Moro. *Kärntner Burgenkunde: Ergebnisse und Hinweise in Übersicht.* Klagenfurt, 1973.

Kohler, Alfred. "Umfang und Bedeutung historisch-geographischer Werke in oberösterreichischen Adelsbibliotheken des 17. Jahrhunderts." *Mitteilungen des Oberösterreichischen Landesarchivs* 13 (1981): 221–237.

———. *Karl V. 1500–1558: Eine Biographie.* Munich, 2001.

———. *Ferdinand I. 1503–1564: Fürst, König und Kaiser.* Munich, 2003.

Königsberger, Helmut G., ed. *Republiken und Republikanismus im Europa der Frühen Neuzeit.* Munich, 1988.

Koops, Tilman Peter. *Die Lehre vom Widerstandsrecht des Volkes gegen die weltliche Obrigkeit in der lutherischen Theologie des 16. und 17. Jahrhunderts.* Kiel, 1969.

Kopal, Wenzel. *Geschichte der Stadt Eferding.* Linz, 1875.

Koser, Reinhold. *Der Kanzleienstreit: Ein Beitrag zur Quellenkunde der Geschichte des dreissigjährigen Krieges.* Halle, 1874.

Kosminsky, Evgeny A. *Studies in the Agrarian History of England in the Thirteenth Century.* Oxford, England, 1956.

Krawarik, Hans. *Exul austriacus: Konfessionelle Migrationen aus Österreich in der Frühen Neuzeit.* Vienna, 2010.

Kreissler, Felix. *Der Österreicher und seine Nation: Ein Lernprozeß mit Hindernissen.* Vienna, 1984.

Kritzl, Johannes. "'Sacerdotes incorrigibiles'? Die Disziplinierung des Sekulärklerus durch das Passauer Offizialat unter der Enns von 1580 bis 1652 im Spiegel der Passauer Offizialatsprotokolle." Th.D. dissertation, University of Vienna, 2011.

Krofta, Kamil. *Majestát Rudolfa II.* Prague, 1909.

———. *Bílá hora.* Prague, 1913.

Krüssmann, Walter. *Ernst von Mansfeld (1580–1626): Grafensohn, Söldnerführer, Kriegsunternehmer gegen Habsburg im Dreißigjährigen Krieg.* Berlin, 2010.

Kučera, Jan P. "Stavovská opozice v Čechách a volba Ferdinanda Štýrského českým králem." *Studia Comeniana et Historica* 14 (1984): 5–42.

Kunisch, Johannes. *Absolutismus: Europäische Geschichte vom Westfälischen Frieden bis zur Krise des Ancien Régime.* 2nd rev. ed. Göttingen, 1999.

Küppers-Braun, Ute. "Zerrissene Familien und entführte Kinder: Staatlich verordnete Protestantenverfolgung im Osttiroler Defereggental (1684–1691)." *Jahrbuch für die Geschichte des Protestantismus in Österreich* 121 (2005): 91–168.

Kurz, Franz. *Versuch einer Geschichte des Bauernkrieges in Oberösterreich unter der Anführung des Stephan Fadinger und Achatz Wiellinger.* Leipzig, 1805.

———. *Beyträge zur Geschichte des Landes Oesterreich ob der Enns.* Vol. 2. Linz, 1808.

Kurz, Marlene, and Thomas Winkelbauer, eds. *Glaubenswechsel.* Innsbruck, 2007.

Lagerquist, Marshall. "Julita gård i Södermanland." *Fataburen* (1957): 29–56.

310 Bibliography

——. "Khevenhüller i dikt och verklighet." *Fataburen* (1960): 53–82.

Landberg, Hans, Lars Ekholm, Roland Nordlund, and Sven A. Nilsson. *Det kontinentala krigets ekonomi: Studier i krigsfinansiering under svensk stormaktstid.* Kristianstad, 1971.

Landwehr, Achim. *Policey im Alltag: Die Implementation frühneuzeitlicher Policeyordnungen in Leonberg.* Frankfurt, 2000.

Langer, Hermann. *Joseph Schaitberger: Ein evangelischer Glaubenskämpfer des 17. Jahrhunderts.* Salzburg, 1985.

Larson, James L. *Reforming the North: The Kingdoms and Churches of Scandinavia, 1520–1545.* Cambridge, England, 2010.

Larsson, Lars-Olof. *Gustav Vasa—landsfader eller tyrann?* Stockholm, 2002.

——. *Arvet efter Gustav Vasa: En berättelse om fyra kungar och ett rike.* Stockholm, 2005.

Laubach, Ernst. *Ferdinand I. als Kaiser: Politik und Herrschaftsauffassung des Nachfolgers Karls V.* Münster, 2001.

Lebow, Richard Ned, Wulf Kansteiner, and Claudio Fogu, eds. *The Politics of Memory in Postwar Europe.* Durham, NC, 2006.

Leeb, Rudolf. "Beobachtungen zu Caspar Tauber: Zur Rezeption reformatorischen Gedankengutes beim ersten Märtyrer der österreichischen Reformation." *Jahrbuch für die Geschichte des Protestantismus in Österreich* 110/111 (1994/95): 21–45.

——. "Das Erbe der Protestantengeschichtsschreibung in Österreich: Die Fragen der Vergangenheit und die Perspektiven für die zukünftige Forschung." *Carinthia I* 189 (1999): 711–723.

Leeb, Rudolf, Maximilian Liebmann, Georg Scheibelreiter, and Peter G. Tropper. *Geschichte des Christentums in Österreich: Von der Spätantike bis zur Gegenwart.* Vienna, 2003.

Leeb, Rudolf, Susanne Claudine Pils, and Thomas Winkelbauer, eds. *Staatsmacht und Seelenheil: Gegenreformation und Geheimprotestantismus in der Habsburgermonarchie.* Vienna, 2007.

Leeb, Rudolf, Martin Scheutz, and Dietmar Weikl, eds. *Geheimprotestantismus und evangelische Kirchen in der Habsburgermonarchie und im Erzstift Salzburg (17./18. Jahrhundert).* Vienna, 2008.

Le Goff, Jacques. *History and Memory.* New York, 1992.

Lehmann, Hartmut, and James Van Horn Melton, eds. *Paths of Continuity: Central European Historiography from the 1930s to the 1950s.* Cambridge, England, 1994.

Lehmberg, Stanford. *The Reformation Parliament, 1529–1536.* Cambridge, England, 1970.

Leidenfrost, Robert. "Religionsbeschwerden der evangelischen Stände von Steiermark, Kärnten und Krain." *Jahrbuch der Gesellschaft für die Geschichte des Protestantismus in Österreich* 4 (1883): 26–30.

Lenz, Rudolf. *De mortuis nil nisi bene? Leichenpredigten als multidisziplinäre Quelle unter besonderer Berücksichtigung der Historischen Familienforschung, der Bildungsgeschichte und der Literaturgeschichte.* Sigmaringen, Germany, 1990.

Bibliography 311

Leppin, Volker, and Ulrich A. Wien, eds. *Konfessionsbildung und Konfessionskultur in Siebenbürgen in der frühen Neuzeit*. Stuttgart, 2005.

Lhotsky, Alphons. *Aufsätze und Vorträge*. 5 vols. Munich, 1970–1976.

Liljegren, Bengt. *Karl XII: en biografi*. Lund, 2000.

Lindberg, Carter. *The European Reformations*. 2nd ed. Malden, MA, 2010.

Lindblom, Andreas. "Anna Regina Khevenhüller till Julita." *Fataburen* (1949): 61–72.

Lindegren, Jan. "The Swedish 'Military State' 1560–1720." *Scandinavian Journal of History* 10:4 (1985): 305–336.

———. *Maktstatens resurser: Danmark och Sverige under 1600-tallet*. Uppsala, 2001.

Lockhart, Paul Douglas. "Denmark and the Empire: A Reassessment of Danish Foreign Policy under King Christian IV." *Scandinavian Studies* 64 (1992): 390–416.

———. "Religion and Princely Liberties: Denmark's Intervention in the Thirty Years War, 1618–1625." *The International History Review* 17 (1995): 1–22.

———. *Denmark in the Thirty Years' War, 1618–1648: King Christian IV and the Decline of the Oldenburg State*. Selinsgrove, PA, 1996.

———. "Dansk propaganda under Kejserkrigen 1625–29." *Historie* (1998): 222–248.

———. *Frederik II and the Protestant Cause: Denmark's Role in the Wars of Religion, 1559–1596*. Leiden, 2004.

Loesche, Georg. *Geschichte des Protestantismus im vormaligen und neuen Österreich*. Vienna, 1930.

Loewen, Harry. *Luther and the Radicals: Another Look at Some Aspects of the Struggle between Luther and Radical Reformers*. Waterloo, ON, 1974.

Löffler, Josef. *Der zweite oberösterreichische Bauernaufstand 1594–1597 im Mühlviertel: Versuch einer systematischen Darstellung*. Saarbrücken, 2009.

Loserth, Johann. "Der Anabaptismus in Tirol: Vom Jahre 1536 bis zu seinem Erlöschen." *Archiv für österreichische Geschichte* 79 (1893): 127–276.

———. *Reformation und Gegenreformation in den innerösterreichischen Ländern im 16. Jahrhundert*. Stuttgart, 1898.

———. "Der Flacianismus in Steiermark und die Religionsgespräche von Schladming und Graz." *Jahrbuch der Gesellschaft für die Geschichte des Protestantismus in Österreich* 20 (1899): 1–13.

———. "Die steirische Religionspazifikation und die Fälschung des Vizekanzlers Dr. Wolfgang Schranz." *Jahrbuch der Gesellschaft für die Geschichte des Protestantismus in Österreich* 48 (1927): 1–57.

Lotz-Heumann, Ute. *Die doppelte Konfessionalisierung in Irland: Konflikt und Koexistenz im 16. und in der ersten Hälfte des 17. Jahrhunderts*. Tübingen, 2000.

Lotz-Heumann, Ute, Jan-Friedrich Mißfelder, and Matthias Pohlig, eds. *Konversion und Konfession in der Frühen Neuzeit*. Gütersloh, 2007.

Louthan, Howard. *The Quest for Compromise: Peacemakers in Counter-Reformation Vienna*. Cambridge, England, 1997.

312   Bibliography

———. *Converting Bohemia: Force and Persuasion in the Catholic Reformation.* Cambridge, England, 2009.

Louthan, Howard, Gary B. Cohen, and Franz A. J. Szabo, eds. *Diversity and Dissent: Negotiating Religious Difference in Central Europe, 1500–1800.* New York, 2011.

Louthan, Howard, and Graeme Murdock, eds. *A Companion to the Reformation in Central Europe.* Leiden, 2015.

Löwe, Hartmut, and Claus-Jürgen Roepke, eds. *Luther und die Folgen: Beiträge zur sozialgeschichtlichen Bedeutung der lutherischen Reformation.* Munich, 1983.

Lowenthal, David. *The Past is a Foreign Country.* Cambridge, England, 1985.

———. *The Heritage Crusade and the Spoils of History.* Cambridge, England, 1997.

———. "Fabricating Heritage." *History and Memory* 10:1 (1998): 5–24.

Luebke, David M., ed. *The Counter-Reformation: The Essential Readings.* Oxford, England, 1999.

Lukinich, Imre. "Geschichte Siebenbürgens, von Baron Georg Erasmus Tschernembl." *Jahrbuch des Wiener ungarischen historischen Instituts* 1 (1931): 133–160.

Lundquist, Sven. "Svensk krigsfinansiering 1630–1635." *Historisk Tidskrift* 86 (1966): 377–421.

Lutz, Heinrich. *Reformation und Gegenreformation.* 5th ed. Munich, 2002.

MacCulloch, Diarmaid. *Thomas Cranmer: A Life.* New Haven, CT, 1998.

———. *The Later Reformation in England, 1547–1603.* 2nd ed. Basingstoke, England, 2001.

———. *Reformation: Europe's House Divided, 1490–1700.* London, 2003.

Macek, Josef. *Tyrolská selská válka a Michal Gaismair.* Prague, 1960.

MacHardy, Karin. "The Rise of Absolutism and Noble Rebellion in Early Modern Habsburg Austria, 1570–1620." *Comparative Studies in Society and History* 34 (1992): 407–438.

———. *War, Religion and Court Patronage in Habsburg Austria: The Social and Cultural Dimensions of Political Interaction, 1521–1622.* Houndmills, England, 2003.

Mączak, Antoni, Henryk Samsonowicz, and Peter Burke, eds. *East-Central Europe in Transition.* Cambridge, England, 1985.

Maleczek, Werner. "Glaube und Heimat: Zur Vertreibung der Zillertaler Inklinanten vor 150 Jahren." *Das Fenster* 42 (1987): 4152–4158.

Maltby, William. *The Reign of Charles V.* Houndmills, England, 2002.

Mamatey, Victor S. "The Battle of the White Mountain as Myth in Czech History." *East European Quarterly* 15 (1981): 335–345.

Mankell, Julius. *Anteckningar rörande svenska regimentars historia.* 2nd ed. Örebro, 1866.

Masaryk, Tomáš G. *Česká otázka: Snahy a tužby národního obrození.* Prague, 1895.

———. *The Meaning of Czech History.* Edited by René Wellek. Chapel Hill, NC, 1974.

Bibliography 313

Mat'a, Petr, and Thomas Winkelbauer, eds. *Die Habsburgermonarchie 1620 bis 1740: Leistungen und Grenzen des Absolutismusparadigmas*. Stuttgart, 2006.

Matschinegg, Ingrid. "Österreicher als Universitätsbesucher in Italien (1500–1630): Regionale und soziale Herkunft—Karrieren—Prosopographie." Ph.D. dissertation, University of Graz, 2008.

McCagg, William O. *A History of Habsburg Jews, 1670–1918*. Bloomington, IN, 1992.

McGrath, Alister. *The Intellectual Origins of the European Reformation*. 2nd ed. Oxford, England, 2004.

McGuigan, Dorothy Gies. *The Habsburgs*. Garden City, NJ, 1966.

Mecenseffy, Grete. "Evangelisches Glaubensgut in Oberösterreich: Ein Beitrag zur Erschließung des religiösen Gehaltes der Reformation im Lande ob der Enns." *Mitteilungen des Oberösterreichischen Landesarchivs* 2 (1952): 77–174.

———. *Geschichte des Protestantismus in Österreich*. Graz, 1956.

Medick, Hans. *Der Dreißigjährige Krieg: Zeugnisse vom Leben mit der Gewalt*. Göttingen, 2018.

Meir, Alice. "Der Protestantismus in der Herrschaft Paternion vom 16. Jahrhundert bis zum Toleranzpatent." *Carinthia I* 162 (1972): 311–343.

Menzel, Josef Joachim, ed. *Geschichte Schlesiens*. Vol. 3, *Preußisch-Schlesien 1740–1945; Österreichisch-Schlesien 1740–1918/45*. Stuttgart, 1999.

Metasch, Frank. *300 Jahre Altranstädter Konvention—300 Jahre Schlesische Toleranz*. Dresden, 2007.

Meyer, Dietrich. *Zinzendorf und die Herrnhuter Brüdergemeine: 1700–2000*. Göttingen, 2000.

Meyerson, Åke. *Läderkanonen från Tidö*. Stockholm, 1938.

Mezler-Andelberg, Helmut. *Kirche in der Steiermark: Gesammelte Aufsätze*. Vienna, 1994.

———, ed. *Festschrift Karl Eder zum siebzigsten Geburtstag*. Graz, 1959.

Miller, Peter N. "Nazis and Neo-Stoics: Otto Brunner and Gerhard Oestreich before and after the Second World War." *Past and Present* 176 (2002): 144–186.

Mitteis, Heinrich. *Die deutsche Königswahl und ihre Rechtsgrundlagen bis zur goldenen Bulle*. 2nd ed. Brünn, 1944.

Mitten, Richard. *The Politics of Antisemitic Prejudice: The Waldheim-Phenomenon in Austria*. Boulder, CO, 1992.

Monod, Paul Kléber. *The Power of Kings: Monarchy and Religion in Europe 1589–1715*. New Haven, CT, 1999.

Mörke, Olaf. "'Konfessionalisierung' als politisch-soziales Strukturprinzip: Das Verhältnis von Religion und Staatsbildung in der Republik der Vereinigten Niederlande im 16. und 17. Jahrhundert." *Tijdschrift voor Sociale Geschiedenis* 16 (1990): 31–60.

Mortimer, Geoff. *Wallenstein: The Enigma of the Thirty Years War*. Houndmills, England, 2010.

Münkler, Herfried. *Der Dreißigjährige Krieg: Europäische Katastrophe, deutsches Trauma 1618–1648*. Berlin, 2017.

314   Bibliography

Murdoch, Steve, and Alexia Grosjean. *Alexander Leslie and the Scottish Generals of the Thirty Years' War, 1618–1648*. London, 2014.

Murdock, Graeme. "Responses to Habsburg Persecution of Protestants in Seventeenth-Century Hungary." *Austrian History Yearbook* 40 (2009): 37–52.

Myers, Alec Reginald. *Parliaments and Estates in Europe to 1789*. London, 1975.

Nagy, László. *Sok dolog próbála Bethlen Gábor*. Budapest, 1981.

Neumann, Wilhelm. *Bausteine zur Geschichte Kärntens*. 2nd ed. Klagenfurt, 1994.

———, ed. *900 Jahre Villach: Neue Beiträge zur Stadtgeschichte*. Villach, 1960.

Nicollier-de Weck, Béatrice. *Hubert Languet (1518–1519): Un réseau politique international de Melanchthon à Guillaume d'Orange*. Geneva, 1995.

Nilsson, Sven A. *De stora krigens tid: Sverige som militärstat och bondesamhälle*. Uppsala, 1990.

Nisbet, Robert. "The Decline and Fall of the Concept of Social Class." *Pacific Sociological Review* 2 (1959): 11–17.

———. *The Sociological Tradition*. New York, 1966.

Nisser, Wilhelm. *Mathias Palbitzki som connoisseur och tecknare*. Uppsala, 1934.

Nora, Pierre. *Les lieux de mémoire*. 3 vols. Paris, 1984–1992.

———. "Between Memory and History: *Les Lieux de Mémoire*." *Representations* 26 (1989): 7–24.

Novick, Peter. *The Holocaust in American Life*. Boston, MA, 1999.

Odhner, Clas Theodor. *Die Politik Schwedens im Westphälischen Friedenscongress und die Gründung der schwedischen Herrschaft in Deutschland*. Gotha, 1877; reprint Hannover, 1973.

Oestreich, Gerhard. "Strukturprobleme des europäischen Absolutismus." *Vierteljahrschrift für Sozial- und Wirtschaftsgeschichte* 55 (1969): 329–347.

Öhman, Jenny. *Der Kampf um den Frieden: Schweden und der Kaiser im Dreißigjährigen Krieg*. Vienna, 2005.

Olson, Oliver K. *Matthias Flacius and the Survival of Luther's Reform*. Wiesbaden, 2000.

O'Malley, John W. *The First Jesuits*. Cambridge, MA, 1993.

———. *Trent and All That: Renaming Catholicism in the Early Modern Era*. Cambridge, MA, 2000.

Opitz, Walter. *Die Schlacht bei Breitenfeld am 17. September 1631*. Leipzig, 1892.

Oredsson, Sverker. *Gustav Adolf, Sverige och Trettioåriga kriget: Historieskrivning och kult*. Lund, 1992.

———. *Gustav II Adolf*. Malmö, 2007.

Östergren, Stefan. *Sigismund: en biografi över den svensk-polske monarken*. Ängelholm, Sweden, 2005.

Packull, Werner. *Hutterite Beginnings: Communitarian Experiments during the Reformation*. Baltimore, MD, 1995.

Palacký, František. *Dějiny národu českého v Čechách a v Moravě*. 5 vols. Prague, 1848.

Pálffy, Géza. *The Kingdom of Hungary and the Habsburg Monarchy in the Sixteenth Century*. New York, 2009.

Bibliography 315

Parker, Geoffrey, ed. *The Thirty Years' War*. 2nd ed. London, 1997.

Parkin, Frank, ed. *The Social Analysis of Class Structure*. London, 1974.

Patrouch, Joseph F. *A Negotiated Settlement: The Counter-Reformation in Upper Austria under the Habsburgs*. Boston, MA, 2000.

Patry, Raoul. *Philippe Duplessis-Mornay: Un huguenot homme d'État*. Paris, 1933.

Pauli, James. *Adliga Ätten Pauli: En släkts öden under fyra århundraden, 1500–1920*. Stockholm, 1920.

Peball, Kurt. "Zur Quellenlage der 'Annales Ferdinandei' des Grafen Franz Christoph Khevenhüller-Frankenburg." *Mitteilungen des Österreichischen Staatsarchivs* 9 (1956): 1–22.

Pekař, Josef. *Bílá hora: Její příčiny i následky*. Prague, 1921.

Perjés, Geza. *The Fall of the Medieval Kingdom of Hungary: Mohacs 1526–Buda 1541*. Boulder, CO, 1989.

Peterson, Luther D. "Justus Menius, Philipp Melanchton, and the 1547 Treatise, *Von der Notwehr Unterricht*." *Archiv für Reformationsgeschichte* 81 (1990): 138–157.

Petersson, Erik. *Den skoningslöse: en biografi över Karl IX*. Stockholm, 2009.

Petráň, Josef, and Lydia Petráňova. "The White Mountain as a Symbol in Modern Czech History." In *Bohemia in History*, ed. Mikuláš Teich, 143–163. Cambridge, England, 1998.

Petrin, Silvia. *Die Stände des Landes Niederösterreich*. St. Pölten, 1982.

Petry, Ludwig, and Josef Joachim Menzel, eds. *Geschichte Schlesiens*. 3rd ed. 3 vols. Stuttgart, 1999–2000.

Pettegree, Andrew, ed. *The Reformation of the Parishes: The Ministry and the Reformation in Town and Country*. Manchester, 1993.

Piringer, Kurt. "Ferdinands III. katholische Restauration." Ph.D. dissertation, University of Vienna, 1950.

Plaschka, Richard Georg. *Von Palacký bis Pekař: Geschichtswissenschaft und Nationalbewußtsein bei den Tschechen*. Graz, 1955.

Pojar, Miloš. *Jindřich Matyáš Thurn—muž činu*. Prague, 1998.

Polišenský, Josef V. *The Thirty Years War*. London, 1971.

Politi, Giorgio. *Gli statuti impossibili: La rivoluzione tirolese del 1525 e il programma di Michael Gaismair*. Torino, 1995.

Porshnev, Boris Fedorovich. *Muscovy and Sweden in the Thirty Years' War, 1630–1635*. Edited by Paul Dukes. Cambridge, England, 1995.

Pörtner, Regina. "Gegenreformation und ständischer Legalismus in Innerösterreich, 1564–1628." *Zeitschrift für Historische Forschung* 27 (2000): 499–542.

———. *The Counter-Reformation in Central Europe: Styria 1580–1630*. Oxford, England, 2001.

Preger, Wilhelm. *Matthias Flacius Illyricus und seine Zeit*. 2 vols. Erlangen, 1859–1861.

Preinfalk, Miha. *Auersperg: Geschichte einer europäischen Familie*. Graz, 2006.

———. "Evangelische, Lutheraner, Accatholici: Die Familie Auersperg und der Protestantismus in Niederösterreich." *Jahrbuch für die Geschichte des Protestantismus in Österreich* 123 (2007): 219–228.

316 Bibliography

Press, Volker, ed. *Alternativen zur Reichsverfassung in der Frühen Neuzeit.* Munich, 1995.

Prestwich, Menna, ed. *International Calvinism, 1541–1715.* Oxford, England, 1985.

Priestly, Tom M. S. "Slovene Protestants in Carinthia." *Slovenian Studies Journal* 6 (1984): 177–189.

Pühringer, Andrea. *Contributionale, Oeconomicum und Politicum: Die Finanzen der landesfürstlichen Städte Nieder- und Oberösterreichs in der Frühneuzeit.* Vienna, 2002.

Pursell, Brennan C. *The Winter King: Frederick V of the Palatinate and the Coming of the Thirty Years' War.* Aldershot, England, 2003.

Quillet, Jeannine. "Tyrannie et tyrannicide dans la pensée politique médiévale tardive (XIV-XVe siècles)." In *Actes du Colloque La Tyrannie, mai 1984,* ed. Centre de publications de l'Université de Caen, 61–73. Caen, 1984.

Rainer, Johann. "Der Prozeß gegen Kardinal Klesl." *Römische Historische Mitteilungen* 5 (1961/62): 35–163.

Raitière, Martin N. "Hubert Languet's Authorship of the *Vindiciae contra Tyrannos.*" *Il pensiero politico* 14 (1986): 395–420.

Rak, Jiří. *Bývali Čechové: české historické mýty a stereotypy.* Jinočany, Czech Republic, 1994.

Ranum, Orest A. *The Fronde: A French Revolution (1648–1652).* New York, 1993.

Rapp, Francis. *L'Église et la vie religieuse en Occident à la fin du Moyen Âge.* Paris, 1980.

Raschzok, Klaus, and Reiner Sörries, eds. *Geschichte des protestantischen Kirchenbaues: Festschrift Peter Poscharsky zum 60. Geburtstag.* Erlangen, 1994.

Rauscher, Peter, ed. *Kriegführung und Staatsfinanzen: Die Habsburgermonarchie und das Heilige Römische Reich vom Dreißigjährigen Krieg bis zum Ende des habsburgischen Kaisertums 1740.* Münster, 2010.

Rauscher, Peter, and Martin Scheutz, eds. *Die Stimme der ewigen Verlierer? Aufstände, Revolten und Revolutionen in den österreichischen Ländern (ca. 1450–1815).* Vienna, 2013.

Rebel, Hermann. *Peasant Classes: The Bureaucratization of Property and Family Relations under Early Habsburg Absolutism, 1511–1636.* Princeton, NJ, 1983.

Reingrabner, Gustav. *Adel und Reformation: Beiträge zur Geschichte des protestantischen Adels im Lande unter der Enns während des 16. und 17. Jahrhunderts.* St. Pölten, 1976.

———. "Adelige Grundherrschaft und Reformation." *Heimatkundliches Jahrbuch des Waldviertler Heimatbundes* 2 (1978/79): 43–64.

———. "Zur Geschichte der flacianischen Bewegung im Lande unter der Enns." *Jahrbuch für Landeskunde von Niederösterreich* 54/55 (1990): 265–301.

———. "Gegenreformation in Niederösterreich: Das Protokoll der Reformationskommission für das Viertel ober dem Wienerwald von 1657–1660." *Jahrbuch der Gesellschaft für die Geschichte des Protestantismus in Österreich* 113 (1997): 9–115.

Bibliography 317

———. "Die kirchlichen Verhältnisse im Waldviertel im Jahre 1544." *Das Waldviertel* 49 (2000): 9–36.

———. "Die Beschlagnahme adliger Güter in der Gegenreformation." *Österreich in Geschichte und Literatur mit Geographie* 45 (2001): 259–280.

———, ed. *Evangelisch: Gestern und Heute einer Kirche*. St. Pölten, 2002.

Reinhard, Wolfgang. "Zwang zur Konfessionalisierung? Prolegemona zu einer Theorie des konfessionellen Zeitalters." *Zeitschrift für historische Forschung* 10 (1983): 257–277.

———. *Geschichte der Staatsgewalt: Eine vergleichende Verfassungsgeschichte Europas von den Anfängen bis zur Gegenwart*. Munich, 1999.

Reinhard, Wolfgang, and Heinz Schilling, eds. *Katholische Konfessionalisierung*. Gütersloh, 1995.

Reissenberger, Friedrich. "Das Corpus evangelicorum und die österreichischen Protestanten (1685–1764)." *Jahrbuch der Gesellschaft für die Geschichte des Protestantismus in Österreich* 17 (1896): 207–222.

Reiterer, Albert. "Die konservative Chance: Österreichbewußtsein im bürgerlichen Lager nach 1945." *Zeitgeschichte* 14 (1986/87): 379–397.

Repgen, Konrad, ed. *Krieg und Politik 1618–1648: Europäische Probleme und Perspektiven*. Munich, 1988.

Rheinwald, Georg Friedrich Heinrich. *Die Evangelischen Zillerthaler in Schlesien*. Berlin, 1838; new ed., Brixlegg, Austria, 2012.

Ričan, Rudolf. *Dějiny Jednoty bratrské*. Prague, 1957.

Richmond, Anthony H. "Ethnic Nationalism and Postindustrialism." *Ethnic and Racial Studies* 7 (1984): 4–18.

Ridderstad, Wilhelm. *Gula Gardet, 1526–1903*. Stockholm, 1903.

Rigby, Stephen H. *Marxism and History: A Critical Introduction*. Manchester, 1987.

Rill, Bernd. *Kaiser Matthias: Bruderzwist und Glaubenskampf*. Graz, 1999.

Ringmar, Erik. *Identity, Interest and Action: A Cultural Explanation of Sweden's Intervention in the Thirty Years War*. Cambridge, England, 1996.

Roberts, Michael. *Essays in Swedish History*. London, 1967.

———. *The Early Vasas: A History of Sweden, 1523–1611*. Cambridge, England, 1968.

———. *Gustavus Adolphus*. 2nd ed. London, 1992.

Robitsch, Matthias. *Geschichte des Protestantismus in der Steiermark*. Graz, 1859.

Rösener, Werner. *The Peasantry of Europe*. Oxford, England, 1994.

Ross, Hartmut. *Für ein anderes Europa: Fürst Christian I. von Anhalt-Bernburg*. Oranienbaum, Germany, 2003.

Rudert, Otto. *Die Kämpfe um Leipzig im großen Kriege 1631–1642*. Leipzig, 1937.

Runciman, Walter Garrison. *A Treatise on Social Theory*. 3 vols. Cambridge, England, 1983–1997.

Ruppert, Karsten. *Die kaiserliche Politik auf dem Westfälischen Friedenskongreß (1643–1648)*. Münster, 1979.

318 *Bibliography*

Rusam, Georg. *Österreichische Exulanten in Franken und Schwaben.* Munich, 1952; 2nd ed., rev. and enl. Neustadt a. d. Aisch, Germany, 1989.

Sachsenhofer, Günther. *Die Bibliothek des Freiherrn Georg Erasmus von Tschernembl: Eine Rekonstruktion.* Unpublished Hausarbeit für die Grundausbildung für die Verwendungsgruppe A im Bibliotheks-, Dokumentations- und Informationsdienst. Linz, 1992.

Sakrausky, Oskar. *Agoritschach: Die Geschichte einer protestantischen Gemeinde im gemischtsprachigen Südkärnten.* Klagenfurt, 1960.

———. "Der Flacianismus in Oberkärnten." *Jahrbuch der Gesellschaft für die Geschichte des Protestantismus in Österreich* 76 (1960): 83–109.

Salaba, Josef. "Slavatova apologie Jesuitů." *Český časopis historický* 4 (1898): 324–332.

Sandgruber, Roman. *Ökonomie und Politik: Österreichische Wirtschaftsgeschichte vom Mittelalter bis zur Gegenwart.* Vienna, 1995.

Santifaller, Leo, ed. *Festschrift zur Feier des zweihundertjährigen Bestandes des Haus-, Hof- und Staatsarchivs.* 2 vols. Vienna, 1949–1951.

Satzinger, Friedrich. *Vöcklabruck Stadtgeschichte: Von den Anfängen bis 1850.* Vöcklabruck, Austria, 2006.

Sauser, Ekkart. *Die Zillertaler Inklinanten und ihre Ausweisung im Jahre 1837.* Innsbruck, 1959.

Scheichl, Franz. *Aufstand der protestantischen Salzarbeiter und Bauern im Salzkammergute 1601 und 1602.* Linz, 1885.

———. "Glaubensflüchtlinge aus den österreichischen Gebieten in den letzten vier Jahrhunderten." *Jahrbuch der Gesellschaft für die Geschichte des Protestantismus in Österreich* 14 (1893): 134–184.

Schieche, Emil. *J. A. Comenius und Schweden.* Stockholm, 1968.

Schieffer, Rudolf. "Von Mailand nach Canossa: Ein Beitrag zur Geschichte der christlichen Herrscherbuße von Theodosius dem Großen bis zu Heinrich IV." *Deutsches Archiv für Erforschung des Mittelalters* 28 (1972): 333–370.

Schilling, Heinz. "Die Konfessionalisierung im Reich." *Historische Zeitschrift* 246 (1988): 1–45.

———. *Religion, Political Culture and the Emergence of Early Modern Society: Essays in German and Dutch History.* Leiden, 1992.

———. *Konfessionalisierung und Staatsinteressen: Internationale Beziehungen 1559–1660.* Paderborn, 2007.

———, ed. *Die reformierte Konfessionalisierung in Deutschland—Das Problem der "Zweiten Reformation".* Gütersloh, 1986.

Schimert, Peter George. "Péter Pázmány and the Reconstitution of the Catholic Aristocracy in Habsburg Hungary, 1600–1650." Ph.D. dissertation, University of North Carolina, 1990.

Schindling, Anton, and Walter Ziegler, eds. *Die Territorien des Reichs im Zeitalter der Reformation und Konfessionalisierung.* 7 vols. Münster, 1989–1997.

Schlachta, Astrid von. *Die Hutterer zwischen Tirol und Amerika: Eine Reise durch die Jahrhunderte.* Innsbruck, 2006.

Bibliography   319

Schlaich, Klaus. "Corpus evangelicorum und Corpus catholicorum: Aspekte eines Parteienwesens im Hlg. Römischen Reich Deutscher Nation." *Der Staat* 11 (1972): 218–230.

Schlumbohm, Jürgen. "Gesetze, die nicht durchgesetzt werden—ein Strukturmerkmal des frühneuzeitlichen Staates?" *Geschichte und Gesellschaft* 23 (1997): 647–663.

Schmid, Franz. *Bischof Martin Brenner (1548–1616)*. Dietenheim, Germany, 1984.

Schmid, Peter, and Heinrich Wanderwitz, eds. *Die Geburt Österreichs: 850 Jahre Privilegium minus*. Regensburg, 2007.

Schmidt, Georg. *Geschichte des Alten Reiches: Staat und Nation in der Frühen Neuzeit 1495–1806*. Munich, 1999.

Schmidt, Hans. "Konversion und Säkularisation als politische Waffe am Ausgang des konfessionellen Zeitalters: Neue Quellen zur Politik des Herzogs Ernst August von Hannover am Vorabend des Friedens von Nymwegen." *Francia* 5 (1977–78): 183–230.

Schmidt, Heinrich Richard. *Konfessionalisierung im 16. Jahrhundert*. Oldenburg, 1992.

———. *Dorf und Religion: Reformierte Kirchenzucht in Berner Landgemeinden der Frühen Neuzeit*. Stuttgart, 1995.

Schnabel, Werner Wilhelm. *Österreichische Exulanten in oberdeutschen Reichsstädten: Zur Migration von Führungsschichten im 17. Jahrhundert*. Munich, 1992.

Schober, Friedrich. "Zur Geschichte des Bauernaufstandes 1632." *Mitteilungen des Oberösterreichischen Landesarchivs* 2 (1950): 77–174.

Schoenstedt, Friedrich. *Der Tyrannenmord im Spätmittelalter: Studien zur Geschichte des Tyrannenbegriffs und der Tyrannenmordtheorie, insbesondere in Frankreich*. Berlin, 1938.

Scholz, Oscar. *Hubert Languet als kursächsischer Berichterstatter und Gesandter in Frankreich während der Jahre 1560–1572*. Halle, 1875.

Schönfellner, Franz. *Krems zwischen Reformation und Gegenreformation*. Vienna, 1985.

Schragl, Friedrich. *Glaubensspaltung in Niederösterreich: Beiträge zur niederösterreichischen Kirchengeschichte*. Vienna, 1973.

Schraml, Carl. *Das oberösterreichische Salinenwesen vom Beginne des 16. bis zur Mitte des 18. Jahrhunderts*. Vienna, 1932.

Schreiber, Arndt. *Adeliger Habitus und konfessionelle Identität: Die protestantischen Herren und Ritter in den österreichischen Erblanden nach 1620*. Vienna, 2013.

Schubert, Friedrich Hermann. *Ludwig Camerarius 1573–1651: Eine Biographie*. Kallmünz, Germany, 1955.

Schulenburg, Otto. *Die Vertreibung der mecklenburgischen Herzöge Adolf Friedrich und Johann Albrecht durch Wallenstein und ihre Restitution: Ein Beitrag zur Geschichte Mecklenburgs im dreissigjährigen Kriege*. Rostock, 1892.

320   *Bibliography*

Schulze, Hagen. *The Course of German Nationalism: From Frederick the Great to Bismarck, 1763–1867.* Cambridge, England, 1991.

Schulze, Winfried. "Zur politischen Theorie des steirischen Ständetums der Gegenreformationszeit." *Zeitschrift des historischen Vereins für Steiermark* 62 (1971): 33–48.

———. *Landesdefension und Staatsbildung: Studien zum Kriegswesen des innerösterreichischen Territorialstaates (1564–1619).* Vienna, 1973.

———, ed. *Friedliche Intentionen—kriegerische Effekte: War der Ausbruch des Dreißigjährigen Krieges unvermeidlich?* St. Katharinen, Germany, 2002.

Schulze Wessel, Martin. "Tschechische Nation und katholische Konfession vor und nach der Gründung des tschechoslowakischen Nationalstaates." *Bohemia* 39 (1997): 311–337.

Schuster, Leopold. *Fürstbischof Martin Brenner: Ein Charakterbild aus der steirischen Reformations-Geschichte.* Graz, 1898.

Schwartz, Barry. *Abraham Lincoln and the Forge of National Memory.* Chicago, IL, 2000.

Schwarz, Karl, and Peter Švorc, eds. *Die Reformation und ihre Wirkungsgeschichte in der Slowakei.* Vienna, 1996.

Scott, Tom. *Thomas Müntzer: Theology and Revolution in the German Reformation.* New York, 1989.

Scribner, Bob [Robert W.], and Gerhard Benecke, eds. *The German Peasant War of 1525: New Viewpoints.* Boston, MA, 1979.

Senkenberg, Renatus Karl von. *Versuch einer Geschichte des Teutschen Reichs im siebenzehnten Jahrhundert.* Vol. 5. Halle, 1795.

Simon, Thomas. *Grundherrschaft und Vogtei: Eine Strukturanalyse spätmittelalterlicher und frühneuzeitlicher Herrschaftsbildung.* Frankfurt, 1995.

———. *"Gute Policey"—Ordnungsleitbilder und Zielvorstellungen politischen Handelns in der Frühen Neuzeit.* Frankfurt, 2004.

Šindelář, Bedřich. "Slezská otázka na mírovém kongresu vestfálském 1643–1648." *Sborník prací Filozofické fakulty brněnské univerzity.* C, Řada historická 10:8 (1961): 266–295.

———. "Comenius und der Westfälische Friedenskongreß." *Historica* 5 (1963): 71–107.

Sittig, Wolfgang. "Die Schröffl in der Pfarre Gröbming." *Zeitschrift des Historischen Vereines für Steiermark* 46 (1955): 162–190.

Skinner, Quentin. *The Foundations of Modern Political Thought.* 2 vols. Cambridge, England, 1978.

Skowron, Ryszard. *Olivares, Wazowie i Bałtyk: Polska w polityce zagranicznej Hiszpanii w latach 1621–1632.* Kraków, 2002.

Šmahel, František. *Husitská revoluce.* 4 vols. 2nd ed. Prague, 1995–1996.

Soden, Franz von. *Gustav Adolph und sein Heer in Süddeutschland von 1631 bis 1635.* 3 vols. Erlangen, 1865–1869.

Söderberg, Bengt G. *Slott och herresäten i Sverige: Södermanland.* 2 vols. Malmö, 1968.

Bibliography 321

Sommer, Wolfgang, ed. *Kommunikationsstrukturen im europäischen Luthertum der Frühen Neuzeit.* Gütersloh, 2005.

Spitz, Lewis W. *The Religious Renaissance of the German Humanists.* Cambridge, MA, 1963.

Srbik, Heinrich von. *Deutsche Einheit: Idee und Wirklichkeit vom Heiligen Reich bis Königgrätz.* 4 vols. Munich, 1935–1942.

Stadler, Barbara. *Pappenheim und die Zeit des Dreißigjährigen Krieges.* Winterthur, Switzerland, 1991.

Stadler, Karl. *Österreich 1938–1945.* Vienna, 1966.

Stark, Rodney. "Secularization, R.I.P." *Sociology of Religion* 60 (1999): 249–273.

Starkey, David. *The Reign of Henry VIII: Personalities and Politics.* London, 1985.

Staszewski, Jacek. *August II Mocny.* Wrocław, 1998.

Steiner, Jürgen. *Die pfälzische Kurwürde während des Dreißigjährigen Krieges (1618–1648).* Speyer, 1985.

Steiner, Stephan. *Reisen ohne Wiederkehr: Die Deportationen von Protestanten aus Kärnten 1734–1736.* Vienna—Munich, 2007.

———. *Rückkehr unerwünscht: Deportationen in der Habsburgermonarchie in der Frühen Neuzeit und ihr europäischer Kontext.* Vienna, 2014.

Stella, Aldo. *Il "Bauernführer" Michael Gaismair e l'utopia di un repubblicanesimo popolare.* Bologna, 1999.

Stevenson, David, and David H. Caldwell. "Leather Guns and Other Light Artillery in Mid-17th-Century Scotland." *Proceedings of the Society of Antiquaries of Scotland* 108 (1976–1977): 300–317.

Stieve, Felix. *Der oberösterreichische Bauernaufstand des Jahres 1626.* 2 vols. Munich, 1891.

Stloukal-Zlinský, Karel. *Karel z Lichtenštejna a jeho účast ve vládě Rudolfa II. (1569–1607).* Prague, 1912.

Stockhorner von Starein, Otto. *Die Stockhorner von Starein: Versuch der Darstellung der Geschichte dieses Geschlechtes.* Vienna, 1896.

Stögmann, Arthur. *Die Konfessionalisierung im niederösterreichischen Weinviertel: Methoden, Erfolge, Widerstände.* Saarbrücken, 2010.

Stollberg-Rilinger, Barbara. *Des Kaisers alte Kleider: Verfassungsgeschichte und Symbolsprache des Alten Reiches.* 2nd ed. Munich, 2013.

———. *Maria Theresia: Die Kaiserin in ihrer Zeit.* Munich, 2017.

Straub, Dietmar, ed. *Der oberösterreichische Bauernkrieg 1626: Ausstellung des Landes Oberösterreich, Linzer Schloß, Schloß zu Scharnstein im Almtal, 14. Mai bis 31. Oktober 1976.* Linz, 1976.

Strnadt, Julius. *Der Bauernkrieg in Oberösterreich.* Wels, 1924.

Strohmeyer, Arno. *Konfessionskonflikt und Herrschaftsordnung: Widerstandsrecht bei den österreichischen Ständen (1550–1650).* Mainz, 2006.

Strom, Jonathan, Hartmut Lehmann, and James Van Horn Melton, eds. *Pietism in Germany and North America 1680–1820.* Farnham, England, 2009.

Stülz, Jodok. "Zur Charakteristik des Freiherrn Georg Erasmus von Tschernembl und zur Geschichte Oesterreichs in den Jahren 1608 bis 1610." *Archiv für Kunde österreichischer Geschichts-Quellen* 9 (1853): 169–226.

322   Bibliography

Sturmberger, Hans. *Georg Erasmus Tschernembl: Religion, Libertät und Widerstand.* Graz, 1953.

———. *Ferdinand II. und das Problem des Absolutismus.* Munich, 1957.

———. *Aufstand in Böhmen: Der Beginn des Dreißigjährigen Krieges.* Munich-Vienna, 1959.

———. *Adam Graf Herberstorff: Herrschaft und Freiheit im konfessionellen Zeitalter.* Munich, 1976.

———. *Land ob der Enns und Österreich: Aufsätze und Vorträge.* Linz, 1979.

Suárez Fernández, Luis. *Fernando el Católico.* Barcelona, 2004.

Suvanto, Pekka. *Die deutsche Politik Oxenstiernas und Wallenstein.* Helsinki, 1979.

Svalastoga, Kaare. *Social Differentiation.* New York, 1965.

Svalastoga, Kaare, and Preben Wolf. *Social rang og mobilitet.* 2nd ed. Copenhagen, 1972.

Svalenius, Ivan. *Gustav Vasa.* Stockholm, 1950.

Svensson, Axel, ed. *Karl XII som fältherre.* Luleå, 2001.

Swanson, Robert N. *Religion and Devotion in Europe, c. 1215–c. 1515.* Cambridge, England, 1995.

Swatos, William H., Jr., and Kevin J. Christiano. "Secularization Theory: The Course of a Concept." *Sociology of Religion* 60 (1999): 209–228.

Sydow, Jürgen. "Die innerösterreichische Zuwanderung nach Regensburg im 16. und 17. Jahrhundert." *Blätter für Heimatkunde* 29 (1955): 63–66.

Tacke, Andreas, ed. *Ich armer sundiger Mensch: Heiligen- und Reliquienkult am Übergang zum konfessionellen Zeitalter.* Göttingen, 2006.

Tai, Hue-Tam Ho. "Remembered Realms: Pierre Nora and French National Memory." *American Historical Review* 106 (2001): 906–922.

Teich, Mikuláš, ed. *Bohemia in History.* Cambridge, England, 1998.

Teige, Josef, et al., eds. *Na Bílé hoře.* Prague, 1921.

Thaler, Peter. *The Ambivalence of Identity: The Austrian Experience of Nation-Building in a Modern Society.* West Lafayette, Ind., 2001.

———. *Of Mind and Matter: The Duality of National Identity in the German-Danish Borderlands.* West Lafayette, Ind., 2009.

Tham, Wilhelm. *Den svenska utrikespolitikens historia.* Vol. 1:2, *1560–1648.* Stockholm, 1960.

Thyresson, Bertil. *Sverige och det protestantiska Europa från Knäredfreden til Rigas erövring.* Uppsala, 1928.

Tikhomirov, Mikhail Nikolaevich. "Soslovno-predstavitel'nye uchrezhdenia (zemskie sobory) v Rossii XVI veka." *Voprosy istorii* 1958:5 (1958): 3–22.

Tolloi, Philipp. "Aspekte der Rezeptionsgeschichte des Tiroler Bauernkrieges und Michael Gaismairs von 1525 bis 1945." Master's thesis (Diplomarbeit), University of Vienna, 2006.

Tomek, Ernst. *Kirchengeschichte Österreichs.* 3 vols. Innsbruck et al., 1935–1959.

Tracy, James D. *Europe's Reformations, 1450–1650.* Lanhan, MD, 1999.

———. *Emperor Charles V, Impresario of War: Campaign Strategy, International Finance, and Domestic Politics.* Cambridge, England, 2002.

Bibliography 323

Trencsényi, Balázs, and Márton Zászkaliczky, eds. *Whose Love of Which Country? Composite States, National Histories and Patriotic Discourses in Early Modern East Central Europe*. Leiden—Boston, 2010.

Troeltsch, Ernst. *Die Soziallehren der Christlichen Kirchen und Gruppen*. Tübingen, 1912.

Tropper, Christine. *Glut unter der Asche und offene Flamme: Der Kärntner Geheimprotestantismus und seine Bekämpfung 1731–1738*. Vienna, 2011.

Tropper, Peter G. *Staatliche Kirchenpolitik, Geheimprotestantismus und katholische Mission in Kärnten (1752–1780)*. Klagenfurt, 1989.

———. "Emigriert—missioniert—deportiert: Protestanten und Geheimprotestantismus in Österreich und Salzburg zwischen Gegenreformation und Toleranz." *Rottenburger Jahrbuch für Kirchengeschichte* 13 (1994): 179–189.

Tschopp, Silvia Serena. *Heilsgeschichtliche Deutungsmuster in der Publizistik des Dreißigjährigen Krieges: Pro- und antischwedische Propaganda in Deutschland 1628 bis 1635*. Frankfurt, 1991.

Turchetti, Mario. *Tyrannie et tyrannicide de l'Antiquité à nos jours*. Paris, 2001.

Uhl, Heidemarie. *Zwischen Versöhnung und Verstörung: Eine Kontroverse um Österreichs historische Identität fünfzig Jahre nach dem "Anschluß"*. Vienna, 1992.

Utgaard, Peter. *Remembering and Forgetting Nazism: Education, National Identity, and the Victim Myth in Postwar Austria*. New York, 2003.

Van Scheelven, Aart A. "Der Generalstab des politischen Calvinismus in Zentraleuropa zu Beginn des Dreißigjährigen Krieges." *Archiv für Reformationsgeschichte* 36 (1939): 117–141.

———. "Beza's De Iure Magistratuum in Subditos." *Archiv für Reformationsgeschichte* 45 (1954): 62–83.

Van Ysselsteyn, Gerardina Tjaberta. "L'auteur de l'ouvrage 'Vindiciae contra tyrannos' publie sous le nom de Stephanus Junius Brutus." *Revue historique* 167 (1931): 46–59.

Vardy, Steven Béla. *Modern Hungarian Historiography*. Boulder, CO, 1976.

Vierkandt, Alfred, ed. *Handwörterbuch der Soziologie*. Stuttgart, 1931.

Villstrand, Nils Erik. *Sveriges historia 1600–1721*. Stockholm, 2011.

Visser, Derek. "Junius: The Author of Vindiciae contra Tyrannos?" *Tijdschrift voor Geschiedenis* 84 (1971): 510–525.

Völker-Rasor, Anette, ed. *Oldenburg Geschichte Lehrbuch: Frühe Neuzeit*. Munich, 2000.

Wadl, Wilhelm, ed. *Glaubwürdig bleiben: 500 Jahre protestantisches Abenteuer*. Klagenfurt, 2011.

Wagner, Murray L. *Petr Chelčický: A Radical Separatist in Hussite Bohemia*. Scottsdale, PA, 1983.

Walker, Mack. *The Salzburg Transaction: Expulsion and Redemption in Eighteenth-Century Germany*. Ithaca, NY, 1992.

Wallin, Sigurd. "Palbitzki i vapenlunden." *Fataburen* (1962): 97–108.

Wandruszka, Adam. *The House of Habsburg: Six Hundred Years of a European Dynasty*. New York, 1964.

324 Bibliography

Weben, Violaine, ed. *Théodore de Bèze: Un grand de l'Europe*. Paris, 2000.

Weber, Max. *Wirtschaft und Gesellschaft*. 2nd ed. Tübingen, 1925.

Weigl, Andreas. *Bevölkerungsgeschichte Europas*. Vienna, 2012.

Weiss, Rudolf. *Das Bistum Passau unter Kardinal Joseph Dominikus von Lamberg (1723–1761): Zugleich ein Beitrag zur Geschichte des Kryptoprotestantismus in Oberösterreich*. St. Ottilien, Germany, 1979.

Welsersheimb, Madeleine. "Hans Ludwig von Kuefstein (1582–1656)." Ph.D. dissertation, University of Vienna, 1970.

Westerburg, Ernst-Joachim. *Fürst Christian I. von Anhalt-Bernburg und der politische Calvinismus*. Thalhofen, Germany, 2003.

Wetterberg, Gunnar. *Kanslern: Axel Oxenstierna i sin tid*. 2 vols. Stockholm, 2002.

Whaley, Joachim. *Germany and the Holy Roman Empire*. 2 vols. Oxford, England, 2012.

Wheatcroft, Andrew. *The Habsburgs: Embodying Empire*. London, 1995.

White, Hayden. *Metahistory: The Historical Imagination in Nineteenth-Century Europe*. Baltimore, MD, 1973.

——. *Tropics of Discourse: Essays in Cultural Criticism*. Baltimore, MD, 1978.

Widter, Anton. "Die Teufel zu Winzendorf." *Berichte und Mittheilungen des Alterthums-Vereines zu Wien* 23 (1886): 104–114.

Wiedemann, Theodor. *Geschichte der Reformation und Gegenreformation im Lande unter der Enns*. 5 vols. Prague, 1879–1886.

Wilflingseder, Franz. "Martin Laimbauer und die Unruhen im Machlandviertel, 1632–1636." *Mitteilungen des Oberösterreichischen Landesarchivs* 6 (1959): 136–202.

Wilson, Peter H. *Absolutism in Central Europe*. London, 2000.

——. *Europe's Tragedy: A History of the Thirty Years War*. London, 2009.

Winkelbauer, Thomas. "Krise der Aristokratie? Zum Strukturwandel des Adels in den böhmischen und niederösterreichischen Ländern im 16. und 17. Jahrhundert." *Mitteilungen des Instituts für Österreichische Geschichtsforschung* 100 (1992): 328–353.

——. "Sozialdisziplinierung und Konfessionaliserung durch Grundherren in den österreichischen und böhmischen Ländern im 16. und 17. Jahrhundert." *Zeitschrift für historische Forschung* 19 (1992): 317–339.

——. *Fürst und Fürstendiener: Gundaker von Liechtenstein, ein österreichischer Aristokrat des konfessionellen Zeitalters*. Vienna-Munich, 1999.

——. *Ständefreiheit und Fürstenmacht: Länder und Untertanen des Hauses Habsburg im konfessionellen Zeitalter*. 2 vols. Vienna, 2003.

Wisner, Henryk. *Zygmunt III Waza*. 2nd ed. Warsaw, 2006.

Wissgrill, Franz Karl. "Teüfel von Krottendorf Freyh: zu Gunderstorf, Eckhartsau etc." *Berichte und Mittheilungen des Alterthums-Vereines zu Wien* 23 (1886): 131–136.

Wodak, Ruth, et al., eds. *The Discursive Construction of National Identity*. 2nd ed. Edinburgh, 2009.

Bibliography 325

Wodka, Josef. *Kirche in Österreich: Wegweiser durch ihre Geschichte*. Vienna, 1959.

Wolf, Adam. *Geschichtliche Bilder aus Österreich*. Vol. 1. *Aus dem Zeitalter der Reformation (1526–1648)*. Vienna, 1878.

Wolf, Eric C. *Peasants*. Englewood Cliffs, NJ, 1966.

Wolff, Fritz. *Corpus Evangelicorum und Corpus Catholicorum auf dem westfälischen Friedenskongreß: Die Einfügung der konfessionellen Ständeverbindungen in die Reichsverfassung*. Münster, 1966.

Wolfsgruber, Cölestin. *Kirchengeschichte Österreich-Ungarns*. Vienna, 1909.

Wolgast, Eike. *Die Wittenberger Theologie und die Politik der evangelischen Stände*. Gütersloh, 1977.

———. *Die Religionsfrage als Problem des Widerstandsrechts im 16. Jahrhundert*. Heidelberg, 1980.

Wolkan, Rudolf. "Die Ächtung der Horner Konföderierten und die Konfiskation ihrer Güter." Ph.D. dissertation, University of Vienna, 1913.

Wopfner, Hermann. "Bäuerliches Besitzrecht und Besitzverteilung in Tirol." *Forschungen und Mitteilungen zur Geschichte Tirols und Vorarlbergs* 4 (1907): 390–405.

———. *Die Lage Tirols zu Ausgang des Mittelalters und die Ursachen des Bauernkriegs*. Berlin-Leipzig, 1908.

Wurm, Heinrich. *Die Jörger von Tollet*. Linz, 1955.

Zeeden, Ernst Walter. *Die Entstehung der Konfessionen: Grundlagen und Formen der Konfessionsbildung im Zeitalter der Glaubenskämpfe*. Munich, 1965.

Zöllner, Erich. *Geschichte Österreichs: Von den Anfängen bis zur Gegenwart*. Vienna, 1990.

Zwiedineck-Südenhorst, Hans von. *Fürst Christian der Andere von Anhalt und seine Beziehungen zu Innerösterreich*. Graz, 1874.

———. *Venetianische Gesandtschaftsberichte über die böhmische Rebellion (1618–1620)*. Graz, 1880.

Index

absolutism 46, 234; concept 112, 140n7, 232, 270; Habsburg Monarchy 11, 253, 254, 269; and social discipline 48
Albert/Albrecht VII (archduke of Austria) 94, 95, 96, 125
Albrecht I (German king) 3, 21n4
Albrecht II (Holy Roman Emperor) 4, 21n4
Altdorf, university 90, 167, 207
Altenhauser, Hans 207
Althan (family) 82
Altziebler, Kaspar 207
Amalie Elisabeth (landgravine of Hesse-Kassel) 168
Amann von Ammansegg, Christoph 164
Amann von Ammansegg, Georg Sigmund 164
Amlacher, Bartholomäus 153
Amsdorf, Nikolaus von 116
Anabaptists 39, 57, 250
Andreæ, Jakob 235
Andreæ, Johann Valentin 257n19
Anhalt, Christian of 92
Anna of Bohemia and Hungary 4, 8, 9
Aragon 5
Arminius 15
Arnim, Hans Georg von 157
Arundel, Thomas Howard Earl of 213
Assmann, Aleida 13
Assmann, Jan 13, 16
assurance of 1571 43, 44
Augsburg, diet of 8, 9
Augsburg Confession 8, 41, 43, 132, 236, 238
Augsburg Interim 9, 116

Augustus I (elector of Saxony) 122
Augustus II the Strong (king of Poland) 104n52, 231, 248
aulic council 54
aulic war council 83
Austria, archduchy: Counterreformation 52–56; Reformation 40–41; see also individual territories
Austria, republic: historical memory 1, 2, 16–19, 21n1, 21n2, 233, 255; national identity 2, 16–19, 250–252, 255; political parties 16
Austrian Catholicism: and Austrian identity 18–19; and landownership 195–197; literature 270, 272–273; peasantry 195; political role 247, 250
Austrian estates: composition 73–75, 101n29; internal divisions 94, 96; literature 270; nature 20, 70–71; political role 38, 43, 50–51, 70–71, 83–84, 86, 96, 230, 232; towns 76–77
Austrian hereditary lands: population 192; religious conditions 11; social structure 192; territorial divisions 39; see also individual territories
Austrian Protestantism: cultural impact 239; current distribution 263n86; education 52; emigrants 35, 136, 153–160, 162, 164–171, 173, 207–208, 209, 239–240, 273; international connections 151; legal situation 43–44, 234; literature 270, 271–272, 274–275; modern image 233; nobles 37, 52, 75, 150,

161–162, 238–240; Ottomans 38; Peace of Westphalia 160, 167, 168–170, 239, 247; peasants 37, 240–246; resistance 70–71, 86–87, 125, 161, 193–196, 207–211, 214–217, 231, 233, 235, 274–275; submersion 237–240; and Sweden 153–160, 162, 164–171, 173, 193, 207–211, 215; towns 32–34, 37, 43, 44, 87, 150, 161, 237–238

Bad Aussee 34
Bahlcke, Joachim 270
Baltic-German nobility 158, 167, 173
Bamberg, prince-bishopric 33, 74
Banér, Johan 159
Barbaro, Francesco 33
Barclay, William 118
Baron, Hans 113
Baroque 17, 18, 47, 65n83
Baroque Catholicism 80, 216, 233, 238, 272
Barton, Peter 270, 272
Barudio, Günther 274
Bavaria 165, 250; and Habsburgs 4, 20, 21n6, 44, 50, 97, 230, 251; Innviertel 61n37; occupation of Upper Austria 77, 97–98, 129, 135, 136, 201–206, 215; political role 20, 38, 50, 53, 55, 97–98, 130, 249, 251; religious conditions 35, 36, 38, 39–40, 47, 249; Thirty Years' War 95, 97–98, 136, 201–206, 210, 211, 230; see also Munich; Wittelsbach (dynasty)
Berger, Stefan 14–16
Berlin 164
Bernardin, Andre von 164
Berne 48
Bernhard of Weimar 157, 165
Bethlen, Gábor 93, 108n103, 135, 208
Beza, Theodore 119, 120–122, 124
Bibl, Victor/Viktor 270
Bible of Kralice 81
Bielefeld school 48
Bierbrüyer, Alexander 156
Bireley, Robert 68n116, 271
Bismarck, Otto von 208
Blahoslav, Jan 81
Bohemia: arrival of Habsburgs 4; conflict with Habsburgs 94, 95, 99, 112, 130; emigrants 158, 164, 165, 169, 171, 173, 209, 226n105, 253;

estates 87–88, 94, 230, 232; Peace of Westphalia 169; population 192; Reformation 30–31; religion 81–82, 87–88, 94, 129, 272; Renewed Land Ordinance 232; resistance 75, 231; Saxon occupation 209; and Sweden 152–153
Bohemian Confederation 95
Bohemian Confession 31, 87
Bourges 120
Brandenburg 6, 8, 84, 163, 207
Brandi, Karl 270
Breitenfeld, battle of 157, 159
Bremervörde 170
Brenner, Martin 41, 51–52, 197
Bruck 44
Bruck an der Leitha 102n37
Brunner, Otto 72
Brunswick-Lüneburg 169
Brutus, Stephanus Junius 119, 122–123
Bugenhagen, Johann 115–116, 141n29
Burgenland 246, 263n83, 263n86
Burgundy 3, 4, 5, 11
Burkert, Günther 270
Burkhardt, Johannes 274

Calvin, John 115, 117, 120
Calvinism: Altdorf 90; Austrian lands 236, 246, 275; Bohemia 129, 133; Bohemian Brethren 81; confessionalization 48; France 29, 118–124, 137; Germany 152, 172, 230; Hungarian lands 93; legal status 10; Netherlands 117; Palatinate 94; resistance 113–114, 115, 117, 118–124, 137, 172, 235–236; Scotland 117; Tschernembl 90, 127, 132, 136, 137, 235
Camerarius, Ludwig 164
Canisius, Peter 53
capitulation resolution 86–87, 106n79
Capuchins 46
Carinthia: Counterreformation 51–52; emigrants 153–155, 159, 160–162, 164–170, 173, 207, 240; estates 38, 51, 74, 150; Habsburg rule 3, 252; Inner Austria 39; literature 269, 271, 273; nobility 150, 162, 275; religion 41, 42, 51–52, 75, 161, 195, 197, 218n15, 237, 238, 243,

328   *Index*

245–246, 263n86; resistance 197, 237; Slavophones 41
Carniola 3, 38, 39, 51, 89, 162
Casimir IV (king of Poland) 4
Casparus 205
Catholicism: appeal 80; Croatia 28; Habsburgs 30; Middle Ages 27–28; and monarchy 111; Spain 28, 30; *see also* Austrian Catholicism
Catholic League (Holy Roman Empire) 97, 109n119, 134, 166, 173, 230
Catholic reform 46, 48, 49, 272
Charles II (archduke in Inner Austria) 42, 44, 50, 52
Charles IV (Holy Roman Emperor) 3
Charles V (Holy Roman Emperor) 4, 5–11, 23n25, 45, 116, 270
Charles VI (Holy Roman Emperor) 21n6, 245
Charles VII (Holy Roman Emperor) 21n6
Charles IX (king of Sweden) 151–152, 155, 172
Charles XI (king of Sweden) 170, 189–190n190
Charles XII (king of Sweden) 248
Charles Emmanuel I (Duke of Savoy) 133
Chelčický, Peter 81
Chemnitz, Bogislaff 162
Christian II (elector of Saxony) 84
Christian IV (king of Denmark) 133, 136, 153, 208, 224n81, 225n85
Christina (queen of Sweden) 157, 167, 168, 169, 170
Christina of Holstein-Gottorp 152, 157
church guardianship 33, 36, 197, 219n19
church patronage 33, 36–37, 194, 197
Clauss, Hermann 273
Cologne 6, 53
Comenius, John Amos 169
Commendone, Giovanni Francesco 33
Compacts of Basel 4
Confessio Carinthica 42
confessionalization: foreign policy 274; peasants 197, 214; stages 171–172, 193; theory 47–49, 65n80, 66n89, 231; Thirty Years' War 98
confessional oath 245, 262n71, 262n72

Convention of Altranstädt 248–249
conversion 79–82, 103n48, 245, 273
Copenhagen 170
corpus catholicorum 247
Corpus Christi, guild of 32
corpus evangelicorum 247–248
Council of Constance 30
Council of Trent 45–46
Counterreformation: archduchy of Austria 52–56, 75–78, 98, 150, 156, 201–202; and Austrian identity 18; Hungary 5; Inner Austria 49–52, 98, 132, 150, 155, 160–162; literature 272–273; societal debate 30; spiritual effects 212; terminology 46
Crinesius, Christoph 207
Croatia 3
Croats 28, 157, 179n61
Crowne, William 213
crypto-Protestantism 241–247
Czech identity 253, 255
Czech language 4, 81

Danube 34, 198, 211
Dedic, Paul 162, 207, 271, 273
Defereggen Valley 243–244, 261n60
de Geer, Louis 157
Denmark: foreign policy 136, 152, 208, 248; and Holy Roman Empire 135; Protestantism 29; Reformation 29; *see also* Christian IV (king of Denmark)
Derfflinger (family) 207; Georg 207–208, 215, 224n79; Karl 207; Regina 207
Deventer, Jörg 272, 273
Dietrichstein (family): Adam von 194; Bartholomäus von 162, 165, 210, 239; Christian von 166, 239; Gundaker von 239; Rudolf von 166; Sigmund von 33, 78
Dimpel, Wolfgang 34
Dolinar, France 272
Donauwörth 157, 210
Dresden 160
Duby, Georges 71, 73
Duplessis-Mornay, Philippe 122–123, 127
Durkheim, Émile 12, 14

Ebensee 200
Eberhard, Philip 156
Eder, Georg 53–55

Index 329

Edict of Restitution 138, 173
Edict of Worms 7, 32
Egg, Friedrich von 164
Egg, Gottfried von 164, 210
Eggenberg, Ulrich von 80
Elbing (Elbląg) 158, 160
Emling 205
Enenkel, Job Hartmann von 126, 145n88
England: Catholic restoration 118; embassy to Germany in 1636 213; estates 74; foreign policy 152, 153; historical tradition 15; Protestantism 29, 118, 152; Reformation 29
Erik XIV (king of Sweden) 151
Ernst (archduke of Austria) 53, 56, 85
Ernst August (elector of Hanover) 80
estates: and monarchy 1, 70, 111–112, 113, 133; nature 70–73, 101n19, 268n123; see also Austrian estates
estates buildings 32–33, 53, 59n17, 92
Estates-General (France) 73–74
Evangelical Union 97, 109n119, 152, 230
Evans, R. J. W. 269, 270, 271

Fadinger, Stefan 202, 205
Ferdinand I (Holy Roman Emperor): literature 270, 271; political role 4–5, 8, 9–11, 22n17, 23n25; religion 9–11, 32, 41; succession to 42
Ferdinand II (archduke in Tyrol) 42, 50, 66n90
Ferdinand II (Holy Roman Emperor) 2, 66n90, 66n93, 130, 134, 165, 215, 238, 251; Bohemia 129, 131–132, 233–234; literature 271; religious views and policies 49–52, 60n32, 66n94, 88, 99, 137, 138, 150, 155–156, 161, 173, 194, 201, 206, 214, 237; reputation 92–93, 98, 125, 129, 131–133, 137, 233–234; rise to power 92–97, 112, 125, 129, 133, 155–156, 254
Ferdinand II (king of Aragon) 5
Ferdinand III (Holy Roman Emperor) 168, 187n161, 215, 238–239, 271
feudalism 33, 36, 37, 163; attitudes 78, 86, 194; nature 71, 72, 113, 193
Fichtner, Paula Sutter 271
Finland 154
Firmian, Leopold Anton von (prince-archbishop of Salzburg) 244

France 90, 124, 207; absolutism 111–112; constitutional history 119; estates 71, 73, 119; national imagery 15; political role 6, 9, 97, 172, 173; religious conditions 29, 43, 90, 117, 118, 119, 120, 122–123, 137; Thirty Years' War 97, 168; war against Charles V 7, 9
Francis I (Holy Roman Emperor) 21n6
Franconia 19, 33, 90, 166, 167, 241, 273
Frankenberg 212, 213
Frankenburg 201–202
Frankfurt on the Oder 158
Franzel, Emil 195
Fräss-Ehrfeld, Claudia 269
Frederick I (Holy Roman Emperor) 227–228n117
Frederick III (elector of Saxony) 35, 36
Frederick III (Holy Roman Emperor) 3
Frederick V (Elector Palatine, king of Bohemia): Austrian support 96; Evangelical Union 97; loss of Palatinate 136; restitution 135; role in Bohemia 94, 129, 130, 133, 134
Frederick William I (elector of Brandenburg) 207
Frederick William I (king of Prussia) 244
Friedeburg, Robert von 236
Frölich (family) 171, 189–190n190; Eva Margaretha 189–190n190; Hans Christoph 171
Fronde 112
Funkenstein, Amos 14

Gaismair, Michael 194, 215
Garsten 34
Gastein 31
Geneva 90, 119, 120, 122, 136, 137, 236
German liberty 70, 99n2, 134, 162, 163
Germany: language 7, 30, 252; national imagery 15; political leadership 3, 249, 250; see also Holy Roman Empire; individual German territories
Gienger von Grünbühel, Maximillian 164
Gindely, Anton 273
Glete, Jan 172
Glogau (Głogów) 272

330   *Index*

Golden Bull 6
Görz (Gorizia), counts of 89
Gorzno (Górzno) 158
Graz 39, 41, 44; court 234; Estates
  Building 59n17; Jesuits 52; religious
  conditions 44, 51; size 192;
  university 52
Great Peasants' War 193–194
Greece 15, 16, 28, 112
Greek-Orthodox Christians 246
Greifenhagen (Gryfino) 158
Greiffenberg, Catharina Regina von
  239
Greimbl, Jakob 208–209, 210,
  226n95, 226n107
Grieskirchen 36
Grüll, Georg 195, 199, 203
Guelphs (dynasty) 2
Gusow 207
Gustavus II Adolphus (king of
  Sweden): and Austrian exiles
  156, 157–159, 160, 165, 166;
  and Austrian peasants 193, 209,
  210–211, 251; death 166; military
  successes 159; politics 152, 163,
  225n85; Thirty Years' War 151
Gustav Vasa (king of Sweden) 151
Gyllenhielm, Karl Karlsson 156–157

Habsburg (dynasty): branches 39;
  Catholicism 30, 42–43, 70, 247;
  historical memory 16–17, 233;
  intrafamilial conflict 85–88, 98,
  127–128; leadership in Germany
  249, 250; religious policies 39,
  42–43, 70, 150, 233–234; rise 2–5;
  Thirty Years' War 230; *see also
  individual rulers*
Habsburg Monarchy: historical legacy
  1, 16; literature 269; mission 252;
  population 192; *see also* Habsburg
  (dynasty); *individual territories and
  rulers*
Haibacher, Melchior 207
Haider, Siegfried 269
Halbwachs, Maurice 12, 14
Hall (Tyrol) 31
Hallegg, Adam von 164
Hallegg, Paul von 164
Hallein 244
Hallenberg, Mats 172
Hallstatt 200
Hammer-Purgstall, Joseph von 272

Hammerstein (Czarne) 158
Hanau 165, 239
Hård af Segerstad, Brita 155
Hård af Segerstad, Olof 155
Harrach, Leonhard von 103n48
Haugwitz (family) 207
Haydn, Joseph 18
Heidelberg 90, 130, 136
Heilbronn 152
Helsinki 154
Hengerer, Mark 278n19
Henry II (king of France) 7, 9
Henry IV (king of France) 122–123
Henry VIII (king of England) 29
Herberstein (family) 82, 164
Herberstorff, Adam von 201–202,
  203, 204, 205, 206
Hermannstadt (Sibiu) 246
Hernals 33, 56
Herzheimer, Hans 34–35
Herzheimer, Hans Jordan 35
Hesse-Kassel 169
Hintze, Otto 71–72, 74
histoire croisée 2
historical memory 11–19, 233,
  250–255
Hjälmaren (lake) 155
Höbelt, Lothar 190n197, 271
Hobsbawm, Eric 13–14
Hochosterwitz 240
Hofkirchen, Lorenz von 129, 209
Hofkirchen, Wolfgang von 83–84,
  105n72
Hohberg, Melchior Leopold von
  165–166
Hohberg, Wolf Helmhard von 239
Hohenstaufen (dynasty) 2
Hohenwart, Hans Hermann von 165
Hollenburg 162
Holy Roman Empire: constitutional
  conditions 3, 6–7; dissolution
  17–18; high courts 54, 90;
  monarchic succession 3, 6; religious
  conditions 7–11, 249; struggle for
  leadership 249; *see also individual
  territories and rulers*
Horn 86, 96, 253; federation 86, 157;
  grammar school 41
Horn, Gustaf 154, 159
Hotman, François 119–120, 121, 122,
  124, 127, 137
House of Knights (riddarhuset) 155,
  168

Index 331

Hsia, Ronnie Po-Chia 272
Huguenots 117–124; *see also* Calvinism
humanism 28, 90, 120, 126
Hungary 3, 32, 138, 207; Burgenland 246; emigration to 81; estates 5, 74, 85, 125; Habsburg rule 4–5, 39, 86, 93, 95, 135, 248, 252; historical memory 252, 255; Jagiellonians 4; national imagery 15; Ottomans 4, 5, 85, 93; political role 85, 92, 93, 129, 133, 248; population 192; religious conditions 5, 39, 75, 80, 86, 236
Hus, Jan 30
Hussites 30–31, 81, 231
Hutterites 262n74
Hutton, Patrick 12

Iceland 29
Iglau (Jihlava) 189n181
Ignatius of Loyola 47
imperial cameral court 54, 90
Ingolstadt 50
Ingria 160
Inner Austria: Counterreformation 49–52; estates 42; reformation 41–42; *see also individual territories*
Innsbruck 39, 59n17, 91, 192, 234
irenicism 42, 54, 55, 103n48, 172
Isenbunt, Christoph 34
Islam 15, 27, 28
Italy: and Austria 40, 272; Austrians in 83, 90, 155; Catholicism 28, 45, 201; Habsburgs 11; renaissance 28

Jagiellonians (dynasty) 4, 151
Jankau (Jankov), battle of 170
Jews 17, 27–28, 246
Joachim Ernst of Brandenburg-Ansbach 97
Joanna of Castile 4
John I (king of Hungary) 5
John III (king of Sweden) 151
John the Blind (king of Bohemia) 3
John George I (elector of Saxony) 133, 168
Jönköping 155
Jörger (family) 35–36, 61n36, 164, 239; Abraham 36; Christoph II 35–36; Dorothea 35–36; Helmhard 36; Johann Quintin 239; Wolfgang 35
Joseph I (Holy Roman Emperor) 248

Joseph II (Holy Roman Emperor) 246, 250
Judenburg 44, 51
Julita 156–157, 167, 168, 170

Kagg, Lars 165
Kaiser, Leonhard 36
Kann, Robert 269
Karl Philipp (duke of Södermanland) 155
Keller, Jakob 130
Khevenhüller (family) 52, 153, 165, 167, 168, 170, 189n181; Andreas 167, 170; Anna Regina 170; Augustin 167; Bartholomäus (son of Hans) 167, 170; Bartholomäus (son of Paul Sr.) 167, 170; Bernhard 167, 170; Ernreich 239–240; Franz Christoph 19, 80, 167, 209, 225n87; Georg Christoph 167, 170, 189n181; Hans 162, 165–166, 169, 226n97; Paul, Jr. 167, 170; Paul, Sr. 159, 165–168, 169, 173, 207; Regina 167; Sigmund 240
Klagenfurt 41, 44, 51–52, 59n17, 192, 238
Klesl, Melchior 55–56, 83, 85, 93, 171, 194, 272
Knox, John 117
Knyphausen, Dodo von 159, 181n79
Kohler, Alfred 271
Kolberg (Kołobrzeg) 158
Koniecpolski, Stanisław 158
Krainer, Georg 33
Krawarik, Hans 273
Krems 76
Kremsmünster Abbey 209
Kronegg, Hans Christoph von 165
Kuefstein, Hans Ludwig von 160, 209, 212, 227n113

Laimbauer, Martin (Aichinger) 211–214, 227n112, 228n121
Lamormaini, William 50, 271
Landler 245–246
Landskron 162
Langenmantel, Gabriel 153
Languet, Hubert 122–123
Lauingen 157
Lazarists 47
leather guns 156, 157
Leeb, Rudolf 182n96, 270, 271
Leo X (pope) 35

332 Index

Leopold I (Holy Roman Emperor) 207

Leopold V (archduke of Austria, bishop of Passau and Strassburg) 96

Leopold Wilhelm (archduke of Austria, bishop of Olomouc/Olmütz) 224n79

Letter of Majesty (Bohemia) 81–82, 87, 94

Leuber, Johannes 168–169

lex baiuvariorum 27

lex salica 27

libraries 59n17, 90, 126–127, 137, 145n88

Liechtenstein (family) 82; Gundaker von 273; Karl von 80–81

Lilliesvärd, Gabriel 190n191

Linz 34, 41, 59n17, 92, 95, 98, 212, 213

Lista 155

Livonia 158, 167

Ljubljana (Laibach) 44, 51, 64n71

Lobkowicz, Zdeněk 87–88

Löbl, Hans Jakob 76–77, 91–92, 198, 199

Loesche, Georg 195, 270

Löffler, Josef 199

Loosdorf 41

Losenstein (family) 82

Loserth, Johann 274

Louis II (king of Hungary and Bohemia) 4

Louis XIV (king of France) 112

Louthan, Howard 272

Lowenthal, David 14

Lower Austria: estates 43, 74, 82–83, 94, 95–96, 112, 129, 132, 153; literature 270, 273; nobles 79, 82–83, 86–87, 88, 236, 237, 238–240; peasant resistance 199–200; political role 41, 86–87, 88, 95–96; religious conditions 41, 43–44, 53–56, 76, 78, 82–83, 86–87, 88, 150, 160, 169, 194–195, 236, 237, 238–240, 246, 248

Loyola, Ignatius of 47

Loyseau, Charles 71

Luegmayer, Abraham 209, 226n107

Luther, Martin 2, 262n71; Austrian contacts 35, 36; Austrian identity 18; Austrian reception 19, 30, 33; and German language 30; Habsburg views 5; impact 30; and

imperial estates 6–7; and Saxon electors 231; Scandinavia 29; views on obedience and resistance 114, 115, 116, 124, 235

Lutheranism: relationship to Calvinism 90, 113–114, 117, 129, 137–138, 152, 172, 230–231, 235–236; views on obedience and resistance 113–118, 124, 137–138, 235–236, 274–275; *see also* Austrian Protestantism; Luther, Martin; Reformation

Lutter, battle of 136, 153, 208

Lützen, battle of 154, 171, 211

Luxemburg (dynasty) 3

MacHardy, Karin 79, 82, 273

Magdeburg 116, 158

Magdeburg Confession 116–117, 137

Mainz 6

Malaspina, Germanico 41

Malborghet (Malborghetto) 153

Mannheim 154

Mansfeld, Ernst von 156, 208

Maria Gail 33

Maria of Austria (queen consort of Hungary) 4–5

Maria Theresa (queen of Hungary and Bohemia) 21n6, 245

Marchfeld, battle of 3

Marwitz (family) 207

Marxism 72, 73, 226n105

Mary I (queen of England) 118

Maťa, Petr 270

Matthias (Holy Roman Emperor): religious views and policies 39, 86–87, 98, 132, 204; rise to emperorship 86–88; in scholarly literature 271; succession to 93, 94–95, 125, 131, 161; and Tschernembl 39, 92–93, 128, 129, 131; uprising in Salzkammergut 200–201

Maximilian I (duke of Bavaria): aid to Habsburgs 97–98, 230, 251; Catholic League 97; Palatinate 201; political goals 201; Tschernembl 135; Upper Austria 97–98, 201, 204, 205, 215

Maximilian I (Holy Roman Emperor) 3–4, 5, 6

Maximilian II (Holy Roman Emperor) 11, 32, 42–44, 52, 54, 86, 271

Index 333

Mecenseffy, Grete 270
Mecklenburg 8, 158, 164
Meggau, Leonhard Helfried von 126
Melanchton, Philipp 35
Melissus, Paulus 90
Menius, Justus 117
Miklas, Wilhelm 18
Miltitz, Karl von 35
Mitrowitz, Johann Wenzel Wratislaw
    von 248
Mitterauer, Michael 72, 270
Mohács, battle of 4
monarchomachs 118–124, 137, 214
Montgomery, Ingun 172
Moravia 32, 133, 208, 252; Ferdinand
    I 4; Habsburg intrafamilial conflict
    85–86, 128; religious conditions 80;
    see also Bohemia
Mozart, Wolfgang Amadeus 18
Munich 50; court 55, 91, 204, 234;
    Jesuit college 130; Wittelsbachs
    38, 41
Munich Accord 97
Munich Conference 50, 52, 56, 234
Müntzer, Thomas 7
Mur Valley 246
myths 12, 13, 15, 16

Nagerschigg 153, 154
Narva 154
National Socialism 18
Netherlands: emigrants to Sweden
    173; Habsburg rule 94; political
    role 135, 152, 153, 251; religious
    conditions 43, 48, 114
Neuhaus, Adam II von 82
Neuhaus, Lucia Ottilia 82
Nimmervoll, Stephan 209, 226n107
nobility: conversions 79–82;
    Counterreformation 52; economy
    79; ennoblement 78–79; political
    orientation 78, 98–99, 231–232;
    religious orientation 78; service 79;
    size 216n2
Nora, Pierre 12, 14
Norway 29
Novick, Peter 14
Nuremberg: and Altdorf University
    90; exiles in 153, 164, 165, 166,
    170; Upper Austrian peasants 210

Ödenburg (Sopron) 258n29
Oder 158

Oedt, Wolf von 145n88
Oestreich, Gerhard 48, 49
Öhman, Jenny 274
Oredsson, Sverker 162–163
Orleans 120
Ortenburg 38
Otakar II Přemysl (king of Bohemia)
    2–3, 125
Ottoman Empire: Habsburg
    Monarchy 5, 8, 17, 38, 43, 85, 90,
    155, 200, 207, 247, 271; Hungary
    4, 5, 85, 93, 192
Oxenstierna, Axel: German
    connections 173, 191n202; and
    Gustavus Adolphus 163; and
    John Amos Comenius 169; and
    Maximilian Teufel 159, 160; and
    Melchior Wurmbrand 156; and
    Khevenhüllers 168, 170; and Upper
    Austrian peasants 210–211; and
    Wallenstein 274
Oxenstierna, Johan 168

Pacification of Bruck 44, 49–50, 51
Pacification of Graz 44
Padua, university 157
Palatinate: electorship 6, 97, 135, 201;
    territory 97, 201; Thirty Years' War
    97, 130, 136, 152, 164, 206
Palbitzki, Mathias 170
papacy: and monarchy 7, 30, 113;
    political role 45, 80, 131, 133, 137;
    resistance 114
Pappenheim, Gottfried Heinrich zu
    159, 205
Paris 168
Parker, Geoffrey 274
Parkin, Frank 73
Passau 54, 56, 96; bishops 34, 36, 41,
    199, 219n19; diocese 55
Patent of Toleration 246, 247, 250
Paternion 52, 153, 166, 207
Patrouch, Joseph 272
Paul(i) (family) 153–155; Anders 154;
    Andreas 154; Axel 155; Elisabeth
    154; Matthias 154; Michael 154;
    Wolfgang 153; Zacharias 154, 155
Peace of Augsburg 11, 172; Austrian
    Protestantism 38, 42; ground rules
    9–10, 42; Habsburg Monarchy
    38, 39, 44, 49, 151; imperial
    Protestantism 57, 117–118, 151;
    nature 137; promulgation 9–10

334   *Index*

Peace of Kuttenberg (Kutná Hora) 31
Peace of Thorn (Toruń), Second 177n36
Peace of Westphalia: Austrian Protestantism 160, 167, 168–170, 239, 247; Bohemia 168–169; confessional parties 247; France 168; Salzburg 244; Saxony 168–169; Silesia 248–249; Sweden 168–170, 274
peasantry: resistance 20, 40, 91, 193–196, 214–217, 223n60; social conditions 193, 195–197, 223n60
Pfauser, Johann 42
Philip II (king of Spain) 11, 43
Philip of Hesse 9
Philip the Fair (duke of Burgundy) 4
Piarists 47
Pinsdorf 205
Poland: emigration to 81; national imagery 15; Prussia 177n36; religion 43, 81, 231; Saxony 231, 248; Sweden 151–152, 153, 154, 156, 158, 248
Polišenský, Josef 274
Pomerania 8, 155, 158, 163, 167, 168, 170, 207
Porshnev, B. F. 226n105
Prague 4, 130; court 53, 55, 79, 84, 85, 91; executions 135–136; Greimbl 208–209; Hussites 30–31; Lorenz von Hofkirchen 209; Saxon occupation 208–209; Tschernembl 91, 129, 135–136
Přemysl (dynasty) 2, 125
Pressburg (Pozsony, Bratislava) 5, 75, 258n29
Prickelmayr, Andreas 168
printing 30
privilegium minus 17
Poltava 249
Pörtner, Regina 272, 275
Portugal 28, 47
Prokop the Great 31
property registry 195
Protestantism: Bohemia 31; Habsburg family 42–43; Hungary 39; internal divisions 152, 230–231; miners 30–31; *see also* Austrian Protestantism; Reformation
Prunner von Vasoldsberg, Hans Georg von 165

Prussia: aristocracy 207–208; army 207; East Prussia 177n36, 207, 244; negative image 17, 114; Paulus Speratus 32; in Polish-Swedish wars 153, 154, 155; as regional power 245, 249; royal 158, 177n36; Salzburgers 244, 249, 250; Silesia 249; West Prussia 177n36; Zillertalers 250
Puchheim (family) 82, 86

Raitenau, Wolf Dietrich von 201
Ranger, Terrence 13–14
Raupach, Bernhard 19, 271
Rebel, Hermann 196, 203
Reformation: Austria 18, 28–44; Bavaria 38; beginning 2, 7, 28; Bohemia 30–31; church-state relations 111; Denmark 29; England 29; France 29; Germany 7, 8, 30; Hungary 5; and printing 30; social conditions 193–194; students 34; Sweden 29, 30
Regensburg 38, 135; diet 248; exiles 153, 154, 165; Swedish occupation 165
Reingrabner, Gustav 271, 273
Reinhard, Wolfgang 47–48, 49, 65n80, 66n89
Reiter, Ludwig 18
Reiterer, Albert 16–17
religious processions 53, 76, 77, 242
Repgen, Konrad 162
resistance: rural 91, 136, 137, 165, 198–216, 231, 251, 275; theory 112–125, 127, 235–236; urban 76
Retz 96, 132
Rhine 206
Riga 154, 155, 156
right of presentation 36–37
Ringmar, Erik 172
Rome 28, 45, 234
Roth, Joseph 252
Rottal, Georg Ehrenreich von 165
Rudolf I of Habsburg (German king) 2–3
Rudolf II (Holy Roman Emperor) 153; Counterreformation 52–53, 54, 56, 91, 234; Habsburg intrafamilial conflict 85–88, 98, 127–128; Letter of Majesty 81–82; literature 271; and Protestant princes 84

Runciman, W. G. 73
Ruppert, Karsten 274
Rusam, Georg 273

salt mining 34, 192, 200, 202, 243–244
Salvius, Johan Adler 168
Salzburg (prince-archbishopric)
200, 249; political role 74, 201,
247; religious conditions 31, 242,
243–245, 247, 250, 261n64; and
Zillertal 250
Salzkammergut 34, 200–201, 246
Saurau, Ernreich von 161, 182n97
Saxony: and Austrian Protestants 31,
34–35, 36, 84; electoral status 6, 9,
230–231; miners 31; political role
7, 84, 95, 134, 163, 168–169, 173,
230–231, 248
Schaitberger, Josef 242, 243, 244
Scherer, Georg 55
Schilling, Heinz 47–48, 49, 171–172,
274
Schimert, Peter 273
Schladming 31, 37
Schmalkalden, League of 8, 9
Schmalkaldic Wars 9
Schmidt, Heinrich Richard 48–49
Schmitz, Oscar 18
Schnabel, Werner Wilhelm 162, 273
Schönkirchen (family) 89
Schröffl, Ruep 197
Schubert, Franz 18
Schulze, Winfried 48, 270, 274, 275
Schwartz, Barry 13, 254
Schwarz, Karl 272
Schwaz 31, 37, 192, 217n5
Schweidnitz (Świdnica) 272
Schwertberg 89, 91, 126
Siena, university 157
Sierning 198
Sigismund (Holy Roman Emperor) 3,
31, 41
Sigismund (king of Poland and
Sweden) 151–152
Silesia: exiles 171; Ferdinand I 4;
religious conditions 39, 87, 169,
248, 272; and Sweden 158, 169,
248; see also Bohemia
Skinner, Quentin 115–116
Skytte, Johan 156
Slavata (family) 81, 82; Adam 81, 82;
William 81–82

Society of Jesus (Jesuits): and
conversions 82; education 50, 52,
54, 55, 130; Germany 38; libraries
126; mission 46, 47; and monarchs
50; and Tschernembl 126, 130, 138
Södermanland 155, 156
Spain: Charles V 4, 5, 7, 8, 11; Islam
27; Maximilian II 43; monarchy 6;
political role 6, 30, 42, 132, 133,
135, 174n7, 254; Reformation 28;
religious orders 47; Rudolf II 53;
Thirty Years' War 20, 95, 97, 134,
136, 230
Spalatin, Georg 35
Speratus, Paul 32
Speyer 90
Srbik, Heinrich von 252
Stadion, Johann Georg von 33
Starhemberg (family) 89, 164; Barbara
89; Erasmus 89; Gotthard 78, 129,
135, 155, 199; Heinrich Wilhelm
145n88; Reichhard 89
St. Bartholomew's Night 118, 120
Stegger, Michael 207
Sternberg, Stefan Georg von 103n48
Steyr 34, 37, 76–77, 202, 203, 204,
238
Steyregg 213
Stiefel, Michael 36
Stloukal, Karel 80
Stobäus, Georg 52
Stockholm 152; exiles 155, 166, 170,
171; government 152, 164, 169,
248, 249
Stolberg (family) 207
St. Pölten 102n35
Stralsund 155, 164
Strassburg (Strasbourg) 96
stratification theory 72–73
Strein (also Streun) von Schwarzenau
(family) 89, 160; Johann Georg 160
Strohmeyer, Arno 236, 275
St. Sophia's Church (Dresden) 160
St. Stephen's Cathedral (Vienna) 32,
55
Stubenberg (family) 164; Hans
Wilhelm 239
Sturmberger, Hans 235, 273–274, 275
Styria: Counterreformation 83, 98, 99,
132, 133, 161; emigrants 160–161,
165, 167, 171; estates and nobles
38, 44, 50–51, 150, 237, 254, 275;

336 *Index*

Habsburg rule 13; Inner Austria 39; mining 34; religion 31, 41–42, 44, 52, 75, 161, 195, 197, 243, 245, 246
suffering obedience 113–114, 121, 124, 182n96, 235, 236–237, 274–275
Suvanto, Pekka 274
Swabia 2, 166, 241, 273
Sweden: and German Protestants 164; and Habsburg Protestants 153–160, 162, 164–171, 173, 207–211, 215, 226n106; and Poland 151–152, 153, 154, 156, 158, 248–249; politics 152, 168–170, 171–174, 248; religion 151–152; Thirty Years' War 1, 158–160, 162–166, 168–169, 172–173, 208
Switzerland 48, 90, 156, 215, 231, 251

Taborites 81
Tai, Hue-Tam Ho 14
Tauber, Kaspar 32
taxes 127, 130, 162, 172, 196, 201, 232, 235
Teufel (family) 157, 160, 179–180n63; Appolonia 160; Georg 157; Margaretha 160; Maximilian 157–160; Otto Christoph 160
Teuffenbach, Franz Ludwig von 165
Teuffenbach, Johann Friedrich von 165
Teutonic Order 135, 177n36
Thirty Years' War: alliances 97; France 97, 168; literature 273–274; nature 251, 253; outbreak 94; Sweden 1, 151, 158–160, 162–166, 168–169, 172–173, 208
Thurn (family): Franz Bernhard 158; Johann Jakob 165; Heinrich Mathias 94, 158, 164, 253
Tilly, Johann Tserclaes of 97, 136, 158
tolerance 17; religious 10, 38, 43, 48, 96, 138, 245; Transylvania 245; *see also* Patent of Toleration
tolerance congregations 246
Tomek, Ernst 251, 270
Tönnies, Ferdinand 101n19
Tott, Åke 154
transmigrations 245–246
Transylvania: deportations to 245–246; political position 5, 192;

religious conditions 245; Saxons 245; *see also* Bethlen, Gábor
Trauner, Leonhard 34
Trauttmansdorff, Maximilian von 168, 169, 187n161
Treaty of Lieben (Libeň) 86
Treaty of Osnabrück. *See* Peace of Westphalia
Treaty of Passau 9
Treaty of Ulm 97
Trennbach, Urban von 199
Trier 6
Troeltsch, Ernst 113, 235
Truce of Altmark 154
Tschernembl (Črnomelj) 89
Tschernembl (family) 89; Christoph 89; Hans 89; Hans Christoph 90; Heinrich 90; *see also* Tschernembl, Georg Erasmus
Tschernembl, Georg Erasmus: ancestry 89; Calvinism 90, 235; *Consultationes* 130–136; education 90; exile 135–136; household 92; international contacts 92–93; and Jesuits 126, 130, 138; library 126–127; literature 275; peasants 91, 232; political career 90–93, 94–95, 236; political views 20, 127–129, 135, 138, 150, 235, 236, 253–254; as seigneur 91
Tübingen 35
Turks. *See* Ottoman Empire
Tyrol: in Austria Anterior 39; Habsburg rule 13, 42; politics 40, 50, 74–75, 194, 214, 215, 250; Reformation 31, 39–40; religion 31–32, 39–40, 194, 244, 250; social structure 195

Ulm 152
Ungnad, Andreas von 98, 129, 239
Ungnad, David von 239
Union of Calmar 151
United Nations 18
Unity of Brethren (Bohemian Brethren) 31, 81–82, 87, 104n57, 129
Upper Austria: archduchy 39; Bavarian occupation 97–98; estates 74, 90, 91, 92, 95, 97, 125, 162; landownership 195–197; literature 269, 272, 275; noble resistance 86, 92, 95, 96–98, 231; peasant

resistance 136, 165, 198–216,
223n60, 231, 251, 275; political
role 41, 63–64n67, 131; religious
conditions 41, 43, 76, 77, 83, 87,
90, 161, 195, 197, 214–216, 236,
237–238, 243, 245, 246
Usedom 158
Utraquists 31, 81, 87, 129

Vaihingen 136
Vasa (dynasty) 151–152, 163
Velden 162
Vercingétorix 15
Vienna 11, 85, 95, 128, 165, 167,
170, 200; bishop 55; court 41,
42, 53, 79, 91, 92, 168, 169, 204,
237; imperial residence 3; religious
conditions 32–33, 53, 54, 55, 56,
76, 79, 246; size 192; university 35,
54, 55, 270
Villach 33–34, 35, 37, 51, 153, 166,
207
Vingsleör 155
Visatidines 47
Vladislav II (king of Bohemia and
Hungary) 4, 8
Volmar, Melchior 120
Vorarlberg 39, 40, 75
Vösendorf 33, 56
Vult, Elias 171
Vult, Matthias 171
Vultejus, Johannes 171
Vult von Steijern (family) 171,
190n191

Waidhofen on the Ybbs 76
Waldensians 81
Waldheim, Kurt 18
Waldviertel 241
Wallenstein, Albrecht von 80, 210,
274
Wallhof (Valle), battle of 154, 158
War of the Spanish Succession 248
Weber, Max 72–73
Weiberau 209
Weichselmünde (Wisłoujście) 157

Wels 34
Welzer (family) 90; Bernhard 90;
Georg Rupert 90; Johannes 90
Wendish March 89
Werben 158
Wernberg 153
Wettin (dynasty) 9, 230–231
Whigs 15
White, Hayden 15–16
White Mountain, battle of 131,
133, 135, 153, 155, 158; armies
253; Austrian identity 251; Czech
identity 253
Wiener Neustadt 55, 76, 102n35
William V (duke of Bavaria) 50, 56
William V (landgrave of Hesse-Kassel)
164
Wilson, Peter 274
Windegg 89, 91, 107n89, 126
Windhag 197
Windischgrätz, Andre Ludwig von
164
Winkelbauer, Thomas 80, 270, 273
Winter, Ernst Karl 18
Wittelsbach (dynasty) 50; political
position 3, 4, 21n6, 41, 97; religion
38, 44, 49, 53, 55
Wittenberg 33, 36; university 34, 35, 36
Wolfram, Herwig 270
Wolfsgruber, Cölestin 270
Worms, diet of 7
Wrangel, Hermann von 158
Wurmbrand, Hieronymus 156
Wurmbrand, Melchior 156–157, 167,
178n46, 179n54, 179n61, 179n62
Württemberg 8, 136

Zeeden, Ernst Walter 47–48, 49
Zelking, Hans Wilhelm 91
Zeller, Christoph 202, 205
Zenegg, Jakob 153
Zieten (family) 207
Zillertal 250
Žižka of Trocnov, Jan 31
Zöllner, Erich 269
Zurich 156

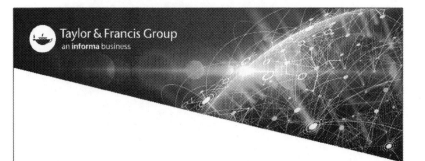